The Border Between Seeing and Thinking

PHILOSOPHY OF MIND SERIES

SERIES EDITOR: David J. Chalmers, *New York University*

The Conscious Brain
Jesse Prinz

Simulating Minds
The Philosophy, Psychology, and
Neuroscience of Mindreading
Alvin I. Goldman

Supersizing The Mind
Embodiment, Action, and Cognitive
Extension
Andy Clark

Perception, Hallucination, and Illusion
William Fish

*Phenomenal Concepts and Phenomenal
Knowledge*
New Essays on Consciousness and
Physicalism
Torin Alter and Sven Walter

The Character of Consciousness
David J. Chalmers

The Senses
Classic and Contemporary Philosophical
Perspectives
Fiona Macpherson

Attention Is Cognitive Unison
An Essay in Philosophical Psychology
Christopher Mole

The Contents of Visual Experience
Susanna Siegel

*Consciousness and the Prospects of
Physicalism*
Derk Pereboom

Consciousness and Fundamental Reality
Philip Goff

The Phenomenal Basis of Intentionality
Angela Mendelovici

Seeing and Saying
The Language of Perception and the
Representational View of Experience
Berit Brogaard

Perceptual Learning
The Flexibility of the Senses
Kevin Connolly

Combining Minds
How to Think about Composite
Subjectivity
Luke Roelofs

The Epistemic Role of Consciousness
Declan Smithies

The Epistemology of Non-Visual Perception
Berit Brogaard and Dimitria Electra
Gatzia

What Are Mental Representations?
Edited by Joulia Smortchkova, Krzysztof
Dołęga, and Tobias Schlicht

Phenomenal Intentionality
George Graham, John Tienson, and Terry
Horgan

Feminist Philosophy of Mind, Keya Maitra
and Jennifer McWeeny

The Border Between Seeing and Thinking
Ned Block

The Border Between Seeing and Thinking

NED BLOCK
New York University

OXFORD
UNIVERSITY PRESS

Oxford University Press is a department of the University of Oxford. It furthers
the University's objective of excellence in research, scholarship, and education
by publishing worldwide. Oxford is a registered trade mark of Oxford University
Press in the UK and certain other countries.

Published in the United States of America by Oxford University Press
198 Madison Avenue, New York, NY 10016, United States of America.

© Oxford University Press 2023

All rights reserved. No part of this publication may be reproduced, stored in
a retrieval system, or transmitted, in any form or by any means, without the
prior permission in writing of Oxford University Press, or as expressly permitted
by law, by license, or under terms agreed with the appropriate reproduction
rights organization. Inquiries concerning reproduction outside the scope of the
above should be sent to the Rights Department, Oxford University Press, at the
address above.

This is an open access publication, available online and distributed under the terms of a
Creative Commons Attribution – Non Commercial – No Derivatives 4.0
International licence (CC BY-NC-ND 4.0), a copy of which is available at
http://creativecommons.org/licenses/by-nc-nd/4.0/.

You must not circulate this work in any other form
and you must impose this same condition on any acquirer.

CIP data is on file at the Library of Congress
Names: Block, Ned, 1942- author.
Title: The border between seeing and thinking / Ned Block.
Description: New York, NY : Oxford University Press, [2022] | Series:
Philosophy of mind series | Includes bibliographical references and index.
Identifiers: LCCN 2022006336 (print) | LCCN 2022006337 (ebook) |
ISBN 9780197622223 (hardback) | ISBN 9780197622247 (epub)
Subjects: LCSH: Cognition. | Perception. | Thought and thinking. | Senses
and sensation.
Classification: LCC BF311 .B554 2022 (print) | LCC BF311 (ebook) |
DDC 153–dc23/eng/20220504
LC record available at https://lccn.loc.gov/2022006336
LC ebook record available at https://lccn.loc.gov/2022006337

ISBN 978–0–19–762222–3

DOI: 10.1093/oso/9780197622223.001.0001

Printed by Integrated Books International, United States of America

The publisher gratefully acknowledges support from New York University
for providing funding for this Open Access publication.

For my grandchildren, Ada, Mae, and Felix.

Contents

Preface		xi
1.	Introduction	1
	Consciousness	16
	Pure perception	17
	What is a joint?	20
	Constitutivity vs. explanatory depth	23
	The contents of perception	27
	Realism about perceptual and cognitive representation	30
	Three-layer methodology	33
	Higher "capacity" in perception (whether conscious or not) than cognition	34
	Armchair approaches to the perception/cognition border	41
	Conceptual engineering	44
	If there is a fundamental difference between perception and cognition, why don't we see the border in the brain?	51
	Interface of perception with cognition	53
	Why should philosophers be interested in this book?	56
	Roadmap	58
2.	Markers of the perceptual and the cognitive	61
	Adaptation	61
	Perception vs. cognition in language	64
	Different kinds of adaptation	69
	Visual hierarchy	83
	The use of adaptation in distinguishing low-level from high-level perception	85
	The use of adaptation in distinguishing perception from cognition	97
	Semantic satiation	101
	Rivalry	104
	Pop-out	109
	Interpolation of illusory contours	111
	Neural markers of perception and cognition	113
	Other markers of perception	115
	Phenomenology	118
	Summary	119

3. Two kinds of seeing-as and singular content — 121
   - Burge and Schellenberg on singular content — 123
   - Attribution and discrimination — 142
   - Ordinary vs. technical language — 152
   - Bias: Perception vs. perceptual judgment — 152
   - Evaluative perception — 157

4. Perception is constitutively nonpropositional and nonconceptual — 166
   - Concepts and propositions — 166
   - Format/content/state/function — 172
   - The nonpropositional nature of perception — 176
   - Conjunction — 180
   - Negation — 182
   - Disjunction — 187
   - Atomic propositional representations — 188
   - Rivalry and propositional perception — 191
   - How do iconicity, nonconceptuality, and nonpropositionality fit together? — 195
   - Laws of appearance — 198
   - Bayesian "inference" — 200
   - Bayesian realism — 204

5. Perception is iconic; cognition is discursive — 215
   - Iconicity, format, and function — 215
   - Iconicity and determinacy — 219
   - Structure — 221
   - Analog tracking and mirroring — 221
   - Analog magnitude representations — 224
   - Mental imagery — 226
   - Holism — 232
   - Integral vs. separable — 234
   - Iconic object-representations in perception — 237
   - Object files in working memory — 246
   - Memory involving perceptual representations — 248

6. Nonconceptual color perception — 265
   - Perceptual category representations — 266
   - Infant color categories — 274
   - Infants' failure to normally deploy color concepts — 278
   - Color constancy — 281
   - Working memory again — 284
   - Experiments on babies' working memory representations — 286
   - Adult nonconceptual color perception — 293
   - Is high-level perception conceptual? — 298
   - Systematicity again — 302
   - Modality — 302

7.	Neural evidence that perception is nonconceptual	306
	"No-report" paradigm vs. "no-cognition" paradigm	308
	Another "no-report" paradigm	319
8.	Evidence that is wrongly taken to show that perception is conceptual	325
	Fast perception	325
	Cognitive access to mid-level vision	333
9.	Cognitive penetration is common but does not challenge the joint	338
	Cognitive impenetrability: Recent history	338
	Perceptual set	347
	Ambiguous stimuli	347
	Spatial attention	354
	Feature-based attention	358
	Dimension restriction	370
	Mental imagery	374
10.	Top-down effects that are probably not cases of cognitive penetration	380
	Figure/ground	380
	Memory color	385
11.	Modularity	394
12.	Core cognition and perceptual analogs of concepts	404
	Perception of causation	404
	Core cognition	410
13.	Consciousness	417
	Phenomenal consciousness vs. access consciousness	419
	Global workspace	423
	Higher order thought	424
	Alleged evidence for higher order thought theories of consciousness	427
	Prefrontalism and electrical stimulation of the brain	442
	Overflow	444
	Biological reductionism	445
	Direct awareness	446
	Teleological approaches	449
	Fading qualia	451
	Consciousness and free will	459
14.	Conclusions	468
	References	475
	Author Index	531
	Subject Index	535

Preface

This book is about the border between perception and cognition—what it is and why it is important. I was drawn to this subject because of the realization that the difference between what I called access consciousness (cognitive access to phenomenally conscious states) and what I called phenomenal consciousness (what it is like to experience) was rooted in a difference between perception—whether conscious or unconscious—and cognitive access to perception.

A bit of the material in this book appeared in one of my four Jean Nicod Lectures in Paris in 2014 (though those lectures were on consciousness rather than the perception/cognition border). I am very grateful to Pierre Jacob and Frédérique de Vignemont for their warm hospitality and wonderful intellectual stimulation.

I am grateful to Jake Beck, Philip John Bold, Tyler Burge, Susan Carey, David Chalmers, Rachel Denison, Santiago Echeverri, Chaz Firestone, E. J. Green, Steven Gross, Chris Hill, Zoe Jenkin, Leonard Katz, Geoff Lee, Bria Long, Eric Mandelbaum, Jessie Munton, Albert Newen, Adam Pautz, Mary Peterson, Ian Phillips, Chris Peacocke, Jake Quilty-Dunn, Susanna Siegel, Barry Smith, and anonymous reviewers for comments on an earlier draft. I am also indebted to discussion groups at Berkeley and NYU that discussed an earlier draft. I am grateful to Templeton World Charities for their support and to Rebecca Keller for preparing both indexes.

My indebtedness to my wife, Susan Carey, and to her book, *The Origin of Concepts*, is visible at many points in the book. The issue I have struggled with most is how to fit core cognition into my picture of the joint in nature between cognition and perception.

Ned Block
Cambridge, MA, November 2021

1
Introduction

What is the difference between seeing and thinking? Is the border between seeing and thinking a joint in nature in the sense of a fundamental explanatory difference? Is it a difference of degree? Does thinking affect seeing, or, rather, is seeing "cognitively penetrable"? Are we aware of faces, causation, numerosity, and other "high-level" properties or only of the colors, shapes, and textures that—according to the advocate of high-level perception—are the low-level basis on which we see them? How can we distinguish between low-level and high-level perception, and how can we distinguish between high-level perception and perceptual judgment? Is there evaluative perception or is evaluation a matter of emotion and perceptual judgment? Is perception conceptual and propositional? Is perception iconic or more akin to language in being discursive? Is seeing singular? Which is more fundamental, visual attribution or visual discrimination? Is all seeing seeing-as? What is the difference between the format and content of perception, and do perception and cognition have different formats? Is perception probabilistic and, if so, why are we not normally aware of this probabilistic nature of perception? Does perception require perceptual constancies? Are the basic features of mind known as "core cognition" a third category in between perception and cognition? Are there perceptual categories that are not concepts? Where does consciousness fit in with regard to the difference between seeing and thinking? What is the best theory of consciousness and does the perception/cognition border have any relevance to which theories of consciousness are best? These are the questions I will be exploring in this book. I will be exploring them not mainly by appeals to "intuitions," as is common in philosophy of perception, but by appeal to empirical evidence, including experiments in neuroscience and psychology.

I will orient the discussion around the question of a joint in nature between perception and cognition resting on differences in format and kind of representation that have been the subject of a great deal of controversy in recent years. Perception is constitutively nonconceptual, nonpropositional, and iconic, but cognition has none of these properties constitutively.

Claims that perception is iconic, nonconceptual, or nonpropositional have been advocated—and opposed—for many years. Stephen Kosslyn is perhaps the most notable advocate of recent years for the iconicity of both perception and mental imagery, but many others have also advocated such views (Block,

1981, 1983a, 1983b; Burge, 2010b; Carey, 2009; Kosslyn, 1980; Kosslyn, Pinker, Schwartz, & Smith, 1979; Kosslyn, Thompson, & Ganis, 2006). Zenon Pylyshyn has been a notable opponent of iconicity for both perception and mental imagery (Pylyshyn, 1973, 2003). Similarly, many have advocated nonconceptual and/or nonpropositional perception (Burge, 2010a; Carey, 2009, 2011b; Crane, 1988; Evans, 1982; Peacocke, 1986, 1989). And there are many opponents (McDowell, 1994; Strong, 1930; Wittgenstein, 1953).

The intended contribution of this book is not that perception is nonconceptual, nonpropositional and iconic, but the elaboration of what that view comes to, engagement with the evidence for and against it; and using this picture of perception to refute widely held theories of consciousness, the global workspace theory and the higher order thought theory, and to argue for a new reason to think there can be phenomenal consciousness without access consciousness. I think I have new evidentially based arguments for other familiar theses. For example, Chapter 6 is devoted to an argument for non-conceptual color perception based on developmental psychology. In the first few chapters, I will be especially concerned with how to distinguish low-level perception from high-level perception and how to distinguish high-level perception from perceptual judgment.

This book is all about evidence. I aim to avoid pronouncements and intuitions. I will also explore the relation between these claims about format, content, and state to modularity and consciousness, and rebut arguments that misconceive the border between perception and cognition. (The content of a representation is the way it represents the world to be, the way the world has to be for the representation to be accurate. The format of a representation is the structure of its representational vehicle.)

I also aim to avoid cherry-picking evidence. When I know of evidence that goes against my claims, I will introduce it.

To say that perception is constitutively X is to say that it is in the nature of perception to be X. The evidence I will present that perception constitutively has certain properties applies most clearly to actual creatures that perceive rather than possible creatures. The evidence I will be talking about concerns the way actual perceptual mechanisms work. Occasionally I will talk about consequences for robot perception, though I am less certain about those claims.

Although I am arguing for certain constitutive properties of perception, my evidence is almost entirely concerned with vision. I believe the points I am making apply at least to all the spatial senses. There is good reason to include smell in the spatial senses (Smith, 2015). Humans can track odors across grass blindfolded, and their tracking deteriorates if they are deprived of the use of one nostril. Humans can also identify the direction of a smell via stereo-olfaction without moving (Jacobs, Arter, Cook, & Sulloway, 2015).

But I will not be talking about the nonspatial senses except in asides such as this one. I will not be talking about proprioception, the sense of balance, thermoception (the sense of temperature, kinesthesia (the sense of movement), chronoception (the sense of time) or others of the perhaps 21 senses (Durie, 2005).

Although there are many types of perception, a wide variety of them obey the same laws of perception such as Weber's Law (that the discriminability of two stimuli is a linear function of the ratios of the intensities of the two stimuli) and Stevens's Power Law (that says that perceived intensity is proportional to actual intensity raised to an exponent, where the exponent differs according to stimulus type). Stevens's Power Law has been shown to apply not only to various forms of visual and auditory intensity but also to many other kinds of perception and sensation. A recent textbook chapter lists the exponents for the following kinds of perception: electric shock, warmth on arm, heaviness for lifted weights, pressure on arm, cold on arm, vibration, loudness of white noise, loudness of 1 KHz tone, and brightness of white light (Zwislocki, 2009). In sum, although my evidence is almost entirely from vision, there is a prima facie case to be made that many of our perceptual modalities have similar underlying natures.

One feature of the treatment of these ideas that will emerge in Chapters 4 and 6 is that perceptual and cognitive states can share the same or at least similar contents, nonconceptual and nonpropositional in the case of perception, conceptual and propositional in the case of cognition. So nonconceptual content is not a kind of content. Chapter 6 will use an extended example in terms of color contents.

Jerry Fodor argued for a joint in nature between perception and cognition based on the distinction between modular (perception) and nonmodular (cognition) processing. The modularity thesis says perception is a fast, inflexible, automatic, domain-specific system that is informationally encapsulated from other systems, has a fixed neural architecture, a characteristic ontogenetic pace of development, and processes that are themselves largely opaque to other systems (Fodor, 1983). This book argues that the joint in nature between perception and cognition does not depend on modularity, and more specifically that there is a joint and there also is considerable penetration of perception by cognition. Still, there is something to the idea that perception is modular, with only restricted kinds of cognitive penetration. In Chapter 9, I will critique a recent proposal in the spirit of modularity by E. J. Green, but I am friendly to the general approach.

How do we know that we are perceiving a face as a face—as opposed to perceiving a face as having certain colors, lines, curves, textures, shapes, and the like—all low-level properties? To answer that question, we need methods of distinguishing high-level from low-level perception.

Something can look blue, look like a face, look expensive, or look like a piano. But are these kinds of looking all perceptual as opposed to judgmental overlays on perception? The perceptual representation of blue is low-level, whereas the perceptual representation of faceness is high-level. Low-level visual representations are products of sensory transduction that are causally involved in the production of other (mid- and high-level) visual representations and include representations of contrast, spatial relations, motion, texture, brightness, and color. (Transduction is conversion of signals received by sense organs into neural impulses.) Another low-level property is spatial frequency (roughly, "stripiness"—see Figure 1.1.). Representations at a slightly higher level, sometimes characterized as mid-level, include representations of shapes that indicate corners, junctions, and contours (Long, Konkle, Cohen, & Alvarez, 2016). High-level representations include representations of recognizable objects and object-parts, but also causation and numerosity. Some think that conscious perception is never high-level, for example Alex Byrne, Adam Pautz, and Jesse Prinz (Pautz,

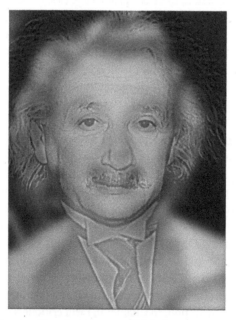

Figure 1.1 Superimposed low-frequency and high-frequency images. From close up you see Albert Einstein (high-frequency image), but from far away (or if you squint) you see Marilyn Monroe (low-frequency image). Any curve can be decomposed into component sine waves. The spatial frequency of the curve depends on the spatial frequencies of those sine waves. See the Wikipedia article on spatial frequency at https://en.wikipedia.org/wiki/Spatial_frequency. Thanks to Aude Oliva for the figure. (See Oliva, Torralba, & Schyns, 2006.)

2021; Prinz, 2002; Siegel & Byrne, 2016) and that what happens when it seems that something looks like a face is that we perceive lower-level properties while judging that certain high-level properties apply. Those who advocate high-level perception are often said to advocate rich as opposed to thin perception (Siegel, 2010; Siegel & Byrne, 2016).

Although I will be arguing at length that we do perceptually represent some high-level properties, I agree with the skeptics that it is a mistake to postulate rich content solely on the ground that a perceiver can visually recognize something. For example, I can visually recognize that something is a pipe wrench without seeing it as such.

One view of the rich/thin debate that is not the one I am endorsing is that the thin view is one in which we perceive low-level properties "directly" and high-level properties "indirectly." This picture, sometimes called the "layering" conception, is that "we see more abstract and worldly things in and by seeing simpler and more primitive ones" (Lycan, 2014, p. 7). I think we visually attribute faceness, causation, and numerosity directly.

High-level perception is to a large extent causally dependent on low-level perception but not totally dependent on low-level perception. For example, there are direct connections between subcortical structures like the amygdala and the high-level fusiform face area (Herrington, Taylor, Grupe, Curby, & Schultz, 2011). The amygdala is activated by fearful faces by a pathway that skips the low-level perceptual analysis of early visual cortex (McFadyen, Mermillod, Mattingley, Halász, & Garrido, 2017). Further, even to the extent that high-level perception is causally dependent on low-level perception, that doesn't make high-level perception indirect in the sense that high-level percepts are composed of low-level percepts. High-level perception in the sense I am using is just the perceptual attribution of high-level properties.

What is the evidence that we visually represent some high-level properties? I will be addressing this question in more detail later, especially in Chapter 2, but I will give one line of evidence here having to do with visual agnosia (a term due to Freud). My argument will be superficially similar to one given by Tim Bayne (2009), and one reason for introducing the argument in the introductory chapter is that the difference between my argument and Bayne's illustrates a key feature of the methodology of this book.

A nineteenth-century classification system of agnosias due to Lissauer (Shallice & Jackson, 1988) that is still useful distinguishes between apperceptive agnosia, in which subjects have problems with grouping of perceptual elements, and associative agnosia, in which grouping is normal or close to normal but recognition is not. Apperceptive agnosia is now more commonly referred to as "visual form agnosia." (The latter term is used in the second [but not the first] edition of Martha Farah's classic book [Farah, 2004].) Apperceptive agnosics can often see color and texture but cannot see shapes and often have trouble telling whether they are seeing one object or two objects. They have difficulty copying drawings even when they can draw from memory with their eyes closed.

Associative agnosics can often copy drawings well without knowing what they are copying. Associative agnosia is characterized by failure to apply high-level visual properties, even though associative agnosics often have normal recognition through nonvisual sensory modalities and intact low-level vision. For example, an associative agnosic might be unable to visually recognize that something is a dog despite being able to recognize that something is a dog haptically and despite having the concept of a dog. Hans-Lukas Teuber described associative agnosia as "percepts stripped of their meaning" (quoted in Goodale & Milner, 2005, p. 13).

In addition to broad visual associative agnosia there are also specialized associative agnosias such as prosopagnosia, the inability to recognize faces despite intact low-level perception. Color agnosia, a type of associative agnosia, is discussed in Chapters 4 and 6. A recent paper reported an even more specific agnosia, agnosia for the digits '2' through '9'. The patient could recognize '0' and '1' and letters of the alphabet. The patient was an engineering geologist with a degenerative brain disease. Although he could not recognize the eight mentioned digits, he could do mental arithmetic. He came up with a different system of representing the eight digits and set up his computer to use the new numerals on the screen so that he could keep working (Kean, 2020; Schubert et al., 2020).

Apperceptive agnosics don't demonstrate the existence of low-level without high-level perception, since what they lack is a kind of low-level perception involving low-level grouping. However, patients whose perceptual grouping is normal but have associative agnosia have low-level perception without high-level perception. The existence of associative agnosics is an excellent reason to believe that there is high-level perception and high-level perceptual content.

I think this point establishes that there is high-level perceptual content, but it does not show that there is high-level perceptual phenomenology, that is conscious high-level content (cf. Bayne, 2009). But separating the issue of high-level perceptual phenomenology into the question of high-level perceptual content and whether that content can be conscious allows us to get a grip on the latter question. And this is the point of methodology that I am illustrating here.

It is widely agreed among those who study the neuroscience of consciousness that specific phenomenal contents are based at least in part in the brain circuits that process that kind of content. For example, visual brain area MT+ processes motion perception, both 3D and 2D motion. The evidence is partly correlational—even illusory motion and motion aftereffects involve activation in MT+ (Tootell et al., 1995), but the conclusion is also supported by stimulation to MT+. Indeed the experience of specific directions of motion is produced by stimulation to distinct subareas of MT+ (Salzman, Murasugi, Britten, & Newsome, 1992).

Although we know that activation in MT+ is part of the neural basis of motion experience, what we don't know is *what else has to happen* for (conscious) motion experience to occur. Though we don't know, theorists do make claims about what else has to happen. For example, the global workspace theory (to be discussed in detail in Chapters 4 and 13) says that the motion representational contents must be "globally broadcast."

What is global broadcasting? Perception sparks competition among neural "coalitions" in perceptual areas in the back of the head. (See Koch, 2004, for a readable account of neural coalitions and (Dehaene, 2014) for a readable presentation of the global workspace account.) These coalitions involve feedback/feed-forward loops known as recurrent activations. The recurrent activations in the back of the head trigger "ignition," in which a winning neural coalition in perceptual areas links up with frontal circuits via "workspace neurons" that link the front and back of the head. The result is a systemwide mutually supporting neural coalition that advocates of the global workspace model describe as broadcasting in the global workspace. See Figure 1.2. According to the global workspace theory, representations of motion based in MT+ being globally broadcast is constitutive of perceptual consciousness of motion.

The "global workspace" model of consciousness (Dehaene, 2014) is illustrated in Figure 1.2. The outer ring indicates the sensory surfaces of the body. Circles are neural systems and lines are links between them. Filled circles are activated systems and thick lines are activated links. Activated neural coalitions compete with one another to trigger recurrent (reverberatory) activity, symbolized by the

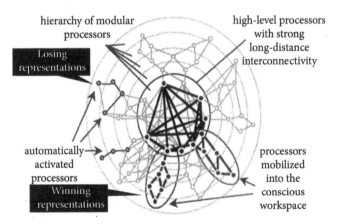

Figure 1.2 Schematic diagram of the global workspace. Dark pointers added. I am grateful to Stan Dehaene for supplying this drawing.

ovals circling strongly activated networks. Sufficiently activated networks trigger recurrent activity in cognitive areas in the center of the diagram and they in turn feed back to the sensory activations, maintaining the sensory excitation until displaced by a new dominant coalition. Not everyone accepts the global workspace theory as a theory of consciousness (including me), but it does serve to illustrate one kind (again, not the only kind) of competition among sensory activations that in many circumstances is "winner-takes-all," with the losers precluded from consciousness. (As we will see in Chapter 7, there is a revised version of the global workspace theory, the global playground theory, that is arguably superior.)

I have argued that recurrent activations confined to the back of the head can be conscious without triggering central activation. Because of local recurrence and other factors, these are "winners" in a local competition without triggering global workspace activation (Block, 2007a). Strong recurrent activations in the back of the head normally trigger "ignition," in which a winning neural coalition in the back of the head spreads into recurrent activations in frontal areas that in turn feed-back to sensory areas. See Figure 1.2. As Dehaene and colleagues have shown, such locally recurrent activations can be produced reliably with a strong stimulus and strong distraction of attention (Dehaene, Changeux, Nacchache, Sackur, & Sergent, 2006). (Since I am concerned in most chapters of this book with normal perception, I won't say much about my disagreement with the model until we get to the chapter on consciousness. But for the record, I think the global workspace model is a better model of conceptualization than of consciousness.)

Here is the point: What is true for low-level perceptual representations such as the representation of motion is also true for high-level perceptual representations, such as face-representations based in the fusiform face area. When high-level perceptual representations are broadcast in the global workspace they give rise to high-level conscious phenomenology—according to the global workspace theory. So the global workspace account plus the fact that there is high-level perceptual content leads to the conclusion that there is high-level perceptual phenomenology. (I am assuming that the high-level representations are sometimes broadcast in the global workspace, but that is obvious enough.) So *if we assume the global workspace account of consciousness*, we can move from the high-level perceptual content shown by the agnosia evidence to high-level perceptual phenomenology.

The first-order recurrent activation account of conscious content is basically a truncated form of the global workspace account: It identifies conscious perception with the recurrent activations in the back of the head without the requirement of broadcasting in the global workspace (Block, 2005b; Lamme, 2003). First-order theories do not say that recurrent activations are by themselves sufficient for consciousness. These activations are only sufficient given background conditions. Those background conditions probably include intact connectivity with subcortical structures. (The cortex is the thin sheet covering the brain, the "gray matter.") This kind of connectivity is disrupted under general anesthesia (Alkire, 2008; Golkowski et al., 2019).

That is, according to the first-order recurrent activation account, the active recurrent loops in perceptual areas plus background conditions are enough for conscious perceptual phenomenology. So long as high-level representations participate in those recurrent loops, conscious high-level content is assured. So *if we assume the first-order recurrent activation account of consciousness*, we can move from the high-level perceptual content shown by the agnosia evidence to high-level perceptual phenomenology.

I favor the first-order point of view. If the first-order point of view is right, it may be conscious phenomenology that promotes global broadcasting, something like the reverse of what the global workspace theory of consciousness supposes. ("Something like": First-order phenomenology may be a causal factor in promoting global broadcasting; but according to the global workspace theory, global broadcasting constitutes consciousness rather than being caused by it.)

I believe that the same line of thought will apply to any neuroscientific theory of consciousness. All will have to agree that perceptual representation of motion in MT+ plus something else—e.g., certain relations to other brain activations or to behavior—are the basis of conscious experience of motion. It is difficult to imagine a remotely plausible candidate for the "something else" that applies to low-level representations such as activations in MT+ but does not apply to high-level activations such as activations in the fusiform face area. This point is the core of my argument for high-level phenomenology.

Some will reject the application of this idea to high-level phenomenology, but that rejection will have to be based on an independent doctrine that there is no high-level perceptual phenomenology. For example, Jesse Prinz's AIR theory (attended intermediate level representation) holds that conscious perception is a matter of mid-level perceptual representations being modulated by attention in a way that allows for availability to working memory—albeit indirectly, via encoding of high-level representation (Prinz, 2012). (Working memory will be discussed later in this chapter and in Chapters 5 and 6.) My point here is that Prinz's theory fits the mold I have described for low-level contents such as motion contents, and he is only able to avoid the extrapolation to high-level phenomenology by explicit stipulation that only mid-level representations can be conscious.

Representationists (also known as representationalists or intentionalists) among philosophers, such as Alex Byrne and Michael Tye, would also be committed to high-level perceptual phenomenology if they accept my argument that there is high-level perceptual representation (Byrne, 2001; Tye, 2019). Representationists hold that the phenomenology of perception is grounded in or determined by its representational content, so high-level content requires high-level phenomenology. (They require further conditions, e.g., that the high-level representations are poised for a role in thought and report, but there is no reason to suppose that these conditions do not apply to high-level representations.)

In sum, many widely accepted perspectives in both neuroscience and philosophy support the move from the existence of high-level perceptual content to the conclusion that there is high-level perceptual phenomenology.

Adam Pautz has argued that the hypothesis of visually representing clusters of low-level properties is methodologically superior to the hypothesis of representing high-level properties. The low-level account is alleged to be more uniform, applying both to faces and to Byrne's "greebles," invented stimuli that are used to study object perception. And the low-level account is alleged to be more parsimonious since the high-level account postulates an extra layer. However, these arguments can't explain the evidence of the sort just presented from agnosias for specific high-level representation. Further, as mentioned earlier, high-level perception has causal sources that are causally independent of low-level perception so high-level perception cannot be reduced to low-level perception.

Now we can return to the use of associative agnosias in arguing for high-level phenomenology. As I mentioned, Tim Bayne (2009) uses associative agnosia to argue for high-level phenomenology. He notes that associative agnosics have low-level perceptual phenomenology, but that it is "extremely plausible" to suppose that the result of the agnosia is that "the phenomenal character of his visual experience has changed" (p. 391). However, introspective judgments about high-level phenomenology are hard to agree on, as anyone who has argued with an opponent about them realizes. How sure can anyone be that they have the experience of visually attributing faceness as opposed to visually attributing colors, shapes, and textures?

Further, as Robert Briscoe (2015) points out, those who do not believe in high-level phenomenology (such as Prinz) will regard this argument as question-begging. They will think that the associative agnosics have lost recognition of high-level properties without having lost any alleged phenomenology that is specific to high-level properties.

Note however, that my argument is not subject to the problem that Briscoe raises. I have used associative agnosia and its difference from visual form agnosia to argue for high-level perceptual representation—without assuming anything about phenomenology or consciousness. Then I have added that all the main contenders for scientific accounts of how phenomenology relates to perceptual representation have the consequence that there is high-level perceptual phenomenology.

I think this two-step argument for high-level phenomenology is more convincing than other arguments with the same conclusion (Peacocke, 1983; Siegel, 2010). At least it replaces reliance on intuitions about the phenomenology of experience with appeal to the scientific literature.

I am mentioning this issue in the introductory section of Chapter 1 because it illustrates the utility of the methodology of this book. I am discussing perception without consideration of consciousness or phenomenology, and then, once certain conclusions about perception are "established," I will be arguing—in Chapter 13—that they provide arguments against "cognitive" theories of consciousness such as the global workspace and higher order theories.

More discussion of what the distinction between low-level and high-level comes to in terms of the visual hierarchy will come in the discussion in Chapter 2 and in the section of Chapter 4 on Bayesian inference.

I will be giving further arguments that there is high-level perception, though I do not think we have high-level representation of every observable property—observable in the sense that we can detect its presence perceptually. For example, we can often tell visually whether something is expensive but I doubt that expensiveness is visually represented. My main focus, however, is the difference between seeing something as, for example being a face, and forming a *minimal immediate direct perceptual judgment* that it is a face, the latter being the most perception-like of cognitive states. (More on this below.) The main issue of this book is what that difference is and why it is explanatorily important. The difference between high-level and low-level perception mainly comes in because it can often be hard to distinguish cognitive representations from high-level perceptual representations.

One feature of the scientific approach to perception that frustrates some readers is that there are observable properties that probably are not represented in perception. I just mentioned the property of expensiveness. Other such properties are being a baseball bat or a CD case. Endre Begby describes Burge's view that probably we don't perceptually represent these properties as "oddly reductive" (Begby, 2011). I think that what seems odd to many people is that we can tell pretty well by looking whether something is a baseball bat and whether it is a CD case. We can even do a visual search for baseball bats and CD cases. The reader should keep in mind that the issue here is whether, when one searches for a baseball bat, one is searching on the basis of low-level properties such as color, shape, and texture or whether a representation of baseball bats functions directly in visual search. This is a real experimental issue in many cases. For example Rufin van Rullen argues on the basis of experimental evidence that when one searches for a face in a scene, one uses representations of low-level properties and does not use a high-level face representation directly in search (VanRullen, 2006).

The cognitive state that is hardest to distinguish from a perception is a minimal immediate, direct perceptual judgment based on that perception. If I am perceiving a face, I often simultaneously judge on the basis of that perception that there is a face. When I speak of *immediate* perceptual judgment, I am talking about a cognitive state that is noninferentially triggered by perception. A direct perceptual judgment is based solely in the perception with no intermediary, inferential or otherwise. I can have a direct immediate perceptual judgment that the two lines in the Muller-Lyer illusion are unequal even when I know that they are actually equal. Thus in the case of known illusions, we have opposite cognitions. We have a perceptual judgment that the lines are unequal and knowledge that they are equal.

Of course, the content of an immediate perceptual judgment has to do with the way the world presents itself in perception. More specifically, what I mean is a *minimal* immediate direct perceptual judgment. A minimal perceptual judgment conceptualizes each representational aspect of a perception and no more. Later in this book I will use "perceptual judgment" to mean minimal immediate direct perceptual judgment, often leaving out everything but the "perceptual judgment."

Given my definition of "perceptual judgment," you may wonder whether there really is a difference between perception and perceptual judgment. This whole book is aimed at showing that there is such a difference and what that difference is. Chapter 2 concerns markers of perception that are not markers of perceptual judgment. And the penultimate section of Chapter 3, "Bias: perception vs. perceptual judgment," gives a simple nontechnical example of how one could get empirical evidence that a mental state is a perceptual judgment rather than a perception. That issue stems from some shootings by police of unarmed Black men in which the police seemed to be saying that they "saw" a gun. This section presents one item of evidence that such reported states were perceptual judgments rather than perceptions. Readers who are especially interested in that issue could read that section now, since it does not presuppose anything in the book that comes before it.

A concept of something in my terminology is a representation that functions to provide a way of thinking of what it is a concept of. Oedipus had at least two concepts—i.e., two ways of thinking of his mother, one we could describe as "Mom," and another when he married her (perhaps Greek analogs of "Jocasta" or "Sweetie"). He then found out that, tragically, the two ways of thinking of her, the two concepts of her, were ways of thinking of the same person. Some uses of the term "concept" link it to discrimination and others to categorization (Connolly, 2011). As we will see in Chapter 6, there is perceptual categorization in the absence of the ability to use a representation in thought and reasoning. In my terminology, these cases exhibit nonconceptual perceptual categorization. The ways of representing that are involved in concepts play a role in propositional thought or reasoning—that is definitional in my use of the term "concept."

What is meant by "cognition"? A prescientific characterization is that it constitutively involves capacities for propositional thought, reasoning, planning, evaluating, and decision-making. (I won't be talking about the conative attitudes [e.g., wanting] or emotions.) Some insects—for example, the nonsocial wasp—can perceive but are not good candidates for propositional thought. Perceptual judgment (i.e., minimal immediate direct perceptual judgment) can be unconscious and automatic. (I will have little to say about emotions, moods, and other mental states that are neither a matter of just perception nor just cognition.)

My usage of the terms "cognition" and "perception" is consonant with much of the recent literature on perception (Firestone & Scholl, 2016a; Pylyshyn, 1999), but some restrict the term "perception" to what I am calling low-level perception (Linton, 2017) and others use "cognition" to encompass mid-level and high-level perception as both perception and cognition (Cavanagh, 2011). This usage is responsible for the term "visual cognition" to mean mid- and high-level vision. For example, here is how Patrick Cavanagh defines "visual cognition" (Cavanagh, 2011, p. 1538):

> A critical component of vision is the creation of visual entities, representations of surfaces and objects that do not change the base data of the visual scene but change which parts we see as belonging together and how they are arrayed in depth. Whether seeing a set of dots as a familiar letter, an arrangement of stars as a connected shape or the space within a contour as a filled volume that may or may not connect with the outside space, the entity that is constructed is unified in our mind even if not in the image. The construction of these entities is the task of visual cognition.

Cavanagh seems to exclude low-level perception with the phrase "base data," and the example of a familiar letter brings in high-level perception.

Consider the Necker cube (pictured in Chapter 2). It can be seen as having a front surface pointing to the lower left or, alternatively, the upper right. These are mid-level differences since they have to do with computation of surface representations. By Cavanagh's definition, the difference counts as cognitive—and also a difference in mid-level vision. This way of talking would preclude a joint in nature between perception and cognition, so I will stick with an anchor for "cognition" in propositional thought, reasoning, planning, evaluating, and decision-making. (See the section on conceptual engineering later in this chapter for a discussion of principles of clarifying the notions of perception and cognition.)

Conceptions of cognition that link it to thinking and reasoning have been called the conservative approach by Cecilia Heyes (Bayne et al., 2019). Of the conservative view, she says (p. R611) it "has a venerable history in Western thought but it's out of kilter with contemporary scientific practice. It implies that much of the research done by those who identify as cognitive scientists—for example, work on the behaviour of plants, shoals of fish and swarms of bees—has nothing to do with cognition."

Although using the term "cognition" in the "liberal" manner that Heyes prefers may have some advantages and it might identify some kind of a joint in nature, it won't be the joint between seeing and thinking. Individual bees may have some thought, but the swarms of bees and shoals of fish don't and plants don't.

Perhaps the most significant difficulty for the perception/cognition joint has been "core cognition," systems that appear to constitute a mental kind that is both paradigmatically perceptual and paradigmatically cognitive. The existence of a third category does not in itself impugn a joint. Glasses are normally rigid in the manner of solids but have the amorphous structure of liquids. Glasses do flow, more quickly at some temperatures than others, and they do not have the "shear" properties of solids. Glasses have a level of molecular organization intermediate between that of liquids and that of solids (Curtin, 2007). Indeed, one newly discovered form of glass resembles solids in that the molecules cannot change orientation but resembles liquids in that the molecules can move freely (in the sense of translational motion) in all directions (Roller, Laganapan, Meijer, Fuchs, & Zumbusch, 2021). No one would think that the existence of these intermediate types impugns the important explanatory significance of the division of matter into gas, liquid, and solid.

However, the problem posed by core cognition goes beyond providing a third category. The problem is that perception and cognition each are defined by a set of properties that have their own explanatory unity and core cognition purports to spoil that unity by combining fundamental features of both perception and cognition.

Two of the most dramatic cases of core cognition are mental representation of causation and approximate numerosity (Carey, 2009; Carey & Spelke, 1994). I will argue in Chapter 12 that in these cases there are perceptual analogs of our cognitive representations of causation and numerosity and that some of the key phenomena can be seen as simply perceptual. Also, some can be seen as cognitive phenomena that utilize perceptual materials, as when we think about something by thinking about what it looks like. In their writings on core cognition, Susan Carey and Elizabeth Spelke have advanced a view of core cognition as combining both perceptual and cognitive features in a single type of representation. I will be arguing for a different view, in which the category of "core cognition" is best thought of as mixing fundamentally different kinds of representations in a single system. In a homogeneous mixture, like air or sugar water, the distinct kinds are not easily discernable. In a heterogeneous mixture, like smoke (gases plus particles) or salad dressing (oil plus vinegar), there are different kinds that are discernable. I am saying that core cognition may be a heterogeneous mixture of perception and cognition.

There are other heterogeneous mixtures of perception and cognition. Here is an example of the use of perceptual materials in cognition: when we use a perceptual simulation involving perceptual representation of a sofa and a doorway to think about whether the sofa will fit through the doorway. It is well established that we use the mental imagery system to do something often described as "mental rotation" in such reasoning, and the mechanisms of mental imagery are substantially (but not completely [Kaski, 2002]) shared with perception (Block, 1983a). Another example: the use of perceptual color representations to consider the question of which green color is darker, that of a Christmas tree or that of a frozen pea. In this case, the reasoner uses two different perceptual concepts of color shades. These perceptual concepts are conceptualized percepts, i.e., percepts that have been incorporated into a conceptual structure. Another type of conceptualized percept would be a descriptive concept with a slot for perceptual materials (Balog, 2009b; Block, 2006; Papineau, 2002).

But why don't these examples and the existence of conceptualized percepts show there is no joint in nature? The answer is that the joint is between perception on the one hand and types of states that may use perceptual materials, but not constitutively, on the other. This argument will be explored in greater detail later in the section Conceptual Engineering (p. 46). I will argue that perception should be restricted to what might be called pure perception, perception that does not occur as part of a judgment or as part of a working memory representation. (Working memory is a mental scratch pad that will be described in detail later, mainly in Chapters 5 and 6.) Pure perception is perception without any cognitive envelope.

Perceptual simulations used in cognition do not have all the properties of perception. I will present evidence in Chapter 2 that a basic kind of competition between perceptual representations that is characteristic of perception does not obtain with perceptual representations in working memory. Further, there is reason to believe that the perceptual representations of colors used in working memory representations do not allow for fine-grained colors, the minimal shades of perception.[1] Finally, perceptual simulations used in working memory do not have the phenomenology characteristic of conscious perception.

---

[1] There is, however, evidence that spatial resolution is not decreased in working memory (Tamber-Rosenau, Fintzi, & Marois, 2015). At the neural level, Zhao et al. used an orientation working memory task while the subjects were undergoing fMRI scanning. They found that the earliest cortical representations (in V1) on the opposite side from the stimulus lost precision over time, but oddly the representations on the same side as the stimulus did not lose precision. Thus it may be that there are two different kinds of spatial representations involved in spatial working memory (Zhao, Kay, Tian, & Ku, 2021).

(Compare hearing a phone number and rehearsing it while you look for your phone.) These three points indicate deep differences between perception and perceptual materials used in working memory.

One consequence of the thesis of this book is that certain kinds of machine "vision" are not really cases of vision or even of perception. This issue will be explored in Chapter 6, where I will discuss a robot whose cameras output propositional representations concerning the properties of pixels in the camera's sensor. If those representations are treated as premises in inferences on the basis of which the robot infers the environmental causes of those stimulations, then the robot would have direct sensory production of thought without perception.

One upshot of the ideas in this book for epistemology is that it is a mistake to think of the way perception justifies perceptual belief in terms of inference from perceptual contents to belief contents. Another upshot has to do with intentionality. The kind of intentionality involved in perception is different from although perhaps the source of the intentionality of belief (Neander, 2017; Shea, 2018).

Consciousness

As noted earlier, throughout most of this book, I will be concerned with perception rather than conscious perception. The border I am talking about is the border between perception—whether conscious or unconscious—and cognition—whether conscious or unconscious. In part, this focus stems from the perception literature (cf. Teufel & Nanay, 2017). Much of the experimental work on perception and cognition does not address the issue of whether the effects are conscious or unconscious. But in part this focus reflects the view that perception is a natural kind that includes both conscious and unconscious perception (see Block, 2016a; Block & Phillips, 2016; and Phillips, 2015, for both sides on this view). (A similar idea applies to the relation between conscious and unconscious control of behavior (Suhler & Churchland, 2009).)

In endorsing the methodological priority of perception over conscious perception, I am not endorsing a view that perception is metaphysically and explanatorily prior (Miracchi, 2017) to consciousness. There are many conscious states that are not perceptual. Perception and consciousness are overlapping natural kinds, neither of which has priority over the other.

Of course the phenomenology of perception is conscious and is part of . . . perception! Some visual phenomena occur in both conscious and unconscious perception, for example the phenomenon of binocular rivalry to be described in Chapter 2. Also, illusory contours probably are present in unconscious vision, since, as will be described in Chapter 2, they occur in insects, and occur so early in visual processing in primates that they probably partially precede conscious perception. However, other perceptual phenomena may only occur in conscious vision, for example, perceptual pop-out.

In Chapter 6 I will argue for nonconceptual color perception in children. Then in Chapter 13 I will leverage that point to argue that these children have phenomenal-consciousness of color without access-consciousness of color.

Pure perception

Any perception that we notice will inevitably involve conceptualization—as part of the cognitive process of noticing the perception. But there may be creatures whose perceptions are always pure, never involving cognition. Wasps have well-developed visual systems. For example, wasp vision exhibits many of the standard visual constancies. Peter Godfrey-Smith has noted that despite their excellent vision, wasps have short lives with highly stereotyped action patterns and show little or no sign of a cognitive or affective life (Godfrey-Smith, 2017).

This is true of the solitary wasp species, for example the sphex wasp. There are thousands of wasp species, with the social wasps being more sophisticated. One social wasp (the paper wasp) has been shown to be capable of a kind of transitive inference-like behavior (Tibbetts, Agudelo, Pandit, & Riojas, 2019). Bees have been shown to learn matching relations between numerosities of 3, 2, and 1 items and symbols, and also between symbols and numerosities (Howard, Avarguès-Weber, Garcia, Greentree, & Dyer, 2019a). But bees trained on matching symbols to numerosities did not generalize to matching numerosities to symbols. And conversely. Although bees have been shown capable of such kinds of symbolic associations with number, they failed the transitivity test. Tibbetts et al. speculate that sensitivity to transitive relations evolved in the paper wasp because its social structure involves dominance hierarchies among individuals. Bees do not have social ranks of the same sort, and of course solitary wasps have no social ranks. My discussion below concerns solitary wasps, not social wasps.

Jumping spiders have been shown to distinguish between biological and nonbiological motion (De Agrò, Rößler, Kim, & Shamble, 2021). De Agrò et al. used displays of 11 moving dots. If the dots are on human joints, displays look like moving humans to human observers. De Agrò et al. constructed similar displays based on spider joints and presented spiders with those displays as well as displays based on moving geometrical figures and random displays. They found that the spiders looked longer at the nonbiological motion. This difference may reflect high-level perception as shown in humans of biological motion. Alternatively, it could reflect cognition.

Flying insects are subject to evolutionary pressure to reduce the size of their brains (Godfrey-Smith, 2017). Godfrey-Smith speculates (in a talk at NYU) that the lifestyle of wasps, combining excellent vision, short lifespan, and limited capacity for learning, pairs with perceptually controlled stereotyped action sequences rather than cognition.

Wasps are capable of "classical" ("Pavlovian") associative conditioning but have not been shown to be capable of the kind of instrumental or operant conditioning in which a reward (or punishment) affects the probability or strength of the behavior that led to the reward (Godfrey-Smith, 2017; Perry, Barron, & Cheng, 2013). In classical conditioning, a light stimulus paired with food can lead to an appetitive response in the presence of the light without the food. In operant (or "instrumental") conditioning, a *voluntary* response that leads to food is then used by the animal to get food, as when a rat learns to press a bar to get a reward. Operant conditioning is more complex than classical conditioning; indeed it is usually considered to include classical conditioning as a component (Perry et al., 2013). (The pairing of the food with the bar press elicits an appetitive response that the animal voluntarily harnesses to get food.) A creature that does not have operant conditioning may have no cognition either.

The stereotyped action patterns of the sphex wasp were famously described by Wooldridge (Dennett, 1984; Hofstadter, 1979; Wooldridge, 1963).

> When the time comes for egg laying, the wasp Sphex builds a burrow for the purpose and seeks a cricket which she stings in such a way as to paralyze but not kill it. She drags the cricket into the burrow, lays her eggs alongside, closes the burrow, then flies away, never to return. In due course, the eggs hatch and the wasp grubs feed off the paralyzed cricket, which has not decayed, having been kept in the wasp equivalent of a deepfreeze. To the human mind, such an elaborately organized and seemingly purposeful routine conveys a convincing flavor of logic and thoughtfulness—until more details are examined. For example, the wasp's routine is to bring the paralyzed cricket to the burrow, leave it on the threshold, go inside to see that all is well, emerge, and then drag the cricket in. If, while the wasp is inside making her preliminary inspection, the cricket is moved a few inches away, the wasp, on emerging from the burrow, will bring the cricket back to the threshold, but not inside, and will then repeat the preparatory procedure of entering the burrow to see that everything is all right. If again the cricket is removed a few inches while the wasp is inside, once again the wasp will move the cricket up to the threshold and re-enter the burrow for a final check. The wasp never thinks of pulling the cricket straight in. On one occasion this procedure was repeated forty times, always with the same result." (Wooldridge, 1963, pp. 82–83)[2]

---

[2] Keijzer (2013) argues that Wooldridge exaggerates. In the most systematic study he describes, using 31 wasps, 10 repeated until the end of the experiment, 10 broke the loop, and the others seem a grab-bag of cases. However, no single stereotyped action patterns should be expected to operate exceptionlessly. Perhaps different stereotyped action patterns are mixed, probabilistically. Keijzer

Sphex wasps lay their eggs in crickets but apparently are not able to count the crickets they have placed in the nest. They drag the crickets into the nest by the antennae but if the antennae are cut off they do not drag the cricket in by the legs.

Wasps show no sign of "wound tending," in which a damaged animal will protect and groom the affected part, making them good candidates for zombies with no phenomenal consciousness (Godfrey-Smith, 2016b). If a wasp tears a part of its body, it carries on, taking no notice of and without favoring the affected part. This suggests that wasps do not feel pain. Of course, the lack of pain mechanisms is compatible with other forms of consciousness attaching to mechanisms that wasps do have—such as perception. But given that consciousness may have evolved originally as a motivating force, the lack of that force in its most salient use is an indication of lack of consciousness. Bees have been shown not to prefer water with morphine in it when part of a leg is chopped off, though as far as I know this has not been tested with wasps (Groening, Venini, & Srinivasan, 2017). Still, the result with bees does suggest that pain may not be part of insect physiology.

Ants show "social" wound tending (Frank, Wehrhahn, & Linsenmair, 2018) in the sense that nest-mates groom the injuries of other ants, greatly decreasing the chance of infection. Interestingly, lightly wounded ants will adjust their behavior, acting as if their injuries are worse than they are around nest-mates. Note that social wound tending does not indicate conscious pain on the part of the wounded ant.

Given all this, the likelihood that (solitary) wasps have anything that we could call concepts seems low, so they are excellent candidates for nonconceptual perception. (Cf. Burge, 2010a; Peacocke, 2001a). (Disagreements about related issues can be found in Bermudez, 1994, and Peacocke, 1992b, 2002.) At the very least, the susceptibility to evidence of the claim that the wasps have perception without cognition shows it is not a conceptual truth that perception requires concepts or cognition. Of course I am assuming that there is no hidden contradiction in the claim that solitary wasps have perception without concepts or cognition.

To avoid misunderstanding, note that I am not arguing that we *know* or even have very good reason to think that wasps have perception without concepts, cognition, or consciousness. Rather, wasps are candidates for such a status.

I expect that some philosophers will be tempted to deny that wasps perceive at all, if it really is true that their perception is not conscious and if they have no cognitive states that could be thought of as perceptual judgments. However, common sense and science both tell us that wasps perceive (Burge, 2010b). The

---

also argues that in certain cases, fixed action patterns may be useful from an evolutionary point of view. However, stereotyped behavior that is evolutionarily selected is still stereotyped behavior.

wasp has a visual system that in rough outline is like ours. It uses its eyes to see its prey and uses vision to track and ambush it. The wasp sees that the cricket is no longer on the threshold of the burrow and that is why the wasp moves the cricket to the threshold. There have been debates about whether humans have unconscious perception, but those debates revolve around the issue of whether unconscious perceptual representations are at the "individual" level or whether they are subindividual (Block & Phillips, 2016; Peters, Kentridge, Phillips, & Block, 2017; Phillips, 2018). In the case of the wasp, I don't see how it could be claimed that the wasp's visual states are not at the individual level, given their role in guiding the wasp's actions.

If I am right that wasps perceive colors and shapes and that their perceptions have color contents and shape contents, then there is a kind of perception that is not dependent on or derived from concepts.

As we will see in Chapter 5, there are some views of concepts that can accept that the Sphex wasp has no cognition but still maintain that it has perceptual concepts in virtue of the wasp's ability to perceptually identify and track objects (Green & Quilty-Dunn, 2017; Mandelbaum, 2017; Quilty-Dunn, 2020). The disagreement here is not merely verbal but reflects different views of what empirical science tells us are the right categories for understanding the mind. I do agree with Green, Quilty-Dunn, and Mandelbaum, though, and disagree with advocates of a cognitive view of concepts (Camp, 2009) on the importance of stimulus independence as a rough guide to what representations are concepts. More on that topic later in this chapter.

What is a joint?

A joint is a fundamental and explanatorily significant difference between the kinds that are separated by the joint. Perception and cognition function differently in the mental economies of organisms that have them and in how they themselves are to be explained. For example, cognitive states—but not perceptual states—are formed by processes of reasoning and affect other states by processes of reasoning. The formation of perceptual states—but not cognitive states—involves direct effects of "constancy" mechanisms (Burge, 2010a). Perception functions to provide us with information about what is happening in the nearby environment now, whereas cognition functions in reasoning about the news provided by perception so as to decide what to do and to plan for the future.

To understand a difference in kinds, it may help to know what a kind is. There are many theoretical disputes about kinds (Franklin-Hall, 2015; Kitcher, 2007; Taylor, 2020, 2022). Rather than start with any theoretical position on what a joint is, I propose to frame the discussion of joints around actual examples of joints. Examples: gravitational/electromagnetic forces, hydrogen/helium, lepton/quark, liquid/solid, animals/plants. These examples show us that a joint is compatible with considerable causal interaction across the joint. Plants and animals interact and even co-evolved. For example, colors of flowers co-evolved with color vision in bees. And as mentioned earlier, a joint is compatible with intermediate or indeterminate cases. Red algae, mushrooms, slime mold, and giant kelp are neither plants nor animals. Viruses are neither alive like animals nor inanimate like rocks. Joints can be a matter of clusters of properties. For example, both animals and plants have vacuoles, storage bags of the cells, but plants tend to have one large vacuole whereas animal cells have one or more small vacuoles. There are some binary differences though. Both animal and plant cells have a cell membrane but only plants have a cell wall. And animal cells do not have chloroplasts, except temporarily when they eat plants. Although the joint between liquids and solids is explanatorily important, its role in explanations in physics and chemistry is background not foreground in current disputes and I expect that the same is true of the joint between perception and cognition.

Perception is iconic, nonconceptual, and nonpropositional, constitutively, or at least these features are explanatorily deep properties of perception. (See the next section.) These properties are necessary but not jointly sufficient for perception. For example, hallucination has all these properties but is not perception. And imaginings—visual simulations— with all three properties can be used to decide which peg fits in the hole. Perhaps the cognitive process of deciding what fits in the hole could not have occurred without the visual simulation and in that sense that particular token cognitive process essentially has all three properties. But cognition per se does not require any of the three properties.

I will list cases of the three properties that are not cases of perception in this footnote so as to easily refer back to it later.[3] The project of this book is to

---

[3] Hallucinations and visual imaginings are iconic, nonconceptual, and nonpropositional without being perception (because of the absence of the normal causal relation to objects perceived). That normal causal relation could be included in an analysis of the ordinary concept of perception, but I do not regard it as part of the fundamental scientific nature of perception. See the section on conceptual engineering in this chapter. Another kind of failure of the sufficient condition has to do with the distinction between sensation and perception, the difference being that sensation lacks the objective import of perception, argued by Tyler Burge to involve perceptual constancies (Burge, 2010a). The representation-like states of sensation are iconic, nonconceptual, and nonpropositional without being perceptual. So, if perception is a natural kind, an additional requirement of constancies would have to be imposed.

Thought can perhaps use mental maps, perceptual memories, and perceptual anticipations without conceptualization of them (Burge, 2010a; Fridland, 2014), though see the discussion later in this chapter for evidence that maplike structures may be the foundation of conceptual thinking. In Chapter 5, there will be a discussion of iconic representations used in cognition, such as iconic representation of number. Perceptual simulations can be used in cognition though perhaps only by being conceptualized. Standard imagistic cognition tasks include deciding if the tip of a horse's tail goes below the horse's "knees," whether there is a letter formed by rotating a capital 'N' 90 degrees (either clockwise or counterclockwise). One can use perceptual simulations in all sorts of cognitive tasks, for example, imagining the layout of one's apartment in order to decide how many paint shades are needed.

elucidate some characteristics that are fundamental to perception that are not fundamental to cognition. I am not aiming at conditions that are both necessary and sufficient for perception—nor conditions that are necessary and sufficient for cognition.

Although I am not aiming at conditions that are both necessary and sufficient I am not ruling out such conditions at least for perception. And I firmly reject views such as the "cluster concept" view of perception that are incompatible with necessary and sufficient conditions.

William Alston offered a cluster concept view of the concept of religion (Alston, 1967). He noted a number of elements that are common to religions, belief in a supreme being, a distinction between sacred and profane, rituals and morality based in the sacred, religious feelings, prayer, a worldview, an organization of life based on the worldview, and a social group based on elements of the cluster. As he noted, for each these elements, there are actual and possible religions that lack that element. For example, some forms of Buddhism do not involve belief in a supreme being and Quakers have no sacred objects.

My objection to the cluster concept account of perception is that it does not allow for necessary conditions. I have the same objection to Richard Boyd's homeostatic property cluster view of natural kinds (Boyd, 1989, 1991; Taylor, 2020). As I will be arguing, iconicity, nonconceptuality, and nonpropositionality are necessary and fundamental to perception.

The architecture of a computer is a matter of relatively fixed structural organization of computational components. It is commonly said that architecture is a matter of hardware as opposed to software. That isn't quite right since Macs and PCs have different hardwares but can both be programmed to have modules that only accept one kind of input, say an input with a certain tag.

One architectural division of the mind is that there are properties that are representable by cognition but not perception. For example, cognition but not perception can represent that an action is justified (Green, 2020a). Arguably, there are features of the world that perception can represent, e.g., according to some philosophers but not others, fine-grained colors are not representable by cognition (Evans, 1982; McDowell, 1994; Raffman, 1995). It isn't clear how deep these differences are. One can certainly imagine a creature whose cognition and perception are more aligned than ours.

One could perhaps fashion an ungainly necessary and sufficient characterization of perception in terms of being constitutively nonconceptual, nonpropositional, and iconic, while having objective import (unlike sensation) and involving actual objects in an appropriate causal relation to the perceptual state (unlike hallucination, mental maps, perceptual memories, perceptual anticipations, and perceptual simulations). I am offering this characterization only in a footnote instead of the text because I am not in the business of offering necessary and sufficient conditions. The conditions just sketched depend on a list of problematic kinds of cases that may not be complete.

I will be arguing that there are deeper differences in format and type of state that would still persist even if there were no differences in what properties are represented.

Constitutivity vs. explanatory depth

I am claiming that iconicity, nonconceptuality and nonpropositionality are constitutive, or at least explanatorily deep properties of perception. What is the difference between constitutivity and explanatory depth? The difference is not very important to the themes of this book, so I will be brief. There is a case for constitutivity but a stronger case for explanatory depth.

The difference between what is constitutive of perception and what is an explanatorily deep property of it concerns what kind of a concept the concept of perception is. I have tried to steer clear of arguments based solely on "intuitions" in this book, but when the question is what kind of a concept our concept is, intuitions are relevant. I'll focus on two alternatives: whether perception is a natural kind concept or a functional concept. These are not the only possibilities, but they are the best candidates.

Issues about concepts can be discussed in terms of the words that express those concepts. This issue about the concept of perception can be discussed in terms of the question of whether the word "perception" has a "natural kind" or a "functional kind" semantics. Hilary Putnam famously imagined that there could be a planet, "Twin Earth," in which a there is a chemical XYZ that has no hydrogen or oxygen but is still "watery" in Chalmers's (1996) sense of having the observable properties of water, including being colorless and odorless, sustaining life, falling from the sky, and occupying rivers and streams and oceans (Putnam, 1975). Although the denizens of Twin Earth—whom we can imagine to be neural duplicates of us—use their term "water" to refer to the watery XYZ in their oceans, *our* word "water" and our concept of water do not apply to XYZ. We should say rather that the liquid in their oceans is the functional equivalent of water but is not water. If this is right, the concept of water is said to be a natural kind concept and the semantics of the term "water" involves natural kind semantics.

The natural kind semantics of "water" contrasts with the functional kind semantics of "mousetrap" and "philosopher." The mousetraps and philosophers of Twin Earth might be constructed differently from and composed of different materials from our mousetraps and philosophers, but if they are the functional equivalent of our mousetraps and philosophers, then they are genuine mousetraps and philosophers. Philosophers who disagree with Putnam's view that "water" has a natural kind semantics can hold that "water" has a functional semantics—any watery liquid is water.

Metaphysicians distinguish between possible worlds considered as counterfactual and possible worlds considered as actual (Chalmers, 1996; Davies & Humberstone, 1980). I will explain—assuming Putnamian views about water as a natural kind. In considering Putnam's Twin Earth world as counterfactual, we hold fixed the actual composition of water, considering whether the stuff in the counterfactual ocean is water. The stuff in the counterfactual ocean is water if and only if it is H_2O. We can say that the term "water" is metaphysically "rigid," denoting water (i.e., H_2O) in every world in which it exists. When we think about a counterfactual world, we use our term "water," anchored in H_2O, to consider whether the world contains water. If the oceans in the counterfactual world are filled with XYZ and not H_2O, they are not filled with water.

A world considered as actual is an actual world candidate. Instead of holding the actual composition of water fixed, we ask ourselves what we should say if we discovered that the actual watery stuff in our oceans is XYZ. We should say that water turns out to be XYZ. We can put this by saying that the term "water" is epistemically nonrigid in that it does not denote the same stuff in every world considered as actual. In Putnam's Twin Earth considered as an actual world candidate instead of as a counterfactual world, "water" would refer to XYZ. See Chalmers (2012a, pp. 238ff, 318ff).

Although XYZ is not water, if Twin Earth is merely distant in space rather than being counterfactual, and if we had regular travel between earth and Twin Earth, we might broaden the concept we attach to the word "water" to cover both H_2O and XYZ. Since I am a Putnamian who thinks "water" has a default natural kind semantics, I think this would be a change of meaning and concept. The changed concept would dictate that whatever functions like actual water is water.

In my view, "perception" is like "water" in having a default natural kind semantics. When I discussed my book at Chris Hill's and Adam Pautz's seminar at Brown in October 2020, Pautz pressed me on this, both in the seminar and in our discussions afterward, arguing that I had not given reason to prefer the view that perception is a natural kind to the view that it is a functional kind.

How can the reader decide whether "perception" has a natural kind or functional semantics? (I am ignoring the possibility both are wrong.) A good way to proceed is to consider what to say about various candidates for perceivers. Would creatures that process stimulation in a way that is roughly functionally equivalent to our visual perception but via representations that are conceptual, propositional, and discursive be seeing or even perceiving? I say no, but a functionalist about perception should say yes.

Let us focus on the claim I will be making in Chapters 4 and 5 that perception is constitutively nonpropositional and iconic. One consideration that I will be appealing to in arguing for the constitutive nonpropositionality of seeing is that the contents of perception cannot be logically complex. We can see something as a mixture of red and blue or as indeterminate between red and blue but not as *simply red or simply blue*, i.e., as having the disjunctive property of being simply red or simply blue. We cannot see something as *if red then round*, that is, as having the conditional property of being round if red. And, I will argue, that although this case is less straightforward, that perceptual contents cannot be negative and they cannot be conjunctive.

Consider the possibility of a robot that has digital cameras whose outputs are pixel array representations that the robot treats as premises in inferences and uses them to reason about the causes in the environment of those arrays. Let us suppose that the robot can "visually" represent something as having the conditional property of being if red, then round. The robot can also "visually" represent something as having the disjunctive property of being red or blue. And let us suppose that it "visually" represents the disjunctive property using discursive representations rather than iconic representations. For concreteness, we could suppose the representations are strings of words. Would that robot have visual perception? I would describe the robot as having light transducers that directly produce discursive thought, skipping the stage of perception.

To be clear, the issue concerns seeing-as, not seeing-that. Seeing-that includes the products of inference from seeing-as. As Fred Dretske once commented, I can see that the gas tank is empty by looking at the gas gauge, even though the gas tank is not visible. Seeing-that can have logically complex contents, inferred from seeing-as. I can see that either the tank is empty or the gas gauge is broken.

I am not talking about seeing-that in that sense. I am talking about perceptual attribution, i.e., seeing-as; and in particular, the putative perceptual attribution of the conditional property of being if red, then round. It is in that sense that I am saying it is wrong to suppose anyone or anything could literally see something as if red, then round, or as having the disjunctive property of being simply red or simply blue.

I am appealing here to my own intuitions about the application of the concept of seeing. Imagine a conversation with the robot who claims to see the moon as if gray, then round. You say "You mean you see it as gray and then expect it to be round? Or do you mean you see it as gray and also as round?" It says "No neither of those is what I mean. I see it as having a conditional property."

I haven't said anything about whether the robot is conscious, but if one brings in consciousness, the point seems more convincing. If we ask the robot, "You mean it looks conditional?" And it answers, "Yes, it looks this way: if gray, then round," one might naturally conclude that the robot is misapplying the concept of seeing.

It is hard to imagine what it would be like to see something as if gray, then round. It may be said, though, that this point about visual imagination can be explained by appeal to the deep explanatory nature of perception rather than its constitutive properties. I can't imagine seeing with conditional contents, because in trying to imagine it I must use my visual system, which is not capable of conditional contents. So, according to the objection, my failure of imagination is due to a deep explanatory property of human perception, not a constitutive property of all perception.

In reply I say that although I am incapable of bat-style sonar, I can in some reasonable sense understand it. So I doubt that it is restrictions on imagining that make the robot just described seem to be a nonperceiver.

How can we distinguish between the actual properties of perception that are constitutive and those that are not? One method is to use thought experiments like the one described above involving robots that process stimuli in a way that deviates from actual processing of stimuli. We see via light, electromagnetic radiation with wavelengths of 400–700 nm (a nanometer being a billionth of a meter). But one can imagine a robot with a visual system much like ours that sees or at least perceives via electromagnetic radiation of much shorter (e.g., X-rays) or longer wavelengths (e.g., microwave radiation). And one can imagine perception using many other propagating signals.

Compare the case of our building robots whose vision uses X-Rays instead of light with our chemists producing small quantities of XYZ. In the former case, one would be imagining robots that see but in the latter case we would be imagining watery stuff that is not water.

Just as water being identical to H_2O precludes a watery substance that is not H_2O from being water, so the fact that perception is a form of iconic and nonpropositional representation precludes the robot described as having visual perception. Deciding to call the robot camera system "perception" would be deciding on a change of meaning.

I agree that it may be that the language would develop so as to give "perception" a functional kind semantics, but I believe that if it does, the term "perception" will have changed its meaning so as to denote a functional kind, just as "water" would change its meaning if we were to merge language communities with the residents of Twin Earth. Whether the language does develop in that way I think will depend on the social role of robots. If their social role involves our conceiving of them as not at all like us, then we may think of their cameras as writing directly into thought, skipping the stage of seeing. But if they are regarded as just a different kind of person, then it will be natural to conceptually engineer the term "visual perception" to encompass the conversion of light stimulation into cognitive representations.

Sometimes the issue of whether we are referring to a natural kind or a functional kind is framed in terms of the intentions of normal speakers of the language in question. David Lewis held that natural kinds are "reference magnets" and this has been explained in terms of the intentions of speakers. If speakers intend to refer to natural properties, then speakers must have the concept of naturalness, which seems most unlikely. Even less likely is the supposition that ordinary speakers who talk about seeing have the concepts of format, concept, or proposition. It cannot be that ordinary users of words like "see" and "perceive" intend to refer to a capacity with a certain format or a capacity that is nonconceptual.

What makes much more sense is that speakers' implicit intentions drive them in the direction of treating natural properties as the reference of kind-terms, even though subjects do not have the requisite concepts. Thus, naturalness would have a theory-external role, as Lewis thought (Chalmers, 2012b; Lewis, 1984; Sider, 2011).

Although I am defending the idea that "perception" and in particular "vision" has a natural kind semantics, I don't have a high level of certainty about this. As Gareth Evans emphasized (1982), there is a good deal of indeterminacy in the referential intentions of common-sense reasoning. For this reason, I want to emphasize my fall-back position that the properties of perception that I am delineating are explanatorily deep rather than constitutive.[4]

The contents of perception

Views of perception differ in whether they acknowledge that perception has representational content. Many "naïve realists" think of perception as a direct awareness relation to objects and properties in the world (Brewer, 2011; Campbell, 2002). Some naïve realists allow representational content in unconscious subpersonal states (Travis, 2004). Naïve realists struggle with perceptual illusions in which we perceptually misrepresent the world. Naïve realists also struggle with the effects of attention on perception, in which attention makes stimuli look higher in contrast, faster, stripier (higher in "spatial frequency"), or higher in color saturation (Block, 2019a; Brewer, 2019).

I have discussed naïve realism elsewhere (Block, 2010, 2019a) and will not be repeating those discussions here. Except for a short discussion in Chapter 13, I won't be discussing naïve realism here since I am presupposing an orientation shaped by the science of perception. The science of perception is deeply committed to perceptual representation (though see French and Phillips, 2020). In the next section, I will give a few examples of how practice in vision science presupposes representation and representational content.

One argument for perception having content appeals to perceptual experience. Susanna Siegel notes that there is a powerful argument from the fact that something looks red to the conclusion that the perception is accurate if and only

---

[4] I am indebted to conversation with Adam Pautz concerning this section.

if what is seen is red (Siegel, 2010), in which case the accuracy condition can just be taken to be the content of the perception.

The content of a representation, as I am using the term, is the way it represents the world to be. Contents are indexed by accuracy conditions. My perception as of a red object at a certain location represents a red object at a certain location and is accurate just in case there is a red object in that location (Siegel, 2006, 2016). Note that the category of accuracy conditions is wider than that of truth conditions. For example, noun phrases have accuracy conditions but not truth conditions. The noun phrase "that red object in that location" is accurate just in case the "that" singles out a red object in that location. Although I reject the claim that perceptual content is constitutively singular, I do agree with Crane and Burge that the content of perception is more like the content of a noun phrase than like the content of a sentence (Burge, 2010a; Crane, 2009).

The reader may wonder what the cash value is of the difference between "That red object" and "That is a red object." Tim Crane says what is important is that accuracy admits of degrees but truth does not (Crane, 2009, p. 458: "Accuracy is not truth, since accuracy admits of degrees and truth does not"). This is not my view. Degree-related talk is somewhat more natural for accuracy than for truth, but this is not a principled difference. One could also use degree-related talk for truth. For example, people describe one theory as a closer approximation to the truth than another.

What is important from my point of view is that propositional representations can be used in content-based transitions in which the representations can serve as premises or conclusions in reasoning. The use of "is" and the term "true" as opposed to "accurate" are markers for that deeper difference. (By reasoning I mean a certain kind of content-based rational transition in thought in which propositional representation can serve as premises or conclusions.)

Of course, one can move from a perception that something is red to the judgment that it is red. Why isn't that "move" the right kind of content-based rational transition in thought? That issue is the burden of Chapter 4 and to some extent Chapter 6.

It is often assumed that the content of perception is propositional content, that is, that in perception one bears the perception relation to a proposition (Byrne, 2005; Pautz, 2009). This view was famously endorsed by John McDowell, who claimed that the propositional and conceptual nature of perceptual content is required in order to understand how perception can justify perceptual belief when a perceptual experience is taken at face value (McDowell, 1994). McDowell says (p. 26), "That things are thus and so is the content of the experience, and it can also be the content of a judgement: it becomes the content of a judgement if the subject decides to take the experience at face value. So it is conceptual content." (See McDowell, 2019, for a somewhat different view.) However, epistemologists should want a conception of perceptual content that is not contradicted by the science of perception.

A distinction is often made between intrinsic and derived intentionality (Haugeland, 1980; Searle, 1980). Words on paper have derived intentionality in that their representational contents depend on the minds that use those representations. The representations that the minds use do not themselves depend for their contents on representations other than other mental representations, so they have intrinsic intentionality.[5] If there were no minds, marks on paper that happened to look just like words would have no content. Indeed, there was no doubt a time in the history of the human race when there was mental representation without external representation. In these terms, the content of perception is intrinsic, not derived.

The treatment of perceptual contents in terms of accuracy conditions contrasts with treatments of perceptual contents that are grounded in the phenomenology of conscious perception, for example the "appears/looks" conception and the view that the content of a perception consists in the properties that the object presents to us (Chalmers, 2006; Pautz, 2009). When an unconscious perception becomes conscious, a content of an unconscious perception becomes a content or part of a content of a conscious perception, so the most basic account of the content of perception will apply both to conscious and unconscious perception. Many accounts of perceptual content do not even purport to apply to all perception, conscious and unconscious. For example, Adam Pautz's "identity" conception of content says that experiential properties are relations to contents, thereby giving a theory that does not apply to both conscious and unconscious perception (Pautz, 2009).

Fred Dretske (2007, 2010) argued that there was a kind of seeing that is nonconceptual and requires no noticing, attending, or classification of the item seen. He contrasted this "simple" seeing with fact-seeing or seeing-that. I do not recognize any such kind of seeing, though I think we can speak of seeing in a way that makes no commitment to classification. I think all seeing is seeing-as (Block, 2014c) in that vision always attributes properties. (This issue is taken up in Chapter 3.) I do agree with Dretske that seeing is nonconceptual and requires no noticing. (The jury is out on attending.) But I also think that seeing often involves something that can be called categorization, something over and above the mere attribution of properties. This thesis will be spelled out and evidence provided in Chapter 6 in discussing categorical perception of color without concepts of color.

---

[5] As far as I know, this distinction was first introduced into the literature in John Haugeland's comment on Searle's "Minds, Brains and Programs." In his response to Haugeland (the references in the text are to these two publications), Searle gives the distinction his own terminology, which I have used here. Haugeland used "original" and "derivative."

Realism about perceptual and cognitive representation

I will be assuming that there are genuine perceptual representations. I will give some arguments for representations here and there will be a brief discussion of opposed views such as naïve realism and enactivism in the context of debates about consciousness in Chapter 13.

I am a realist about representation and representational content—in contrast to J. J. Gibson (1979) on representation generally and Frances Egan (2014) on representational content. I do not, however, assume that these mental representations have their contents essentially—that is, that a mental representation could not change its content without becoming a different representation or that if a mental representation had had a different content it would have been a different representation. And I will not be assuming that there is a reductive account of representation. So I am not assuming hyperrepresentationalism about mental content in Egan's terms (2014, 2018).

In my view, realism about mental representation and representational content is baked into the practice of perceptual psychology and cognitive science, as is especially clear in discussions of illusory perception. Where there is misrepresentation, there is representation because perceptual misrepresentation shows that perceptual representation cannot be thought of along the lines of Gricean "natural meaning." As Grice (1957) noted, we can say that the spots mean measles, but it would be contradictory to say that the spots mean measles but the spotted person doesn't have measles. Natural meaning in Grice's terminology contrasts with nonnatural meaning. We can say that the three bells mean the bus is full, and that allows for error. There is no contradiction in saying the three rings mean that the bus is full but it isn't. Perceptual illusions are cases of nonnatural meaning: They are cases of error.

It may be said that illusion can be glossed without representation: An antirepresentation advocate may say that an illusory perception is one in which the visual system gives its usual response to a certain feature in a situation in which the feature is not instantiated. But that antirepresentational gloss cannot explain the fact that the practice of vision science does not assume that perception is usually veridical.

It may be said that representation is reducible to a concoction of responsivity, functional role, and teleology. If so, that does not show there are no representations. Water is reducible to H_2O, but no one will conclude that there is no water. Reduction as applied to water, heat, temperature, light, etc., is distinct from elimination as applied to caloric, phlogiston, and witches.

I will describe a controversy in vision science that does not assume that perception is usually veridical. It is particularly useful because neither the problem nor its solution can be understood without assuming that perception is representational.

The controversy involves "peripheral inflation," a phenomenon to be discussed in more detail later in Chapter 13. Acuity, contrast sensitivity, and color sensitivity decline exponentially in the peripheral visual field, although most people do not report a decline in colorfulness or sharpness across the visual field. Galvin and colleagues (Galvin, O'Shea, Squire, & Govan, 1997) showed that when subjects matched the appearance of peripheral with foveally viewed edges, an blurrier edge in the periphery tended to be matched with a sharper edge in the fovea. Galvin et al. concluded that there is an illusion of sharpness in the peripheral visual field and there have been similar claims for colorfulness.

It should be obvious that we cannot understand the idea of ubiquitous illusions of sharpness and colorfulness in the peripheral visual field without assuming that perception is representational.

But are there really such illusions? Galvin et al. were implicitly adopting foveal appearance as veridical and anything that deviates from it as illusory. But neither foveal nor peripheral vision should be regarded as "the" standard of veridical perception. A perceptual ability cannot tell us about properties to which it is not sensitive (Anstis, 1998; Haun, 2021). In foveal vision, we can't see spatial frequencies above 50 cycles per degree. (See the caption and text surrounding Figure 1.1 for an explanation of spatial frequency.) In peripheral vision, our sensitivity is lower, but that is not a defect any more than it is a defect of foveal vision to not be sensitive to 70 cycles per degree. Nor is it a defect of color vision that it is not sensitive to ultraviolet or infrared light.

Colorfulness and sharpness are perceptual qualities that arise in different portions of the visual field in a way that is dependent on what kinds of sensitivities exist in *that part of the visual field*. An edge that would look blurry in foveal vision would look sharp in peripheral vision if the spatial frequency sensitivity required to see the blur was above the sensitivity of that part of peripheral vision. Then that edge would be matched in subjective sharpness to a sharper edge in foveal vision, explaining the Galvin et al. result.

Blurriness and sharpness have to be understood as *relative to grain of representation*. And that fact shows that blurriness and sharpness cannot adequately be discussed in a framework that eschews representation.

We have to distinguish physical properties like reflectance spectra from subjective properties like perceived colorfulness and sharpness (Haun, 2021). Subjective representation of sharpness and colorfulness depends on what the perceptual channel is sensitive to, and there are differences in that regard between peripheral and foveal vision.

This point does not make vision always veridical. Visual representation of a colorless display as colorful would of course be illusory. Representation of a sharp edge would be illusory if there is no edge. The point rather is that the veridicality of a representation of an edge in the periphery depends only on the low spatial frequencies that can be detected in the periphery and not on the high-spatial frequencies that can be detected in the fovea.

In sum, at least one aspect of the phenomenon of so-called peripheral inflation cannot be understood without appeal to visual representation.

Still another representational debate concerns the "tilted coin." Do we see the tilted circular coin as circular, as elliptical, or as both? It is hard to get a handle on this debate except via consideration of what is represented in vision. The controversy concerns the question of whether we have two representations of the shape of the tilted coin, of both the circular and elliptical shapes, or whether we have only one, of the circular shape. The naïve realist would have to say that the controversy concerns whether we are directly aware of both the circular and elliptical shapes. But that construal is inadequate to understanding the experimental reasoning.

For example, Morales, Bax, and Firestone (2020) did experiments that suggest that a representation of a tilted circular coin interferes with a representation of an elliptically shaped coin seen head-on, the upshot being that the representation of a tilted circular coin also involves a representation of its circular shape. The explanation here concerns interference of representations and is not adequately construed in terms of direct awareness of shapes.

I don't mean to endorse the reasoning of Morales, et al. The fact that children find it difficult to master the ability to report perspectival shapes and that even professional artists take longer to report perspectival than objective shapes suggests that the perspectival shape may be only postperceptually represented [Perdreau & Cavanagh, 2011].) (See Burge and Burge, 2022, for a reply to Morales, et al. and the reply by Morales, et al. in the same issue.)

Another type of finding that supplies direct evidence of visual representation comes from single case deficit studies. Michael McCloskey and his colleagues examined a subject who made bizarre errors of mislocation of visual targets. By analyzing her errors, McCloskey was able to show that she separately represented distance and direction from an "origin" whose location was dictated by the location of spatial attention (2009). She was much more accurate on distance from the origin than on direction from the origin, suggesting separate representations of these quantities. The reasoning involved here and its support of representational realism is very nicely spelled out in Chapter 2 of Karen Neander's (2017) book. Her treatment explains in detail why the subject's perceptual representations are intensional.

It may be said by those who reject realism that the practice of the science of perception embeds pragmatic decisions that have to be accepted by anyone who wants to join the field so that what the field takes as representation is not objectively representation. But what the field accepts is the task of understanding perception, what it is, how it works, and how it fits into the rest of the mind. That should be enough for real representation.

Three-layer methodology

Here is the methodology used in this book for assessing whether there is a joint in nature between perception and cognition and what constitutes it if it exists. Recall that minimal immediate direct perceptual judgment is the kind of cognitive state that is hardest to distinguish from perception, so my focus will be on distinguishing perception from that kind of perceptual judgment.

1. Use prescientific ways of thinking of the perception/cognition border to make a preliminary classification of representations, states, and processes as definitely perceptual, as definitely cognitive, and as not definitely either. As explained below, one armchair approach appeals to the idea that perception has the function of being stimulus-dependent in a way that cognition is not; others focus on immediate warrant, and others focus on observable properties.
2. Look for scientific indicators that make sense of the pretheoretic classifications while being aware that the scientific indicators may not always agree with the prescientific classifications. The main scientific indicator to be used below is perceptual adaptation, but also rivalry, pop-out, illusory contours, and speed of processing. Many other scientific indicators could have been chosen. Each of these indicators is dependent on the others, in a benign circular dependence I will argue that the scientific indicators give a better picture of what is perceptual and what cognitive than the armchair methods.
3. Consider whether the scientific indicators of perception/cognition are constitutive of perception/cognition or rather symptoms of constitutive features. I will suggest that the use of adaptation, rivalry, pop-out, illusory contours, and speed of processing have more to do with the functions of perception and cognition rather than their underlying natures.
4. Using the scientific indicators as indexes of what states and representations are perceptual and which cognitive, try to isolate the underlying constitutive features.

The prescientific indicators will be discussed in this chapter, the scientific indicators in Chapter 2, and the constitutive features in Chapters 4, 5, 6, and 7. Of course, this process can derail at any stage and the possibility that there are no explanatorily important differences to be found has to be kept in mind.

I am going to start in Chapter 2 with a first pass at the scientific indicators of perception and cognition and the problem of circularity in so doing. Focusing on perception, the problem of circularity is that the rationale for any indicator as an indicator of perception rather than cognition depends on the verdicts of other indicators. I will argue that the circularity is benign so long as there is a set of indicators that converge on the cases we are most sure of, classifying some cases as perceptual, others as cognitive, and none as both perceptual and cognitive.

The picture that I am assuming is that reality has an objective structure and one of the roles of science is to lay that structure bare. We have a pretheoretic grip on a distinction between perception and cognition, but the methods of Chapter 2 help us to refine those categories, putting some borderline cases on one side or the other and none on both sides. Once we have refined these categories, we can examine whether they have deeper natures and, if so, what they are. That is the topic of Chapters 4–8. Of course, the terms of refinement that I will be using— "nonpropositional," "nonconceptual," "iconic"—will no doubt themselves have borderline cases. I do not propose to characterize the border between perception and cognition in a way that eliminates all borderline cases.

Higher "capacity" in perception (whether conscious or not) than cognition

As I mentioned, the program of this book is to start with a discussion of the nature of perception and how it differs from cognition, putting aside issues of consciousness and phenomenology until the penultimate chapter of the book, Chapter 13. One of the advantages of this approach is that I can adapt arguments first used— ineffectively— with respect to consciousness and apply them with much greater effect as applied to perception. In this section I will describe one such approach.

Fragile visual short-term memory

Victor Lamme's laboratory at the University of Amsterdam demonstrated fragile visual short-term memory in a series of articles starting with Landman, Spekreijse, and Lamme (2003). In many of these experiments, the subject is shown briefly a circle of rectangles that can either be vertical or horizontal. There is a dot in the middle of the screen which the subject is supposed to fixate in the sense of pointing the eyes at it. The array is replaced by a blank screen for a variable period.

Then another array appears in which one of the rectangles may or may not have changed orientation. A line pointing to one of the locations—the cue— can appear at any one of three times; the subject's task is to say if the rectangle that the line points to changes orientation between the first array and the second array. In Figure 1.3, the rightmost box of the top sequence shows the cue at the last stage, the leftmost box of the middle sequence shows the cue at the beginning, and the third shows the crucial case in which the cue comes in the blank period after the first display has disappeared but the last display has not yet appeared.

Using statistical procedures that correct for guessing, Landman et al. (2003) computed a standard capacity measure showing how many rectangles the subject is able to track. When the cue comes at the beginning, subjects unsurprisingly are close to perfect. In the bottom part of Figure 1.3 there is a graph with three bars: The middle bar indicates that subjects have a capacity of nearly all eight of the rectangle orientations when the cue is at the beginning. (Similar results are obtained if the cue appears within 10 ms from the offset of the first array.) When the cue comes at the end, with the second array, subjects show the classic working memory capacity of roughly four items. (See the next subsection below and Chapters 5 and 6 on working memory.) Lamme and his colleagues argue that the second array has obliterated the ongoing perceptual representation of the first array. Thus, the subjects are able to deploy working memory so as to access only half of the rectangles despite the fact that subjects reported seeing all or almost all of the rectangles. This is a classic "change blindness" result.

The crucial manipulation is when the indicator comes on during the blank period after the original rectangles have gone off but before the new array has appeared. If the subjects are continuing to maintain a visual representation of the whole array and reading their answers off of it—as subjects say they are doing, the capacity measure should be higher than four items. The finding is that the capacity is between six and seven for up to about 4 seconds after the first stimulus has been turned off, suggesting that subjects are able to maintain a visual representation of all or most of the rectangles. This result backs up what the subjects say. Note that the rightmost and middle bars of the graph at the bottom of Figure 1.3 are nearly the same. Similar results using different types of stimuli were obtained by Jeremy Freeman and Denis Pelli at NYU (Freeman & Pelli, 2007).

Lamme has argued that a conscious memory image of the first array persists in the blank period before it is wiped out by the appearance of the second array. According to that point of view, what is both conscious and accessible during the blank period is *the impression of a circle of rectangles with their tilts specified clearly enough to distinguish vertical from horizontal*. In the blank period the orientations and shapes of the specific items are conscious but there is a

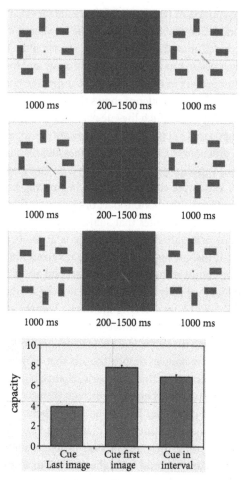

Figure 1.3 The paradigm of the Amsterdam group led by Victor Lamme. A circular array of eight rectangles is presented for 1 second. There is a blank period of up to 1.5 seconds, followed by a second array of eight rectangles. The second array may or may not contain a rectangle at a different orientation from the first array. One rectangle is cued by a line either in the last array, in the first array, or in the blank period in the middle. There is a free pdf on the Oxford University Press web site that has the color version of this and all the other figures. Thanks to Victor Lamme for this figure.

limitation on access: Necessarily, not all are accessed. None are inaccessible. Necessarily, most lottery tickets lose but there are no tickets that cannot win. Similarly, necessarily, many specific shapes are not accessed though none are inaccessible. The upshot is "overflow": The capacity of conscious perception overflows cognition.

Lamme's argument has been rejected by many critics on the ground that he has not provided any direct evidence that the fragile visual short-term memory representation is actually conscious (Byrne, Hilbert, & Siegel, 2007; Cohen & Dennett, 2011; de Gardelle, Sackur, & Kouider, 2009; Grush, 2007; Kouider, de Gardelle, & Dupoux, 2007; Kouider, de Gardelle, Sackur, & Dupoux, 2010; Phillips, 2011a, 2011b; Van Gulick, 2007). The critics say that what is conscious is *that there is a circle of rectangles*, but without the specification of the tilts. The idea is that the tilts are dredged up from unconscious memory when there is a cue. (See Sergent, et al., 2013.)

Advocates of Lamme's argument (Block, 2007a, 2008, 2011c) have argued that unconscious memory is too weak to support the high capacity revealed in the experiments by Lamme and colleagues. The critics' retort is that experiments on unconscious short-term memory require very degraded stimuli in order to make the perceptions unconscious, whereas the stimuli used by Lamme and colleagues are not degraded. The reply to that is that unconscious perception in normal subjects may require such degraded stimuli. Still, I think it is fair to say that this debate is at something of an impasse.

However, the use I am making of Lamme's results in this chapter is not vulnerable to this criticism. My point is that what the work by Lamme and his colleagues does show is that *perception has a higher capacity than cognition*. This shows that perception is fundamentally different from cognition, independently of issues of consciousness. This point is another illustration of the utility of my methodology of discussing perception independently of consciousness. In that way we can divide the question of greater capacity in conscious perception than in cognition into two questions: Is there a greater capacity in perception than cognition? Here the answer is clearly yes. And that answer strongly supports the thesis of this book that there is a joint in nature between perception and cognition.[6] The second question is, Is the excess capacity conscious? I will take up that question in Chapter 13.

A further point is that the limit of 3–4 items in working memory are, as Jake Quilty-Dunn noted, an "item effect," in which each item is encoded by a distinct vehicle, requiring more resources to represent more items (Quilty-Dunn, 2019a). Jerry Fodor, who coined the term "item effect" puts the point this way: "It is a rule of thumb that, all else being equal, the 'psychological complexity' of a discursive representation (for example, the amount of memory it takes to store it or to process it) is a function of the number of individuals whose properties it independently specifies. I shall call this the 'item effect' " (Fodor, 2007, p. 111).

---

[6] That the overflow argument can be given in a form that does not mention consciousness was also noted by Peter Carruthers (Carruthers, 2015, 2017).

Thus the 3-4 item limit in working memory suggests the discrete constituents typical of language of thought models.

There is one problem that has been raised concerning Lamme's argument that also applies to mine, and I will discuss that argument in the next subsection.

Slot vs. pool models

These experiments have been criticized for presupposing a "slot" model of working memory in which working memory has a limited capacity—roughly four items for many of the standard stimuli used in experiments like those described above (Gross, 2017, 2018; Gross & Flombaum, 2017). The calculation that allows capacities to be computed assumes limited capacity of working memory.

It is true that slots in working memory may not be part of the most basic level of explanation. At the most basic level, working memory allows for many representations at reduced levels of precision. But in certain conditions, slot-like behavior can emerge. When unfamiliar items that don't fit into a smallish set of categories are used, subjects do not show any clear limit in working memory. Instead, they show decreasing memory precision for larger sets. For example, the pictures (e.g., boat on a beach, narrow street, children holding hands) used in an experiment by Potter and her colleagues (2014) to be described in Chapter 8 show decreased memory precision for 12 items compared to 6 items but there is no sign in her data of any capacity limit. Fougnie, Cormiea, Kanabar, and Alvarez (2016) have shown that if given incentives to remember more items, subjects remember more items at decreased precision. By contrast, familiar closed class items that are easy to discriminate from one another, like digits, letters of the alphabet, and rectangles that can take a small set of cardinal orientations show working memory limits of up to four items.

Whether or not the representations of perception and working memory are probabilistic, there are notable types of slot-like behavior in working memory experiments (Adam & Serences, 2019; Adam, Vogel, & Awh, 2017; Bouchacourt & Buschman, 2019; Donkin, Kary, Tahir, & Taylor, 2016; Pratte, Park, Rademaker, & Tong; Xie & Zhang, 2017; Xu, Adam, Fang, & Vogel, 2018). Susan Carey has explored extensive slot-like working memory systems—the "parallel individuation" system—in infants who tend to have three rather than four slots (Carey, 2009).

One explanation of slot-like behavior has to do with the role of inhibition in suppressing less probable representations. Endress and Potter (2015; Endress & Siddique, 2016; Endress & Szabo, 2017) explain slot-like behavior in terms of an underlying variable precision model in which interference from long-term memory representations imposes slot-like processing. This slot-like behavior is often neglected in current controversies, for example by Gross and Flombaum (2017).

Hilary Putnam famously noted (1974) that a square peg of slightly under 1 inch on a side will fit through a 1-inch square hole in a board but not a 1-inch diameter round hole. The explanation of why the peg will fit through one hole but not the other need appeal only to the rigidity of the peg and the board and the geometry of the situation. Descending further to the level of the clouds of particles that make up the peg and the board will yield an explanation that is more general in one respect, since it can explain the cases in which the peg or the board deforms. But the explanation in terms of geometry and rigidity is more powerful in that it gives a simple explanation of why the square peg won't fit through the round hole, an explanation that would only be obscured by describing the peg and board as clouds of elementary particles. The geometry and rigidity explanation is more general in a way since it applies to rigid pegs and boards made of cellular substances like wood, lattice structures like ice or diamond and amorphous structures like glass.

Explanation in terms of "slots" in working memory is like explanation in terms of rigidity and geometry. The slots in working memory are as real as the rigidity of the board and pegs. The pool of resources model is more general in a respect, since it can explain both the cases in which there is slot-like behavior and those in which there is not. But the slot model gives a simple and elegant explanation of the special cases in which slot-like behavior emerges.

Although the slot vs. pool debate has been ongoing for some time, the pool model is often simply ignored in articles comparing different forms of memory, even in the best journals. For example, a recent article in *Current Biology* on iconic memory says, "The most stable form of short-term visual memory is working memory. Working memory is resistant to masking . . . , but it has a limited capacity of only a few items" (Teeuwen, Wacongne, Schnabel, Self, & Roelfsema, 2021).

Gross and his colleagues (Gross, 2017, 2018; Gross & Flombaum, 2017) see the difference between iconic memory, fragile short-term memory and working memory not in terms of a difference in capacity but in terms of how "flat" the probability representations of the items are. They think iconic memory and fragile memory have relatively flat curves, representing many things at decreased precision, whereas working memory tends to represent a few things at high precision and many other things at lower precision. This picture ignores the role of suppression in slot-like behavior as described in the Endress and Potter model described above. Gross et al. see these kinds of memory as basically the same, whereas because of the role of suppression, there are qualitative differences.[7]

The most fundamental point about the difference between working memory and iconic/fragile memory, however, is that they are different in format. As will be argued in detail in Chapter 5, iconic and fragile memory have the format of perception, namely iconic format. Working memory, by contrast, is discursive.

A recent experiment provides fairly direct evidence for a difference in format between iconic memory and working memory. Michael Pratte (2018) presented subjects with 10 colored squares, and after a retention interval that could be as short as 33 ms or as long as 1 s, one location was cued. Subjects were asked to indicate the color of the square at that location by moving a cursor to the appropriate point on a smoothly varying color wheel. As Pratte notes, many previous experiments used stimuli that do not allow for measurement of the precision of what is retained. But, following (Zhang & Luck, 2008) Pratte used color stimuli and color wheel responses that do allow for measurement of the precision of memory. See Figure 1.4.

Pratte was interested in comparing a "sudden death" model of decay of the icon with a gradual decay model. He found that the sudden death model predicted the results much better than the gradual decay model. As time went on, subjects remembered fewer of the colors, but the ones they did remember were remembered with as much precision at the end of the delay period as at the beginning. Over time, the guessing rate increased as the memory capacity decreased, but the precision stayed about the same. See Figure 1.5. A similar result was found in Experiment 2 of Pratte (2019), except in this experiment, subjects were given the color and gave a graded response as to the location that color had in the first

---

[7] Interested readers may want to consult the increasingly baroque controversy between advocates of models of working memory that are more partial to slot-like aspects and models that emphasize a pool of resources (Adam & Serences, 2019; Adam, Vogel, & Awh, 2017; Bays, 2018; Brady, Konkle, & Alvarez, 2011; Donkin et al., 2016; Ma, Husain, & Bays, 2014; Pratte, 2019; Suchow, Fougnie, Brady, & Alvarez, 2014; Xie & Zhang, 2017; Z. Xu et al., 2018).

I argued in the previous section that perception (whether conscious or unconscious) has a higher capacity than cognition. There is a result however that may be thought to undermine that conclusion. Wu and Wolfe did an experiment involving multiple object tracking (Cohen, 2019; Wu & Wolfe, 2018). The multiple object tracking paradigm is described in Chapter 4. In Wu and Wolfe's experiment, a number of animal pictures move around the screen. (They used from 6 to 32 animals at a time.) At a randomly chosen time, the animals are replaced by gray disks and the subject is asked to move a cursor to a specified animal, e.g., the horse. Earlier experiments calculated a capacity to track of about 2.7 items, but Wu and Wolfe collected multiple guesses, reasoning that later guesses might reveal approximate knowledge of the locations. And that is what they found: approximate knowledge of the locations of up to 9.9 items. This result may seem to challenge my argument, because if the capacity of working memory is much larger than we had thought, then the capacity of perception may not be larger than the capacity of cognition.

However, there is a flaw in this objection. Slot-like behavior only emerges with closed-class items, such as letters or rectangles, that can have only a few orientations. This experiment involves continuous values of locations, so the slot reasoning does not get a grip.

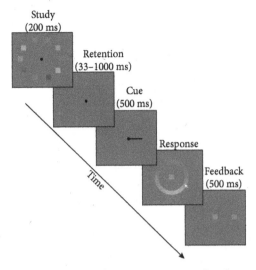

Figure 1.4 In Pratte's experiment, subjects were presented with 10 colored squares, then just a fixation point for a period between 33 ms and 1 second, then a cue indicating one of the 10 locations. They were tasked with identifying the color at that location by moving a cursor to the appropriate part of a color circle. Then they got feedback, showing what they had picked and what the correct color was. There is a free pdf on the Oxford University Press that has the color version of this and all the other figures. Thanks to Michael Pratte for this figure.

display. Again, the decay of memory capacity was due to an increase in guessing, rather than a change in precision.

The upshot is that iconic memory decays differently than working memory. Iconic memory decay is not compatible with the "pool" model, in which decay is loss of precision, suggesting that iconic memory and working memory have different formats, given that the pool models do appear to fit working memory.[8]

Armchair approaches to the perception/cognition border

It is commonly said that perception is more dependent on stimuli than are thoughts, beliefs, and judgments (Beck, 2014; Camp, 2009; Phillips, 2019; Prinz, 2002; Shea, 2014). However, the cognitive state that is most directly dependent on perception, minimal immediate direct perceptual judgment, is also dependent

---

[8] This point is also made in (Quilty-Dunn, 2019a). As we will see in Chapter 5, Quilty-Dunn holds that object representations in perception and working memory are discursive, so if the representations of the colored squares in this experiment are object representations, Quilty-Dunn owes us an explanation of why two discursive representations have such different properties.

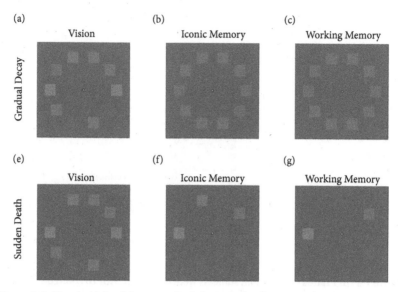

Figure 1.5 Two models of decay, gradual decay in the top row and sudden death in the bottom row. Items d and f have been omitted from this diagram. There is a free pdf on the Oxford University Press that has the color version of this and all the other figures. Thanks to Michael Pratte for this figure.

on stimuli. Perceptions are causally sustained by current proximal stimulation, but so are perceptual judgments. How can we distinguish perception from this kind of perceptual judgment?

Jake Beck (2018) says the key is that all representational elements of a perception have the function of being stimulus-dependent, whereas in a perceptual judgment, that is not necessary. I can see the spots on a bird as it flies by but still formulate the perceptual judgment that it has spots even when it is a dot on the horizon with no visible spots. And that judgment is fulfilling its function.

Recall that a minimal perceptual judgment conceptualizes each representational aspect of a perception and no more. An immediate perceptual judgment conceptualizes a perception with no inferential step. A direct perceptual judgment is based on the simultaneous perception with no intermediary. On the face of it, minimal immediate direct perceptual judgment would seem to be as stimulus-dependent as the perception it conceptualizes. Beck formulates an amended criterion that dictates that if the concepts in perceptual judgment can be applied outside of activation of transducers, they are not individually stimulus dependent and the judgment isn't stimulus dependent. However, as Jake Quilty-Dunn notes (2020), that rules out conceptual perception by fiat. As we will see in

Chapter 6, conceptual perception is an empirical issue and there are some empirical reasons to take it seriously—although ultimately, as I will argue, the best empirical case goes against conceptual perception.

It is often said that perception is fast, automatic and noneffortful and cognition has none of these properties. It is true that there are many cognitive states that are slow, effortful and require a decision and this can often be explained by the fact that cognition often requires global broadcasting, and that its formation takes at least 270 ms. But the minimal immediate direct perceptual judgments I have been talking about are plausibly cognitive and are automatic, seemingly noneffortful and perhaps faster than much of cognition. Further there are some perceptions that are slow, decisional, and effortful, for example perceptions that are the result of "free fusing" two images to make a single stereo image. (For instructions on how to do this, see the Wikipedia article on Stereoscopy or http://www.starosta.com/3dshowcase/ihelp.html.)

Perhaps the right armchair approach is via the epistemological role of perception. Perceptions are often regarded as justifiers that do not themselves require justification. Perceptions provide immediate prima facie warrant for de re beliefs about particulars where immediate warrant is warrant that is not mediated by warrant for something else. (Thanks to Ram Neta for conversation on this topic.) What is a de re belief? Oedipus has a de re belief, of his mother, that he is married to her. That is, he has a belief concerning a certain person (who—unknown to him—happens to be his mother) that he is married to her. The contrast is with a de dicto belief: Oedipus does not believe (de dicto) that he is married to his own mother. For example, he does not have a belief that he could express as "I am married to my mother." The epistemic view may be right, but it won't help much in deciding which representations are perceptions since in any real case in which there is a doubt about whether a state is a perception or a perceptual judgment, there will be a corresponding doubt about warrant.

Here is an example of a real dispute for which the epistemological approach does nothing to help us. Experimental results purport to demonstrate that desirable objects appear nearer (Balcetis & Dunning, 2010). After eating salty food, subjects' judgments about the distance between them and a bottle of water were lower than after drinking water. Did they really perceive the distance differently or was the difference only in a postperceptual cognitive judgment?

Frank Durgin and his colleagues (Durgin, DeWald, Lechich, Li, & Ontiveros, 2011) provide evidence that these results really concern perceptual judgment rather than perception. If desirable objects really do appear nearer, then those distance perceptions provide immediate prima facie warrant for belief in the shorter distance; but if desirability affects perceptual judgment without affecting perception, then the distance perceptions do not. No appeal to immediate prima facie warrant will help adjudicate between Balcetis and Dunning (2010) and Durgin et al. (2011), since we can only decide the warrant question by deciding the perception question.

Another approach to distinguishing perception from cognition would be to appeal to the phenomenology of perception (Montague, 2018) as compared with the phenomenology of cognition—or the phenomenal properties ascribed by perception as compared with the phenomenal properties ascribed by cognition (Glüer, 2009; Kriegel, 2019; Nes, Sundberg, & Watzl, 2021).

Perception could be said to be particularly phenomenally fine-grained or rich or to ascribe fine-grained or rich phenomenal properties. However, minimal immediate direct perceptual judgments may share the fine-grainedness of the perceptions they are based on. Further, it is not of the essence of the phenomenology of perception to be fine-grained. Larry Weiskrantz noted that blindsight patient DB had greater acuity in portions of his blind field in some circumstances than in the patient's sighted field (Weiskrantz, 1986/2009). (Here I assume, controversially, that blindsight is truly blind.)

It may be said that there are properties that can be phenomenally represented in thought but not in perception. But that observation won't help us with distinguishing a perceptual and a cognitive representation of the same property (Kriegel, 2019).

I am not going to pursue the phenomenological issue further, in part because I am looking for a characterization of the natural kind common to conscious and unconscious perception.

Some have argued that there is no one privileged way of delineating a border between perception and cognition (Beck, 2014; Phillips, 2019). I will be arguing for a way of drawing the border that has fundamental explanatory significance. It is always open to others to try to find some other way of drawing the border that has equal explanatory significance.

Conceptual engineering

Joints are discovered, not stipulated. Fundamental structural divides are not a matter of convention. However, there is a role for what might be called conceptual engineering in the discovery of joints. What I have in mind is that to the extent that there is vagueness in the concepts of perception and cognition, they should be understood so as to home in on a joint if there is one. I'll discuss four cases, perceptual learning, the superimposition of imagery on perception, the use of perceptual materials in cognition, and dual component views. (See Cappelen, 2018.)

Perceptual learning

There are many types of perceptual learning ranging from associative learning to more sophisticated forms of Bayesian updating. It is commonly said that perceptual systems are shaped by perceptual experience. For example, chess players often say that they can see patterns of strength and weakness. What is controversial is whether there is a direct effect of cognition on the shaping of perceptual systems or whether the shaping of perceptual systems is a matter of exposure, subsequent familiarity, and sensorimotor training.

The reason this issue is controversial is that it is difficult to separate the effects of training and exposure from the effects of conceptualization of that exposure. As Ellen Fridland (2014, p. 4) puts it, "In fact, proponents of cognitive penetrability often appeal to cases of perceptual learning and expertise in order to support their position. It is in cases of, e.g., expert radiologists, chess players, chicken sexers, artists, musicians, and athletes that changes in perception seem plausibly to occur. But in these cases, the change in perception results from regular, long-term exposure to and training with a certain class of perceptual stimuli."

Perceptual categories can be learned, even in an hour of training. Ester, Sprague, and Serences (2020) trained subjects in categorizing tilted lines as on one side or another of a standard orientation (chosen arbitrarily for each subject; see Figure 1.6). Subjects became adept at this categorization and then two forms of brain scanning showed that representations in early vision of the orientations were repelled by the boundaries. That is, orientations near the boundaries were represented as comfortably on one side or the other. These categorical biases emerged at the earliest stages of visual processing.

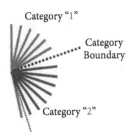

Figure 1.6 Tilt categorization task from (Ester et al., 2020). An arbitrary tilt was selected for each subject, indicated by the category boundary in the figure. Orientations on the clockwise side of the boundary were classified as category 2 and categories on the other side were 1. There is a free pdf on the Oxford University Press web site that has the color version of this and all the other figures. This figure is from the *Journal of Neuroscience*, which does not require permission.

Note that there is no evidence in this experiment for a cognitive effect on perceptual categorization. The mechanism by which these perceptual categories emerge may be entirely sensorimotor.[9]

I know of only one published study that makes a serious attempt to separate the effects of exposure from a direct cognitive effect (Emberson, 2016; Emberson & Amso, 2012). They argue for a cognitive effect that is distinct from exposure, but in my view the case is underwhelming.

Some argue from categorical perception to cognitive penetration of perception (Emberson, 2016; Gerbino & Fantoni, 2017). In categorical perception, discrimination is faster and more accurate when stimuli are on different sides of a category boundary: that is, better across than within categories. For example, children are born with equal discriminatory capacities for all the world's languages, but as they learn their own languages, they lose sensitivity to differences within—and gain sensitivity across—phonological categories of the home language. It is well established that perceptual categories can be influenced by training. For example, training with new color categories can reshape color category boundaries (Özgen & Davies, 2002).

If categorical perception can be acquired in part on the basis of knowledge in addition to mere exposure, then there is "diachronic" (over time) cognitive penetration. (Categorical perception will be discussed in detail in Chapters 6 and 12.)

Pylyshyn (1999, p. 360) discusses some cases of perceptual learning, arguing that "none of these results is in conflict with the independence or impenetrability thesis as we have been developing it here." Pylyshyn, following Fodor (1983), is taking the cognitive impenetrability thesis to hold only synchronically (at a time), not diachronically.[10]

This dispute can seem rather verbal, but there is an approach to a principled response: draw the borders between kinds that will reveal a joint if there is one. Suppose there are direct diachronic cognitive effects that change the structure of perceptual systems and, even more doubtfully, that those effects challenge a joint. Both assumptions are highly controversial (and I don't subscribe to either), but let's suppose they are true for the sake of the example. My proposal is that if excluding cognitively driven structural changes in perception homes in

---

[9] There are category repulsion effects in other perceptual paradigms that are partly perceptual and partly postperceptual. See Fritsche and de Lange (2019).

[10] Fodor isn't that clear about the matter, but in a discussion of the diachronic modification of associative connections, he says, "to put the matter somewhat metaphysically, the formation of interlexical connections buys the synchronic encapsulation of the language processor at the price of its cognitive penetrability *across time*" (Fodor, 1983, p. 82). What I am calling the diachronic/synchronic distinction is sometimes referred to as the off-line effect/on-line effect distinction (Lupyan, Rahman, Boroditsky, & Clark, 2020).

on a joint, then we should understand the concept of perception so as to exclude those diachronic effects (Block, 2016b). To be clear, I am not claiming that perception is only synchronic. Perception takes time and there are diachronic perceptual effects such as adaptation. Perceptual tracking is constitutively temporal. What I am suggesting might be excluded (on the basis of highly controversial premises) from perception is cognitively driven diachronic structural effects on perception if there are any.

One might call this a clarification of the concept, but not a clarification in a sense that counts as changing the concept, any more than realizing that whales are not fish was part of a change in the concept of fish. Many types of concepts contain within them a pressure toward natural kinds. By age 5, children understand that if you paint a stripe on a racoon and implant stink glands the result is still a racoon and not a skunk (despite being shown a "before" picture depicting a racoon and an "after" picture that looks like a skunk) (Gelman, 2003; Keil, 1989). And they do not reason in the same way for artifactual kinds. If shown a "before" picture depicting a coffee pot and an "after" figure depicting a bird feeder, 5-year-olds tend to regard the operation as having changed a coffee pot into a bird feeder. Five-year-olds know that something can look more like coal than gold but be gold nonetheless. Even if they are unsure of how to classify something, they judge that there is a correct answer that an expert would know. And they take internal constitution as a better inductive base than external properties. These results have been replicated cross-culturally including with Native Americans (the Menominee), the Vezo in Madagascar, Yucatec Mayans, Yoruba in Nigeria, and the Torguud of Mongolia. (For a more skeptical spin on this issue, see Leslie, 2013.)

Just as realizing that whales are not fish clarifies what a fish is without changing the antecedent concept of a fish into a different concept, so the decision to exclude perceptual learning from perception clarifies what perception is without changing the concept of perception. We could call it clarification of the concept of perception but understanding "clarification" so as not to require conceptual change. The scientific concept of fish, excluding as it does, marine mammals, better captures the natural kind intent of the concept than a description based on shape. The "fish-shape" concept doesn't even help with generalizations about modes of swimming, since true fish swim differently than warm-blooded marine mammals. The fact that it is so natural to use the phrase "true fish" expresses that implicit commitment to a natural kind element in the concept. The hope of clarification of the concepts of perception and cognition to home in on the natural kinds is to achieve a success of the same sort as the natural kind concept of fish.

It is worth noting that this kind of conceptual clarification can result in giving up part of what had earlier seemed essential. People sometimes think of the property of water of sustaining life as part of some kind of a definition of "water." However, water is a mixture of "light" and "heavy" water, where heavy water involves an isotope of the more familiar form of hydrogen. This isotope (deuterium) has a nucleus with a neutron and a proton instead of the more usual lone proton. Heavy water is poisonous. So, the property of being able to sustain life is not a necessary condition of being water.

Superimposition of imagery on perception

Another example: Mental imagery can be superimposed on perception. Is the resulting state a perception? An example will make this issue more concrete.

Brockmole, Wang, and Irwin (2002) used a "locate the missing dot" task in which the subject's task is to move a cursor to a missing dot in a 5 by 5 array. A partial grid of 12 dots appears briefly and then disappears followed soon after by another partial grid of 12 different dots in the same location that stays on the screen until the response. If the time between the two stimuli is short enough, subjects can fuse the 2 partial grids and move the cursor to the missing dot, remembering nearly 100% of the dots on the first array. However, if the second array is delayed to 100–200 ms, subjects' ability to remember the first array falls precipitously (from nearly 12 dots down to 5 dots). Brockmole et al. explored extended delays—up to 5 seconds before the second array appears. The amazing result is that if the second array of 12 dots comes more than 1.5 seconds after the first array has disappeared, subjects become very accurate on the remembered dots. Instructions encourage them to create a mental image of the first array and superimpose it on the array that remains on the screen. This experiment will be described in more detail later in the section on mental imagery (p. 339).

We can call the resulting superimposition of imagery on perception, a "quasi-perceptual state." If quasi-perceptual states are counted as perception, would this be cognitive penetration of perception? And if it is cognitive penetration, would it challenge a joint? I don't think cognitive penetration challenges a joint (see Chapter 9 for many cases of cognitive penetration that do not challenge a joint). But those who think it does have a reason to exclude the quasi-perceptual states that result from superimposition from the category of perception. There is also an "ordinary language" reason: We do not normally count perceptual imagery as perception, since imagery does not function to be stimulus-dependent.

I believe that many quasi-perceptual states of this sort have routinely been counted as perception. Effects of this sort are involved in many of the phenomena used to criticize a joint in nature between cognition and perception. Many of the effects of language and expectation on perception cited by opponents of a joint in nature seem very likely to involve superimposition of imagery on perception. For example, Gary Lupyan notes that in a visual task of identifying the direction of moving dots, performance suffers when the subject hears verbs that suggest the opposite direction (Lupyan, 2015). The plausibility that this result involves some sort of combination of imagery and perception is enhanced by the fact that hearing a story about motion can cause motion aftereffects (Dils & Boroditsky, 2010).

Another example: Delk and Fillenbaum (1965) showed that when subjects are presented with a heart shape and asked to adjust a background to match it, the background they choose is redder than if the shape is a circle or a square. As Fiona Macpherson (2012) points out, there is evidence that subjects are forming a mental image of a red heart and superimposing it on the cut-out. Macpherson regards this as a case of cognitive penetration. But whether it is cognitive penetration depends on whether the resulting quasi-perceptual state is a genuine perceptual state (see the discussion in the section on mental imagery in Chapter 9).

In a recent article in *Nature Human Behaviour*, Chunye Teng and Dwight Kravitz (2019) showed that holding a color or orientation in mind while doing a perceptual task biased the perceptual classification toward a distractor if the mental image was similar to the distractor. Again, whether this is cognitive penetration depends on a prior decision as to whether quasi-perception is perception.

There is also evidence that visual imagery is involved in ordinary perception where subjects are not asked to imagine anything. Tarr and Pinker (1989) taught subjects to recognize line drawings and then examined recognition of the objects depicted at unfamiliar angles. They showed that the time it took to recognize an object at an unfamiliar angle depended on the angular distance that would be required to rotate the object to the familiar view. This suggests that perceptual object representation can involve coordinated representations from different vantage points, at least some of which can be characterized as mental images.

Fodor's and Pylyshyn's notion of "cognitive penetration" requires a direct effect of cognition on perception in the sense of no intermediate causal link that is a person-level mental state. (See Chapter 9 for further discussion.) By that criterion, these imagery effects will count as cognitive penetration only if quasi-perception is perception.

Cognitive states that use perceptual materials

The issue of drawing borders to home in on a joint if there is one arose earlier in connection with the question of why I was counting perceptual simulations used in cognition (e.g., to determine whether the couch would fit through the doorway if rotated) as cognition. In such process, there are iconic, nonconceptual, and nonpropositional representational elements and these elements are deployed in reasoning. I said that because they are deployed in reasoning, these elements are enclosed in a cognitive envelope. I argued that what makes a perceptual representation perceptual is not just being iconic, nonpropositional, and nonconceptual but also whether those properties are constitutive of the state.

Earlier in this chapter, I mentioned three important differences between perceptual representations in perception and similar representations in working memory. First, perceptual simulations used in cognition may not use the fine-grained representations of true perception, at least with regard to color representations. I mentioned minimal shades of colors that may require being driven by bottom-up world-driven information flow. Second, there are computational differences between perceptual representation in perception and perceptual representation in working memory having to do with "divisive normalization," a notion that will be explained in the next chapter. Finally, working memory representations do not have the phenomenology of perception.

Still, one should have an open mind about whether the best way of thinking about perceptual simulations is by treating them as part of the same natural kind as perception, that natural kind being what one might call perceptual representation. This would handle perceptual simulations and superimpositions of imagery on perception in a uniform manner. And if perceptual memories, perceptual anticipations, and mental maps constitutively involve iconic, nonconceptual, and nonpropositional representations, the same proposal may classify these representations as perceptual representations. (However, see the section below on whether map-like structures are actually conceptual, and indeed are the basis of thought.)

The constitutive iconic format and nonconceptual and nonpropositional nature of perceptual representation provide necessary conditions of perceptual representation but more is required to provide a sufficient condition. As mentioned earlier, to distinguish between perception and sensation, we may require that the perceptual representations involve the constancies of perception (Burge, 2010a).

Dual component views

Some theorists hold "dual component" theories of perception (Smith, 2002) in which a perceptual experience is a complex state that has a nonconceptual nonpropositional component and, at least sometimes, a conceptual/propositional component (Peacocke, 1992b). The conceptual/propositional component is usually supposed to be caused by the nonconceptual component. According to some, the conceptual/propositional component is a belief (Quilty-Dunn, 2015), according to others it is a "seeming," a propositional attitude that is formed automatically and persists despite not being endorsed by the subject (Brogaard, 2014; Reiland, 2014; Tucker, 2010). Is there any substantive difference between such views and the one that I will be advocating?

Someone might argue that the disagreement is just a matter of how expansive we wish to be about what to include in perception, and in particular whether to include the propositional component in perception. I reject such views and not just on the ground of conceptual engineering that I have been talking about. In Chapter 4, I will be arguing that perceptual representations do not have the logical properties required of propositional representations.

If there is a fundamental difference between perception and cognition, why don't we see the border in the brain?

Here is part of a recent interview by Jordana Cepelewicz of Lisa Feldman Barrett and other psychologists and neuroscientists (Cepelewicz, 2021b):

> "Scientists for over 100 years have searched fruitlessly for brain boundaries between thinking, feeling, deciding, remembering, moving and other everyday experiences," Barrett said. A host of recent neurological studies further confirm that these mental categories "are poor guides for understanding how brains are structured or how they work." Barrett is giving voice to a widespread view that the real mental categories are the ones that neuroscientists discover."

This is a view famously put forward by Paul and Patricia Churchland (P. Churchland, 1986; P. M. Churchland, 1981).

I certainly agree with the Churchlands that the categories of folk psychology will be refined and in some cases eliminated by neuroscience, but importantly—and this is often left out—many of our folk categories can be validated by neuroscience, although perhaps not current neuroscience. Further, as Cepelewicz goes on to say, "However, often neuroscientists can only discover crucial mental categories once they are identified by psychology." Indeed the categories neuroscientists validate are often categories that are provided by psychology with no help from folk psychology. The opponent process theory of color perception was discovered in the nineteenth century by Ewald Hering and further elaborated by Dorothea Jameson and Leo Hurvich in the 1950s, all on the basis of behavioral data and introspection. Then the theory was validated by finding opponent cells in the lateral geniculate nucleus and later refined using both neural and behavioral data.

The absence of a clean spatially specific border in the brain is illustrated by a study in which subjects were asked to make similarity judgments of many pairs of pictures (Bracci & Op de Beeck, 2016). The pictures fit into six categories: animals, vegetables/fruit, minerals, musical instruments, sports items, and tools. They also differed along nine shape dimensions. For example, some instruments, vegetables, and minerals were long and thin, others roughly circular. Early visual areas were dominated by shape-based similarity judgments, prefrontal areas were dominated by category-based judgments, but most of the brain showed a mix of responses to shape and category. Albert Newen recently argued that studies of this sort show that neuroscience dictates a third category in between perception and cognition and hence that there is no joint in nature between perception and cognition (Newen, 2021).

It would be natural to interpret both Newen and Barrett as saying that no one has discovered boundaries in the brain between perception and cognition so there is only a superficial reality to the difference.

But the problem with this argument is that there can be a basic difference that is not realized spatially. There is a basic difference between data and program representations in computers, and early computers stored data and program in separate registers, but modern computers often use distributed representations. In distributed representations, the separate parts are defined by functional relations rather than physical areas. Two data registers are linked not by adjacency but by pointers.

Further, a bottom-up analysis of the chips in a computer would not easily lead to an understanding of basic principles of organization. This point was famously made in an article in *PLOS Computational Biology* titled "Could a Neuroscientist Understand a Microprocessor?" applying standard neuroscience techniques to a primitive Atari chip (also used in the first Apple computer) (Jonas & Kording, 2017). The authors conclude (p. 14), "However, in the case of the processor, we know its function and structure and our results stayed well short of what we would call a satisfying understanding." Of course, given that the difference between perception and cognition is real and fundamental, it will be in principle possible to find its neural implementation. But no one should expect that it will be easy to find using current techniques.

Interface of perception with cognition

The main interface of perception with cognition is when perceptual materials are retained in working memory, as described earlier in this chapter and in greater detail in Chapters 5 and 6. But there are two other cognitive systems that are not closely associated with working memory, to be described briefly in this section.

I'll start with the system that is most unlike perception, the language of thought system, long discussed in the philosophical literature, including in the late medieval period by William of Ockham (Rescorla, 2019), and revived more recently by Jerry Fodor and Gilbert Harman (Fodor, 1975; Harman, 1973). Perhaps the leading property of language of thought systems is the independence of syntactic roles and the lexical items that are fillers of those roles (Frankland & Greene, 2020a, 2020b). This kind of independence does not apply to iconic representations where a smudge that represents a hand in one part of one picture could represent a foot in another part, a claw in another part or a flipper in another part.

A somewhat different emphasis involves tree structures. Tecumseh Fitch proposed the "dendrophilia hypothesis that 'humans love trees,'" more specifically, "that 'humans have a multi-domain capacity and proclivity to infer tree structures from strings' even in the simplest cases, to a degree that is difficult or impossible for most nonhuman animal species" (2014, p. 352).

Stanislas Dehaene and his colleagues have provided strong evidence for the first part, that humans love trees, and more specifically that humans have a proclivity to code sequences into recursive tree structures (Planton et al., 2021). What is meant here by "recursive"? If you concatenate an adjective (e.g., "big") with a noun phrase (e.g., "green egg") you get a new noun phrase ("big green egg"), and that new noun phrase can itself be concatenated with an adjective to form still another noun phrase (e.g., "expensive big green egg"). This is an example of one kind of recursion. Applied to procedures, a recursive procedure is one whose implementation requires that very procedure.

As Dehaene notes (2000; Planton et al., 2021), current neural networks cannot represent truths that involve recursion, such as "Every number has a successor." Humans learn such rules easily. Four-year-old humans can learn to reverse the sequence ABCD to DCBA in five trials, but nonhuman primates take tens of thousands of trials. Thus, human cognition seems importantly different from the cognition of nonhuman primates and the computations of current neural networks.

George Miller famously proposed that working memory has 7, plus or minus 2, "slots." (Recall as explained earlier in this chapter, slots in working memory are real but not fundamental.) Later work suggested that the evidence for Miller's estimate did not control for "chunking." For example, as will be noted in Chapter 2, the series of letters "FBI CIA KGB" is much better recalled than "KBA GFI BFC" (Rosenberg & Feigenson, 2012). Chunking is a data compression mechanism. As Planton et al. propose, the complexity of a sequence of stimuli can be indexed by the length of its compressed form using an internal language that allows for nesting. The internal language relevant to the binary stimuli involves a term for "stay" and a way of representing change. For example, AAAA would be represented as four stays, whereas ABAB would be an item plus three repetitions of a change.

Dehaene and his colleagues explored how subjects process sequences of stimuli. They gave subjects sequences of auditory and visual stimuli that were binary in the sense of being composed of two types of items that repeated in sequences. The items could be high and low tones or red and green dots, for example. Assuming that subjects coded the stimuli using two instructions, "same" and "change," they tested subjects' ability to detect sequence violations in five different experiments, finding that "data compression" coding schemes using recursive tree structures explained subjects' behavior for all but the shortest sequences. The psychological complexity of the sequences were indexed by the size of the most compressed mental representations of them as shown by the subjects' detections of violations of the sequence rules, but also by subjects' complexity ratings.

One surprising prediction that was borne out concerned A^nB^n patterns. For sequences of 16 items, these sequences could be two chunks of 8 (i.e., AAAAAAAABBBBBBBB), four chunks of 4 (i.e., AAAABBBBAAAABBBB), eight chunks of 2, or 16 chunks of 1. These sequences all have the same model complexity (the log number of repetitions) and were found to have the same psychological complexity.

A similar model also predicted subjects' behavior in a task involving spatial locations on a regular octagon (Amalric et al., 2017). The experimenters found that a language of nested sequences of geometrical primitives of rotation and symmetry explained subjects' behavior in judgments of regularity, in completion of sequences, and in an eye-tracking task. Sequence complexity also predicted brain activity in the inferior frontal cortex. Results were similar among three very different groups, French adults who had been through school, French kindergarteners, and the Munduruku, indigenous Amazonians who had no schooling and very limited language concerning numbers and geometrical terms, suggesting that the "language of thought" as applied to geometry is a basic human ability that does not depend on culture.

Later experiments by the same group (Sablé-Meyer et al., 2021) used a methodology that required subjects to detect an "odd one out" among six quadrilaterals. This task is suitable both for nonlinguistic subjects and subjects with language. The behavior of unschooled members of the Himba tribe, French kindergarteners, and French adults were predicted by the language of thought model, but that model did not predict the behavior of baboons in this task. Baboon behavior was best modeled by a convolutional neural net model, not by the language of thought model. As the authors note, this result suggests that symbolic abstraction with nested structures is a basic human capacity that distinguishes humans from other primates.

Steven Frankland and Joshua Greene have identified different brain regions connected with different cognitive systems (Frankland & Greene, 2020a, 2020b). They take the language of thought system grounded in the dorsolateral prefrontal cortex to code instructions for thoughts, and "grid-like" representations in the default mode network (DMN) to serve as the "canvas" for these thoughts. The dorsolateral prefrontal cortex, the top/side of the prefrontal cortex, is widely thought to be the center of thought, the control of working memory, and executive function. The DMN involves the "inside" of the prefrontal cortex, where the hemispheres face each other; the posterior cingulate cortex, also on the midline of the brain; and the angular gyrus, on the border of the parietal and temporal lobes. The DMN was originally identified as a wakeful rest area implicated in mind-wandering, but Frankland and Greene review very different functions in mental maps involving both physical space and conceptual spaces.

The DMN is implicated in conceptual combination both in fMRI results and in lesion studies. For example, patients with low gray matter density in the angular gyri, parts of the DMN, show impairment in conceptual combination tasks but not in single word tasks. According to Frankland and Greene (2020a, p. 295), "Research on the timing of semantic processing indicates that the DMN is where semantic production begins and semantic comprehension ends."

Grid cells, centered in the DMN, are involved in spatial navigation but also play a role in the use of spatial abilities in conceptual combination. Grid cells as used in spatial navigation represent space via representation of equilateral triangles combined to form hexagons, six triangles to a hexagon. Each of the six triangles assembled in the hexagon occupies one-sixth of the hexagon, spanning 60°. This 60° structure is revealed in greater grid-cell activity for spatial changes of 60° than other changes. Remarkably, this difference can be observed in fMRI recordings at various parts of the DMN during spatial navigation (Doeller, Barry, & Burgess, 2010; Frankland & Greene, 2020a).

Constantinescu, O'Reilly, and Behrens (2016) used the Doeller procedure on tasks involving a two-dimensional space in which one axis was the length of a bird's neck and the other was the length of the bird's legs. They observed the same 60° signature. Frankland and Greene suggest that when conceptual representations involve magnitudes, vector displacement representations in the grid-cell network may be used in conceptual combination. These grid-cell representations are iconic in the sense to be introduced in chapter 6 of analog mirroring, in which relations among represented environmental properties are mirrored by instantiations of brain-analogs of those relations.

Frankland and Greene review a great deal of literature on the uses and limitations of the grid-cell network in cognition. What is relevant for the purposes of this book are first that the uses they review are conceptual, involving conceptual combination in thought. The grid cell system is not a perceptual system. Unlike "place cells" that remap according to perceptual input, grid cells are relatively insensitive to perceptual input. Second, given that grid-cells involve iconic representation it is natural to suppose that they interface with the iconic representations of perception. Third, as Frankland and Greene make clear, this work is in its infancy and much of what they say is framed in the language of speculation. As we will see, the speculative nature of this work contrasts with what we know about perception, as explored in later chapters of this book.

Why should philosophers be interested in this book?

Here are some reasons why philosophers should be interested in this book.

1. The relevance to epistemology is significant, given that perception but not perceptually based cognition is often supposed to provide unjustified justifiers. If perception is conceptual, propositional, and discursive, then a compelling view of how perception justifies belief is just that we believe what we see—or hear, feel, etc. But if I am right that perception is none of those things, then a different model of perceptual justification is required. Traditionally, the philosophy of perception has been geared toward illuminating the epistemology of perceptual judgment—what justifies the judgments about the world that we base on perception (Stoljar, 2009). This project has often ignored the science of perception. The presumption of this book is that epistemologists would do well to find out what perception is from the science of perception and to base the epistemology of perception on that scientific answer.

2. If perception is nonconceptual, nonpropositional, and iconic, then certain kinds of robots will not be perceivers. Specifically, if a camera output writes directly into cognitive representations, the robot would have data-driven cognitive states that are not perceptual.
3. The conclusions of this book are relevant to issues concerning the synthetic a priori. I'll give an example from a recent controversy.
4. Most importantly, the conclusions of this book concern the nature of minds.

Paul Boghossian and Timothy Williamson have debated whether there are synthetic a priori truths that are justifiable by intuition, more specifically, justified by intellectual seemings (Boghossian & Williamson, 2020). The kind of intellectual seeming at issue would include, for example, the appreciation of the truth of the proposition that it is morally wrong to inflict pain merely for one's own amusement. Boghossian argues that such intellectual seemings are similar to perceptual seemings in that they are "predoxastic" in the sense of prior to actual belief and also that these intellectual seemings dispose us to believe. He argues further that the considerations that show that perceptual seemings justify perceptual belief apply also to the claim that intellectual seemings justify intellectual beliefs. Williamson opposes predoxastic seemings in both cases. According to Williamson, we have a visual seeming that the Müller-Lyer lines are the same length, but it is not predoxastic because it is constitutively tied to the "felt visually-based inclination to judge that one line is longer" (pp. 232–233).

Similarly, according to Williamson, an inclination to judge that it is morally wrong to inflict pain for one's own amusement does not present itself to him as based on its seeming true. If asked why he is inclined to judge that p, an appeal to p seeming true "sounds forced and feeble" (p. 233) because the explanans is too close to the explanandum.

In my view, both Boghossian and Williamson are mistaken. Boghossian is mistaken because intellectual seemings are not predoxastic and Williamson is mistaken because perceptual seemings are predoxastic. More specifically:

1. Perception is plausibly nonconceptual and nonpropositional, and so are perceptual seemings, but intellectual seemings have to be conceptual and propositional since the contents cannot be appreciated without thought.
2. Perception is iconic, while cognition, including intellectual seemings, is largely discursive, the exception being map-like representations.
3. Perception is subject to large adaptation effects. If I look at a red square for more than a few seconds, it will look slightly less red, as the perception

shifts toward the green end of the red/green opponent process channel. (See Chapter 2.)

Because of adaptation, perception of ambiguous stimuli results in rivalry, as explained in detail in Chapter 9. If I look at a Necker cube, one face will appear to come toward me. That perception will then weaken due to adaptation, and then the other way of perceiving it will win out and another face will come forward. This can continue indefinitely. An ambiguous figure/ground display yields comparable oscillations in how we see it because of adaptation. (Again, see Chapter 2.) But there is no comparable oscillation in intellectual seemings. People disagree as to whether XYZ is water or not, but we do not experience oscillating views of the sort we do with perception.

4. Perception is to a large extent architecturally separate from cognition and so to a large extent functions autonomously of the subject's theories. The main exception is for ambiguous stimuli. See Chapters 9–11. We cannot say the same however of intellectual seemings. They are part of the cognitive system and so not architecturally distinct from it. There is every reason to think that they are highly influenced by the subject's theories. Cognitive penetration of perception is limited, but cognitive penetration of intellectual seemings is likely to be relatively unconstrained.

This last item is by far the most significant of the four points for the Boghossian/Williamson debate. The epistemic value of intellectual seemings is likely to be greatly reduced compared to the epistemic value of perceptual seemings. Susanna Siegel (2017) argues that the epistemic status of a perceptual seeming is affected by how it is formed. For example, wishful seeing or fearful seeing weaken the epistemic force of the perception. But a similar point applies to intellectual seemings that are influenced by one's theoretical views. To allow intellectual seemings to support conclusions that play a role in producing the intellectual seeming in the first place would be a kind of "double counting" and so the intellectual seeming should be epistemically downgraded.

Roadmap

- Chapter 2 is concerned with markers of the perceptual.
- Chapter 3 is concerned with whether the content of perception is singular, whether perception is attributional, and whether there are two kinds of seeing-as. It ends with a brief discussion of racially biased perceptual responses by way of illustrating how we can distinguish between perception and perceptual judgment.

- Chapters 4–7 make the positive case that perception is constitutively iconic, nonconceptual, and nonpropositional. Then Chapter 8 makes the negative case—that arguments to the contrary are mistaken.
- Chapter 6 describes a special kind of perceptual representation, a perceptual category representation. These representations are often conflated with concepts—wrongly, I will argue. This is the central chapter for my argument that perception is nonconceptual and the basis for my new argument for "overflow".
- Chapter 7 discusses evidence from neuroscience that perception is nonconceptual.
- Chapter 8 discusses evidence that is wrongly taken to show that perception is conceptual.
- Chapter 9 describes fundamental machinery of perception that determines direct content-appropriate effects of the content of cognition on the content of perception—i.e., cognitive penetrations (by many common standards). The idea here is that once one sees what the joint between perception and cognition is, we can see that feature-based attention, imagery, and other ubiquitous phenomena involve cognitive penetration. Then I will observe that from what we can tell so far, the mechanisms of cognitive penetration (and the representations produced by these mechanisms) divide into the perceptual and the cognitive; so, there is no reason to believe that interpenetration of perception and cognition show any problem with the joint.
- Chapter 10 discusses top-down effects that have been mistakenly supposed to be effects of cognition on perception.
- Chapter 11 discusses modularity. I will argue against modularity in the sense of Fodor and Pylyshyn, but also that there is substantial truth in the modularity thesis.
- Chapter 12 discusses core cognition, arguing against the view that representations of causation and numerosity form a third category intermediate between perception and cognition.
- Chapter 13 discusses the consequences of the joint for cognitivist and conceptualist theories of consciousness.

This book presents a certain conception of perception, of cognition, and of the difference between them. I give evidence and argument for some but not all of the details. I am hoping that the plausibility and coherence of the picture presented will carry some of the burden of argument. I take it to be generally agreed that cognition is paradigmatically conceptual, propositional, and discursive (noniconic), though I will say a bit more in what follows in contrasting perception with cognition.

As the reader will see, I focus much more on perception than on cognition. The reason for that is that the psychology and neuroscience of perception is vastly better developed than the psychology and neuroscience of cognition. The perceptual systems all have fairly similar tasks—of making the output of sense organs useful to the organism. And phenomena discovered in one sensory modality often appear in others. For example, "change blindness," first discovered in vision, also appears in auditory and haptic perception. By contrast, the aspects of the mind that use conceptual propositional discursive representations are a disparate lot with little uniformity. The best developed of the sciences of cognition are those, as with the psychology of language, that are most like perception.

2
Markers of the perceptual and the cognitive

In this chapter, I will describe some indicators that a representation is perceptual and not cognitive.[1] Some of these indicators are also useful in distinguishing high-level perception from low-level perception. But the justification of each indicator inevitably appeals to other indicators. Circularity looms. A skeptic could say the whole edifice is rotten. However, it is a far from insignificant fact that there are indicators that classify the cases we are surest of correctly and these same indicators agree with one another. The overall strategy is self-correcting in that if the methods fail to converge, we know our assumptions are bad. We do have such methods, lots of them. A critic could allege that there is another set of methods that satisfies all the same desiderata but that classifies differently. Good luck to anyone who takes on that task.

Perhaps the most useful of the methods that are widely used exploits perceptual adaptation. I will start with a long discussion of perceptual adaptation, followed by much shorter discussions of other methods: rivalry, pop-out, speed of perceptual processing, and illusory contours. Note that adaptation, rivalry, pop-out, speed, and illusory contours are all indicators and are not intended to be constitutive of perception. Chapters 4–6 concern what is constitutive of perception.

Adaptation

Perceptual adaptation is an effect of perceiving one stimulus on the perception of another stimulus. John Frisby called the perceptual adaptation methodology the "psychophysicists' microelectrode" (Frisby, 1979; Mollon, 1974). Just as the neuroscientist can first raise, then reduce a neuron's firing rate by direct stimulation with a microelectrode, the psychophysicist can first raise, then reduce a neural system's activity by stimulating it with its preferred stimulus. Perceptual

---

[1] Parts of this chapter and some other chapters contain material from (Block, 2014a, 2014c, 2016b).

adaptation was known to Aristotle,[2] who described (in "On Dreams") what we now call the "waterfall illusion": "when persons turn away from looking at objects in motion, e.g., rivers, and especially those which flow very rapidly, things really at rest are seen as moving" (Aristotle, 1955, p. 731). Staring at something moving down raises the threshold for detecting downward motion, biasing the percept toward upward motion, so stationary things look like they are moving upward.

Because of this kind of effect, adaptation is often characterized as "repulsive" in the sense that exposure to one property biases another perception away from that property. Perception of the downward-moving waterfall raises the threshold for seeing downward motion: a downward-moving stimulus must be higher in contrast to achieve the same degree of apparent motion. Hence in looking at a stationary item afterward, the percept is biased toward upward motion.

The most familiar kind of adaptation for many people is adaptation to color. You can experience this in dramatic fashion with Figure 2.1. If you fixate the dot in the top picture for 30 seconds, then move your gaze to the corresponding point in bottom picture, it will briefly look like a color photograph. Areas that contain yellow (e.g., the sky) will seem to contain blue in the corresponding areas of the bottom photo.

You saw the bottom photo as blue in the sky area. That is perception. But no doubt you also judged that it was blue or at least looked blue, and judging is cognition. So the question arises of whether adaptation is a perceptual phenomenon, a cognitive phenomenon, or both? Adaptation would be of little use as an indicator if we cannot nail down what it indicates.

We could think of this case in terms of Susanna Siegel's "method of phenomenal contrast" (2010). The experience of the bottom picture when you first saw it compared with a few seconds later after the effect of adaptation has faded provides a phenomenal contrast. We can inquire what the best explanation is of that phenomenal contrast. Is the phenomenal contrast a matter of the different phenomenologies of perceptual judgment or, alternatively, of perception itself? The obvious explanation is that the difference in judgment is due to a difference in perception itself. The sky area of the bottom picture looks blue briefly and that is why you judge it to be blue.

If the difference in judgment was primary—i.e., not due to a difference in perception, why would it be so brief? We can explain the time course of perceptual adaptation and its fading in terms of a temporary shift in a perceptual opponent process system to be described below. But how do we know that the opponent process system is part of perception rather than cognition? That is the benign circularity to be discussed throughout this chapter. The opponent process

---

[2] But there is an issue as to whether he was reporting apparent motion in the same or opposite direction from the stimulus (Sekuler, 1965).

Figure 2.1 Color adaptation demonstration. First, fixate on the small dot in the middle of the top picture. Stare at it for 30 seconds. Then fixate the corresponding spot on the bottom picture. What subjects with normal color vision report is that the bottom picture looks colored for a brief period. This figure requires color. There is a free pdf on the Oxford University Press web site that has the color version of this and all the other figures. Used with permission of Peter Reid, The University of Edinburgh.

systems explain adaptation, and adaptation, rivalry, pop-out, speed, and illusory contours all converge on a single set of perceptual mechanisms.

The utility of adaptation can be exhibited by an approach to a phenomenon that allows simultaneous investigation of both perception and cognition, the "phonemic restoration effect" (Warren, 1970) (also known as the "phoneme" restoration effect). The next section is a case study in aspects of language that are perceptual and aspects of language that are cognitive and not perceptual.

Perception vs. cognition in language

In the phonemic restoration effect, individual phonemes are removed from words and replaced by white noise that shares an acoustic envelope with the phonemes (Warren used coughs). Subjects nonetheless say they hear the phonemes (with noise in the background). For example, the /s/ sound in "legislature" is replaced by noise ("legi#lature"), but the subjects say they hear "legislature" with a noise (which I am representing as "#") occurring at the same time as the /s/ sound. You can experience the effect for yourself by playing this 18-second YouTube video: https://www.youtube.com/watch?v=UlJs24j3i8E. It has been shown repeatedly that subjects cannot distinguish reliably between the perception of a word with a real phoneme (plus white noise) and perception of the same word in which the phoneme has been replaced by noise (e.g., between "legislature" with # and "legi#lature") (Samuel, 1997, 2001). (The effect is strongest for stops (/p/, /t/, /k/, /b/, /d/, /g/) and fricatives (/f/, /s/, /v/, /z/) near the ends of long words.)

The major theoretic issue concerning the phonemic restoration effect concerns the distinction that is at the heart of this book. The competing theories are:

1. <u>Restored phonemic perception</u>. When the stimulus is "legi#lature," the subject hears the /s/ sound plus white noise, i.e., "legislature" together with #.
2. <u>Perceptual judgment</u>: The subject does not hear the /s/ sound, i.e., the subject hears "legi#lature" but perceptually judges that the stimulus was "legislature" together with #, failing to report the missing sound.

The interest of this phenomenon from the point of view of this chapter is, first, that the effect can be shown to be perceptual rather than cognitive, using adaptation. That is, option 1 is correct. Second, there is a strong adaptation effect for phonemes but none for spoken words, suggesting that spoken words are not perceptually represented (though of course they are cognitively represented). This is one of few negative adaptation results in the literature. (Negative results are generally not publishable.) Third, neuroscience methods give converging evidence for some of the same conclusions. Fourth, the example will be useful for our later discussion of cognitive penetration since in some cases, the effect reveals a strong effect of cognition on perceptually ambiguous stimuli. (One caution: for simplicity, I will speak of restoration of phonemes, though actually results often don't distinguish clearly among a number of sublexical levels, e.g., between phonemes and phonetic features.)

One experimental paradigm (developed by Arthur Samuel) uses pairs of words in which a removed phoneme makes the resulting stimulus ambiguous. For example, "faster" and "factor" differ in one phoneme. (Other contrasting pairs included "novel"/"nozzle" and "babies"/"rabies.") The key difference in the "faster"/"factor" example is that between the "fricative" (/s/) sound in "faster" and the "plosive" (/k/) sound in "factor." Replacing those phonemes by noise with an appropriate acoustic envelope yields an ambiguous stimulus that can be primed for disambiguation by an appropriate sentential context, e.g., "On the highway, he drives the car much _____."

Leonard et al. (2016) recorded from a high-density multi-electrode electrocorticography array on the surface of the cortex of patients whose brains were being examined in order to localize seizures. This method (known as ECoG) has a high signal-to-noise ratio and excellent temporal and spatial resolution. Direct recording from the brain is methodologically superior to brain-imaging techniques in many respects. Further, the high resolution for both space and time contrasts to standard forms of brain imaging that are good at one but not both.

Subjects virtually always reported hearing either "faster" or "factor." Leonard et al. were able to show that the sounds were recreated in the auditory cortex in the same area (superior temporal gyrus) that discriminates between the real /k/ and /s/ sounds and, amazingly, at about the same time after the stimulus as hearing the unambiguous words "faster" and "factor." The authors provide evidence that the processes that use the context to disambiguate the sounds were based in a cognitive area, the left inferior frontal cortex, but they did not see any actual frontal registration of the phonetic features that differentiate /k/ from /s/. They conclude (p. 7), "More generally, the observation of a warping of the acoustic-phonetic representation in STG [NB: the superior temporal gyrus] that is preceded by predictive effects in a higher-order cognitive region (left inferior frontal cortex) is inconsistent with models of speech perception that posit post-perceptual decision processes as the locus of restoration."

To summarize: A cognitive area that processes sentence context (but does not itself code phonemic information) biases an auditory perceptual area toward replacing an ambiguous stimulus by the contextually appropriate phoneme. This is a clear content-specific effect of cognition on perception ("cognitive penetration"). And it is empirical support for concrete versions of some of the theses of this book, that there is a joint between cognition and perception, that individual cases can be placed on either side of the joint, and that the joint is compatible with cognitive penetration of perception by cognition.

Of course, the reasoning just described is dependent on other experimental paradigms that classify the brain regions involved as cognitive or auditory-perceptual. So, the benign circularity noted earlier is not sidestepped. However, this is yet another convergent result that suggests that the methods discussed so far really are isolating distinct perceptual and cognitive representations.

Some readers may be familiar with the controversy over "filling in" in the visual field. When one looks at something with one eye, there is a "blind spot" created by the dead space where the optic nerve goes though the retina. (This is needed because the human eye—unlike the octopus eye— is constructed backward, with the wiring in the way of the light.) The issue arises as to why we don't notice a hole in our visual field. Dan Dennett (1991) famously argued: "The fundamental flaw in the idea of 'filling in' is that it suggests that the brain is providing something when in fact the brain is ignoring something" (p. 356). But P. S. Churchland and V. S. Ramachandran showed that in fact the brain does provide early visual activity to make up for the missing signal, "filling in" the hole in the visual field (Churchland & Ramachandran, 1996). The phonemic restoration effect is an analogous form of "filling in."

The Dennettian approach fits with a picture of cognition and perception as of the same fundamental type. For cognitive purposes, ignoring can be a quicker and easier approach than providing something. If perception followed the same rules as cognition, Dennett's suggestion would make sense. But perception follows its own rules.

Similar conclusions can be drawn from a behavioral psychological paradigm involving adaptation. Samuel (1997, 2001) reasoned that if the phonemic restoration effect is a perceptual effect, the "restored" phonemes should have the same adaptational effect on *subsequent* stimuli that real phonemes have. Just as seeing many dots causes a subsequent set of dots to look like fewer dots, hearing repeated /d/ sounds makes an ambiguous stimulus sound like /b/. (/d/ and /b/ are on opposite sides of a phonemic border.)

In the version used in (Samuel, 1997), four-syllable words were used in which the target phoneme was in the third syllable. (I'll give examples based on the contrast between /b/ and /d/. The /d/ words were "academic," "armadillo," "confidential," "psychedelic," and "recondition." The /b/ words were "alphabet," "Caribbean," "cerebellum," "exhibition," and "inhibition." Subjects heard 24 words from one list, say the /d/ words, and then had to classify eight ambiguous stimuli that had had the phoneme replaced by noise. The result was repulsive: that is, when the /d/ words were repeated, they gave higher-than-baseline categorizations of the ambiguous stimuli as /b/ words and lower as /d/ words, a classic effect of adaptation. (Higher than baseline means higher than when no words were presented before the ambiguous stimuli.) The corresponding result occurred when /b/ words were repeated and with other cases.

Then came the big test: Instead of /d/ words in the stimulus, they used the same words ("academic," "armadillo," "confidential," "psychedelic," and "recondition") but with the /d/ sound replaced by white noise, e.g., "aca#emic." The repulsive effect was the same, though smaller. In other words, *the percept involving the internally generated phonemic representation functioned rather like the percept of the real phoneme in its effect on later stimuli.* This result goes beyond previous work on phonemic restoration in that it isn't only that subjects can't reliably tell the real from the internally generated but also that the percepts have *similar effects on subsequent states.*

I said that the paradigm allowed for simultaneous investigation of perception and cognition. The paradigm shows perceptual effects for phonemes but not for words, even though words are cognitively represented. (For example, speakers of English know that "kiss" and "gift" are words but "giss" and "kift" are not words.) Samuel tested for adaptation effects for words in a number of ways. One was to use the words with the missing phonemes, but without the white noise, e.g., "arma_illo" rather than "arma#illo." Subjects report hearing a /d/ sound in the second but no /d/ sound in the first. And that report is borne out in the data. Although subjects are aware that "arma_illo" is a variant of the word "armadillo," it has no repulsive effect on subsequent stimuli, an absence of a cognitive adaptation effect.

A second experiment involved matching words (e.g., "kiss" and "gift") with nonwords ("giss" and "kift"). The nonwords (e.g., "giss") were produced by splicing the /g/ sound in "gift" onto the front of "kiss." The aim of the paradigm was to approach the issue of whether there would be any extra adaptational oomph from the words as compared with the matched nonwords. Samuel's question was whether the adaptational effects are based on sublexical (below the level of the word) representations rather than lexical representations. The result was that "gift" was no more effective than "giss," and "kiss" was no more effective than "kift." All the adaptational oomph comes from the sublexical components. "Gift" and "giss" have equivalent adaptational oomph because they are alike in the relevant sounds, even though they are different at the level of word syntax and word semantics, showing the presence of a phonemic effect and the absence of effects having to do with cognitive representations involving the syntactic and the semantic properties of words.

Another result along the same lines makes use of the fact that the initial consonants used in the previous experiment varied along a well-specified dimension—in this case "voice onset time." If you feel your throat in saying words with /b/, /d/, and /g/, you will hear a vibrational difference from similar words with /p/, /t/, and /k/. This parameter can be varied to produce a set of stimuli that vary from "gift" to "kift." It has long been known that if a subject hears repeated voiced syllables, that will have a repulsive effect, pushing the perception of a sound in such a series in the nonvoiced direction. Samuel asked the question as to whether, in such a continuum, tokens at the lexical end of the continuum ("gift") would adapt less than tokens at the nonlexical end ("kift"). The result: There was no differential effect of lexicality on adaptation. Again, the upshot was the demonstration of perceptual effects involving phonemes with the absence of effects having to do with cognitive representations involving the syntactic and the semantic properties of words.

Samuel (1997) summarizes (p. 125): "The results of the current study indicate that adaptation effects do not operate at the lexical level. . . . The results are best accounted for by the view that lexical activation, together with an appropriate masking noise, produced a perceptually-restored phonemic code, and that this sublexical representation produced the observed adaptation."

Interestingly, an experiment has been done focusing on written lexical items using a methodology very similar to what Samuel used to show that there is no adaptation for spoken lexical items (Hanif, Perler, & Jason, 2013). Hanif found a robust effect for written lexical items, a result in tension with Samuel's. Perhaps this is not surprising, since there is a brain area on the left fusiform gyrus, called the "visual word form" area, that corresponds to the fusiform face area on the right fusiform gyrus. Lesions to this area cause "pure alexia," the inability to visually recognize words while still being able to visually recognize letters. Apparently, the right fusiform area plays a role in face recognition in children until they learn to read, when it is co-opted for written word perception (Dehaene & Cohen, 2011).

Recall that the discussion of this section started with two competing theories of the phonemic restoration effect:

1. <u>Restored phonemic perception</u>. When the stimulus is "legi#lature," the subject hears the /s/ sound plus white noise, i.e., "legislature" together with #.
2. <u>Perceptual judgment</u>: The subject does not hear the /s/ sound, i.e., the subject hears "legi#lature" but perceptually judges that the stimulus was "legislature" together with #, failing to report the missing sound.

A number of different experimental approaches converge on the first of these theories. Further, the cognitive level of words did not show auditory adaptational effects except via the perceptual appreciation of the sublexical components of the words. Words did show visual adaptational effects, however.

We have discussed two kinds of cases of phonemic restoration, the multisyllabic cases like "legi#lature" and the ambiguous word cases like "fa#tor." In both cases, we have strong evidence for the effect being an effect on perception. But only in the "fa#tor" case do we have evidence for cognitive penetration. In the "legi#lature" case, the possibility remains that it is a top-down effect *within* the language system.

In sum, in the phonemic restoration effect we have clear evidence of perceptual adaptation effects together with the absence of adaptation effects involving cognitive properties having to do with the syntax and semantics of words. These results show that adaptation methodology is powerful enough to distinguish between perception and cognition.

In the next section, I will delve deeper into adaptation, in part to make a case for my side of a controversy with Tyler Burge on what we can learn from adaptation.

Different kinds of adaptation

One item of evidence that adaptation is perceptual is that it is often retinotopic. Adaptation is shown to be retinotopic when if you move your eyes you move the locus of adaptation. Color adaptation is always retinotopic and this fact is partly explained by decreased sensitivity in cones in the retina but also by decreased sensitivity in retinotopic cortical areas in the visual system.

Retinotopic adaptation is generally regarded as conclusive evidence for the perceptual nature of an effect. For example, Jonathan Kominsky and Brian Scholl say, in a discussion of adaptation, "This strikes us as a largely unambiguous and uncontroversial way to identify visual processing, since we know of no type of higher-level judgment that yields any sort of retinotopically specific effect" (Kominsky & Scholl, 2020, p. 3).

Both retinotopic and spatiotopic (see below) visual areas are organized in a similar manner to the retina (at least within each half visual field), with neighboring areas of space represented by neighboring chunks of cortex; and activations correspond to activations on the retina. Each point in the retina or in retinotopic cortex corresponds to a point in the visual field that that retinal or cortical location is sensitive to. Many neuroscientists say that the retinotopic organization of visual areas facilitates linking representations at different levels of the visual hierarchy that involve direction toward an area of space, though this is hard to show experimentally.

A distinction is often made between a retinotopic and a spatiotopic/topographic area or effect. (I will use the term "spatiotopic" rather than "topographic.") The difference is usually understood as: A retinotopic effect will move as the eyes move, whereas a spatiotopic effect preserves retinal neighborhood relations but need not move with the eyes. A spatiotopic effect (that is not also retinotopic) will depend on cortical areas that are organized in the manner of the retina. For both retinotopic and spatiotopic cortical areas, spatial relations on the cortex correspond at least roughly to spatial relations in the world relative to the viewer. Many adaptation effects are mediated by the first cortical visual area, V1, and are retinotopic. Motion perception depends on a higher area MT and is spatiotopic but not retinotopic (Astle, 2009). I will describe an adaptation effect below in which there was no attempt to control eye movements but nonetheless both the adapting and adapted stimulus had to be on the same side of the subject's fixation point for the adaptation to work. Thus, this adaptation is spatiotopic but may not be retinotopic. Low-level adaptation effects are retinotopic or spatiotopic, though that may not be true for some high-level adaptation.

Gender adaptation for faces has been shown to be retinotopic (Afraz & Cavanagh, 2009). (See later in the chapter for a gender adaptation effect.) And other face adaptation effects are also at least partly retinotopic (Afraz & Cavanagh, 2006). Individuals have preferred fixation points on faces, some lower, some higher on the face. Suppose your preferred fixation point is higher and mine is lower. If you are forced to fixate where I do and I where you do, our abilities to identify faces can fall 20% (Peterson & Eckstein, 2013), showing a surprising extent of retinotopic processing in normal face perception.

Color vision is complex, but the most fundamental basis for it is an opponent process system in which there are three channels, red/green, blue/yellow, and dark/light. A channel is defined by two pools of neurons, each of which responds maximally to one end of the channel. The repulsive effects of adaptation for such cases is a matter of shifting the balance of one or more of these channels. Thus, adapting to the yellow in the sky area in the first picture causes one to see blue in that area in the second picture.

Opponent processes also obtain for many other perceptual dimensions. For example, viewing a very blurry image makes a neutral stimulus look sharper and viewing a very sharp image makes a neutral stimulus look blurry.

I mentioned the red/green and blue/yellow channels. Actually, the so-called red/green channel is cherry/teal and the so-called blue/yellow channel is violet-chartreuse (Skelton, Catchpole, Abbott, Bosten, & Franklin, 2017). People often speak of the three kinds of cones in the retina as sensitive to red, green, and blue, but attaching those color names to the peak sensitivities of the three kinds of cones is also a gross oversimplification. The points about the channels and cones are important because it shows that our color categories emerge at a later stage of visual processing than the retina or channels (Siuda-Krzywicka, Boros, Bartolomeo, & Witzel, 2019; Witzel, 2019).

Color adaptation is an instance of what is called "norm-based" adaptation, in which there is a neutral norm (gray in the case of color). Norms exist because of channels in which there are two pools of neurons that are activated by the two ends of a channel. When the two pools have activations that are equal, the perception is of the norm. Adaptation occurs when one of the pools is more active than the other and so its threshold for firing decreases, shifting the balance toward the other end of the channel. Hence, the "repulsive" effect. Although the norm is usually considered to be the point at which both channels respond equally, some models of norm-based coding involve an explicit representation of the norm (Jeffery, Burton, Pond, Clifford, & Rhodes, 2018). The norm can shift with each perception.

In norm-based perception, subjects classify the norm as "neutral" with respect to the relevant dimension. Hence my use of the term "neutral" to describe the blurry/sharp norm three paragraphs ago. Some sample norm-based domains are the aforementioned blur and certain kinds of distortions in arrays of faces. For example, when viewing expanded and compressed faces, subjects update a norm for a prototypical face. Evidence of neural correlates for this process has been found (Kloth, Rhodes, & Schweinberger, 2017).

A different kind of adaptation is found in the tilt aftereffect. See Figure 2.2. If you fixate the rightmost (clockwise) grid for at least 30 seconds and then glance at the middle grid, it should look slightly tilted counterclockwise. Fixating the leftmost (counterclockwise) grid in the same way should make the middle grid look to be tilted slightly clockwise, another repulsive effect. In this case, the explanation has to do not with opponent channels but with separate channels tuned to slightly different orientations. Staring at the slightly clockwise tilt of the rightmost grid lowers the sensitivity of the channels for clockwise perception, so when you look at the middle grid, the preponderance of neural activation is in the counterclockwise channels. The tilt aftereffect is complex, and I will say more about it later. Other multichannel effects involve color contrast, stripe density (more exactly, spatial frequency), and viewpoint direction of a face. (See the caption and text surrounding Figure 1.1.)

Opponent and multichannel adaptation are both paradigmatically repulsive effects, but we can tell them apart on the basis of various differences in how they work. One obvious difference is that in norm-based (opponent) adaptation, there is a norm, e.g., gray in the case of color adaption. That norm does not show a standard repulsive adaptation effect. (If you stare at gray, the adaptation effect will be to make any other color look more extreme in one or another opponent direction. More on this later.) Perhaps the most useful difference, though, is that in opponent adaptation, the biggest effects happen when the first ("adapting") and second ("test") stimulus are far apart (Burton, Jeffery, Calder, & Rhodes, 2015), whereas the opposite is true in multichannel adaptation. Hence, in Figure 2.1, the adapting and test stimuli look very different from each other, whereas in Figure 2.2, they look quite similar. Many standard adaptation cases are mixtures of the two kinds of adaptation.

The phrase "perceptual adaptation" is used to describe many different phenomena. For example, as one ages, the lens of the eye yellows considerably. But white things continue to look white, not yellow. The process of accommodation to the changing lens is often called perceptual adaptation. But it is quite different from what I am talking about here. I am talking about brief and temporary changes in perceptual sensitivity and the effects on subsequent perception (Webster, 2015). As so often in science though, definition is difficult, since there is often a member of the intended natural kind that does not fit because of a weird difference in conditions.

For example, consider the McCollough effect. (See the Wikipedia article on this effect for examples of the stimuli.) The subject stares at red and black stripes oriented horizontally and also green and black stripes oriented vertically for a few minutes. After that adaptation, the white part of a black and white striped stimulus with vertical and horizontal components will look colored with the "opposite" colors from the adapting stimulus. The effect is thought to be a result of norm-based adaptation in cells that are sensitive to both color and orientation. This effect can last for months if an appropriate releasing stimulus is not encountered. (The effect occurs in pigeons, where it can last for 24 hours [Lea, Earle, & Ryan, 1999].) Thus, one can see that the brief nature of the other cases

Figure 2.2 The tilt aftereffect. Stare at the rightmost grid for 30 seconds, fixating the dot in the middle. Then look briefly at the center grid. It should look slightly tilted to the left. Now stare at the leftmost grid for 30 seconds, fixating the dot in the middle. When you look briefly at the center grid, it should look tilted slightly to the right. Thanks to Marisa Carrasco for this diagram. The effect works, though at a reduced level, when the adapting stimulus is shown to one eye and the test stimulus is shown to the other eye. This shows that the effect is partly based in binocular and partly based in monocular processors.

of perceptual adaptation I have been talking about is contingent on the fact that almost anything can be a releasing stimulus.

The explanation of both norm-based and multichannel adaptation has been said to be "fatigue" of neurons or neural circuits. Circuits that register a slight clockwise tilt are fatigued by exposure and so do not respond as sensitively as before. Fatigue of red-registering circuits shifts the balance toward green. Fatigue is wrong in many ways (Solomon & Kohn, 2014). One failure of the fatigue idea is that it fails to explain how adaptation can sometimes have attractive rather than repulsive effects. (I said adaptation is "paradigmatically" repulsive, meaning that paradigms of adaptation are repulsive.) Another failure will be mentioned below.

In multichannel adaptation, there is often a mix of repulsive and attractive effects. Adapting to an oriented grid lowers sensitivity in neurons tuned to that orientation, but it also shifts the tuning curve away from that orientation by as much as 10° (Jin, Dragoi, Sur, & Seung, 2005). This effect can work in opposition to the lowered sensitivity. The mix of attractive and repulsive effects in adaptation can lead to overall attractive effects.

In the tilt aftereffect, staring at a right-tilted grid makes a subsequently presented vertical grid look left tilting. This effect works for orientations from 0° to 50°, but for larger angles, especially between 75° and 80°, the effect is attractive. That is, a line tilted at 75° to the right makes a vertical line look tilted to the right. These effects can be explained on the basis of perceptual mechanisms of centering and scaling, mechanisms that increase the information content of population responses (Cliffor, Wenderoth, & Spehar, 2000). When you look closely at how a case of adaptation works, the details can make it clear that it is perceptual.

If you fixate the dot in Figure 2.3 for 30 seconds, then immediately move your gaze to the dot at the center of Figure 2.4, you will find that it looks, initially and briefly, as if there are more dots on the right even though the stimuli on the right and left are identical. The explanation is that we have perceptual representations of numerosity. Channels for high numerosity on the left side of your visual field decrease sensitivity, so when you look at Figure 2.4, the balance on the left shifts toward dominance of channels for low numerosity. Something similar happens on the right with respect to low numerosity, making the dominant channels on the right shift toward high numerosity. The combination of both effects results in the right side looking more numerous. This is a norm-based adaptation and the norms are context-relative, shifting with ambient numerosities. Adaptation to numerosity has been shown across the animal kingdom, including in insects.

There is a well-known methodological issue with a wide variety of psychophysical experiments. Perhaps it is easiest to illustrate it with the example of a subject being asked to say whether a stimulus is present or absent. If the subject's responses shift in different circumstances, that could be due to a change

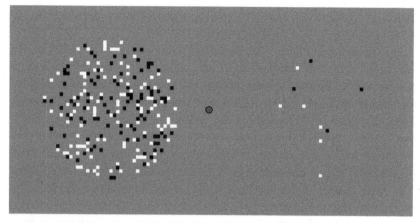

Figure 2.3 Point your eyes at the dot in the middle for 30 seconds. Then, immediately, move your gaze to Figure 2.4. Look at the dot in the middle of Figure 2.4, asking yourself whether there is a difference in apparent numerosity between the left and right sides. (See Burr & Ross, 2008.) Thanks to David Burr for this figure.

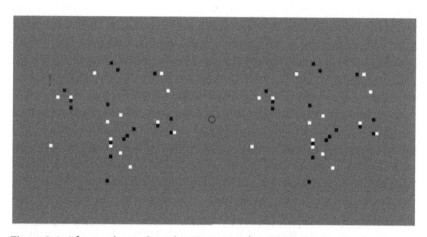

Figure 2.4 After you have adapted to Figure 1, immediately switch your gaze to this figure. You will find that it appears, initially as if there are more dots on the right than the left. Actually, there are 30 dots on both sides. (See Burr & Ross, 2008.) Thanks to David Burr for this figure.

in whether the subject sees the stimulus, or, alternately, in what is called the "decision-criterion," a matter of the degree of certainty the subject requires to report that stimulus was present. The criterion can be manipulated in many ways. For example, if there is a reward for correct detections and no penalty for false alarms, the subject may adopt a strategy of saying the stimulus was there if the subject feels that there is even a slight chance that it was there. Criterion levels also shift in response to numbers of "catch trials" in which there is no stimulus. As the proportion of catch trials decrease, the criterion tends to decrease as well. Sometimes adaptation experiments are criticized from the point of view of "signal detection theory" for inadequate attention to criterion effects (Smortchkova, 2020; Storrs, 2015). One standard approach is to show a difference in adaptation between one location in the visual field and another. No criterion effect has ever been shown to be retinotopic or spatiotopic. Since many perceptual adaptation effects, including high-level effects, are retinotopic or spatiotopic to some degree, criterion effects can often be ruled out.

However, standard psychophysical approaches fail to consider an obvious way of avoiding criterion issues. In the numerosity experiment just described, it briefly *looks* as if there are more dots on the right than on the left. I have shown these displays in many classes and I have to assure the audience that I have not tricked them with a video that starts with more dots on the right and shifts to equal numbers of dots. There is no reason to expect criterion effects to fade. This is not the first-person experience of a criterion effect. It is a robust effect that you can experience for yourself despite the absence of laboratory conditions. This point might fall on deaf ears in the psychophysics community because of suspicion of "introspective" reports, but a rational reader should be persuaded by it.

It is an interesting question how far we can go with first-person experience in adjudicating the difference between perception and perceptual judgment. It is obvious that the adaptation effect just described (and the ones described earlier) are effects on the subjects' experiences. I don't think any normal perceiver could follow the instructions given and not agree with that. Sometimes it is supposed that we cannot tell whether such effects on experience are on the experience of *perception* rather than *perceptual judgment* (Helton, 2016). But the experience of seeing Figure 2.1 after adapting is a *color* experience. That is a matter of perceptual experience, not just perceptual judgment. A similar point can be made about the experience of tilt in Figure 2.3 and of numerosity in Figure 2.4.

It is sometimes said that gender and emotion adaptation effects are likely to be criterion effects (Briscoe, 2015). Joulia Smortchkova suggests that they might be criterion effects that have been modularized (2020). Whether or not they are criterion effects, they are clearly effects on perceptual experience. For example, the effects of Figure 2.5 and Figure 2.6 clearly involve the way the center picture looks. (For the strongest effect, use pieces of paper to cover the pictures that you are not supposed to be looking at.) Similar effects to those shown in Figure 2.5 and Figure 2.6 have been shown with morphs of human hands and either robot hands or animal paws (Conson et al. 2020). Subjects who adapted to animal

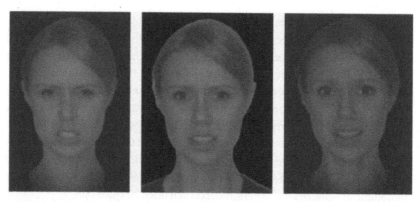

Figure 2.5 Stare at the picture on your right for 60 seconds while covering the other pictures. Look very quickly at the center picture, noting your first reaction as to whether it looks more fearful or more angry. Then stare at the picture on the left for 60 seconds. Then look very quickly at the picture in the middle, noting your first reaction. You should see the center picture differently, first more angry, then more fearful. This is the classic "repulsion" effect of adaptation. From Butler, Oruc, Fox, and Barton (2008, p. 118), with permission of Elsevier.

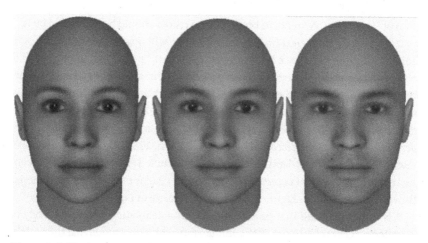

Figure 2.6 The instructions here are analogous to those of the previous illustration. Stare at the picture on your right for 60 seconds while covering the other pictures. Look quickly at the center picture, noting your first reaction as to whether it looks more feminine or more masculine. Then stare at the picture on the left for 60 seconds. Then look quickly at the picture in the middle, noting your first reaction. You should see the center picture differently, first more feminine, then more masculine. This is the classic "repulsion" effect of adaptation. Modified from Figure 2 of Javadi and Wee (2012). Reprinted under the terms of a Creative Commons Attribution License.

hands or robot hands were more likely to see morphs as human hands, exhibiting the classic repulsion effect.

In the case of low-level phenomenology we can often be sure whether an effect is merely perceptual rather than an effect on perceptual judgment. The problematic cases are cases of high-level phenomenology. A language sounds different before and after one learns it. No doubt that difference in part has to do with low-level perception as a result of increased perceptual expertise and differences in attention but is there a difference in high-level semantic phenomenology as well? I don't think this can be answered on the basis of introspection. A pine tree looks different before and after learning to recognize pine trees (Siegel, 2010). Is that a matter just of the changes in low-level perception or is it due to perceptual attribution of the high-level property of being a pine tree?

When we see emotional faces and gendered faces as in Figure 2.5 and Figure 2.6, are we visually attributing emotions and genders or are we visually attributing certain low-level facial appearances? That is, are we seeing emotions and genders or are we seeing certain low-level appearances that are typical of those emotions and genders? This is a tricky question that can be approached both experimentally and conceptually.

Pursuing the conceptual approach, the primary question is whether the functional role of a visual representation could support treating it as a representation of an emotion or a gender. According to my view of nonconceptual perception, the role within the visual system could not support such a categorization, but it remains possible that a wider functional role could do so, including the role of the visual representation in producing a perceptual judgment about the emotion or gender. Especially if the formation of a minimal immediate direct perceptual judgment is automatic, I can see a fairly good case for regarding the visual representation as a nonconceptual representation of the emotion or gender.

In a commentary on an earlier version of some of this material (at a meeting on my manuscript organized by Ophelia Deroy at Venice International University in Fall 2018), Albert Newen argued that some emotions involve cognitive states and so perception of such emotions must be partly conceptual. I understand Newen to have argued that since the emotion requires a cognitive background, perceptual recognition of it would require some perceptual appreciation of that cognitive background and so involve concepts. Of course, recognition of something with a certain essence can proceed without engaging conceptually with that essence. Someone can be trained to recognize a tumor on an X-Ray film while knowing little or nothing about cancer. The concept of cancer will come in at the level of perceptual judgment, not as part of the perceptual content. So my response would be again that nonconceptual representation of emotion may be possible in the case of automatic or nearly automatic production of a minimal immediate direct perceptual judgment with the right conceptual content.

The experimental approach might explore other body parts that express the same or "opposite" emotions or genders. So if body part X can be feminine or masculine, one could ask whether fixating on a masculine face would make a subsequent presentation of X seem more feminine than it would otherwise appear.

The evidential route from adaptation to perception is complex. Adaptation is a sensory phenomenon, encompassing preperceptual sensation as well as perception. As mentioned earlier, Burge (2010a) identifies the perceptual constancies as constituting the dividing line between sensation and perception. There can be sensory but preperceptual adaptation even without either perception or cognition. As mentioned earlier, perceptual materials can be used in concepts so there can be a kind of perceptual adaptation in conceptual thought. For example, motion aftereffects like the waterfall illusion can be induced by imaging motion in one direction (Winawer, Huk, & Boroditsky, 2010). Although perceptual materials function in cognition, it is only in virtue of these perceptual materials that cognition shows adaptation effects. (More on this topic below.)[3]

The upshot is that adaptation is not sufficient evidence for perception even if it is sufficient for perceptual materials—whether in sensation or perception or used in cognition. One consequence is that we should be cautious in supposing that adaptation in recognition of emotion (Marchi & Newen, 2015; Newen, Welpinghus, & Juckel, 2015) shows that recognition of emotion is purely perceptual. The adaptation may be due to perceptual materials functioning in a nonperceptual state.

A distinction is often made (and often criticized) between basic emotions and secondary emotions. Basic emotions are often said to be characterizable neurobiologically (Celeghin, Diano, Bagnis, Viola, & Tamietto, 2017). By this sort of criterion, there is a case that we share at least some basic emotions with fruit flies (Gu, Wang, Patel, Bourgeois, & Huang, 2019). It is the secondary emotions that are alleged to involve cognition and motivate the idea that their recognition involves concepts. I don't know whether there are adaptation effects for representing secondary emotions, but there is one result that suggests maybe not (Palumbo, D'Ascenzo, Quercia, & Tommasi, 2017). Palumbo et al. showed subjects valenced scenes that did not contain faces from the International Affective Picture System, e.g., polluting smokestacks as a negatively valenced

---

[3] A reviewer wondered whether the retinotopic nature of much of adaptation shows that it is preconstancy and therefor preperceptual. However, there is no one "level" of constancies in vision. Some constancies are even computed in the retina. Many retinotopic and spatiotopic areas have been discovered in different levels of the visual system (Silver & Kastner, 2009; Silver, Ress, & Heeger, 2005).

scene. (The valences were determined in a separate experiment by ratings of other subjects.) They did not find any standard "repulsive" adaptation effect. For short presentations they got no effect and for long presentations, they found that negative scenes biased subjects toward a more *negative* response toward a subsequent scene and positive scenes biased subjects toward a more *positive* response toward a subsequent scene. If the scenes elicited secondary emotions, then this experiment suggests a lack of adaptation effects for secondary emotions. It also provides evidence against evaluative perception. Further arguments are to be found in Chapter 3.

Further, even if there are adaptation effects for secondary emotions, perhaps they can be attributed to basic emotions that are involved in the secondary emotions, as for example the basic emotion of sadness might be involved in some cases of the secondary emotion of grief. Grief requires understanding that someone has died, whereas sadness does not require any such cognitive background.

Newen also argued that work on expert perception and in particular perception of chess board configurations (Bilalić, Turella, Campitelli, Erb, & Grodd, 2012) shows that perception is conceptual. Chess experts, he argued, can see whether the white knight is under attack, whether knights are present on the board, whether there are four threats of black to white, and whether the number of bishops and knights on the board add up to four.

I agree with Newen that there is a perceptual component to chess expertise. For example, chess novices require foveation of chess pieces for recognition of them, whereas experts can perform as well with the pieces in parafoveal vision. Chess experts have a big advantage over novices in recognizing realistic chess configurations, though not for pieces randomly placed on the board. But the role of concepts in *improving* perceptual capacities does not entail that the resulting perceptual capacities are even in part conceptual. Concepts can be used to train up perception without permeating perception. More generally, we must distinguish factors involved in the origin of something from that thing's fundamental nature. Emotion also plays a role in improving perceptual capacities, but that does not show that the resulting perceptual capacities are in part emotional. Electricity plays a role in improving perceptual capacities but that does not show that the resulting perceptual capacities are in part electrical.

Newen notes that the temporoparietal junction is more active in experts than novices in evaluating complex chess positions (Rennig, Bilalić, Huberle, Karnath, & Himmelbach, 2013), arguing that the temporoparietal junction is responsible for gestalt recognition and that in the case of chess, that the gestalt recognition involves concepts. But the temporoparietal junction has many nonperceptual cognitive functions including for example, recognizing other peoples' mental states from stories about them (Saxe, Whitfield-Gabrieli, Scholz, & Pelphrey, 2009).

The articles I have read by the group that Newen cites (Bilalić, 2018; Bilalić, Langner, Erb, & Grodd, 2010; Bilalić et al., 2012; Huberle & Karnath, 2006; Rennig et al., 2013) do not suggest that the abilities of experts to tell whether the white knight is under attack are purely visual. The time it takes experts to respond—nearly 2 seconds—leaves plenty of room for cognition to operate on perceptual inputs.

Newen also cites experiments that varied shape and category membership of pictures so as to isolate the brain areas that process category and shape information (Bracci & Op de Beeck, 2016). As mentioned earlier in this chapter, Bracci et al. found shape processing in early visual areas in the back of the head and category processing in prefrontal cortex. As mentioned earlier, there were many areas in mid- and high-level vision that involve both shape and category. Newen suggests that representations in these processing areas are neither purely perceptual nor purely conceptual but a mixture of the two, throwing shade on the joint in nature between perception and cognition.

However, as will be explained in Chapter 6, there are perceptual category representations that are not conceptual. (In fact in my view, no perceptual category representations are conceptual, but my case for that is weaker than for the former claim.) Chapter 6 is devoted to explaining in detail that there are perceptual categories for color in infants between 6 and 11 months even though they do not possess color concepts. I also note that infants have perceptual categories for phonemes despite the obvious lack of phoneme concepts. As we will see below, high-level perceptual representations need not be conceptual.

Newen and Vetter (2016) distinguish between pure perception, pure cognition, and "everyday perception," which they take to be conceptual perception. Their example of pure perception is black and white dots that don't form any objects.

> The middle ground includes the majority of everyday perceptual experiences: to describe the content of these experiences, it seems adequate to use a combination of descriptions of non-conceptual, spatial organizations of dots intertwined with high-level and abstract conceptual contents to create a meaningful percept. Everyday perceptual experiences can have rich contents . . . but nevertheless can be clearly distinguished from perception-based judgments. Our suggested account of distinguishing paradigmatic pure perception from paradigmatic pure cognition with the majority of perceptual phenomena as everyday rich perception as a middle ground presupposes the possibility of rich

perceptual contents and allows for both: that these rich contents are produced by perceptual learning or by cognitive penetration.

However, as I will be arguing in detail in this book, rich contents can be purely perceptual. Further, as I will describe later in this chapter, the method of adaptation can be used to distinguish rich perceptual contents from the conceptual contents of cognition.

To be clear, adaptation is not sufficient for perception, and it may not be necessary either. (I have been interpreted as saying that adaptation is a "criterion" for perception [Smortchkova, 2020], but I meant an evidential criterion, not a necessary or sufficient condition.) There may be structural features of the visual field that preclude some kinds of spatial adaptation. Chaz Firestone (in correspondence) has given me a list of properties that are candidates for being both perceptual and not adapting: near/far, left/right, connectedness, symmetry, heterogeneity. For example, repeated viewing of something far away might not make a mid-distance item look closer. (I don't know of any test of this.) Repeated viewing of symmetrical things might not make things look less symmetrical, though as we will see in the discussion of perceptual norms later in this chapter, it might make items look to have more "extreme" properties in opponent channels. In some of these cases, there may be structural features of the visual field that preclude adaptation: For example, nature might have been expected to disfavor creatures who, after seeing many things on the left, saw food that is right in front but seen as on the right.

In some of these cases, there is actual evidence. Ron Finke put prism glasses on subjects that shifted their world view slightly to the right or to the left. When subjects donned the right-shifting glasses and were asked to point to a red marker, they pointed 5 cm to the right of it. Once they had a few hours of experience, including seeing the finger pointing to the wrong place, they were able to point normally. Then, when the glasses were removed, they pointed 5 cm to the left of the red marker (Finke, 1989), a classic repulsive adaptation effect. (He got similar effects—though smaller—when he merely asked subjects to imagine seeing their finger pointing 5 cm to the right.) Of course, this result does not show that seeing many things on the right will bias perception toward the left, since it may be the discrepancy between the percept of the thing and the percept of the finger that drives the effect.

It is known that low-level visual mechanisms in humans and animals can detect symmetry. For example, animals and people prefer symmetrical mates (Rhodes, Louw, & Evangelista, 2009). Further, there are specialized high-level mechanisms for detecting facial symmetry (Rhodes, Peters, Lee, Morrone, & Burr, 2005). For example, symmetry detection is better for upright than for inverted faces and better for normal face pictures than for contrast reversed face pictures. And face symmetry detection is more vulnerable to tilt than symmetry detection in nonfaces. Gillian Rhodes and her colleagues have shown adaptation to certain kinds of facial asymmetries (Rhodes et al., 2009). Whether there would be adaptation to symmetry in general is another matter.[4]

I think the right conclusion is that it is not known whether adaptation is necessary for perception. I don't know of a case of a property known to be perceptual by another test that has failed to show adaptation. (I have asked a number of vision scientists who study this kind of thing about this and have not found a plausible case.) But we lack a principled reason to think adaptation is necessary.

Replying to my (2014c), Tyler Burge (2014) argues that adaptation data cannot provide even prima facie evidence for visual representation of high-level properties. He argues that since the visual registration of high-level properties is always based on the visual registration of low-level properties, the adaptation one sees in these cases could be low-level adaptation together with the (high-level) numerosity content being conceptual.

I noted in Chapter 1 that subcortical structures like the amygdala are actively connected to the fusiform face area (Herrington et al., 2011). So a perception of a fearful face is partially a matter of a pathway that skips the low-level perceptual analysis of early visual cortex. So Burge is relying on a false premise. I will put the falsity of that premise to one side, though, in further discussion of his argument.

On Burge's view, it will be impossible to disentangle—using just adaptation—the following:

1. high-level visual representation of numerosity,
2. low-level visual representations (e.g., of density or surface area) plus (cognitive) judgments of numerosity.

I argued (2014c) that one could always find "baroque congeries of low-level properties" that are coextensive with a high-level property. (I am no longer so sure of that, given the point just made that some of the sources of information in high-level areas do not pass through low-level analysis, but I will put this concern to one side.)

The big problem in distinguishing high from low is that for any high-level property, e.g., being a face, there will be a set—maybe a highly disjunctive set—of low-level properties on the basis of which one recognizes the high-level

---

[4] Of course the experiments I have been talking about use pictures of faces rather than actual faces, and the gender and emotional expressions involved in Figure 2.5 and Figure 2.6 are depicted rather than real. I don't know of any reason to think that the results of using real faces would be any different, so I will ignore the difference.

properties. I described the set of low-level properties as recognitionally equivalent to the high-level property.

Burge responds to the evidence I give for high-level representations (including the Susilo study to be explained in the next section) by saying that congeries of low-level representations, including generic shape representations, might seem baroque from the point of view of physics and geometry but not from the point of view of vision science. He says (footnote 4):

> Relevant generic shapes are usually not of interest to physics or geometry. It would be a mistake, however, to think of the shape type as "disjunctive," except relative to explanation in those sciences. The groupings are associated with shape-patterns that signal faces. They have an objectivity like that of the North Sea, to use Frege's example. The objectivity is not in any general sense "disjunctive." The fact that a grouping or kind is systematically relevant to shipping routes and territorial claims, or to recognition of faces, suffices to give it objective-kind status, even if the sciences of physics and geometry do not refer to it.

I agree that the objectivity of the North Sea is not disjunctive, but the analogy is not apt, as I will explain in the next two sections.

Burge's argument raises two issues: (1) how, using perceptual adaptation, we can distinguish low-level from high-level perceptual properties and (2) how, using perceptual adaptation, we can distinguish perception (whether high or low) from cognition. (Recall that low-level visual representations are products of sensory transduction that are causally involved in the production of other [high-level] visual representations and include representations of shape, spatial relations, motion, texture, brightness, and color.) I will discuss these in order. But first, I must clarify the issues by just briefly summarizing some of the facts about what the difference is between high-level and low-level perception.

Visual hierarchy

As is often noted, as one ascends the visual hierarchy there are fewer eye-specific cells. When the adapting stimulus has the same effect whether the test stimulus is in the same or different eye, the effect is on middle- or high-level vision (Webster, 2015, p. 552). So, assuming a specific adaptation that has been observed is perceptual, transfer between eyes indicates it is not low-level perceptual.

The visual hierarchy is divided into a ventral (bottom of the brain) part and a dorsal (top of the brain) part. Inputs to the ventral stream go from the retina to lateral geniculate nucleus in the middle of the brain to cortical areas V1 to V2 to V3 to higher occipital areas, to processing in temporal cortex. The dorsal stream takes input from V1 and subcortical areas and includes parts of occipital and parietal cortex. The ventral stream is usually considered to end in the front part of the temporal cortex in area TE (Setogawa, Eldridge, Fomani, Saunders, & Richmond, 2021; Suzuki, 2010). When TE and the immediately preceding area, TEO, are removed from monkeys (in both hemispheres), the result is "severe, long-lasting impairment in categorization" with sparing of low-level visual abilities and no decrease in acuity (Setogawa et al., 2021, p. 1).

Each of the stages of the hierarchy receives signals mainly from the areas above and below it in the hierarchy. Information flows both up and down, so, unsurprisingly, there are different views as to what should be thought of as the "main" direction of information flow (Clark, 2016; Lee & Mumford, 2003; Orlandi & Lee, 2018).

The higher in the visual hierarchy, the larger the receptive fields of individual neurons. (The receptive field of a visual neuron is the area of space that the neuron responds to.) The receptive fields of V4 neurons are four times as large as the receptive fields of V1 neurons and in the highest level areas in the temporal cortex, receptive fields cover much of the visual field (Lee & Mumford, 2003). Receptive field size is one way of defining the visual hierarchy. Another way is in terms of what features are being registered, orientations and edges in lower areas, surfaces in somewhat higher areas, and objects, agency, causation, and faces at the highest areas (Orlandi & Lee, 2018).

This hierarchical picture is widely accepted (e.g., Yantis, 2005) even though there are disagreements between classical and predictive coding views about the primary direction of information flow (Clark, 2016). (The predictive coding approach will be discussed later.) But it is also widely acknowledged that information flow takes many pathways with substantial information flow in all directions, up, down, and laterally. See Shea (2014) for further discussion.

Compare the visual hierarchy to the "phylogenetic scale," as in "Where in the phylogenetic scale does consciousness arise?" This is a much vilified notion (Godfrey-Smith, 2017), since so-called lower animals such as jellyfish are the products of as much evolution as "higher" animals. Evolution does not proceed in the direction of more complexity. But complexity of properties processed and receptive field size does show more of a directional component.

This section contained a brief refresher on high- vs. low-level perception. Now on to my reply to Burge and a discussion more generally about how we can tell high-level perception from low-level perception and both from cognition.

The use of adaptation in distinguishing low-level from high-level perception

Some say that the contents of conscious perception are never high-level (Brogaard, 2013; Prinz, 2013), whereas others acknowledge high-level content (Bayne, 2009, 2016; Block, 2014c; Burge, 2010a, 2010b; Fish, 2013; Peacocke, 1983; Siegel, 2010). The discussion among philosophers has to a large extent been based on armchair considerations, though there has been some discussion of experimental results involving perception of gists or ensemble properties such as the average expression of faces and adaptation (Bayne, 2016; Fish, 2013; Marchi & Newen, 2015). (Ensemble properties/gists are defined in Chapter 4 in the section "Atomic propositional representations.") However, the same issues arise with respect to gists as with other putative cases of high-level perception. How do we know that a subject is perceiving an average facial expression rather than averages of low-level shape properties such as orientations, texture gradients, contrasts, etc.?

When one sees a dog, there are many different instantiated properties one could be said to be seeing: the property of being a fuzzy black and white thing, the property of being long and waggly, the property of being a labradoodle, the property of being a dog. It is sometimes argued that there are answers to such questions only if perception is conceptual (Gauker, 2011). However, there are often answers even though perception is nonconceptual. The topic of this section is how to use adaptation to distinguish between perceptual representation of low-level properties like colors, shapes, and textures from high-level properties like being a dog.

Similar issues have been discussed in philosophy with regard to the phenomenology of experience. For example, do we experience a nonconceptual sense of ownership of our body or is the sense of ownership a conceptual and judgmental overlay on nonconceptual experiences of "pressure, temperature, position, balance, movement, and so on" (de Vignemont, 2018, p. 13)?

One line of reply to Burge takes advantage of the different temporal properties of high- and low-level adaptation. Position in the visual hierarchy is correlated with differences in how long it takes to adapt to a stimulus. There is evidence that low-level features are slower to adapt than high-level features (Suzuki, 2005). As Suzuki notes, cells in the earliest visual cortical area (V1) do not show adaption for stimuli presented for 500 ms or less, taking seconds to adapt. But neurons higher up the hierarchy that register global properties like aspect ratio and relative size do adapt to stimuli of 500 ms or less. As Suzuki notes, this difference can allow for the separation of high- from low-level adaptation. A property that adapts to a brief stimulus is likely to be high-level.

Another reply to Burge is that many of the details of the different kinds of adaptation reveal aspects of perceptual systems that show whether the perception is high or low and also show that the adaptation effect derives from perception rather than cognition. For example, in norm-based adaptation we can find a norm, a stimulus that exemplifies a neutral point in an opponent process, as with the case of gray in the case of color. The fact that gray is a color norm is in the first instance a fact about perception, not cognition.

Some say the norm in norm-based adaptation might show little or no adaptation effect. For example, Webster seems to suggest that there will be no adaptation to the norm in a norm-based system, e.g., no adaptation for a neutral gray (Webster, 2015; Webster & MacLin, 1999). Even if there are some particular values of a perceptual parameter that don't show adaptation, still the parameter does in general show adaptation.

I mentioned earlier that if you stare at gray, there is a subtle adaptation effect in which other colors will look more extreme in one or another opponent direction. More specifically, exposure to norms tends to change the slope of the tuning function. Nichola Burton and her colleagues found evidence for this kind of adaptation to high-level norms (2015). They used a fear/antifear case in which adapting to a fearful face makes faces look less fearful and adapting to an antifear face makes faces look more fearful. The neutral face is defined as the face in which the neural responses to the fear and antifear faces are equal (along the same lines as all norm-based coding). Is there adaptation to the neutral face? Burton et al. found that the adaptation effect of adapting to the neutral face was to steepen the slope of the tuning functions for both ends of the spectrum, pushing perceptions toward the extreme directions, making faces look either more fearful or more antifearful.[5] (Note that the absence of simple repulsive effects for the norms in norm-based coding is another indication that the "fatigue" idea of adaptation is wrong.)

When we see a signature of a norm in adaptation we can ask what defines that norm. In color adaptation, it is color, a low-level property that defines the norm. In the case of emotional faces, it is the emotional expression that defines the norm. The signature properties of norm-based adaptation show perception rather than cognition, with their invocation of opponent processes and channels, and then consideration of what the norm or channels are indicates whether the adaptation is based on high-level or low-level perceptual properties. Fear and antifear are high-level, so this phenomenon suggests high-level adaptation that has many of the same properties as low-level adaptation.

A similar point can be made about multichannel adaptation. In the tilt aftereffect described earlier, the signature properties of multichannel adaptation show

---

[5] I am assuming that subjects are seeing the fearfulness (i.e., perceptually representing fearfulness), even though of course they know they are looking at a picture, not a face. One item of evidence for this is that fearful face pictures cause physiological indications of arousal, including skin conduction and activation of the amygdala.

the adaptation is perceptual rather than cognitive and the tuning of the channels to tilt show low-level perception. Of course, typing tilt as low-level and emotional expression as high-level requires more than adaptation.

Part of my reply to Burge, then, is that when we apply principles of scientific simplicity to the signature properties of the various kinds of adaptation, we can see that there is strong reason to regard adaptation of these kinds as perceptual, and then the details of the norms and channels can tell us whether the adaptation is high or low.

Another line of reply to Burge also appeals to scientific simplicity, especially the principle that we should try to explain similar effects by appeal to similar causes.

I will explain by reference to an experiment in which subjects adapted to the numerosity of their own finger-tapping (Anobile, Arrighi, Togoli, & Burr, 2016). They were instructed to tap quickly on some trials and slowly on others. They then made judgments of the numerosity of clouds of dots or alternatively of number of light flashes, judging the numerosities of the cloud of dots or light flashes as high or low. There were substantial adaptation effects in both cases with nearly identical adaptation curves relating perceived numerosity with actual numerosities. Tapping slowly increased numerosity judgments for both the dots and the flashes; tapping quickly decreased numerosity judgments for both the dots and the flashes. This adaptation experiment shows two types of adaptation effects:

- cross-modal, i.e., tactile/visual
- cross-format, i.e., sequential flashes vs. synchronic (simultaneous) judgment of dots.

These adaptation effects were similar in magnitude and slope for both cases, cross-modal and cross-format. See Figure 2.7 for further explanation.

E. J. Green suggests (2021) that we should not conclude that there is a single representation of numerosity accessed by the different modalities, since the result could be explained by causal relations among distinct modality-specific representations. For example, a visual representation of high numerosity might causally produce a tactile representation of high numerosity. But that hypothesis makes the similarities of slope and magnitude mysterious.

It is difficult to think of an explanatorily adequate low-level account, even a highly baroque and disjunctive account. Why would the adaptation effect be so similar in magnitude and slope despite differences in kind in low-level parameters (auditory/visual, synchronic/diachronic) if it were not primarily based on perceptual representation of numerosity? So even though the path to high-level representation is often (though not always, as I noted) via low-level

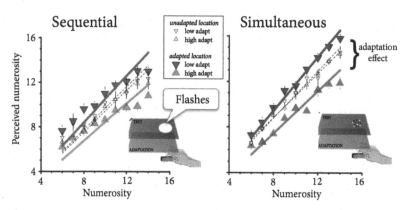

Figure 2.7 Perceived numerosities vs. actual numerosities for sequential (on left) and simultaneous cross-modal comparisons. The upward facing triangles show adaptation effects to high numerosities. Notice that on both the left and the right the upward triangles are below the diagonal line, indicating that when subjects experience high numerosities in the form of fast tapping, they perceive both sequential flashes and dot clusters as having lower numerosities than they would without any adaptation. The reverse is true for adaptation to low numerosities. The open triangles indicate the cases in which the tapping and the visual stimuli were on opposite sides. In those cases, there was virtually no adaptation effect, showing that the adaptation was spatiotopic. The lack of effect in the opposite hemifield also shows that the effect is not an effect of shifting decisional criterion (Storrs, 2015). There is a free pdf on the Oxford University Press web site that has the color version of this and all the other figures. Thanks to David Burr for this figure. (See Anobile et al., 2016.)

representation, appeal to low- and high-level representation may differ—as in this case—in explanatory significance.

I described the representations as cross-format on the ground that in one case the perception is sequential and the other simultaneous. Although this shows the formats are different at one stage of processing, it does not rule out that the formats are the same at another stage of processing.

In addition—and this goes beyond the evidence of adaptation itself—if the tapping was on the right, there were adaptation effects only for visual stimuli on the right. Likewise for the left, showing either retinotopic or spatiotopic adaptation. Of course, no experiment can prove that the adaptation was to numerosity, but this is pretty strong evidence against a cognitive interpretation.

The application of explaining similar effects by similar causes is that the effects on different modalities in different formats can all be explained by multimodal perceptual representation of numerosity. My admonition against disjunctive "baroque congeries of low-level properties" might have been better cast as an invocation of the similar effects–similar causes principle. We should favor the uniform explanation of the similar effects despite differences of format and modality. Of course there is always a possible disjunctive competitor to a "similar cause" explanation, but an advocate of such a competitor would have to explain why the curves for different formats and modalities are so similar.

The multimodal representation of numerosities has been shown to develop in infants by 4 months of age. Lisa Feigenson and her colleagues used looking time habituation to show that 4-month-olds could visually detect a 4 to 1 difference in numerosities but not a 3 to 1 difference. But when the infants were provided with redundant auditory information about the numerosities, their discrimination improved to the point where they could differentiate a 3 to 1 difference (Wang & Feigenson, 2021). In sum, the fact that the adaptation was cross-modal and cross-format suggests it was high-level perceptual and the fact that it was retinotopic or spatiotopic suggests it was not cognitive. (The latter point is not relevant to my disagreement with Burge since it goes beyond just adaptation.)

I can imagine someone claiming that because this effect was cross-modal, it wasn't really perception, since it might be alleged that perception is always in a single modality. But cross-modal effects are so ubiquitous in spatial perception that on that understanding of perception, there would be little spatial perception. Consider, for example, the motion aftereffect in which adapting to a moving stimulus makes a stationary stimulus seem to be moving in the opposite direction. Talia Konkle and her colleagues showed that adapting to haptic motion causes a visual motion aftereffect and adapting to visual motion causes a haptic motion aftereffect. In addition it has been shown that visual adaptation to motion causes an auditory motion aftereffect (Kitagawa & Ichihara, 2002). As Konkle et al. note, a number of spatial perception modalities rely on "shared representations that dynamically impact modality-specific perception" (Konkle, Wang, Hayward, & Moore, 2009, p. 745). Evidence for this thesis has been accumulating over many years. See an earlier brief summary in Block (2003b).

There are also cross-modal effects of perception of facial expression (Matsumiya & Shiori, 2008). Matsumiya had subjects view a series of faces that started with happy expressions and ended up with sad expressions. The task was to say where the border between happy and sad was. In another version, the subjects felt the facial features on a happy mask that was out of sight. The effect of feeling the happy mask was a classic repulsion effect, the border shifted toward the sad faces, again suggesting adaptation for a high-level property. (This might however be a criterion-shifting effect in which subjects are using the strategy of classifying doubtful cases as different from the mask (Storrs, 2015). Recall that such an explanation is ruled out in the numerosity experiment cited above because of its spatiotopic localization and very noticeable phenomenal character.

Konkle explains the cross-modal motion effect in terms of multimodal representations, that is, representations that are shared by different modalities. There is an argument against this explanation, though. Visual representations have a visual phenomenology whereas haptic representations have a haptic phenomenology. That observation motivates an alternative account to the effect that what may be shared is subpersonal mechanisms that underlie structural similarities in representations in different modalities but not the representations themselves.

I don't find this alternative persuasive. Spatial perceptual representations may always have nonspatial aspects, and the phenomenology may be contributed in part by those nonspatial aspects. Compare the visual representation of a corner of a cube and a haptic representation of the same corner (Block, 1995c). Are we sure from introspection that there is no shared spatial phenomenology? Of course there are differences—the visual representation represents color whereas the haptic representation represents texture and temperature (Tye, 2000). But that is independent of the issue of whether anything spatial is shared. I would further suggest that it is worth investigating whether the phenomenal representation of space in perception is tied in with the representation of affordances, all based in dorsal visual representations (Jacob & de Vignemont, 2010; Jacob & Jeannerod, 2003; Milner & Goodale, 2008). (An affordance is a possibility of action [Gibson, 1979; Siegel, 2014].)

Some evidence for perceptual representation of numerosity could be explained in terms of correlated variables such as item density, size, brightness, and surface area. However, numerosity and item density involve different discrimination curves and different perceptual thresholds (Castaldi, Piazza, Dehaene, Vignaud, & Eger, 2019). Further, Castaldi et al. were able to show direct effects of attention to numerosity on neural representations of numerosity in visual areas in the dorsal visual stream compared to attention to average item size.

I don't mean to give the impression that everyone agrees that we perceptually represent numerosity. There is an active debate concerning whether experiments involving visually based numerosity judgments can be explained away on the basis of correlated variables such as dot density (Abdul-Malak & Durgin, 2009; Briscoe, 2015; Durgin, 2008; Picon, Dramkin, & Odic, 2019). I have summarized some of this debate elsewhere (Block, 2019e), and won't repeat it here, in part because the controversy seems irrelevant given the results mentioned above about cross-modal and cross-format numerosity effects. I don't see how these visual correlation-based approaches can explain the cross-modal effects described above. (This point is also made by Smortchkova [2020].)

In Chapter 5 I will describe in detail a distinction between integral and separable pairs of dimensions. For now, let us say that for integral pairs of dimensions such as height and width or speed and direction, one can't attend to one dimension without attending to the other. Numerosity paired with surface area constitutes an integral pair of dimensions (Aulet & Lourenco, 2021), and numerosity may be integrally paired with other spatial dimensions. Integrality is a perceptual phenomenon and the dimensions that are integral are perceptual. This fact provides another item of evidence that we perceive numerosity.

Another line of evidence that provides problems for Burge's view comes from "face space." Subjects can be presented with a large number of pairs of (pictures of) faces and asked to rate the similarities of the various pairs. Using these similarities, a face space can be constructed in which there are dimensions that allow for faces that are in some sense the antifaces of other faces (Johnston, Milne, Williams, & Hosie, 1997; Valentine, 1991; Valentine, Lewis, & Hills, 2016). Subjects adapted to a face show enhanced recognition of its antiface, a classic adaptation result. Eyeballing a face and its antiface, one can typically see some low-level features that are in some sense opposite. E.g., if the first face has wide-set eyes, its antiface might have close-set eyes. Although the face space described here was not constructed on the basis of such features, oppositional relations between them emerge from the similarity judgments. So perhaps the adaptation effects can be ascribed to those low-level features?

There are two significant problems for that view. First, these adaptation phenomena are robust under affine transformations of the faces, i.e., transformations that preserve collinearity and ratios of distances. These transformations change many low-level features such as size and orientation (Jiang, Blanz, & O'Toole, 2007). Second, such adaptation effects transfer substantially even when the adaptor and adapting faces differ in viewpoint, for example from frontal to 30° rotated (Jiang et al., 2007). A 30° rotated face will differ from a frontal face in many low-level features.

Joulia Smortchkova has argued that high-level adaptation is not of the same kind as low-level adaptation. In this section, I have described very detailed similarities between low-level and high-level adaptation. But there is one dissimilarity that I agree with Smortchkova about. I don't know of any low-level adaptation that depends on consciousness. To the extent that this has been investigated, adaptation effects occur in unconscious perception. But face identity adaptation effects depend on the perception being conscious. Moradi et al. (Moradi, Koch, & Shimojo, 2005) used two different methods of making face perception unconscious, continuous flash suppression (a relative of binocular rivalry) and another kind of inattentional suppression. (In continuous flash suppression, a stimulus—e.g., a face—is presented to one eye while the other eye is shown rapidly moving brightly colored patches that command attention. In these conditions, the visual representation of the face is reliably suppressed for periods up to a minute. Having experienced this a number of times, I can testify that for long periods, all one is aware of is the rapidly moving brightly colored stimulus. (See the discussion in connection with Moradi et al.'s footnote 56 on the issue of whether the suppressed perception really is unconscious.) What Moradi found was that the face adaptation effects disappeared when the face was seen unconsciously, whereas adaptation effects for a low-level property, tilt, were preserved in unconscious perception.[6]

Another approach to distinguishing high from low using face adaptation is based on two ideas (Susilo, McKone, & Edwards, 2010). The first idea is to compare adaptation effects between inverted and upright faces on the assumption that adaptation effects that work for inverted faces are likely to derive from low-level representations, whereas extra adaptation for upright faces is likely to involve high-level perceptual representations specific to faces. The second idea is that adaptation for stretching in general and elongation and squatness in particular transfers from one shape to another. For example, staring at a tall thin ellipse (the "adapting" stimulus) makes a square ("test" stimulus) look like a rectangle that is wider than it is tall, and staring at a squat adapting ellipse makes a test square look like a rectangle that is taller than it is wide. Susilo et al. designed an experiment that examined transfer of adaptation from the letter 'T' of various heights to faces whose eye to mouth distance also varied as shown in Figure 2.8 and also the reverse transfer of adaptation. They used adapting items (both 'T's and faces) of three different elongations, testing the effects of these differences in adaptings on a variety of elongations of "test" faces and 'T's.

The technique was to ask the subject to stare at a face or a 'T' of one of the three elongations for 4 seconds, then to view a face or a 'T' of one or another elongation, judging whether the test item was longer or shorter. A subject who has adapted to an elongated stimulus will see another stimulus as shorter than it would otherwise have looked, so to the extent that perception of upright and inverted faces is low-level, transfer of adaptation *within* stimulus types should be the same as *between* stimulus types. Using 'F-F' to mean transfer from face to face, there are four types of transfers that should all be the same if perception is entirely low-level, i.e., F-F = F-T = T-T = T-F. But if upright face perception and aftereffects derive only from face-specific (high-level) representations, there should be no transfer in either direction between faces and 'T's. (Of course, when upside down faces were used, the 'T's were upside down as well—and conversely.)

The results were that for inverted stimuli, F-F, F-T, T-T, and T-F were nearly the same, only 8% of the aftereffect was face-specific (high-level). Inverted faces are seen almost entirely via shape-general (low-level) representations. In the case of upright faces, 55% of the aftereffect was face-specific and so high-level and

---

[6] Ian Phillips has argued in a number of articles that putative cases of unconscious perception are either weakly conscious or if genuinely unconscious, not perception. (See Peters et al., 2017; Phillips, 2015, 2018; Phillips, 2020a.) Of course, if the supposed unconscious perception in these experiments is really weakly conscious, then it may be that all adaptation requires conscious perception.

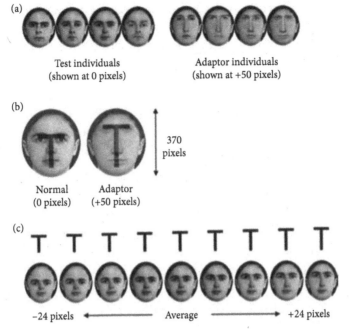

Figure 2.8 The most elongated faces are shown in right side of (A). The pixels mentioned corresponded to .29% of full head height. A short and long face and 'T' are shown in (B). (C) has 'T's and faces of various different elongations used as the tests. From Susilo, McKone, et al. (2010), with permission of the Association for Research in Vision and Ophthalmology. This figure was also used in Block (2014c).

45% was low-level. So, high-level face-specific representations play a slightly larger role than low-level representations in the perception of upright faces.

Note that the overall shape of the face does not change between the elongated and squat faces. It is the shape of the central features that change. But this is equally true of the inverted and upright faces, so the low-level effects exhibited in the inverted faces show that the internal shape can dominate adaptation responses.

Of course, no single result can rule out that the result is due to differences between low-level features of right-side-up and upside-down faces (e.g., the downward rather than upward curve of the eyebrows). Further experiments could be done to rule out further low-level responses. Eventually we would reach the point where the evidence is strong enough so that experimenters feel it is not worth the time and effort to rule out still further low-level hypotheses.

The appeal to scientific simplicity in this case can perhaps best be put in terms of questions that can be answered on the high-level account but not on the low-level account. Why does adaptation transfer from F to T almost completely for inverted faces but not for upright faces? On the high-level account, there is an answer in terms of a high-level representation for faces in the upright case but not the inverted case. Opponents should try to come up with an answer in low-level terms.

Stephen Yamamoto objected that there might be a low-level visual template for the upright but not inverted faces and the template might impede adaptation.

According to template theories, the process of categorizing something one perceives is supposed to be a matter of matching a stored perception to an input. Template-matching is used successfully in some computer vision applications, for example the recognition of account numbers on checks. But success here depends on a standard size, distance, and orientation. As has often been pointed out, storing a separate template for each illumination, angle of vision, distance, and other aspects of viewing conditions would involve far too many templates for real-time recognition, though it may be that for some ultra-low-level representations such as those used in edge detection and spatial frequency detection, the visual system actually does have enough storage (Palmer, 1999, pp. 377–383). (See the caption and text surrounding Figure 1.1 for an illustration of spatial frequency.)

One attempt to avoid combinatorial explosion takes the stored templates to be partial perceptions. For example, an attempt to explain the pattern recognition abilities of expert chess players assumes that what is stored is some rather than all of the positions on a chess board. But this method depends on the 8-by-8 grid structure of the chess board and so cannot be used as a general approach. Perception textbooks often discuss and reject template theories on the ground of computational intractability. As Stephen Palmer puts in in a widely used textbook, "if all possible shapes people can discriminate had to be repeated in every position, orientation, size and sense, the proliferation of templates that would result—called a combinatorial explosion—boggles the mind. Replication of templates therefore is not a tractable solution to the general problem of shape representation, although it may indeed suffice for a minimal set of very simple templates such as lines and edges" (Palmer, 1999, p. 380). Prototype theories appeal to stored averages of representations, but prototype accounts are more suited to theories of concepts than theories of percepts.

Sometimes it is objected that associations among low-level properties for upright but not inverted faces can explain such results (Yamamoto, 2018). Would squatness of a face fail to make a 'T' look elongated because the squatness is associated with other face properties? Why would squatness be associated with other face properties given that faces are only sometimes squat? Perhaps a face template or prototype could be used in such an argument, but as we have just seen, there are reasons not to take them seriously as theories of percepts.

In sum, template theories are not very useful in vision science and there is no particular reason to invoke them in this case. In any case the invocation of a template does not favor low-level perception, since a template can involve whatever levels of perceptual representation actually obtain.

What is a high-level representation? Is it just a matter of associations among low-level properties? Associations are not enough. First, one of the tests of high-level adaptation involves varying low-level properties. If a substantial chunk of the adaptation effect persists despite variation of low-level properties, that is indicative of high-level representation. Associations among low-level properties would not engender an adaptation effect that is independent of the low-level properties. Second, the presence of such associations for upright faces and the absence of them for inverted faces cannot explain the Susilo experiment. Why would associations among low-level properties decrease the squat and elongation adaptation? Third, why would associations be localized to one side of the field of vision while still generalizing between different formats and modalities? As so often with associationistic accounts, the appeal to associations piles one ad hoc consideration on another.

The evidence given in this section and the reasoning based on it is an example of reasoning from what are called "adaptation metamers" (Webster, 2015). Metamers are pairs of stimuli that differ in fundamental ways but nonetheless have the same effect on an aspect of perception. (Color metamers have different reflectance profiles but look the same in hue.) Adaptation metamers are designed to be the same at some specific level of processing but different in others. The stimuli just described are the same in their effect on the perception of approximate numerosity but different in other respects. The idea of adaptation metamers is to separate out the level of processing at which the effect of adaptation is found.

In sum, part of my reply to Burge invokes the signature properties of norm-based and multichannel adaptation. These signature properties, with their appeal to opponent processes and channels of sensitivity, strongly suggest perception rather than cognition. And then the details of the channels—what the norm is and what the channels are sensitive to—indicate high-level vs. low-level. There is some vagueness, though, in what exactly counts as going beyond adaptation itself, but I will not be concerned with that issue. Other lines of thought that appeal to the details of specific experiments (numerosity and elongation) point in the same direction.

Although the discussion in this section and the next are focused on adaptation, I will digress for the rest of this section to discuss a result that has been taken to impugn higher-level representation of faces. Doris Tsao and her colleagues have shown that there are six face-sensitive regions in the temporal lobe of rhesus macaque monkeys (Chang & Tsao, 2017; Hesse & Tsao, 2020a; Quian Quiroga, 2017; Tsao, 2019). These face patches are tightly connected, as shown by the fact that stimulating one face patch results in activation of the other face patches without activation of areas in between. Two regions in the middle of the temporal lobe were viewpoint sensitive, with different activations depending on whether the face was presented in profile or straight on. But in the most anterior part of the temporal lobe, the face area known as 'AM' responded independently of viewpoint. Tsao describes AM as the "end of the network" (2019, p. 26). Tsao and her colleagues showed that a 50-dimensional space was enough to specify the perception of any given face. The response of each neuron in the face patches could be approximated by a linear combination of the dimensions. And using the same dimensions, they could predict what the face stimulus was given the activations of neurons.

This result has been taken by some philosophers as evidence against high-level perception. For example, Chris Hill turns a skeptical eye on high-level representation:

> To be sure, we are clearly capable of visually discriminating the gazelles from the lions at the watering hole, and the Fords from the Ferraris on the highway. We are also capable of responding to stimuli differentially in ways that reflect such discriminations. But it by no means follows that we perceptually represent gazelles as members of the kind *gazelle*, or that we perceptually represent lions as members of the kind *lion*. It is possible to explain our discriminative abilities by supposing that we simply represent gazelles and lions as possessing congeries of low-level properties, such as shape, that are strongly correlated with kind membership. (Hill, 2022)

He goes on to say that Chang and Tsao showed

> that all human faces can be represented by points in a fifty-dimensional space, where each dimension corresponds to the degree to which a face instantiates a certain low-level feature. . . . It appears that perceptual stereotypes are all we need to explain perceptual discrimination among specific kinds and differential responses to kinds. I see no advantage in the more ambitious hypothesis that we perceptually represent members of kinds *as* members of kinds.

I do not think "low-level" is right for Chang and Tsao's feature dimensions, but let me put that point on hold briefly to note that, for any particular high-level property there may be a congery of low-level properties that is "recognitionally equivalent" to the high-level property. Finding the low-level properties that produce a given high-level property representation does not eliminate the high-level representation in favor of low-level representations. Experiments such as those discussed earlier in this section are evidence for the reality of high-level representation.

Let us return to the question of whether the features isolated by Chang and Tsao are "low-level. Chang and Tsao came up with two kinds of features, shape and "appearance." In the case of the shape parameters, they placed 58 dots on what seemed to them intuitively to be key features of the face, what they called "landmarks." The dots specified, for example, the hairline, the eyes, the nose, the mouth. As Chang and Tsao say, "a set of landmarks were labeled by hand" (Chang & Tsao, 2017, p. 1015). Or, as they say in another publication, "To generate these shape and appearance descriptors for faces, we started with a large database of face images. For each face, we placed a set of markers on key features" (Tsao, 2019, p. 27). Eyes and hairline are themselves high-level features, so reducing the overall appearance of a face in terms of them is explaining high-level features by high-level features. Further, as Chang and Tsao note, their parameters are holistic: "Most of the dimensions were 'holistic,' involving changes in multiple parts of the face; for example, the first shape dimension involved changes in hairline, face width, and height of eyes" (Chang & Tsao, 2017, p. 1015). In sum, I don't think the Chang and Tsao results challenge the reality of high-level perception.

The preceding discussion concerned distinguishing high-level from low-level perception as well as distinguishing both from cognition. I now focus on the latter.

The use of adaptation in distinguishing perception from cognition

If adaptation is to be useful in distinguishing perception from cognition, there would have to be adaptation for perception but not cognition. What would cognitive adaptation be? Recall that adaptation is primarily a repulsive effect. So, we could look for repulsive effects in cognition. Do thoughts of prime numbers bias one toward thinking sample numbers are nonprime? That seems unlikely, but other cases seem more plausible: Maybe thoughts about expensive things make one think that moderately priced things are cheaper than they are. Maybe thoughts about right-wing views make one think centrist views are left wing?

A recent study (Kim, Burr, & Alais, 2019) asked subjects to judge the attractiveness of paintings and compared judgments with previous judgments. They had a set of 100 paintings of scenery and still life, using 40 randomly selected paintings from the group of 100 for each subject. These paintings were presented twenty times each at different sizes and different places, and the subjects had to indicate attractiveness with a slider. The findings went opposite to what an adaptation account would predict: Judgments were positively correlated with judgments of the recent past. The judgment of the currently viewed painting resembled the judgment of the previously viewed painting. This is an example of an effect involving judgment that does not show the pattern characteristic of adaptation.

In a recent paper, Grace Helton (2016) argues that adaptation can be nonperceptual. She asks the reader to consider a case in which thinking about large houses causes one to regard a normal size house as small. She says this may be a cognitive rather than a perceptual phenomenon. Could such an effect, if it exists, be perceptual? If one is looking at pictures of big houses one might perceptually adapt to size. As noted earlier, even imagining can produce perceptual aftereffects (Finke, 1989; Winawer et al., 2010). Perhaps one judges the normal house as smaller because it looks smaller and it looks smaller because of perceptual adaptation to size.

If the phenomenon Helton describes exists, it could be a result of regression to the mean. In regression to the mean, a performance (in anything) that deviates from the mean is likely to be followed by a performance that is closer to the mean. In a famous example, instructors at an Israeli pilot training program claimed that negative reinforcement for a bad performance was effective whereas positive reinforcement for a good performance was counterproductive. They had noticed that good flights tended to be followed by worse ones and bad flights tended to be followed by better ones (Kahneman, Slovic, & Tversky, 1982). The explanation of regression to the mean is that performance is a consequence of systematic and unsystematic (random) factors. The systematic factors are likely to persist from one performance to another, but the unsystematic factors will vary randomly. An outstanding performance is likely to be partly due to luck, and luck is likely not to persist. Hence more average performance is likely to ensue. Once one understands regression to the mean, one sees that it is quite a different matter from adaptation, applying, for example, to performance by machines.

Shifting standards have been shown in employment experiments (Wexley, Yukl, Kovacs, & Sanders, 1972). For example, one study used taped interviews in which actors answered 10 employment-relevant questions, e.g., "What leadership positions did you attain in college?" The actors acted scripts for three levels of suitability for the job, high (H), average (A), and low (L). Subjects watched a series of three such videos and gave rankings (in some conditions on 9-point scales, so there were roughly 3 points within each division). They saw all eight combinations of H, A, and L. The result was that there was a tendency to give "repulsive" responses. For example, if they saw an H, followed by an H, the next one was likely to be downgraded. However, the biggest effects were on the A (average) interviews. That is, the downward shift in the 9-point scale for HHA was bigger than for HHH and HHL. Similarly, the upward shift for LLA was bigger than for LLL or LLH. The authors note that other studies had gotten similar results.

Recall that perceptual adaptation effects are either norm-based or multichannel. Recall that one signature of these types is a matter of whether the size of the effect is larger or smaller depending on the difference between adapting and test stimuli. As explained earlier, a larger effect when the difference is large would suggest norm-based adaptation and the other way around would suggest multichannel adaptation. The interview experiment just described does not fit either of these models. The biggest effects were for intermediate differences. Further, it is not clear what an "average" would be in the case of multichannel adaptation. For example, there is no average angle of a line.

The authors suggest two interpretations, neither of which has the flavor of adaptation. For example, one of their suggested explanations is that subjects tend to attend more to answers that are novel, so in the HHA case they may have focused on the answers that were different from those they had just seen. In the HHH case, nothing was novel about the third video and in the HHL case everything was novel, so none of the responses merited special attention.

In any case, let us suppose, no doubt contrary to fact, that there is cognitive adaptation. We can still distinguish cognitive adaptation from perceptual adaptation by consideration of the specific features that I have been mentioning of perceptual adaptation. For example, I mentioned the following features of perceptual adaptation:

1. Many if not most perceptual effects are retinotopic or spatiotopic, even multimodal high-level effects.
2. As just noted, the interview experiment just described does not fit the models of either multichannel or norm-based adaptation.
3. The size of the adaptation effect is a logarithmic function of the duration of the adapting stimulus, and decay of adaptation is exponential. One type of logarithmic increase would be if in increasing the time of adaptation from 1 ms to 10 ms to 100 ms to 1,000 ms to 10,000 ms—each increase has the same effect. (This is not an extremely high bar, since many effects are logarithmic [Storrs, 2015].)
4. Whether there are both attractive and repulsive effects and whether the balance can be explained by known visual properties like centering and scaling.

In brief, even if there were cognitive adaptation, it may differ in ways that allow a specific kind of adaptation to be used as an assay for perception.

Helton suggests that cognitive effects of the sort she is talking about might involve System 1 processing. System 1 processes are said to be fast, high-capacity, parallel, unconscious, contextualized, biased, automatic, associative, intuitive, effortless, experience based, often emotionally charged, difficult to control, and independent of intellectual ability. System 1 is supposed to contrast with System 2, the slow, serial, effortful, analytical processing found in reasoning. As has often been pointed out, the clusters of properties used to define System 1 often do not occur together, and likewise for System 2. And the characteristics that define System 1 often co-occur with the characteristics that define System 2. For example, intuitive thinking can be slow and effortful (Carruthers, 2014). For this reason, some former supporters have been equivocal about whether the System 1/System2 terminology should be abandoned (Evans & Stanovich, 2013).

Sometimes people say that adaptation applies to every neural representation. If so, why wouldn't it apply equally to cognition as to perception? The mechanism that leads to that claim is spike frequency adaptation, a widespread feature of neurons—both sensory and nonsensory neurons—in which spiking frequency decreases upon repeated stimulation. However, it is not clear to what extent spike frequency adaptation is involved in perceptual adaptation. Many of the mechanisms of adaptation are known to be network mechanisms rather than cellular mechanisms like spike frequency adaptation (Benda & Herz, 2003; Gutkin & Zeldenrust, 2014; Webster, 2012). Spike frequency adaptation makes more sense in the case of multichannel adaptation than for norm-based adaptation. Recall the point made earlier that there is no simple repulsive adaptation effect for the norm in an opponent process pair (e.g., gray in the opponent processing response to hue.) But even for multi-channel adaptation, there are attractive as well as repulsive effects, suggesting mechanisms that are not at the cellular level.

In some cases, we know the neural mechanisms of adaptation and they are not spike frequency adaptation. For example, in olfaction, activation of olfactory receptor neurons affect a subpopulation of neurons in the olfactory bulb that release dopamine, inhibiting sensitivity in the olfactory bulb. The amount of dopamine released functions as volume control. For example, when a person has a cold, dopamine decreases, thereby increasing sensitivity in the olfactory bulb. This adjustment of "volume" is a very different phenomenon from the perceptual adaptation discussed here. I am discussing aftereffects, not setting of the volume control. Note that the dopamine release does not cause an "opposite" effect on later perception.

It sometimes happens that property x adapts property y but y does not adapt x. This suggests mechanisms that go beyond the cellular level. For example, in olfaction, adaptation to pentanol has a strong repulsive effect on smelling propanol, but only a minimal transfer in the other direction. What explains such asymmetries? Often the asymmetries are due to an inclusion relation between the features. Again, this has nothing to do with spike frequency adaptation.

The issue of the utility of adaptation as an index of perception is tied in with another issue, whether perception is nonconceptual or conceptual. I will be arguing for the nonconceptual nature of perception, and that conclusion will figure in my approach to the aforementioned two kinds of core cognition that have been alleged to be a problem for a joint in nature between perception and cognition: numerosity and causation. Those who think perception is conceptual have a reason to downplay the perception/cognition border since both are alleged to involve concepts. (They have a reason, but it is defeasible since they can believe in a robust border defined by modularity.)

I have argued (2014c) that if there was cognitive adaptation, you would expect cases of cognitive without perceptual adaptation—and there is no good evidence for such a thing. Henry Shevlin (2016) argues that perhaps there is no adaptation for nonperceptual concepts but nonetheless there is adaptation for perceptual concepts. One might use perceptual materials in reasoning about whether a horse's tail comes below its knees. The perceptual concepts used in such exercises can show adaptation. So, reasoning from adaptation to perception is complex. The real issue is whether there can be *purely* cognitive adaptation—adaptation when no perceptual materials are involved? That is the test that I had in mind. I know of no evidence for purely cognitive adaptation.

I mentioned that one kind of evidence that adaptation is perceptual is that it often is retinotopic, i.e., dependent on the two stimuli—the one that causes the adaptation and the one that shows the effect of adaptation—being projected to the same spot on the retina. Retinotopy shows that the neural basis of the adaptation of the stimulus is in one of the perhaps 25 retinotopic or spatiotopic brain areas in the visual system. As I mentioned retinotopy is widely accepted as ruling out a cognitive interpretation. For example, Rolfs et al. note (2013, p. 4): "Cognitive boundary shifts are common and may even be contingent on location in the world—what looks like steam over a pot will look like smoke over a chimney. Never, however, will cognitive boundary shifts be specific to a particular location on our retina, independent of location in the world."

Recall that the method of avoiding vicious circularity that I am advocating is to focus on clear cases of perceptual phenomena with an eye to what makes them clear cases. Of course, I am not arguing that adaptation is constitutive of perceptual states, though I think it is related to the purpose of perceptual systems (as will be described later). The topic of the moment is to illustrate a method of discovery—how we can tell whether a given phenomenon is perceptual.

One candidate for cognitive adaptation is "semantic satiation," a phenomenon that is the topic of the next section.

Semantic satiation

One candidate for a cognitive and conceptual adaptation effect is semantic satiation. It has been repeatedly reported at least since the early twentieth century that when a person says a word over and over again, the word begins to sound meaningless (Warren, 1968). The phrase used to describe the phenomenon, "semantic satiation," might suggest a cognitive and conceptual form of adaptation. I think not, and I'll say why. In brief, the point to be made in this section is that there are a number of different phenomena grouped under the heading of "semantic satiation." All seem primarily modal, and although some may involve a kind of representation of a semantic "space," none has the flavor of a phenomenon in which thinking of prime numbers makes a subsequently considered number seem nonprime.

One obvious experimental issue about semantic satiation is how to separate whatever semantic effect there is from perceptual adaptation to the visual or auditory presentation of the word. One straightforward item of evidence for perceptual adaptation to auditory representation of the words is an experiment where subjects were required listen to a stream of words through headphones while speaking the words as they heard them. In one case (Warren, 1968) a subject heard the word "tress" repeated many times. A string of the subject's responses was this: "stress, dress, stress, dress, Jewish, Joyce, dress, Jewess, Jewish, dress, floris, florist, Joyce, dress, stress, dress, purse." Clearly, the phonological representation was affected by repetition.

There have been many attempts to partial out the effects due to perception of the auditory or visual vehicles of the words from the meanings of the words. Balota and Black (1997) showed subjects words on a screen repeated either 2, 12, or 22 times while the subjects read the words aloud. They then asked subjects to make repeated judgments about whether pairs of words were related. The pairs included among many others, "royalty"–"queen" (related) and "royalty"–"box" (unrelated). They measured the time it took to answer and the accuracy of the answers. The key issue was whether the difference between "royalty"–"queen" and "royalty"–"box" decreased with an increasing number of repetitions. And the answer is it did. Balota and Black took this to show that the semantic representation on which relatedness judgments were based had weakened. A further feature of their study was that the effect was preserved even when the subjects did not read the words aloud. And the effect was not present when subjects made rhyming judgments. Since rhyming judgments focus on nonsemantic features, the authors took this result to indicate that when semantic processing was decreased, the effect decreased.

However, though the effect was strong in young adults (average age 20) in older adults (average age 70) there was no effect. This reveals a gulf between semantic satiation and perceptual adaptation. Perceptual adaptation is a basic feature of perception that is present in all known perceptual systems. There is age-related deterioration in many aspects of vision, especially in the eye, but the cortical component of perceptual adaptation does not change much with aging

(Webster, 2011). Balota and Black give an account of their results that suggest that they have more to do with the organization of the language system than anything that is similar to perceptual adaptation.

Another study involving 3 or 30 repetitions of words (Pilotti, Antrobus, & Duff, 1997) found what they took as semantic satiation when 30 repetitions were in the same voice but not when there were a variety of different voices. Compare this with the results described above for the perceptual representation of approximate number (e.g., as diagrammed in Figure 2.7) in which varying the low-level formats allows isolation of a high-level perceptual effect. Why would a cognitive effect be so phonologically specific?

Another paradigm in which words are repeated showed again that subjects have a subjective sense of loss of meaning of repeated words, but that the actual effect on semantic representations depend on what the subjects take themselves to be doing. Specifically, the semantic satiation is present in incidental learning but absent when subjects are trying to learn associations (English & Visser, 2014; Kuhl & Anderson, 2011). This is quite different from perceptual adaptation, in which so long as subjects are attending to the stimuli, perceptual adaptation is, apparently, independent of task.

Another line of research used EEG to examine effects of repetition of words in both visual and auditory modalities (Kounios, Kotz, & Holcomb, 2000). They found semantic effects, but they were restricted to one modality.

Another phenomenon that seems closely related to these effects is the speech to song illusion (Deutsch, Henthorn, Fau-Lapidis, & Lapidis) discovered by Diana Deutsch. When a phrase is repeated a number of times, it begins to sound as if it is sung rather than spoken. You can hear this for yourself by playing the examples at http://deutsch.ucsd.edu/psychology/pages.php?i=212. The effect only works if the repetitions are exactly the same as one another. Again, this is quite different from the adaptation discussed in this chapter, in which standard methodology is to have repetitions that change some properties of the stimulus but not others so as to isolate an effect at a certain level in perceptual systems.[7]

---

[7] Steven Gross (Gross, 2022) mentions a study by Tian and Huber (2010) that pits three theories against one another: word adaptation, meaning adaptation, and adaptation of the relation between word and meaning. They did an experiment that they regard as providing evidence against word adaptation and meaning adaptation and for adaptation of the relation between word and meaning. The methodology—which I won't describe—assumes that presentation of words like "apple" or "orange" activates the meanings of the superordinate "fruit," but they don't justify that assumption. Also, as Gross notes, they did not take into account the fact that adaptation to lower-level features can take longer than adaptation to higher-level features. Also the absence of word adaptation for printed words is in conflict with the Hanif study mentioned earlier.

To conclude the discussion of semantic satiation: There are many interesting aspects of the phenomena grouped under the heading of "semantic satiation," but none of them provide evidence for adaptation to meanings.

This concludes my discussion of perceptual adaptation as an indicator of perception as opposed to cognition. I now move to a much briefer discussion of other indicators, including rivalry, pop-out, and illusory contours. Then I will turn from indicators of perception to the topic of the fundamental nature of perception.

Rivalry

I now move to other markers of the perceptual, starting with a marker that is very closely related to adaptation, rivalry.

Figure 2.9 shows a Necker cube, a figure that exhibits monocular rivalry, i.e., rivalry that obtains even if viewed with one eye. (This example introduced ambiguous figures into the scientific literature in 1832, though there were reversible figures in Euclid's work [Long & Toppino, 2004].) The image is ambiguous, but we do not normally see a "mixed" version of the two interpretations. First one face appears in the foreground, then another, then the first face again. Of course, one's perceptual judgment shifts too, but that is because the perception shifts. And in that sense, the rivalry is perceptual.

How do we know the rivalry is perceptual? After all, there is another interpretation: that the perception stays constant, with perceptual judgment shifting back and forth (Nanay, 2009). That is, the perception stays the same but one

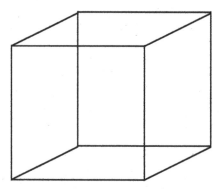

Figure 2.9 Necker cube. On initial viewing, especially from below, the left facing face is usually in the foreground. After staring at the stimulus, especially from above, that face will recede and the right facing face will be in the foreground.

judges first that there is a cube with a left-facing front and then that there is a cube with a right-facing front.

One item of evidence that it is a perceptual phenomenon is that adaptation to one size of Necker cube does not carry over to another size or to another location in the visual field. In addition, if one views two Necker cubes in different parts of the visual field, the adaptation processes are independent of one another. These results suggest the effect is due to processes in early vision (Long & Toppino, 2004). Another argument that the rivalry is perceptual is that it occurs in afterimages. See Figure 2.10.

There are further problems with the perceptual judgment account. Why would one judge one's own unchanging afterimage to be changing if it was not actually changing? In the reversal for Figure 2.9, one is viewing something in the environment, so the reversing judgment is about what one is seeing. But for Figure 2.10, the judgment would have to be about one's own experience, a much more sophisticated matter. Given that aftereffects have long been known to occur in animals (Scott & Powell, 1963), the perceptual interpretation is preferable.

Another point in favor of the perceptual interpretation is that rivalry also obtains between the eyes, and why would perceptual judgment involve competition between the eyes? Between-eye rivalry is one kind of binocular rivalry, a visual phenomenon in which two "incompatible" stimuli are projected to each of a subject's eyes. For example, one eye might get a face, the other eye a house. What the subject consciously sees is first a face filling the whole visual field, then

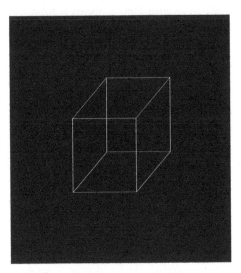

Figure 2.10 To get a reversing afterimage, fixate the dot for 20 seconds, then project the afterimage on a white piece of paper. The imaged cube will often reverse. From Long and Toppino (2004).

a house filling the whole field, and so on, alternating for as long as the experiment goes on. Subjects are aware of intermediate mixtures between a face and house occasionally but very briefly. (See Chapter 4 on what makes stimuli "incompatible" and Chapter 9 for more on the face/house alternation.)

Binocular rivalry is in part rivalry between processing streams specific to each eye but also in part rivalry between the perceptual contents represented by those streams. Hesse and Tsao (2020b) decoded neural activations during binocular rivalry on a trial-by-trial basis, revealing that the same neurons code for both the conscious percept and the suppressed percept at the same time. This shows that rivalry cannot just be between neural regions or processing streams and in part must be between the neural bases of perceptual contents themselves.

Another part of the case for rivalry being a perceptual phenomenon is that it is widespread in the animal kingdom. For example, binocular rivalry in fruit flies works much as does between-eyes rivalry for humans (Miller, Ngo, & van Swinderen, 2012). See the illustration in Figure 2.11. Fruitflies are not known for cognition.

The traditional dynamical systems explanation of rivalry is that vision is a winner-takes-all faculty. Pools of neurons representing each eye's processing stream, or alternatively, each of the incompatible stimuli, inhibit one another. (Recall the point just mentioned about the finding of Hesse & Tsao.) In the presence of neural noise, one pool wins temporarily, the winning pool inhibiting the losing pool (Drew et al., 2021). Then that pool is weakened by adaptation and the other pool representing the other alternative takes over (Alais, O'Shea, & Blake, 2010; Blake & He, 2005; Brascamp, Sterzer, Blake, & Knapen, 2018). The inhibition of one pool on another is presumed to operate via inhibitory interneurons (interneurons are neurons that modulate the interactions of other neurons) (Mentch, Spiegel, Ricciardi, & Robertson, 2019).

Because of the impact of neural noise, the time of the transitions cannot be predicted on the basis of past transitions. This model is supported by evidence from psychophysical experiments, brain imaging, and neuropharmacology (Brascamp et al., 2018). However, some data on rivalry suggest a complementary mechanism in which each of the pools of neurons is an "attractor" that competes in the presence of noise (Theodoni, Panagiotaropoulos, Kapoor, Logothetis, & Deco, 2011).

Predictive coding accounts also purport to explain binocular rivalry (Hohwy, Roepstorff, & Friston, 2008), but it is unclear to what extent these accounts simply frame the very same explanation differently. As (Brascamp et al., 2018, p. 84) note, "For example, accumulation of unexplained prediction error in the predictive coding account parallels the buildup of adaptation in the traditional dynamical systems account." Jakob Hohwy argues (2013) that the predictive

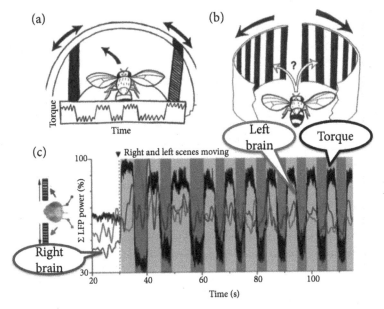

Figure 2.11 Binocular rivalry in fruit flies. The flies are tethered to a device that measures the torque produced by motion in the left and right directions as shown in A. The fly is presented with rightward moving stripes in the right eye and leftward moving stripes in the left eye, as shown in B. In the diagram in C, the torque goes first in one direction then the other, and so on, as indicated by the black traces. At the same time, left brain and right brain responses show a tendency to opposite activations. There is a free pdf on the Oxford University Press web site that has the color version of this and all the other figures. Reprinted under the terms of a Creative Commons Attribution License. See Miller et al. (2012).

coding view explains why we have adaptation, but if that is true it would be more of an evolutionary than a processing account.

One potential difference is that while dynamical systems models involve local sensory circuits, predictive coding models can appeal to higher levels of processing, including cognitive representations in frontal cortex (Brascamp et al., 2018). As we will see in Chapter 7 in a further discussion of binocular rivalry, this degree of freedom of predictive coding models may run into conflict with the fact that the explanation of when perception is rivalrous rather than involving merging is strongly localist. Predictive coding theorists may have to resort to ad hoc appeal to one level in the hierarchy insulating lower levels from influence (Drayson, 2017).

Logothetis and Leopold (1999) describe three properties of binocular rivalry. (1) Exclusivity: The multistable percepts are not active together, though there are sometimes unstable piecemeal transitions. (2) Inevitability: Eventually one interpretation will replace another. And (3) Randomness: The duration of one dominant percept does not predict the duration of the next (Logothetis & Leopold, 1999).

Monocular rivalry is involved in figure/ground perception. In shapes on a white background such as those of Figure 2.12, the black area tends to be seen as figure and the white as ground. The figure area has a definite shape whereas the ground appears shapeless, in part because it often seems to continue behind the figure. As Mary Peterson has shown (Peterson & Cacciamani, 2013), there is a competition between the white shapes and black shapes, in which the losing shape is inhibited. As she says (p. 449), "The losing candidate object is not perceived; its side of the border is simply perceived as a shapeless ground to the object." (In this context, "perceive" is meant as "consciously perceive"; the shape of the ground is unconsciously perceived—as with other forms of rivalry. The evidence for this will be discussed later.) As with other forms of rivalry mentioned

Figure 2.12 Gestalt principles favor the black central area as figure, but subjects nonetheless processed the content of the white background to the semantic level even if they showed no conscious recognition of what the white items are. See Cacciamani et al. (2014). Thanks to Mary Peterson for this figure.

here, staring at the picture for 60 seconds or so will result in the figure becoming the ground and the ground becoming the figure.

I doubt that these three properties obtain for ambiguous cognitive "stimuli," since cognition is not a winner-takes-all faculty. Using cognition, we are happy to entertain mixtures of views. There are many conundra in philosophy for which adherents line up on either side. Perhaps there are philosophers who find themselves going back and forth, but in perception going back and forth is inevitable for every normal observer, a very different matter. In binocular rivalry, "the two monocular stimuli are seen alternately in a never-ending cycle" (Freeman & Li, 2009, p. 174).

Of course, immediate perceptual judgment is as winner-takes-all as perception. But, this fact about perceptual judgment is parasitic on perception and is not an independent cognitive characteristic. One judges that first one face of the Necker cube seems to be facing forward, then another is facing forward because the perception changes. In binocular rivalry one judges that one is seeing a face, then one judges that one is seeing a house. The judgments follow on and are caused by the perceptions.

Adaptation can obtain with preperceptual states, but rivalry shows the state is perceptual and so in that sense is more useful than adaptation. I also doubt that rivalry can occur in a perceptual concept without some influence of actual perception. Although visual imagery is in many ways similar to vision, the cognitive processes required to produce a mental image seem to make it difficult to produce a fully ambiguous mental image (Chambers & Reisberg, 1985). Rivalry can occur in afterimages that are themselves products of perception, but I don't know of any case of rivalry for internally generated mental images. Further, binocular rivalry seems to require the two processing streams of the eyes.

In Chapter 4, I will argue that the details of rivalry provide evidence that perception is not propositional. Rivalrous stimuli have to be "incompatible" (in a sense to be explained) in order for rivalry to take place—otherwise perception can "blend" the stimuli. The difference between rivalrous and nonrivalrous stimuli in what counts as incompatibility provides evidence for nonpropositionality.

Pop-out

"Pop-out" is a phenomenon in which a visual feature immediately comes to the fore as distinct from its background. Pop-out is likely an additional sufficient condition of perception. (If pop-out occurs in hallucination, that is another reason to focus on perceptual representation rather than perception.) Pop-out as I am using the term does not require any task. If you look at the left side of Figure 2.13, the red dot leaps to the foreground. Pop-out occurs even without any task,

110 THE BORDER BETWEEN SEEING AND THINKING

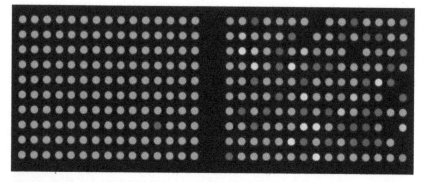

Figure 2.13 Example of pop-out. The red dot leaps to the eye on the left but not on the right. It is very easy to find the red dot on the left but slow and laborious to find it on the right. This figure requires color. There is a free pdf on the Oxford University Press web site that has the color version of this and all the other figures. Thanks to PsyToolkit, https://www.psytoolkit.org/fa, and Gijsbert Stoet for this picture.

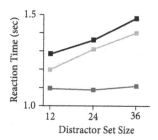

Figure 2.14 The time it takes to find a target vs. the size of the set of nontargets. The blue curve is for high similarity between target and distractors, whereas the red line is for a low degree of similarity—as on the left in Figure 2.13. These curves are for pigeons, suggesting that pop-out does not involve heavy use of cognition. There is a free pdf on the Oxford University Press web site that has the color version of this and all the other figures. Redrawn from Blough (1992, p. 295). Reprinted with permission from Springer *Nature*.

including in 4-month-old infants (Quinn & Bhatt, 1998). For other examples of pop-out, see Chapter 4, where the point is made that when a feature pops-out, its absence does not pop-out.

However, a behavioral index of pop-out has to do with a task: visual search. In visual search, when the target is such a visual feature and is highly visually dissimilar to the distractors, as in the left side of Figure 2.13, the number of distractors does not matter much, as shown in Figure 2.14 in the bottom curve of time to find the target mapped against number of distractors. The relevant dissimilarity is *visual* similarity not cognitive similarity. The items can be as cognitively similar or dissimilar as you like and that will not factor in except to the extent that those cognitive similarities and differences are reflected in visual similarities and differences. What counts as a visual similarity as opposed to a cognitive similarity? That is a matter for determination using other techniques. Benign circularity again! The curves in Figure 2.14 are for pigeons, revealing again that creatures of widely varying cognitive abilities can nonetheless have visual systems with very similar properties. (Recall the point made earlier about adaptation in fruit flies!)

What would show cognitive pop-out? One example is if there were an array of digits with pop-out for digits representing prime numbers. I know of no published cases that are plausibly construed as cognitive pop-out, but there are a number of cases in which cognition can be ruled out as a source of pop-out.

Bria Long did a series of experiments (Long & Konkle, 2017; Long et al., 2016; Long, Störmer, & Alvarez, 2017) that examined pop-out in cases where the subjects had no cognitive appreciation of what made something pop-out. This work will be described in detail in Chapter 8. Very briefly, Long "texturized" pictures of common large objects, small objects, animals, and artifacts, resulting in "texforms" of these pictures. The texforms were all the same size on the screen. The texturization process had the effect that subjects could not guess the categories of the original pictures from the texforms. Nonetheless subjects were faster to search for texforms of large objects among texforms of small objects (and vice versa) than when the texforms were of the same size; and faster to search for texforms of animals among texforms of artifacts (and conversely). There were other indications of perception rather than cognition (including Stroop effects, to be described in Chapter 8). All these results add up to suggesting that pop-out effects are perceptual rather than cognitive.

Interpolation of illusory contours

Another perceptual phenomenon that probably does not occur in cognition— even cognition with perceptual concepts— is "interpolation" of illusory contours, in which properly aligned and spaced edge elements are seen as connected by an illusory edge (Keane, 2018). See Figure 2.15. Interpolation takes place in many creatures with limited cognition, for example insects and sharks. What does occur in cognition is inference—for example inference that the back side of the laptop I am typing on now still has a scratch on it. (By "inference" I mean a psychological process of content-based reasoning of which the paradigm cases are processes of reasoning from premises to conclusions.) The difference is that the illusory contours... well... look like contours. But we don't have to rely just on that.

Figure 2.15 Kanizsa Triangle. The edges of the triangle whose vertex points down are "modally" completed (you have a perception as of edges) whereas the edges of the triangle pointing up are amodally completed. From the Wikipedia article "Illusory Contours," under a creative commons license.

Experiments with single-cell recording in monkeys show that neurons in V1 and V2 respond strongly to both real and illusory contours, though more strongly to real contours (Keane, 2018; Lee & Nguyen, 2001). V1 and V2 are low-level visual areas, showing the effect is perceptual and visual. Interestingly, the effect of illusory contours depended on the stimuli being placed in the center of the neuron's receptive field (Keane, 2018). How could that be if the effect were not a perceptual effect? (As explained earlier, the receptive field of a visual neuron is the area of space that the neuron responds to.) Further, illusory contour effects on V1 and V2 occur in fully anesthetized animals. Since anesthesia eliminates much if not all of cognition, that is further evidence that these effects are perceptual.

Effects on V1 have been observed at 50 ms after the stimulus (Keane, 2018) though some experiments have reported that illusory contours are not observed until 200 ms (Anken, Tivadar, Knebel, & Murray, 2018). Both speeds are fast enough to suggest that there is no inference going on—at least no cognitive inference. It is usually thought that cognition—at least conscious cognition—requires global workspace activation, something that takes at least 270 ms. after the onset of the stimulus. If so, then the computation of illusory contours is faster than thought.

Illusory contours are due to top-down influences, but these influences are within the visual system. For example the area that computes visual form affects V1 and V2 (Wokke, Vandenbroucke, Scholte, & Lamme, 2012).

Look at the "occlusion illusion" in Figure 2.16. The occluded semicircles on the right and left are exactly the same, but the one on the left looks larger. The effect persists even when one sees that it is illusory. This is typical of perceptual but not cognitive illusions. But wait—how can we be sure that the apparent size

Figure 2.16 Occlusion illusion. The semicircles are the same size, but the occluded one looks larger. From Palmer et al. (2007, p. 651). Reprinted by Permission of SAGE Publications, Ltd.

difference is perceptual? Well we can appeal to other aspects, but in the end we are confronted with the benign circularity I keep mentioning. Similarly with the fact that illusory contours have effects on other visual properties (Palmer, Brooks, & Lai, 2007).

Neural markers of perception and cognition

"Divisive normalization" is a characteristic computation in perceptual circuits in which the perception of an item and its neighbors influence one another (Carandini & Heeger, 2012; Heeger, 1992). (See Chapter 2 of Wu [2014] for an account of how normalization works in attention.) A classic example of the effect of normalization is the center-surround suppression illustrated in Figure 2.17. Normalization is feature tuned. More specifically, cortical area V1 reacts to orientation, and center-surround suppression is much larger when the orientation and surround are collinear than when they are orthogonal. In Figure 2.17, the center patches are identical in contrast but the patch that is collinear with the surround looks lower in contrast. Bloem et al. asked whether the center-surround suppression of the sort illustrated in Figure 2.17 would also obtain in visual working memory (Bloem, Watanabe, Kibbe, & Ling, 2018).

The question is motivated by the fact that visual working memory uses perceptual representations in the service of cognition. In perception, the perceptual representations are maintained by bottom-up perceptual processes, whereas in working memory, the perceptual representations are maintained by a top-down process, but the representations are known to be similar. For example, when a brain imaging (fMRI) classifier is trained on perceptual representations of orientation or contrast in V1, it can also detect those representations reasonably well in V1 in visual working memory. Harrison and Tong trained a classifier on

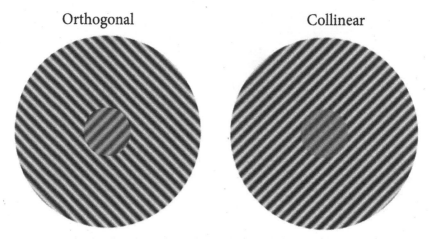

Figure 2.17 Illustration of the effect of divisive normalization. The center disk is the same on both sides but looks lower in contrast on the right because of surround suppression that depends on similar orientation of the disk and its surround. Thanks to Sam Ling for this figure.

perceptions of orientation and found that they were 80% accurate in predicting which of two orientations subjects were holding in visual working memory (Harrison & Tong, 2009). Similar results hold for contrast (Xing, Ledgeway, McGraw, & Schluppeck, 2013). These results reveal that there is some similarity in the representations of vision and visual working memory.

Bloem et al. presented subjects with stimuli containing a center disk and a surround donut in which the orientations were either collinear or orthogonal. The center and the surround could each be of five different contrasts, and the contrasts were varied independently. The center and surround could either be presented simultaneously or sequentially, separated by 1 second. After both center and surround were presented, subjects were given a probe that they were supposed to adjust by turning a knob to match either the center or the surround in contrast as they remembered it. They did not know whether they would be expected to make the probe match the center or the surround until the probe appeared so they had to remember both. The result was that there was robust center-surround suppression (of both the center and the surround) when the stimuli were presented simultaneously, but there was no center-surround suppression when they were presented sequentially and maintained in visual working memory. As the authors note (p. 10), "While visual memory representations modulate activity within early visual cortices... they follow a different set of computational rules, bypassing contrast normalization."

The upshot is that there is a basic neurocomputational difference between perceptual representations in perception and perceptual representations in working memory.[8]

Other markers of perception

There are many other markers of perception that I could have explored in depth. One that will be discussed in other chapters is Weber's Law. Weber's Law stipulates that relative discriminability of two stimuli is a linear function of the ratio of the intensity of the stimuli. Doubling the intensity of a stimulus will double the just noticeable difference in intensity. Thus, the just noticeable difference for change in a given stimulus is proportional to the intensity of the stimulus. For example, the just noticeable difference for discriminating pressure on the skin in one case is a 12% difference in pressure intensity (Pardo-Vazquez et al., 2019). If you double the intensity, you double 12% of the intensity, so the more intense stimulus requires double the intensity difference. Perception is subject to Weber's Law, but there is reason to doubt that cognition is subject to it.

A development of Weber's Law, the Weber-Fechner Law, tells us that perceived intensity of a stimulus is a logarithmic function of the actual stimulus intensity (above a threshold). We can use this law in providing additional evidence on whether numerosity can be perceived. An indication that it is perceived (over and above the evidence given earlier about adaptation) is that if kindergarteners are asked to put the digits from 1 to 10 on a line they give more space to the smaller numbers, roughly in accord with a logarithmic representation. On average, 3 is at the midpoint of the line. The Munduruku, an Amazonian group with limited formal education, do the same (Varshney & Sun, 2013).

Another marker that plays a role in recent experiments is closely related to pop-out: search efficiency. Searching for an object among perceptually similar objects is slower than searching for that same object among perceptually dissimilar objects. For example, searching for an animate thing (or rather a picture of an animate thing) is slower if the distractors are other animates than if they are artifacts (Long et al., 2017). Searching for a prototypically large thing e.g., elephants, among prototypically small things, e.g., mice (with the pictures all equal

---

[8] Results that may seem to conflict with this result appeared in Fang, Ravizza, and Liu (2019). However, Fang et al. do not seem aware of the distinction between visual working memory and fragile visual short-term memory. Their results seem to involve the latter and the latter is a much more perceptual form of storage. Fragile memory was discussed briefly in Chapter 1 and will be discussed again in Chapter 5.

116 THE BORDER BETWEEN SEEING AND THINKING

in size) is faster (Long et al., 2016). But when searching for a food item, it does not matter whether the distractors are food or not, suggesting that these are not perceptually represented properties (Long, Moher, Konkle, & Carey, 2019). These results indicate that animacy and prototypical size are visually represented, and other results point in the same direction. Indeed, recent results indicate that the dimension of perceptual similarity involved in such search tasks is closely related to divisions in the architecture of the visual system (Cohen, Alvarez, Nakayama, & Konkle, 2017).

One marker of perception that is worth more discussion is innateness and innate functional role. In the experiment indicated in Figure 2.18, Reid et al. projected red laser lights on the bellies of pregnant women in their 3rd trimesters (Reid et al., 2017). (Only red light can penetrate the abdomen.) Using ultrasound, they found that fetuses were more than twice as likely to turn toward stimuli of

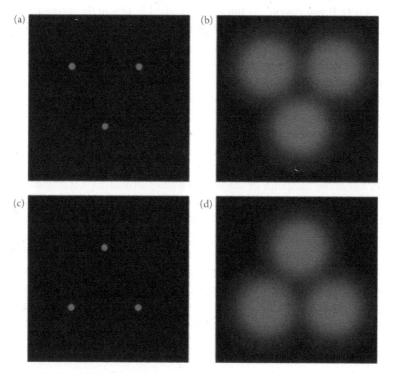

Figure 2.18 A and C represent the stimuli aimed at fetuses. B and D represent what the authors calculate that those stimuli would look like to an observer inside the womb after penetrating 30 cm of maternal tissue. There is a free pdf on the Oxford University Press web site that has the color version of this and all the other figures. From Reid et al. (2017)

the sort of A and B than stimuli of the sort of C and D. These results are the same as that of similar experiments involving newborn babies. A and B are more like faces than C and D along a number of different dimensions, mainly being top-heavy. Both stimuli are, like faces, symmetrical and high in contrast.

Is the fetus's differential response based on perception or on perception plus perceptual judgment? One consideration is that these are, well . . . fetuses. In fetuses, there is very little development of frontal cortex—the neural home of thought—compared with sensory cortex. The number of synapses in perceptual areas is much higher and the degree of myelination of neural fibers is much higher than in frontal cortex (Huttenlocher & Dabholkar, 1997). (Myelin speeds neural conduction and so is an index of processing speed.) Glucose metabolism in perceptual areas is much stronger than in frontal areas (Gazzaniga, Ivry, & Mangun, 2002, p. 642). All these measures reverse by about age 3. Again, we see how decisions as to what is perceptual and what is cognitive are holistic, based on other decisions as to which parts of the cortex are specialized for perception and which for cognition.

Another consideration pointing in the same direction is that these representations interact with exogenous attention, itself a perceptual process. Once infants are born, their attention is drawn to stimuli like A much more powerfully than to stimuli like C. Further, these responses show multisensory integration, in which visual and olfactory clues are integrated in helping the newborn to turn toward the mother.

Another marker is perspectival sensitivity, explored in a recent article by Greyson Abid (2021). As Abid concedes, perspectival sensitivity is a rather imperfect guide to perception. Mere sensation exhibits perspectival sensitivity even if it falls short of perception. According to Burge (2010a), smell and taste might be sensory without being perceptual if they lack perceptual constancies. Also, some forms of cognition may exhibit perspectival sensitivity without being even partly perceptual. A verbal description of a scene—or a thought that encodes that verbal description—can describe the scene from a perspective. One can imagine a cognitive system with no perception that has a GPS that informs it of its position and access to the internet, informing it of the positions of other things from which it computes perspectival representations. So perspectival sensitivity is not sufficient for a state to be even partly perceptual.

It may not be necessary either, since there are viewpoint-neutral perceptual representations. Perceptual representations are a mix of allocentric and egocentric representations (Tarr & Hayward, 2017) but one can imagine purely allocentric perceptual representations. (Allocentric frames represent objects relative to one another, whereas egocentric frames represent objects in a coordinate system based in the perceiver.) For example, the most anterior of the six face patches in the macaque face system in the temporal lobe has allocentric face representations (Moeller, Crapse, Chang, & Tsao, 2017). Such representations may be active in hallucination and dreaming. And one can imagine a situation in which all the other face patches in the temporal lobe are inactivated, leaving only the most anterior one.

Phenomenology

Another way of pinpointing whether a mental state is perceptual or cognitive is that some states determinately have the phenomenology of perception. Consider the simultaneous contrast illusion. In Figure 2.19, the two disks in (a) and the two bricks in (b) are of equal luminance but look different in brightness. (Brightness is perceived luminance.) How do we know that this is a perceptual rather than a cognitive effect? The most obvious answer is that the disks just look different. But how do we know that the difference is in perceptual phenomenology rather than cognitive phenomenology? It is unmistakable that the difference is visual rather than, say, auditory or the phenomenology of thought or reasoning.

But it is always useful to have experimental confirmation, and in this case we do. Pawan Sinha runs Project Prakash, in which children in India who are

Figure 2.19 Simultaneous contrast illusion. The two disks in a and the two bricks in b are the same in luminance while looking quite different in brightness. There is a free pdf on the Oxford University Press web site that has the color version of this and all the other figures. From Sinha et al. (2020, p. 42), with permission of Elsevier.

blind because of congenital cataracts have a cataract operation that restores their sight. Sinha found that the newly sighted children gave the same responses to stimuli like those in Figure 2.19 as normally sighted children. Since the newly sighted children would not have had the experience that would motivate thought processes about such stimuli, this provides evidence that the phenomenon is perceptual.

Summary

I have mentioned a number of psychological indicators of perception: adaptation, rivalry, pop-out, speed, automaticity, search efficiency, and interpolation. The justification of any one of these methods as indicative of the perceptual rather than the cognitive will inevitably appeal to other perceptual phenomena. These phenomena classify cases in the same way. Or in cases where they don't, there have to be explanations of why not that do not suggest that the method is breaking down. For example, as I mentioned, Chaz Firestone speculates that there may be no adaptation for near and far because of structural features of the visual field that resist adaptation. And in the case of phenomena classed as cognitive these converging tests give the opposite verdict. The methodology here is to find phenomena that group together, that apply to cases we are sure are perceptual and don't apply to cases we are sure are nonperceptual cognition.

What do the indicators have to do with what perception is at the most fundamental level? Are they mere symptoms of perception or are they more deeply connected with what perception is? In the case of adaptation, one connection is very likely evolutionary. The evolutionary purpose of perception is acquiring information about what is happening here and now. Call that "news."

Any feature of the visual system that produces a constant effect has to be filtered out in order to focus on news. This evolutionary explanation of adaptation is commonly cited. "Sensory adaptation allows us to tune out stimuli that do not provide us with new information needed to cope with the environment. This is the property of adaptation that is generally used to define adaptation in textbooks" (McBurney, 2010, p. 406). Another important evolutionary feature of perception is the need for the news to be timely, and of course that is relevant to the faster speeds of perceptual analysis than for the application of concepts in cognition and for the automaticity of perception. Of course, one can reason one's way to what is happening now, given appropriate premises, and on the predictive coding approach, that is part of how perception works (Clark, 2016; Hohwy, 2013). But even on the predictive coding approach, predictions are compared with sensory inputs, so there is a news component as well.

Another important feature of adaptation is that for both multichannel and norm-based adaptation, adaptation changes the tuning of neurons in the visual system. In the case of the norm-based adaptation described above, adaptation shifts the range of sensitivity. This range-shifting is especially noticeable for adaptation to ambient luminance. We have all had the experience of entering a darkened room and needing a brief period of adaptation to see in the low light (McBurney, 2010).

The winner-takes-all aspect of perception is required because the perceiving subject has to act, often quickly. It won't do for perception to wallow in ambiguity as with the more leisurely activity of cognition. By contrast, for cognition, facts that are not news are important too. We want to continue to know that tigers are dangerous, for example. In short, the psychological indicators for distinguishing the perceptual from the cognitive that I have described may be mere indicators of perception/cognition, but they are closely related to the different functions of perception and cognition.

I also mentioned a perhaps deeper difference between perception and cognition in connection with divisive normalization as instantiated in center-surround suppression. As I mentioned, there is evidence that while center-surround suppression obtains in vision, the preserved visual representations in visual working memory do not show this effect (Bloem et al., 2018). Center-surround suppression is a kind of competition and is related to the winner-takes-all nature of perception, but this kind of competition need not obtain in cognition.

Although the markers I mentioned are important to perception, and we can explain why perception should have these properties, they do not seem fundamental to perception. We can imagine a robot whose perceptions are slow, not automatic, and do not show adaptation, pop-out or illusory contours. I will argue that there are deeper properties of format, content, and kind of state that are fundamental to perception. Perception is iconic in format, and nonconceptual and nonpropositional, where these latter two properties can be regarded as properties of content or of content-related kind of state. I think it is just obvious that format, content, and kind of state are more fundamental than adaptation, rivalry, pop-out, speed, automaticity, search efficiency, and interpolation. Of course not every difference in format, content, and kind of state is a fundamental difference. I will be arguing that the iconic/discursive difference is a fundamental difference in format, a difference in kind, not just a difference in contingent properties. And likewise for the conceptual/nonconceptual and propositional/nonpropositional differences. I think the arguments for these differences will make clear how basic they are.

The markers of perception discussed in this chapter are relevant to some controversies in the philosophy of perception about the extent to which perception requires attribution, discrimination, and singling out, as will be discussed in the next chapter.

3
Two kinds of seeing-as and singular content

What is it to see something as red or to see something as a cat? On the account of perception that I am advocating, there are two distinct kinds of seeing-as. Tyler Burge's model of perception (2010a) will be my jumping off point. I will explain what I think is right and what is wrong with it and I will compare it to some similar views of Susanna Schellenberg (2018).[1]

What is depicted in Figure 3.1 is—starting on the left—a circular object (a plate); sensory registration stimulated by the object; a perception of the object as circular via a visual demonstrative that singles out a particular; and a basic perceptual judgment with the content that that particular (the referent of the visual demonstrative) is circular that involves a conceptualization of the perceptual representation of circularity. A basic perceptual judgment is one that conceptualizes the attributional element of a percept. (A useful precisification of Burge's "basic perceptual judgment" would be the minimal immediate direct perceptual judgment that I explained in Chapter 1.) The "That X" in the diagram is meant to indicate that the perceptual content has a structure analogous to that of the content of a noun phrase, with singular and general aspects to the content. The "that" is analogous to the singular element.[2] Burge holds that the property representation (indicated by the 'X') functions in identificational reference—i.e., in picking out the particular that the perception is about—and also to make an attribution to the particular referred to, in this case the plate. The predication in the "that X" is what Burge calls "impure predication" because of the dual role of the property representation in identificational reference and also attribution (Burge, 2010b). The basic perceptual judgment "That is circular" is produced via the application of the concept of circularity to yield a structured propositional

---

[1] Thanks to Joseph Gottlieb, Chris Hill, Ali Rezaei, Mark Sainsbury, and Susanna Schellenberg for comments on an earlier draft of this chapter.

[2] I am simplifying Burge's view for purposes of intelligibility. (See footnote 28 in Burge, 2010b.) One simplification: Burge emphasizes that the "that" is to be understood as a context-bound singular application depending on the causal factors involved in the particular case. He usually indicates this point by putting a subscript on the "that." Another kind of simplification is that the example does not cover perception of relations. Another is that a more complex perception can be plural rather than singular, i.e., directed toward more than one particular. His footnote 28 goes into other respects in which this gloss is a simplification.

122 THE BORDER BETWEEN SEEING AND THINKING

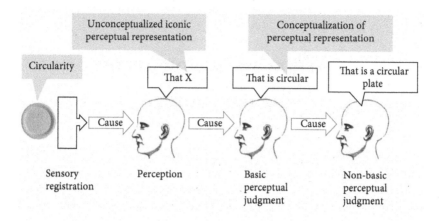

Figure 3.1 A depiction of Burge's model of perception (Burge, 2010a). From Block (2014a). Feedback connections are not shown.

mental representation. In the basic perceptual judgment, the property representation ("circular") functions to attribute a property but not within the scope of identificational reference. In the judgment that this (contextually indicated thing) is circular, the attribution of circularity to the referent of the demonstrative is pure predication, because the predication functions independently of the identificational reference. As we will see below, I think that singular representation is not a constitutive feature of perceptual representation (although it is a feature of many perceptions).

Although I will be arguing in Chapter 4 that perception is nonpropositional, I do not endorse one of Burge's arguments for this. Burge argues that pure predication is required for propositional structure but that the attributives of perception, being used in identificational reference, are never cases of pure predication—hence perception is not propositional. I agree with E. J. Green's and Jake Quilty-Dunn's arguments (Quilty-Dunn & Green, forthcoming) that the attributives of perception need not be used in identificational reference. As they note, perceptual attributives are flexibly used in identificational reference or in predication, depending on context. Indeed, the role of an attributive—whether it is predicative or used in identification can shift within a single perception (Quilty-Dunn & Green, forthcoming).

The first kind of "seeing-as" is nonconceptual *perceptual* seeing-as in which the property indicated by 'X' is attributed to a particular. In the case illustrated, the particular is a physical object. In other cases of perceptual seeing-as, a property can be attributed to other types of particular, an event, a temporal moment, or a position in space, or even such made-up entities as a property instance or a trope (the specific redness of a specific red thing)—if such entities exist at all. The second kind of seeing-as is *cognitive* rather than perceptual. In the example, it is the conceptual attribution of circularity. Burge doesn't actually say that there are two kinds of seeing-as, but he did not object to it in his response (2014) to my suggestion of it (2014c).

It may be that some cases of cognitive attribution are nonconceptual. Nonconceptual thinking can perhaps use mental maps (though see Chapter 1 on grid-cells) and they may be involved in attribution (Burge, 2010a). Sometimes the word "cognition" is anchored to conceptual thinking. For example, Tim Bayne says "thinking, reasoning, perceiving, imagining, and remembering are cognitive processes to the extent that they involve the use of concepts." (Bayne et al., 2019, p. R 608) But I am using the term somewhat differently—excluding perception (which in my view is in any case nonconceptual) and including nonconceptual thinking that uses nonconceptual elements.

Does "That X" represent satisfactorily? That is, for there to be reference at all must the referent of "that X" actually have the property represented by 'X'? Burge's answer is: "Most of the attributions can go wrong even if a particular is perceived" (Burge, 2010b, p. 34). He explains the "most" by saying that some aspect of the attributive (i.e., the representation of the property) must be accurate and gives the example of certain topological conditions of connectedness. He is clear, though, that a particular can be misperceived and that the misperception will fail to fulfill the accuracy function of perception, where the accuracy function is distinct from its evolutionary function (Burge, 2010a, p. 302).

Burge and Schellenberg on singular content

According to Burge, perception constitutively and necessarily functions to single out what is seen, namely a particular (Burge, 2009). (Of course, as indicated in the last paragraph, perception does not require successful singling out.) I listed some different sorts of particulars above. For example, Burge (2010a, p. 542) says, "Perception is essentially, at every point, context-bound singling-out of particulars. Its attributions function in presenting particulars." Susanna Schellenberg (2018) uses "particular" in roughly the same sense as Burge and also holds that perception is constitutively a matter of discriminating and singling out particulars. She emphasizes that perception involves discriminating and singling out property instances but also objects and events. (Terminological note: An "object of perception" can be anything that is perceived, not just physical objects. Sometimes Burge uses the term "object" where it is clear that he means any particular that is an object of perception.)

I once subscribed to the singular content view (Block, 2014c), but will argue here that while physical object perception is usefully construed as singular, there are other kinds of perception that are more usefully construed as existential. The most plausible examples of existential perception are those that do not involve figure/ground separation. On my view, even for object perception, there is no objective fact about singular content but only a pragmatic issue of how best to think about object perception for certain purposes. On my diagnosis, Burge and Schellenberg go wrong trying to fit perception into a framework that is appropriate to language.

Burge holds that perception has singular content, but he does not claim that perception has singular format. Singular format requires an element of the representational vehicle whose function is to pick out a single thing. Linguistic demonstratives like "that" have both singular format and content. Burge's analogizing of a perception to "that F" is meant to be at the level of content. I agree with him that perception need not involve any singular format element. I will say why in Chapter 5 in a discussion of the view of E. J. Green and Jake Quilty-Dunn to the effect that object perception does require a discursive format element.

Burge (2010a) argues that "perception is clearly constitutively of concrete particulars, and thus has singular elements in its representational content" (p. 167). Burge's (2010a) book introduces the idea here (p. 83):

> Take a visual perceptual state as of a cylindrical solid. There are two aspects of perceptual representational content of the state—general and singular. The singular aspect functions fallibly to single out (refer to) perceived particulars. When successful, the perceptual state refers to a particular cylindrical solid, and perhaps particular instances of cylindricality and solidity. The general aspect in the representational content functions fallibly to group or categorize particulars by attributing some indicated kind, property, or relation to them. (Burge, 2010a)

By contrast, Schellenberg holds that perception is singular in both content and format. For example, she says that, "while perceptual capacities are general, the representations yielded by employing general perceptual capacities are not only syntactically singular, in the good case, they are moreover semantically singular" (Schellenberg, 2018, p. 67).

The term "singular content" is ambiguous. In the weak sense of the term, it means content that is directed toward a particular, and whose accuracy conditions depend on that particular. If I think that (contextually indicated) apple is locally grown and you think that (indicating a different but qualitatively identical apple) apple is locally grown, the truth value of your thought and my thought can differ depending on the origin of our respective apples. There are many perceptions that plausibly single out in the sense of being directed toward objects and having accuracy conditions that depend on those objects. Both scientists and philosophers have argued for that conclusion. For example, Pylyshyn's "fingers of instantiation" are perceptual demonstratives postulated by Pylyshyn to account for multiple-object tracking (Pylyshyn, 1989) (discussed in the next section and more extensively in Chapter 4.)

However, there are stronger uses of the term "singular content." One such use is what philosophers call "object-involving content."[3] Object-involving content includes the object seen as a constituent of the content. Another use that is stronger than the weak use of the last paragraph is one in which the referent of the singular content "constitutes" the singular content. "Constitutes" can be understood in terms of the content being grounded in the referent or metaphysically determined by the referent. Schellenberg regards perceptual content as constituted by its object in this sense (p. 16). (See also Davies, 1996/7.) I will lump together these stronger kinds of singular content, calling them "strong singular content" and describing the strong view as saying that perception is constituted by its object. That object can be any kind of particular, including a temporal moment or spatial location, or even a property instance if such there be, so they would more accurately be called "particular-involving" content. (I will stick with "object-involving," since that is standard.)

Burge takes perceptual content types of the sort studied by science to be nonsingular and not constituted by the particulars seen. (This much I agree with.) On his view, it is the individual perceptual tokens that are singular (in at least the weak sense; he doesn't explicitly endorse or reject the strong sense). Thus, he regards perception as a "hybrid" in which perceptual tokens are singular but there are types that are not. Here is how he puts it: "Thus, although seeing is in a sense a natural kind, it is a hybrid kind. It is a psychological state that, *in each instance*, depends for being a seeing on entities and causal relations beyond the psychology of the individual.... The representational contents of perceptual states include context-bound applications—demonstrative *occurrences*. These applications' identities hinge on the particular contexts and particular times in which they occur" (2010a, pp. 389–390).

---

[3] Some readers will be familiar with the controversy over naïve realist views of perception (Brewer, 2019; Campbell, 2002; Martin, 2002). I won't be discussing naïve realism in this book except in this footnote and briefly in Chapter 13. See my (2010) for some science-based arguments against such views, Bill Brewer's reply (Brewer, 2019) and my rejoinder (Block, 2019a). Naïve realists often hold that the phenomenology of a veridical perception and a subjectively indistinguishable hallucination will have "no common factor." For example, Mike Martin (2004) claims that there is no "distinctive mental event or state common to these various disjoint situations" (p. 37). I agree with Burge that there are non-object-involving perceptual types that capture the contents of perception of objects, specifically what veridical and subjectively indistinguishable hallucinatory perceptions have in common. (See Burge, 2005; Campbell, 2011; McDowell, 2010.)

Burge says that whether token perceptions are particular-involving is "not fundamental." What is fundamental is that there are scientific types that are not particular-involving. (See p. 364 of Burge, 2010a, and footnote 70 in Burge, 2005.[4])

Schellenberg (2018) distinguishes between phenomenological particularity and relational particularity. The former applies to a perception when it seems to be of a particular but the latter requires an actual particular that partly constitutes the perception. She notes that we can have particular-constituted singular thoughts and argues that the best explanation of our ability to think those singular thoughts is that they are based on and justified by particular-constituted singular perception. However, as she also notes, those who reject particular-constitutive singular perception can try to explain how we can have such singular thoughts by appeal to the causal relation of the perceiver to the perceived particular (p. 21).

That concludes my exposition of Burge's and Schellenberg's views. I now move toward explaining why I don't accept them.

Perception having singular content even in the weak sense has a seemingly odd consequence. If I am seeing a tree, the content of my perception would not be the same if the tree were imperceptibly switched with a different but qualitatively identical tree. (This is a "seamless transition" case [Johnston, 2004; Pautz, 2011].) In the seamless transition case, one could regard the perception as continuing throughout the changing of the trees while changing content mid-way through. The weak kind of singular content would allow an ongoing perception with changing content. But on the strong kind of singular content (and also the weak kind if content is taken to individuate perceptual states), the perception itself would have to change when the tree is switched. That is, when

---

[4] What Burge says (p. 76) is, "Whether one individuates application *tokens* in terms of their distal causes is, I believe, not fundamental." In other words, whether token perceptions are particular-constituted is not fundamental. He explains, "I believe that there is a natural and defensible understanding of representations marking such events that accords with human and animal fallibility: One's perceptual belief could have been based on illusion if abnormal conditions had been substituted, indiscernibly, for the actual causal conditions. But even if applications were object-based, the same explanatory perceptual state kind (and the same belief kind) would have been involved." I take his term "object-based" to mean what I am calling "particular constituted." So he is saying there is a natural understanding of the perceptual representation of say a red ball in which the perception could have been based on seeing a different red ball. If one allows that this very perception could have been a perception of a different object, one is treating the perception as not object-constituted. This interpretation is further backed up by the passage to which footnote 70 is attached (p. 54): "I have maintained that there are reasons to acknowledge a way of individuating perceptual applications that leave them, in their essential identities, independent of the object referred to or perceived. That is, the same application could have been caused by another object or by processes that stemmed from no object. In that way, the application is *independent,* for its identity, of the perceived object." Burge quotes this passage and elaborates on it in the footnote of (Burge, 2010a, pp. 362–364).

one tree is imperceptibly switched with a different but qualitatively identical tree, one perception is replaced by another perception even though the perceiver has no way of knowing that one of the perceiver's internal states has ended and another begun.

Suppose you are looking at a scene involving a red ball on a white background for 2 seconds. After the first second, the red ball is seamlessly replaced during an eye blink by a different but indiscernible red ball. Your visual system receives no indication that a switch has been made and it looks to you as if you have been seeing the same red ball for 2 seconds. (Brian Loar's lemon example adds a third stage in which after seeing first one lemon, then another lemon, the subject hallucinates a lemon without being aware of any subjective change. [See Loar, 2003; Sainsbury, 2019].) According to Burge, because of the different objects of perception, you have two distinct perceptual states and in that sense two different perceptions, though perceptions of the same explanatory type. He says (2010a, p. 393):

> Although the two state instances refer to different balls—and the states' contents have different token singular demonstrative applications—the kind of state formed (the attributional kind) is the same in all other respects.

What is suspect about the consequence of a change from one perception to another is not that it sounds strange. I don't take that to be problematic. Rather, perception has no access to the distinction between qualitative and numerical identity. So why should the difference between qualitative and numerical identity figure in the individuation conditions of perceptions? Further, it would seem that if my conscious perceptual state is replaced by a different conscious perceptual state, then I should be able to know that this replacement has taken place from the first person point of view, at least in principle. Alternatively: If am not able to know that the replacement has taken place, there should be a causal explanation of why that knowledge is not available to me. But a seamless transition case precludes any such knowledge.

To be clear, I don't take this point to be much of an argument against the singular content view. Indeed, there is a contrary intuition that appeals to an analogy with thought: we are prepared to suppose that the causal history of my term "Moses" determines a reference even if virtually all of our beliefs about that referent are false—e.g., that Moses was an itinerant Egyptian fig merchant who spread false stories about splitting the Red Sea, seeing the burning bush, etc. (Kripke, 1972). And it could be argued that perception, being the epistemic basis of thought, must also be individuated by its causal source. A counter-reply to this argument would be that thought, unlike perception, has access to the distinction between qualitative and numerical identity.

The singular side on this issue is Burge's and Schellenberg's view that perception is constitutively singular—in at least the weak sense (Burge) and the strong sense (Schellenberg). Opposed to that are the "existentialists" like Christopher Hill (2019, 2021) and perhaps Mark Sainsbury (2019). I say that Sainsbury is perhaps an existentialist since he argues for existentialism about object perception and does not extend the argument to other forms of perception (Sainsbury, 2019). But since object perception is the best candidate for singular perception, his arguments might be taken to support existentialism about all perception. (See also Davies, 1992.)

A well-known argument for existentialism is that it allows for a common content to a veridical perception and a subjectively indistinguishable hallucination. Indeed, a veridical perception can match a hallucination not only subjectively but also in terms of the neural processing involved. Of course the particularists can insist that a veridical perception and a subjectively and causally indistinguishable hallucination are fundamentally different kinds of states, thereby undermining the argument for existentialism.

I don't see a strong reason to favor either existentialism or singularism or the "pluralist" view that all perceptions have both singular and existential content (Logue, 2021). Further, the existence of perceptual states that are not on the face of it about particulars at all (to be described below) suggests that singular content in neither the strong or weak senses is constitutive of perception, even if object perception is singular in the weak sense.

Whether or not one accepts Burge's and Schellenberg's intuitions about seeing concrete objects like a ball, their view looks less plausible when applied to the example, to be discussed in detail below, of seeing motion in the periphery without seeing any object moving. Consider such a case of seeing motion in the periphery for 2 seconds. After the first second, the object that is moving is replaced by a distinct but identical object during a blink—still in the periphery. Your visual system receives no indication that a switch has been made. Should we conclude that there are two perceptions? But how could there be two perceptions given that the objects whose change requires the two instances of motion were never visible to the perceiver? If the content of the perception is existential—e.g., that there is motion in such and such a place in such and such a direction—then there is one perception. (I'll consider later in this chapter the objection that one can see or at least be visually aware of invisible objects and their shapes.)

A defender of constitutive singular content could say that in these cases one is perceiving instances of properties (i.e., particulars that are identical instantiations of properties). Schellenberg construes causation in terms of property instances. In her view, properties are always to be understood in terms of their instances. (See 2018, p. 15 and p. 70 and two paragraphs below.) One indication that Burge might also appeal to perceiving instances is that he notes that spatial perception occurs throughout the animal kingdom, including in arthropods. But, he argues, there could be an animal that was incapable of spatial perception, seeing only lightness or color. However, he argues, even the perceptions of such a primitive animal would have a singular content element. He says (2010a, p. 496) "A representational content of the state would be something like that₁ red!" (where the '1' indexes a token application of the demonstrative). Here the most obvious referent of the demonstrative would be an instance (or a trope).

I find appeal to entities such as property instances or tropes rather suspicious, especially given that Burge and Schellenberg agree that the philosophy of perception should be based on the science of perception. The science of perception does not appeal to such entities and has no need to do so. (See Byrne, 2019; Schellenberg, 2019).

In any case, Burge does not give an argument for the conclusion about the primitive animal. Why couldn't the content of the animal's perception be the existential content that there is redness? What abilities or tendencies of the primitive animal would determine the difference between the singular content and the existential content? Sometimes intuitions about the causal source of a perception seem to be paramount in Burge's and Schellenberg's reasoning. But as we will see, an existential view of the content of perception can also accommodate these intuitions.

A defender of singular content can certainly postulate that all the apparent counterexamples in which one perceives a property without an object are cases of perception of a particular that is an instance of the property, but this postulation makes one wonder whether the thesis of singular content as constitutive of perception is stipulative rather than a substantive thesis. The perceptual attribution of a property can always be viewed as the singling out of a property instance, but if the particularists rely on this, they must tell us why one of those construals is the right one. Note that I am not insisting on the attributional construal. Rather my position is that the issue of whether perception is constitutively singular has no factual answer.

To be fair to Schellenberg, she offers an argument that we see instances of properties. Her argument is that when we perceive the shape of the cup, the shape must be causally efficacious since we cannot see what does not causally impinge on us (Schellenberg, 2018, pp. 145–150). However, this argument assumes her view of causation as based in property instances. There are alternative pictures of perceiving the shape of the cup, some of which postulate instances of shapes and others of which do not.

One alternative picture is that I see the cup, attributing a shape property to it. It is in virtue of the shape property of the cup that I see it as having that shape. What is causally efficacious in this case is the cup's having a certain shape, or, alternatively, the cup itself, and it is causally efficacious in producing the perception in virtue of some of its properties but not others. There is no need to appeal to property instances on these accounts.

I said it is in virtue of the shape property of the cup that I see it as having that shape. This way of thinking derives from some basic considerations about causation. Suppose I throw a red brick at a window, breaking the window. It is in virtue of the mass and velocity of the brick that it breaks the window, not in virtue of the brick's red color. In that sense, mass and velocity are causally efficacious properties but the color is not. I suppose Schellenberg could maintain that the instances of mass and velocity cause the window to break, but an alternative is that the brick breaks the window in virtue of its mass and velocity. The soprano's high C "Help!" may shatter the glass but the meaning of the word "help" is not causally efficacious in shattering the glass; rather it is the intensity and pitch of the sound that are causally efficacious (Dretske, 1988; Sosa, 1984).

Schellenberg thinks that vision scientists are committed to property instances in that they talk about "features" being causally efficacious and spatiotemporally located. But as just noted, properties can be causally efficacious and one can speak of locating them in space and time by locating objects that have those properties during certain temporal periods. We can understand features to be properties, not instances of properties.

We have two different ways of thinking of the metaphysics of causation, one based in properties, the other in instances of properties. Without some good reason for favoring one rather than the other there is no compelling reason to accept constitutive strong singular content. This point contributes to my sense that the issue of constitutive singular content of perception is not a factual issue.

There are three issues under discussion:

1. Is perception constitutively singular in the weak sense? That is, is perception constitutively directed toward a particular and does that particular figure in the perception's accuracy conditions?
2. Is perception constitutively singular in the strong sense? That is, is perception constituted by the particular that is perceived?
3. Are there some perceptual contents that are existential?

Burge and Schellenberg say yes to 1 and no to 3. Schellenberg says yes to 2 and Burge does not endorse or reject 2, saying, as mentioned earlier, that the issue of whether token perceptions are object-involving is "not fundamental." I say that there is no good reason to accept either 1 or 2 because I don't think the categories involved in the question apply neatly to perception and because of the equal plausibility of a yes to 3: The content of the perception of motion in the periphery and some other cases to come is usefully construed as existential.

Schellenberg has another argument for strong singular perceptual content that is based on the claim that perception is constituted by perceptual capacities that function to discriminate and single out particulars (2018, 24–28). She puts it this way:

> ... perceptual states are constituted by employing perceptual capacities that function to discriminate and single out particulars, and in the case of an accurate perception, they in fact discriminate and single out a particular of the right kind. Now if singling out a particular has any significance, then the subject's perceptual state is constituted by the particular when she perceives that particular. To think otherwise would be to sever the link between the function of the capacity and its output. After all, mental states are outputs of employing capacities with a certain function, and these outputs are individuated by the particulars on which the capacities operate. A perceptual state of perceiving α is constituted by α in virtue of the perceptual state being constituted by employing a perceptual capacity that functions to single out particulars of the type under which α falls.

Of course, the premise of this argument, that "perceptual states are constituted by employing perceptual capacities that function to discriminate and single out particulars," is as controversial as the conclusion and I would not accept it. As far as I can see, Schellenberg gives no argument that perceptual states must have this function. Further, as Michael Martin notes (2020), a capacity that functions "to discriminate and single out particulars" could be construed to single out *whatever* item is suitably related to the subject. In order to leverage this capacity to support singular content, weak or strong, one has to interpret the phrase in a de re manner and that itself would need justification.

Analogously, "the tallest spy" singles out whoever is the tallest of the spies if there are spies and no ties. My capacity to discriminate and single out M&Ms for purposes of eating them is a capacity to discriminate and single out whatever M&Ms are ready to hand and would make suitable snacks. When this capacity successfully singles out a particular M&M, the resulting state is not constituted by that particular M&M, since the same capacity might have singled out a different M&M.

What is meant in this argument by singling out a particular? This passage looks to be an argument from singling out in something like the weak sense (in an accurate case) to singling out in the strong sense: "Now if singling out a particular has any significance, then the subject's perceptual state is constituted by the particular when she perceives that particular." The "Now if singling out a particular has any significance" seems to involve a sense of "singling out" that is neutral on the object-constituting nature of singling out. The link would seem to be intended to ground the transition from the weak to the strong sense. I will argue against singling out in both senses below.

I will move now to a more detailed discussion of the case of seeing motion in the periphery without seeing a moving object. Although there are many anecdotal reports of seeing motion in the periphery without seeing a moving object, I have been unable to find any direct test. There are however, reasons for thinking that this happens.

1. Motion discrimination in the periphery is nearly as strong in the periphery as in the fovea, but acuity in the periphery is much weaker than in the fovea. McKee and Nakayama (1984, p. 25) note, "Velocity discrimination ($\Delta V/V$) [NB: difference in velocity divided by velocity] is as precise in the periphery as in the fovea, amounting to about 6% for the optimum velocity range." Note, however, that this is velocity discrimination (that is, discrimination between different velocities), not velocity detection, and in the experiments reported, the moving objects were visible.
2. When acuity is weak, objects may not be distinguishable from their background. For example, a grid of black on white stripes that can be resolved with good acuity may not be distinguishable from a uniform gray field with low acuity. If acuity is too poor to distinguish the moving object from the background, the visual system would be unable to ascribe motion to it. Thus, seeing motion of an object that cannot be resolved would be a case of perception in which the object that is moving cannot be distinguished from the background.
3. The peripheral retina is dominated by rods, not cones, and rods feed preferentially to the motion-sensitive area of visual cortex, area MT/V5.

These are reasons for believing that one can see motion without seeing a moving object. One plausible construal of such perceptions is that they are existential: there is motion there.

As I mentioned, some have argued that one can see or at least be visually aware of things, light from which does not reach the eye (Ganson, 2021; Lande, 2022; Munton, 2021). Consider for example, the "tunnel effect," in which an object disappears behind an occluder that is no wider than the object and emerges from the other side. (This effect is described in detail in Chapter 5.) If the trajectory is smooth and the motion is sufficiently speedy, observers have the impression of motion behind the occluder. Jessie Munton (2021) argues that one can see the object behind the occluder and that more generally one can see "invisible" objects. Kevin Lande (2022) partially disagrees, arguing that one is visually aware of the object and its shape behind the occluder even though one cannot see it. He makes a strong case for visual awareness of the occluded parts as well as the shapes of partially occluded objects in cases of amodal completion of the sort discussed in Chapter 2.

Even if one agrees with either Lande or Munton, the point does not generalize to the cases of seeing motion without seeing a moving object that I have been describing. In the occlusion cases that Munton and Lande are concerned with, there is some kind of visual representation of the occluded part or shape and that is crucial to their arguments. As mentioned in Chapter 2, Churchland and Ramachandran showed that at least in some cases there is detectable "filling in" in early visual processing and similar results have been shown in other visual phenomena (Churchland & Ramachandran, 1996; Spillman, Otte, Hamburger, & Magnussen, 2006). See the article by Lande for an impressive marshalling of empirical evidence that in amodal completion, the occluded parts are represented in the visual system. Further, in the discussion of the phonemic restoration effect in Chapter 2, we saw evidence of an auditory form of such "filling in" in which the filled in syllable was represented in the auditory system, as shown by its effect on adaptation. But in the cases of seeing motion in the periphery, the visual system has no information about the shape or other local properties of the moving object.

A different sort of case of seeing motion without singling out a moving thing may involve a visual phenomenon known as "crowding." The further into the periphery, the more prevalent the crowding. One subject in a crowding experiment was quoted as saying, "It looks like one big mess.... I seem to take features of one letter and mix them up with those of another." Another subject said: "I know that there are three letters. But for some reason, I can't identify the middle one, which looks like it's being stretched and distorted by the outer flankers" (Pelli, Palomares, & Majaj, 2004, p. 1139). See Figure 3.2 for an example of crowded perception.

In crowded perception, there is more than one object in an "integration field," making the perception bewildering. I will explain. Perception of objects involves

Figure 3.2 If you fixate the '+' you will very likely find the perception of the letters on the right to look to have features that are jumbled together in a way that is hard to describe. Subjects are often unsure of how many letters there are in a case of crowding. The letters on the left "escape" crowding because the features that are jumbled together are the same. Thanks to Denis Pelli for this figure. (See Block, 2012, 2013; Pelli et al., 2004.)

134   THE BORDER BETWEEN SEEING AND THINKING

assigning features to objects. This process is known as "binding." If one sees a blue triangle moving to the right and a green square moving upward, the visual system has to assign the shape, color, and motion to the right objects. This process involves "windows of integration" in which shape, color, and motion are bound to one another and to an object representation. (These windows may be receptive fields at the level of V2 or other levels of the visual system.) However, the size of the windows of integration grows larger with peripherality to the point where often there is more than one object in a single window of integration. See Figure 3.3 for an indication of the size and shape of these windows and how they increase in the periphery of vision.

The reason I am mentioning crowding is that if there are a number of moving objects in an integration field, the visual system may have little or no information about which motions go with which objects. This phenomenon may underlie some cases of the sense of seeing motion without determinately seeing a moving object. In such cases, there can be no singling out of the moving object.

Further, even when the crowded objects are not moving, the visual system often does not have information about how many objects there are or which shapes go with which objects. Michael Tye (Tye, 2010, 2014a) has argued that consciously seeing an object must put the perceiver in a position to have a de re

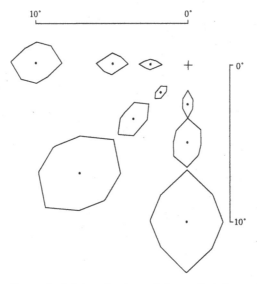

Figure 3.3 If one fixates the '+' sign, the size and shape of windows of integration as they change with eccentricity are indicated by the roughly oval figures. As indicated, the size of the windows of integration increase with increasing peripherality. What is not shown in this diagram is that the windows are overlapping. Thanks to Denis Pelli for this figure. (See Pelli & Tillman, 2008.)

thought about what is seen. As he puts it (Tye, 2010, p. 413), "I am conscious of a thing just in case my experience has a phenomenal character *directly* on the basis of which I can at least ask myself 'What's that?' with respect to the thing (or form some singular belief about it)." I objected (Block, 2014b) that a creature—say a spider—can see things without the capacity for de re thought, but Tye's condition remains quite plausible as applied to creatures that do have the capacity for de re thought. This condition dictates that in crowded perception one is not seeing the crowded items. My suggestion is that we can plausibly construe perception of crowded objects as existential.

An advocate of the Burge/Schellenberg position may argue that there is visual reference to crowded objects that are moving in such cases—just defective visual reference. But an equally good construal is that there is jumbled existential perception with no visual reference. And of course they always have the recourse of appeal to perception of instances of motion, thereby moving in the direction of trivialization.

Another case that is sometimes said to involve the experience of motion without a moving thing is the phi phenomenon, a variant of apparent motion. In the phi phenomenon, fast alternation of one item and another nearby creates a sense of motion from one place to the other. If the alternation is slowed down to roughly half the frequency for phi, one sees a clearly moving thing. This is called beta motion (Steinman, Pizlo, & Pizlo, 2000). See the discussion in Chapter 5.) However, in the phi phenomenon *there is apparent motion without the appearance of a moving object.* As Steinman et al. put it (p. 2263), one might call it "a pure, objectless, movement."

Another case in which there are reports of seeing motion without seeing a moving object is Riddoch syndrome or Type 2 blindsight. In Type 1 blindsight, subjects are said to not consciously see objects in a portion of their visual field. But when an object moves, they often can see the motion consciously. This is Type 2 blindsight (Hayashi et al., 2017; Weiskrantz, 1986/2009). (There is a controversy over whether blindsight is really blind. See the discussion and references in Chapter 13 below.)

In sum, there are a number of cases that may be perception of motion without a moving object.

Another candidate for nonsingular seeing is ensemble perception. (Ensemble perception, sometimes called gist perception, was mentioned in Chapter 2 and will be discussed repeatedly in this book. The phenomenon will be defined in Chapter 4 in the section "Atomic propositional representations.") In ensemble perception one can see the average tilt and the average size of lines or the average expression of faces without being able to see any particular face. (For evidence that one sees average properties without seeing the particulars that exhibit the properties that are averaged, see Ariely, 2001; Bayne & McClelland,

2019; Openshaw & Weksler, 2019.) Of course the particularist can claim that one visually singles out the group itself. It is not clear, however, that in seeing the average expression of a sea of faces that one does single out any particular group. As before, it is open to the particularist to say that vision singles out an instance of the average expression. As before, this may save the thesis at the cost of trivializing it.

Here is another putative case in which perception may not be singular: The frequency at which flickering light fuses so that the flicker is no longer seen is higher in the periphery of vision for many subjects than in the center of vision, and in that sense we can be more sensitive to flicker in the periphery. As a result, one can see flicker in the entirety of the peripheral visual field without localizing it to any one place (Seiple & Holopigian, 1996). I have experienced this myself when looking at a TV screen head on, close enough so that the edges are in peripheral vision where the flicker fusion threshold is higher. A particularist might say this is perception of an everywhere-in-the-periphery object but I would describe it as a perception of some flickering in the periphery.

Another case is the "ganzfeld" perception. This footnote, which will be referenced later, explains the ganzfeld perception, in which one sees fog-like light.[5] In the ganzfeld perception, the perception of flicker in disparate parts of the visual field described above, and the perception of motion, there is perception without figure/ground segregation, so there is no figure to be singled out.

Is the ganzfeld perception accurate or is it illusory? An experience as of fog-like light is accurate just in case there is fog-like light—it is not obvious that it has to be any particular fog-like light. An experience as of light is naturally taken to be an experience of *some* light, not of any concrete particular. I would say the same for the flicker perception I described. It can reasonably be construed as a perception of some flicker. I would say the same for some experiences of motion in the periphery without determinate perception of any moving object. I see no point in shoehorning these perceptions into a model that is based on object perception.

A defender of singular content as constitutive of perception might say that the ganzfeld perception has to have some way of specifying *which* surfaceless fog-like

---

[5] In a ganzfeld perception, what one perceives can often be described as a "space-filling surfaceless fog" (Hochberg, Triebel, & Seaman, 1951, p. 153). You can get a pretty good version of this by cutting a ping pong ball in half and putting a half on each eye (Wackermann, Pütz, & Allefeld, 2008). Having done this myself, I would describe it more as fog-like light than as a fog. Hochberg et al. found that after a few minutes of ganzfeld color perception, color perception faded out. Many of the subjects "were unwilling to believe that the lights had not been changed or shut off" (p.156). When the color illumination of the ganzfeld was cut off, almost all subjects experienced the complementary color, showing the expected effect of visual color attribution. Similar effects have been reported for luminance adaptation, with subjective luminance fading almost to the minimum level after 5–7 minutes (Knau & Spillmann, 1997). (The minimum level is the "eigengrau" level, defined as what is experienced in a totally dark room after dark adaptation.)

light is the one seen. That might be true for linguistic reference to a fog-like light, but perceptual reference is constrained by direct causal relations to what is seen in ways that linguistic reference is not constrained. Perception can take advantage of such direct causal proximity to what is seen without *having* to build in such specifications. Remember: I am not denying that one *can* construe the content as that instance of fog-like light or that fog-like light trope; my point is that there is no compelling need to construe the content as singular, and no objective fact that the content is singular.

I can imagine the objection: "But isn't it clear that the surfaceless fog-like light is the one *here*?" Sure, but perception has no need to build that condition into the content. Perception is always as of the here and now, so there is no need for here and now to be explicitly represented.

Perceptions constitutively have accuracy conditions. What is the accuracy condition of the ganzfeld perception? Perhaps Burge and Schellenberg would say the content of the perception is something like "that surfaceless fog-like light" and its accuracy condition is that the referent of "that" is a surfaceless fog-like light. But why prefer that view to the view that the content is existential, that there is a surfaceless fog-like light or some surfaceless fog-like light? (Compare Burge's discussion of Evans [2010a, pp. 184–185].)

John Bengson mentions a case derived from Susanna Siegel's "pink glow that you have when your eyes are closed" (Siegel, 2010, p. 209):

> "... you are out for a walk on a dark, cloudy night, without a flashlight (torch); you look around, gazing intently, and you find yourself confronted with a peculiar shade of black (perhaps ebony, bean, or jet) in all directions: as they say, it is *pitch black*. In these cases, you are no doubt presented with a color: a shade (or shades) of blue-green or black, respectively. But it is not presented to you as being the case that something is that shade (or shades), that that shade is (or shades are) instantiated by anything (not the water, not the boat, not the road, not the surrounding landscape, not the color properties themselves, not "the night," not anything). (Bengson, 2013, p. 801)

One could interpret Bengson as saying that one is presented with an object, a shade. I would not agree with that, but I would agree with him on an interpretation in which what he describes is not object perception or instance perception but rather perception of *some* blackness.

Burge could reply that in the cases I mentioned there is no perception, only sensation. Burge claims that perceptual constancies are required for perception. The rationale for this claim is that perceptual constancies are what give perception its objective import. Without them we have mere sensation with no objective import or real representation.

I don't know whether constancies are involved in any of the cases I mentioned. There are constancy mechanisms in the eye and in subcortical structures that process visual input prior to cortical processing (Chen, Sperandio, Henry, & Goodale, 2019). So the ganzfeld perception, the blackness perception, and the perception of motion without perception of a moving object may after all involve constancies. Perception of motion typically involves motion constancy. However, whether or not these cases involve constancies, they all clearly involve objective import in the sense of perception as of something in the world. When I see motion in the periphery without seeing a moving object, I am visually representing motion in the world—it seems to me visually that the environment involves motion. The same is true of visual attributions of flicker, blackness, and fog-like light. If no constancies are involved in these perceptions, so much the worse for the appeal to constancies in distinguishing perception from sensation.

One problem with appeal to constancies is that there are distinct neural bases of constancies in perception and perceptually guided action. This has been shown repeatedly in the work of Milner and Goodale and was recently demonstrated cleanly in a patient, MC, with a damaged ventral visual stream combined with an intact dorsal visual system. This patient judged the size of objects at different distances according to retinal size—in other words, without size constancy. But MC's grip aperture for picking up objects at different distances reflected normal constancies (Whitwell, Sperandio, Buckingham, Chouinard, & Goodale, 2020), showing constancies in visually guided action without constancies in visual judgment. If constancies make the difference between sensation and perception, we need to know *which* constancies and *why* those constancies. The fact that MC can grasp objects that he is consciously aware of suggests that he does consciously see them and that his conscious vision has objective import—whether or not his conscious vision has the relevant constancies.

There are well-known objections to existential content of perception, having to do with an illusory experience of one object when another object that one is not seeing satisfies the misrepresenting content. In Grice's famous "veridical illusion" example (1961), a pillar of a certain location, shape, size, color, texture, etc., is in front of me but is occluded by a mirror that reflects an exactly similar pillar to my side. My experience (and retinal image) is qualitatively the same as if I were seeing the pillar in front of me. If perceptual content were existential, my perception would be veridical since "there is a pillar in front of me that has such and such a location, shape, size, color, texture, etc." is true, but intuitively my perception is illusory. The pillar I am actually seeing is not in front of me. (It could be termed a "veridical illusion" in the sense that the content is satisfied [veridical] but by something other than what one is seeing [illusion].)

However, existentialism has the option of a causal condition. Chris Hill (2019) suggests an account along the following lines (p. 2):

A subject S is perceptually aware of an object O just in case (i) S's experience E represents that there is a (single) object with such and such perceptible qualities in such and such a location, (ii) O is causally responsible for E, and (iii) O comes closer than any of the other causes of E to satisfying its representational content.

Such an account could dictate that in Grice's example, I am seeing the pillar on the side and also that the perception is illusory because I am mislocating it. Of course, causal accounts have a notorious sort of problem: Without any specification of the type of causal connection required, they are vulnerable to counterexamples that involve nonstandard causal chains.

How can an existential view account for "phenomenological particularity" in perception—that it seems to the subject, perceptually, that there is a particular present (Schellenberg, 2018)? As Hill notes, there are a number of ways of interpreting the phrase. If it just amounts to saying that in perception one is often aware of a particular object, then the existential account, offering as it does an analysis of that awareness relation, does account for the impression of particularity. Hill challenges the particularist: "But a theorist who claims that particularized phenomenology is different than existential phenomenology should specify a differentiating feature, or at least, provide a set of instructions for introspectively discriminating one" (p. 14). However, the particularist can say that they do not allege that there is a difference between the phenomenology of a perception of *this particular object* and a perception of *an object* with the same properties—but rather that there is no such thing as the phenomenology of a perception of *an object*.

Michael Tye has a more elaborate version of Grice's example (2019). Suppose you are seeing a pair of cubes, a red cube on the right and a green cube on the left. Call them "RedRight" and "GreenLeft." You are wearing color inverting and spatial inverting goggles, so RedRight looks to be on the left and also green, and GreenLeft looks to be on the right and also red. If your perceptual content is existential, then the existential content might be "There is a red cube on the right and a green cube on the left." But if that is the content, the experience is veridical, which is the wrong result, since vision misrepresents the stimuli but in a way that preserves existential content. A causal existential account may be able to handle this sort of case. The cubes that one sees are causally responsible for the percepts of those particular cubes, and nothing else that is a cause remotely satisfies the perceptual content.

Some of the examples that I gave are immune from Gricean objections even independently of the existential proposal. There is no possibility of seeming to see one ganzfeld while seeing another ganzfeld or seeming to see one blackness filling the whole visual field while seeing another. The ganzfeld and blackness experiences do not involve objects that can be mislocated. (For a related complication, see the discussion four paragraphs below about veridical hallucination.) Flickering may be different if flickering in the entire periphery of the visual field has the phenomenology of attribution to an area of space rather than to the visual field itself as with the ganzfeld and the blackness examples. On the former understanding, one can imagine an experience of flickering in the entire periphery of the visual field in which what is flickering is a screen in a mirror. One apparently sees the flickering as being in front of one, but really it is off to the side, as in Grice's example.

Suppose one has an experience as of seeing upward motion on the left side of the periphery and downward motion on the right side of the periphery. Perhaps there could be an apparatus with mirrors creating an illusion in which the actual downward motion is on the right side and the actual upward motion is on the left side in a way that preserves existential content, as in Tye's example. So it looks as if the content of the experience of motion in the periphery might not be an existential content.

Mark Sainsbury has suggested a somewhat different existential content that that can be applied to these cases if they are construed as cases of perception of particulars (2019). He thinks of it as a general theory of perceptual content that is mid-way between simpler existential content and singular content.

The key to his view is the thesis that the perceptual content of a perceptual experience is correct if and only if "there are perceived objects of which it is nonaccidentally true." Because of the "there are" this is a kind of existential account. But what is it to perceive an object? Sainsbury argues, plausibly, that we cannot perceive something unless it plays a causal role in producing our perception. In Grice's pillar example, the perceiver does not perceive the occluded pillar because it does not play a causal role in producing the perception. In addition, the perceptual property representations (such and such a location, shape, size, color, texture, etc.) apply to the occluded pillar, but only accidentally in virtue of the coincidental fact that the same shape, size, color, texture, etc. apply to the pillar one perceives in the mirror and the attributed location is the apparent location of the reflected pillar. So the "nonaccidental" condition rules out the occluded pillar as the one to which the perceptual property representations nonillusorily apply. And the causal condition rules out the occluded pillar as the object of perception. The only candidate then that satisfies both conditions is the pillar on the side.

Further, since the pillar one is seeing is mislocated, the locational part of the perceptual attribution is not true of it, so it is a case of illusion. This is the right result, so Sainsbury's version of the existential content survives Grice's argument. (I won't go through the details of Tye's case since the idea is the same.) And the same reasoning applies to the perception of motion in the periphery if one construes each episode of motion as an event that falls under the category of "object" in Sainsbury's sense. And the same reasoning applies to the perception of flicker in the periphery of the visual field if one similarly construes the flickering as an object.

Sainsbury's account applies best to object-perception, but a variant of it has some advantages with regard to the other cases I mentioned such as the ganzfeld perception and perception of motion. I mentioned the "veridical illusion" issue, but another standard objection to existential contents is the possibility of "veridical hallucination." Suppose, for example, that a subject is wearing the ping pong balls in illumination conditions that would normally result in the ganzfeld experience but that the signals from the eyes are blocked before they get to the brain. At the same time the subject is having electrical stimulation of the visual cortex that reproduces the experience the subject would be having if a real ganzfeld perception were underway. A natural thing to say is that the subject is having a ganzfeld hallucination. But if the content of the experience is existential, then it follows that the subject is having a veridical perception of fog-like light, contrary to what many would want to say about this case. However, Sainsbury's account can preclude the conclusion of veridical perception, since neither the causal nor the nonaccidental application condition are satisfied.

In discussing this point in my philosophy of perception class, Bar Luzon noted that if a situation were set up so that there were *systematic* veridical hallucinations, the "nonaccidental" condition would no longer apply. (For example, an evil demon arranges it so that everything one sees is a "veridical hallucination.") Although the accuracy of the existential contents in such a case is not accidental, it lacks the "right kind" of systematicity. If "the right kind" cannot be spelled out, the causal condition might dictate that all perceptions are of evil demon states. Perhaps for this case, Hill's partially descriptive form of existentialism will work better. I should also add that as these odd scenarios move into the domain of the bizarre, it becomes harder to justify putting much weight on intuitions about them.

It is often supposed in debates about the alleged singular content of perception that the phenomenology of seeing a specific object exhibits "specific phenomenological particularity" (French & Gomes, 2019) in the sense that it gives us an impression of uniqueness (Gottlieb & Rezaei, under review). Hill tries to explain away this impression of uniqueness from an existentialist point of view by appealing to the fact that object perception can be very fine-grained in its representation of shape, size, color, and other properties (Hill, 2019).

I don't favor either side in this dispute. I think existential content is plausible for some perceptions, notably those that don't involve figure-ground segregation, and singular content has at least some plausibility for object perception.

In sum, I have given some examples of perception that does not involve figure-ground segregation that support existential content as at least equally good as singular content for some cases and explained how a more sophisticated existential content thesis can avoid a standard kind of counterexample even to object-perception. To be clear, my overall view is not that there is strong support for existential construals of perception but that there is no fact of the matter as between the rival views.

In response to my points about nonsingular content, I often hear the following objection: "You concede that singular content is plausible for object perception; but given that we should have a uniform account of all perception, we should favor singular content for ganzfeld and motion perception as well." One problem with this reasoning is that the sensory modalities other than vision are less plausibly singular than vision. For example, I can experience roughness with tactile perception. An enveloping tone that pervades the local environment is an audio version of a ganzfeld. Of course, it is always open to the objector to claim that these perceptions are singular perceptions of tropes or instances, e.g., instances of roughness rather than some roughness. Still, the pressure to adopt a uniform account could lead to a uniform existential account once the full array of senses are taken into account. The point is even more plausible if one regards smell and taste as perceptual senses (but see Burge, 2010b, p. 415.)

This section has mainly been devoted to my disagreement with Burge and with Schellenberg about whether perception constitutively singles out particulars. I want to end the section though with the aspect of my view that is compatible with Burge's—the two distinct kinds of seeing-as: (1) nonconceptual seeing-as, in which a property is attributed by vision, and (2) conceptual seeing-as, in which a concept is applied. The conceptual seeing-as is not perception but rather perceptual judgment. It is often what is meant in talk of seeing-as. The border between them is the joint in nature between perception and cognition.

Attribution and discrimination

This section is about attribution in perception and its relation to perceptual discrimination. Perceptual attribution is perceptually ascribing a property; perceptual discrimination is perceptually distinguishing between two properties or particulars.

The issues of this section concern whether perception constitutively involves discrimination, or, alternatively, attribution, and whether attribution requires discrimination or whether discrimination requires attribution. It might be useful to start with a very simple pair of examples of artificial devices that do analogs of one without the other.

A simple attributor could be a device whose sole sense organ is a light-sensitive photocell. If a photon hits the light-sensitive element it fires. And we can imagine that downstream mechanisms use the firing as an indication of light. One could regard this mechanism as attributing without discriminating. It could be said that the detector attributes but does not categorize and so makes a poor comparison to perceptual attribution. Instead of a photocell, we could consider a telephone keypad. There are 12 buttons, each of which emits a distinct tone. A defender of discrimination as basic could claim that pressing one of the buttons discriminates between that button and others—or no buttons. And the defender of discrimination could say that the photocell detector discriminates between something and nothing. But then the claim that discrimination is basic would seem more of a postulation than a claim about what is substantively fundamental to perception.

A simple discriminator could be an exclusive-or gate that fires when its two inputs are different and does not fire when its inputs are the same. A see-saw (teeter-totter) would be an example if we take one of the sides moving into the air as firing.

A real-world illustration of the difference are two common methods of evaluating a subject's color constancy abilities. One method is attributional: show subjects color samples under different illuminations and ask the subject to name the colors. (Of course, this involves cognition as well as perception.) Another method, favoring discrimination, involves color matching: Subjects are shown a color sample under one illumination and asked to choose among samples under a different illumination which one matches the first sample in color.

The signal detection theory framework treats perception as a choice between alternatives. Detection is treated as a comparison between the signal distribution and the noise distribution and so a form of discrimination.

But the Bayesian framework treats attribution and discrimination as distinct processes, neither of which is more fundamental. From a Bayesian perspective, attribution is a matter of posterior probability of a range of hypotheses about the environment, given sensory evidence. Discrimination can be thought of in terms of a comparison of likelihoods, the extent to which one environmental hypothesis predicts sensory evidence differently than another hypothesis (Jazayeri & Movshon, 2006). The posterior probability is proportional to the product of the likelihood and the prior probability. So on that analysis, attribution requires taking prior probabilities of the environmental hypotheses into account. The idea behind that analysis is that the visual system should be biased against attributing a very rarely instantiated property. But priors do not figure in a comparison of likelihoods since the rarity of instantiation of one or another property should not be relevant to detecting a difference between the properties. A comparison of likelihoods need not play a role in attribution, and priors need not play a role in discrimination. The upshot is that on the Bayesian approach, attribution and discrimination are computationally different, with neither required for the other.

(See the discussion of Bayesian approaches in Chapter 4 for an explanation of prior and posterior probabilities.)

I would summarize the preceding discussion by saying that a number of considerations suggest that there is no strong reason to favor either attribution or discrimination as more basic than the other.

Burge holds that perception is constitutively attributional, but Schellenberg disagrees (2018, p. 69). (My view is closer to Burge's than Schellenberg's and will be explained below.) Schellenberg objects to this kind of view on the ground that it overintellectualizes perception.

> The thesis that experiences have attributional structure over-intellectualizes perception in that it posits that perception necessarily involves seeing something as something. The thesis that perception necessarily involves seeing something as something posits that perception has a sentential or proto-sentential form. But there are many cases of perception that do not have any such sentential or proto-sentential form. If I see a green leaf, I am not necessarily aware of the leaf as green. I may just be aware of green at a particular location.

As I will be arguing, nonconceptual seeing-as does not require sentential or proto-sentential form—indeed it requires iconic format. Conceptual seeing-as may involve sentential format, but conceptual seeing-as is not perception.

As indicated in the last section, there is a moderately good case that one can perceive motion without perceiving any moving object. When Schellenberg speaks of being "aware of green at a particular location," the object of awareness is supposed to be an instance of or instantiation of green. As mentioned in the last section, if perception of instances is introduced solely to save the view that perception is constitutively of particulars, one does wonder why the view should be seen as substantive rather than a stipulation. And if perception of instances is a consequence of a general view of the metaphysics of causation—that causation is a matter of property instances causing other property instances—one wonders why a view that is supposedly based on the science of perception should instead be based on the metaphysics of causation.

All of the markers of perception discussed in Chapter 2 involve perceptual attribution. The mechanisms of the repulsive effects of adaptation described earlier (in Chapter 2) all depend on attribution. In adaptation to red, an extended period of *attribution* of red or repeated attributions of red shifts the balance of the red/green channel toward green. An extended period of *attribution* of high numerosities raises the threshold for *attribution* of high numerosities, biasing perception toward low numerosities. An extended period of *attribution* of clockwise tilt raises the threshold for *attribution* of clockwise tilt, biasing perception toward the counterclockwise. These mechanisms operate all over the animal kingdom including in insects. They also operate in unconscious perception.

In rivalry, there is a conflict between one *attribution* and another *attribution*. In pop-out, some *attributions* take precedence over other *attributions*. (For example, nonconjunctive *attributions* take precedence over conjunctive *attributions*.) In interpolation, *attributions* involve "filling in." The winner-takes-all nature of perception involves conflict between competing *attributions*. In sum, many of the most fundamental perceptual phenomena involve attribution.

How do we know that it is extended or repeated attributions that lead to the repulsive effect—rather than extended or repeated discriminations? One answer is that attribution leads to the repulsive effect even when there is no discrimination. Perception of redness causes a repulsive effect even when there are no other colors. Most impressively, adaptation occurs in a ganzfeld perception in which one sees a homogenous field of light as surfaceless fog-like light. (See footnote 5, earlier in this chapter, on what a ganzfeld perception is.)

Of course, it is always open to an objector to insist that in a ganzfeld perception there is discrimination between something and nothing, between one color and another or between the portion of surfaceless fog on the left and the portion of surfaceless fog on the right or between the surfaceless fog now and the surfaceless fog a second ago. (See Schellenberg, 2018, p. 27, for this line of thought.) But without some actual evidence for mechanisms of discrimination in the ganzfeld perception, this sounds more like postulation than like a substantive thesis.

One of the functions of attribution is generalization. To use a standard example, if a bird eats a toxic butterfly it needs to abstract the category of the butterfly so as not to eat that kind again. An overly narrow category can lead to further toxicity, whereas an overly wide category can lead to hunger. Roger Shepard proposed a "universal law" of perceptual generalization in terms of categories as volumes in a psychological similarity space, a law that has more recently been explained in terms of efficiency of coding (Block, 1997a; Shepard, 1987; Sims, 2018). These categorical representations are part of the mechanism of attribution.

As I mentioned, Schellenberg denies that perception is constitutively attributional and claims that perception can involve discrimination without attribution (2018, Section 3.2.1). She advocates "capacitism" (2018, p. 67), a view that holds that attribution is grounded in discrimination.

> Denying the attribution thesis is compatible with allowing that there are cases that cannot be analyzed without positing that the perceiving subject is attributing properties. After all, in denying the attribution thesis I am denying only that perception is constitutively a matter of attributing properties to her

environment. According to capacitism, any attribution of properties will be grounded in discrimination.

Her capacitism bases perception in perceptual capacities. "What are perceptual capacities? A perceptual capacity is a mental capacity that functions to differentiate, single out, and *in some cases* classify particulars of a specific type, such as instances of red" (2017, p. 4, italics added). I agree that perception paradigmatically involves such capacities, but that does not show that they are necessary or constitutive of perception or that attribution is grounded in discrimination.[6]

Zenon Pylyshyn has long denied that attribution is required for perception. He bases this claim on multiple object tracking (MOT), in which many people can visually track roughly four objects that change color and shape and other visible properties without disrupting tracking. (See the discussion of MOT in Chapter 4.) Pylyshyn says (2007b, p. 40) "It appears that nothing is stored in the object-files under typical MOT conditions, which suggests that targets are not being picked out under a description—they are not picked out as things that have certain properties or satisfy certain predicates." Pylyshyn's "visual indexes" or FINSTs (for "fingers of instantiation") are not supposed to require any property representations. Pylyshyn's picture gains plausibility from experiments that combine MOT with "change blindness." For example, Bahrami and colleagues showed that if subject's attention is distracted (by "mud splashes"), subjects miss changes of color and shape in the objects that they are tracking (Bahrami, 2003).

However, the figure/ground structure of object perception requires a difference between what is attributed to the figure and to the ground. Perception of the figure and the ground requires not only distinguishing figure from ground but also perceiving the figure as having a particular shape—and that requires

---

[6] Schellenberg's analysis of perceptual consciousness in terms of capacities doesn't seem to allow for unconscious perception, since many if not all of those capacities are exercised in unconscious perception. Her approach to this issue appears to be to claim that there is no unconscious perception in the sense of perception without phenomenal consciousness, interpreting cases of perception without phenomenal consciousness as really being a matter of phenomenal perception without access (or access consciousness) She says, "Indeed, I argue that unconscious perception is a matter of being in a mental state with phenomenal character without having access to that phenomenal character" (2018, p. p. 186). (I introduced the notion of access consciousness in Block, 1990. See also Block, 1994 and Stoljar, 2019.)

Schellenberg's view has difficulties with regard to cases of conscious perception in which there are unconscious aspects. For example, a famous visual form agnosic DF has conscious percepts in which she sees color and texture with little or no consciousness of form. She can see an object in front of her that has a slot in it but has little or no conscious perception of the angle of the slot. (I fill in the details in my contribution to Peters et al., 2017.) What DF sees consciously is color and texture. What she sees mainly unconsciously is a slot at a particular angle and that unconscious perception allows her to post the card into the slot with virtually the same accuracy as a normal person. If Schellenberg says that perception of the slot and its angle is entirely conscious, she has to explain why DF is only slightly above chance in saying what the angle of the slot is and cannot guess much above chance as between horizontal and vertical; and she cannot even mime the angle with a card.

attribution. Attribution of shapes occurs "automatically and obligatorily" (Baker & Kellman, 2018, p. 1295), even when there is no task that requires such attribution. Recent work has shown that shape attribution is quite abstract, allowing perceivers to see shapes as the same even when one is composed of dots and others of curves. And subjects see shapes as identical even when the orientations and sizes differ.

Although the figure/ground structure of object perception requires perception of the shape of the figure, conscious perception of the ground treats it as shapeless (Peterson & Cacciamani, 2013), as noted in Chapter 2. As Peterson and Cacciamani also show, the shape of the ground is at least sometimes represented, but unconsciously. Further, segmenting the perceptual representation requires differences of attribution to different segments. (Cf. Burge 2009, p. 282; 2010a, pp. 455–456.) In sum, Pylyshyn's claims about no attribution in object perception go against a great deal of evidence to the contrary. Indeed there is a good case that attribution is fundamental to perception of objects.

Here is an argument that attribution is more fundamental than discrimination. If two items are different, they have to be different in some specific property. Discrimination is always discrimination with respect to some specific property and it is hard to see how there can be discrimination with respect to a given property without that property being attributed.

But wait, a see-saw does not attribute weight. And, one can imagine a special purpose color-difference detecting module that fires when it sees a color difference, without attributing the property of being colored. However, it cannot be that every discrimination is accomplished by such a modular mechanism since there are far too many possible and actual discriminations. And it is hard to envision a more general mechanism for discrimination that does not depend on attributions.

To see this point, consider the process of habituation described briefly in Chapter 2 and to be discussed in detail in Chapter 6. In habituation, someone looking at a screen in which the same property is instantiated again and again becomes bored and looks elsewhere. When looking time at the screen falls by a fixed amount, e.g. half, the subject is said to be habituated to the property, and when a different property instantiated on the screen leads looking time to go back up again, the subject is said to be dishabituated. Of course habituation and dishabituation depend on discrimination since perceived sameness leads to habituation and perceived difference leads to dishabituation.

Here is the key point: the amount of habituation and dishabituation can be based on discrimination of different properties. Here is a real world illustration. Leslie and Keeble (Leslie & Keeble, 1987) habituated six month olds to images of a disk seemingly causing another disk to move. (As will be explained in Chapter 12, some such "billiard ball" sequences look causal whereas other very similar sequences in which there is a slight delay or a small gap between the disks look non-causal.). The babies dishabituated to a similar non-causal sequence in the opposite direction. Leslie and Keeble were able to show that the difference underlying the dishabituation was a combination of two differences, one in respect of the difference in direction and the other in the perception of causality. It is hard to see how to explain this without adverting to perceptual attribution of both direction and causality.

To be clear: I am not saying that in order to discriminate red from green one has to visually represent red or visually represent green. That is, I am not saying that discrimination is a matter of attributing properties to two items and comparing them. The point rather is that to discriminate red from green one must in the general case, visually attribute color.

As noted earlier, perceptual discrimination and perceptual attribution are based in at least somewhat distinct neural mechanisms. (See the discussion in Block, 2015a, Section 10; Goodman, 2013.) Different perceptual systems can prioritize attribution and discrimination in different ways. For example, the mantis shrimp has 12 kinds of photoreceptors as compared with our 3 kinds. But they are not part of an opponent process system. Rather they function as a simple fast recognition system, resulting in excellent attribution combined with poor discrimination (Thoen, How, Chiou, & Marshall, 2014).

I know of one experiment that provides evidence that at least for one kind of perception, discrimination may be required for attribution. Picon, et al. compared discrimination and attribution of numerosity to displays of dots (Picon et al., 2019). Picon et al. used stimuli that combined dot displays with standard illusions. One illusion they used is the plug/hat illusion, illustrated in Figure 3.4. The line and circumference of the circle are the same length, but the line looks longer. Picon et al. contrasted discrimination judgments in which subjects judged whether there were more dots on the left or the right with estimation judgments in which subject estimated the number of dots (e.g., 15 dots). The dots were arranged either in straight lines or in curves. They found that in the discrimination task, the illusion interfered with the judgments. If given a straight

Figure 3.4 A version of the plug/hat illusion. The straight line is the same length as the circumference of the circle but seems longer. Thanks to Donald Simanek for this picture.

line and a curved line with an equal number of dots, subjects tended to judge the dots in the line as more numerous. However, the illusion did not affect estimation judgments. Some other illusions, however, affected both discrimination and estimation. They do not mention, however, any cases in which illusions affect estimation without affecting discrimination. A double dissociation would have shown complete independence. I would not jump to conclusions about attribution being more basic than discrimination. Ventral system illusions that are not dorsal system illusions are common but the reverse is hard to find—even though neither system is more basic.

I will move now to a discussion of whether there can be attribution without discrimination or discrimination without attribution.

It is tempting to think that in discriminating between property X and property Y, one must perceptually attribute a relational property that entails a difference between X and Y. It is also tempting to think that the attribution of this relational property depends on comparing different attributions to each of X and Y. Will Davies (2020) calls this dependence of relational attribution on monadic attribution the monadic determination thesis. (Cf. also Morrison, 2015; Papineau, 2015.)

One can certainly imagine a very special purpose difference detector that discriminates X from Y without attributing either X or Y. For example, if there are two adjacent flat surfaces, such a detector could detect a difference in height by detecting a vertical segment or edge. Of course, this detector would discriminate between X and Y by attributing something else: a vertical segment or edge. So it does not suggest discrimination without attribution. Davies (2020) describes evidence for the representation of different contrast between two regions without attribution of color to either region, but even if he is right, the perception he describes involves attribution—namely of contrast.

I mentioned one moderately convincing case of perceptual attribution without discrimination, the ganzfeld perception. I have been unable to find any convincing cases of perceptual discrimination without perceptual attribution of different properties to the items discriminated or perceptual attribution of a relational property. (The example at the beginning of this section of the discrimination involved in one form of color constancy testing involved the attribution of a relational property.) I will mention some failed cases.

One case that I have used to illustrate discrimination without attribution, I now think wrongly (2007b, p. 450), is of "beats," the alternating sounds caused by interference between the vibrations of instrument strings that vibrate at slightly different frequencies. (Note, this is not the sense of "beat" in which there is a certain number of beats to a measure.) When strings have only one vibration frequency, the frequency of beats is the difference between the frequencies of the two strings. One can have identical perceptions of two pitches, yet discriminate them via beats. This is an unconvincing example of perceptual discrimination because hearing beats is not the same as simply perceptually discriminating between 2 sounds. The whole process is cognitive and conceptual in that one has to know that beats indicate a difference in pitch.

Another somewhat different kind of failed example is being able to discriminate between two slightly different color shades via border effects such as Mach Bands. Two color chips can look exactly the same when separated by a few millimeters but then when brought together so that they are touching, color border effects allow for discrimination. This example is unconvincing because the border effect introduces inhomogeneous apparent color of the chips.

Jeremy Goodman uses the example of two trees that can be discriminated from one another by slight differences in how far they stick up above the tree canopy even if, in viewing each tree individually, one's visual attribution of height to each would be the same (Goodman, 2013). I can see two ways of understanding this example, neither of which yields a successful example of discrimination without attribution. On one analysis, one sees the height of each of the trees and how far they stick up above the canopy, the latter being part of what grounds the former. In that case there is both attribution and discrimination, so it is not a case of discrimination without attribution. The alternative picture is that one sees something sticking up above the canopy, say twigs, but one does not see either of the trees. Perhaps one infers that the trees are of different heights. On this picture, there is attribution to whatever is sticking up (the twigs) but no perceptual discrimination between trees: Any discrimination would have to be inferred. Neither is discrimination without attribution.

Geoff Lee suggested a case in commenting on a version of this chapter: With very short temporal separation of sounds, people can sometimes tell that there are two sounds rather than one but subjects don't know which one came first (Hirsh, 1959). This is temporal discrimination without attribution of a specific temporal location to each of the discriminated sounds. In this case though, it may be that discrimination involves the attribution of a relational property involving a relation between the items that are discriminated—namely temporal difference.

The difficulty of finding even one convincing case of discrimination without attribution is notable.

Causally speaking, attribution and discrimination affect one another. Practice in attribution even without reward can aid discrimination. For example, in the classic "preexposure" or "predifferentiation" effect, exposure to a meaningless shape facilitates later discrimination of those shapes from others (Goldstone, 1994). And there is also evidence that perceptual categorization facilitates discrimination (Harnad, 1987a).

Training in discrimination can also improve attribution. Rats that were trained on a black/white discrimination were better able to use a black or white color as in an attributional task in which a color was paired with a directional response and the rat had to identify the color in order make the correct response (Lawrence, 1950). These causal facts suggest a linkage between attribution and discrimination. However, a recent study of absolute pitch showed that the ability to discriminate tones is a poor predictor of the ability to identify them (Reis, Heald, Veillette, Van Hedger, & Nusbaum, 2021).

There are differing approaches to the subjective intensity of perceptual magnitudes, one associated with Weber, based in discrimination, "just noticeable differences," the other based in part in various kinds of attribution. S. S. Stevens's power law is the most famous of the partially attribution-based approaches.

As explained in Chapter 2, Weber's Law says that the discriminability of two stimuli is a linear function of the ratio of the intensities of the two stimuli. Weber's Law is about discrimination, but a related law, the Weber-Fechner Law is about attribution. The Weber-Fechner Law says that the perceived intensity of a stimulus is a logarithmic function of its physical intensity.

Steven's psychophysical method was in part attribution-based because rather than asking subjects to discriminate magnitudes, he asked them to assign a numerical ratings to them. For example, a subject might rate the brightness of a light as a 7. Subjects were shown stimuli that varied in intensity and asked to assign numbers to them. This is an attribution. Of course assigning numbers to other stimuli inevitably involved comparison to previously rated stimuli. These assignments could be considered relational attributions but also involve discrimination. Many have been skeptical about this procedure because it seems that assigning a numerical magnitude would be completely arbitrary. But as Stevens showed, reliable results allowed for the construction of a ratio scale of subjective magnitudes. Although Stevens's approach is based largely on attribution, his ideology was firmly in the discrimination-is-basic camp. Schellenberg quotes his famous 1939 statement at the start of Chapter 1 of her book (p. 13): "When we attempt to reduce complex operations to simpler and simpler ones, we find in the end that discrimination or differential response is the fundamental operation. Discrimination is prerequisite even to the operation of denoting or 'pointing to.'" (Stevens, 1939). But despite this ideology, Stevens's approach is more in the attribution camp than the Weber method. The relative merits of Weber, Fechner, and Stevens are much debated (Beck, 2019). I think a conservative conclusion would be that discrimination and attribution both contribute to subjective magnitudes, again suggesting close linkages between attribution and discrimination.

To sum up this section, attribution and discrimination are both paradigmatically involved in perception and are at least somewhat distinct abilities with at least somewhat distinct neural bases. Some evidence points to attribution as more basic and some to discrimination as more basic. It may be that there are different answers to the basicness question for different types of perception.

Ordinary vs. technical language

Is the sense of "see" used here (and the distinction between two kinds of seeing-as) merely technical and so not relevant to what we ordinarily mean? Tim Williamson asked me in a presentation of this material (in my 2013 John Locke Lectures) whether in this sense of "see" one can see New College. It is useful to distinguish primary from secondary seeing. We can take primary seeing to be the application of a nonconceptual visual representation to a "visual object," i.e., an object that is itself picked out by a nonconceptual perceptual demonstrative of the sort described earlier. Secondary seeing involves hybrids of primary visual representations and concepts applied to objects of primary seeing and complexes of them in states that put together perception with perceptual judgment. Such hybrids can represent things that are not visual objects (i.e., not the referents of the demonstrative aspects of perceptions) on the basis of visual objects that compose them. Thus, the notion of seeing in which we see New College is secondary seeing and it can be reconstructed in terms of the sciences of perception and cognition (Block, 2014c).

I have been defending the view that there are two very different mental relations to the world that have been described as seeing-as, visual perception of something as having a certain property and perceptual judgment that something has a certain property. The difference in these attributions has been investigated in some recent cases of social concern involving bias, a topic that is discussed in the next section. The next section illustrates one way of telling the difference between perception and perceptual judgment.

Bias: Perception vs. perceptual judgment

Some readers may be skeptical about whether there really are two kinds of seeing-as. Indeed, some readers may be skeptical about whether there is really any difference between perception and minimal immediate direct perceptual judgment. In this section, I will mention an issue of whether a certain phenomenon that has been much in the news involves perception or, alternately, perceptual judgment, and I will describe some evidence that the effect hinges on perceptual judgment rather than perception. The evidence I will present is not strong, and there are some indications in the opposite direction, but the point of what I will be talking about is really (1) that there is a conceptual difference between perception and perceptual judgment and between the two kinds of seeing-as and (2) that these differences can be empirically investigated. The evidence I will mention is particularly useful because it is so simple and straightforward.

There has been a steady stream of cases in which police have killed unarmed Black people while claiming that they saw the victims as having weapons. Is one of the two kinds of seeing-as involved in this case, and if so, which one? There have been many studies that have suggested to some that racial stereotypes have influenced the perceptions of the police officers (Correll, Park, Judd, & Wittenbrink, 2002; Correll, Urland, & Ito, 2006; Eberhardt, Goff, Purdie, & Davies, 2004; Payne, 2001). Paradigms for studying this issue vary in their degree of "realism," that is, similarity to the actual circumstances in which biased behavior occurs. I will be talking about a highly "unrealistic" paradigm whose compensating advantage is better isolation of the causal factors in a laboratory setting. The opposite approach, trying for a high degree of realism using police personnel as subjects with realistic videos as stimuli, has been investigated by Lois James at Washington State University (James & Vila, 2016).

Susanna Siegel has argued that if such stereotypes affect perceptual experience, the epistemic status of the perception is downgraded. Stereotypes may engender irrationality in perception (Siegel, 2017). I won't discuss the epistemic issue, but rather the question of how one could find out whether the effect of stereotypes is an effect on perception rather than perceptual judgment. This is a book about the difference between perception and cognition, not about bias, so the discussion of this issue will be in the service of exploring that distinction. In the discussion to come, the meaning of "bias" is an effect of racial stereotypes on either perception or perceptual judgment.

I will discuss Keith Payne's paradigm in which subjects see a Black or White face, then, very briefly, a weapon or a tool and then a noise mask whose purpose is to prevent an ongoing visual icon of the weapon or tool. Then subjects are instructed to press one button if they saw a weapon and another if they saw a tool. See Figure 3.5.

The standard result in Payne's paradigm is that subjects make biased judgments in the sense of stereotype congruent judgments. They are more likely to mistakenly say they saw a tool if primed with a White face and they are more likely to mistakenly say they saw a weapon if primed with a Black face. But are these stereotype congruent responses due to biases in perception or perceptual judgment (or both)? Which kind(s) of seeing-as is (are) involved?

We get some clarity on this from a more articulated version of the paradigm (Stokes & Payne, 2010). They presented the stimuli very briefly so as to make them very hard to see. The point of making the stimuli hard to see is that the best cases for cognitive penetration of perception are widely thought to be cases of ambiguous or ambiguously presented stimuli. It is widely thought that when the

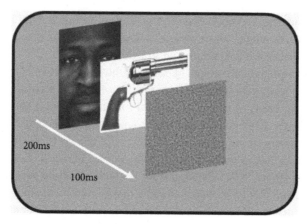

Figure 3.5 Basic shooter paradigm. First subjects see a Black or White face, then a weapon or a tool and then a noise mask. The purpose of the noise mask is to prevent on ongoing memory image of the weapon or tool. I am grateful to Keith Payne for this figure.

bottom-up signal is strong, cognitive factors have a smaller chance of affecting perception. Thus, it is a good policy in trying to encourage cognitive penetration to use ambiguous or ambiguously presented stimuli.

Subjects gave a speeded response that shows the standard stereotype congruent responses as depicted on the left side of Figure 3.6. Subjects mistakenly classify tools as guns when preceded by a Black face and to a smaller degree they mistakenly classify a gun as a tool when preceded by a White face. However, in this study, subjects were allowed to correct their response with no time limit. And as you can see from the right side of Figure 3.6, the error rate greatly decreases and stereotype congruent responses disappear. As Payne and his colleagues note, in a standard illusion, the illusory perception persists despite our knowledge that it is an illusion. The fact that the responses change so radically suggests that this is a result of an effect on judgment rather than real perceptual seeing-as.

This conclusion was bolstered by another version of the experiment in which subjects were given plenty of time but the stimuli were presented so briefly that they were on the threshold of conscious perception. They set presentation times separately for different subjects so as to achieve 65% correct scores on a pretest. The idea was to make sure there were plenty of errors in order to see what kind of errors there were. In an additional task, subjects were asked to indicate whether they were confident and saw details such as the barrel of a gun or handles of pliers. This was the "see" response in Figure 3.7. They were to respond "know" if they were confident but did not see such perceptual details. And "guess" was the

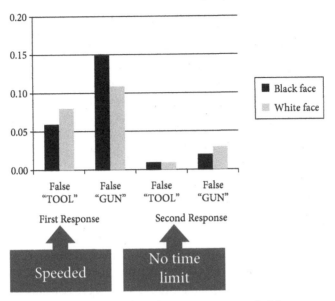

Figure 3.6 Results of one of Payne's studies comparing speeded first responses with an opportunity to correct those responses with no time limit. I am grateful to Keith Payne for this figure. (See Stokes & Payne, 2010.)

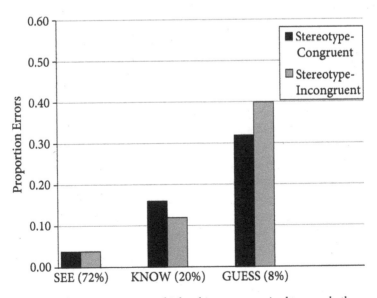

Figure 3.7 Another experiment in which subjects are required to say whether their response was based on perceptual details (see), knowledge without perceptual details (know), or guessing (guess). I am grateful to Keith Payne for this figure. (See Stokes & Payne, 2010.)

alternative when they were not confident. As you can see from Figure 3.7, biased (in the sense of stereotype congruent) responses tended to be in the "know" category. That is when subjects said they could see the perceptual details, they tended not to give stereotype congruent responses. When they gave confident stereotype congruent responses—a mistaken "gun" after a Black face or a mistaken "tool" after a White face—they tended to say they did not see details. And interestingly, guesses went in the opposite antistereotype congruent direction. This result suggests that the stereotype congruent responses were based on the second kind of seeing-as, perceptual judgment, rather than the first kind of seeing-as, perception itself.

But how does a conceptual bias interact with a nonconceptual perception to affect perceptual judgment? Let us ask a prior question: How does a nonconceptual perception become conceptualized so as to form a perceptual judgment? In terms of the diagram at the outset of this chapter, how does perceptual seeing-as lead to conceptual seeing-as? I think the most promising theory of how this happens is the global workspace theory discussed in Chapter 1 and to be discussed further in Chapters 4 and 13. The global workspace theory is offered by its proponents as a theory of consciousness, but as I mentioned, I think it serves better as a theory of conceptualization. What happens to a percept in conceptualization according to this account is that it becomes linked via "ignition" in a reverberating circuit connecting the perceptual representation with cognitive representations in frontal cortex. (See Jeannerod & Jacob, 2015.)

If this is right, it may explain the observation (Raftopoulos, 2010) that nonconceptual representations cannot be stored in working memory, for if they could, we would be able to recognize fine grained shades (in conditions that preclude iconic memory and fragile visual short term memory). It has often been noted that people have a hard time doing this, though I don't know that there has been any experimental test of this point.

Three cautions about this section:

1. Does it matter for social purposes whether the effect is on one kind of seeing-as or the other? It might be relevant to how the effects of stereotype congruent responses can be meliorated (Siegel, 2017).
2. Other articles have made something of a case—though not a strong case in my view—for an effect of bias on perception (Amodio, 2014; Correll, Wittenbrink, Crawford, & Sadler, 2015; Eberhardt et al., 2004). (But see Francis, 2015.)
3. Even if there are effects of stereotype congruency on perception, their mechanisms may be limited to those that are either perceptual or cognitive, as I will argue in Chapter 9 with regard to other better understood effects of cognition on perception. Further, many of the more dramatic effects that

have been alleged are better seen as effects on perceptual judgment rather than perception.

What higher order properties are represented perceptually must be decided on a case-by-case basis. Evidence suggests that faceness, gender, age, attractiveness, race, and emotional expressions are perceptually represented. Are artifact kinds perceptually represented? I mentioned evidence from the work of Talia Konkle that they are. Indeed, the evidence to be mentioned in Chapter 8 indicates that visual cortex contains artifact representations that are organized by prototypical size of the artifact (Konkle & Oliva, 2012).

Evaluative perception

Humans are evaluating creatures. But is evaluation part of perception itself? If it is, then the distinction between cognition and high-level perception may be in trouble. Which side of the border can we place evaluative perception on? Evaluation seems conceptual, so how can it be part of perception?

We have many experiences that may seem to show there is evaluative perception. For example, we experience food smelling and looking disgusting and a face looking scary. Given this intuitive basis, the view that there is evaluative perception has been popular among philosophers (Audi, 2018; Fulkerson, 2020; Jacobson, 2021; Noordhof, 2018; Stokes, 2018) and among scientists (Barrett & Bar, 2009; Lebrecht, Bar, Barrett, & Tarr, 2012).

However, these evaluative experiences may be cases of perception of non-evaluative properties combined with evaluative emotions and judgments. The overall "experience" comprising both the perception and the judgments may be describable as both perceptual and evaluative, but it does not follow that the perception is evaluative.

Frédérique de Vignemont notes that one model of the relation between perception and evaluation is binding, as when the visual representation of an edge is bound together with a tactile representation of the same edge (de Vignemont, 2021). But as de Vignemont notes, where there is binding, there can be misbinding, as in the McGurk effect (to be discussed in Chapter 6). But it is not clear that anyone has reported such affective misbinding. That would be when, for example, you perceive something as chocolate and also disgusting. Further, as we will see in the discussion of binding in Chapter 4, there are two kinds of binding, direct and indirect binding. There is evidence that the only direct binding is to location. Orientation and spatial location are bound together directly, but color and orientation are bound together only indirectly, via binding of each of them to location. If information about location is lost, so is information about which orientations go with which colors. But one wonders whether location is really crucial to affective responses to perception. Does one have to be aware of where the disgusting thing is in order to smell something disgusting?

Still, the analogy offered by de Vignemont between affective perception and multisensory perception is worth investigating. What needs to be shown though is that the affective part is genuinely perceptual.

Some philosophers have suggested a layered conception of content in which nonevaluative features of the environment constitute one layer and evaluative features constitute another layer (Audi, 2018). The danger in talk of layers of representation is that the evaluative layer will turn out to be cognitive or emotional rather than perceptual. Audi speaks of a "feeling of integration" between the layers, but a feeling of integration does not provide any reason to think that perception represents evaluative properties.

Other philosophers have favored a composite nature of evaluative perception. For example, Matthew Fulkerson (2020, p. 22) suggests that emotional perception has two elements. "One of these elements is sensory-discriminative, focused on tracking and providing awareness of objective sensible qualities. The other is affective-motivational, relating perceptual objects directly to the needs and present state of the subject." But why think that the affective-motivational element is actually a kind of perception or that perception represents evaluative properties?

Fulkerson supports this view by appealing to a wide range of experiments in which sensory-discriminative pathways are associated with affective-motivational pathways, but the evidence he provides is not evidence that the affective-motivational pathways are perceptual. He quotes Edmund Rolls on the basic architecture, noting that while Rolls's "focus is on somatosensory [touch] and thermal awareness, the points generalize" (Fulkerson, 2020, p. 24).

Here is what Rolls says:

A principle thus appears to be that processing related to the affective value and associated subjective emotional experience of somatosensory and thermal stimuli that are important for survival is performed in different brain areas to those where activations are related to sensory properties of the stimuli such as their intensity. An implication of the principle is that by having a system specialized for the affective or reward aspects of stimuli it is possible to modify goal oriented behaviour, and to do this independently of being able to know what the stimulus is (its intensity, physical characteristics, etc.). Thus even if a stimulus has lost its pleasantness because of for example a change of core body temperature, it is still possible to represent the stimulus, recognize it, and learn about where it is in the environment for future use. This is a fundamental aspect of brain design. (Rolls, 2010, p. 230)

What Rolls emphasizes here is the physiological and functional distinctness of the perceptual and evaluative systems. Nothing in this perspective about the basic architecture of the system underlying "emotional perception" suggests that the emotional part is itself perceptual.

Perception and evaluation are very tightly intertwined and in such entwining cases it may not be easy to say whether there are two systems or one. One very concrete way of understanding it is in line with the topic of this chapter: Do we perceive events or things as good or praiseworthy or as having other evaluative properties? That is, does perception attribute evaluative properties? If there is perceiving-as having evaluative properties, it should manifest itself in some of the phenomena described in Chapter 1 such as adaptation, pop-out, and rivalry.

There is a large literature in social psychology alleging that there is a phenomenon of "moral pop-out." Recall from Chapter 2 that pop-out is a visual phenomenon in which a visual feature immediately comes to the fore as distinct from their background. However, the term "pop-out" is not used in this sense in the literature on moral pop-out. To see what "moral pop-out" is supposed to be, it suffices to look at the experimental methodology (Gantman, Devraj-Kizuk, Mende-Siedlecki, Van Bavel, & Mathewson, 2020; Gantman & Van Bavel, 2014). Anna Gantman and colleagues presented subjects with a series of degraded words and letter strings presented in conditions in which subjects were correct on indicating that they were words as opposed to nonword letter strings only 75% of the time—50% would be at chance. Techniques for degrading included making the font small, presenting the words very briefly, changing the background color to be similar to the font color and masking (described in Chapter 8). The words could be moral words or nonmoral words, and the letter strings were scrambled versions of those moral and nonmoral words. Subjects were asked to press one button for a word and another button for a nonword. (This is known as a lexical decision task.) The result reported in the 2014 article and replicated in the 2020 article was that moral words were somewhat more likely than nonmoral words to be identified as words. The effect worked for degraded words but not for clearly presented words which is the opposite of what one would expect for a perceptual phenomenon. In normal visual pop-out, degrading the stimuli hinders the effect. Further, the words were presented one after the other instead of all at once—so the moral words did not "pop" out from the background. I conclude that this phenomenon is quite different from the kind of pop-out described in Chapter 2 that is a clear indicator of perception.

Gantman et al. (2020) also showed, using a temporally sensitive form of brain imaging (ERP for event related potential, based on EEG), that the differentiation of moral words from nonmoral words started, at the earliest, 300 ms after presentation, about 100 ms after differentiation of words from nonwords. The ERP signature was what is called the P3 or P3b, which is usually considered as showing broadcasting in the global workspace. Gantman et al. (2020, p. 243) construed this result as follows: "We tentatively interpret this finding as a threshold effect: the emergence of differential P3 activity for moral vs non-moral words suggests that moral words may receive and maintain a preferential gateway into conscious awareness. As such, it appears that the moral pop-out effect is likely not a perceptual pop-out, but perhaps a pop-in, to awareness." They are of course assuming that the global workspace account of consciousness is correct, claiming that while there is no pop-out during the initial perception, there is an ascension into consciousness during the global broadcasting cycle.

The global broadcasting theory was discussed in Chapter 1 and will be discussed further in Chapters 4 and 13. My claim that it is best seen as a theory of conceptualization rather than consciousness has recently been bolstered by a result showing that what the P3b indexes is not conscious perception but rather reported conscious perception (Cohen, Ortego, Kyroudis, & Pitts, 2020). A recent survey showed that in many studies in which a perception was not task-relevant, conscious perception occurred without the P3b and so without global broadcasting (Dembski, Koch, & Pitts, 2021). Sergent, et al. (2021) got similar results using a "no-report" paradigm. (See Chapter 7 on no-report paradigms.) Dembski et al. also survey a range of results that show that what does correlate with conscious perception in an EEG signal is the "perceptual awareness negativity" that occurs much earlier (120 ms to 200 ms after stimulus presentation) and that is based in the brain circuits that process the relevant modality, visual areas for sight and auditory areas for hearing. So I regard the Gantman et al. result taken at face value to indicate that the moral effect is not perceptual per se but is rather an effect of bringing concepts to bear on perception.

My conclusion had the qualifier of taking the result at face value. My reason for that qualifier is that Chaz Firestone and Brian Scholl hypothesized that the result was actually due to spreading activation in the semantic system, a phenomenon known as semantic priming (Firestone & Scholl, 2015). As Firestone and Scholl note, subjects are faster to identify "nurse" as a word in a lexical decision task if "nurse" was preceded by "doctor" than if it was preceded by "butter." Semantic priming is a well-known phenomenon whose mechanism is thought to be spreading activation in a memory network.[7] Activation of the "doctor" node

---

[7] Priming is an unconscious modification of subsequent processing by an earlier stimulus. When a subject sees a word during an experiment, the subject is more likely to later complete a word stem so as to match the previously seen word. For example, if the subject has seen the word "reason," the subject is more likely to complete the stem "rea" with "son" (rather than, e.g., "der") than baseline (i.e., when no word is presented before the stem). Priming can be a matter of associations. For example, presentation of the word "doctor" makes it easier for a subject to recognize the word "nurse" as a word, even if "doctor" is presented subliminally. But priming can also be semantic. In semantic priming, a word primes a semantically related word: e.g., "dog" makes "wolf" easier to recognize. A subliminally presented digit, "4," makes the processing of the word "four" more efficient. Priming

partially activates the "nurse" node, lowering the threshold for later identifying it as a word. Firestone and Scholl noted that in Gantman et al.'s list of moral and nonmoral words, the moral words were closely related semantically to one another. For example, the moral words included "justice," "law," "illegal," "crime," "convict," "guilty," and "jail," whereas the nonmoral words such as "exchange," "rule," "limited," "steel," "confuse," "tired," and "house" were not chosen because of any semantic relation to one another. Firestone and Scholl go on to note that the moral words could have primed one another. As they put it (p. 410),

> Thus, just as the word "doctor" primes semantically related words such as "nurse," words such as "crime" may have primed semantically related words such as "convict"—whereas words such as "steel" would not have primed unrelated words such as "confuse." In that case, "moral popout" would simply be another demonstration of semantic priming, with no implications for the relationship between perception and cognition.

And they went on to confirm their speculation by doing an experiment like that of Gantman et al. in which moral words were replaced by words that were related by a fashion theme, like "pajamas" and "stiletto." They got a "fashion pop-out" effect of about the same magnitude as Gantman et al.'s "moral pop-out" effect. And they reported similar results for transportation-related words.

Firestone and Scholl's article was followed by a number of other papers raising many issues that I won't discuss here (Firestone & Scholl, 2016c; Gantman & Van Bavel, 2015, 2016). Whether or not Firestone and Scholl are right that the Gantman et al. result is due to semantic priming, I think it is clear that the result does not show pop-out for moral properties in the sense used in Chapter 2, in which pop-out is a visual phenomenon in which some visual features immediately come to the fore and in which pop-out is a strong indicator of perception.

To be clear, Firestone and Scholl are concerned to rebut allegations of effects of cognition on perception—they are defenders of modularity of perception. I accept effects of cognition on perception, especially in the case of ambiguous stimuli such as those used by Gantman et al. (See Chapter 9 for more on this.) Firestone and Scholl (2016c) object to Gantman et al.'s claim (Gantman & Van Bavel, 2015, p. 631) that "perception is preferentially attuned to moral content." I accept that moral evaluations can attract attention, changing perception, as detailed in Chapter 9.

---

often taps into long-term memory systems. For example, the name of a person can make a subject faster in recognizing a picture of an associated person. In one study, "Prince Charles" made recognition of Lady Di faster. All these effects operate cross-modally, e.g., from sound to sight. Priming works via "spreading activation". It is not inferential or cognitive.

The effect of evaluation on attention has been demonstrated by Antoine Barbot and Marisa Carrasco (Barbot & Carrasco, 2018), who showed that emotional stimuli such as fearful faces attracted involuntary attention early in the perceptual process, resulting in increased apparent contrast and improved performance. Carrasco's paradigm will be explained in detail in Chapter 9. Briefly, many factors can attract attention to a stimulus, affecting perceptual properties such as apparent contrast, and improving performance. The attraction of attention by a fearful face shows that it affects attention, but does not show that perception has evaluative content.

I have claimed (Block, 1995c) that in seeing an edge and tactually feeling an edge, phenomenally different percepts can have the same content. As de Vignemont notes, one proposal would be when one sees something disgusting, it isn't that vision attributes disgustingness to the object but rather vision has a prescriptive modality, rather like an affordance. Or perhaps the modality applies to the experience itself, a prescription for less of this kind of experience. I find these proposals intriguing, but they seem to have the problem of the composite theories just discussed. The onus though would be on proponents of the attitude view to show that the states that have evaluative content are genuinely perceptual. Otherwise, it will be natural to see these cases as perception accompanied by evaluation.

One important issue with regard to evaluative perception is the extent to which emotional and narrowly perceptual systems interact. Lisa Feldman Barrett and Moshe Bar argue on the basis of neuroanatomical considerations involving the OFC—i.e., the orbitofrontal cortex (so called because it is close to the eye sockets) for the following thesis (Barrett & Bar, 2009, pp. 1331–1332):

> We have proposed that a person's affective state has a top-down influence in normal object perception. Specifically, we have proposed that the medial OFC participates in an initial phase of affective prediction ("what is the relevance of this class of objects for me"), whereas the lateral OFC provides more subordinate- level and contextually relevant affective prediction ("what is the relevance of this particular object in this particular context for me at this particular moment in time"). If this view is correct, then personal relevance and salience are not computed after an object is already identified, but may be part of object perception itself.

Barrett and Bar are right that affect influences perception, but it does not follow that evaluative properties are actually represented in perception.

A more recent paper by the same authors plus others (Lebrecht et al., 2012) argues that evaluative representations should be thought of as high-level visual attributions: "valence can be considered a higher-level object property. . . .

Thus, valence is not a label or judgment applied to the object postrecognition, but rather an integral component of mental object representations" (p. 1). This article argues that the literature on evaluative properties in perception has been excessively driven by perception of objects to which people have extreme reactions, e.g., blocks of gold and blood-stained weapons, and instead should focus on "micro-valences" involving ordinary objects such as clocks, chairs, and lamps. They refer to studies that show that perceivers attribute valences to ordinary objects: People have "gut reactions" to objects that involve preferences for some objects over others, for example, curved over jagged objects. But I didn't notice any studies cited that clearly separate perception from perceptual judgment.

When experiments have focused on perception itself, results have not supported evaluative perception. Sophie Lebrecht's PhD thesis involved an experiment (Lebrecht, 2012) in which subjects were presented with 120 pictures, three at a time. On some trials, the instructions were to pick one of the three objects that they would most like to "keep" if offered as a present. On other trials, they were asked which object they would most like to "return" if offered as a present. Each object was presented a total of five times across the experiment. A point was added for "keep" responses and subtracted for "returned" objects. This procedure yielded a subject's "micro-valence score" for each object from + 5 to –5. They found that subjects gave either consistently positive or consistently negative scores to about half the objects, showing consistent preferences. But were the preferences *perceptual* or *postperceptual*? Or some combination of perceptual and post-perceptual?

That issue was addressed by another experiment using some of the stimuli from the first group, most of which were in these categories: armchairs, cameras, teapots, and telephones. These categories were chosen because they had roughly the same numbers of positively and negatively valenced objects. Subjects were presented briefly with one picture and then another picture, the task being to say if the objects were same or different. I like this design since if valence is really part of what is attributed in perception—if objects look valenced—that should have some effect on their response times. For example, it should be easier to tell that two teapots are different if they are of different valences since that would be like ascertaining that teapots are different when they are of different colors.

The results were hard to interpret. If the pictures were from the same category, e.g., both teapots, subjects were slightly faster to answer if the pictures had different valences for that subject. I will describe the same category task as the two teapot task and the different category task as the teapot/camera task to make it easier to visualize the results. So the first result was that for the two teapot task, subjects were faster if the valences were different. However, on the second result, the teapot/camera task, the *opposite* result was found, i.e., it took slightly longer to answer if the pictures had different valences, one positive the other negative.[8] It is these opposite results that make it hard to interpret the experiment.

Hilla Jacobson (Jacobson, 2021) follows Lebrecht in arguing that there is a way of seeing these results that supports the affective perception claim. I will get to their interpretation in a moment, but first I want to observe that this is the best of the experiments I have found that has a design that stands a chance of ascertaining whether or not valences are actually perceived, as opposed to being postperceptually ascribed. And here is my main point: Even if a story can be told that looks like it supports affective perception, this is a weak reed for supporting affective perception. It is often possible to construct "just so" stories to "make sense" of results whatever the results. Further, this is a hot topic with many articles claiming affective perception, referenced above. It is embarrassing for the affective perception view if the best evidence was in a thesis and not published in experimental articles. If many advocates of affective perception thought this line of research was worth pursuing, I would have expected a number of published articles on it by now.

How are these results supposed to support affective perception? The first result was that if the objects were both teapots, subjects were faster when the valences were different. That result, taken on its own, would seem to support affective perception. Just as it would be easier to tell that two teapots are different if they were different colors, it should be easier to tell they are different if one is "colored" positively and the other is "colored" negatively. The problem is how to fit the first result with the second: that liking a camera and disliking a teapot made the subjects slower in distinguishing the camera from the teapot. The same reasoning just described would seem to apply. Distinguishing a red camera from a blue teapot should be faster than distinguishing a red camera from a red teapot.

Lebrecht and Jacobson try to explain the pattern of results by appealing to "affective priming" a well-known phenomenon in which a valenced stimulus makes one faster in processing another affective stimulus if the valence direction is the same (Klauer & Musch, 2003). Affective priming would be a force for making subjects faster when they like both items whether the items are both teapots or whether they are a teapot and a camera. Affective priming fits with the second result, but now the problem is the first result. Why doesn't affective priming have the same impact for two teapots? It looks like the reasoning analogizing valence to color fits with the first result but not the second, and the affective priming story fits with the second but not the first. However, it is not clear that there is a single framework that handles both results and also ascribes valences to perception itself. Perhaps a story can be told that fits with affective perception, but to repeat the point made earlier, this is a weak reed for supporting affective perception.

---

[8] Also, subjects were slightly faster on the teapot/camera task than on the two teapot task.

Another line of thought in favor of evaluative perception comes from work on core cognition, the topic of Chapter 12. Hamlin et. al (Hamlin, Wynn, & Bloom, 2007) presented situations to infants that were intended to depict a climber repeatedly trying to get up a hill. After numerous attempts, another character either helped the climber get up or hindered, pushing the climber further down the hill. All three characters were geometric figures made of wood with eyes. After seeing a number of presentations in which one character, e.g., a triangle, was a helper and another, e.g., a circle was a hinderer, the infants were given a choice of reaching for the triangle or the circle. Both 6-month-olds and 10-month-old preverbal infants reliably chose the helper. Further experiments along the same lines suggest that infants prefer the helper and have a negative preference for the hinderer. The upshot for evaluative perception is that the system appears early enough to be plausibly innate and to have a perceptual basis.

These infant preferences are part of core cognition. As I will argue in Chapter 12, core cognition has both a perceptual and a cognitive component. An indication of the cognitive component in the experiments just mentioned is that infants like a hinderer of a hinderer. This sounds more like cognition than perception.

I have been considering whether there is perceptual attribution of evaluative properties but another possibility suggested by de Vignemont and advocated by Jacobson is that what is evaluative about perception is not its content but its mode. As de Vignemont puts it, there may be affective coloration of perception, mental paint (Block, 2003a; de Vignemont, 2021). On one model, the idea would be that perception has descriptive content and an evaluative aspect that is prescriptive or imperative.

There are problematic aspects to this proposal. In the case of perceptual attribution, any property that can be represented consciously can also be represented in unconscious perceptual processing. (I say "unconscious perceptual processing" rather than "unconscious perception" to sidestep issues raised by Ian Philips about whether unconscious perceptual processing is really at the personal level that is required for a state to be perception (Block & Phillips, 2016; Peters et al., 2017). But if there is an evaluative mode of perception, can it obtain in unconscious processing? If so, I would need to be convinced that it is not a content property. If not, I wonder how to explain how it pops into existence when a perception becomes conscious. I see the mode idea as more of a glimmer of a proposal than a real proposal.

This chapter has been concerned with two kinds of seeing-as, nonconceptual perceptual attribution and conceptual perceptual judgment. I contrasted my view with the views of Burge and Schellenberg, and applied the ideas to two issues involving seeing-as.

4
Perception is constitutively nonpropositional and nonconceptual

Chapter 2 discussed indicators of perception; this chapter introduces some of the properties that underlie those indicators. I will give an overview of the positive case that perception is constitutively nonpropositional and nonconceptual, focusing on nonpropositionality, though discussion of propositionality inevitably involves discussion of conceptuality. Chapter 5 will argue that perception is constitutively iconic as contrasted with cognition, which is paradigmatically discursive. Then in Chapters 6 and 7, I'll go into the nonconceptual nature of perception in more detail. Chapters 4–7 make the positive case for a joint between perception and cognition and its nature, then Chapter 8 makes the negative case, replying to arguments on the other side.

I will not be claiming that iconicity, nonpropositionality, and nonconceptuality are sufficient for perception, since they are shared with hallucination and some cognitive states that use perceptual materials, for example perceptual simulations in cognition. (Some other such cases are listed in Chapter 1, footnote 3.)

Concepts and propositions

The term "concept" is sometimes used in a representational sense and sometimes in the sense of what concepts in the representational sense express or mean. In the representational sense, the sense that I will be using, concepts are representational (paradigmatically predicative) elements that constitutively function in propositional thought, reasoning, problem-solving, evaluating, deciding, and other cognitive processes and states. On my usage of the term, concepts might be described, redundantly, as conceptual representations and propositions as propositional representations.

Concepts of something provide ways of thinking of it. Oedipus had at least two ways of thinking of his mother and two concepts of her, which, he came to realize, tragically picked out the same person. Perceptual concepts provide perceptual ways of thinking of something. For example, visual and tactile concepts of the same curved edge can use perceptions in the different modalities to ground thinking of that curved edge in different ways.

This representational notion of concept is widespread in cognitive science, and for good reason, given its role in psychological explanation. A proposition in the representational sense is a syntactic-like structure composed of concepts. The representational sense of "concept" is more common than the representational sense of "proposition." The term "proposition" is not as much used in cognitive science as "concept," but it is a natural pair with the notion of concept that is so used since both are representations. Whenever I think there is a chance of misunderstanding, I will use the redundant phrases "conceptual representation" and "propositional representation."

To fix ideas, it may be helpful to consider Bruno Latour's infamous claim that Ramses II could not have died of tuberculosis since tuberculosis was discovered by Robert Koch in 1882. Latour said, "Before Koch, the bacillus had no real existence. To say that Ramses II died of tuberculosis is as absurd as saying that he died of machine-gun fire" (Latour, 1998). What mistake was Latour making? As was common in postmodernist thinking of the 1990s, he confused the concept of tuberculosis with tuberculosis itself. What happened in 1882 is that a representation of tuberculosis (that is, the bacillus) came into existence. It is that kind of representation that am calling a concept.

Some use the term "concept" in a sense more tied to the ability to use language (Gupta, 2013; Sellars, 1956; 1997). Given how clear it is that nonlinguistic animals and human babies have perceptions with perceptual contents, the claim that their contents are nonconceptual because they lack language would be of no interest. So a linguistic notion of concept would not be appropriate for my purposes.

Others use a notion of concept that is grounded in belief (Byrne, 2005; Davidson, 1999). Alex Byrne mentions a sense of "concept" in which "Someone possesses the concept F iff she believes that ... F ... (for some filling of the dots). So, for example, someone who believes that Seabiscuit is a horse, or that horses are birds, or that all horses are horses, possesses the concept *horse*" (Byrne, 2005, p. 232; Martin, 1992; Peacocke, 1983; Tye, 1995b). On this notion of "concept," talking about concepts is really a way of talking about beliefs. I think grounding what a concept is in terms of propositional attitude states is right, but the category of belief is too narrow. Some animals may be able to reason with evanescent mental representations, using them to infer evanescent but useful consequences, without having the kind of standing states that would qualify as a belief. Further, anyone who hopes that horses are birds has the concept of a horse even though they do not believe that horses are birds.

A second problem with Byrne's characterization is that what it is to have a concept should be thought of in terms of *potential* propositional states, not just actual beliefs as in Byrne's formulation. Someone who is capable of hoping that horses are birds, can question whether horses are birds and can muse that horses are birds has the concept of a horse independently of actual hoping, questioning, and musing.

I said concepts paradigmatically function in propositional cognition. Why paradigmatically? Because of the possibility that concepts, established in propositional thought, could also function in some other way outside of propositional thought. For example, the concept of a bird, having been grounded in thoughts concerning birds, can play a role in imagining something as a bird. One can follow a command "Imagine a bird" without having propositional thoughts about birds.

My account comports with Peacocke's proposal that possession conditions are important to what a concept is. Peacocke says, "There can be nothing more to the nature of a concept than is determined by a correct account of the capacity of a thinker who has mastered the concept to have propositional attitudes to contents containing that concept (a correct account of 'grasping the concept')" (Peacocke, 1992b, p. 5). On my account, the capacities of the thinker who has mastered a concept are a matter of the function of that thinker's propositional attitudes involving that concept in reasoning, problem-solving, evaluating, deciding, and other cognitive processes.

This picture of concepts is often called the epistemic or pragmatic notion of what a concept is, as opposed to atomistic accounts such as Fodor's (Fodor, 1998; Newen & Bartels, 2007) (although Fodor's account is also a representational account). And it contrasts with views such as Jesse Prinz's (2002) and that of Albert Newen and Andreas Bartels (2007) in that both allow perceptual concepts without propositional abilities.

Jake Quilty-Dunn (2020) advocates an antipragmatic view of what concepts are, what he calls "possession-as-storage." Having a concept is simply storing a certain symbol in memory, according to this view. But what makes the symbol express the concept? We pragmatists give a pragmatic answer: In order for a symbol to mean what it does, it must have a certain function. Quilty-Dunn regards even Fodor's atomism as too pragmatist, since according to Fodor, what makes a concept the concept of a dog is that it enables thinking of dogs as such, but thinking of dogs as such requires memory retrieval, and that is a kind of function. On functional accounts of what a concept is, there may be borderline cases of concepts in which the function is disabled by, for example, working memory limitations or even failures that are built into the architecture and so cannot be regarded as malfunctions. Whether the representations in such cases are concepts must be decided one by one, but there is no problem of principle for pragmatists in refusing to ascribe a concept to a creature whose abilities are too meager.

Atomistic representations certainly are not what we normally think of as concepts. Could someone really think about dogs as such while denying that dogs are living things, that they are smaller than planets, larger than viruses, that they are born and die, have limbs? Such a person might not be able to distinguish dogs from fire hydrants.

Quilty-Dunn's critique of pragmatism depends on a view of what pragmatism requires (p. 279), namely "a primary motivation for pragmatism is that it ties concept possession to verifiable cognitive tasks and thus furnishes us with diagnostic tests of conceptuality emanating from a "practically useful account that captures the core set of cognitive tasks that we expect concepts to perform (Camp, 2009, p. 276)."

That may be Camp's motivation, but it isn't mine. I think the functional notion of concept is the one that makes sense for cognitive science and the one that is used in practice. Diagnostic tests are seldom if ever dispositive in science since we can always find a better test.

Although concepts in the sense used here are constitutively cognitive in the sense that their identities are based on their cognitive function, that does not preclude nonconceptual and nonpropositional cognition, as may occur in the use of mental maps in guiding behavior (Burge, 2010a; Newen & Bartels, 2007). And concepts can function cognitively in hybrid representations that have perceptual elements. Mental maps are often hybrid representations, as with maps on paper. A map on paper may represent relative distances between cities geometrically but represent elevations via conventional colors and the names of the cities via discursive labels, both conceptual elements.

One line of evidence that concepts and percepts are fundamentally different derives from color agnosia, an associative agnosia in the sense of Chapter 1. I will discuss a case of color agnosia later in Chapter 6 after I have introduced the idea of categorical perception. But I will briefly mention one line of evidence. Color anomia or agnosia (I'll use the latter term) is the inability to conceptualize color—for example, to name colors, point to the green one, say whether the blue banana or the yellow banana is the odd one, and to color black and white drawings of common objects with the usual color. Color agnosia is distinct from achromatopsia, the inability to see color. Color agnosia can co-occur with normal color perception. The locus of brain damage for color agnosia in adults is the left hemisphere (Miceli et al., 2001; van Zandvoort, Nijboer, & De Haan, 2007), whereas color perception is based in both hemispheres. So substantial destruction of the neural basis of color concepts is compatible with unscathed color perception.

Wait, you may ask: How do we know that color agnosics who have little or nothing in the realm of color concepts can nonetheless see colors perfectly well? Chapter 6 describes a number of nonverbal methods of investigating color perception without using language. Briefly, the simplest method is to show the subject a uniform screen of one color with a disk of another color. Subjects who can see the difference will typically move their eyes to the differently colored disk. Agnosics who do not understand color well enough to color a gray-scale banana yellow will nonetheless move their eyes to a yellow disk on a different color background. Also color agnosics can often pass the Ishihara color blindness test, in which symbols and shapes are visible to people with normal color vision but not those with red/green color blindness.

Turning from concepts to propositions: It is often noted (McGrath, 2014) that "the conception we associate with the word 'proposition' may be something of a jumble of conflicting *desiderata*" (Lewis, 1986, p. 54). Two of those conflicting desiderata are as the primary bearers of truth value and as the contents of cognitive states such as those involved in thought and reasoning.

One approach to the truth value desideratum individuates propositional contents in terms of the possible worlds in which they are true. The propositional content that Trump lost is the set of possible worlds in which Trump lost. But this coarse-grained propositional content is often said not to be useful in the context of explaining what people do and think in terms of what they think and perceive. For example, the propositional content that all bachelors are unmarried and the propositional content that $2 + 2 = 4$, both being true in all possible worlds, would be the same propositional content (Stalnaker, 2014).

Another coarse-grained view of content is the Russellian view of propositional content in which the proposition that Oedipus is married to Jocasta is an ordered set of 3 items whose members are Oedipus and Jocasta and the marriage relation. The identity of that set does not depend on how its members are designated, so the propositional content is the same propositional content as the propositional content that Oedipus is married to Mom (as we can imagine that Oedipus called her), although those contents are different from the point of view of psychological explanation.

Similar points apply to perceptual content if we count the ways we perceive things as part of the perceptual content. To use an example given earlier, we can perceive the corner of a cube as sharp either visually or haptically. These two types of percepts differ in modes of presentation, and those modes of presentation have different phenomenologies. Assuming that a difference in phenomenology entails a difference in content, then the Russellian contents are too coarse-grained for psychological explanation.

But does a difference in phenomenology entail a difference in content? I don't think there is a factual answer here—only a question of what notion of content one wants to use.

Michael Tye (2005) advocates Russellian contents of perception. As I mentioned in Chapter 2, he holds that the phenomenological difference between the haptic and visual perception of the sharpness of the cube is that one percept represents other visual properties, e.g., color, whereas the other percept represents other tactile properties, e.g., roughness. I argue that this difference is not sufficient to explain the phenomenological difference between haptic and visual perception (Block, 1995a, 1995c).

In the rest of this section, I will consider the question of whether conceptual and nonconceptual representations can have the same contents. It is widely thought that contents are by their nature conceptual or nonconceptual (Peacocke, 1994). An alternative conception ties conceptuality to states of mind (Heck, 2000, 2007). I think that conceptuality is best thought of as applying to states of mind rather than contents as Richard Heck has argued (2000, 2007). If Heck is right, that opens the door to conceptual and nonconceptual states having the same contents. My position is that while nothing in the nature of perception or of cognition precludes conceptual and nonconceptual states having the same contents, in practice this probably never happens.

In Chapter 6, I will argue in more detail that perception is nonconceptual, using the example of color perception and conception in children. I will argue that children between 4–6 months and 11 months of age have color perception without color conception and that the nonconceptual nature of color perception in infants is a model for all perception. To the extent that infants' perceptual color representations and adult conceptual color representations represent the same colors, then their contents are alike in at least reference, if not in the modes of presentations of those referents.

Don't get me wrong. I acknowledge that infant color categories differ from adult color categories in a number of ways that would make for differences. For example, adult color concepts almost certainly do not divide up the colors in as fine-grained a manner as color percepts.

In Chapter 6, I will mention evidence for the conclusion that the child's nonconceptual representations of color are based in the right hemisphere whereas adult color concepts are based mainly in the left hemisphere and are closely connected to color language. As we will see, the left and right hemisphere representations divide up the colors somewhat differently. One would expect the change in role that comes with conceptualization to make for differences in content, but that may not always be the case. In principle a predicational content-element can be conceptual when used in thought and nonconceptual in perception.

So, conceptual and nonconceptual representations are fundamentally different, and different in their neural bases, but in principle they could have the same referential contents. For example, we can conceptually represent red. If we could nonconceptually represent red—which I doubt given the fine grained content of color perception—there could be conceptual and nonconceptual representations with the same referent. And in principle they could have the same phenomenal modes of presentation. But there are many factors that suggest that in practice there will be substantial differences between the contents of conceptual and nonconceptual representations. In addition, as I will argue later in this chapter, there are certain kinds of logically complex contents cannot be the contents of perception.

To sum up this section, concepts are representational (paradigmatically predicative) elements in structured representations. Those structured representations, propositions, paradigmatically and constitutively function in propositional thought, reasoning, problem-solving, evaluating, deciding, and other cognitive processes and states. In the next section, I will say a bit more about propositions (that is, propositional representations).

Format/content/state/function

As I have been saying, what makes propositional representations propositional is their role in content-based transitions in cognitive processes such as reasoning, inferring, thinking, and deciding. In my terminology, judgments are occurrent propositional states that affirm something, and whose representations can be premises or conclusions in reasoning and have inferential relations to other mental representations (Block, 1980). Although propositional representations are paradigmatically structured, they do not have to be structured. The propositional role in reasoning is compatible with lack of internal structure.

As noted earlier, the solitary wasp has perceptual representations without having any representations at all that are good candidates for conceptual or propositional functions. It is the presence or absence of those functions that determine whether the representations are conceptual or propositional.

It might be said that even if the wasp does not actually reason, still its perceptual representations might be apt for reasoning, and so would be propositional. The claim would be that if cognitive machinery of reasoning was added to the wasp's brain, its perceptual representations would be able to function as premises or conclusions. However, I am doubtful that counterfactuals about what representations would do if neural circuits were added to the wasp brain make much sense (Kripke, 1982). Talk of "adding" cognitive machinery to a brain runs into this problem: A brain that lacked cognitive machinery would have to be reorganized in order for cognitive machinery to be integrated into the information processing of the system. So the truth of the counterfactual would depend on what kind of a reorganization is supposed to be involved. Talk of adding machinery to a functioning apparatus would make sense, however, for certain kinds of modular systems. One can add RAM to a computer, but that is because it is designed in a modular way that allows for that change. There is no reason to believe that a wasp brain is modular in that sense.

Any representation at all could in principle function in reasoning if circuits were added that used that kind of representation in reasoning. As I noted, an image of an isosceles triangle could function as a concept of triangularity if used in a certain way. No doubt, pennies could function in reasoning as premises and conclusions in a machine if the machine's processing was arranged so as to use the pennies in the right way. That fact does not license speaking of pennies as propositional representations, simpliciter. In this way, the concept of a propositional representation is like the concept of a gene. Pennies are genes in some conceptually possible system that uses the coins in the right way. As with genes, propositional representations are only propositional relative to a system in which they function or are apt to function.

Although the functions that make a representation propositional also make some of its components conceptual, there can be propositional representations that contain some nonconceptual representations. For example, if samples of phenomenology can be quoted, as in some recent theories of phenomenal concepts (Balog, 2009b; Block, 2002b; Papineau, 2002), the samples themselves would be nonconceptual components of the resulting propositional representation.

Turning now from function to format, the format of a representation is the structure of the representational vehicle, where the vehicle is the bearer of the content. A single format can express different contents in different representational systems. To take a common example, one pronunciation of 'Empedocles leaped' in English is the same as one pronunciation of 'Empedocles liebt' in German, though they have different contents, as Donald Davidson noted (1968, p. 135). An English sentence in TimesRoman type provides one format, but its content could be expressed in other languages. For example, according to Google translate, the content that kittens are cute can be expressed as

子猫はかわいいです or as بلی کے بچے پیارا ہیں

in languages other than English.

Format can reveal or hide the structure of content. The letter 'p' could be used to represent the propositional content that grass is green. A symbol with no structure is used here to represent a structured content. "They are eating apples" can express two different contents, corresponding to the more elaborated formats "They [[are eating] apples]" and "They [are [eating apples]]."

Iconic representations of approximate numerosity, amount, and spatial dimensions are structured at the level of content since they involve both a designation of an area of space (or an object at an area of space) and also a property or magnitude placed at that area of space. The format of these representations is iconic. The structure of iconic representations will be discussed in the next chapter.

On some views of content, for example, contents as sets of possible worlds, it is not easy to see how contents can be structured. On other views of content, the structure of the content of a representation derives from the structure of its vehicle (Beck, 2012; Heck, 2007).

Contents are often said to be nonconceptual or nonpropositional. Contents are said to be nonconceptual if they are not "composed" of concepts. Byrne (2001) holds that perceptual contents are nonconceptual in something like this sense but are also propositional because they have truth value. However, treating contents as nonconceptual would not make sense if conceptual and nonconceptual states can share content, as I have suggested. For this reason, I will take conceptuality and nonconceptuality to be properties of states rather than contents. Two states can represent the same content, one conceptually, the other nonconceptually.

I can acknowledge propositional representations that have some nonconceptual components, but there can't be entirely nonconceptual propositional representations, since the characteristic inferential role that determines that a representation is propositional will inevitably determine conceptuality for some of the proposition's constituents.

It is representational elements of the states that have content that determine whether a state is conceptual or propositional (Heck, 2000). One formulation that gives a role to states is that a nonconceptual content is a content that cannot be the full content of a paradigm cognitive state such as a belief or thought (Peacocke, 2001a; Siegel, 2016). But this definition still treats content as the primary bearer of the property of being conceptual or nonconceptual.

What is it about a representational state that makes it nonconceptual or nonpropositional? It is sometimes said that what it is for a state to be nonconceptual is that the subject of the state need not possess the concepts required to characterize the state's content from the subject's point of view (Byrne, 2003; Crane, 1992; Heck, 2000; Siegel, 2016; Stoljar, 2009). But a being who had a concept corresponding to every perceptual representation might still have nonconceptual perception, as I will explain.

Recall that a concept in the sense that I am using the term is a representational (paradigmatically predicative) element that functions in propositional thought, reasoning, or other cognitive states. The point about a nonconceptual representational state isn't so much that the subject does not possess these representational elements or even that the state doesn't include them, but rather that they don't play a role in determining the content of the state. That is, what makes a state conceptual isn't just that the subject possesses an appropriate concept, but that the concept is deployed so as to determine the content. A nonconceptual state is one for which concepts play no role in determining the representational content. Conceptuality is a matter of role. This point about nonconceptuality will loom large in Chapter 6, where I will argue that infant color perception between 6 and 11 months is typically nonconceptual.

Although contents are not in themselves propositional or conceptual, we can speak of a content of a given representation as propositional or conceptual if it is part of a conceptual or propositional state. In terms of format and state, I am arguing that perceptual representations are iconic in format and that perceptual states are nonconceptual and nonpropositional. Nonconceptuality and nonpropositionality are not properties of format. It is natural to think that a single format item can in principle if not in practice function as a nonconceptual perceptual representation in one system but as a concept in another system. As mentioned earlier, one might suppose that a perceptual representation of an isosceles triangle can be used as a concept of a triangle—as in Berkeley's famous example. I will argue in Chapter 6 that this natural line of thinking is not quite right.

At this point I will just say that iconic format is ill-suited for the systematicity that is characteristic if not constitutive of conceptual and propositional representations, so it is no accident that the iconic formats of perception are nonconceptual and nonpropositional. (There is further discussion of this point later in this chapter and in Chapter 6.)

Although iconic format is the topic of the next chapter, I will briefly describe the notion of iconic format that I will be using. It is often said that iconic representation is "natural" as compared with arbitrary symbolic representation (Giardino & Greenberg, 2015), and my notion of iconicity is in that tradition. I will give evidence that in perception there is representation of properties by representational analog mirrors of them. The notion of iconicity that I will be using is constituted by analog tracking and mirroring. Analog tracking and mirroring obtains when there is a set of environmental properties and a set of representations of those environmental properties such that:

1. Certain differences in representations function as responses to differences in environmental properties in a way that is sensitive to the degree (and also kind) of environmental differences. For example, as objects like the ones depicted in Figure 4.1 are rotated, perceptual representations function to alter in a way that corresponds to that rotation and is sensitive to that degree of rotation.
2. Certain differences in representations function to alter the situation that is represented in a way that depends on the degree (and also kind) of representational change.
3. Certain relations (including temporal relations) among the environmental properties are mirrored by representations that instantiate analogs of those relations.

176   THE BORDER BETWEEN SEEING AND THINKING

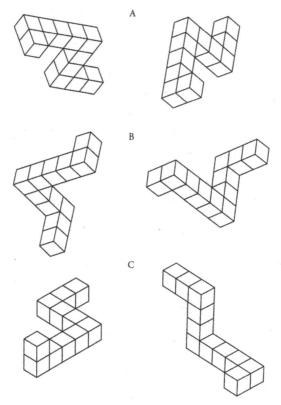

Figure 4.1 Shepard rotation. Subjects are asked whether the pairs depicted are superimposable. Thanks to Adrian Twissell for this figure. The answer is yes for A and B and no for C.

Function determines both format and content, though different aspects of function figure in these two determination relations. One cannot judge format from a snapshot of a representation. Something that we might classify as a picture on the basis of a snapshot representation might function in another context as a discursive symbol.

The nonpropositional nature of perception

Many theorists think that perception (or at least object perception) is propositional (Byrne, 2005; Glüer, 1999; Green & Quilty-Dunn, 2017; Matthen, 2005; McDowell, 1994; Quilty-Dunn, 2016a, 2019b; Siegel, 2010; Speaks, 2005; Tye,

1995b). Some philosophers hold that perception is conceptual and propositional because their best account of how we can know via our senses requires perceptual contents as premises in reasoning (McDowell, 1994; Tucker, 2010).

We sometimes speak of perceptions as being reasons for action. One might say that my perception of the chocolate cookie that you are offering me is a reason for me to reach out and take it. But this way of talking is also compatible with the perception being a ground of a reason rather than an actual reason (Burge, 2010a, p. 435).

Consider the propositional content that corresponds to a simple declarative sentence, say the propositional content that pigs fly. There is also a content expressed by the negation of that sentence, the propositional content that it is not the case that pigs fly. And there are corresponding disjunctive and conditional propositional contents, that pigs fly or angels weep and that if pigs fly, then angels weep.

The claims that are the basis of the argument of this chapter are (1) that these operations do not apply to perceptual contents and (2) that perceptual contents do not have internal structures that reflect these operations. One can see something as nonblue by seeing it as red, but one cannot see anything simply as not-blue. One can see something as intermediate or indeterminate between red and blue (e.g., purple) but not as having the disjunctive property of simply being red or being blue. Note that something that is indeterminate between red and blue does not satisfy the accuracy condition for being red or being blue; to satisfy that disjunctive accuracy condition, something must be red simpliciter or blue simpliciter. Further, one can see something as red but not as if red then blue. (A previous version of the points about logical structure appeared in my replies to Putnam [pp. 452–453] and to Siegel & Silins [p. 507] in Pautz & Stoljar [2019].)

It is obvious enough that we can't perceive something as if red, then green; or perceive something as red or green. I think the same holds for negation, disjunction, and conjunction, but it is easier in the case of these logical operations to be misled, hence I will focus on them in the next three sections.

After writing a draft of this chapter, I discovered that Tim Crane (2000, 2009) has argued for a similar view (cf. also Burge, 2010a, 2010c).

> In the previous section I claimed that pictures do not have propositional content because propositions can be asserted or denied, and they can stand in logical relations. The only sense in which pictures stand in logical relations is when someone uses a picture along with some non-pictorial representation to make some claim. Similarly, if a proposition were the content of a perceptual experience, then it should be capable of being negated, disjoined, conjoined, etc. But

it seems that just as one cannot do these things to the content of pictures, one cannot do them to the contents of experiences either. (Crane, 2009, p. 462)

What Crane says here can be given two interpretations, one involving internal and the other involving external logical relations. His main point concerns external logical relations: Perceptual contents cannot be negated, disjoined, conjoined, etc. The internal interpretation is that the contents themselves cannot have an internal structure involving negations, disjunctions, conjunctions, etc.

Of course, perceptual contents can be negated, disjoined, and conjoined in the sense that one can judge that the content of a perception does not obtain or that either the content of this perception obtains or the content of that perception obtains. But these are judgments, not perceptions. More importantly for my point is that it isn't just that we can't conjoin, disjoin, or negate seeings but also that in the sense in which one can conjoin, disjoin, or negate seeings—in judgment—what results is not seeings with conjunctive, disjunctive, or negative contents. Logically complex perceptual contents are what is most directly relevant to the question of whether perception is propositional. If perceptual contents cannot be disjunctive in content or have the content of a negation, then, as will be explained below, perceptions cannot be premises in the disjunctive syllogism. External logical relations are also relevant to propositionality since disjunctions of perceptions and negations of perceptions cannot be premises in the disjunctive syllogism.

Wait, why am I talking about logical structure of contents and logical relations among contents, when the sense of "nonconceptual" I am using concerns states, not contents? In my view, contents are grounded in the functional roles of representational aspects of states. Further, whether a state is nonconceptual or nonpropositional is also grounded in the functional roles of representational aspects of states. In particular, propositionality is a matter of whether representational aspects of states are apt for use in reasoning and other cognitive processes. So content, conceptuality, and propositionality are all ultimately functional.

Don't perceptions have truth conditions? And doesn't that show they are propositional? Siegel (2010) proposes identifying propositional content with accuracy conditions. On my notion of a proposition, having accuracy conditions does not guarantee propositionality. There are two issues here, a minor issue of the difference between accuracy and truth and a major issue: What makes a representation propositional is its role in reasoning. Accuracy conditions or even truth conditions do not guarantee a role in reasoning.

First, the minor issue of the difference between accuracy and truth. As Crane (p. 464) notes concerning Jacques-Louis David's painting of Napoleon crowning himself, what the picture represents is Napoleon crowning himself, and "Napoleon crowning himself" does not express a proposition; rather it is a noun phrase referring to an event.

Note that the noun phrase "that F" is accurate just in case the referent of "that" has the property that is the referent of 'F.' So, accuracy conditions need not be propositional. Consider a singular perception of something as green. The perception is accurate just in case the thing that I see—i.e., the thing that is singled out by my perception—is in fact green (Burge, 2010a; Crane, 2009; Siegel, 2010). So a perception can place a property at an object or location via a structure that is analogous to that of a noun phrase. Of course perceptions are not linguistic; rather they often involve singling out together with an attribution (Burge, 2010a). The important difference is that noun phrases are not suitable to act as premises or conclusions in reasoning and so do not have propositional content. Although I am skeptical about Burge's noun phrase model as a model of all perception, it does have the advantage of revealing that we cannot reason from the fact that perceptions involve attribution to the conclusion that perceptions are propositional.

As I mentioned, the major issue is that perceptions do not have the logical properties that are required for a role in reasoning. That point—to be discussed in the rest of the chapter—is what makes them nonpropositional. However, in Chapter 3, I also expressed some sympathy with the possibility of perception having existential content. Am I contradicting myself? The key point is that the "existentialist" view does not require that it is possible for there to be a nonexistential perceptual content that is then existentially quantified. Indeed, the generalist viewpoints in the sense of Chapter 3 (including existentialism) are typically held for all perception.

Susanna Siegel (2017) has argued that Jill's fear that Jack is angry can lead her to experience Jack's neutral expression as angry. She sees this as at least analogous to inference. She says (p. 100), "Here, experiences are responses to other experiences, just as conclusions are responses to inferential inputs." However, it is not clear that the experience of Jack's neutral expression as angry is a perception rather than a perceptual judgment. And in any case being analogous to inference is not the same as inference, so even if the experience is a perception, it does not follow that a perception can be a conclusion of a chain of reasoning.

Assuming I am right that perceptual contents do not admit of negation, disjunction, conjunction, and conditionalization, does that show they are nonpropositional? No, because they might be atomic propositional contents. In the next two sections I will discuss conjunction and negation. Then in the following section, I will argue that perceptual contents are not atomic propositional contents.

Conjunction

One principle governing conjunction is that conjoining well-formed propositional representations yields a well formed conjunctive propositional representation. Another principle is that if the conjuncts are true, so is the conjunction. Further, if the conjunction is true, so is each of the conjuncts. Conjunction can conjoin propositions but also predicates. From the proposition that this is round at t and this is square at t, one can deduce the conjunctive proposition that this is round at t and this is square at t, and (given anaphora), we can conclude with the predicate conjunction that this is round and square at t. Our cognitive faculty can conjoin any two propositional representations or predicate representations, and though the result will be syntactically well formed it need not be semantically well formed. For example, combining the predicates "weighs 700 pounds" and "is a prime number" yields a conjunction that arguably is not semantically well formed.

Perception does not adhere to these principles. For example, conjoined visual attributions of being spherical and cubical as applied to the same thing at the same time may not be possible, and the same for the conjoined attribution of pure red and pure green. So principles applying to conjunction may not hold for perception.

Of course, we can adopt a convention that restricts conjunction. Dave Chalmers mentioned an analogy in my class on this chapter: Fish 'n chips. The apostrophe-'n' connective is a form of conjunction but perhaps limited by convention. "Justice 'n equality" isn't a good use of that connective. But the restrictions of conjunction for perception are not limited by convention but by the nature of perception itself.

In some cases, we understand something about why certain combinations cannot be perceptually ascribed. Color works via opponent channels, as elaborated in Chapter 2. Opposite ends of these channels cannot be activated at once. Hence one cannot see something as pure red and pure green at the same time. (Interestingly, a slight activation of both sides of the channel can be accomplished by projecting an image to the retina that moves with the eye, creating a "stabilized" image. This leads to a deterioration of the percept in which "the colors of the image diffuse into one another." Some subjects describe the resulting percept as momentarily greenish and reddish (Billock, Gleason, & Tsou, 2001, p. 84).

If there is a language of thought, I guess we can imagine a being whose sentential conjunction was similarly limited. Perhaps certain symbols in the language of thought would make the belief box malfunction. That would be genuine conjunction with limitations.

The kind of perceptual combination under discussion could be said to be a form of perceptual binding. (See this footnote for a description of what binding is.[1]) On that understanding, what we have been discussing is whether binding is a form of conjunction.

The mechanism by which one property is bound to another in perception is thought to involve temporal synchronization of the representations that are bound together. For example, if motion is bound to color, activations in the motion areas of the cortex (MT/V5) are synchronized with color activations (V4 and V8). This mechanism imposes limits on what can be bound to what.

One mark against thinking that binding is a kind of conjunction is that there are basic properties of binding that have no analog with regard to conjunction. As mentioned in Chapter 3, there are two kinds of binding, direct and indirect binding. Orientation and spatial location are bound together directly, but color and orientation are bound together only indirectly, via binding of each of them to location (Schneegans & Bays, 2017). If information about location is lost, so is information about which orientations go with which colors. So, vision can represent rectangle R as red and also represent rectangle R as oriented at 45°, but that is not enough to ensure a representation in which redness and orientation at 45° are bound together in a representation of rectangle R, since they must also be represented as having locations and those locations must be the same. There is no comparable distinction between direct and indirect conjunction.

A defender of binding as a form of conjunction might want to regard the limitations on binding that I have been discussing as features of "performance" rather than "competence." In other words, it might be said that there are no limits on well-formedness of bindings, but only "performance" limits on what we can bind together. However, it is unclear why fundamental properties of the visual system such as the opponent processes that operate in many domains should be regarded as performance limitations.

We have been discussing conjunction introduction. What about conjunction elimination? If a conjunction is well-formed, so are the conjuncts. From well-formed conjunctions, one can often form the conjoined propositions on their own and the conjunctive proposition entails the components. I can bind red and triangular in perception, but I can't just un-bind these aspects of the perception,

---

[1] "Binding" is the process in which different properties are attributed to a single object in a perception of that object. For example, motion, represented in one part of the brain, shape represented in another, and color in another are put together to represent an object with a certain shape and color moving in a certain trajectory. Suppose one sees a red square moving to the right and a green circle moving to the left. How does the visual system "know" that the redness, squareness, and leftward motion go together whereas the greenness, circularity, and rightward motion go together? This is known as the "binding problem" (Schneegans & Bays, 2017; Treisman, 1998).

seeing something as just red or just triangular. There are many cases in the neuropsychological literature of mis-binding (e.g., Balint's Syndrome [Kanwisher & Wojciulik, 1998]), but I know of no cases of unbinding. Given the points made above about direct and indirect binding and now the lack of unbinding, the idea of binding as a form of conjunction begins to look rather strained.

Another kind of case in which the visual system puts properties "together" in some sense is when there are ambiguous stimuli such as the Necker cube or the face/vase picture. But those are cases of rivalry (discussed in Chapter 2). In binocular rivalry, there can be blends of the two percepts. For example, if a masculine face is presented to one eye and a feminine face to the other, the subject can perceive either an androgynous face that does not preserve the original masculine and feminine faces, or alternations of the masculine and feminine faces that does not bind the two together at the same time (depending on what is attended). (These cases will be discussed later in this chapter.) None of these is a conjunctive percept.

Analogous points apply to whether anything that could be called perceptual uncertainty is really a kind of disjunction or whether perception of uniformity is really a kind of universal quantification.

Negation

What is the difference between predicate negation and propositional negation. The difference is, to take a standard example, the difference between asserting that Socrates has the property of being not-wise and asserting that it is not the case that Socrates is wise. The former but not the latter entails that Socrates exists. Ruth Millikan has argued that for nonlinguistic creatures, predicate negation is crucial because they tend not to have direct evidence against a proposition. They discover that the proposition that x is F is false by finding positive evidence for the proposition that x is G, where G is incompatible with F (Millikan, 2004).

I have brought up predicate negation because it may seem more plausible for perception than propositional negation. In particular, Anya Farennikova (2013) has claimed that we can see absences. She gives a number of cases of putatively seeing absences: you leave your laptop on a table in a café, go out briefly and when you return you (allegedly) see its absence. You (allegedly) see the absence of milk in the refrigerator, the absence of your colleague at a meeting, the absence of the keys from the drawer.

Further, magic tricks often make use of "illusions of absence" in which, for example, an object is put into the magician's hand but when the hand opens, there is only ... absence. Recently, an article has explored magic tricks in which there

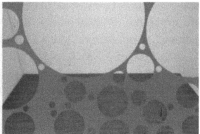

Figure 4.2 The figure on the right results from superimposing a complex shape on the photograph on the left. From Svalebjørg et al. (2020).

is an illusion of absence (Svalebjørg, Øhrn, & Ekroll, 2020). It was discovered that subjects' awareness of absence was resistant to finding out how the trick was done, in a manner similar to what occurs in amodal completion. In the left photograph (Figure 4.2), a table with objects is presented. Then in the right, a complex shape is placed over the first photograph in such a way that all the objects are occluded. Svalebjørg et al. note (p. 3) that it is difficult to "imagine that the objects on the table . . . are really hidden behind the violet 'bubbled' occluder." I agree with what they say—but note that the process of comparing the pictures on the right and left clearly has a strong cognitive element, and so one should be suspicious of it as a justification of a perception of absence.

To the extent that these cases have plausibility as perceptions of absence, they look more like predicate negation than propositional negation. (Cf. Burge, 2010a, p. 540.) However, there is no requirement of negation in nonlinguistic practical reasoning (Bermudez, 2007). A nonlinguistic reasoner can get by with mastering what Bermudez calls "proto-negation" in the form of pairs of contraries such as present/absent, safe/dangerous, and up/down. Suppose the reasoner knows that if the gazelle is present, the lion is absent. Seeing that the lion is present, the conclusion can be drawn that the gazelle is absent—on the basis of the fact that present/absent are contraries. With specific contraries, no negation is needed. Perhaps Farennikova's cases are proto-negations, where proto-negation does not require propositionality.[2]

To be clear: I am not denying that there are perceptual expectations. What I am denying is that the result of a perceptual expectation that is not satisfied is predicate or propositional negation. Recall the discussion in Chapter 2 of pop-out, a visual phenomenon in which a visual feature leaps to the eye in a sea of distractors. Features that pop out attract attention. Pop-out is immediately

---

[2] See, Burge (2010c), Cavedon-Taylor (2017), and Martin and Dokic (2013) for further discussion.

apparent, but has been tested in the experimental literature mainly via examining the properties of visual search. However, it is important to keep in mind that pop-out occurs even without a search target (including in 4-month-old infants) (Quinn & Bhatt, 1998), so pop-out is not the same as efficient search. The main behavioral test of pop-out is visual search that is extremely efficient in the sense that the number of distractors matters little so long as the distractors are visually dissimilar to the pop-out feature. See Figure 2.13 and Figure 4.3. Color, shape, motion, orientation, size, depth, and being a closed figure can all pop-out but, other salient items cannot, e.g., your name (Wolfe & Horowitz, 2017).

Features that pop out can be *directly* used in visual search in the sense that the feature can itself guide search and not via some other properties that correlate with the feature. For example, it is easy to search for faces in a sea of nonfaces (Hershler & Hochstein, 2006). However, doubts have been raised about whether it is faceness per se that is responsible for the pop-out effect of faces or whether the low-level properties that are the basis for recognizing the face are responsible, as claimed by Van Rullen (2006). I think the evidence is strong on the side of faceness per se as the basis of pop-out, but I mention the dispute to illustrate the difference between a feature being used directly in visual search rather than

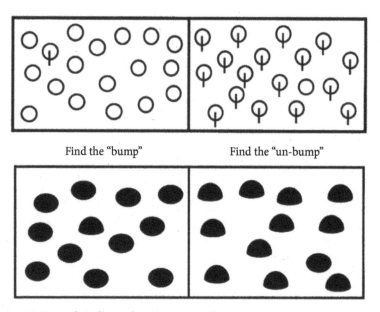

Figure 4.3 Examples where a feature pops-out but its absence does not. In the top picture, search for the circle with the line on the left and search for the absence of such a circle on the right. In the bottom picture a bump pops-out among nonbumps, but not vice versa. Thanks to Jeremy Wolfe for these figures. (See Kristjánsson & Tse, 2001; Wolfe & Horowitz, 2017.)

indirectly used (as in effect claimed by Van Rullen). If a feature can be directly used in visual search then that the feature is actually represented in vision.

There is plenty of evidence that when a feature pops out, its absence cannot be expected to pop out (Treisman & Gormican, 1988). See Figure 4.3 for some examples of asymmetric visual search in which an X pops out among Ys but a Y does not pop out among Xs. In the top of the figure, the presence of a line pops out but its absence does not. In the bottom, a discontinuity in curvature pops out but its absence does not. The explanation in the latter case is that curvature discontinuities are represented in vision but their absences are not (Kristjánsson & Tse, 2001). The asymmetric pop-out paradigm has the advantage that the visual similarity between target and distractor is the same in both cases, since in both cases it is the similarity between X and Y.

An orange object is easy to find among a sea of red objects, but a red object is not easy to find among a sea of orange objects. This asymmetry can be explained in terms of the failure of absences to pop out. It is thought that the explanation for this is that when one spots an orange item among red things, one is seeing the yellow in the orange (orange is a "binary" color, seen as composed of yellow and red), whereas one does not see the absence of yellow in a red object among orange objects (Wolfe, 2001). Again, absences do not pop out.

Absences cannot be used in direct search, but they can be used in indirect search. We can see this using negative cuing, i.e., presentation of a stimulus that in the context of a task induces subjects to divert attention from something. If subjects are told, truthfully, that a target will not appear on a red object, the result is more efficient search, but the advantage of negative cuing appears only very late in the perceptual process, arguably after the percept is already formed. Negative cuing makes search *less* efficient early in the perceptual process because the effect of telling subjects not to attend to X is to increase attention to X in early perceptual processing (Kawashima & Matsumoto, 2018). Indirect search may be more of a cognitive than a perceptual process.

Direct use in visual search may not be an all or nothing thing, and all visual search depends on the distractors, features of the scene, the value of what is being searched for, and prior history of search (Treisman & Gormican, 1988; Wolfe, 2001). And pop-out is a sufficient condition of a property being visually represented, but it may not be necessary. Still, the fact that absences do not pop out suggests that when we "see" absences, what is really happening is that a cognitive category is imposed on a visual representation that does not represent anything missing.

In a recent presentation in the City University of New York Cognitive Science series, Jorge Morales presented unpublished data on seeing absences (Morales & Firestone, 2020). Morales and Firestone used four figures that were presented in both an intact form and a form with a missing part: a butterfly without the one wing, a shirt without one sleeve, a bicycle without a wheel and a pair of trousers with a missing leg. They presented dots at various positions asking subjects to press one button if the dot was on an object and another button if the dot was on empty space. They found that subjects were fastest if the dot was on an object, slowest if on empty space not on a missing object part, and in between on a missing object part, e.g., the missing wing of a butterfly.

These results can be explained by appeal to object-based attention, a phenomenon to be discussed in Chapter 5. The basic idea of the phenomenon is that attention spreads within an object so that subjects who are attending to part of an object are faster at answering questions about another part of that object than they are about equidistant points that are not on the object. To apply this phenomenon to the Morales and Firestone result, one has to postulate that there is some kind of amodal completion of the missing part so that a dot on that part is attended to faster than if it was on empty space. The upshot is that this experiment better supports amodal completion of missing parts than perception of absence.

Returning to the case for perception being nonpropositional, my argument has partly been based on the fact that perception exhibits absence of what I called internal propositional structure.

Thus, perceptual contents could not be premises in the disjunctive syllogism. Suppose I reason from

1. Either perceptual content x obtains or perceptual content y obtains
2. It is not the case that perceptual content x obtains
3. So, perceptual content y obtains.

Premise 1 could not be a perceptual content because, as pointed out above, perceptual contents cannot have disjunctive internal logical structure. And premise 2 cannot be a perceptual content because perceptual contents cannot be negations. Premises 1 and 2 only make sense as judgments or beliefs. Anyone who thinks that perceptual contents can function in reasoning owes us an argument showing why we should understand the supposed premises in such reasoning as perceptual contents rather than as the contents of perceptual judgments.

A further problem for the view that perception has propositional content is that at least for some perceptual contents, children can have those contents or approximately those contents without any ability to reason with them. As I mentioned, I will present detailed evidence for perception of color in babies from 4–6 months to 11 months old without any sign of an ability to reason with color contents in that 4–6 to 11-month-old period.

If perception really were propositional, those propositional contents would lend themselves naturally to reasoning. At the same ages at which babies cannot use color information in reasoning, they can use size, shape, and kind properties in reasoning, so the fault does not lie in general reasoning abilities.

Disjunction

In the last two sections, I argued against conjunctive and negative perceptual contents. I will now very briefly tackle disjunctive perceptual contents. My line of thought here is that children 2 years old and under show no sign of disjunctive contents in decision-making or other forms of cognition, but if there really were disjunctive perceptual contents, one would expect that they would in some way be applied in cognitive processing.

First, I should acknowledge that 2-year-olds and many animals appear—at first glance—to use disjunctive reasoning. If a desirable object is put in one of two containers that are partially occluded so that the subject cannot see which one it is in, and then one container is shown to be empty, the children and animals will reliably search in the nonempty container. Many animals can pass this test (Völter & Call, 2017), though in some cases they have been found to pass only under very restricted conditions. Asian elephants have been shown to pass using olfactory cues but not visual cues. Great apes, some monkeys, ravens, and Clark's nut-crackers pass with no training. African gray parrots and dwarf goats pass only with repeated testing. Sheep and squirrel monkeys don't pass at all. Human children fail at 15 months but pass at 17 months (Mody & Carey, 2016). Indeed, using eye tracking, there is some sign of success on this task at 12 months (Cesana-Arlotti et al., 2018; Halberda, 2018).

However, as Mody and Carey (2016) and Leahy and Carey (2020) point out, this success could be due to a strategy of avoiding searching in a container that has been seen to be empty and does not show disjunctive reasoning. And they found many other items of evidence that these children do not exhibit disjunctive reasoning. One item is illustrated in Figure 4.4. There are three places a sticker can be hidden. A sticker is hidden in one of two cups on the right and in the cup on the left, in both cases behind a screen. The screen comes up and the child gets one chance to look in one of the cups. Three-year-olds and great apes only search in the left-hand cup 50% of the time despite the fact that they were shown that a sticker is certainly there. They divide the remaining 50% evenly among the two cups on the right. Even 4- and 5-year-olds are well below adult levels on this test. Another line of experimentation that exhibits failure to use disjunctive representation derives from an experiment by Redshaw and Suddendorf (2016). They constructed an inverted Y-shaped apparatus in which a desired item (stickers for children, a food for apes) was dropped in the tube so that it could come out on either branch of the Y. The subjects could keep the desired object if they caught

188 THE BORDER BETWEEN SEEING AND THINKING

Figure 4.4 Three cups are presented. A screen goes down and a sticker is put into one of the pair of cups on the right. A screen goes down on the left and a sticker is put into the one cup that is on the left. Children can turn over one cup to get the sticker but if they guess wrongly, they fail. Three-year-olds and great apes search the left hand cup 50% of the time, even though there is certainly a sticker in it. And they apportion their searches to the right side cups in equal proportion. Thanks to Susan Carey for this diagram. (See Leahy & Carey, 2020; Mody & Carey, 2016.)

it but if they missed it, it fell into an inaccessible place. Two-year olds and apes just put one hand under one of the openings instead of putting both hands under both. After nine trials, only 10% of the apes hit on the two-hand strategy. After eight trials, only 20% of the 2-year-olds were using two hands. And the successes may be due to reinforcement rather than actual understanding, since even 3-year-olds often regress to using just one hand. By contrast almost all the 4-year-olds used two hands from the start.

The point here is that if the children could see the inverted Y apparatus as involving a disjunctive route, one would expect them to use two hands. So they fact that they don't suggests lack of disjunction in perception. This is not strong evidence, but it is evidence.

Atomic propositional representations

Earlier I postponed treatment of the objection that my arguments have only ruled out certain kinds of logically complex propositionality but that perception might be restricted to propositionality that lacks that kind of complexity. I appeal to lack of logical complexity because it removes a reason for thinking that perceptions have the kind of inferential role that would ground their propositionality. The fundamental issue is inferential role. I will be examining the best case for such inference in perception, Bayesian inference, below in this chapter.[3] In the rest of this section, I will try to make an independent case against atomic propositional states in perception.

If perception is propositional, we should ask why there are no logically complex contents. Perhaps the logical limitations of perception are not due to its being nonpropositional, but rather to its sensory source? The idea would be this: Perception gets its information from the senses, and the senses only supply the materials for atomic propositions. So, according to this view, perception is propositional but the propositions of perception are always atomic because the architecture of the mind limits perception to information from the senses.

One problem with this explanation of putative atomic propositions in perception is that it is not true that the sole source of information in perception is sensory. There are substantial effects of cognition on perception, as will be discussed in Chapter 9. These effects are especially noticeable in the case of ambiguous perception. Another source of information in perception is the history of the species. Using controlled rearing experiments, Giorgio Vallortigara and his colleagues have shown many kinds of innate perceptual information in chicks (Vallortigara, 2021).

Another flaw in this this putative explanation of atomic propositions in perception is that many (if not all) stimuli are ambiguous. We don't see disjunctions in the case of ambiguous stimuli; rather, we have one percept or the other: Perception is a winner-takes-all faculty, where the winning perception can be a merger. (See Chapter 9 for examples of ambiguous stimuli.)[4]

Further, the world can supply perception with conditional inputs in which X is always followed immediately by Y. The information is there for perception to register that if X, then Y. Likewise, for conjunction: X and Y can always appear together in perception. I think a similar case can be made for negation and some forms of quantification. The information can be in the input, but perception nonetheless eschews the structured contents that would reflect such structured inputs. In sum, there is no good case for blaming the lack of logical complexity in perception on limitations in the sensory input.

Those who hold that perceptual contents are propositional and atomic must confront the fact that perceptual contents can be complex in many respects other than logical complexity. One such respect is relational perception. One can see something as next to something else or on top of something else or as twice as big as something else. Further, one can see what I referred to earlier as "ensemble" properties. Some examples are: average size, orientations, speed, colors, facial expressions, and level of diversity of

---

[3] On some views of inference, an inference is a kind of judgment and therefore cognitive rather than perceptual. For example, Ram Neta argues that inferences are judgments of the form "Premise, and therefore Conclusion" (Neta, 2013).

[4] Smell may not be a winner-takes-all sense but it may not be a perceptual sense either. (See Burge, 2010b.)

orientations, colors, and expressions (Bronfman, Brezis, Jacobson, & Usher, 2014; Haberman, Brady, & Alvarez, 2015b). For example, one can see average tilt of a group of tilted grids, but also average expression of a group of faces (Haberman, Brady, & Alvarez, 2015a). Some of these ensemble properties (also known as gists and as summary statistics) are processed at early to intermediate stages of the visual hierarchy, notably cortical areas V2 and V4 (Okazawa, Tajima, & Komatsu, 2015).

And ensemble properties can be coupled with relational perception. One can see one cloud of dots as more numerous but less dense than another. One can see a point as the centroid (average position) of a cloud of dots. Subjects can track the centroid of a group of disks, even under conditions in which attention is drawn off by a difficult task. I'll say a bit more about this latter point.

In the multiple object tracking paradigm, a group of figures (e.g., disks) are presented. See Figure 4.5. Some of the disks blink or are otherwise indicated. The subject is supposed to track those objects as they move about in a random way. Most subjects can track about four objects if they do not move too quickly or up to eight objects if they are moving more slowly (Alvarez & Franconeri, 2007). Subjects occasionally noted that they could see the average position of both the disks they were tracking and those they were not tracking and this was verified (Alvarez & Oliva, 2008).

In sum, there is a lot of structure in perception, but the logical structure that is characteristic of propositional representation is notably missing. This is a puzzle for those who say perceptual content is propositional. They have to explain why complexity is present in perceptual content but not the kinds of complexity that would be characteristic of propositional representation.

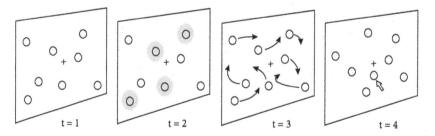

Figure 4.5 Sequence of events in a basic multiple object tracking experiment. Eight disks appear on the screen, four are indicated as the ones the subject is supposed to track, the indications of the four disappear, the disks move randomly. At the end the subject is asked to identify the four that were first cued. Most people can track four objects fairly reliably. From Pylyshyn (2007a), under a Creative Commons license.

Rivalry and propositional perception

The last section focused on the claim that perception is propositional but atomic. This section won't concern atomic propositional perception per se. The discussion below will use the phenomenon of binocular rivalry discussed in Chapter 2. In order to explain why binocular rivalry is relevant to propositional perception, I will have to explain some of the details of binocular rivalry.

The point I will make derives from rivalry between processing streams specific to the individual eyes, but similar points apply to monocular rivalry (i.e., rivalry between different parses of a stimulus seen with one eye). As noted in Chapter 2, rivalry, both binocular and monocular, involves competition between contents as well as, in the case of binocular rivalry, eye-specific processing streams.

Chapter 2 explained that rivalry requires "incompatible" stimuli. In cases of conflict between the actual properties of the stimulus and perceived properties of the stimulus, what counts is perceived properties (Chopin, Mamassian, & Blake, 2012) so what is required for rivalry is not "incompatible" stimuli but "incompatible" representations. The winner-takes-all nature of perception comes into play even if there is no relevant conflict. If there is no conflict, subjects "fuse" the percepts, but that is still a kind of winner-takes-all percept, since the individual percepts lose out to a merged percept.

What is the nature of this incompatibility? One major divide is between global and local differences of stimuli. It turns out, interestingly, that *local* differences are what mainly count for incompatibility. A key fact needed to understand what follows is that mere luminance differences don't contribute to incompatibility so long as the items of different luminance are of the same shape and contrast polarity. Contrast polarity is a matter of being lighter or darker than the background. Both the 'X' and the 'O' of Figure 4.6 are light shapes on a darker background and so the 'X' and the 'O' are the same in contrast polarity. The items of Figure 4.6 are compatible locally because the squares are of the same shape and contrast polarity but differ globally ('X' vs. 'O'). And all the subjects in (Carlson & He, 2004) experienced fusion of these items rather than rivalry. Similar results were obtained by stimuli that differed in global motion but were matched in local properties. And other experiments using more complex setups have also reported that global differences don't matter if there are no relevant local differences (Freeman & Li, 2009). The point I am making here is that if your picture of "incompatible stimuli" is what would be natural to a theorizer who assimilates perception to perceptual judgment, you should be troubled by this result. The natural judgment on seeing the 'X' conflicts with the natural perceptual judgment on seeing the 'O,' so why aren't they "incompatible"?

Part of the explanation is that some properties are represented in monocular circuits in the visual cortex, that is, circuits in visual cortex that process signals

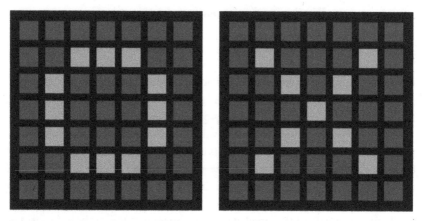

Figure 4.6 These are sample stimuli used in a binocular rivalry experiment. Each image is projected to a different eye. Thanks to Thomas Carlson for this figure. See (Carlson & He, 2004)

from only one eye. Other properties—more holistic properties—are processed in binocular circuits. The binocular processing tends toward higher visual areas where receptive field sizes are much larger than in monocular areas. (As explained in Chapter 1, the receptive field of a visual neuron is the area of space that it responds to.) The receptive field size of the earliest visual cortex can be as little as half a degree, whereas the receptive field size in higher level areas of cortex can be 30°. Binocular rivalry is partly rivalry between the streams specific to the eyes, so it depends in part on monocularly represented features, whereas what we naïvely think of as the contents of perception, e.g., seeing an 'X' vs. seeing an 'O,' are represented binocularly in higher areas.

This point is accentuated by experiments on faces shown in Figure 4.7. A masculine and feminine face are presented, each to a different eye. If the subject attends to local features or to parts of the faces, such as the eyes, the subject experiences standard binocular rivalry, as indicated in the diagram by "Alternating percepts." Standard binocular rivalry also occurs if the faces are presented upside down. However, if the subjects attend to holistic features such as gender, there is fusion instead of rivalry: the subject sees an androgynous face that blends masculine and feminine features (Klink, Boucherie, Denys, Roelfsema, & Self, 2017). Although binocular rivalry is in part rivalry between holistic representations, the local features play a strong role in determining the difference between rivalry and merger.

Why is this relevant to the issue of the propositionality of perception? Many advocates of propositionality of perception seem to be thinking of perception as much like what I am calling perceptual judgment. A natural propositional

PERCEPTION IS NONPROPOSITIONAL AND NONCONCEPTUAL 193

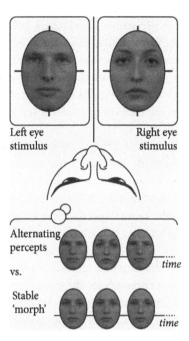

Figure 4.7 Binocular rivalry stimuli. The masculine face is presented to the left eye and the feminine face to the right eye. If the subject is attending to local features or parts such as the eyes, standard binocular rivalry ensues. This is indicated by the label "alternating percepts. If the subject is attending to holistic features such as gender or the identity of the person, the subject sees a morphed androgynous face, as pictured. Thanks to Chris Klink for this figure. See (Klink et al., 2017).

judgment concerning the item on the right of Figure 4.6 occupying the whole visual field would be that there is one thing, an 'X' in front of me; and that conflicts with the natural propositional judgment concerning the item on the left that there is one thing, an 'O' in front of me. So, if the content of perception matches the content of perceptual judgment, the question arises as to why rivalry isn't determined by that conflict? The extent to which perception is "local feature placing" in which properties are attributed to areas of space and objects allows for rivalry to be determined by tiny detailed features.

Moreover, if the propositionalist thinks of the contents of perception along the lines of "There is one thing, a feminine face in front of me" and "There is one thing, a masculine face, in front of me." Then it is hard to explain why there should ever be fusion, since the propositions remain the same, whatever one is attending to. The effect of attention to details is to favor the amplification of monocular features, but that is irrelevant to the global propositional conflict. Certainly the concern of propositionalists to see perceptual beliefs as justified via inference from perceptions (McDowell, 1994; Munton, 2016; Pautz, 2011) suggests that sort of propositional content rather than contents about the third pixel from the left in the middle row, or other details. This is not a knockdown argument against propositionalists. Propositionalists are free to adopt propositional contents involving details in response to the very criticisms that I have been raising. However, such contents would undermine much of the motivation for propositionalism.

The local nature of binocular rivalry creates difficulties for many theories of perception. For example, the "predictive processing" approach (Clark, 2016) regards perception as a matter of "controlled hallucination," in which hypotheses—including hypotheses involving general knowledge of what might be seen—confront the data. As mentioned earlier, a commonly used binocular rivalry stimulus is one in which a face is shown to one eye and a house to the other. What the subject experiences is an alternation between a face and house perception, in which each fills the whole visual field for a brief period. Advocates of the predictive processing approach see the issue in terms of conflict between a face hypothesis and a house hypothesis, fed by the general knowledge that nothing is both a face and a house. Andy Clark, following Hohwy et al. (2008), puts the reasoning as follows:

> But why, under such circumstances, do we not simply experience a combined or interwoven image: a kind of house/face mash-up for example? Although such partially combined percepts do occur, and may persist for brief periods of time, they are never complete (bits of each stimulus are missing) or stable. Such mash-ups do not constitute a viable hypothesis given our more general knowledge about the visual world. For it is part of that general knowledge that, for example, houses and faces do not occupy the same place, at the same scale, at the same time. This kind of general knowledge may itself be treated as a systemic prior, albeit one pitched at a relatively high degree of abstraction (such priors are sometimes referred to as "hyper-priors"). In the case at hand, what is thereby captured is the fact that "the prior probability of both a house and face being co-localized in time and space is extremely small." ... This, indeed, may be the deep explanation of the existence of competition between the higher-level hypotheses in the first place—these hypotheses must compete because the system has learned that "only one object can exist in the same place at the same time." ... The constant switching that characterizes our subjective experience in binocular rivalry cases is thus explained. The switching is the inevitable result of the probabilistic prediction error minimizing regime as constrained by the hyperprior that the world in which we live and act is one in which unitariness and coherence are the default. (Clark, 2018, p. 80)

But as we have seen, general knowledge hypotheses about faces being different from houses and one thing in one place at one time play little or no role in determining the difference between compatible and incompatible stimuli. The main determinants are low-level local features. To be clear, I am not claiming that the low-level local nature of binocular rivalry refutes the predictive coding point of view. The high-level explanations of the sort described above are natural but not inevitable on a predictive coding approach.

The prevalence of local over global features in perception is not limited to binocular rivalry. Biological motion using point-light displays in which dots represent key positions on the body such as the head and the joints is very recognizable. Indeed people can easily discriminate gender, emotion, and intention from these displays as well as activities such as crawling, jumping, rowing, walking, and waving (Sun, Wang, Huang, Ji, & Ding, 2021). Further, babies show preferential attention to biological point light displays in the first few days of life and newly hatched chicks do the same (Sun et al., 2021). We can distinguish global from local biological motion, e.g., by scrambling global motion, leaving local motion intact. Automatic global processing turns out to be diminished or absent in autistic people. Sun et al. showed that local biological motion is more important than global biological in "breaking through" the masking effect of continuous flash suppression. (See the discussion in Chapters 2 and 9 of continuous flash suppression for an explanation of "breaking through.")

To summarize where we are in the discussion: I argued that perception lacks internal and external logical structure and then discussed the issue of whether perception's lack of internal logical structure could be due to perceptual representations being propositional but atomic. I noted that sensory input exhibits regularities and complexities that could lead to internal logical structure if the system allowed for it. These points were intended to undermine the idea that impoverished input could support atomic propositional perception. I then noted various kinds of complexities in perceptual representations such as representations of relations, means, and variances, noting that perceptual representations are not atomic in nonlogical respects. I then launched into a long discussion of binocular rivalry, the point of which was to show that perception cannot be assimilated to perceptual judgment as it is normally conceived.

How do iconicity, nonconceptuality, and nonpropositionality fit together?

It may seem that one could move from the claim that (1) perception is nonpropositional and (2) conceptual representations are constituted by their roles in propositional representations to (3) the conclusion that perception is nonconceptual. As mentioned earlier, this inference would be oversimple. It is their function in propositional representations that constitute concepts, but that does not preclude concepts functioning outside of their constitutive role in propositional representation. Perception might for all I've said be conceptual though nonconstitutively so. Although the reasoning just presented is not dispositive, it does put the burden on advocates of conceptual perception to present evidence for it, evidence I have seen no hint of. I will discuss this point further in connection with my main argument for nonconceptual perception in Chapter 6.

The systematicity and generality of conceptual and propositional thought requires discursive format. Iconic representations have structure, but iconic structure is inadequate to fully explain the degree and kind of systematicity and generality of thought. Gareth Evans argued that conceptual thought required certain sorts of combinations of concepts. More specifically, if one can think that a is F and that b is G, one must also be capable of thinking that a is G and that b is F (Evans, 1982). Jerry Fodor argued that thought is systematic: If you can think the thought that John loves Mary, you can also think the thought that Mary loves John. These ideas have much truth in them, though there are limits (Beck, 2012; Block, 1995b). In order to explain how our cognitive representations can have systematicity and generality to the extent that they have them, we need to allow that thought has discursive format. See Hartry Field's "Mental Representation" for an argument in that vicinity (Field, 1978).

Iconic representations can be used as concepts, as noted earlier in connection with Berkeley's notion of the function of an image of a particular triangle in representing all triangles. Further, nothing precludes a system in which nonconceptual representations have discursive format. Still, we can expect discursive representations to be conceptual and we can expect iconic representations to be nonconceptual. Discursive format is a natural fit with conceptuality (and propositionality) because of the way representations have to function to be conceptual and propositional. Similarly, iconic format is a natural fit for nonconceptuality and nonpropositionality.

If, contrary to what I am arguing for, perception is in part conceptual, would the concepts have to be the same concepts as used in thought? If there were perception-specific concepts, they would have to have a role in reasoning or inference of some kind; otherwise what would make them concepts at all? In the section after next, I will examine the best candidate for perceptual inference, Bayesian updating. If Bayesian updating is inferential—contrary to what I will be arguing for—the propositional and conceptual representations involved might concern perceptual processing that is not accessible to conscious thought. I will argue that Bayesian updating does not support the use of perceptual representations in any kind of specifically perceptual reasoning and so does not support perception-specific concepts.

I keep saying that perception is nonconceptual, but then I also acknowledged percepts that are—as I said—conceptualized in the sense of incorporated into a conceptual structure. How is it possible for there to be conceptualized percepts? Why isn't that incoherent? One example is the use of perception-based concepts to determine whether any object is revealed by turning a capital 'D' counter-clockwise 90° and placing it on a capital 'J.' In answering that question, you have to take perceptual representations and use them in thought. I am describing that as conceptualizing the perceptual representations. This is not incoherent because it involves the embedding of perceptual representations in a cognitive envelope.

What would a conceptualized percept be? As will be explained in Chapter 5, conceptualized representations in working memory can involve considerable abstraction from perceptual representations, to the point where two quite different percepts can be conceptualized in the same way. Kwak and Curtis (2022) show that how a perception is conceptualized in working memory depends on the task. In particular, a cloud of moving dots and an oriented grid can be conceptualized in the same way given the right task.

Still, the dependence of conceptualization on task does not reveal what the format is of conceptualized representations. In Kwak and Curtis (2022) the conceptualized version of the perception of both moving dots and oriented grid is an iconic representation of an angle that they depict as an oriented stripe. Another possibility, mentioned earlier, is a descriptive concept that has some kind of a slot for perceptual materials (Balog, 2009b; Block, 2006; Papineau, 2002). Another is the addition to a percept of a descriptive tag.

These formats though don't tell us how conceptualization can occur. As I will explain in Chapter 5, a model of what it is to conceptualize a percept is provided by the global workspace theory.

What is the difference between a conceptualized percept used in thought and a nonconceptualized percept used in thought? I mentioned earlier that we cannot store raw unconceptualized color shades in working memory, as shown by the fact that once a fine-grained shade has disappeared from the screen in conditions that discourage iconic memory and fragile visual short term memory, subjects cannot easily identify which fine grained shade they saw (Raftopoulos, 2010).

Another difference is in function. A concrete example may help. Consider a sentence written down with two slots: "__ is more vivid than __." If I had sample color patches, I could insert them into the slots in the sentence without forming concepts of the colors. But what if the samples were mental images—could they just be stuck into slots in a representation in the belief box?

Suppose that is possible. Suppose perceptual image 1 is in the first slot and perceptual image 2 is in the second slot. Suppose that there is another sentence in the belief box with the same format, but perceptual image 2 is in the first slot and perceptual image 3 is in the second slot. Is this setup sufficient for the subject to draw the conclusion that perceptual image 1 is more vivid than perceptual image 3? If so, then the perceptual images are functioning in a conceptualized manner. If not, then at least some of them are not functioning in a conceptualized manner. This function in thought and reasoning provides an important difference between a conceptualized perceptual image and a nonconceptualized perceptual image.

The fact that perception cannot be conjunctive, disjunctive, conditional, negative, or universal is tied to the iconic format of perception. To have *productive* disjunction, conjunction, etc., there must be format elements that play the role of logical constants. One can certainly imagine using pictures as logical constants, but in so doing we would be giving them a function that treats them as discursive symbols. Part of what analog mirroring involves is a correspondence between degrees of difference in representational parameters and what is represented. It is hard to see how a representation that is iconic by that standard could be a logical constant.

Laws of appearance

Adam Pautz has argued for what he calls "laws of appearance." These "laws of appearance" may seem similar to the points about lack of logical structure in perception earlier in this chapter. Pautz (2017a, 2017b) gives eight examples, which I will paraphrase, shortening when appropriate. (See also Pautz, 2020.)

 I. It's impossible to have an experience with the content *something is pure blue and also greenish blue*.
 II. It's impossible to have an experience with the content *something is spherical and cubicle*.
 III. It's impossible to have an experience with the content *blue is intrinsically overall more like green than purple*.
 IV. It's impossible to have an experience whose only content *is* a wildly disjunctive content—for example, *that thing is round and green and directly in front of me or it is square and purple and 45 degrees to the left*.
 V. It's impossible to have an experience whose *only* content is *that thing's facing surface is round* (i.e., without any information about the chromatic or achromatic colors of the thing or its background).
 VI. It's impossible to have an experience that only has the content *that thing is cubicle*, but that doesn't have any de se content about the thing's apparent shape from a particular point of view (as it were, a "God's eye" visual experience of a cubicle object, from no point of view).

VII. It's impossible to have a single experience whose content is *a is red all over and b is wholly behind a*.

VIII. It's impossible to have a visual experience in which one *phenomenally* represents a "high-level" content like *that is a pine tree* or *that is a Republican*, but in which one phenomenally represents *no* "low-level" content at all.

None of these are quite the same as my claim that perception cannot be conjunctive, disjunctive, conditional, negative or universal. The closest is IV, the law that rules out wildly disjunctive content. In my view, wildly disjunctive content is ruled out only because disjunctive content is ruled out. I agree with some of these cases, but I think others are not truths at all. Their plausibility stems from the difficulty we have in imagining the kind of perceptual experience that would be involved (Speaks, 2017). But that is because visual imagery is conditioned by normal perception. I will go through these one by one, more or less in order.

I believe that the perceptual ascription of pure blue and also greenish blue (Pautz's (I)) is difficult to imagine for the reasons discussed earlier in this chapter. They are "contraries" because of the opponent structure of color vision. Prior to Billock et al., I think that one might have suggested a law of appearance that nothing could look both reddish and greenish all over at the same time. The overall lesson is that difficulty in imagining is a problematic guide to the limits of perception.

Pautz's (I) may be true of us but not fundamental to all perception. In the case of (II), the perceptual ascription of being spherical and being cubical, there may be a known phenomenon that qualifies. Seeing a cube and a sphere in the same "integration field" in the periphery of vision might be such a case. The visual system registers sphericity and cubicality but has no information sufficient to determine which property goes with which object. The result would be a percept that combines the attribution of sphericalness and cubicness in a confused way. See the discussion of crowding in Chapter 3.

Perceptual representation of *blue is intrinsically overall more like green than purple* (III) is ruled out for the same reason as logically complex contents: they are not possible in an iconic system. The predicate '__ is more like __ than __' may not be representable in an iconic system, and adding "intrinsically" doesn't change that. In this case we have a prohibition that applies to all perception, not just conscious perception.

As I said, I agree with Pautz's IV. Since disjunctive contents are ruled out, so are wildly disjunctive contents.

Pautz's V rules out ascription of just shape—without any color information. (This is also discussed in (Pautz, 2017b; Speaks, 2017). We can perceptually experience movement in the periphery of vision without any chromatic or achromatic color, so I doubt that shape without color can be conclusively ruled out.

Pautz's VI rules out allocentric without egocentric content. (Allocentric frames represent objects relative to one another, whereas egocentric frames represent objects in a coordinate system based in the perceiver. The egocentric coordinate systems are most directly linked to action.) Allocentric and egocentric content are to some extent separately computed in vision. I would not be shocked if it were discovered that certain kinds of brain damage (to egocentric systems) could result in this kind of perception. There are two visual systems in mammals, dorsal and ventral. The dorsal system is probably entirely egocentric (Dijkerman, Milner, & Carey, 1998) whereas higher levels of the ventral system are allocentric. (See Chapter 2 on the visual hierarchy.) So, in principle, stimulation of higher levels of the ventral system in the temporal lobe might produce purely allocentric experience, contrary to Pautz's VI.

I am also skeptical about the truth of VII. Given that vision involves a multiplicity of systems, nothing rules out some kind of representation of objects, one of which occludes the other.

I would say something similar about VIII. Normally, high-level activation requires low-level activation. When we form an image involving a high-level content, e.g., an image of a face of someone we know, we activate the high-level face representation by activating low-level representations, including representations in V1. It seems that we do not have the ability to directly activate high-level visual areas. But a high-level representation without low-level activation might in principle be produced by neural stimulation to high-level areas.

I concede that these cases are difficult, and I am not that confident of my responses. I am sure that Pautz's suggestions will stimulate a great deal of discussion.

Bayesian "inference"

Recall that I am anchoring "inference" to content-based reasoning transitions among representational states, the paradigm instances of which involve the presence of identifiable premises and conclusions in which the conclusions are derived by reasoning from the premises. (Of course, vagueness in "inference" may be reflected in vagueness in "premise," "reasoning," and "conclusion.") Unsurprisingly, I don't think that perceptual representations are ever the premises or conclusions of inferences. In this section, I will start with some general remarks about inference in perception and then move to rebutting arguments based on the Bayesian point of view for inference in perception.[5]

It is often assumed that perceptions are premises or conclusions of inferences. For example, in a recent article, Chris Frith (2017, paragraph 7) describes the perception of convexity and concavity this way: "Our brain creates the illusion because we expect light to come from above, and so we can infer the 3D shapes from the shading." Endorsement of inference in perception is often found in the predictive coding paradigm. For example, Lupyan and Clark discuss the Cornsweet illusion in which two tiles that are the same in color look to be different in color because of misleading illumination. They say that "the brain uses what it has learned about typical patterns of illumination and reflectance to infer (falsely, in this case) that the two central tiles must be different shades of gray" (Lupyan & Clark, 2015, p. 280).

Following Herman von Helmholtz (1866), Richard Gregory (1974), Irving Rock (1983), and David Marr (1982), many philosophers and psychologists endorse inference in perception.[6] Marr divided perception into measurement and inference. Patrick Cavanagh (2011, p. 1539) concedes that not much is known about the supposed inferences, using "measure" in Marr's sense:

> Deconstructing the mechanisms of inference is difficult and not yet very rewarding. There are too many plausible alternatives and too many flinty-eyed reviewers who can see the obvious shortcomings. So one goal of this review is to underline the difficulty of research in high-level vision as well as its importance. . . . it became clear that many models were premature and underconstrained by data. Rather than risk the gauntlet of justifiable skepticism, most vision research turned to the more solid ground of how vision measures the world, putting off to the future the harder question of how it draws inferences.

Inferences are sometimes postulated to explain perceptual constancies. Jerry Fodor (2015, p. 205) argued that all perception is conceptual as follows:

> on the one hand, there is *no perceiving* without *perceiving as*; and, on the other hand, there is no *perceiving as* without conceptualization; and, on the third hand, there is no conceptualization without concepts.

---

[5] The rest of this chapter is much shortened and revised version of Block (2018), as modified in response to criticisms from Michael Rescorla (2020) and Steven Gross (2020).
[6] Helmholtz repeats what ibn al-Haytham said in 1024 about inference in perception, along with the anecdotes used to justify it, and without attribution (Cavanagh, 2011).

So, he concludes, perceiving is inherently conceptual. Fodor (2007, p. 114) justified the idea that there is no perceiving as without conceptualization on the ground that "all the perceptual representations that are accessible to consciousness exhibit constancy effects and, by pretty general consensus, constancy effects are the products of inferences." Fodor's argument that perception is conceptual is based on the idea (one that I agree with and that is presupposed in this book) that concepts are constitutively connected to propositions and the hallmark of propositions is inference.[7]

If retinal stimulation could be due to a concave object illuminated from below or from a convex object illuminated from above, the visual system is built to prefer the latter perception. (Indeed it is built to prefer the perception that assigns the direction of the light source as above and slightly to the left [Mamassian, Landy, & Maloney, 2002].) According to one point of view, the tendency to see light as coming from above stems from inference from an explicitly represented propositional representation—an assumption—that light comes from above (Rock, 1983). Other examples of supposed premises in the visual system are that nearby objects block the view of objects that are further away but not vice versa and that objects are typically convex.

However, the fact that the visual system respects a regularity does not show that it uses a premise concerning that regularity, for example, a premise that light comes from above. As Nico Orlandi has observed, one might as well suppose that a smoke detector that relies on the fact that smoke particles block light uses a premise to the effect that smoke particles block light (2014).

In some cases in which the visual system respects a regularity, we know the mechanism by which this happens and we can see that the mechanism cannot be regarded as inferential. For example, the primate retina involves two kinds of sensors, cones and rods. The cones feed to an intermediate layer of bipolar cells, and they in turn feed to retinal ganglion cells. Ganglion cells have been shown to compute predictions of the motion of objects (Liu, Hong, Rieke, & Manookin, 2021). Are these motions inferred? Liu et al. showed that the mechanism is that when a bipolar cell is activated, that activation spreads to neighboring bipolar cells. Those adjacent bipolar cells are "primed" so that if they are then activated by cones, they send a very strong signal to the ganglion cells that they are connected to. As a result, the effects of motion can "ripple" across the network of bipolar cells. This is an "analog" mechanism that on its face does not involve any states that could be considered premises or conclusions. If this process is considered a

---

[7] In the same 2007 article, Fodor appears to be saying that iconic representations are nonconceptual and that some perceptual representations are iconic. Kati Balog (2009a) argues that the only way to make sense of this view is that what Fodor means is that unconscious subpersonal representations of perception are nonconceptual. If so, Fodor would seem to have been unaware that constancies operate in unconscious perception. (See also Margolis & Laurence, 2012.)

case of inference, then the notion of inference has been cheapened to the point where it cannot be regarded as closely tied to premises and conclusions.

Recently, inferential accounts of perception have relied on an alleged form of inference based on Bayesian updating. Idealized Bayesian accounts of visual perception compute the probabilities of various configurations of stimuli in the environment on the basis of prior probabilities of those environmental configurations and likelihoods of retinal stimulation if those environmental configurations obtain. Bayes' theorem states that the probability of a hypothesis about the environment (e.g., that there is a certain distribution of colors on a surface) given retinal stimulation is proportional to the prior probability of that hypothesis multiplied by the probability of the retinal stimulation given the hypothesis. If h is the environmental hypothesis, e is the evidence from retinal stimulation and $p(h|e)$ is the probability of h given e, then $p(h|e)$ is proportional to $p(e|h) \times p(h)$. $p(e|h)$ is the "likelihood" (of the retinal stimulation given the environmental hypothesis), and $p(h)$ is the prior probability of the environmental hypothesis. (An equivalence rather than a statement of proportionality requires a normalizing factor so that probabilities sum to 1.)

In idealized Bayesian updating, the system uses the previous probability assigned to the environmental hypothesis as the prior in changing the hypothesis about the environment in response to new retinal stimulation. So, idealized Bayesian updating requires multiplying one's current prior probability estimate times one's current estimate of likelihood to get the probability of the environmental hypothesis, given current stimulation. Then the probability of the environmental hypothesis becomes the new prior. The most plausible versions of these theories are hierarchical in that the visual system is divided into stages with distinct priors and likelihoods at each stage, as explained in the section of Chapter 2 on the visual hierarchy. I say "idealized" because it is known that Bayesian calculations of the sort described having to do with perceptual hypotheses cannot be performed in real time by a system that is as computationally limited as we are. Many different sorts of approximations to idealized Bayesian computations have been proposed.

The problem, though, with approximations to Bayesian computations is that they need not involve the slightest use of Bayesian reasoning. An example from a recent article by Brian Leahy and Susan Carey will help to make this point (Leahy & Carey, 2020). Suppose I am looking for my keys. Suppose further that I find it easier to imagine locations in proportion to previously seen locations of my keys. I may tend to look in the easiest location to imagine. If the keys are not there, I may tend to look at the next easiest place to imagine. We can suppose that previous observed locations of my keys reflect the probability that the keys are in one of those locations now. So my behavior reflects the probability of locations of my keys, but not as a result of any sort of probabilistic representation. Indeed, a person could be able to engage in successive simulations of this sort without any ability to conceptualize alternative possibilities. In fact, as Leahy and Carey argue, this process characterizes the behavior of 2-year-olds in some experimental situations. They argue further that 2-year-olds are incapable of representing alternative possibilities, a prerequisite for probabilistic reasoning.

I mentioned earlier in this chapter in the section on disjunction some of the evidence that 2-year-olds cannot represent alternative possibilities. Recall that Redshaw and Suddendorf showed that 2-year-olds failed to hold both hands under an inverted Y apparatus. Apparently, they visually simulated the desired object going one way or the other instead of representing both possibilities (Leahy & Carey, 2020).

The subject I am discussing is probabilistic representation in perception, not cognition (thinking, reasoning, deciding). And it is probabilistic representation, not representation of probabilities. Let me explain the difference. The probabilistic perceptual representations at issue here are of this sort: <red, there$_i$, .7>, to be read as a representation of redness at the location indicated by "there$_i$," with a .7 probability. But what if what is represented in perception is not redness but itself a probability, say that the probability is .3 that something is red? This is a representation *of a probability*. Humans certainly have cognitive representations of probabilities. We know that if A causally engenders B, then the presence of A makes B more probable. And we use such representations in reasoning and problem solving (Gopnik et al., 2004; Griffiths & Tenenbaum, 2006). Randy Gallistel and his colleagues have provided some evidence of representations *of probabilities* in perception (Gallistel, Krishan, Liu, Miller, & Latham, 2014), though I am not persuaded that this study concerns perception as opposed to perceptual judgment. If there is perception of probability, the question arises as to whether there could be a *probabilistic representation of probability*, for example, a representation of the form: <probability of redness of .3, there$_i$, .7>. (If this seems unintelligible, note that I can have a .9 credence that the probability of decay of a certain subatomic particle is .1.) In any case, the discussion in the rest of this chapter concerns probabilistic representation, not representation of probabilities; and in perception, not cognition.

Bayesian realism

Often, Bayesian theories of perception are held as computations in an ideal observer, an observer who uses Bayesian principles to optimally compute what is in the environment on the basis of retinal stimulation. Ideal observer theories are instrumentalist in that they are not committed to the representation in real visual systems of priors or likelihoods or computations using them within the system.

Further, even when actual data approximate to the predictions of ideal observer models, we cannot infer Bayesian realism. For example, Maloney and Mamassian show how non-Bayesian reinforcement learning can result in behavior that comports well with an ideal Bayesian observer (Maloney & Mamassian, 2009). So Bayesian models, construed from the ideal observer point of view, do not license attributions of inference in perception (Colombo & Seriès, 2012; Rescorla, 2015a).

It is common for those who emphasize Bayesian processes in perception to appeal to global optimality. For example, Lupyan and Clark (p. 280) seem to try to justify the claim about inference quoted above on the basis of a more general appeal to Bayes optimality of perceptual processing. They say, referencing (Brown & Friston, 2012): "In the world we actually live in, these particular prior beliefs or neural expectations are provably 'Bayes optimal'—that is, they represent the globally best method for inferring the state of the world from the ambient sensory evidence." Many perceptual processes are Bayes optimal, but many are not. As Dobromir Rahnev and Rachel Denison note in a review of suboptimal processes in perception, there is an extensive literature documenting suboptimal performance (Rahnev & Denison, 2018). In any case, Bayes optimality is neutral between instrumentalist and realist construals.

What would show that something that deserves to be called Bayesian inference actually occurs in perception? In the crudest implementation, there would be a representation of prior probabilities, a representation of likelihoods, and computation over these values. (Additional arithmetic complexity would be added by utility functions that compare the utility of the various environmental hypotheses.) Dobromir Rahnev suggests that any realist model of Bayesian perceptual computation would require a set S of stimuli, a set r of internal responses, and a model of the probability of each internal response given one of the stimuli (Rahnev, 2019). As he notes, Bayes' theorem can invert this model to compute the likelihood of each stimulus for a given internal response. And these likelihoods multiplied by the prior probabilities of each stimulus would yield the posterior distribution. In practice, realism about Bayesian calculations can often be quite elusive, since the various forms of approximation have varying kinds of relations to the idealized computations. It can be difficult to know what is required for Bayesian realism.

Recent debates about Bayesianism in perception have appealed to David Marr's famous three levels of description of perception. The top level, the computational level, specifies the problem computationally, whereas the next level down, the algorithmic level, specifies how the input and output are represented and what processes are supposed to move from the input and output. To use one of Marr's examples, in the characterization of a cash register, the computational level would be arithmetic. One variant of the algorithmic level would specify a base 10 numerical system using Arabic numerals plus the techniques that elementary school students learn concerning adding the least significant digits first. An alternative to this type of algorithm and representation might use binary representation and an algorithm level involving AND and X-OR gates (Block, 1995b). The lowest level, the implementation level, asks how the algorithms are implemented in hardware. In an old-fashioned cash register, implementation would involve gears and in older computer implementations of binary arithmetic, magnetic cores that can be in either one of two states (McClamrock, 1991).

Many prominent Bayesians say that Bayesians are working at the computational level. For example, Griffiths et al.: "Most Bayesian models of cognition are defined at Marr's (1982) 'computational level,' characterizing the problem people are solving and its ideal solution. Such models make no direct claims about cognitive processes—what Marr termed the 'algorithmic level'" (Griffiths & Pouget, 2012, p. 417). Further support for the computational level comes from the fact that many of the algorithms that approximate the normative Bayesian computation presuppose only probabilistic transitions among states and so do not use probabilistic representations (Gross, 2020; Sanborn & Chater, 2016).

In an argument for Bayesian realism, Michael Rescorla notes the variety of models that he counts as realist. He says (2020, p. 48): "One might ask why these diverse physical implementations all count as credal states. What do the implementations have in common, such that they count as ways of attaching subjective probabilities to hypotheses?" As he notes, to answer that question we would need to know what it is to attach a subjective probability to a hypothesis, and the literature on that subject is "disappointing." Although there are models that are not clearly realist or instrumentalist, there are also many models whose status is clear. I don't aim to refute Bayesian realism, but I will be suggesting that instrumentalism is a viable alternative to it. According to instrumentalism, Bayesian computations are useful, but should be thought of in an "as-if" mode. My aim is to argue that there is no compelling reason to prefer realism to instrumentalism.

Rescorla has ably defended Bayesian realism. I think his best arguments involve the predictive value of assuming that perceptual systems represent certain prior probabilities (Rescorla, 2015a, 2015b, 2020). For example, the assumption of a "slow motion prior," in which slow distal speeds are favored, predicts that in situations of low contrast or low luminance, the prior probability is given greater weight relative to sensory evidence, so speed is underestimated (Culham, 2012; de Bellis, Schulte-Mecklenbeck, Brucks, Herrmann, & Hertwig, 2018; Gross, 2020). (That is, the likelihood function will predict very similar sensory evidence for a wide range of stimuli, so the importance of the likelihood will decrease compared to the importance of the prior in comparing one speed with another

[Gross, 2020].) And it does appear that there are conditions in which drivers will drive faster in low light conditions (though apparently not in fog [Pretto, Vidal, & Chatziastros, 2008]). Rescorla also discusses a phenomenon known as motion-induced position shift that involves objects moving translationally—e.g., from one side of the screen to the other while at the same time a pattern inside the object is also moving. The overall result is that the perception of the translational motion is shifted in the direction of pattern motion. What is most impressive about this case is that model assumptions keyed to one case explained many other cases.

Another of Rescorla's arguments notes that we have good Bayesian models of how priors evolve in response to changing environmental conditions. For example, such models predict that if one exposes a subject to stimulation in which luminance and stiffness are correlated, the priors will change so that stiff objects are seen as more luminant. And this prediction is born out. In another such case, subjects in a shape task were exposed to lighting that did not come from above and priors changed as expected, including in a new task environment in which they were judging lighting. These results argue for representations of prior probabilities. Other results argue for representations of likelihoods (van Bergen, Ma, Pratte, & Jehee, 2015; Walker, Cotton, Ma, & Tolias, 2020). (See Block, 2018.) These predictive successes demand explanation. The question is: Is the right explanation that the models are approximately true?

Overall, Rescorla says, a realist interpretation yields explanatory and predictive generalizations that would be missed on an instrumentalist interpretation. His reasoning here seems similar to Richard Boyd's "miracle" argument: that the best explanation of successful prediction is that the entities referred to in the theories that generate the prediction really exist and to a first approximation really have the properties ascribed to them in the theory (Boyd, 1989). The specific application here is that our ability to predict how priors will change supports the hypothesis that priors are really represented in perception.

Rescorla sums up his realist case this way (2020, p. 57):

In my opinion, instrumentalism about Bayesian cognitive science is no more plausible than instrumentalism regarding physics, chemistry, biology, or any other successful science. Just as the explanatory success of physics provides evidence for gravity, or the explanatory success of chemistry provides evidence for the chemical bond, or the explanatory success of biology provides evidence for evolution by natural selection, so does the explanatory success of Bayesian cognitive science provide evidence for credal states and transitions across a range of psychological domains. In particular, the striking explanatory success of Bayesian perceptual psychology provides strong evidence for subpersonal credal states figuring in perception.

From Rescorla's point of view, instrumentalists about Bayesian cognitive science are like the logical empiricists, a discredited movement that came to fame in the Vienna Circle and lasted from the 1920s through the 1950s. The logical empiricists—notably Moritz Schlick, Rudolf Carnap, Otto Neurath, and, later, A. J. Ayer—argued that we can explain results in the hard sciences without postulating "unobservable" entities that causally impact our observations (Ayer, 1936/1971). This movement died out as our knowledge of such "unobservable" entities as subatomic particles grew, as our reasons for believing in them became unassailable, and as the category of "unobservable" began to look like a confusion. Its former proponents abandoned the view.

Why revive instrumentalism now? What is wrong with Rescorla's argument is that there is a major relevant difference between historical instrumentalism and Bayesian instrumentalism and that difference is evolution by natural selection. Evolution is a pro-instrumentalist mechanism. There is no doubt that behaving according to Bayesian norms is enormously valuable for an organism and we can expect strong evolutionary pressure toward behavior that *fits the norms of Bayesian rationality*. But Bayesian rational behavior does not have to be implemented using the conceptual apparatus that is best suited to describing Bayesian rational processes by the theorist. The problem with Rescorla's argument is that it is not clear that the way evolution chose to produce behavior that adheres roughly to Bayesian norms involves the representation of probabilities in the perceptual system.

An example illustrates my point. A recent study of pea plants shows that growth of roots of pea plants involves sensitivity to uncertainty in nutrients and mean values of nutrients (Dener, Kacelnik, & Shemesh, 2016).

Individual pea plants had their roots separated into different pots as indicated in Figure 4.8. The conditions could be rich (lots of nutrients) or poor, and variable (i.e., fluctuating) or constant. In rich conditions, the plants grew a larger mass of roots in the constant pot; in poor conditions, the plants grew a larger mass of roots in the variable plot. As the authors note, the plants were risk prone in poor and risk averse in rich conditions, fitting the predictions of risk sensitivity theory. Were the plants monitoring the uncertainty in nutrients reaching their roots or the mean richness in the environment? The plants have no nervous system and no one has found anything that could be called a representation of uncertainty or a representation of richness. Any talk of plants "monitoring" uncertainty would have to be regarded as "as if" talk unless there is evidence to the contrary.

The conclusion of Dener et al. (2016, p. 1766) fits with my methodological suggestion:

PERCEPTION IS NONPROPOSITIONAL AND NONCONCEPTUAL 209

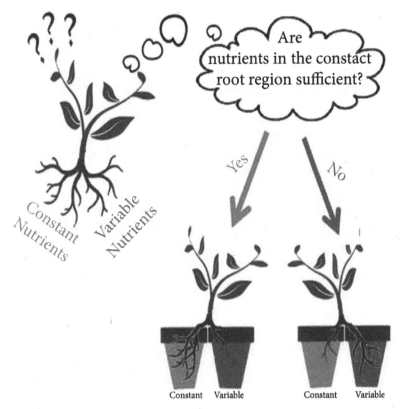

Figure 4.8 This is the "graphical abstract" for Dener et al. (2016). Reprinted with permission from Elsevier.

Plants' risk sensitivity reinforces the oft-repeated assertion that complex adaptive strategies do not require complex cognition (adaptive strategies may be complex for us to understand, without necessarily being complex for organisms to implement). Bacteria ... fungi ..., and plants generate flexible and impressively complex responses through "decision" processes embedded in their physiological architecture, implementing adaptive responses that work well under a limited set of ecological circumstances (i.e., that are ecologically rational).

In sum, sensitivity to uncertainty does not require representation of *anything*, and certainly not representation of uncertainty.

Here is the application to Rescorla's scientific realist arguments. Our perceptual systems certainly act as if they represented prior probabilities. But the pea plant behaves as if it represented mean levels of nutrients and their degree of uncertainty. Since the pea plant lacks a nervous system, we can be pretty sure that there are no such representations. Somehow, natural selection has found a way for plants to behave according to some of the norms of Bayesian rationality without those representations. The challenge to Rescorla's reasoning is that we have to allow for the possibility that the same is true of *our perceptual systems*.

Rescorla notes that one encoding of a full probability distribution that avoids computational intractability is the special case in which the probability distribution fits the "bell curve" or Gaussian distribution. In that case, the entire probability distribution can be characterized by its mean and variance. If someone knows the mean and the variance and that the distribution is Gaussian, they can easily calculate any probability value. But wait—even if the visual system represents the mean and variance, does it also represent that the distribution is Gaussian? A natural answer is that the visual system does not need to represent that the distribution is Gaussian. If it is built to compute in ways that only make sense given that the distribution is Gaussian, and if it is Gaussian, then there is no need to explicitly represent that fact. However, once we see that the visual system can be built to act *as if* it represented that the distribution is Gaussian without actually representing that fact, we can ask whether something similar might be true for the representations of mean and variance. Why can't the system act as if it represented the mean and variance without actually doing so, as with the pea plant described above? I think the answer is that without knowing more about what the exact mechanisms are, we cannot be confident in a realist interpretation being better than an instrumentalist interpretation.

Rescorla (2020) cites me saying that many Bayesians favor the computational level (Block, 2018) and responds with a rhetorical question (p. 62): "Why should we regard a Bayesian model as approximately true when its own creators decline to do so?" He answers: "I reply that the dispute between realism and instrumentalism is not about what scientists believe, any more than the dispute between Platonism and nominalism regarding mathematical entities is about what mathematicians believe. The dispute is about what we have *reason* to believe." Of course he is right that the dispute is not about what cognitive scientists believe, but the cognitive scientists in this case are not best construed as in amateur philosopher mode. I believe they are responding to the situation described above, that Bayesian behavioral norms have been selected for but that whether the mechanism by which they are implemented actually involves Bayesian inference is up for grabs. Steven Gross calls my challenge (from Block, 2018) the "mere sensitivity" challenge: Mere sensitivity to probabilities does not entail representation of probabilities (Gross, 2020). One of Gross's suggestions is that we can use the distinction between the content of a representational state and its mode or manner of representation to see how representation of probabilities is not necessary. The distinction between content and mode can be hard to get a grip on so I will illustrate it.

I mentioned in Chapter 2 that I have had a disagreement with Michael Tye about the difference between the tactile perception of a corner of a cube and a visual perception of the same corner. I proposed that the two representations have the same content but are in different modalities, the visual modality vs. the tactile modality. Tye held that the difference is in the contents: the visual state and the tactile state represent the shape of the corner but differ in other represented features, e.g., hardness rather than color of the material the cube is made of. I countered that even apart from color and hardness there is a difference in the phenomenology of the perceptual representation of the corner itself (Block, 1995a; Tye, 1995a). This is a dispute about whether a certain phenomenal difference that Tye and I agree obtains is best explained in terms of a difference in mode—tactile vs. visual—or a difference in content.

But the difference between content and mode of representation can be considered independently of phenomenology. Consider for example, Fodor's "belief box" account of belief: that what it is to believe that grass is green is to have a sentence that means that grass is green in one's belief box. (The belief box metaphor is due to Schiffer, 1981.) What it is to believe that it is not the case that grass is green is to have a sentence that means that it is not the case that grass is green in the belief box. But an alternative account is that one has a belief box and also a belief-not box. What it is to believe that it is not the case that grass is green is to have the sentence that means that grass is green in the belief-not box. The boxes are the modes, whereas the contents of the sentences in the boxes are the representational contents under discussion. Of course the box metaphor is a way of talking about the functional role of the representations. The contents themselves can be given a functional interpretation (Block, 1986).

We certainly accept the notion of a graded attitude in cognition. Instead of the sophisticated belief that there is a .7 probability that it is cold out, we can have the much less sophisticated graded belief that assigns a .7 credence to the proposition that it is cold out. The latter is less sophisticated because it does not require a propositional content that makes use of the concept of probability.

One consideration against Gross's proposal derives from Nicholas Shea's criterion of reusability (Shea, 2018, 2020). Shea suggests that a condition of representation is that the vehicle of representation be reusable. As Gross notes, there could be a reusable perceptual representation of redness in front of one that has a .6 probability attitude or a .8 probability attitude, so the representation of red is reusable. But what would it be for the probabilistic attitude to be reusable? It is not clear that this idea makes sense.

What is the application of Gross's suggestion to the issue of Bayesian realism? I argued that there is a difference between mere sensitivity to probabilities and representation of probabilities and that the evidence can be handled by the former, so the latter is not required. Gross replies that if we allow probabilistic representation by mode, my argument is sidestepped because there is no difference between sensitivity and representation when it comes to mode. However, if Gross is right that there is no difference between sensitivity and representation when it comes to mode, it is not clear what to conclude. Calling it "probabilistic representation by mode" doesn't seem right if there is no difference between sensitivity and representation. "No difference" is a symmetrical relation. I am tempted to think that if the probabilistic aspect of perception is in the mode of representation it is in an important respect implicit and is compatible with instrumentalism about probabilistic contents. Further, as Shea notes (2020), even if attitude and content are both functional, they depend on different aspects of function rather than total functional role. (I pointed this out long ago [Block, 1986, 1987].) As Shea notes, priming is part of the total functional role of a representation without affecting either content or mode of representation. More to the point, a representation can have sensitivities to the environment that do not affect the aspect of functional role that determines mode.

There are two aspects of the issue discussed in this section for the overall thesis of this book. First, if there is inference in perception, then, according to the notions of proposition and concept being used here, perception would be conceptual and propositional, knocking out two of the three hallmarks of the joint in nature. Further, if as I have claimed the iconic nature of perception supports the nonpropositional nature of perception, the iconicity thesis would be brought into question.

Second, if perceptual representations are constitutively probabilistic and cognitive representations are not, that is a potential feature of the border. Griffiths et al. argue that Bayesianism has no consequences for probabilistic representation and although the topic of inference doesn't come up explicitly, it would seem as if the same point applies to inference. As an example, they note (p. 417) that

> ... certain classes of Bayesian models can be approximated with an exemplar model, a traditional form of psychological process model. The idea behind this approximation is that people store examples of past events in memory, which act like samples from the prior, and then activate these stored exemplars based on their similarity to observed data, which acts like the likelihood function. Priors and likelihood functions appear in proving that this algorithm approximates Bayesian inference but disappear into familiar psychological notions of memory and similarity in defining the algorithm itself. Although this is just one example, we believe that there need be nothing intrinsically "Bayesian" about algorithms that approximate Bayesian inference."

If they are right, Bayesianism does not support the view that perception is probabilistic.

I have mentioned the predictive coding framework a number of times. It is often treated as if committed to a realist interpretation of priors and likelihoods and is usually thought of as an implementation of traditional hierarchical Bayesian theories, as claimed by (Clark, 2016). What are hierarchical Bayesian theories?

The visual system can be thought of in terms of a stream of processing, starting at the sensory transducers, moving to representations in V1 of zero-crossings, then, still in the occipital lobe, of lines and edges and surfaces. In the temporal lobe part of the stream, we have representations of objects, including faces. This stream can be thought of as a series of perceptual stages. (See the section of Chapter 2 on the visual hierarchy). Traditional Bayesian theories portray information flow as "upward" from sensory stages to hypotheses about the world. Predictive coding advocates think of the information flow as "downward," with hypotheses about the activation at the next lowest level corrected by the upward signal, the last (bottom) stage being prediction of sensory stimulation. According to traditional pictures, what is transmitted "upward" is an ever-more articulated representation of the world, corrected by priors from higher levels. According to the predictive coding perspective, what is transmitted downward is predictions about the next lowest level whereas what is transmitted upward is the difference between the current representation and the prediction from the next level higher up, the error. As I mentioned earlier in this chapter, Andy Clark describes perception as "controlled hallucination" (Clark, 2016).

As Nico Orlandi and Geoffrey Lee note, it is unclear how information flow can really be different in predictive coding models from in traditional models if they are just alternative implementations of the same hierarchical Bayesian model (Orlandi & Lee, 2018). Since everyone acknowledges that there is constant information flow in the visual system in both directions, the issue of whether information flow is upward or downward is misconceived. One can think of the bottom-up signal as correcting the hypothesis embodied in the prior; but one can equally think of the prior as correcting the signal from the senses. These different formulations just reflect a different spin on the same facts. The only issue of fact is the relative role—in a given case—of the prior and sensory stimulation in determining the percept. Both perspectives agree that in certain circumstances—e.g., when the perceiver wakes up after being knocked out, not knowing where they are or whether it is day or night—the role of priors in determining the percept will inevitably be much less significant than the role of sensory stimulation (Orlandi & Lee, 2018).

Consider the case in which the downward "prediction" is perfect and so, on the predictive coding model, there should be nothing sent upward. (In the predictive coding terminology, the signal is "explained away.") As Orlandi and Lee argue, whether a signal is sent upward depends on how one cuts up the stages.

(See also Cao, 2018, for a different argument to the same conclusion.) In sum, there is no solid argument from the use of Bayesian ideal observer models in either the traditional formulations or the predictive coding versions to the conclusion that perception is inferential and therefor conceptual.

In this chapter, I have made the initial case that perception and perceptual representation are constitutively nonpropositional and nonconceptual. There will be more on the nonconceptual nature of perception and perceptual representation in Chapter 6. I turn now to the thesis that perception is iconic.

5
Perception is iconic; cognition is discursive

In the last chapter, I explained the difference between state, content, and format and argued that perception is constitutively nonconceptual and nonpropositional in the state sense. In this chapter, I argue that perception is constitutively iconic in format (cf. Burge, 2010a; Carey, 2009; Dretske, 1981; Tye, 1995b, 2002). Cognitive representation has none of these properties constitutively. Though cognitive representations are not iconic constitutively, they nonetheless can use iconic representations as, for example, when one plans how to get the couch through the doorway. In this chapter, I will characterize the "analog mirroring" notion of iconicity I am using, contrast it with other conceptions and give a variety of lines of evidence that perceptual representations are iconic in that sense. I will also argue against the "pluralist" view that some perceptual representations are iconic and some discursive.

However, before I get to that, I will talk about two issues that can be discussed independently of the specific notion of iconicity that I am using. The two issues involve arguments against iconic representation as involved in all of perception. First, E. J. Green and Jake Quilty-Dunn have argued that perceptual object representations must have a syntactic constituent that accomplishes singular reference, and as a consequence, perceptual object representations are discursive. They argue for the "pluralist" position that although perceptual object representations are discursive, other perceptual representations are iconic (Green & Quilty-Dunn, 2017; Quilty-Dunn, 2016b, 2019a, 2019b, 2020). Second, it has been alleged that iconic representations must always be ambiguous, that perceptual representations are not ambiguous, and so perceptual representations cannot be wholly iconic. As I will explain in the next few sections, both of these arguments neglect the functional role of iconic representations. And then I will move on to the analog mirroring and tracking notion of iconicity.

Iconicity, format, and function

As I mentioned in Chapter 3, the term "singular content" is ambiguous. In the weak sense of the term, it means content that is directed toward a particular, and whose accuracy conditions depend on that particular. If I perceptually represent an apple as red and you perceptually represent a different but exactly similar apple as red, the accuracy conditions of our perceptions differ. I mentioned that there is a stronger sense of "single out" involving content that is constituted by its object. Chapter 3 focused more on the stronger sense, but this chapter will focus on the former, weaker sense.

Although I think much of perception has singular content in the weaker sense of directedness toward a particular, in Chapter 3 I mentioned some reasons for skepticism about whether singular content in that sense is of the essence of perception, using the examples of the ganzfeld experience, the perception of flicker in the periphery of vision, and the perception of motion without perception of a moving thing. In the case of object perception though, I agree that content is singular in the weak sense. My disagreement with Green and Quilty-Dunn concerns whether perception of objects requires a format constituent that singles out the object and more specifically whether perception of objects requires a noniconic format constituent.

According to Green and Quilty-Dunn, multiple object tracking shows that perceptual object representations have an indexical format-constituent. They say, "Subjects can reliably track objects in MOT despite significant changes in colour, shape, and size during a trial (vanMarle and Scholl, 2003; Zhou et al., 2010). Thus, we contend that, at minimum, there is a syntactic separation between indexical constituents and feature representations in object-files." (See the earlier discussion in connection with Figure 4.5 for an explanation of multiple object tracking.) As they make clear, they think the indexical constituent is noniconic (discursive). Although I don't agree that a nonindexical discursive format element is required for tracking, I do think that iconic representations often have structure and there can be iconic elements in an iconic structure that track objects.

There are many cases in which an iconic representation singles something out and in which there is demonstration at the level of content but not vehicle. A map for example singles out what it is a map of. What determines the reference is how the map is used, not any format element. A painting of the Empire State Building can single out the Empire State Building because of the intentions of the painter and the causal role of the Empire State Building in producing the painting—without any indexical format constituent. For many such paintings it would not make sense to say the whole painting is such a format element since the painting may depict other things, e.g., the sky. The defender of the format constituent idea could say a portion of the painting is the singular format element. But not all styles of painting allow for the neat separation of such a portion.

Although I have emphasized the similarity between perceptual representation and maps, I also pointed out in Chapter 1 that maplike structures may be part of the conceptual basis of cognition. Further, one way in which perception is not maplike is that perception involves a complex mix of allocentric and egocentric reference frames. As mentioned in Chapter 4, allocentric frames represent objects relative to one another whereas egocentric frames represent objects in a coordinate system based in the perceiver. The egocentric coordinate systems are most directly linked to action. The egocentric aspect of perception is itself complex, integrating vision, touch, and audition with proprioceptive and vestibular inputs (Nakashima, Iwai, Ueda, & Kumada, 2015). Jake Quilty-Dunn (2017, 2019b) describes my position as a "hybrid" because, he says, I allow for an indexical element in perception that represents noniconically together with iconic representations of properties. He says that I have to explain how different formats can compose with one another. He seems to be supposing that I postulate a singular format element and that it has to compose with other format elements. (To be fair, early drafts of this book may have been unclear on this point.)

As I have been saying, the demonstrative element in some perceptions can be a *content* element only: No indexical format element is required. But even when there are different formats involved in one representation, there need be nothing that deserves to be called a mechanism of composition. Maps contain discursive labels for roads, towns, rivers, and the like without any mechanism of interaction with the iconic format of maps other than the implementation of the convention that, unlike the Hollywood sign on a map of Hollywood, they do not depict. In a map of the United States, the label "Mississippi River" does not denote a geographical feature in the shape of the letters. Labels function differently from iconic representations on maps that indicate, for example, the shape of a river. As noted earlier, maps are hybrid representations. The shape of a representation of a river designates the shape of the river whereas the label tells us the name of the same river: The two formats function differently.

In discussion of an earlier version of this chapter in a philosophy of perception course that Ian Phillips and I taught at NYU in Spring 2018, it was said that perhaps a map with labels is really two distinct representations, an iconic representation that represents, e.g., rivers and their shapes, and a set of discursive labels. Phillips noted, however, that the shape of a river could be denoted on a map by a shaped string of letters spelling out the river's name.

To be clear: I am not opposed to distinct iconic format elements in perceptual representations. Many theories of vision postulate compositional structure at the level of vehicle, for example Marr's 2.5D sketch and Nakayama's surface representations (Marr, 1982; Nakayama, He, & Shimojo, 1995; Palmer, 1999). Biederman has long advocated 2D and 3D visual components he calls "geons" such as cylinders, cones, and rectangles. Shape recognition is supposed to depend on combinations of perhaps 30 such geons (Biederman, 1987). For example, a mug would be decomposable into a cylindrical shape plus the half torus of the handle. No version of the thesis that perceptual representation is iconic should be interpreted to be incompatible with compositional structure.

As noted earlier (see Figure 4.5 and the discussion of slot models in Chapter 1), Zenon Pylyshyn and Brian Scholl (Pylyshyn, 1984; Scholl & Pylyshyn, 1999) have shown that we can track roughly four moving objects, even as they change properties in various ways, and even as they go behind occluders. Does tracking behind occluders show that the perceptual representations must have a singular format element and so are not iconic?

A dynamic conception of iconic representations would embody constraints on iconic object representations like those on "Spelke objects": (1) cohesion, (2) contact, and (3) continuity (Spelke, 1990). Cohesion states that "objects maintain their connectedness and their boundaries as they move." Contact states that "distinct objects move together if and only if they touch." (Note: this does not apply to animate objects.) Continuity states that "An object traces exactly one connected path over space and time."

These constraints were first formulated by Elizabeth Spelke on the basis of experiments on infants, but the same constraints apply to multiple object tracking in adults, suggesting that they are built into the visual system. When objects fail these constraints, multiple object tracking fails, suggesting that perceptual attribution is important in multiple object tracking. On a dynamic conception of iconic representation, an iconic representation can persist through changes that do not destroy its dynamic integrity.

The belief that if a representation has a singular content it must also have a singular format element may stem from the general supposition that a difference in content for a representation must be due to a difference in format. This principle was defended explicitly by Fodor in (1980): "mental representations are distinct in content only if they are also distinct in form"(p. 68). He says that differences in content have causal consequences and "to put it mildly, it is hard to see how internal representations could differ in causal role *unless* they differed in form" (p. 68). Fodor is alluding to the idea that the mind is a semantic engine driven by a syntactic engine in which every content difference gets its causal powers from a corresponding syntactic difference (Block, 1995b).

However, there is a trade-off between format and processor in system design. Recall the discussion in Chapter 4 of the "belief box" theory. Fodor argued that what it is to believe that grass is green is to have a sentence that means that grass is green in one's belief box. What it is to believe that it is not the case that grass is green is to have a sentence that means that it is not the case that grass is green in the belief box. As I mentioned, an alternative account is that one has a belief box and also a belief-not box. What it is to believe that it is not the case that grass is green is to have the sentence that means that grass is green in the belief-not box. There could even be a poorly designed system that has a belief-that-it-is-not-the-case-that grass-is-green box and that box can have a '1' or a '0' in it. Of course, talk of boxes is a way of talking about functional role of a representation. So, what the examples suggest is that what can be done by format can also be done by processor. The application to the case at hand is that what accomplishes singular reference could be a feature of processing rather than a singular format element.

I've been considering Green and Quilty-Dunn's argument based on singular content to the conclusion that perception cannot be wholly iconic. I will return to Green and Quilty-Dunn later in the chapter, but I will now switch to a different argument with a similar conclusion based on the supposed indeterminacy or ambiguity of iconic representation.

Iconicity and determinacy

The iconic nature of perception has been thought to be incompatible with the determinacy of perceptual representation (Fodor, 1975; Quilty-Dunn, 2016a; Shevlin, 2016). Jerry Fodor says that a picture of a man walking uphill is ambiguous between walking uphill frontward and walking downhill backward. He also says (and here I agree) that perceptions do not normally exhibit anything that can be called ambiguity. If you catch a glimpse of a man walking uphill without perceptual information about motion, you see it as a man walking uphill. From these two premises, Fodor concludes that images could function as mental representations only if they were accompanied by descriptions that disambiguated them (Fodor, 1975). Fodor did not suppose that we are aware of the descriptions but that they determined how we interpreted the icons. I will refer to these descriptions as "captions."

As Fodor could acknowledge, still photographs of a person walking uphill look like a person walking uphill. Still photographs of moving creatures—e.g., an athlete throwing a discus or a fish jumping in the air out of the water—showed motion aftereffects (like the waterfall illusion mentioned earlier) that would be expected from the fish jumping forward rather than backward (Kourtzi & Kanwisher, 2000). Note that these aftereffects involve the subject's knowledge of what a discus is and how it is thrown, and knowledge of what direction fish jump in. This knowledge "penetrates" perception, as will be discussed in Chapter 9.

On one version of Fodor's view, these facts could be explained by postulating that although the pictures are intrinsically ambiguous, the ambiguity is resolved by the internal caption.

Wittgenstein famously says, "I see a picture; it represents an old man walking up a steep path leaning on a stick.—How? Might it not have looked just the same if he had been sliding downhill in that position?" This is followed by, "Perhaps a Martian would describe the picture so. I do not need to explain why we do not describe it so" (Wittgenstein, 1953, p. 54e).

There are two accounts of how we differ from the Martians. On Fodor's sort of account, we have the caption and the Martians do not. But there is another account in terms of built-in functional roles. What is most important about these roles is something Wittgenstein might not have acknowledged, their use in thought in addition to their use in public interchanges.

Fodor seems oblivious to this possibility. Here is what he says (1975, p. 190):

> But if pictures correspond to the same world in too many different ways, they also correspond in the same way to too many different worlds. A picture of John with a bulging tummy corresponds to John's being fat. But it corresponds equally to John's being pregnant since, if that is the way that John does look when he is fat, it is also, I suppose, the way that he would look if he were pregnant. So if the fact that John is fat is a reason to call a picture of John with a bulging tummy true, then the fact that John isn't pregnant is as good a reason to call a picture of John with a bulging tummy false. (A picture which corresponds to a man walking up a hill forward corresponds equally and in the same way to a man sliding down the hill backward; Wittgenstein, 1953, p. 139.) For every reason that we might have for calling a picture true, there will be a corresponding reason for calling it false. That is, there is no reason for calling either. Pictures aren't the kind of things that can have truth values . . . what refers aren't images but images-under-descriptions.

Fodor's argument goes from the potential ambiguity of pictures to the conclusion that iconic representation requires a caption, neglecting the fact that the function of mental representations can have the effect of resolving what might be an ambiguity for a Martian. The point here is related to one made in Chapter 4 concerning Berkeley's observation that an "idea" (i.e., a mental image) of one particular triangle can function so as to represent triangles in general. In the case of perceptual icons, there are in-grained functional roles (often biologically preferred) that render the caption approach superfluous.

Someone might object that if there is a preferred functional role, then the format properties are superfluous. The objector might say, "The functional role will determine what concept is represented whether the representation is iconic in format or discursive in format, so the format is irrelevant." But this objection ignores the role of format in determining that the functional role is what it is. Format is part of the implementation of the functional role. Consider the use of mental imagery to figure out whether a sofa will fit thought a doorway. The image has a certain functional role, but the format properties are not incidental to that role. The iconic information can be used in the application of percepts in thought.

"But doesn't the preferred functional role make iconic representations propositional?" Recall that one cannot see something as not blue or as having the disjunctive property of being blue or red. That is the main kind of datum in the argument against perception being propositional and the point about functional roles does not change it. The point about preferred functional roles applies equally to "discursive" or language-like mental representations. A sentence on paper can be ambiguous. Given that each term can mean something different in different languages, it could be said to be infinitely ambiguous. It is the functional role of the discursive representations that makes them determinate in meaning. The upshot is that representational properties of both iconic and discursive representations are grounded in functional role and that attention to functional role can defang some arguments for indeterminacy of perceptual representation.

Structure

Iconic and discursive representations are similar in many respects. Both have structure and both can (but need not) involve parts, including atomic parts. Fodor and Pylyshyn argued that the "systematicity" of thought derives from discursive representation (Evans, 1982; Fodor, 1987; Fodor & Pylyshyn, 1988). If you can think the thought that John loves Mary, you can think the thought that Mary loves John. If you can infer from the thought that Mary and John are nice to the thought that Mary is nice, you can also infer to the thought that John is nice.

However, iconic representations allow for forms of systematicity as well. If you can see the square as above the triangle you can see the triangle as above the square (Block, 1995b, p. 411). Further, iconic representations can be structured. The floor plan of an apartment can have subelements that represent rooms (Haugeland, 1991). A map of a state can have subelements that represent counties, and those can have subelements that represent cities. Although iconic and discursive representations can both be structured, discursive representations do not exhibit the analog mirroring that I take to be definitive of iconicity and to which I now turn.

Analog tracking and mirroring

Moving now to the nature of iconic representation, there are a number of notions of iconicity and even within cognitive science, there are two main notions. The one I find most useful is what might be called analog tracking and mirroring. Analog tracking and mirroring obtains when there is a set of environmental properties and a set of representations of those environmental properties such that:

1. Certain differences in representations function as responses to differences in environmental properties in a way that is sensitive to the degree of environmental differences. For example, as objects are rotated, perceptual representations function to alter in a way that corresponds to that rotation and is sensitive to that degree of rotation.
2. Certain differences in representations function to alter the situation that is represented in a way that depends on the degree of representational change.
3. Certain relations (including temporal relations) among the environmental properties are mirrored by representations that instantiate analogs of those relations.

The first two conditions characterize tracking, whereas the third is concerned with mirroring. Of course, a form of tracking is shared between iconic and discursive representations. The key difference comes in with the role of *degrees of difference*. The tracking involved in perception involves changes in representation keyed to differences in the environmental magnitude that are above the threshold for making a perceptual difference in the particular observational and attentional circumstance. Perception tracks differences that are as fine-grained as can be registered in those observational and attentional circumstances, whereas cognition tracks only cognitively relevant differences. Of course, the mirroring condition also involves degrees—mirroring of degrees by degrees.

One common criterion for iconic representations (Camp, 2018) is that the representations are "dense" in the sense that given any two values of a parameter there is another value in between. Analog mirroring in the sense that I am using the term does not require density. Two magnitudes can be mirrors of each other even if both are "digitized."

Without some characterization of "certain," "analog" and "mirror," these conditions are admittedly rather vague. Rather than try for defining these terms, I'll show the reader some of the evidence for these claims, thereby narrowing down the vagueness to some extent.

Roughly this picture of iconicity has been much discussed in the philosophical and psychological literature (Beck, 2015; Block, 1983a, p. 515; Burge, 2018; Goodman, 1976; Hill, 2013; Kulvicki, 2004; Lewis, 1971; Maley, 2011; Peacocke, 1986, 2019; Quilty-Dunn, 2016b), though its major source is Roger Shepard's notion of second-order isomorphism (or mirroring) (Shepard, 1978; Shepard & Chipman, 1970). First-order similarities between representations and what they represent are a matter of the same properties applying to both, e.g., distance being represented by distance; second-order isomorphisms—as they use the term—are a matter of structures of systems of representational properties corresponding to structures of systems of properties that are represented.

Analog mirroring is widely used in cognitive science discussions of iconic representation. Another notion of iconicity that is also often used in cognitive science appeals to parts. Some—but not all—iconic representations have systematic parts that represent parts of what the whole represents and relations among the parts represent relations among the parts of what the whole represents. In addition, each part represents many properties. Perceptions have a canonical decomposition into parts at the level of content if not at the level of vehicle, but the parthood notion just describe requires concerns format parts at the level of vehicle.

Versions of the part conception have been proposed many times, though one of the most influential treatments has been that of Stephen Kosslyn (Block, 1983a, 1980; Kosslyn et al., 1979; Sloman, 1978; Sober, 1976; Tye, 1991). John Kulvicki traces it back to Alberti (Alberti, 1435/1991; Kulvicki, 2015; Quilty-Dunn, 2019a). Kosslyn's definitions tend to say that for a representation to be pictorial, *all* of its parts must represent parts of what the whole represents. If points on the surface of a picture count as parts, this would make many actual pictures noniconic. (For example, a newspaper iconic depiction of an orange object is often composed of red and yellow dots, but these parts are not representational in themselves.) In my "Mental Pictures and Cognitive Science" (1983a, 513), I said "at least one part" to cope with this problem. Another approach would be to distinguish between "constituents," the semantically significant parts, and the other parts (Echeverri, 2017). What is especially useful about the part notion is that it allows for the specification that each part represents many properties.

The part notion does have some problems, though. One problem is that if there are smallest parts, it is not clear how they can fit the definition, since they do not themselves have parts. A more significant problem is that the characterization of iconicity in terms of parts excludes what is by my lights one of the major kinds of iconicity discussed in cognitive science, analog magnitude representations, the topic of the next section. Iconicity as used in cognitive science is probably best regarded as a cluster concept. The part conception and the analog mirroring conception are two elements of the cluster. I think the analog mirroring conception is more important in cognitive science, especially the study of perception, so I will be using that conception. The next section explains what analog magnitude representations are and why they are important.

Analog magnitude representations

One kind of representation that is iconic by my definition and that does not easily lend itself to discussion in terms of parts involves the "analog magnitude system," a system that tracks physical size, luminance, durations of time, distances, amounts of food, and many other quantities. The system that tracks these spatial and temporal magnitudes also tracks numerosities. The system is common to many animals, including invertebrates and human infants. Representations in this system obey Weber's Law, which you may recall from Chapter 2, stipulates that relative discriminability of two stimuli is a linear function of the ratio of the intensity of the stimuli. Doubling the intensity of a stimulus will double the just noticeable difference in intensity. Tripling the intensity of a stimulus will triple the just noticeable difference in intensity, and so on.

A key feature of iconic representation of magnitudes, one that is exhibited in the analog magnitude system, is a tracking relation (Beck, 2015; Gallistel, 2011; Gallistel & Gelman; Maley, 2011). For example, an increase of sufficient size in luminance functions to cause a corresponding change in the analog magnitude representation of luminance. We have already seen an example in Chapter 2 of operation of the analog magnitude system in the perceptual representation of approximate numerosity. (See Figure 2.7.) The representations of approximate numerosities reveal their iconic nature in conforming to Weber's Law even when the stimuli are digits rather than amounts of anything (Dehaene, 2011; Moyer & Landauer, 1967). One such task asks subjects to indicate whether a given number is larger or smaller than 5 (by pressing one or another of two keys). Subjects are faster for the digit '9' than they are for the digit '6' and also less likely to make a mistake. Similar results apply to the task of saying which of two digits represents the larger number. The explanation is that the ratio of 9 to 5 is larger than the ratio of 6 to 5, so Weber's Law applies even in the absence of visible numerosities. Further, damage to brain areas involved in analog processing of number (e.g., the angular gyrus) cause dyscalculia, difficulty in digital arithmetic (Dehaene, 2011). It seems that analog representations of number are involved even in digital computation. If this seems surprising to you, think about how difficult it is to do arithmetic using the binary system. Purely formal calculation when you don't know how the symbols map onto the approximate number system can be very difficult.

The neural mechanisms of analog representation are not well understood. A recent review of 93 articles shows that circuits in parietal and frontal lobes constitute a generalized magnitude system (Sokolowski, Fias, Bosah Ononye, & Ansari, 2017). The left superior parietal lobule appears specialized for symbolic numerical magnitudes (e.g., Arabic digits), with representation of approximate numbers of dots in the precuneus. It appears that approximate numerosities are represented both in the general magnitude system (Newcombe, Levine, & Mix, 2015) and in a system that is specialized for number (Sokolowski et al., 2017). Recent work on dogs suggests that the areas of the parietal lobe that subserve approximate numerosity perception in humans also subserve approximate numerosity perception in dogs (Aulet et al., 2019). Plausibly, approximate numerosity perception is part of our vertebrate heritage.

Drafts of this book for some years now have made the point that analog magnitude representations need not have parts of the sort suitable for the part conception of iconicity. Many others have noticed this point as well (Ball, 2017; Beck, 2019; Clarke, forthcoming; Peacocke, 2019). Peacocke illustrates it with this example: Suppose that firing rates of certain neural circuits represent time duration. Although one duration has another duration as a part, a firing rate of 50 times per second does not have a firing rate of 17 times per second as a part (p. 58).

It is sometimes supposed that analog magnitude representations do have parts and that what makes the difference between representing one magnitude and another is the number of parts. This picture gained support from the Meck and Church theory of analog magnitude representation, which postulated a stream of neural pulses modulated by a gate that opened and closed (Meck & Church, 1983). In a mode for counting individuals, the gate might open briefly every 200 ms. The energy accumulated was supposed to be an analog representation of the number of individuals. (See also Beck, 2015.) However, this theory makes the prediction that representing larger magnitudes should take more time than representing smaller magnitudes, and Justin Wood and Elisabeth Spelke showed that it did not take subjects longer to encode 16 dots than it took to encode 4 dots (Wood & Spelke, 2005). Current theories do not support any kind of a part model of analog magnitudes. So the part notion of iconicity is inapplicable to some standard cases of iconicity.

Analog mirroring alone applies to analog magnitude representations such as representations of length, duration, numerosity, luminance, and loudness. But much of the most dramatic evidence for analog mirroring in perception comes from spatial representations, many of which satisfy the part conception of iconicity as well.

In sum, I prefer the analog tracking and mirroring conception of iconicity to the parts conception, but there are representations of both types in perception and to a large extent the two conceptions apply to the same perceptual representations. I have not yet given evidence for iconic representations in perception. That is the subject to which I now turn. I will start with evidence for iconicity that involves mental imagery.

Mental imagery

One form of evidence in favor of perceptual representations being iconic stems from experiments on mental imagery. There are two relevant properties of mental imagery.

1. The representations of perceptual imagery are of the same kind as perceptual representations but produced in a different way, top-down rather than bottom-up (Block, 1983a, 1983b).
2. Imagery representations are iconic.

One can conclude from these two premises that at least those perceptual representations that can be produced in imagery are iconic. A small selection of the vast evidence for both premises will be presented below.

Evidence that imagery uses representations of the same type as perception appeals both to the neuroscience and psychology of perception and perceptual imagery. I'll describe a few of the very many items of evidence that the representations of imagery are perceptual representations generated top-down. One line of evidence comes from the "oblique effect." In a variety of tasks, oblique lines are harder to resolve than vertical or horizontal lines. For example, it is harder to make comparisons among stripes (e.g., comparing widths) when the stripes are oblique than when they are vertical or horizontal (Figure 5.1). And the same holds for imagined stripes (Kosslyn et al., 2006, pp. 68–69). The

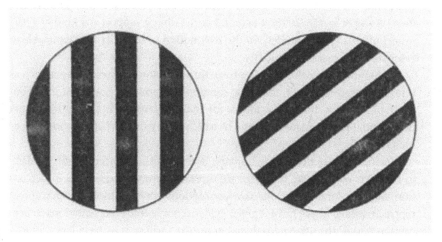

Figure 5.1 Grids of the sort used in demonstration of the Oblique Effect. Thanks to Steve Kosslyn for the figure.

behavioral oblique effect has been shown widely across vertebrates (e.g., in pigeons), suggesting that the design of visual cortex favorable to vertical and horizontal may be baked into the vertebrate genome (Donis, 1999).

A related aspect of the oblique effect is that if one moves a grid further from the subject, the stripes will begin to blur at shorter distances for oblique stripes than for vertical or horizontal stripes. Kosslyn and Pennington demonstrated this effect with one group of subjects. Then, a different group of subjects was asked to memorize grids of various sizes, either in vertical or in oblique orientation. They asked subjects to image a grid in one orientation, then rotate it to the other orientation, then to imagine walking back from the grid until the stripes began to blur. They found that imagined oblique stripes blurred at shorter imagined distances than imagined vertical stripes. And the difference between vertical and oblique was the same for real grids as for imagined grids (Kosslyn, 1983, pp. 82–83). Further, another group of subjects that read the description of the experiment could not predict the result. Many parallels between vision and visual imagination of this sort are described by Finke (1989).

These observations can be explained by the fact that orientation tuning in the parts of the visual cortex used in both imagery and perception is less sensitive for diagonal orientations than for vertical or horizontal orientations (Kosslyn et al., 2006, p. 68). It has been shown that cortical responses to tilted grids in early visual cortex (V1, V2, V3) are less variable for horizontal and vertical grids than for oblique grids (van Bergen et al., 2015).

A second line of evidence that imagery uses perceptual representations is that subjects are slower for peripheral visual tasks compared to the same tasks done foveally and the same is true for visual imagination. (Subjects can imagine two objects directly in front, and maintain the image of one in front while the other moves to the side.) Further, subjects are faster in making judgments for stimuli that are more luminant or higher in contrast and the same holds for the same judgments on imagined stimuli (Broggin, Savazzi, & Marzi, 2012).

A third line of evidence that imagery representations are perceptual representations involved repetitive transcranial magnetic stimulation (TMS), in which an electromagnetic pulse is applied to the scalp, creating a burst of neural noise. If applied to early visual areas, a visual task involving stripes is impaired relative to a sham pulse of repetitive TMS. (In the sham pulse, a coil is placed on the head that makes the same noise as with the real pulse.) And a similar impairment occurred when subjects were imagining doing the visual stripe task (Broggin et al., 2012).

A fourth line of evidence that imagery representations are perceptual is that deficits in one of perception/imagery are often—but not always—mirrored by deficits in the other. For example, one patient had deficits in both perception and imagery only for faces and colors; another, only for facial expressions; another, only for spatial relations (Kaski, 2002).

A fifth line of evidence is that the phenomenology of perception and imagery are sufficiently similar that subjects can confuse one for the other (Dijkstra & Fleming, 2021). In the early years of the twentieth century, Cheves West Perky did an experiment in which subjects were asked to form a mental image projected on a ground glass screen. Unknown to the subjects, Perky often projected an image from behind the screen at a level that was independently ascertained to be at threshold. When asked to describe their images, subjects often added details from the pictures but nonetheless insisted that they were reporting their own imagery (Perky, 1910). Perky's methodology was basically a matter of interviewing subjects, a method known to be subject to many extraneous factors. Attempts to replicate this experiment using modern methods suggested that the imagery actually raised the thresholds for perception so that subjects may not have been perceiving the pictures after all (Reeves & Lemley, 2012).

Dijkstra and Fleming did a conceptual replication of Perky's experiment using a twist on her methodology. They showed subjects shapes on a screen at threshold level and at the same time asked them to imagine shapes. They asked subjects to say how vivid their image was and also whether they were seeing something real or whether any element of the shapes they reported experiencing was due to imagery. One might expect that subjects would be more likely to say they were seeing a picture when the picture was of a different shape from what they had been asked to imagine, for example a picture of a circle when they were trying to imagine a square. But the opposite was found. They were more likely to say they saw a circle when they were also imagining a circle. Further, when there was no picture on the screen, subjects were more likely to say they saw a real picture if they also reported a more vivid experience. One suggestion for how to explain these results is that the phenomenology of seeing something real is simply a more vivid version of visually imagining.

I don't mean to give the impression that perception and perceptual imagery are perfectly aligned. I will mention some examples of failure of alignment:

1. There are fine-grained color and grid representations that apparently cannot be produced in imagery (though see Pearson, 2020). More generally, imagery representations lack detail present in visual representations. Recall that the receptive field of a visual neuron is the area of space that it is sensitive to. As noted in the discussion of the visual hierarchy in Chapter 2, receptive field size increases as one goes up the visual hierarchy to the point where at the highest level neurons respond to all or most of the visual field. V1 receptive fields are small and allow for the representation of detail that higher areas can't match. A recent study showed that the effective receptive

field size of imagery representations in V1 were much larger than visual receptive fields and more akin to visual representations of high-level vision (Breedlove, St-Yves, Olman, & Naselaris, 2020). However, there is no reason to think that the finer-grained representations of vision have a different format from the imageable representations. In perception, signals from the environment drive perceptual representation even in the absence of large top-down effects. In imagery, representations are produced via top-down influence. People can form images of something they have just seen but also of things that they have never seen. There has been controversy over the role of early visual cortex in visual imagery (Bartolomeo, Hajhajate, Liu, & Spagna, 2020; Pearson, 2019, 2020). Pearson (2020) proposes that some of the disagreements can be resolved if it is shown that visual imagery generated in patients with lesions in early visual areas can involve vivid images but images that lack the detail provided by early vision.
2. Subjects are faster in making perceptual judgments about low-spatial-frequency grids (coarse stripes) than for high-frequency grids (fine stripes). But no reliable effect of this sort has been observed for imagined stripes. One explanation is that subjects have difficulty forming images of high-frequency grids. Again, there is no reason to think that fineness of grain makes a difference to format.
3. There are deficits in vision that do not correspond to deficits in visual imagery. Often, such deficits are due to damage in the eye or in one of the waystations between the eye and visual cortex. Thus, differences in deficits between imagery and perception appear to have more to do with differences in the way these representations are produced (top-down rather than bottom-up) than in the types of representations themselves.

In sum, the representations of perceptual imagery show many of the same properties shown by perception itself, lending plausibility to the claim that the representations are of the same type. There are exceptions, but they appear to have more to do with the way representations are produced than the nature of the representations themselves.

I now move to a second premise of the argument: that the representations of mental imagery are iconic.

In the pairs of figures like the three pairs of Figure 5.2, subjects are asked whether one can be superimposed on the other. The time taken to answer (when the answer is yes) is a linear function of the angular distance between them both for cases like A, in which one item could be cut out and rotated to put on top of the other, and for cases like B, which involve rotation in depth. (The items in C are not superimposable.) Subjects described themselves as rotating images in their minds in order to get the answer. Different subjects rotated at different

230 THE BORDER BETWEEN SEEING AND THINKING

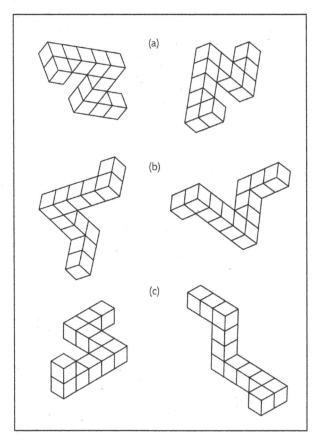

Figure 5.2 Shepard rotation. This is Figure 4.1 reproduced here for convenience. Subjects are asked whether the pairs depicted are superimposable. Thanks to Adrian Twissell for this figure. The answer is yes for A and B and no for C.

speeds but the average rate of rotation was about 60° per second. The upshot of these experiments is that there are mental analogs of physical rotation in which intermediate representational stages correspond to intermediate stages of physical rotation.

This experiment suggests analog mirroring between representations and objects in the world.

A different sort of experiment that also suggests mirroring, done by Ronald Finke and Steven Pinker (see Figure 5.3), showed subjects four dots placed randomly. Then the dots disappeared and one second later an arrow was presented. The task was to say whether the arrow pointed to a location previously occupied by a dot. The rightmost box represents the former locations of dots with open

Figure 5.3 Random dots were presented for 5 seconds as in the leftmost box. Then, 1 second after the dots had disappeared, subjects were shown an arrow, as in the middle box. Their task was to say whether the arrow had pointed to where one of the dots (now gone) had been. The rightmost box is an artist's depiction of the scanpath from the arrow to where one of the dots had been that the eye would have followed if the dots had been physically present. The locations of the dots are represented by open circles. Response times were proportional to distance between the arrow head and the dots. Thanks to the late Ron Finke for the figure. (See Finke, 1989.)

circles and the supposed scanpath by a dotted line. For yes answers, the time it took to answer was a linear function of the distance to the dot. If the arrow was presented first, before the dots, there was no effect of the distance (Finke, 1989; Finke & Pinker, 1982). Finke's interpretation is that when the arrow was presented after the dots disappeared, there was a mental analog of scanning in which the time of scanning depended on the mental analog of spatial distance. Although there were no instructions to use imagery, the majority of the subjects in the condition in which the arrow came after the dots disappeared reported that they had done the task by imagining that they were scanning along the direction of the arrow to mentally "see" whether it pointed to where the dots had been. When the arrow came before the dots, the majority of subjects did not report imagery. The analog of scanning in this experiment suggests analog mirroring, in which mental processes involving representing dots in space mirror the motion of the eyes along a trajectory involving real dots.

To recap, the argument just given is that imagistic representation is iconic; visual imagery uses the representations of the same type as perception; so, perceptual representation is iconic. As noted, some visual representations do not correspond to imagery representations. And I certainly have not shown that all representations of imagery are iconic. These are loose ends that would have to be nailed down in a more detailed treatment of this argument. Rather than develop this argument further, I will move to a discussion of some doubts about the iconicity of at least some perceptual representations. Some of these doubts are based on the fact that a single iconic representation often represents many properties at once. This feature of iconic representation—known as holism—is sometimes taken as part of the definition of iconicity and that claim is then used to argue that some perceptual representations are not iconic. I will argue that it is a mistake to treat holism as necessary to iconic representation.

Holism

E. J. Green and Jake Quilty-Dunn use the "part" conception of iconic representation: "Parts of the representation represent parts of the scene represented by the whole representation." I don't reject the part conception, but as I noted, there is a rationale for a different notion of iconicity because analog magnitude representations have no parts and analog magnitude representations are commonly regarded as iconic in the cognitive science literature (for example Carey, 2009, p. 8). An analog magnitude representation can represent numerosity, size, luminance, duration, distance, amount of food, and many other quantities. No parts of representations of numerosity, size, luminance, duration, distance, or amount of food are required.

Green and Quilty-Dunn favor a definition of iconic format that includes "holistic" representation, in which multiple features are represented by the same part of a representational vehicle (Green & Quilty-Dunn, 2017; Quilty-Dunn, 2019b). Green and Quilty-Dunn define "holism" this way (p. 11): "Holism: Each part of the representation represents multiple properties at once, so that the representation does not have separate vehicles corresponding to separate properties and individuals." They suppose that holistic representation "glues" properties together. So, it may seem that there is no substantive disagreement here, just different senses of the term "iconic." They use "iconic" so that holism is required for it but I use the term in accord with analog mirroring. I don't think the issue is purely verbal and will explain why I think the holism requirement is defective.[1]

Green and Quilty-Dunn give an argument against iconicity of certain perceptual representations based on an experiment by Daryl Fougnie and George Alvarez (2011).

Let us focus for the moment on part A of Figure 5.4, which shows a working memory experiment that concerns color and orientation. Subjects were shown a fixation point, diagrammed in the lower left corner of part A, for one second. Then, as depicted in the next box, there was a 1200 ms presentation of five colored triangles. Then there was a blank screen for 900 ms, followed by five boxes where the triangles had been. One of the boxes was filled, the others were empty. The subject's task was to indicate the color and orientation of the triangle that had been at the location of the filled box. Both color and orientation were

---

[1] Green and Quilty-Dunn concede that some philosophical accounts of iconicity do not require "holism," but they contend that "holism" is involved in "the notion of iconic mental representation that is operative within cognitive science." In an implicit acknowledgment of "holistic" representation not being part of a common notion of iconicity, they define "iconicity" in terms of the parts principle ("Parts of the representation represent parts of the scene represented by the whole representation") and then define "iconic format" as "iconicity plus holism," supporting this move with the claim that "iconicity leads to holism." (Quilty-Dunn, 2019a, gives slightly different definitions, including both the parts principle and holism in the definition of an iconic representation.)

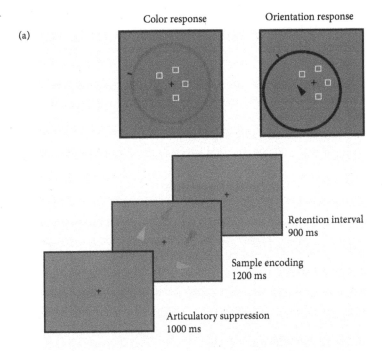
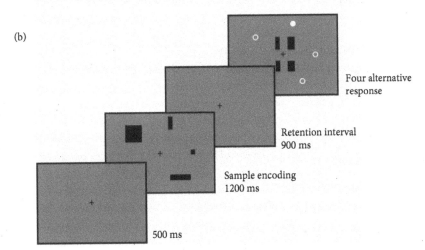

Figure 5.4 Two experiments by Fougnie and Alvarez. Part A indicates that color and orientation are not integrated into a holistic iconic representation. The timeline starts with a fixation point in the lower left box in A. Colored triangles are presented next, then boxes where the triangles had been. One of the boxes is filled. The subject's task is to pinpoint the color and orientation of the triangle that was in the location of the filled box. See the text for an explanation of B. This figure requires color. There is a free pdf on the Oxford University Press web site that has the color version of this and all the other figures. Thanks to Daryl Fougnie for the figure.

indicated by moving a cursor to a point on a wheel of colors/orientations. (The experimenters varied whether color or orientation was reported first.) The result was that subjects very often remembered color without orientation and orientation without color.

Green and Quilty-Dunn use this result to argue that the perceptual representations involved were not holistic and therefore not iconic. To see what is wrong with this reasoning, we need to understand the distinction between integral and separable dimensions of perception.

Integral vs. separable

When a single iconic representation represents many properties, pairs of those properties can be "integral" or, alternatively, "separable." An integral pair of dimensions (Garner & Felfoldy, 1970) can be defined as a pair of dimensions such that one cannot attend to one dimension without attending to the other. Separable pairs are those that are not integral. Thus, height/width, hue/saturation, hue/brightness, brightness/saturation, speed/direction, loudness/pitch, and saturation/lightness are all integral pairs, whereas height/speed, brightness/size, and color/shape are represented separably. Integrality is sometimes ascribed to integrally represented dimensions in the world and sometimes to the mental representations of them. Representation is primary, but to avoid constant repetition of the word "representation" I will often put this in terms of integral and separable dimensions, as I have in this paragraph.

Integrality has a number of important psychological aspects. First, as just mentioned, one cannot attend to one of a pair of integrally represented dimensions without attending to the other. Second, integral dimensions are unified. We often have names for relations between integral dimensions and these relations often are psychologically significant independently of the dimensions themselves. One example is aspect ratio, the ratio of height to width. For example, adaptation has been shown for aspect ratio (ratio of height to width) that is independent of adaptation to height and adaptation to width (Dickinson, Morgan, Tang, & Badcock, 2017). There is a phenomenal dimension to this unity as well. As W. R. Garner put it (1974), "Psychologically, if dimensions are integral, they are not really perceived as dimensions at all . . . and do not reflect the immediate perceptual experience of the subject" (p. 119).

One item of evidence for integrality is that integral dimensions "interfere" with one another in a variety of tasks. For example, a visual task involving one of a pair of integral dimensions is hampered (as indicated by, for example, slower responses) by task-irrelevant variation in the other. If the subject is asked to judge the hue of a stimulus, variation in the size of stimuli does not slow the subject but variation in saturation does. (This is known as Garner interference, named for W. R. Garner, who first formulated these ideas.) (See Algom & Fitousi, 2016b; Palmer, 1999, pp. 550–554.)

Whether the perceptual system treats pairs of dimensions as integral or separable determines degree of visual similarity. One experimental paradigm involves objects that differ in values along two dimensions, e.g., height and speed. If subjects are asked to rate how similar two items are, their judgments reflect adding similarity in height plus similarity in speed—since height and speed are separable dimensions. But if the dimensions are integral, the two dimensions have to be integrated together as in the simplest case, the hypotenuse of a right triangle. (The metric for integral dimensions is Euclidean [hypotenuse], whereas for separable dimensions it is City Block [sum of the sides]. See the brief tutorial on this difference, p-. 1365–1366 of Algom & Fitousi [2016a].)

Whether a specific pair of dimensions is integral is not an intrinsic property of iconic representation. For example, dimensions that are integrally represented in perception need not be integrally represented in the representations of art. Length and width are paradigmatically integrally represented in perception. But a pictorial representation may represent one without the other (Block, 1983b). See Figure 5.5, in which, given the intentions of the "artist" (me), there is a determinately represented width of a column of liquid but no determinately represented length or surface angle.

I will now explain why the distinction between integral and separable dimensions is relevant to the argument by Green and Quilty-Dunn argument that is based on the experiment by Fougnie and Alvarez.

Recall that Green and Quilty-Dunn (Green & Quilty-Dunn, 2017, 2019a; Quilty-Dunn, 2019b) argue that this experiment shows working memory representations are not iconic. Recall that Green and Quilty-Dunn require that iconic representations are holistic, where "holism" is defined as "parts of icons represent multiple properties simultaneously" (Quilty-Dunn, 2019a, p. 3). Quilty-Dunn (2019a) reasons from the Fougnie and Alvarez result as follows, using "VWM" to mean visual working memory (p. 16):

Figure 5.5 Illustration of depiction of mass of liquid in a beaker without a representation of the surface angle or the length of the column of liquid. From Block (1983b).

In cases where subjects were very far away from the correct value on one dimension (i.e., when they lost information about that feature), they were nonetheless typically able to produce accurate responses on the other dimension. That is, storage of color in VWM doesn't necessarily correlate with storage of orientation (nor vice versa). . . . These effects imply a lack of holistic binding in representations in VWM, and therefore suggest that representations in VWM have a discursive format and employ distinct symbols to represent distinct feature dimensions. Since these dimensions are represented by means of distinct symbols (i.e., not in an icon that satisfies HOLISM), the fact that one is lost should not be expected to tell you whether the other is lost as well.

The experiment just discussed supports the separability of color and orientation in working memory, but the experiment illustrated in B of Figure 5.4 supports the opposite (integral) conclusion about height and width. The procedure is very similar to the one just described. Five rectangles were presented that varied in height and width, then there was an interval of 900 ms. After the interval, four rectangles appeared together with five circles where the rectangles had been. One circle was open and one closed. Subjects were to match for height and width of the target rectangle, i.e., the one that had been at the location of the filled circle. Two of the rectangles among which they could choose matched in either height or width, one rectangle matched in neither and of course one (the best answer) matched in both. The result is that subjects rarely got the height without the width or the width without the height. In other words, the result for the two spatial properties, height and width were the opposite of what happened in the first experiment, involving a spatial and a nonspatial property.[2] This is evidence that height and width are represented integrally. This makes intuitive sense since, as mentioned earlier, height and width seem intuitively to be part of a single shape-factor, sometimes known as aspect ratio.

What is the point of the integral/separable distinction and how is it relevant to holism? The integral/separable difference is a difference in the relation between pairs of represented features of perceptual icons, not to the icons themselves. For perceptual representations, typically some pairs of properties are integral and some separable, as we saw in the Fougnie et al. experiment. If iconicity required integrality, there would typically be no answer as to whether a representation was an icon. Or perhaps the answer would be: Some pairs of features are represented integrally and some are not. The claim that icons are integral is a kind of category mistake: Typically, some pairs of features are integral and some not.

---

[2] Note that spatial and nonspatial properties can form integral pairs. There is evidence that numerosity and surface area are an integral pair (Aulet & Lourenco, 2020).

A revised version of the holism requirement might be that a representation is holistic if it has even one integral pair of feature representations. Note however that this version of holism would count against the "pluralist" view of Green and Quilty-Dunn, specifically their view that perceptual object representations are discursive. Perceptual object representations often involve both integral and separable dimensions. For example, they sometimes have height, width, color, and orientation, as when one sees a street sign. Height and width are an integral, but height and color are not.

Instead of regarding a representation as holistic if it has even one pair of integral feature dimensions, we might consider regarding a representation as nonholistic if it has even one separable pair. But then it will be hard to find any holistic representations. Either way, holism does not seem a very useful criterion for iconicity.

In the last section, I gave evidence for imagery representations being iconic and then argued that imagery representations are of the same kind as perceptual representations—but produced in a different way. This is an indirect argument in that it makes use of imagery representations to argue for the iconicity of perceptual representations. I now turn to evidence of iconicity deriving from perceptual representations of objects. Although there is ample evidence that perceptual object representations are iconic, to be presented in the next section, there is also a great deal of evidence that has been taken to support the view that perceptual object representations are discursive. That evidence will be discussed later in the chapter.

Iconic object-representations in perception

In much of the literature, perceptual object representations are known as object-files. An object-file is often defined as a representation of mid-level vision that maintains reference to an object, including a moving object, over time, storing and updating information about the object (Kahneman, Treisman, & Gibbs, 1992). A theme of the rest of this chapter is that the term "object-file" is an ambiguous term used to denote representations of two different kinds, one perceptual, one cognitive. Thus the term "object-file" is a trap for the unwary, contributing to confusion about the border between perception and cognition.

Seeing an object as such is a matter of visually representing it as an object. That requires representation that goes beyond low-level representations of properties: color, shape, texture, motion, and the like. What capacities are involved? I have emphasized a number of perhaps overlapping capacities: visually singling

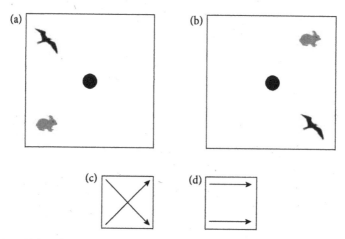

Figure 5.6 If A and B are quickly alternated, one sees apparent motion, usually as depicted in D. Thanks to Susan Carey for the figure. (Cf. Carey, 2009, p. 73.)

out the object, visually detecting the object (in the sense of distinguishing between the object's presence and its absence), visually differentiating the object from the background, visually discriminating the object from other objects, and visually categorizing the object (Block, 2012, 2013). I believe that these abilities help to pinpoint a natural kind. However, all of them are controversial.[3] In this section, I won't appeal to these capacities. Instead, I will bring in phenomena that suggest that object-perception is iconic whether or not these capacities can be used to characterize object-perception.

One line of evidence for the iconic nature of object-perception exploits apparent motion, a phenomenon discovered in the early twentieth century (Wertheimer, 1912). Apparent motion occurs if a subject is shown A in Figure 5.6, followed by B, then A again, then B again, and so on. Subjects report seeing motion. At high rates of flicker between A and B, motion will be seen without intermediate stages. (This is called "phi.") At slower flicker rates, subjects see the trajectories of the moving objects with intermediate stages clearly visible. Subjects report seeing objects of one color or shape transforming into objects of another color or shape. (That phenomenon is called beta motion.) It should be said that subjects do not confuse apparent motion with real motion, but apparent motion still looks like motion (Sperling, van Santen, & Burt, 1985).

---

[3] Fred Dretske argued for a concept of seeing——simple seeing—that does not require visual categorization or singling out (Dretske, 1969). In his later work he claimed one can see a perfectly camouflaged object (2007).

Most subjects will see the motion in D rather than the motion in C because the primary determinant of the motion is minimizing the distance between the items. The effect on apparent motion of path length has been estimated to be 15 times the strength of the effect of the shapes of the items involved (Flombaum & Scholl, 2006). The visual system prefers not to see a bird turning into a rabbit, but that preference is balanced against the preference for shorter distances of motion. So, they will see a bird crossing the screen from left to right, gradually changing into a rabbit at the top right, and the opposite transformation on bottom. The larger the difference between the paths, the more likely the subject is to see the shorter motion (Nakayama et al., 1995). However, if the paths are roughly equal, shape counts.

Path length and shape work together in an integrated manner. The direction of motion depends on a smooth way on the distance between the items. See Figure 5.7, in which the gradual nature of this type of transition is graphed. The gradual transitions are indicative of the analog mirroring of iconic representation. The integration of smoothly varying spatial factors with factors involving object representations suggests that these are not fundamentally different kinds of representations, as would be expected if object representations in perception are discursive whereas other representations are iconic. (This is the "pluralist" view of Green and Quilty-Dunn, to be discussed later in the chapter.) It would be possible to combine discursive representation of objects with a spatiotemporal

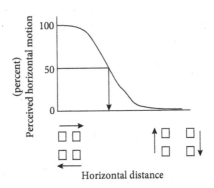

Figure 5.7 The likelihood of seeing horizontal (rather than vertical motion) in apparent motion displays that are variants of the one in the previous figure. The horizontal axis shows horizontal distance, whereas the vertical axis graphs the likelihood of perceiving horizontal motion rather than vertical motion (i.e., the bird on the top left turning into the rabbit on the top right and the corresponding transformation across the bottom of the screen). What the graph shows is that as horizontal distance gets greater, subjects are less likely to see horizontal motion. From Nakayama et al. (1995). Thanks to Ken Nakayama for this figure.

representation system, but to the extent that spatial and spatiotemporal effects saturate object representations, that view is less attractive.

The apparent motion stimuli just described are ambiguous in the sense that there are two very different representations that the visual system can compute from them. As we will see in Chapter 9, when stimuli are ambiguous in this sense, cognitive and conceptual factors can affect which representation the visual system computes. This is cognitive penetration in the sense described in Chapter 1 and at greater length in Chapter 9. So, one should not be surprised if cognitive information influences which kind of motion the subject sees.

In this section, we are discussing evidence for iconicity of perceptual object representations. So why does apparent motion constitute evidence for iconic object-seeing as opposed to just seeing of shapes? One relevant manipulation uses pairs of white bars that protrude from their black background and differ in orientation by 90° between the left and right displays, as in Figure 5.8. Subjects see the bars as rotating back and forth (instead of birds changing into rabbits). Note that the bars appear to rotate gradually. That is, the subject sees the intermediate orientations. The fact that subjects see intermediate stages of rotation suggests that the representations are part of a system that mirrors rotation operations on actual objects—analog mirroring. See Figure 5.8.

The display is viewed via an apparatus that allows for independent manipulation of what is sent to each eye. Whether the white bars emerge from the background in the manner of objects is manipulated by changing binocular disparity cues. If the bars look like parts of a squarish shape instead of like protruding objects, then there is a visual experience of vertical motion but no visual experience as of rotation (Nakayama et al., 1995). If there is no apparent object,

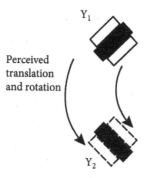

Figure 5.8 A clockwise oriented bar can be seen to rotate to a counterclockwise oriented bar in apparent motion. From Nakayama et al. (1995). Thanks to Ken Nakayama for this figure.

then there is no rotation. To the extent that shapes are involved, they are not 2D shapes, since the 2D outline is the same whether or not the display looks like parallel bars.

To be clear: what makes these representations perceptual is that the bars look like they are moving and rotating. What suggests they are iconic is the presence of intermediate stages of rotation and translation (i.e., vertical movement).

The apparent motion results are direct evidence for the iconicity of object perception because they exhibit the smooth variation indicative of analog mirroring. I now turn to indirect evidence that perceptual object representations are iconic. More specifically, I will consider evidence that object representations in perception are integrated with other representations in perception, notably spatial representations, arguing against the "pluralistic" view that perceptual object representations have different formats from other perceptual representations. None of this evidence conclusively excludes pluralism but it does suggest a kind of spatiality of object perception that should make pluralists uncomfortable.

The first type of evidence I will consider involves object-based attention. (See Scholl, 2001, for a review.) Perceptual attention can be divided into three types, depending on what is attended to: object-based attention, in which what is attended to is an object; spatial attention, in which what is attended to is a region of space; and feature-based attention, in which what is attended to is a property of objects or regions of space. The word "attention" is used in many different ways, including speaking of attention to items that cannot be perceived directly, for example, an idea, a social movement, or a moral failing. But the kind of attention being discussed here is perceptual in that it is tightly integrated into perceptual systems and it obeys perceptual regularities such as divisive normalization (Bloem & Ling, 2019). (See the discussion at the end of Chapter 2 surrounding Figure 2.17 for a brief account of divisive normalization.) For example, divisive normalization governs the effects of attention on perception having to do with the size of the attentional field as compared with the size of the stimulus (Reynolds & Heeger, 2009).

Subjects show faster and more accurate processing for features belonging to the same object than for features belonging to different objects, showing that perceptual object representations are involved in the control of attention. The basic type of experiment that shows this is illustrated in (a) in Figure 5.9. If subjects see a cue at C, they are faster at detecting a target on the same object at S (for "same") than an equidistant target on another object, D (for "different"). And this holds whether or not there is an occluder, as in (b). The fact that the result does not depend on whether there is an occluder indicates that the subjects are seeing the

242 THE BORDER BETWEEN SEEING AND THINKING

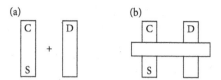

Figure 5.9 If cued to C, subjects are faster to detect targets at S than at D even though S and D are equidistant from C. Thanks to Brian Scholl for this figure. (See Scholl, 2001.)

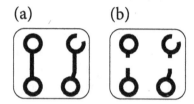

Figure 5.10 Subjects were asked to categorize the ends of the wrenches. From Scholl (2001). Thanks to Brian Scholl for this figure.

occluded objects as objects. This is not in itself evidence for iconicity, but that is coming below.

Object representation and object-based attention can persist even in the absence of retinal stimulation as with the tunnel effect described at the end of this chapter.

Object-based attention can be used to characterize what constitutes a visual object. Watson and Kramer gave subjects brief presentation of wrench-like stimuli including those shown in Figure 5.10. Subjects were tasked with making two judgments about each stimulus, categorizing the ends of the wrenches as "open" as in the top right of both (a) and (b) and "bent" as in the bottom right of both (a) and (b). Watson and Kramer reasoned that if both features were on the same "visual object," subjects would be faster. Subjects were faster for the objects in (a) than in (b) because of the gaps in b.

Here is the evidence for iconicity: Object-based attention is a matter of degree. Objects such as the vertical rectangles of Figure 5.9 show less of an object effect if the rectangles are altered so as to be less "good" as objects, for example if the bottom horizontal bar of the rectangle is deleted (Marino & Scholl, 2005). If there was a radical format difference between object-perception and other perception, one would not expect such gradual effects. The difference between discursive and iconic representation is not a matter of degree. It is unclear how pluralists can explain these effects.

Another feature of object-based attention that goes against pluralism is that attention "spreads" within an object from a cue at one end of the object (as in Figure 5.9) (Richard & Vecera, 2008; Zhao, Kong, & Wang, 2013). Spreading would make no sense if there were no representational analogs of the spatial extent of the object that mirror the spatial properties of the object.

A similar point about the integration of perceptual object representations with spatial representation applies to a phenomenon known as inhibition of return. Inhibition of return was first demonstrated in a paradigm in which there are three boxes, a central box and two flanking boxes. If one of the flanking boxes (say the one on the right) is cued (e.g., it suddenly brightens), attention is drawn to it. Then the central box was cued. If a target was presented in the right box within 150 ms, there is a detection advantage (due to the residual attention to the right box), but if a target is presented in the right box after 300 ms, there is a disadvantage in detection. The upshot—now verified in many paradigms—is that the attention system is inhibited from attending to *something* that has recently been attended for as long as 3 seconds.

But what is that something? Is it an area of space, a scene, an object, or what? The answer is areas of space and objects both show inhibition of return, not surprising since there is both object-based attention and spatial attention. The object-based effect is exhibited when what is inhibited is a return of attention to the object in which the cue originally occurred (Tipper, Jordan, & Weaver, 1999). This is verified by varying other properties such as location, showing an independent effect of same object.

With inhibition of return as with object-based attention, there is a gradient of effects within an object, with the strongest effect at the cued location within the object, and weaker effects in the same object but further away from the cue (Klein & Ivanoff, 2008). This shows integration of object-based effects with spatial effects, again providing evidence against the view that there is a difference in kind between object perception (allegedly discursive) and other perception (iconic). Again, object perception is integrated seamlessly with spatial attention, something that would call for explanation if they involved representations of different formats as the pluralists claim.

To avoid misunderstanding, I am not saying that iconic and discursive elements cannot be combined in a single representation. An iconic depiction of the shape of a street can be combined on a map with the name of the street. But notice that this is possible because the name has spatial properties: its location, orientation, and size. Indeed, the name of Doyers Street, a curvy street in southern Manhattan, is often curved like the street on maps of Manhattan. By comparison, the effects of perception of space and objects combine in inhibiting return in a kind of vector summation.

A different kind of support for iconicity in object-perception involves visuospatial neglect, a syndrome in which subjects fail to attend to objects on one side of the body. The point of discussing visuospatial neglect is that it reveals that object representations, spatial representations, temporal representations, and numerical representations are tightly coupled in overlapping systems, counting against the claim that object representations have a different kind of format from other perceptual representations.

In one kind of visuospatial neglect, subjects ignore or fail to consciously see the left side of the visual field. Patients fail to eat the food on the neglected side of their plates, fail to dress the neglected side of the body, and so on. This kind of neglect is based in one form of egocentric perception. When left-sided neglect patients are asked to bisect a horizontal line, they put the bisecting mark to the right of the midpoint. Interestingly, some left-sided neglect patients show the same effect for imagined lines, further bolstering the imagery argument given earlier in this chapter. The size of the rightward drift in bisecting lines is proportional to the length of the line, i.e., larger displacements with larger lines. This dependence on degrees is indicative of iconic representation. These effects are all matters of degree and interact with many spatial visual features, again providing problems for pluralism. For example, for very short lines, there is an effect in the opposite direction, the "crossover effect" (Zorzi et al., 2012).

Neglect involves inattention to, and perhaps lack of perception of, one side of space. But it often applies to one side of individual objects that have salient axes, showing again that the control of attention depends on spatial aspects of perception, showing integration of object representations with spatial representations. That integration would require explanation if the two kinds of representations were of different formats, one iconic, one discursive. Many patients neglect the left sides of objects all over the visual field, showing some influence of allocentric spatial representation (Beschin, Cubelli, Della Sala, & Spinazzola, 1997; Tipper & Behrmann, 1996). And patients often neglect the initial letter or segment of a word, even if the word is presented vertically; neglect the Western Hemisphere even in an upside-down map; or neglect the left side of a face even in an upside-down photograph (Bisiach & Luzzatti, 1978; Caramazza & Hillis, 1990). Again, these effects are matters of degree and interact with spatial features.

A classic demonstration of object-based neglect involved barbells, two circles connected by a line. Neglect patients had trouble with detecting targets on the left circle, but when the barbell was rotated so that the left circle had moved to the right, many patients showed flipped results, with more trouble on the right circle. This effect was only observed if the barbell was a single object: if the line between the circles was omitted, there was no such effect (Tipper & Behrmann, 1996).

PERCEPTION IS ICONIC; COGNITION IS DISCURSIVE   245

Again we see seamless integration of object perception with spatial perception, a surprising result if the two have entirely different formats. Another classic demonstration of object effects in neglect is shown in Figure 5.11. A patient who was asked to copy a picture left out the left side some of the individual objects in the picture. See (Walker, 1995) for other examples. This is a commonly observed phenomenon. Once again we see that the perception of objects is part of a spatial representation system, something that would be in need of explanation if object representations were discursive but spatial representations were iconic.

As just mentioned, neglect also extends to "numerical space." Left-sided neglect patients asked what number is halfway between 2 and 6 skew their answers toward 6. Strikingly, the crossover effect just mentioned also applies to numerical space (Zorzi et al., 2012). Similar results apply to temporal estimation problems for neglect patients (Bonato, Saj, & Vuilleumier, 2016). A further crossover effect is that normal subjects who were asked to estimate additions or subtractions of dots showed a leftward bias on the number line (that is, they underestimated) for small numbers of dots, but a rightward bias for large numbers (overestimating)

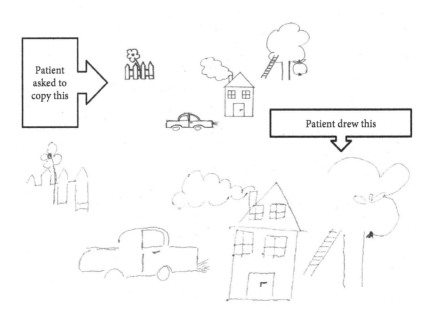

Figure 5.11 A visuospatial neglect patient was asked to copy the top picture. The bottom picture is the patient's attempt. Note that the patient leaves out some of the left side of some of the individual objects in the picture. Thanks to James Danckert for this picture.

(Zorzi et al., 2012). The explanation usually given for this kind of result is that spatial representation is co-opted for the numerosity system.

I will be urging caution about drawing conclusions about perceptual representations from evidence about the remnants of perceptual representations in working memory. To the extent that inhibition of return involves working memory, that caution applies to the results just mentioned. One way in which working memory would add perceptual features rather than subtract them is via the imposition of perceptual imagery, but it would have to be shown that imagery is involved in the experiments I am talking about.

Finally, as I mentioned in the last chapter that in the multiple object tracking paradigm, not only can subjects track about four disks but also they can also track the average position of the disks. See Figure 4.5. A reminder: A number of disks (eight in the figure) are shown on a screen. Four of the disks blink or are otherwise indicated and then the disks move randomly. The subject is supposed to track those objects as they move about in a random way. Most subjects can track about four objects if they do not move too quickly. Subjects turned out to be able to track the centroid of the target disks, but they could also track the centroid of the distractor disks. And they could do this even if their attention was drawn off by a difficult secondary task of counting the number of times the disks crossed some lines on the screen (Alvarez & Oliva, 2008). This experiment suggests that perceptual object representations integrate with spatial representations even though working memory is also involved in multiple object tracking. In sum, there is plenty of evidence that perceptual object representations are of a piece with other sorts of spatial perception, putting pressure on the view that object representations are different in format from other sorts of perception.

Object-files in working memory

Susan Carey (Carey, 2009; Feigenson, Spelke, & Carey, 2002) and her colleagues have shown that object representations in working memory can code continuous variables. Babies who are shown varying amount of graham cracker pieces deposited separately in two buckets will crawl toward the container with more cracker stuff—when the difference in surface area is large enough—and if there are equal amounts, the babies are at chance on which to crawl to. If the experimenter puts one very large piece in one bucket and two small pieces in the other bucket, babies tend to crawl to the bucket with more cracker. Results of this sort would be expected if the representations are iconic.

But why think the babies are using perceptual object representations in this experiment? This experiment shows the "slot" signature of object representation, namely that the working memory representations have a limit of three objects. Babies can compare the surface areas if the number of items is three in one bucket and two in the other, but if there are four pieces in one bucket and two in the other, they are at chance. And they are also at chance for four vs. one (Carey, 2009; Feigenson et al., 2002). (See the section of Chapter 1 on slot vs. pool models of working memory.)

Another variant is also governed by numerosity. Instead of two buckets, this experiment uses a single closed container into which the experimenter deposits objects, one at a time and into which the baby must reach to get the objects. The top of the container is covered with a flexible material with a slot that allows the baby to reach into it without seeing what is inside. The dependent variable is how many times the baby reaches. If three objects have been ostentatiously placed in the bucket, the baby tends to reach three times, whereas if the number of objects is four or more, babies' reaching is at chance. "Infants search no longer upon having seen four go in and having retrieved only one than if they have seen just one go in and have retrieved only one. It's not that the child represents nothing in the box when he or she saw four go in; the infant does reach in and retrieve one. Infants represent something in the box, but they cannot form a representation of a set of four items under these circumstances" (Carey, 2009, p. 84). This is the signature of working memory "slots." As explained in Chapter 1, adult humans and monkeys tend toward four slots whereas babies tend toward three slots. A variant of this closed container experiment varied the size of the objects. If infants saw two objects—say small cars—placed in the container, they searched for exactly two even if the first car retrieved had twice the surface area and four times the volume of the car they saw hidden.(Carey, 2009, pp. 84–85, 142–146). These experiments reveal iconic object representations in working memory. And again we see that working memory representations are task dependent.

A principle that I am using in interpreting these experiments and that will be discussed in the remainder of this chapter is this: If the remnants of perceptual representations in working memory show iconicity, then very likely that iconicity is inherited from perception—unless there is evidence of mental imagery, which, as explained earlier in this chapter, shares representational types with perception. However, if the remnants of perception in working memory do not show iconicity, then the iconic properties may have been lost in the process by which perceptual representations are transferred into and maintained in working memory. So lack of iconicity in working memory does not show lack of iconicity in perception.

Memory involving perceptual representations

The reader may be wondering at this point why anyone would favor noniconic perceptual object representations. What convinces many people I think is the singular element in perception and perceptual attention discussed in Chapter 3. What may be especially impressive is the use of perceptual attention to track objects, as in the multiple object tracking experiments described in Chapters 3 and 4. It may seem that object-tracking requires a format element, a "this" that "follows" the objects. The appeal here seems to be to a vague sense of a mechanical model involving a "finger of instantiation" (Pylyshyn's term) that somehow follows the object, as your finger could follow a moving object on a screen. This appeal to a "Cartesian Theater" (Dennett, 1991) loses its attraction once one starts thinking of how such a finger could work in the brain where there is no screen and no finger. One way to dissolve the appeal is to ask yourself how surprised you would be if a deep neural net could do object tracking. We now have deep neural nets that can do many very impressive perceptual tasks. See, for example, Dall-e-2 on the openai web site. We should not be surprised if such a neural net can do object tracking and it would be a stretch to suppose the deep neural net architecture allows for a singular format element.

The evidence provided by E. J. Green and Jake Quilty-Dunn (Green & Quilty-Dunn, 2017; Quilty-Dunn, 2016b, 2019b, 2020) is based on the "object-specific preview benefit" or OSPB (Kahneman et al., 1992). They use the OSPB to argue that the format of perceptual object representation is discursive rather than iconic, and that object perception is propositional. They are pluralists about perceptual format, arguing that the formats of perceptions that are not perceptual object representations are iconic. By contrast, I have argued that all perceptual representation is iconic, and in the last section I noted that some working memory object representations are iconic too.

The OSPB involves representations in working memory. In order to understand the issues, it is helpful to understand working memory in comparison with two other kinds of short-term visual memory, iconic memory and fragile visual short-term memory. These forms of memory are more like perception than working memory, but it is hard to do experiments of the sort needed to demonstrate iconicity with them. Working memory is longer lasting and robust and so easier to do experiments on, but does not preserve all the properties of perception. The main reason for introducing iconic memory and fragile visual short-term memory is their contrast with working memory. I will be arguing that there is a difference of kind between the "object-files" of working memory and the "object-files" of normal perception. On my view, the use of the term "object-file" to refer to the full perceptual representations used in tracking and also the conceptualized remnants of perception in a cognitive envelope working memory sets us up for confusion.

Iconic memory

Immediately after the presentation of a stimulus, reverberating retinal activity and activity in V1 grounds perceptual representation of low-level properties, what is often called "visual persistence" (Coltheart, 1980). For another couple of hundred ms, there is a genuine form of memory, "iconic memory," that also represents higher level properties (Pratte, 2018).

The classic experiment demonstrating iconic memory was done by George Sperling. In the Sperling experiment, there is a brief flash of an array of letters separated into rows, e.g., three rows of four letters each (Sperling, 1960). Subjects report seeing all or almost all the letters but can recall only three or four of them once the display has gone off. However, if one row is cued by a tone within a few hundred milliseconds after the stimulus disappears (a high tone for the top row, low tone for the bottom row, etc.) subjects can recall three or four from any given row, suggesting that they did have a brief visual representation of all the letters. The ratio of total capacity (roughly 3.5 in each of three rows) to capacity without a cue is called the "partial report superiority." The phenomenology of a version of the experiment was described by William James in his *Principles of Psychology*: "If we open our eyes instantaneously upon a scene, and then shroud them in complete darkness, it will be as if we saw the scene in ghostly light through the dark screen. We can read off details in it which were unnoticed whilst the eyes were open" (James, 1890).

Fragile visual short-term memory

As I mentioned in Chapter 1, Victor Lamme's laboratory at the University of Amsterdam demonstrated fragile visual short-term memory in a series of articles (starting with Landman et al., 2003). The experimental paradigm combines the "iconic memory" paradigm of the Sperling experiment with "change blindness." This paradigm shows a greater capacity in fragile visual short-term memory than in working memory but a smaller capacity than in iconic memory. See Chapter 1 for details.

As I noted in Chapter 1, a recent experiment (Pratte, 2018) suggests that representations in iconic memory undergo a "sudden death" decay, in which the surviving representations maintain the same level of precision rather than decaying in precision as "pool of resources" models would predict. Since the memory capacity found by Pratte decays smoothly from 33 ms to 1000 ms, and since iconic memory does not last more than a few hundred ms, both iconic and fragile visual short-term memory would appear to be involved in this experiment. Since working memory *does* fit the pool of resources model, it would appear to be of a different kind than the earlier stores, as would be predicted by the claim of a format difference.

Working memory

Working memory is a kind of cognitive scratch pad that can be used to manipulate information for cognitive purposes. For example, if you want to reason from the proposition that p and the proposition that if p, then q, you must hold the premises in working memory in order to make the deduction. There can be cognition without working memory, but working memory is necessary for reasoning in which a premise is retained for later use. Presence of a representation in working memory is not "storage" but rather active maintenance.

Working memory is far more robust than either iconic or fragile visual short-term memory. Ilja Sligte found that a white screen (a so-called light mask) obliterated iconic memory but not fragile visual short-term memory or working memory. A pattern mask obliterated fragile visual short-term memory but not working memory.

Working memory is generally taken to be controlled by prefrontal cortex on the outside mid-level surfaces (dorsolateral prefrontal cortex). Transcranial magnetic stimulation (TMS) is the application of an electromagnetic pulse to a brain area, creating neural noise. Transcranial magnetic stimulation to visual areas (notably V4) impaired fragile visual short-term memory, and TMS to a cognitive area, the dorsolateral prefrontal cortex, impaired working memory but not fragile visual short-term memory (Sligte, Scholte, & Lamme, 2008; Sligte, Vandenbroucke, Scholte, & Lamme, 2010; Sligte, Wokke, Tesselaar, Scholte, & Lamme, 2011). So these different forms of memory are distinct both at the psychological and neural levels.

There have been many proposals for further fractionating working memory. For example, Justin Wood has argued that working memory can be divided into a view-dependent store with a capacity of roughly four items and a more abstract view-independent store of about two items (Wood, 2009). However, it is unclear whether the view-dependent store might involve fragile visual short-term memory.

When working memory representations do not show iconicity, one cannot be sure whether the iconicity was lost in the conceptualization process, but when they do show iconicity, the iconicity derives from the iconicity of perception in many paradigms. As mentioned earlier, the only way in which perceptual features get into working memory aside from perception is via the imposition of perceptual imagery. Mental images take about a second and a half to generate (Kosslyn et al., 2006), and that fact can often be used to rule out the presence of imagery.

A recent experiment showed how two quite different perceptual representations can be converted into the same working memory representation if the subject's task is appropriately similar. Yuna Kwak and Clay Curtis (2022) used two kinds of stimuli on different trials, oriented gratings (Gabor patches) and clouds of moving dots. Subjects' task was to indicate the orientation of the grating or the direction of the moving dots after a delay period. They scanned the subjects using fMRI during the delay period prior to doing the tasks. The first result was that decoding trained on the grating task also worked on the dot task and vice versa. This fact shows that the working memory representation was sufficiently abstract as to be common between the two perceptions. The second result homed in on what the actual shared representations were. They developed a visualization technique that allowed them to transform the brain representations into a display on a screen that would have produced that brain activation. And the result was that both the representations of the grid and the dot motion transformed to an oriented stripe. The representation of the cloud of dots abstracted away from the representations of the individual dots and the representation of the grating abstracted away from the spatial frequency and contrast of the grating. What this experiment shows is that working memory representations depend not only on the stimulus but also on the task. A similarity in task can lead to a similarity in working memory representation even if the percepts differ. I mentioned another kind of task dependence of working memory earlier in this chapter: whether size is represented in working memory depends on the task.

I have mentioned four items of evidence that perceptual representations differ from working memory representations:

1. As described in Chapter 2, perception exhibits a canonical computation, divisive normalization. One manifestation of this computation is center-surround suppression, in which perception of a central disk is suppressed by similar properties in a doughnut surrounding it. This is illustrated in Figure 2.17. When the disk and the doughnut were presented one at a time, with the first stimulus maintained in working memory, there was no center-surround suppression (Bloem et al., 2018). The upshot is that a basic computational feature of perception is absent in perceptual working memory.

2. As just explained, the number of items that a subject can hold in more perceptual forms of memory is greater than in working memory.
3. Perception allows for finer-grained representations than working memory.
4. Working memory representations are based not only on the stimulus but also on the task that the stimulus is used for.

Arguments against perceptual iconicity that are based on perception and memory of objects

Zenon Pylyshyn famously argued against iconic representations in the mind, based on his criticisms of Stephen Kosslyn's work on mental imagery (Kosslyn et al., 2006; Pylyshyn, 1973, 2002). But current opposition to iconicity is confined to perceptual object representations, and the locus of controversy is the object specific preview benefit, i.e. the OSPB. In one version of the OSPB, two boxes are on the screen containing pictures, for example, pictures of an apple or a loaf of bread. The pictures disappear and the boxes move. Then a picture appears in one of the boxes, either of an apple, a loaf of bread, or something else. The subject's task is to name the object. Subjects are faster in naming an apple if (a picture of)an apple was in one of the boxes. (So far, that is just "priming," a phenomenon whereby something just seen or related in certain ways what something just seen is easier to recognize.) However, and this is the OSPB, subjects are faster still if the apple is in the very box that it started in, even if that box has changed sides.

Another version of the OSPB is illustrated in Figure 5.12, Words are presented in boxes. Then the words disappear and the boxes move as indicated for 1.5 seconds. Then a picture appears in one of the boxes which the subject is supposed to name. The result is that the subject is faster to name the apple if the box the apple is in was the one in which the word "apple" had appeared. Green and Quilty-Dunn take this result to indicate that the perceptual representation—the "object-file" that underlies this ability—is a symbol that has the content apple and is bound to semantically linked information in a separable, nonholistic fashion. For example, the object-file might simply be a discursive list of linked properties. As Green and Quilty-Dunn note: There is also an OSPB from lowercase words to uppercase versions of the same word, e.g., from "bread" to "BREAD." That, they say, shows that the perceptual representation of the word abstracts from shape properties and so cannot be iconic. This is part of the abstractness argument against iconicity.

In another variant, pictured in Figure 5.13 (Jordan, Clark, & Mitroff, 2010), two boxes are presented with pictures in them, say a hammer and a whistle. The pictures disappear and the frames then move so that the boxes can end up on a different part of the screen from which they started a second later. Then the

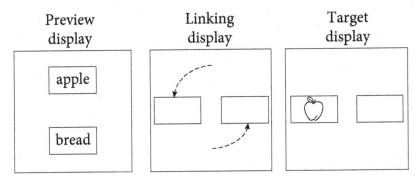

Figure 5.12 Version of the object specific preview benefit that shows that object-files contain both linguistic and pictorial information. From Quilty-Dunn (2016b), based on Gordon and Irwin (2000). Thanks to Jake Quilty-Dunn for the figure.

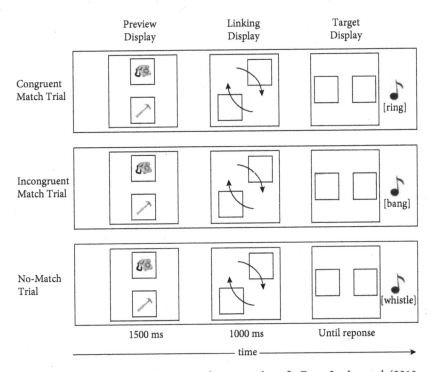

Figure 5.13 Version of the object-specific preview benefit. From Jordan et al. (2010, p. 495), with permission of Taylor & Francis, http://www.tandfonline.com

subject hears a sound and has to say whether the sound matches one of the pictured items. Subjects are faster if the sound matches the object that was in the box that is now on the side that the sound is coming from. For example, in the top row of Figure 5.13, the sound of ringing matches the picture of a telephone.

Subjects are fastest for the "congruent" situation in the top row. The sound of banging in the second row does not match but was present (bringing with it the speed increment of priming. See footnote 7 in Chapter 3.). That row comes in second. The slowest is the bottom row in which the sound—a whistle—does not match either of the pictures.

Green and Quilty-Dunn conclude that perceptual object representations are discursive symbols that abstract away from modality-specific information in an amodal format.

How do we know that the representations involved in the OSPB are working memory representations? In the experiments pictured in Figure 5.12 and Figure 5.13, there is a delay between the first stimulus and the last stimulus. In the experiment with the word "apple" and the picture of the apple, the delay is 1.5 seconds. In the experiment with the sounds matched to objects, the delay is 1 second. A further experiment showed that the OSPB was preserved even if the blank period lasted as long as 8 seconds (Noles, Scholl, & Mirtroff, 2005).

However, iconic memory of the perceptual kind exhibited in the classic Sperling experiment lasts only a few hundred milliseconds. As I mentioned earlier, there is another kind of perceptual memory, "fragile visual short-term memory" (Lamme, 2016). (See earlier in this chapter for an explanation of fragile visual short-term memory.) Fragile visual short-term memory has been shown to last up to 4–5 seconds, but never longer. In addition, fragile visual short-term memory has been shown in static displays but never moving displays. Further, fragile visual short-term memory is, well, fragile, and easily overwritten. The motion in these displays may be enough to damage fragile visual short-term memory representations. These considerations strongly suggest that the kind of memory involved in the OSPB is working memory, the least perceptual of the three kinds of visual short-term memory.

Now we get to the crux of the disagreement: Green and Quilty-Dunn take the abstractness shown in the experiments just described as applying to perception because they think the OSPB involves full perceptual representations. I think the OSPB concerns working memory representations that have conceptualized *remnants* of perception in a cognitive envelope and that there is no evidence that the abstractness shown in the OSPB can be ascribed to perception as opposed to the cognitive aspects introduced by the conceptualization and the cognitive envelope. So the crucial disagreement concerns whether the OSPB involves *full perceptual representations* of just the sort that are involved in perception itself.

The first thing to note about the OSPB is that after the picture or word disappears, *the subject is no longer seeing them.* They see the boxes that are rotating, not what was originally in the boxes. I have looked at OSPB displays. Once the letters disappear one just sees the boxes moving with no awareness of the letters. The fact that the subject does not see the picture or word by itself shows that we should be suspicious of any claim that in the blank period the subjects have real perceptual representations of the items that were originally in the boxes. Indeed, there is no reason to think that the subjects in this experiment have any visual phenomenology of the items in the boxes during the blank period. The iconic memory and fragile visual short-term memory mentioned above are said by subjects to be phenomenal, but I don't know of any reports of phenomenology of working memory in experiments that contrast iconic memory, fragile visual short-term memory, and working memory, such as the experiments by Victor Lamme's group in Amsterdam (Lamme, 2003, 2004, 2006, 2016, 2018; Landman et al., 2003; Pinto, Sligte, Shapiro, & Lamme, 2013; Pinto, van Gaal, de Lange, Lamme, & Seth, 2015; Sligte, 2011; Sligte et al., 2008; Sligte, Scholte, & Lamme, 2009; Sligte et al., 2010; Sligte et al., 2011). Further, it takes 1.5 seconds for a subject to generate a mental image. In the 1 second that the boxes are rotating as depicted in Figure 5.13 there would be no time to generate a mental image of the hammer or telephone. Both of these points suggest a difference in kind between the "object-files" of working memory and the "object-files" of perception. As I noted earlier in this chapter, the use of the term "object-file" to refer to the full perceptual representations used in tracking and also the conceptualized remnants of perception in a cognitive envelope sets us up for confusion.

Consider the top row of Figure 5.13. On the left we see a box with a telephone on the top and a hammer on the bottom. Then the pictures disappear and the boxes move. They move for 1 second as depicted in Figure 5.13, but as I mentioned the time lag can be as long as 8 seconds. Then a sound plays. As I mentioned, the subjects are not seeing the telephone or the hammer. They just see the empty boxes moving. If the representations of the telephone and the hammer are real perceptual representations, perhaps they would be *unconscious perceptual representations*. Now I happen to be a fan of full perceptual representations in unconscious perception (Block & Phillips, 2016; Peters et al., 2017). But one lesson of recent work on unconscious perception is that it is harder to produce than was earlier thought. Megan Peters and Hakwan Lau (Peters & Lau, 2015) did an informal survey of people who work on perception and found that though most thought unconscious perception exists, most also thought that unconscious perception had not been demonstrated to exist.

Note the contrast with the evidence presented earlier for iconic object representations in perception. Recall the apparent motion case, in which a bird is seen to be moving and then changing into a rabbit. The trajectory and bird/rabbit shapes are consciously experienced even though they are not on the screen. And in the Nakayama experiment, the moving object is seen to rotate even when nothing is rotating on the screen. Paradigmatic perceptual object representations are conscious in that we consciously see objects as having certain properties. But no evidence has been given that subjects have any visual experience in the blank period in the OSBP.

We can see the difference via a phenomenon known as the tunnel effect, in which an object disappears behind a narrow occluder (the "tunnel") and an object emerges from the other side of the tunnel. The second object may differ in color, shape, and kind from the first (e.g., a lemon goes in and a kiwi goes out). If the tunnel is narrow enough relative to the size of the object moving through it (best results are achieved when the occluder is the width of the object) and the motion is fast and smooth enough, subjects see a single object going behind, changing shape and color and emerging from the other side.

If there is a brief pause in the motion of the object behind the screen, it looks as if one object is replaced by another with the first object remaining behind the screen. For adult human observers, we have subjective descriptions, but the experiment has also been done with monkeys. The version done with monkeys had two occluders. Occluder 1 was the tunnel and Occluder 2 was a screen that the object coming out of the tunnel went after emerging briefly in full view from the tunnel. When a lemon turned into a kiwi with smooth motion the monkeys looked only behind Occluder 2. However, when there was a brief pause, resulting in motion that human observers described as the lemon being replaced by the kiwi, the monkeys looked behind both occluders. See (Flombaum & Scholl, 2006; Scholl & Flombaum, 2010). The upshot, of course, is that the monkeys saw the sequences as we do.

An early article on the effect from the days in which first-person descriptions were routinely used in perception journals, says that "an absolutely compelling impression of continuous and uniform movement can be produced . . . all the observers agree that the movement behind the tunnel is as 'real' as" motion without the occluder (Burke, 1952, p. 124). As the relative length of the tunnel increases and the speed decreases, subjects can still track the moving object using a working memory representation, but they no longer experience motion. My point is that when the representation becomes a working memory object representation rather than a perceptual representation is when consciousness fades. I have seen no report of awareness of the objects in the OSPB.

In the tunnel effect, one sees a continuous path linking the object coming out from the screen to the object that went in. By contrast, when one matches the train noise with the box the train was in, one does not see the box as containing the train—rather one remembers that it did contain the train more than a second ago. This difference adds to the considerable case that the object representations of perception are importantly different from the conceptualized versions of them used in working memory.

In the OSPB, perceptual representations are conceptualized in working memory. As we saw in the Kwak and Curtis experiment described earlier in this chapter, we can expect that conceptualization in working memory will produce a format difference that is keyed to the task. Kwak and Curtis describe a format change in the direction of abstraction. Another format change may just be augmentation, as when a discursive tag is appended.

In paradigm cases, what happens when a perceptual representation is conceptualized is that it is broadcast in the global workspace. "On top of a deep hierarchy of specialized modules, a "global neuronal workspace," with limited capacity, evolved to select a piece of information, hold it over time, and share it across modules" (Dehaene, Lau, & Kouider, 2017, p. 489). When a piece of information is held and shared in the global workspace, perceptual format may not be preserved. Given this situation, it is unfortunate that the field often uses the term "object-file" to refer both to the perceptual object representations and to whatever remnants of them are used in working memory object representations.

In the paradigm case, full perceptual representations are conscious but no evidence has been given that paradigms of working memory representations, including object representations in working memory are conscious, suggesting important differences between the two types of object representations and adding to the evidence presented earlier that working memory representations that are derived from perception differ from perceptual representations in important ways. Further, as mentioned earlier, the divisive normalization of perception does not obtain in the perceptual representations of working memory.)

Subjects are not seeing the telephone and hammer in Figure 5.13, but let us reconsider whether they are having mental imagery of the telephone and hammer? As noted earlier, mental imagery takes about a second to 1.5 seconds to generate, as confirmed in many experiments by Stephen Kosslyn (Kosslyn et al., 2006). Kosslyn's experiments involve top-down imagery, but a different paradigm examined bottom-up imagery and got approximately the same time lag (Brockmole et al., 2002). (Brockmole's experiment is discussed in Chapters 1 and 9.) Brockmole's experiment was then redone by Kosslyn with similar results (Kosslyn et al., 2006). In the light of the time it takes to generate a mental image, note that the delay period in many OSPB experiments was only 1 second.

It is also noteworthy that mental imagery does not seem to be necessary for much of working memory. Aphantasia is a syndrome defined as follows: "Individuals affected by aphantasia cannot experience the sensory qualities of objects that are not physically presented to them" (Jacobs, Schwarzkopf, & Silvanto, 2018, p. 61). If you want to find out more or take an aphantasia test, go to https://aphantasia.com.

About .7% of people seem to be extremely aphantasic (Milton et al., 2021). They have poor autobiographical memory, e.g., the colors and shapes of items on their breakfast table that day and poor face recognition. However, they can answer questions that most people say they answer using mental imagery, for example, whether grass or pine needles are darker green. Normal peoples' pupils constrict when asked to imagine a white triangle, but not aphantasics. Jacobs et al. found that an aphantasic patient performed about as well as normal subjects on a variety of working memory tasks. The one working memory exception was a task in which subjects were shown a figure (a diamond, parallelogram, or square) and then, about 4 seconds after the figure disappeared, they had to say whether a dot on the screen would have been inside or outside the figure if it had stayed on the screen. If the dot was not close to the border of the figure, the aphantasic subject was as good at this as controls, but if the dot was close to the border, she was markedly worse than controls.

My conclusion from the considerations just presented is that there is reason to think there is no mental imagery in the OSPB experiments. To be clear, I am not saying that working memory representations fail to include perceptual materials. Rather, the representations of working memory can preserve substantial perceptual information. Also, I am not saying that working memory object representations are "postperceptual" if that is taken to deny that they include perceptual information and perceptual representations. My point is that working memory object representations ("object-files") are cognitive representations that conceptualize the perceptual materials that they do contain and that the signs of those conceptualizations cannot be used to argue that perception itself is conceptual.

The experiments cited in the last section, especially the experiments on apparent motion, are strong support for the iconicity of perceptual object representations. In defending the opposite view, Quilty-Dunn (2019b) argues that the only real evidence about the format of perceptual object representations comes from—as I would put it—the remnants of them that are preserved in working memory. Quilty-Dunn says (p. 17):

> For Block, there are iconic perceptual object representations and only some of their iconic aspects are inherited by object-files in VWM [visual working memory]. It is not obvious, however, how we can know anything about these representations if not through the OSPB.

I agree with the first sentence but I have just given reasons to doubt the second sentence. The OSPB is a working memory phenomenon, but the apparent motion results are a matter of vision, not working memory. They provide evidence for the iconicity of perceptual object representations that is independent of evidence from working memory. And their perceptual nature is revealed by the fact that subjects can have a visual experience of the bird turning into a rabbit and in the rotation experiment they have a visual experience of the apparent rotation.

(Both of these effects depend on the frequency of stimulus alternation being in the "beta" range rather than the "phi" range, as explained earlier in this chapter.) Further, the perceptual individuation of objects is quite different from our conceptual ways of individuating objects in which we do not think that the bird and the rabbit are the same object. The fact that the apparent motion results concern objects rather than mere 3D shapes is shown by the point made in connection with Figure 5.8 that if there is no visual object, there is no rotation.

One reflection of the fact that working memory representations that contain perceptual materials are more abstract than perceptual representations is a difference in "tolerance." Tolerance is a term used in the memory literature to describe whether the subject in a memory experiment regards an object as the same as one that was seen earlier. Visual long-term memory in humans is famously tolerant, especially in comparison to artificial intelligence programs that have a great deal of difficulty recognizing an object as the same one seen earlier but from a different vantage point angle (Schurgin & Flombaum, 2018). Schurgin and Flombaum showed that visual working memory is very tolerant, indeed substantially more tolerant than visual long-term memory. But perceptual representations are viewpoint-specific.

An indication that the relevant features of object representations that is exploited in these experiments are cognitive aspects of the representations is that the links adverted to via the term "match" above may involve inference. The sound of a piano is said to "match" the picture of the piano. The sound of a dog barking is said to "match" the picture of the dog. Likewise, for a "match" between a sound and a picture of a train. Matching in this sense is inferential rather than perceptual. Jordan, et al. are aware of this possibility and they tried to hamper one form of inference by asking the subjects to memorize 4 digits presented before each trial. After the subjects give the matching response, they were to repeat the 4 digits. This was supposed to interfere with a strategy of coding the pictures verbally. But the matching can be inferential even if that inference is not accomplished in a verbal system. The subject does not have to state the premise and conclusion explicitly for the process to be inferential.

Jordan et al. end up seeming to favor the hypothesis that I am suggesting, that the result concerns the working memory aspect of object-files rather than their perceptual aspects:

> Alternatively, object file representations may not be intimately tied to any particular sensory modality. In this sense, object files should not be conceived of as visual or auditory, but rather as abstract amodal representations. Although no evidence to date can conclusively tease apart these alternatives, the existence of nonvisual object processing . . . may support the latter hypothesis. Such

multisensory information could be bound in working memory via the episodic buffer's linking of visual and verbal material. (Jordan et al., 2010, p. 501)

Jordan, et al. seem to be thinking that the results reflect abstract amodal aspects of working memory rather than perception.

Quilty-Dunn (2016b, 2019b) responds to a version of the argument I just gave (from an earlier version of this book). One example that Quilty-Dunn gives of the perceptual nature of the object representations involved in the OSPB suggests that the perceptual representations involved in the OSPB can be unconscious. Mitroff et. al. (2005) did an experiment much like the ones just described, but with one twist. The motion of the boxes was ambiguous: It could be seen as the boxes streaming through one another or it could be seen as the boxes bouncing off one another. The boxes started off in the top corners. Subjects almost always report them as having moved through the center of the screen, crossing paths and ending up in the opposite (kitty-corner) corners. (This is called "streaming.") In a small minority of cases (as few as 3%) subjects describe the boxes as meeting in the middle and bouncing off one another, ending up on the same side as they started on. Remarkably, although the streaming percept was almost always reported, the OSPB suggested that the percept was almost always the bounce percept. Quilty-Dunn concludes that the bounce percept was usually unconscious.

What does this result show? The subjects' reports reflect bouncing, but the OSPB suggests streaming. Quilty-Dunn concludes that the explanation for this effect is that the information in cognition and perception are not enough in contact to resolve the discrepancy. Quilty-Dunn takes this result to exploit the informational encapsulation of vision—the claim that the visual system's sole source of information is sensory transducers, and not cognitive systems. And he takes that to support the idea that the representations involved in the OSPB are representations of perception.

I do not dispute that these representations are perceptual, but note that I have been maintaining that working memory object-files use perceptual materials. The perceptual materials can exhibit perceptual effects even when enclosed in a cognitive and conceptual envelope. It should not be disputed that these perceptual materials used in a working memory representation can be unconscious. Unconscious perceptual materials used in a working memory representation are enough to explain the finding.[4] So I don't think this result casts doubt on my claim that OSPB representations are conceptual and remnants of perception.

---

[4] Another possibility is that a conscious perceptual representation of a bounce can be misconceptualized as a case of streaming.

That concludes my main reply to Green and Quilty-Dunn. I have presented evidence that perceptual object representations are iconic—as are other perceptual representations. And I have rebutted evidence that is supposed to show that perceptual object representations are different from other perceptual representations in being discursive and conceptual.

There are a number of remaining issues however. One involves "multiple object tracking" experiments. (See the diagram in Figure 4.5.) A refresher: On one version, eight disks are on the screen. Four of them briefly change color, and the disks move about. The subject's task is to attend to the four that were first cued and then pick them out when the disks finally stop. Most people can follow four such disks through large changes in shape and color (Scholl & Pylyshyn, 1999). Perceptual object-files are said to be part of the tracking mechanism. Following Pylyshyn, Green and Quilty-Dunn conclude that a syntactic representation of the object is needed to explain why tracking is not derailed by large changes in perceptual properties, and so perceptual object representations have to be discursive rather than iconic.

However, there is reason to think that multiple object tracking requires working memory. The most obvious indication is that in many versions of multiple object tracking, subjects can track only about four moving items. This limit is the same as the number of "slots" in working memory for some kinds of materials. (See Chapter 1 on slot vs. pool models and the section of Chapter 5 on working memory.)

Another type of evidence presented by Quilty-Dunn (2019b) involves transsaccadic memory. A saccade is a fast, ballistic movement of the eye, usually occurring 2–3 times per second. Visual processing is greatly reduced during a saccade, so the visual system must rely on memory to encode which objects in the scene after the saccade are the same as the ones in the scene before the saccade. If I am watching a horse race, my visual system must keep track of which horse is which as I saccade back and forth between them.

There are indications that the same kind of object-files that figure in the OSPB also have a role in the transsaccadic memory representations that are involved in tracking objects and guiding eye movements to them (Schut, Fabius, Van der Stoep, & Van der Stigchel, 2017). Quilty-Dunn takes this to show that the object representations that are indexed by the OSPB are perceptual.

However, there is ample evidence that transsaccadic memory representations are working memory representations. For example, Irwin (1992) did an analog of the Sperling experiment (described earlier) for transsaccadic memory. You will recall that in Sperling's experiment, subjects could recall only 3 or 4 items from an array of 12 but they could also recall 3 or 4 from any given row if cued after the stimulus had disappeared. Their iconic memory capacity was roughly 3 × 3.5, i.e., 10.5 letters. In Irwin's transsaccadic memory version, subjects saw an array of letters at one fixation but were not given the cue until after they had moved their eyes to the new location. The result was that their memory capacity was about a third of that revealed in Sperling's experiment. That suggests that the kind of memory involved is working memory, since that is a typical working memory performance for letters as stimuli.

Irwin found that a mask presented within 40 ms of the stimulus had a significant impact, but there was no effect at periods longer than 40 ms (120 ms and 950 ms), suggesting that a visual icon is present but only very briefly, being wiped out by the saccade. (In the Sperling phenomenon, iconic memory lasts 200–300 ms.) Irwin concludes (p. 311), "It appears that transsaccadic memory retains visual aspects of a stimulus but perhaps for a brief time only."

Irwin and Andrews (1996) used a different procedure with similar results. Subjects saw an array of 6–10 colored letters in the center of the visual field together with a peripheral target to which subjects were supposed to move their eyes. The subjects saccade to the peripheral target at which time the central array disappeared and the peripheral target was replaced by an indicator of one of the positions that had been occupied by a letter. Subjects were supposed to report the letter and its color. The subjects can only do this via memory of the presaccade fixation, so this task uses transsaccadic memory. They could report the letter and its color for only 3–4 locations, the typical signature of working memory.

The fact that transsaccadic memory contains only some perceptual elements is widely appreciated. For example, Gordon et al. (2008) describe the Irwin and Andrews experiment as follows (p. 667):

> Contrary to what would be expected if transsaccadic memory had a very high capacity, Irwin and Andrews found that the subjects could report the color and identity of only 3–4 of the letters in the array. Interestingly, this capacity was very similar to that reported by Irwin (1992), who required subjects to report letter identity alone. Irwin and Andrews concluded that transsaccadic memory consists primarily of integrated object representations (which may include a number of object features), along with residual activity in the feature maps that underlie sensory processing. Subsequent work in which more complex stimuli were used also suggests that transsaccadic memory consists primarily of representations of a small number of objects in the scene).

The point by Gordon et al. that the result by Irwin and Andrews (1996) and Irwin (1992) both come up with the limit of 3–4 even though one involved reporting two properties and the other reporting just one property comports with a well-known property of working memory, namely that its limit of 3–4 is a matter of 3–4 items, independently of the number of features of those items. (See the discussion in Chapter 1 of slot models of working memory in comparison with models that appeal to a pool of resources.)

There is also evidence of long-term memory involvement in transsaccadic memory. Hollingworth and Henderson (2002) did an experiment in which subjects fixated naturalistic scenes while their fixations were being tracked with an eye-tracker. In one of their experiments, subjects were given a change-detection task. The experimenters decided on one of the objects in the scene as the target object. When subjects happened to fixate on it for more than 90 ms. their attention was drawn to another part of the scene and later a green square appeared, obscuring the object. Subjects had been instructed to fixate the green square and then decide as between two scenes which scene had the original object. Subjects were more than 80% correct even though numerous fixations had intervened between the original fixation and the fixation of the green square. The average number of intervening fixations was 4.6, and even with 9 fixations there was no sign of decreasing accuracy. The upshot is that there is a form of transsaccadic memory that integrates over multiple fixations. In other experiments, subjects retained object-files for as long as 30 minutes. The authors conclude that there can be what they call "long-term memory object files."

Quilty-Dunn takes these transsaccadic memory results to show that the perceptual object representations before the saccade were not iconic. Here is his discussion of the analog of the Sperling experiment for iconic memory (Quilty-Dunn, 2019b, p/ 20):

> Unlike in the Sperling experiments, however, participants only showed storage of three or four letters—the same limit for discursive object representations. This result falsifies the claim that icons are used in deriving object correspondence across saccades. . . . Since object correspondence needs to be computed by the visual system (and not merely by some post-perceptual process—cf. Block ms.), then there must be non-iconic representations in the visual system.

But an alternative interpretation—bolstered by the masking experiment just described in which perceptual information lasts only 40 ms—suggests the opposite, that the perceptual object representations *before* the saccade were iconic and those iconic aspects do not survive the saccade very well. The upshot would be that transsaccadic memory is a form of working memory, or even long-term memory, with remnants of perception. So, it cannot be used in this way to show that perception is noniconic and conceptual.

In this chapter I have argued for iconicity in perceptual representation based on analog mirroring. I also argued that iconic representations need have no format constituent that singles anything out, that iconic representations can be determinate, that conceptions of iconicity based on parts fail to accommodate analog magnitude representations, that perceptual object representations are iconic, and that one must exercise care in drawing conclusions about perception from experiments on working memory. I now turn to the nonconceptual nature of perception.

6
Nonconceptual color perception

This chapter will argue that at least some perceptual representation is nonconceptual, so even if—as I doubt—some perception is conceptual, perception is not constitutively conceptual.[1] The argument will rely on an extended example. Babies between the ages of 4–6 months and 11–12 months have near-adult-level color discrimination—though perhaps without adult-level color constancy—and have perceptual category representations, but, as I will argue, they normally lack color cognition or color concepts (or even color proto-concepts) including the concept of color and the concepts of specific colors. I think a similar argument could be mounted for some other secondary qualities (Locke, 1690) such as, in the case of vision, patterns and luminance, but I will not explore that line of thought here.

My argument in this chapter will depend on a three-way distinction among color category representations:

1. Nonconceptual color category representations. These develop at 4–6 months of age
2. Color concepts. These develop starting around 11–12 months.
3. Linguistic color concepts. These develop starting around 3 years.

First a bit of background.

Philosophers who have a wide variety of theoretical perspectives have converged—wrongly, in my view—on the view that perception is constitutively conceptual. These include thinkers as different as Jerry Fodor (2007) and, apparently, Ludwig Wittgenstein.[2] Brian O'Shaughnessy (2012) says (p. 42) that according to Wittgenstein, "the work of the Understanding lies at the center of visual perceptual experience." (O'Shaughnessy seems to take the Understanding to be conceptual understanding.)

---

[1] Thanks to Anna Franklin for comments on a previous version of this chapter and to Anya Hurlbert for a response to this chapter when it was presented at a satellite of the Vision Science Society in May 2021. Of course they are not responsible for any remaining mistakes. I was also helped by a particularly vigorous discussion in a zoom talk at the Philosophy Department at the University of Texas, Austin, in December 2021.

[2] There are many conceptualists with a cognitive science point of view (Fodor, 2007; Mandelbaum, 2017; Noë, 2004; Prinz, 2006a; Quilty-Dunn, 2016a, 2016b; Shevlin, 2016), as well as a priori conceptualists (McDowell, 1994; O'Shaughnessy, 2012; Sellars, 1956; 1997; Wittgenstein, 1953).

The Border Between Seeing and Thinking. Ned Block, Oxford University Press. © Oxford University Press 2023.
DOI: 10.1093/oso/9780197622223.003.0006

Another tradition takes the opposite point of view—that seeing is constitutively nonconceptual (Burge, 2010b; Crane, 1988; Cussins, 1990; Dretske, 1981; Evans, 1982; Martin, 1992; Sellars, 1997). I am in this camp. Others hold that some perception is nonconceptual and some conceptual (Green & Quilty-Dunn, 2017; Peacocke, 1992b; Siegel, 2010). I will be arguing against these views in subsequent chapters.

As I explained in Chapter 1, perceptual representation often ascribes properties to physical objects, to events, and, in the view of some philosophers, to property instances. This kind of perceptual ascription is often taken to be sufficient for conceptual or propositional perception. For example, C. A. Strong (1930, p. 17) says, "Perception is in effect an implicit proposition: it is as if we said, 'There is an existent whose character is so and so.'" In Chapter 1, I quoted John McDowell saying something similar, though without the implication of existential form: "That things are thus and so is the content of the experience, and it can also be the content of a judgement: it becomes the content of a judgement if the subject decides to take the experience at face value. So it is conceptual content" (McDowell, 1994, p. 26). Thus the mere ascription of properties has been taken to be sufficient for conceptual representation.

As explained earlier, the sense of "conceptual" used in this book may be different from McDowell's because my usage requires a function in thought or reasoning. There is a verbal aspect to the disagreement, but as I hope to show in this chapter, the disagreement has a strong substantive core.

Perceptual category representations

One line of argument that at least some perception is nonconceptual appeals to the perception of animals (Peacocke, 2001a, 2001b). The usual versions of this argument suffer from a lack of evidence that animals do not have the relevant concepts. However, there is one case in which we do have a bit of evidence that the animals do not have the relevant concepts, the case of the solitary wasp that I mentioned earlier. (Recall that the social wasps are more sophisticated.) The key items of evidence were that the (solitary) wasp shows stereotyped inflexible behavior patterns (recall the 40 iterations of the same action), has not been shown to be capable of instrumental conditioning (the most basic mechanism of cognitive learning), has a short adult lifespan with no large benefit of learning; and is subject to evolutionary pressure to reduce brain weight. So long as the wasp does genuinely perceive and has no concepts, the case does support nonconceptual perception.

Of course, it is open to objectors to deny that the wasp genuinely perceives or to claim that the wasp in fact does have and deploy concepts. The very evidence presented earlier that the wasp is not conscious could be used as an argument that it is not "in the space of reasons" and so has subpersonal perceptual processing without actual perception. And those who define concepts behaviorally might suppose that the wasps' ability to select, track, and sting prey, storing them in a burrow shows they have the concept of prey. Thus, objectors may deny perception and/or claim wasp concepts.

Objections of both sorts can be better ruled out in the case to be discussed of infant color perception. On the perceptual side, I will argue that infants show evidence of conscious color perception. They move their eyes to a disk that is a different color from the background, and in another paradigm, they appear to be bored by repeated presentations of the same color. Both suggest conscious perception of color. On the conceptual side, the key is the contrast between infants' concepts or better proto-concepts of size, shape, and kind, and the lack of evidence of such concepts or proto-concepts of color in the very same paradigms. In both respects, the infant case to be laid out is more impressive than the animal cases.

As I mentioned in Chapter 4, two kinds of nonconceptuality are often distinguished, nonconceptual states and nonconceptual contents (Byrne, 2005; Heck, 2000). I mentioned in Chapter 4 that in my view, nonconceptuality properly attaches to states, not contents; and in particular to representational aspects of states. A conceptual and a nonconceptual state could in principle share content, at least referential content, and if that is right, there is no such thing as nonconceptual content. Perceptual contents are typically finer grained than conceptual contents (see below), but it may be that both perception and thought allow for generic contents. If so, perception and thought could have the same generic contents.

Propositional representations paradigmatically have different structures than perceptual representations, so how can they share content? Note that the sentence "That is a circle" has propositional content, whereas the noun phrase "that circle" does not. Yet the truth conditions of the propositional representation and the accuracy condition of the noun phrase representation are the same in that the former is true just in case the referent of the demonstrative is a circle and the latter is accurate just in case the referent of the demonstrative is a circle. There is a shared content despite the different forms.

The difference between "That is a circle" and "that circle"—the word "is"—is not in itself important; what is important is the functional difference indexed by the linguistic difference. The sentence functions in propositional inference, whereas the noun phrase functions in picking something out.

The characterizations of a nonconceptual state that I favor depend on the notion of a paradigm cognitive state. I mentioned earlier a characterization of concepts as representational (paradigmatically predicative) elements of propositional thought, reasoning, problem solving, evaluating, deciding, and other paradigm cognitive processes and states. As mentioned earlier, I use the phrase "paradigm cognitive state" in case there are nonparadigmatic cognitive states that may be nonconceptual and nonpropositional. Burge suggests that there may be nonconceptual mental maps (Burge, 2010a), though, as explained in Chapter 1, the grid-cell system that is involved in mental maps is largely conceptual. Using this notion of concept, a nonconceptual representational state is one that lacks those predicative representational elements.

Another approach to characterizing nonconceptual states appeals to what is required of one in order for one to have those states. One can perceive a banana without having any concept of a banana, but to judge, believe, hope, expect, or decide that a banana is over there, one must have a concept of a banana (Stoljar, 2009). As I mentioned, the focus on concept possession doesn't really get at the heart of what a conceptual state is. What makes a state conceptual isn't just that the subject *has* an appropriate concept, but that the concept functions to determine the content. A nonconceptual state is one for which concepts are not essentially involved in determining the content. This point will be important later in this chapter, where we will discuss the distinction between concept possession and concept activation, i.e., the activation of a previously possessed concept. The evidence I will discuss argues for a lack of color concept activation during a period of infancy. The evidence does not rule out color concept possession without activation of color concepts. But it is lack of activation that is important to nonconceptual perception.

I mentioned earlier that it may seem that in principle one format item can function as a nonconceptual perceptual representation in one system but as a concept in another system. I gave the example of a perceptual representation of an isosceles triangle that can be used as a concept of a triangle—as in Berkeley's famous example. On one interpretation of Berkeley, an "idea" (e.g., a mental image) of an isosceles triangle can function so as to represent triangles in general (Block, 1983a; 2006, fn 31; Szabo, 1995) if the mental image functions in thought so as to not respect the peculiarities of the specific image (Berkeley, 1734, see especially sections XIII to XVI of the Introduction). Thus the idea of a triangle can also be the concept of a triangle.

However, I am not confident that a single-format item can be used both as a percept and as a concept. I can explain by raising the question of what it is about an isosceles triangle representation that tells processors when to take into account the representation of identical sides and when to ignore the representation of identity of the sides. Call the feature of the system that tells processors whether to ignore the isosceles-representing aspect of the triangle representation the C feature ('C' for concept). We can think of the C feature as having binary values. If the C feature has value 1, processors ignore the representation of identity of the sides, and if it is 0, the processors use the isosceles-representing aspect of the representation. Now finally, here is the point: The C feature can itself be considered a format element, with value 1 for concepts and 0 for percepts. So it is not at all obvious that one and the same representation can be used both as a percept and as a concept.

This argument is not supposed to establish that one and the same representation *cannot* be used both as a percept and as a concept. Rather it is an argument that the issue is not so straightforward and may in the end be a matter of decision on the basis of theoretical utility. One relevant consideration is the point mentioned earlier that the iconic format of perceptual representations does not lend itself to the systematicity of conceptual and perceptual representations. Another, as mentioned in Chapter 5, is that the use of perceptual information in the conceptual workspace, working memory, normally involves loss of perceptual information.

This concludes the more general part of this discussion. I now move to more specific points concerning my chief example of this chapter, the example of the perceptual and conceptual representation of color.

Color is the locus of a number of arguments for nonconceptual content, notably the "fineness of grain" argument (Evans, 1982; McDowell, 1994; Peacocke, 1992b, 2001a; Raffman, 1995; Tye, 1995b). Gareth Evans (1982) famously argued that we can discriminate many more colors than we have concepts of. (Actually, he seemed to think we do not understand the claim that there as many concepts as discriminable shades.) The conclusion is supposed to be that perceptions cannot be individuated by the concepts deployed in them because concepts are not sufficiently fine-grained to account for the different perceptual experiences.

Of course, it might be possible to construct fine-grained color concepts from coarse-grained color concepts. If we have the concept of blue and the concept of green, we can construct the concept of 30% closer to blue than to green. However, people and animals can have color experience without such concepts. Indeed, members of the Pirahã tribe lack all number concepts, even the concept of the number one, but their perceptual capacities appear to be the same as other peoples, including their perceptual capacities involving approximate numerosities (Frank, Everett, Fedorenko, & Gibson, 2008). Being able to construct fine-grained color concepts from coarse-grained color concepts might run aground on the required auxiliary concepts.

Some have countered that any shade can be conceptualized with a demonstrative concept, e.g., "that shade," so our perceptual capacities do not outrun our conceptual capacities (Byrne, 2005; Heck, 2007). (This view is often attributed to McDowell, but Peacocke [2001a] notes that this is not actually McDowell's argument.) It seems obvious that the experience of a color shade does not require the concept of a shade. However, it may be that bare demonstratives (*that* rather than *that F*) suffice for conceptualizing fine-grained properties. Peacocke gives the example of a perceptual demonstrative of the timbre of a sound in the absence of any general concept of timbre (Peacocke, 2001a).

Even if Peacocke is right about bare demonstratives, forming a demonstrative concept, even a bare demonstrative concept, is a sophisticated achievement that infants might not be capable of (Roskies, 2008; Tye, 1995b). Even if adults have conceptual abilities sufficient to conceptualize any fine-grained shade, the example of infants suggests that perception does not require such abilities. In addition, there is some plausibility in the claim that one can form a conceptual demonstrative of a color only if one already perceives it, so perception cannot require conceptual demonstration (Heck, 2000; Levine, 2010; Peacocke, 1992b). (But see Brewer, 2005, for another view.) The alternative view—that forming the conceptual demonstrative is simultaneous with and identical to seeing it—leads to a puzzling question of how the demonstrative gets its reference.

McDowell relies on recognitional concepts to disarm the fineness-of-grain argument. Unlike the bare demonstrative approach to conceptualism, the recognitional concept approach runs into the problem mentioned earlier that memories of perception are less fine-grained than perception. See the discussion of mental imagery in Chapter 9, especially of the Brockmole experiment, for an indication of the rapid decay of perceptual information in the first half a second after a perception. See also the discussion of iconic and fragile visual short-term memory in Chapter 5. So recognitional concepts are inadequate to the task.

Even ignoring the fact that perceptual memory is less fine-grained than perception, there is a question of how the very first experience of a new quality would be possible, since the recognitional concept could not already be present (Peacocke, 2001a). I suppose, though, that McDowell could say that the recognitional concept forms at the same time as the perception. However, forming a representation that could function in thought or reasoning takes substantially longer than forming a perception. Recall that cognition requires activations in the global workspace whereas perception can occur prior to these activations. (See the discussion of the global workspace in Chapter 1 and also in Chapters 7 and 13.)

In what follows I will not be talking about arguments for nonconceptuality based on fineness of grain. I am going to be introducing another argument that has not been discussed in the literature as far as I know. (It is not mentioned in recent reviews [Bermudez & Cahen, 2015; Brogaard & Gatzia, 2017a; Margolis & Laurence, 2012]). I will argue that 6- to 11-month-old infants have the abilities indicative of color perception—including, notably, perceptual category representations for color—but normally lack the abilities indicative of color conception—even though these infants have abilities that indicate conception of shape and kind properties. I will start by explaining what a perceptual category representation is.

What is a perceptual category representation? One definition often given is that, for perceptual categories, discrimination across boundaries is more fine-grained (i.e., more sensitive to objective differences) than discrimination within boundaries. This difference is apparent in experience. Pairs of shades that are objectively equidistant look more different when the shades are on opposite sides of a boundary than when they are within the same category. Of course we can distinguish the different shades in both intracategory differences and intercategory differences; but the intercategory differences seem larger to the subject.

Definitions of this sort appeal to an objective dimension such that small differences within that dimension make big differences in perception for stimuli on the borders. Such definitions, though, may be less fundamental than another approach based on perceptual attributions of the categories themselves. Better discrimination across than between borders may be just an index of those categorical representations.

I can explain this with regard to the example of a rainbow, pictured in Figure 6.1 in case you need to be reminded about what a rainbow looks like. When you see a rainbow, it looks like there are rough stripes of different colors despite the rainbow's smoothly changing wavelengths of light (Goldstone & Hendrickson, 2010). Vision imposes color categories on a varying physical substrate that does not itself impose these categories (if the substrate is individuated in the usual way). A full rainbow has seven stripes corresponding to the distinct representations of red, orange, yellow, green, blue, indigo, and violet (hence the grade school mnemonic, "Roy G Biv"). Different points within a single band look slightly different in shade, but they also look to have the same color. Discrimination between points across these bands is better than discrimination of points within bands, but that is because we visually represent the color of each band.

In principle, an objective measure based on subjective judgments might eliminate category effects, suggesting that the definition of categorical perception based on discrimination is in one respect inferior to a definition based on the phenomenology of categories. Some theorists regard the use of a metric based on similarity judgments to determine categorical perception as introducing harmful circularity (Witzel, 2019). But this kind of objection can be raised to any case of categorical perception, including the example given below concerning phonemes. A circle of terms all defined in terms of one another can be totally legitimate.

Before I get to the discussion of color, I will discuss another case of categorical perception, perception of phonemes. In Figure 6.2, the likelihood of perceiving three different phonemes is graphed against a value of a physical stimulus. (That

Figure 6.1 Rainbow. Note that the continuously varying wavelengths look almost as if there are stripes of colors. From Wikipedia. Reprinted under Creative Commons Attribution-Share Alike 2.5 Generic l. This figure requires color. There is a free pdf on the Oxford University Press web site that has the color version of this and all the other figures.

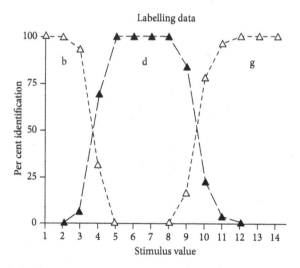

Figure 6.2 The likelihood of perceiving three different phonemes (/b/, /d/ and /g/) as a function of a stimulus parameter that you don't need to know about. (But if you are curious, that stimulus parameter is the difference in frequency between two frequency bands known as the first and second formants. From Goldstone and Hendrickson (2010). Reprinted with permission from John Wiley & Sons.

stimulus value is the difference in frequency between two characteristic sound frequency bands, but understanding this is not required for the example.) For stimulus values between roughly 5 and 8, the difference in frequency bands does not make any difference in the subjects' perceptual categorization of the stimulus as the /d/-sound. And there are similar phenomena for /b/ and /g/ for shorter and longer difference values. In the case of phonemes, the test of categorical perception that is often used is the ABX task, where the subjects are asked whether X is different from A or from B. Subjects are more accurate and faster when A and B are in different categories.

There is a conscious perceptible commonality to /b/-sounds just as there is a perceptible commonality to examples of red in the rainbow of different wavelengths. Subjects hear values between 5 and 8 as somewhat different but as examples of the same phoneme. The auditory system represents these stimuli as a certain phoneme just as the visual system represents as red instances that differ detectibly in wavelength. Indeed, categorical perception of all the world's phonemes is exhibited early in infancy (Goldstone & Hendrickson, 2010). However, in the case of color, we (adults) not only have color perceptual category representations—we also have color concepts. In the case of phonemes, most humans perceive those phonemes without having concepts of phonemes. Only those who have studied some linguistics have the relevant concepts.

As was mentioned earlier, perceptual categories can be learned, even in an hour of training. Ester et al. (2017) trained subjects in categorizing tilted lines as on one side or another of a standard orientation (chosen arbitrarily for each subject). See Figure 6.3 (reproduced for convenience from Figure 1.6). As I mentioned, two forms of brain scanning showed that representations in early vision of the orientations were repelled by the boundaries, suggesting categorical perception. Note that the subjects' perceptions of orientation need not have been

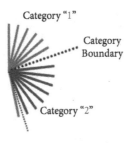

Figure 6.3 Tilt categorization task from (Ester et al., 2020). Reproduced for convenience from Chapter 1. An arbitrary tilt was selected for each subject, indicated by the category boundary in the figure. Orientations on the clockwise side of the boundary were classified as category 2 and categories on the other side were 1. This figure is from *Journal of Neuroscience*, which does not require permission.

categorical before the training (though there is evidence for categorical perception of horizontality and verticality). As I also mentioned, color categories can also be inculcated by brief training (Özgen & Davies, 2002). And of course different languages involve different color categories.

Perceptual categorization is a kind of recognition but does not require anything one might call reidentification. There is no requirement of recognizing the current object or property as like something previously perceived for categorical perception. Another kind of recognition is the formation of a categorical perceptual judgment. The first is entirely perceptual, the second is conceptual and cognitive, though it may include perceptual elements.

Greyson Abid has argued that recognition is neither perceptual nor cognitive (Abid, 2021). My view is that it is both because there are (at least) two kinds, perceptual and conceptual categorization. Abid mentions other states that could be termed kinds of recognition. One is a judgment that one has seen something before. Another makes fewer cognitive demands and might be ascribed to a lower animal: the "registration" that something has been observed before. In addition, a perception can be imbued with a sense of familiarity. And a perceptual judgment can involve a recollection of an earlier perception or perceptual judgment. But all of these states can be categorized as either perceptual or cognitive—or as involving both.

Infant color categories

I will move now to the main example of this chapter: perception vs. conception of color in infants.

Infants of 4–6 months have nearly adult-level color discrimination. How do we know this? There are many ways to assess infants' color discrimination. One of them is presenting colored shapes on a colored background as in Figure 6.4. Infants will typically move their eyes to fixate the shape if it is discriminable from the background, so this technique can be used to measure discriminability at various ages. Infants 2 months old distinguish red from green, and those 3 months old distinguish blue from yellow. The 3-month-olds show spontaneous color preferences (Maule & Franklin, 2019; Skelton et al., 2017).

Infants 4–6 months old have color discrimination capacities that are almost the equal of ours, though there is improvement throughout childhood into adolescence, and color constancy—the ability to see colors as the same despite change in conditions—probably continues to develop (Rogers, Witzel, Rhodes, & Franklin, 2020). Plausibly, these infants are attending to the colors of the different colored shapes, and that is also suggested by the Brouwer and Heeger

Figure 6.4 Infants—and also, adults—who can differentiate the disk from the background will typically move their direction of gaze to the disk. This figure requires color. There is a free pdf on the Oxford University Press web site that has the color version of this and all the other figures.

result mentioned earlier, that inattentive color perception did not exhibit the neural signature of categorical perception.

I will describe evidence that 6- to 11-month-old human infants have color category representations. Much of the evidence I will present for infant color category representations derives from work by Anna Franklin and her colleagues. As I mentioned, infants will move their eyes to a target if it is visibly different from the background, as in Figure 6.4. However, they will move their eyes faster and more accurately across category boundaries than within category boundaries (Franklin, 2015). That is, if we compare two equal objective differences in the stimulus, one across, one within, a color boundary, the responses to differences across boundaries will be faster and more accurate.

The results just mentioned use a variety of objective dimensions such as color space based on Munsell chips and color space based on just noticeable differences. The categorical perception results for infants are robust to these different objective dimensions. (Of course it would be possible to use the data gained from the just noticeable differences to frame an "objective" measure that erases the categorical effect.) The technique just mentioned of measuring the time taken to fixate a target does not depend on language and so works equally well with linguistic and nonlinguistic creatures. Another technique for finding color categories that does not depend on language uses a form of brain imaging to detect a "visual oddball effect," in which a monotonous series of similar stimuli causes attention to flag until one stimulus is perceptually different—in which case there is a measurable increase in attention to the stimulus (Clifford, Franklin, Davies, & Holmes, 2009).

Another technique that does not depend on language uses infants' preferences for novelty as measured by looking time. Infants are more interested in an alternating series of red and green stimuli than they are in a sequence of red stimuli. The interest of an infant can be gauged by measuring how long it takes to stop looking at repeated presentations of a stimulus. When the same stimulus is presented repeatedly, the time spent looking at the stimulus decreases. When looking time decreases by a preset amount (usually by half), the infant is said to be habituated to the stimulus. If a stimulus is presented that looks different to the infant, interest recovers and looking time increases. Habituation paradigms have been shown to reveal the same color categories as the oddball effect and the eye-moving method mentioned above (Aslin, 2007; Bornstein, 1985; Siuda-Krzywicka, Boros, et al., 2019; Skelton et al., 2017).

Note that the *habituation* used in this type of experiment is completely different from the *adaptation* described earlier. Adaptation is an involuntary perceptual aftereffect in which a stimulus subsequent to the adapting stimulus is seen differently because sensitivity is decreased as thresholds rise. Habituation is loss of interest reflected in behavior by *voluntary* action. The baby looks at (for example) their feet instead of at the screen. I will repeat the explanation just given of the difference between habituation and adaptation in this footnote so that it can be referenced later.[3]

One particularly useful looking time technique combines habituation with novelty preference. Pairs of color patches are presented repeatedly with the same color on the left and on the right. After a number of same color pairs are presented, the old color is presented on one side together with a new color on the other side. The extent to which the infant looks at the side of the new color yields a measure of novelty preference (Carey, 2009, p. 41; Maule & Franklin, 2019; Skelton et al., 2017). Note again that the infants' behavior does suggest attention to color.

Habituation and novelty preference have been confirmed as measures of subjective novelty and coordinated with other techniques in hundreds of studies (Carey, 2009). This technique can be used to figure out what stimuli infants treat as stimuli of the same color category. The categories found with this technique

---

[3] When the same stimulus is presented repeatedly, the time spent looking at the stimulus decreases. When looking time decreases by a preset amount (usually by half), the infant is said to be habituated to the stimulus. If a stimulus is presented that looks different to the infant, interest recovers and looking time increases. Note that the *habituation* used in this type of experiment is completely different from the *adaptation* described earlier. Adaptation is an involuntary aftereffect in which a stimulus subsequent to the adapting stimulus is seen differently because sensitivity is decreased as thresholds rise. Habituation is loss of interest. The baby voluntarily looks at (for example) its feet instead of at the screen. (See Carey, 2009, p. 41.)

were the same as those found using the other methods. In sum, a number of completely different techniques yield the same results on infant color categorization. The World Color Survey showed considerable uniformity in the centers of categories of the worlds' languages, both in industrialized and nonindustrialized cultures (Skelton et al., 2017). Skelton et al. (2017) systematically mapped the color categories of 4- to 6-month-old infants using infant novelty preference for colors from one lightness band of the stimulus grid of the World Color Survey. The result is shown in Figure 6.5, row A. The lines link pairs of samples for which there is little or no novelty preference. (That is, after habituation to one, there is little or no recovery of interest to the other.) Pairs of colors for which there are no novelty preference of one over the other can nonetheless often be distinguished when presented simultaneously, as in Figure 6.4. In B, some sample distinctions made in languages are diagrammed with vertical lines.

Infants have five color categories. Labels that make sense from the point of view of an English speaker for those five categories would be reddish, orangish brown/yellowish green, greenish, bluish, purplish. It is hard to see why some of these labels are appropriate from the diagram, since only a few lightness values are visible in the diagram. Lighter versions of 8 are orange and lighter versions of 9 and 10 are yellow. Note that there is one categorical distinction that infants make that is not recognized by English speakers, namely the distinction between greenish brown (12) and green with a slightly brownish tinge (15). Still, there

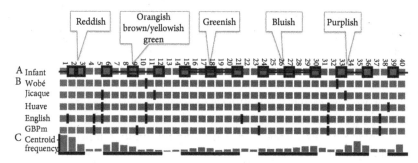

Figure 6.5 A comparison of infant color categories with adult categories from a number of different language groups. Boxes with color labels were added by me. In A, squares indicate sampled stimuli. Horizontal lines linking color patches indicate little or no novelty preference across that boundary. Gaps indicate significant novelty preference and so reveal category boundaries. Note that this is a linear representation of a wheel. There is a single category including 39 and 40 on the right plus 1, 2, and 3 on the left. See the text for an explanation of rows B and C. This figure requires color. There is a free pdf on the Oxford University Press web site that has the color version of this and all the other figures. Thanks to Anna Franklin for the original figure. (See Skelton et al., 2017.)

is substantial overlap between infant color categories and adult color categories. The last line of B is a cluster analysis of languages from the World Color Survey. Four of the five boundaries between infant color categories correspond to borders in the cluster analysis of world languages. This is especially visible in C of Figure 6.5. What you see in C is frequency of category centroids in the World Color Survey for the lightness band in A. Novelty preference categories are indicated by the black horizontal bars in Row C. Gaps between the bars in Row C represent infant category boundaries. The heights of the vertical colored bars in C represent numbers of languages in the World Color Survey that have a centroid at that point. What C shows is that infant color category boundaries are rarely at the centroid of adult color categories and that infant and average world language boundaries tend to coincide. The most notable exception to that rough correspondence is the infant boundary between greenish and bluish. Many cultures have a term that lumps green and blue together. (That is reflected in C by the fact that there is a large range in which there are few high bars.) Taken as a whole, the data in Figure 6.5 shows the respects in which infant color categories influence adult color categories. Adult color concepts tend toward respecting the infant color categories, but the correspondence is far from perfect.

Why do babies have these color categories? Anna Franklin and her colleagues (Maule & Franklin, 2019; Skelton et al., 2017) present evidence that suggests that four of the five infant categories can be explained by the basic opponent channels of early vision, the red/green and yellow/blue channels described earlier. They also note that brain imaging using near infrared spectroscopy (fNIRS), a brain-scanning technology suitable for small children using light, shows localization of the color categories in the classic occipitotemporal visual cortex pathways.

Why are the color category representations or infants from 4--6 months to 11 months not concepts? As I will explain, they normally have no function in cognition.

So far, we have seen that infants have categorical perception for color. In the next section, I will present the case that infants 6–11 months old do not normally deploy color concepts or even color proto-concepts and so their perceptual color category representations are not concepts or proto-concepts. (To avoid repetition, I will usually say "concepts" when the results apply to both concepts and proto-concepts.)

Infants' failure to normally deploy color concepts

If I am right that infants 6–11 months old have categorical perception of color, without, normally, abilities that involve the deployment of color concepts, then, contrary to what many philosophers have said (for example, Connolly, 2011;

Mandelbaum, 2017; Mandik, 2012; Prinz, 2002; Smith, 2002), there can be perceptual categorization that is not conceptual. Eric Mandelbaum (2017, p. 2) puts the conceptualist assumption this way: "It is also often claimed that perceptual representations are nonconceptual. If so, then identification—that is, visual classification—has to occur post-perceptually." As we have seen, color categorization is a form of classification that is perceptual. The identification of categories and color concepts should have been viewed with suspicion since categorical perception occurs throughout the animal kingdom, including in insects (Hoy, 1989). I will be arguing in later chapters that there are perceptual representations of causation and numerosity that are perceptual analogs of our concepts of causation and numerosity, just as the infant's color category representations are perceptual analogs of adult color concepts.

Of course, some may prefer to use the term "concept" so as to classify categorical representations as concepts. But so doing would serve to obscure the fundamental distinction between cognitive categories that function in thought and reasoning and perceptual categories that need have no such function.

To be clear: the reason I am focusing on 6- to 11-month-olds is that by 6 months, infants have adult-level color perception, and starting at 11 months they have faint stirrings of color concepts.

How do we know that the infants we are talking about do not normally deploy color concepts? A preliminary point: It is useful to keep in mind that 6-month-olds are deficient in frontal synapses: Frontal synapse density peaks at 15 months. (By contrast, perceptual synapse density peaks at 3 months.) The frontal cortex of 6-month-olds is also deficient in myelination and glucose metabolism (Gazzaniga et al., 2002, p. 642; Huttenlocher & Dabholkar, 1997). (Myelin is a fatty covering of neurons that is important to transmission of electrical signals.) Their brain bases for concepts are sparse, suggesting that we should be wary of ascribing any concepts to them. As we will see, there is some evidence that babies between 6 months and 12 months have proto-concepts of shape, size, and kind. But even if their representations of shape, size, and kind are not full concepts, they are much further in the direction of concepts than these babies' color representations.

In the last chapter, I mentioned the tunnel effect, in which an object moving smoothly behind a narrow occluder (only slightly larger than the object) is seen to emerge from the other side of the occluder despite the gap in visibility when it is occluded. If a red ball goes behind the occluder and a green ball emerges on the other side, it looks to adults as if a single ball changed color. This effect is less likely to occur to the extent that the screen is wider than the ball. Teresa Wilcox (1999) showed that when 4.5-month-old infants saw a box enter the narrow screen occluder (i.e. a screen the width of the ball) with a ball emerging from the other side (a setup that looks to grownups as the box turning into a ball), they look longer than when the occluder is wider than the object. But they show no increased looking time when a red ball turns into a green ball. At 7.5 months they look longer also when an item of one kind enters and an item of another kind exits (e.g., a duck turns into a truck) but still do not look longer when a red ball turns into a green ball. Finally, at 11.5 months they show increased looking time in changes in all three properties (including color).[4]

Note that my use of the Wilcox experiment does not depend on whether or not the babies see the situation as a single object changing color as opposed to an object of one color being replaced by an object of another color. In either case, the natural interpretation is that there is normally a failure to *notice* the color change—and therefor a failure to deploy color concepts—before 11.5 months.

I say they normally fail to notice the color change. Is noticing just attending? No. There is evidence that categorical perception for color requires attention. As I mentioned, Brouwer and Heeger (2013) compared attentive perception of color with perception of color with attention diverted and found the neural signature of categorical perception only with attention. The sense of "notice" that I am using goes beyond attention, and requires some sort of cognitive classification or entry into a cognitive system. So on my usage of "notice," perceptual categorization and attention are not sufficient for noticing.

I said that they normally fail to notice the color change. Why "normally"? Wilcox found that with training, these children looked longer at a red ball turning into a green ball behind the narrow screen (Wilcox, Hirshkowitz, Hawkins, & Boas, 2014; Wilcox & Woods, 2009). The training consisted in showing the children events in which one colored object had one function and another had a different function. For example, using two identical cups, a red cup was used to pour salt into a box and a green cup was used to pound a peg into a similar box. After two rounds of displaying the difference in function, 9.5-month-olds looked longer when a red ball turned into a green ball. After three rounds of this training, 7.5-month-olds looked longer. For children under 9.5 months, training on red/green tended not to generalize to yellow/blue or purple/orange, but over 9.5 months the training was more likely to transfer. The authors conclude that there is a change in the ninth month in the ability to attend to color generally

---

[4] Jonathan Flombaum and Brian Scholl (Flombaum & Scholl, 2006) have shown change blindness in adults for tunnel effect stimuli. Even adults fail to notice some changes in color. However, they used multiple tunnel effect stimuli—three, four, or five of them———displayed all at once all over the screen. In order for subjects to detect color changes in these stimuli, they have to fixate in the center of the screen, putting all the stimuli in peripheral vision. So the stimuli are seen peripherally and cannot be focally attended since there are a number of them. By contrast, the Wilcox stimuli involve just one tunnel effect event and presumably are focally attended. Flombaum and Scholl show that in conditions in which subjects see one object changing color (as opposed to an object of one color being replaced by an object of another color), change detection of color is enhanced. Still, it is a weakness of my appeal to Wilcox that there are other paradigms in which even adults often don't notice changes in color. See http://perception.yale.edu/Brian/demos/CB-Streaming.html for some demos.

as opposed to specific colors. These results suggest that perhaps the reason that young children do not normally notice color is that in their environment color is not linked to function. Once a function is provided they are more likely to notice color. That also suggests that for other secondary qualities that are linked to function such as taste or smell, attention and noticing are more likely than for color.

Wilcox and Biondi (2015) used the brain-scanning technology suitable for infants mentioned earlier (fNIRS) to investigate the difference between infants who looked longer at changes and infants who did not. They found a signature of detection of change in the front (anterior) portion of the temporal lobe, generally considered the endpoint of the perceptual system as will be explained later in this chapter. Anterior temporal lobe activations in infants has been shown to be reactions to spatiotemporal discontinuities (e.g., in path or speed). They found these activations in children who looked longer at the changes but not those who did not look longer. If my approach is correct, that anterior temporal lobe activation will be part of the neural basis of noticing.

Training can lead infants under 11 months old to notice color, but it does not follow that before training they noticed color or that if they had not received the training they would have noticed color. It certainly does not follow that without training they have concepts or proto-concepts of color even as a temporary property of things. Without training, infants under 11 months do not notice color and so do not have color concepts or protoconcepts and so do not have conceptual perception or protoconceptual perception. With training, they may have protoconcepts of color, but those protoconcepts may only play a role in cognition, not in perception. As we will see in the discussion of adult color perception, there is evidence that adults do not have conceptual color perception and that suggests that the infants who have had the training don't have conceptual color perception either.

Before I go on to discuss the evidence that infants do not normally deploy color concepts, I want to say a bit about color constancy in general as it applies to adults as well as children.

Color constancy

I can imagine someone making the following objection: "You have made heavy weather of the fact that infants below 11 months do not normally notice color, but if their color constancy is poor, then it is just obvious that they would not notice color. Your data can be explained by the constancy facts and so don't support any more expansive conclusion." To see what is wrong with this objection, I need only refer back to the Wilcox experiment on training. The differentiation of function for red and green are enough to enable noticing red and green at a level to induce surprise when a red ball turns into a green ball. So the level of color constancy that *actually exists* in these infants is not at all incompatible with noticing color with a bit of training. And of course the Wilcox experiment also confirms the point that the infants as young as 7.5 months are genuinely perceiving color.

In any case, is it really true that infants have poor color constancy?[5] As I will explain, standard experimental evaluations of color constancy mix together postperceptual color cognition with genuine perceptual color constancy. There are three main methods of evaluating color constancy (in both adults and in children). One method is to simply ask subjects what color something is. To the extent that subjects can identify colors correctly under a range of different lighting, they have color constancy. That method, of course, involves cognitive processes required to cognitively classify the stimuli and so is not a pure test of color perception constancy. The other two methods involve matching samples that are illuminated with different lights. Subjects can be asked to choose which of a number of samples illuminated in one way matches another sample that is illuminated in another way. Alternatively, subjects can be asked to adjust the lighting balance of one sample so as to make it match another sample that is illuminated under different light. All three methods show considerable variation in color constancy from person to person (Radonjic, Cottaris, & Brainard, 2015). One reason for the variation may be what subjects take the task to be, as I will explain.

Adults can make two kinds of color-matching judgments (Arend & Reeves, 1986; Foster, 2003; Norman, Akins, & Kentridge, 2014). One set of instructions leads to matches in "surface color." The instructions are to make the test patch look to be cut from the same piece of paper as another patch. Another kind of instruction is to make the test patch look to have the same hue and saturation and brightness as the other patch. This leads to matches in "reflected color." To the extent that the language of appearance and reality is appropriate here, reflected color is appearance and surface color is reality. Surface color matches show good color constancy for some adult subjects but reflected color matches show little color constancy (Arend & Reeves, 1986). Of course, distinguishing the two kinds of judgments requires considerable conceptual sophistication, including deploying the concepts of brightness, hue, and saturation. So differences in matching scores among adults may involve cognitive differences as well as perceptual differences. One cannot expect small children to be able to make the distinction between the appearance matching and reality matching, so asking children to make color matches risks giving an ambiguous task.

A further concern about color constancy experiments is that although there are color constancy mechanisms in the eye, performance on standard tests of

---

[5] I am indebted to Anya Hurlbert for raising the constancy issue in her comment on this chapter at a satellite meeting of the Vision Sciences Society in May 2021.

color constancy depends on subjects' experience with items with characteristic colors and, for naturalistic stimuli, including what they know about those items (Rogers et al., 2020). What to make of "memory color" effects on perceptual reports will be discussed in detail in Chapter 10. Briefly, some of these effects may be effects on postperceptual judgments rather than on perception itself (Valenti & Firestone, 2019). Alternatively, these effects may be perceptual but reflect associations in the visual system between standard objects and their colors rather than a kind of color constancy that would apply to unfamiliar objects. So some of the variation in performance on color constancy tests reflects factors other than color constancy in perception. Another problem is that color constancy as measured by the usual tests depends on "viewing strategies" (Cornelissen & Brenner, 1995), and these viewing strategies themselves depend on working memory capacity (Allen, Beilock, & Shevell, 2012).

Moving from adults to the constancy abilities of children, Rogers et al. (2020) asked children 33–45 months old to match colors under different illuminations. Children were shown cutouts of two bears with pants and told that that the bears liked to wear pants that matched in color. A bear with pants under one illumination was shown, and children were asked to pick one of four options—all under a different illumination—for another bear to make a color match with the first bear. The result was that a color constancy score for individual children correlated with their ability to use color terms. More specifically, an index of production of color terms correlated .610 with color constancy (though an index of color comprehension correlated only .371 with color constancy).

It would be tempting to conclude that young children have poor color constancy, but that conclusion is unwarranted for a number of reasons, including the doubts about matching as a perceptual test raised in the last few paragraphs. There is a more local reason though: There was no correlation between color constancy and age in this experiment. The older children did not have higher color constancy. Indeed there was no correlation between color naming and age in this sample. Perhaps part of the explanation stems from the fact that there are huge individual differences in color constancy (both in children and in adults) (Allen et al., 2012). Perhaps the individual differences are large enough to swamp developmental effects.

As of 2021, there are no reliable studies comparing infants' color constancy with adult color constancy (personal communication, Anna Franklin). In sum, it is difficult to know what to think about children's perceptual color constancy from the available data. However, I should remind the reader of the Wilcox results on training, in which functions are demonstrated for red and green cups (Wilcox et al., 2014; Wilcox & Woods, 2009). Infants as young as 7.5 months have good enough color constancy to be surprised when a green ball turns into a red ball.

If infants' color constancy turns out to be poor, does that show that the infants are not really perceiving color? Although I once signed on to Burge's view that constancy is the hallmark of perception as opposed to sensation, I no longer do. First, it is not clear what the constancy condition on perception is supposed to be given that there are many constancy mechanisms, including color constancy mechanisms, in the eye. How much constancy is enough for perception? Second, if it turns out that many adults have poor color constancy we should not conclude that they do not perceive colors. We perceive a glass of wine as having a certain taste and smell even if in slightly different circumstances we would perceive it as having a different taste and smell. The poor constancies for taste and smell do not preclude perception.

To sum up this discussion, the Wilcox training experiment shows that the level of constancy that actually exists in 7.5 month old infants is sufficient for noticing color with minor training. (And their experiment involved real objects under illumination, not depictions on a screen for which constancy would not be an issue.) Beyond this fact, the color constancy of infants is unknown at the time of this writing.

I will shift now to discussing the experiments that show that infants under 11 months do not normally use color information in forming expectations or in reasoning or other forms of cognition. To understand the experiments, it will be important to understand that the use of perceptual information in cognition requires a shift of perceptual representations into working memory. To explain the significance of this point, I will say more about working memory in the next section.

Working memory again

Working memory is required for manipulation of information in which some representations are maintained in order to interact with other representations. There can be cognition without working memory, but working memory is necessary for reasoning in which a premise is stored. For example, to reason according to the disjunctive syllogism, one must be able to represent premises of the form p or q and $not\text{-}p$ in order to deduce q.

Working memory is known to be hierarchically organized, coding both "ensemble" properties or "gists" and other global properties along with local properties and their relations to the global properties (Brady et al., 2011). (Ensemble properties have been discussed a number of times in this book and were defined in Chapter 4.) In one recent study (Nie, Müller, & Conci, 2017), geometrical figures (e.g., squares, triangles, diamonds) were themselves composed of geometrical figures—the local figures sometimes being the same as the global figures. By varying the relations between global and local, Nie et al. were able to show that both levels are represented in working memory, that these levels affect one another, that the system tracks the relations between levels (which figures are composed of which figures), and that there is priority to the global level.

It had been thought that there are separate working memory stores for visual/spatial and for verbal information (Baddeley, 2011; Baddeley & Hitch, 1974). The basis for this claim was neuropsychological work on patients suggesting that some patients can lose each capacity without the other and reports of little interference between recall of verbal lists and nonverbal tasks (Morey, 2018). However more recent work has suggested that there may be a single system that underlies both visual and verbal working memory (Morey, 2018).

The central role of working memory in cognition is generally recognized. For example, a recent review in *Nature Reviews Neuroscience* says, "Working memory, which is the ability to briefly retain and manipulate information, is the fundamental basis of cognition" (Nieder, 2016, p. 374). It typically involves activation in the "global neuronal workspace" (Dehaene, Kersgberg, & Changeux, 1998), in which abstractions from perception are made available to mechanisms of reasoning, reporting, evaluating, decision-making, and other cognitive functions. Working memory is controlled by prefrontal areas, especially the dorsolateral prefrontal cortex (Goldman-Rakic, 1987), a brain system that is one of the brain's main centers of executive function. Although working memory representations use perceptual information, these representations are used in the service of cognition and the control of behavior.[6]

A recent review (Christophel, Klink, Spitzer, Roelfema, & Haynes, 2017) notes specifically the abstract categorical representations in the front of the head that are used to control more detailed perceptual representations in the back of the head:

> Taken together, these findings are compatible with a division of labor, in which sensory regions encode low-level details and prefrontal regions encode abstract, categorical information that generalizes across modalities. . . . At the posterior end, the sensory cortices represent incoming sensory information in a relatively pure and detailed form. At the frontal end of the gradient, the frontal cortex represents information that is abstracted and transformed in support of upcoming behavior." (pp. 115–116, 118)

Humans show a working memory storage limit of roughly three items for infants and four items for adults—for certain kinds of materials and certain kinds of tasks. (See the discussion of slot vs. pool models of working memory

---

[6] Note, incidentally, that the brief perceptual memory involved in novelty preference does not require use of working memory. There are two forms of noncognitive sensory memory—iconic memory and "fragile memory" that suffice (Lamme, 2016). See Chapter 2 for a discussion of these types of memory.

in Chapter 1.) However, working memory can retain more items if the items are "chunked" into groups. For example, the series of letters "FBI CIA KGB" is much better recalled than "KBA GFI BFC" (Rosenberg & Feigenson, 2012).

In a series of studies (Zosh & Feigenson, 2009), Lisa Feigenson has explored chunking behavior in infants in which more than three items can be retained if, for example, two are brushes and two are frogs. One paradigm involved searching for items seen to be deposited in an opaque box. If three identical items are deposited in the box in full view, infants will search for a third item after having retrieved two of them, but when four are hidden they show no indication of knowing how many are in the box. When items are chunked, features are lost, or if retained, retained with decreased precision. In one line of experiments, infants appeared to lose all of the kind-specific shape features of the hidden items. They failed to search further when frogs or brushes were hidden and blobs that did not share color, size, or shape with the hidden items were retrieved (Rosenberg & Feigenson, 2012). This level of abstractness indicates conceptual representations. Kibbe and Leslie (2019) provided further evidence of this sort plus evidence that the object files in working memory may involve conceptual information. Six-month-olds can lose all perceptual features of hidden objects while retaining more abstract features such as *human* vs. *artifact*.

To avoid misunderstanding, let me be clear that I am not saying that working memory can never use unconceptualized perceptual representations. Animals may hold perceptual information in working memory about relative size or orientation in guiding behavior. The use of this information may not exploit the predicational structure needed for inference and so may not be conceptual. However, the use of working memory in the experiments just described does suggest some level of conceptual involvement. Perception can represent properties at varying levels of abstraction, from low-level properties like specific shades to high-level properties like impact-causation and individual-agency. However, abstraction from *all* kind-specific shape features suggests the conceptual nature of working memory. From a neuroscience perspective, it is generally agreed that working memory is controlled by brain areas that are strongly implicated in thought, reasoning, and executive function. The function of working memory in reasoning suggests that working memory involves concepts.

Experiments on babies' working memory representations

In this section, I will present evidence that babies in the age range 6 months to 11 months can use shape and kind information in forming expectations but do not normally show any sign of using color information in similar tasks. These data are the heart of my case for the nonconceptuality of color perception.

Earlier I mentioned Wilcox's experiments showing that children look longer when a ball turns into a box and when a duck turns into a truck, but not, until 11.5 months, when a red ball turns into a green ball so long as they have had no special training. That experiment is very unlikely to exploit working memory and so the representations are not good candidates for being conceptual or even being proto-conceptual. The narrow screen is only wide enough for the object to just fit behind it and the occlusion is mostly partial. The object is only very briefly fully occluded. Adults describe the sequence as a red ball turning into a green ball or a ball turning into a box. There is no sign in this experiment of holding a representation in working memory or reasoning with that representation.

Of course, the infant has to have a representation of the ball when it is totally occluded and so no longer visible, but that representation can be in iconic memory and not in working memory. Working memory requires maintenance of a representation by setting up a reverberating loop in which a frontal control state maintains a perceptual representation. (See the discussion of the global workspace in Chapter 1.) These loops take some time to set up and can last for many seconds. By contrast, the perceptual representation of the object behind the narrow screen begins with the percept itself and lasts for milliseconds. Percepts are known to cause persisting activity in V1, the first cortical visual area, and that persisting activity contributes to iconic memory (Teeuwen et al., 2021). Teeuwen et al. showed that the strength of decaying responses in V1 over 100 ms to brief stimuli predicted the accuracy of iconic memory.

An objector may say that the infants do have concepts of color, albeit concepts of color as a temporary property. One item of evidence against concepts of color as a temporary property is that even by 6–8 months, they prefer to look at a normally colored face rather than a blue face (Kimura et al., 2010). (They got similar results for blue bananas and strawberries at 6 months and 8 months but, mysteriously, not at 7 months.) This result also shows lasting object-color associations for color, though I would be reluctant to call this long-term memory for reasons that will be explained later.[7] If they have concepts of colors as temporary properties of things, why prefer to look at normally colored items?

Jean-Remy Hochmann (2010) did an experiment that does not easily fit with the view that these infants have a concept of color as a temporary property. He presented 12-month-olds with pairs of objects that could be the same in shape or color or different in one or the other. In some conditions, there was a rule: Same shape predicted an appearance of an attention-attracting object (a colorful toy)

---

[7] It might be said that the Kimura result shows knowledge of typical colors of things and, since knowledge is conceptual and propositional, infants do have color concepts and their perception may therefore be conceptual. We will see in Chapter 10 in discussion of "memory color" that associations between colors and familiar objects that have those colors are often within the visual system and need not involve anything that could be called knowledge.

in a window on the right (or alternatively on the left). Infants learned to look to the appropriate side for same shape but there was not a significant result for same color. Even if color is taken to be transitory it still could be used to predict something fun and interesting happening on one side rather than the other. Whether a viewer conceives of color as a temporary property or not, same color at a specific time—temporary or not—predicts something interesting, and these infants could not formulate an expectation on that basis.

Their success with shapes may result from genuine inference and if so, the result shows that even at 12 months there is a difference between the ability to reason about shapes and about color. Because the pairs of identical colors were colors on a screen (and did not differ in materials, illumination, viewing angle, or distance), failure of color constancy cannot explain this result.

This is a "null result," always problematic from the point of view of a journal that may reason that a different technique might have shown an ability to formulate the expectation. It is part of a PhD thesis rather than a published article. Still, it is an interesting and useful result and I hope that someone follows it up.

There are, however, plenty of published experimental results that do show that infants below 12 months have trouble forming working memory representations of color. Tremoulet, Leslie, and Hall (2000) showed that even at 12 months, babies have trouble using color information in forming expectations in ways that they can use information about shape and kind. Babies were shown two objects moving out from a screen and back again. When the screen was raised, one of the objects had sometimes changed in shape or color. See Figure 6.6. Infants showed surprise (looked longer) at a change in shape but not in color. Could the babies' expectations be generated by perception alone or is working memory required? The success with shapes has to have involved working memory, because the representations of the objects behind the screen had to be maintained for seconds. Focus on the left side of Figure 6.6. A disk goes out and returns. Then a triangle goes out and returns. The information about the disk must be held in working memory in order to generate an expectation for what happens when the screen is removed. The emergence and return of each object takes 1 second each, and the object stays stationary for 2 seconds. So the disk must be remembered for 1 second while the triangle emerges, another 2 seconds while the triangle is stationary, and another 1 second as the triangle goes back behind the screen, a total of 4 seconds. How long can a perceptual representation be maintained without a working memory representation? Iconic memory lasts at most a few hundred ms. As mentioned earlier, "fragile memory" preserves a perceptual or a quasi-perceptual representation for seconds, but it is, as the name suggests, extremely fragile. In particular, a fragile memory representation of the disk would be destroyed by the perception of the triangle (Lamme, 2003; Sligte et al., 2008).

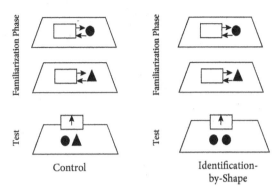

Figure 6.6 The top two rows show two objects emerging from behind a screen and going back inside. Each object emerges and returns twice. Then in the test (lower right) the screen is raised showing two objects, one of which is the same and one different. In the control (lower left) the objects are the same as what the infants saw. The result is that infants are surprised by a changing shape but not color. From Tremoulet et al. (2000, p. 503). Reprinted with permission from Elsevier.

(See Chapter 1 on fragile memory.) So, the representation of the disk must be maintained via working memory.

The upshot is that at 12 months, babies fail to use color information in forming expectations in a circumstance in which they can use shape information. I am not arguing that the use of shape information in forming expectations in these infants exploits predicational structure, that it is genuine reasoning, or that the representations of shape are concepts. The representations of shape may themselves be nonconceptual. The point rather is that even the smidgen of evidence in this experiment for concepts of shape does not apply to representations of color. I will move now to another paradigm that makes the same point.

Infants' expectations about the number of objects behind a screen can be used as a guide to what features of objects use cognitive processing. Figure 6.7 shows a paradigm in which an object emerges from one side of a screen and goes back behind the screen. Then an object that may differ in shape, pattern, or color emerges from the other side and goes back. Then the screen is raised, showing either one or both of the objects. The question is, do infants expect two objects? Summarizing many studies, babies are able to use shape and kind information to form expectations about what will be behind the screen long before they are

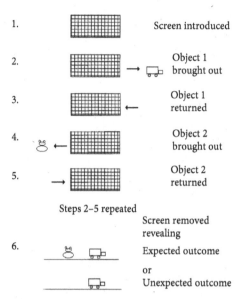

Figure 6.7 An object emerges from one side and goes back behind the screen. An object emerges from the other side and goes back. Then the screen is raised revealing either one or two objects. Thanks to Susan Carey for this figure. Cf. Xu and Carey (1996).

able to use color information for this purpose (Scholl & Leslie, 1999; Xu & Carey, 1996; Xu, Carey, & Welch, 1999), and there is no use of color information prior to 12 months. So expectations about number tell us that infants prior to 12 months can notice and use information about shape and kind but not color in cognitive processes.

How did these experiments test for kind, independently of shape? In one experiment, objects of identical shape moved out from the screen in different ways. One moved on its own, whereas the other was moved out by a hand. In that case, infants expected two objects when the screen went up (Carey, 2009), suggesting that differences in object behavior can be used to generate expectations about kind, independently of shape.

The information about what has come out from each side has to be held in working memory and used in reasoning about number, and so requires working memory representations. Infants are able to form working memory representations that encode shape and kind before they form working memory representations that encode color. That period between success in this paradigm on shape or kind but not yet color is the period in which the babies show abilities with respect to shape and kind that do not reflect conceptualization of color.

Children's tendency not to use color information spontaneously for cognitive purposes prior to 11–12 months contrasts with their ability to use other properties in addition to shape and kind information, notably causal information. Even at 6 months they seem to be able to form expectations that reflect discriminating between causal agents and causal patients. They can use information about the difference to form expectations concerning properties of motion depending on these categories (Carey, 2009, Ch. 6).

It is this difference between what babies do not do cognitively with color categories compared with what they can do with shape, kind, and causal categories that provides reason to believe their perceptual representations of color are nonconceptual. Even those who think that the evidence for conceptual representation of shape, kind, and causation is weak should concede that the difference in 6- to 11-month-olds is striking. Whatever glimmer of concepts of shape, kind, and causation infants have, they do not normally have that glimmer of concepts for color.

The argument is not that infants do not ever have color concepts or protoconcepts of color but rather that in normal circumstances they see colors without activating any such concepts. If the color perception were conceptual, the concepts would have to be activated in color perception.

The results just described involve a contrast between color on the one hand and shape and kind on the other. Perhaps color just isn't as salient as shape and kind? Perhaps... but that isn't an objection. Rather if true it may provide an explanation of why the infants normally lack color concepts and have such a stark case of non-conceptual perception.

I will now switch to a different topic, the difficulty children have in learning color terms, even 2 years after the period we have been talking about and even when they know terms for many other properties of objects. The big problem is in learning the first color word. Once children learn one color term they easily learn others, often on the same day. Interestingly, there has been a marked acceleration over the last 100 years in children's learning of color words. Data from the early years of IQ testing show that at the beginning of the twentieth century, European children did not generally know the four basic color words (the words for red, green, blue, yellow) until age 7. Now they know these terms by 3 years, 3 months (Franklin, 2006). One could speculate that the proliferation of brightly colored toys and programs like Sesame Street that actively teach colors may be the source of the change. Still, even in our era, many children have great difficulty learning color words. Mabel Rice (1980) took a group of 2- to 3-year-olds who knew no color words and taught them the difference between "red" and "green." For most children, learning this difference took over 1,000 trials over several weeks. Even at 2–3 years old, not all of Rice's subjects could even sort by color.

Nancy Soja found evidence that acquisition of the concept of color precedes learning color words (1994). Many 2-year-olds who were at chance on color words were better than chance at using colors to distinguish their toy from the experimenter's toy. And in a game in which the child was expected to imitate the experimenter, many children who were at chance on color words were better than chance at picking the same color item as the experimenter. But no such conceptual abilities have been reported in the 6- to 11-month-olds who have color percepts but no color concepts.

In 1877 Charles Darwin wrote in a letter to a friend, "I attended carefully to the mental development of my young children, and with two or as I believe three of them, soon after they had come to the age when they knew the names of all common objects, I was startled by observing that they seemed quite incapable of affixing the right names to the colors in colored engravings, although I tried repeatedly to teach them. I distinctly remember declaring that they were color blind" (Petzold & Sharpe, 1998). John Campbell mentions a term for this phenomenon coined by an early twentieth-century psychologist, "farbendummheit" (Campbell & Cassam, 2014; Nagel, 1906). (This sort of ignorance of color words in 3-year-olds may be much rarer now than it was in 1980, when Rice did her experiments (Wagner & Barner, 2016). Still, even in 1998, Petzold and Sharpe say (p. 3759), "Although large individual differences occur, it is now well established that the minimum age for accurate and stable performance in color naming is between 4 and 7 years."

One objection to the line of thought of this chapter is: These infants are not in the "space of reasons" (McDowell's term), so they are irrelevant to issues of mentality. Of course, if the infants perceive color without concepts of color, then there can be nonconceptual perception, whether or not they are in the space of reasons. So perhaps the real objection here is that the infants do not perceive color because they are not in the space of reasons. Umrao Sethi suggested in the question period of my talk at the CUNY Graduate Center, February 6, 2019, that McDowell might say that the infants are not conscious of color and so are not perceiving color.

Recall that even 3-month-old infants have color preferences in that they will look longer at some colors than others. And in a variety of paradigms, they have a preference for novel colors. Recall also that infants move their eyes to a disk that they see as a different color from the background; that their attention is increased by an oddball color; that they tire of looking at the same color again, looking instead at other things; and that they look to the side of the screen with the new color. A natural explanation of these facts—especially since we adults show similar behaviors—is that infants are interested in things that have a different color from the background, bored with looking at the same color again and again, and have their interest and attention rekindled by a new color. Boredom and interest and their effects on voluntary action suggest person-level perception, and, somewhat independently, conscious perception. A further item of evidence suggesting that children really do perceive color is the result mentioned earlier that they prefer to look at a normally colored face rather than a blue face (Kimura et al., 2010).

The claim that it is only with consciousness that we enter the "space of reasons" encounters another form of empirical vulnerability, namely the evidence for unconscious reasoning. (See, for example, Part II of Johnson-Laird, 2008, and Garrison & Handley, 2017.) I'm not suggesting that the evidence for unconscious reasoning is overwhelming. Rather I am noting that the view that conceptual mental states have to be conscious takes on an empirical burden. Of course, even if the conceptual has to be conscious, the nonconceptual can be conscious too!

A further point is that we should look to science to tell us what perception is. The characterizations of perception given here are based on what the science of perception tells us about perception. It may be said that perception in the sense that most concerns us is an ordinary notion, not a scientific notion. But that stance ignores the natural kind aspect of our ordinary notions. Since the eighteenth century we have considered whales to be mammals and therefore not fish.

Adult nonconceptual color perception

I now turn to the question of whether adults have nonconceptual color perception. My evidence for nonconceptual color perception in infants is that they do not normally form expectations based on color perception. But after the age of 4, children do form expectations on the basis of color and of course adults do as well. Forming expectations on the basis of color suggests we have concepts of color or at least proto-concepts of color, but those conceptual expectations are cognitive states. The fact that we can form expectations on the basis of color is no evidence at all that our color perception is conceptual. In this section, I will argue that adult color perception is also nonconceptual.

How does language affect adult color categorical perception? Of the many developmental possibilities, we can distinguish between what we might call (1) *Replacement* of nonconceptual categories with concepts and (2) *Preservation* of nonconceptual categories modified by top-down influence. Replacement says that perceptual categories as shown in infants are simply replaced by concepts of colors. Preservation says that the nonconceptual categories of infancy are modified by top-down influences but remain nonconceptual. There is some evidence for replacement, but the weight of evidence supports preservation. Later, I will discuss a third option, *Dualism*, the view that adults have both nonconceptual and conceptual color perception.

I will argue for preservation, but first I want to comment on the objection I always get to my view that adult perception is not conceptual. The objection is based on seeing-as. "I can see something as a dog—and as green. Aren't they both conceptual?" Chapter 3 discusses this issue in detail, but let me just say that it is important to make two distinctions. I can see something as a dog by (1) perceptually attributing certain colors, shapes, and textures, or by (2) perceptually attributing the property of being a dog. The first is low-level perception and the second is high-level perception. In my view neither is conceptual. In addition, there is the state of having a minimal, direct perceptual judgment that something is, say, green based on a perception that is green. This kind of judgment is conceptual, but it isn't perception.

The main evidence for replacement derives from hemispheric specialization. Although there are inconsistent results about hemispheric specialization for color processing in adults (Siuda-Krzywicka, Boros, et al., 2019), infants' color processing is based in the right hemisphere (Franklin et al., 2008). These results are based on an eye movement paradigm like that illustrated in Figure 6.4, in which eye movements between color categories (e.g., blue target on a green background) are compared to eye movements within categories (e.g., blue target on a blue background of a different shade equalized for physical difference). Adults show a slightly larger effect in the right visual field (left hemisphere) whereas 6-month-olds show a significant effect *only* in the left visual field (right hemisphere). This result raises the possibility that color perception in adults, at least the color perception based in the left hemisphere, is conceptual.

However, the time it takes to initiate eye movements to targets that differ across color categories is the same in the right and left visual fields, about 350 ms. If the control of eye movements by the left hemisphere was really conceptual or even proto-conceptual, one would expect control by the left hemisphere to take longer than control by the right hemisphere, since the invocation of color concepts in language areas should take extra time.

Another kind of evidence comes from studies of just noticeable differences for speakers of different languages. Behavioral experiments showing differences in different languages don't distinguish between perceptual and postperceptual effects, but brain imaging can in principle distinguish them. Results, however, are equivocal. Thierry et al. (Thierry, Athanasopoulos, Wiggett, Dering, & Kuipers, 2009) compared speakers of Greek with speakers of English. Greek, unlike English, has distinct color terms for light and dark blue. Using an EEG form of imaging, Thierry et al. found differences between different shades of blue for Greek speakers but not English speakers, and these differences emerged at 100–130 ms after the stimulus, pinpointing early vision. This result suggests influence of linguistic categories on perceptual categories, but that is compatible both with replacement and preservation. (Recall that preservation is: nonconceptual perceptual categories as modified by top-down influences.) Further, there is some evidence that language-specific behavioral color differences disappear when subjects are given a concurrent verbal task. That suggests that the language-specific effects are substantially post-perceptual.

Oddly, this result about Greek speakers conflicts with a similar study about Russian speakers. Forder et al. (2014), using a similar methodology, but with Russian speakers who also make a lexical distinction between light and dark blue, did not find early differences. The differences they found were from 290–320 ms, at about the time that broadcasting in the global workspace is starting and thus the beginning of conceptual processing. It seems unlikely that Greek speakers and Russian speakers would differ in this respect, but even if they do, as I noted, the result for Greek speakers is not incompatible with preservation.

One strong line of evidence for preservation comes from color agnosia. As mentioned earlier, color agnosia is the inability to conceptualize color—e.g., to name colors (color anomia). Color diagnostic objects are objects with a standard color, e.g., a yellow banana, a red strawberry, or a red fire hydrant. When color agnosics are shown pictures of objects such as a strawberry or a fire hydrant, they often have trouble saying whether these color diagnostic objects are appropriately colored or if the pictures are in grayscale, they have trouble coloring them with the diagnostic color.

Color agnosia can co-occur with normal color perception and normal color categorization. The locus of brain damage for color agnosia in adults is mainly in the left hemisphere, the language hemisphere (Miceli et al., 2001; Siuda-Krzywicka, Boros, et al., 2019; van Zandvoort, Nijboer, & de Haan, 2007). Color agnosics often have normal color perception (e.g., they pass the Ishihara color blindness test) but lack specific color concepts. In some cases, they have the generic concept of color and understand the same color relation (van Zandvoort et al., 2007. Normal color perception combined with a lack of color concepts suggests that color perception is not conceptual.

Brain damage in agnosias normally damages both conceptual and perceptual abilities, but recently a stroke patient has been examined who has a striking deficit in conceptual abilities regarding color but with preserved perceptual abilities (Siuda-Krzywicka, Witzel, Chabani, et al., 2019; Siuda-Krzywicka, Witzel, Taga, et al., 2019). The patient—formerly a car paint expert in an insurance company—had a stroke in left hemisphere areas connected to language that damaged his ability to read letters and numbers, though he could name common objects and famous faces. His color knowledge base was nearly normal in the sense that he could verbally give the typical colors of 16 of 20 named color diagnostic objects. For example, he could state that the typical color of cotton is white, that a flamingo is pink, and that a tree trunk is brown.

This patient was severely impaired in naming chromatic stimuli (e.g., a picture of a strawberry) and matching chromatic colors with their names. He was normal with achromatic colors such as black, white, and gray. To the extent that he could say the color of a stimulus, he often used knowledge about the color of common objects. For example, he reasoned (in French) that a sample of red was the same color as blood so it must be red. He never used this technique in naming achromatic colors. The researchers also tested his color categorization.

The experimental paradigm that supports preservation involved presenting the subject with pairs of circles that had one color on the top and another on the bottom. He was asked to pick the circle in which the two colors were in the same category. (He was on the low end of normal for this task.) There were two important results: (1) The patient's correct responses on the task of naming the color of the stimulus did not predict his correct responses on the color categorization task. (2) The patient's color categorization did not predict color naming. This double dissociation of naming and categorization capacities suggests the abilities have independent neural bases. As the authors say, this result "challenges the hypothesis that adult color categorization and color naming depend on the same set of neural processes" (Siuda-Krzywicka, Witzel, Chabani, et al., 2019, p. 2475). This result again suggests that adult perceptual color categories are distinct from color concepts.

Since the patient was on the low end of normal for adult color categorization, it is possible that his color categorization reflected infant categories. If infant categories were used to respond to the stimuli, they would not result in responses that reflect the category system of an adult speaker of French and so might be regarded as deficient in color categorization by adult standards. It would be possible to test this patient to see whether his color categories were those of an adult French speaker or an infant. Kasia Siuda-Krzywicka tells me that just eyeballing the patient's responses, they don't seem to involve clear-cut correspondences with infants' categories.

I mentioned a third option, dualism, the view that adults have both conceptual and nonconceptual color perception. This is not dualism in the sense of the rejection of physicalism and it is distinct from the dualism discussed in the last chapter, the view that we have both iconic and discursive perception.

A recent neural decoding study provides further evidence for preservation and against conceptual color perception in adults and hence against both dualism and replacement (Hajonides, Nobre, van Ede, & Stokes, 2021). Hajonides et al. showed subjects two colored Gabor patches, one on each side of the screen. The patches had randomly different colors and orientations. Subjects wore an EEG mesh on their heads for purpose of decoding the neural signals for color and orientation. The experimenters used methods that isolated the neural activations from which they could best decode the colors that the subjects were seeing. (To make sure that the subjects focused on both patches, they presented a color circle 700 ms later that could be either on the left or on the right and the subjects were tasked with matching the color of the Gabor patch on that side. Another version was focused on orientation and they had to match the orientation.)

The results were decisive: By far the best decoding for both color and orientation was in the visual areas in the back of the head, not in language areas or in frontal conceptual areas. There was little or no decodable signal in frontal areas. In addition, the overwhelmingly best decoding was contralateral to the stimulus (i.e., the right hemisphere coded stimuli on the left). This again pinpoints the visual system rather than conceptual areas. Further, the best decoding was between 150 ms and 350 ms, allowing for little or no conceptual or linguistic coding. (Results for orientation were similar to results for color.) As the authors put it (p.12), "activity in posterior electrodes contralateral to the decoded stimulus were the primary contributors to the decoding of both features, suggesting that visual sensory processing was the main source of decodable signals, ruling out alternative explanations of colour decoding, such as verbal labelling."

Two cautions about this result (emphasized by Jasper Hajonides in correspondence): (1) The result involved averaging over all colors. A color by color analysis might have turned up better decoding from frontal/language areas. (2) EEG is not the most sensitive form of brain scanning so it is possible that other methods might show better decoding. Indeed, a group at Tübingen (e.g. Kapoor, et al., 2022) has been very successful in decoding perception from prefrontal cortex in monkeys. These results though involve spatial stimuli (e.g. moving gratings), not color. And although Kapoor, et al. use a "no-report" paradigm, the results are subject to the "bored monkey" problem to be described in Chapter 7. The bottom line though is that even if color can be decoded from frontal areas, the overwhelmingly strongest decoding is from visual areas.

To summarize, at 4–6 months, infants discriminate colors almost as well as adults (though they may not have adult-level constancy) and they perceptually categorize colors, but they do not exhibit conceptual abilities using color information, even though at the same ages they give a hint of conceptual abilities in the use of information about shape and kind. *Two years later*, many children have an extraordinarily difficult time acquiring color terms, seemingly not realizing what perceptual dimension the adult teachers are trying to indicate. This all adds up to a pretty good case that in young children, color perception is nonconceptual. In addition, I mentioned evidence that adult color perception is nonconceptual too.

Note that the debate about demonstrative concepts of color in connection with the "fineness of grain" argument for nonconceptual color perception does not get a foothold in the argument I have been propounding here. As I mentioned earlier, forming demonstrative concepts is unlikely to be within the abilities of the infants described here.

One consequence of the point I have been making in this chapter is that perceptions are not reasons for belief, though they can be grounds for reasons. That is, we can form the cognitive states that are reasons on their basis without the perceptions themselves being reasons (Burge, 2010a). As I mentioned in Chapter 3, Michael Tye has argued that consciously seeing a thing puts one in a position to have a *de re* thought about it (Tye, 2010, 2014a). Perhaps the perceptions of the infants discussed here put them "in a position" to have *de re* thoughts about the colors they see—in a very loose sense of "in a position." That is, if they were to develop the conceptual apparatus needed for *de re* thoughts, and were they to acquire color concepts, those very perceptions would allow for *de re* thoughts about color. And the same loose sense of "in a position" suggests that in a loose sense of "have a reason" they have a reason to believe that they see colors. It isn't a reason, though, that they can access without further conceptual development. However, if reasons are representations that can be premises in reasoning, then they don't have such reasons.

Is high-level perception conceptual?

We have been discussing color perception, but what about perception of other secondary qualities like taste and smell? And what about primary qualities like shape or size? And what about high-level properties? Recall from Chapter 1 that low-level visual representations are products of sensory transduction that are causally involved in the production of other visual representations and include representations of contrast, spatial relations, motion, texture, brightness, and color. Gradations of high-level representations depend on how much processing of the low-level representations is involved in their production. As a consequence, often position in the visual hierarchy is used as a definition of high-level and size of the relevant "receptive fields" are often used as an index of level. (See the discussion of the visual hierarchy in Chapter 2.)

Even if there is no conceptual color perception, it remains possible that other kinds of perception are conceptual. Is there conceptual perception of faces, causation, agency, gender, and other high-level properties? I have picked color specifically because children's conceptual abilities with respect to color are so meager. One argument against conceptual high-level perception is that high-level perception should allow for negative perception, disjunctive perception, conjunctive perception, and conditional perception, but no such perceptions exist. We can't see a face as *if angry, then masculine*.

If adults have conceptual perception, that would open the door to propositional perceptual contents. Concepts in my terminology are anchored to a role in reasoning, but it isn't clear that adult perception allows for the right kind of role in reasoning. Of course we can conceptualize percepts for use in reasoning. We can reason that if something looks a certain way (using a perceptual experience to specify the way), then such and such will happen. But that kind of reasoning shows only that perceptual experiences can be *brought under a concept* for use in thought, not that perception can itself be conceptual.

Susanna Siegel (2010) advocates conceptual perception in her example of coming to see something as a pine tree via acquiring the concept of a pine tree. However, if seeing a pine tree as a pine tree is really conceptual, why can't we see something as not a pine tree?

Her argument is that there is a phenomenal difference between the experience of seeing a pine tree before and after acquiring the concept of a pine tree and that phenomenal difference is best explained by the role of the concept of a pine tree in representing pine trees. I acknowledge the phenomenal difference but dispute her explanation of it. First, there may be effects of pine tree conception and cognition on perceptual categories, diachronic cognitive penetration, in the lingo of Chapter 9. Secondly, those who have the concept of a pine tree may be attending to different features of the trees and their leaves, engendering different perceptions.

Finally, it is not obvious that we can always easily distinguish which element in an overall state of mind reflects the phenomenology of perception rather than the phenomenology of perceptual judgment. The phenomenal difference involved in perceiving pine trees after acquiring the concept of a pine tree may be in part a matter of the phenomenology of the perceptual judgment with the pine tree content. Siegel combats this sort of idea with the example of finding that the forest has been replaced by an elaborate hologram (2010, p. 105), so what you took to be pine trees are just holographic images. You no longer believe that you are seeing pine trees, but your visual experience is the same nonetheless. So, she concludes, the phenomenology, though conceptual, is not the phenomenology of a cognitive state–like belief.

The problem with this argument is that there is a category of perceptual judgment that is cognitive but does not require believing that things are as they perceptually seem, namely what I described in Chapter 1 as minimal immediate direct perceptual judgment. A perceptual judgment of this sort could be rendered in words as: It visually seems there is a pine tree before me. Thus, the phenomenological difference on acquiring the concept of a pine tree could be a difference in the phenomenology of perceptual judgment.

I have expressed doubt about our ability to distinguish the phenomenology of perception from the phenomenology of perceptual judgment, but in other cases I have expressed confidence that phenomenology attaches to perception. For example, I was confident that the adaptation phenomena described in Chapter 2 were perceptual. And in Figure 6.8 below, I am confident that the modal contours are perceptual. What is the difference? I don't have a general answer to that question but I don't think it is very hard to tell the difference. And our intuitions in these cases are easily backed up by experimental evidence. For example, in the adaptation cases, the effects disappear quite quickly in a way that would be

Figure 6.8 Kanizsa Triangle, reproduced from Chapter 2 for convenience. The edges of the triangle whose vertex points down are "modally" completed (you have a perception as of edges) whereas the edges of the triangle pointing up are amodally completed. From the Wikipedia article on Illusory Contours under a creative commons license.

surprising for a judgment effect that was not perceptually caused. These adaptation effects are repeatable and work on all normal subjects independently of their prior beliefs. In the case of the modally completed triangle of Figure 6.8, the triangle is brighter and appears closer than the background. Why would there be such effects if the phenomenon was not fundamentally perceptual? The amodally completed triangle in Figure 6.8 is equally present in perceptual judgment but its presence in perception is less intuitively obvious. How could this difference be explained if the modal triangle was not perceptual?

Recall the example given earlier of the wasp for which it is plausible that all of its perception is nonconceptual (Chapter 1). That example suggests—but doesn't show—that perception of many other features of the environment *can* be nonconceptual. However, the wasp's perceptions may all be "low-level" in the sense introduced in Chapter 2. One argument that there is nonconceptual perception of high-level features is that high-level perception works in many ways just like low-level perception. In Chapter 2 I explained in detail that for low-level opponent process perception there is a "norm" that is intermediate between the channel extremes. Adapting to the norm steepens the slope of the tuning function in both channels. For example, perception of gray is at the midpoint of the three color channels. Staring at gray produces a subtle adaptation effect of making other colors look to have more extreme opponent channel values. And as I explained, the same is true for perception of emotional expressions. It was found that the effect of adapting to a neutral face was to steepen the slope of the tuning functions for both ends of the spectrum, pushing perceptions toward the extreme directions, making faces look either more fearful or more antifearful. I also noted that there were cross-modal adaptation effects for high-level perceptions of numerosities and facial expressions that were similar to adaptation effects for low level properties such as motion. These items of evidence show substantial commonality between high-level perception and low-level perception.

One item of evidence that could be used to argue for conceptual perception is the finding that when subjects are shown a face together with conceptual information about the person their subsequent recognition of that face improves (Schwartz & Yovel, 2019). Schwartz and Yovel compared asking people to make perceptual judgments at the time of encoding the face (e.g., how round/symmetrical is the face?) vs. conceptual judgments (e.g., how trustworthy/intelligent is the face?). They found a subsequent recognition advantage for the conceptual judgments. One interpretation would be that the perception was conceptual. Another would be that there are perceptual-conceptual associations that enhance perceptual categorization via top-down effects. One reason to favor the latter is that they got enhanced "conceptual" effects just by telling the subjects a name associated with the face. It is hard to see how the name would be a relevant concept.[8]

One strategy that I will use for arguing against high-level conceptual perception will be to discuss two of the best candidates for high-level conceptual perception, perception of causation and of numerosity. These cases are part of the "core cognition" that will be discussed in Chapter 12. (I won't be discussing a third core cognition case, the perception of agency.) Causation and numerosity can be perceived. But in a striking departure from the case of color, even young infants have cognitive abilities involving causation and numerosity (Carey, 2009; Shea, 2014). I have no direct argument for the nonconceptual nature of perception of numerosity and causation, but I will emphasize the similarities between perception of causation and numerosity and low-level perception; and I will be arguing that some of what appear to be cognitive abilities may be perceptual abilities (Burge, 2011).

The point of this chapter is to establish that at least one case of perception is nonconceptual. That puts advocates of *some* conceptual perception in the position of supporting the dualistic theory that some perception is conceptual and some nonconceptual. They would have to justify that view as against the view that in the best cases for conceptual perception (perception of causation, numerosity and agency) what is really going on is that we have both perception of causation, numerosity, and agency and nearly automatic conceptualization of these perceptual representations.

One reason that I have explored infant color perception at length is that disagreements about whether perception is conceptual can seem to be purely

---

[8] For some discussion of this finding in the context of Bruce and Young's theory of face recognition, see Abid (2021).

verbal, with different thinkers characterizing the main terms in different ways. Given that situation, it is useful to anchor the terminology in real phenomena, and infant color perception—with its absence of color conceptual abilities is such a phenomenon.

So far, I have been elucidating one difference between perception and cognition: Perception is nonconceptual. Cognition is paradigmatically conceptual, but that leaves room for nonconceptual elements in cognition. As mentioned earlier, mental maps may (or may not) be forms of nonconceptual nonpropositional cognition. (Rather, the geometrical aspects of mental maps may be nonconceptual; mental maps are hybrid representations with discursive conceptual elements.) Further, perceptual simulations can be used in cognition. See Chapter 1.

Is the existence of possibly nonpropositional nonconceptual forms of cognition such as perceptual memory enough to get in the way of a joint between perception and cognition? Perhaps what these cases show is that it would be best to describe the joint as between on the one hand perception and on the other, propositional and conceptual cognition. See the discussion earlier in Chapter 1 of clarifying the concepts of perception and cognition so as to home in on a joint if there is one. Before I end the chapter, I will just mention briefly two alternative conceptions of conceptual representation, one based in systematicity, the other based in modality.

Systematicity again

What does it take to make a representation conceptual? Many have been influenced by Jerry Fodor's "systematicity" criterion or Gareth Evans' "generality constraint" (Carruthers, 2009; Quilty-Dunn, 2016a, 2016b) mentioned earlier. I do not doubt that if a 4- to 6-month-old infant can see a red square over a blue circle, the infant can also see a blue square over a red circle, thus exhibiting some kinds of systematicity (Quilty-Dunn, 2016b). But despite that kind of combination, the infant cannot use color information in thought and reasoning and the infant cannot use color information in forming expectations in the way it can use shape information. This perceptual variety of systematic combination does nothing to make these representations function in thought and reasoning (Cf. Camp, 2009). Of course, there are many distinct notions of concept but it is hard to see a rationale for using "concept" without grounding it in abilities to think and reason.

Modality

Another account of what it takes to make a representation conceptual postulates that concepts are constitutively nonmodal and that perception is constitutively modal (i.e., a perception is either visual or auditory or . . .). On this basis, some would argue that perception cannot be conceptual. However, there have been many claims that perception, especially high-level perception, is wholly or partly nonmodal and this claim has often been used to argue that perception is conceptual (Fodor, 1975; Quilty-Dunn, 2016b).

Perception is often multimodal. I mentioned the evidence for the multimodality of perception from cross-modal motion aftereffects. In addition, there is evidence that visual perception is affected by inputs from other modalities even at the level of the first cortical stage (V1) of visual processing (Murray et al., 2016). (See also Deroy et al., 2016.)

Everyone has experienced the illusion of upward slope in the cabin of an ascending airplane despite the fact that the visual input is the same as when the airplane is stationary. (Thanks to Barry Smith for the example.) Interestingly, one also has the illusion of upward slope even before the airplane has started the ascent just from the acceleration on the tarmac. These distinct illusions are in the category of "oculogravic" illusions in which forces acting on the body affect vision (Stott, 2013).

Moreover, auditory perception integrates visual and auditory signals, as revealed in the famous McGurk effect, in which the way a subject experiences a speech sound depends on how the speaker shapes the mouth. (Amazingly, when you close your eyes you hear the sound one way and when you open them you hear it another way. You can experience this by typing "McGurk effect" in YouTube.) Charles Spence's group has consistently found effects on perception of sweetness of a drink depending on the color of the mug (Piqueras-Fiszman & Spence, 2012). The general rule is that a sensory modality will be influenced by another sensory modality to the extent that the other modality has more reliable signals for the kind of perception.

It is an interesting fact about perception that people often don't know what modality they are using to perceive something. One wonderful case, very nicely described by Eric Schwitzgebel, is so-called face vision, in which blindfolded people can identify simple geometrical shapes and swatches of cloth as for example velvet or denim. People who could do this had no idea what sensory modality they were using to do it and at one time it was thought that the modality was somehow tactile. It turned out that the modality was hearing—the echoes from different materials sound slightly different from one another (Schwitzgebel, 2011).

The evidence for the multimodality of perception[9] has been ably reviewed recently by Mohan Matthen and Casey O'Callaghan, so I won't review it further

---

[9] Their focus is on the phenomenology of perception, whereas mine is on perception per se, but most of their points apply equally to the two.

here (Matthen, 2016; O'Callaghan, 2016). One case of multimodal perception that many people find dramatic is silent video clips that many people experience as involving sound. In late 2017, there were a number of these things published in online news sites (Murphy, 2017). In an informal survey on Twitter, Lisa DeBruine, a psychologist at the University of Glasgow reported that 70% of people who replied said they heard one of her silent clips as having sound. See https://twitter.com/lisadebruine/status/937302328184594432.

I don't know of any multimodal effect on color perception, but let us suppose for the sake of argument for the moment that such effects exist. Suppose even that color perception in 4- to 6-month-olds is multimodal. Would that suggest that color perception in 4- to 6-month-olds is conceptual? Again, color perception can be multimodal even if it has no role in thought and reasoning. So, a route from multimodality of perception to conceptuality of perception does not look promising.

The terminology for discussing modality can be confusing. Look at Figure 6.8 (reproduced for convenience from Figure 2.15). Most people see a white triangle on top of three black disks that is occluding a black outlined triangle. The white triangle looks brighter than the rest of the figure. The white triangle, disks, and black outlined triangle are seen as complete figures. The perception of the white triangle is said to be an example of modal completion because you see the three edges of the triangle even though they are not drawn on the paper. Perception of the disks and black outlined triangle are described as cases of amodal completion because you see them as complete figures even though you don't see the edges that make them complete and there is no brightness difference as with the triangle that points upward. The occluded backs of objects we see are said to be amodally completed.

Whatever the right modality classification of the shapes in Figure 6.8, these features are clearly perceptual rather than merely cognitive. (This is especially clear in the case of the modal triangle.) One indication of perceptuality is that these kinds of effects occur in cuttlefish, bees, and chicks, organisms that are not known for cognition. Further, as mentioned earlier, completion occurs 50 ms after stimulus onset, faster than thought (Lee & Nguyen, 2001). (The issue of the speed of thought will be taken up in more detail below.)

My argument in this chapter has depended on a three-way distinction between nonconceptual color category representations (that develop at 4–6 months), color concepts (that develop starting at 11–12 months), and linguistic color concepts (that start developing 3 years later). The basic argument is that infants in the middle category have nonconceptual color perception.

I mentioned at the beginning of this chapter that there is a verbal element in the dispute about whether perception is nonconceptual. Some use the word "concept" so that any perceptual category is a concept and others have an even more liberal usage in which any perceptual attribution is an attribution of a concept. But what is not verbal is that there is a substantive issue of whether there is a joint in nature between perceptual representations and cognitive representations of the sort that can function in belief, thought and reasoning. I hope I have made the case that there is such a joint in nature and that perception and perceptual categorization falls on one side and the cognitive representations fall on the other.

To summarize this chapter: I presented strong evidence that normally, 6–11 month olds do not have the abilities diagnostic of color concepts and so their color perception is nonconceptual. I presented weaker evidence that adult color perception is nonconceptual. And that evidence suggests that even the 6–11 month olds who have learned to notice color do not have conceptual color perception. These conclusions do not show that high-level perception or object perception is nonconceptual.

To summarize the conclusion of the book so far, perception is nonconceptual (in the state sense), nonpropositional (in the state sense), and iconic (in format), and there may be an architectural condition as well. These conditions are necessary but not sufficient, as suggested by the putative example of some forms of amodal, nonconceptual, nonpropositional, and iconic cognition such as mental maps (though see Chapter 1 on the role of grid-cells), nonmodal representations of number and more generally, the use of perceptual materials in planning and deciding. Recall that I am not offering necessary and sufficient conditions for a representation to be perceptual. (See Chapter 1.)

The arguments for nonconceptual perception that I have given so far are based more on psychology than neuroscience, but there is neuroscientific evidence as well and it is that subject that I turn to next.

7
Neural evidence that perception is nonconceptual

There is an obvious problem in identifying the neural basis of perception: Experiments typically require responses such as pressing one button rather than another, and it is difficult to see how to separate the neural basis of the perception itself from the neural basis of the cognitive processes involved in classifying the stimulus according to the categories required by the experiment (e.g., present/absent, up/down, horizontal/vertical), maintaining that representation in working memory and deploying those working memory representations in deciding what the response should be. This problem is especially acute when it comes to isolating the nonconceptual ground of perception, since the subjects' cognitive processing will inevitably involve perceptual judgments and the application of concepts required for judgments. It may seem that we cannot possibly tell the difference between the neural basis of the perception and the neural basis of the perceptual judgments.

I introduced this "methodological puzzle" originally with regard to the issue of separating the neural basis of phenomenal consciousness and "access consciousness" (global availability of represented information) (Block, 1995a; 1995c, 2005b; 2007a). But the points apply equally to any mental state or process that has no constitutive connection to behavior, since experiments only inform us about mentality via behavior.

How do the behavioral results of the last chapter avoid the methodological puzzle? The answer is that the experimental paradigms involving babies using looking times and eye movements do not depend on conceptual judgments and so do not present the problem of conflating perception with perceptual judgment. The 4- to 6-month-old infants cannot give reports of what they saw, so the methodology that I described relies on converging evidence from nonverbal techniques that can measure perception without measuring judgment. For example, recall that when looking at a screen containing an object distinct in color from the background (as in Figure 6.4) infants will saccade to (move the eyes to) the distinct object.

We cannot make antecedent assumptions about what mental processes are engaged by a certain behavioral ability such as saccading to the different color object, or the "oddball" neural activation described in the last chapter or the habituation described in the last chapter. The methodological situation is that we must constantly reevaluate what these items of evidence are evidence for, even as we construct theories that use them as evidence.

As it happens, we have good reason to believe that what is going on in all three of the paradigms I mentioned—saccading to a different color, the oddball effect, and habituation—does not involve concepts or cognition. But that fact emerges from the pattern of results and cannot be assumed at the outset. A similar point will be made below about "optokinetic nystagmus" (to be explained). In the rest of this chapter, I will first discuss a case in which evidence from neuroscience has avoided the methodological puzzle in categorizing one cortical area as cognitive and another as perceptual. These two brain areas are the perirhinal cortex and cortical area TE. Then I will turn to two versions of the "no-report" approach that have been applied to consciousness research but can also be used in deciding the question of the conceptuality of perception.

I'll mention a few points from a review paper by Wendy Suzuki that considers the function of the perirhinal cortex and cortical area TE (Suzuki, 2010). As Suzuki explains, evidence from brain lesions was widely interpreted as showing that perirhinal cortex has visual functions. For example, subjects with perirhinal cortex damage had difficulty with visual "oddity" tasks in which they had to pick the oddball among visual stimuli. However, the lesion data is equivocal in part because the exact locus of the lesions is not always clear and because some of the animal work can be explained by the role of the perirhinal cortex in learning the relevant discrimination rather than perceiving the items to be discriminated.

One source of evidence that perirhinal cortex is not a perceptual area has to do with its anatomical connections. Area TE is adjacent to the perirhinal cortex and it is widely agreed that TE is a perceptual area. As I mentioned in the adaptation section of Chapter 2, TE is often thought of as the highest visual area. Whereas the inputs to TE come largely from lower visual areas, the inputs to perirhinal cortex come from many brain areas, including strong connections to areas that are definitely specialized for memory. There are also major cytoarchitectonic differences between TE and the perirhinal cortex. TE has the classic structure of neocortical areas (for example, 6 layers), whereas perirhinal cortex has a quite different allocortical structure with fewer layers and different types of cells. (Neocortex occupies 90% of the cerebral cortex in humans; allocortex is older, supports olfaction, and is shared with nonmammalian species.) Neurophysiological differences tell the same story: Perirhinal cortex encodes various forms of learning, whereas TE acts as a relay to the learning areas, with plasticity involving increased selectivity.

All of these points show the benign circularity that I have been mentioning repeatedly. Massive projections from lower-level visual areas provide part of the evidence that TE is visual whereas perirhinal cortex is not, but that depends on prior classification of those areas as visual. I said inputs to perirhinal cortex include areas that are definitely specialized for memory, but of course that judgment depends on classification of those other areas. As before, the circularity is benign to the extent that different ways of approaching the issue agree with one another and also decide the clear cases appropriately.

I will now turn to the so-called no-report paradigm (Tsuchiya, Wilke, Frässle, & Lamme, 2015). The name is a bit misleading since the idea of it is to exploit reports that come before or after the perception. Reports beforehand can be used to validate a no-report method, and reports afterward can make use of medium-term memory. I will briefly describe two examples. Both of the techniques described below were originally introduced in the context of finding the neural basis of consciousness, but, as we will see, they are similarly relevant to the issue of whether the neural basis of perception must include the neural basis of cognition and conceptuality.

"No-report" paradigm vs. "no-cognition" paradigm

The first example uses binocular rivalry, a phenomenon discussed in Chapter 2 in the "Rivalry" section (recall Figure 2.11, showing binocular rivalry in fruit flies), in Chapter 4, and in Chapter 9. In binocular rivalry, different stimuli are presented to the different eyes and they take turns dominating perception. Although binocular rivalry involves competition between the streams of processing specific to each eye, it also involves competition between the representational contents induced by presenting different stimuli to the two eyes. Indeed the latter competition may be more important, as competition increases as one ascends the visual hierarchy with more inhibition in higher-level visual areas in which monocular neurons are rare (Blake & Logothetis, 2002).

If you put subjects in a brain scanner projecting a face to one eye and a house to the other, asking them to press one button when they are seeing a house and another when seeing a face, you find neural correlates of the differences in visual areas in the back of the head and even more prominently in cognitive areas in the frontal cortex. In an influential 2002 review, the authors conclude, "So, although activity in ventral visual cortex is a consistent neural correlate of consciousness, it might be insufficient to produce awareness without an additional contribution from parietal and prefrontal loci" (Rees, Kreiman, & Koch, 2002, p. 268).

Transitions between rivalrous percepts were detected in both the front and back of the head, but these experiments also isolated the neural basis of the perceptual contents themselves, activations in the fusiform face area in the case of face perceptions and activations in the parahippocampal place area in the case of house perceptions. A conclusion often drawn from these early rivalry experiments by some cognitive theorists was that although the neural basis of the contents of perception such as face content or house content was in the back of the head, what makes those contents conscious was based in the front of the head.

As I mentioned, consciousness is not at issue in this chapter. Rather, what is at issue is whether what has to happen for those contents to be conscious is for those contents to be represented or re-represented in thought areas in prefrontal cortex, as is dictated by most versions of global workspace theories and higher order thought theories of consciousness. For if the dominant percept is represented in thought areas, then the case that the contents are at least partly conceptual would be strong.

There is ample evidence that prefrontal cortex activations are crucial to thought, and especially to what is called "metacognition," cognitive states about other mental states. (Note that "metacognition" is not usually understood to be cognition about cognition, but rather cognition about mental states, including perceptual states.) In one paradigm, bursts of electromagnetic energy (theta-burst transcranial magnetic stimulation) has been found to disrupt metacognition of perception of both low- and high-level properties although perhaps not of emotional expressions of faces, that being centered in the cingulate cortex (Lapate, Samaha, Rokers, Postle, & Davidson, 2020). There is some evidence that the middle of the side part of prefrontal cortex (dorsolateral prefrontal cortex) monitors sensory information that is then relayed to a prefrontal area further toward the front of the head that then combines that information with other information to reach a confidence judgment (Shekhar & Rahnev, 2018). In this chapter, I will tend to speak of prefrontal cortex as the home of thought and more generally as the front of the head being the locus of thought and the back of the head being the locus of perception. A more refined characterization will be presented in Chapter 13 on consciousness.

The rivalry experiments of the early 2000s conflated the processes underlying perception with the cognitive processes involved in doing a task, deciding what the response should be and organizing the response. However, Wolfgang Einhäuser's group used a "no-report" method of determining what the subjects were seeing. (The history of no-report approaches to binocular rivalry is reviewed in Brascamp et al., 2018.) If one eye is shown a grating moving to the left and the other eye is shown a grating moving to the right, the subject is aware of left motion in the whole visual field, then right motion in the whole visual field, then left motion, and so on without apparent limit, as explained in the section on rivalry in Chapter 1. Einhäuser's group showed that a characteristic eye movement called optokinetic nystagmus correlated with the perceived direction of motion as indexed by the subjects' reports. Sharp jerky eye motions to the left correlated with reports of conscious perception of the grating as moving leftward and similarly for rightward motion. In binocular rivalry, there are always brief intermediate states that involve patches of percepts of the two stimuli and aspects of the nystagmus correlated with that too.

Once they had verified the accuracy of nystagmus using reports, they put subjects in the scanner but without giving them any task at all and without asking for reports. They then looked at differences in brain activations when nystagmus indicated a perceptual shift. Of course, subjects could testify after the experiment that their percepts were alternating as usual. The methodology here is that so long as nystagmus predicts perceptual shifts better than chance, the experimenters can use nystagmus to isolate the neural basis of perceptual shifts even when subjects are not reporting anything. The differences between percepts observed using nystagmus instead of reports reflected differences in perceptual areas in the back and middle of the head and not the frontal cognitive areas, suggesting that the perceptions were nonconceptual. The article summarizes: "Importantly, when observers passively experienced rivalry without reporting perceptual alternations, a different picture [that is, different from what happens with report] emerged: differential neural activity in frontal areas was absent, whereas activation in occipital and parietal regions persisted. . . . we conclude that frontal areas are associated with active report and introspection" (Frässle, Sommer, Jansen, Naber, & Einhäuser, 2014, p. 1738). And the article's title reflects this emphasis: "Binocular Rivalry: Frontal Activity Relates to Introspection and Action But Not to Perception."

It is important to distinguish the neural basis of transitions in rivalry from the neural basis of the contents of the rivalrous states themselves (Naber & Brascamp, 2015). If there is no prefrontal difference linked to perceptual transitions, then we can conclude that the perceptual contents cannot be prefrontal and are unlikely to be conceptual. If the prefrontal cortex is representing a face, and then a house, then a face again, there has to be frontal change, even if it is hard to detect. However, if there is a prefrontal difference linked to perceptual transitions, it is much less clear what to conclude. The prefrontal difference might be due to differences in early stages of processing (Overgaard & Fazekas, 2016) or to differential attention to the changing stimulus or changes in working memory rather than changes in perception.

The methodology of some binocular rivalry experiments focus on detecting transitions, not the contents themselves. Often studies of binocular rivalry involve comparisons between binocular shifts and what is called "replay," in which there are real changes between say a face stimulus and a house stimulus. fMRI always involves subtraction of one condition from another. In this paradigm, replay activations are subtracted from rivalry activation. Since both cases involve the same conscious perceptual contents, what is left after the subtraction is correlates of the transitions without any information about the perceptual contents themselves.

However, even though replay subtraction experiments focus on detecting transitions, if contents really are represented frontally, that should show up in the replay subtraction methodology. As noted in Chapters 2 and 4, the standard explanation of rivalry is that pools of neurons representing each eye's processing stream, or alternatively, each of the incompatible stimuli, compete for dominance and also inhibit one another. In the presence of neural noise, one pool wins temporarily. Then that pool is weakened by adaptation (see Chapter 2) and the other pool representing the other alternative takes over (Alais et al., 2010; Brascamp et al., 2018). Because of the impact of neural noise, the time of the transitions cannot be predicted on the basis of past transitions. As noted in Chapters 2 and 4, this model is supported by evidence from psychophysical experiments, brain imaging, and neuropharmacology (Brascamp et al., 2018).

Here is the point: The strengthening and weakening of neural activations that is intrinsic to binocular rivalry distinguishes rivalry transitions from the replay transitions where there is no rivalry. Just changing the stimulus from face to house, then face again, and so on, as in replay, does not produce the strengthening and weakening characteristic of rivalry. Thus when replay activations are subtracted from rivalrous activations, if there is no difference, it follows that the different contents are not represented.

A further point along these lines is that rivalry is a gradual process. There are brief traveling waves of dominance. (See Paffen, et al., 2008 for more on traveling waves.) These traveling waves will be present in rivalry but not in replay, creating another difference between rivalry and replay. This point is significant for higher order theories since they dictate a content difference between rivalry and replay with traveling waves in rivalry and none in replay. That should show up as a difference between rivalry and replay.

One caution: The reasoning just described applies to all methods of brain imaging though of course fMRI may not detect strengthening and weakening or traveling waves that would be detected by microelectrode arrays.

As with the behaviors mentioned in the last chapter (saccading to a different color, the oddball effect, and habituation) one can make no antecedent assumptions as to what exactly the nystagmus behavior is indexing. Nystagmus might have been indexing reported perception rather than perception itself. However, the results suggest that it is perception itself that is being indexed. As with saccading to a different color, we have reason to think that yet another apparently perceptual phenomenon can index just perception.

The Einhäuser result led to a flurry of controversy (Safavi, Kapoor, Logothetis, & Panagiotaropoulos, 2014; Wang, Arteaga, & He, 2013) in which different types of experiments seemed to differ in whether they showed frontal differences in perceptual shifts in binocular rivalry. These results presented serious challenges to the Einhäuser result. Safavi et al. found frontal differentiation in a no-report experiment with monkeys using electrophysiological methods (electrodes inserted in cortical regions) that are known to be more sensitive than the fMRI used by the Einhäuser group. Impressively, the Safavi et al. group used monkeys that had not been trained on a discrimination task, ruling out covert decision-making that would have been expected to make a frontal difference (personal communication from Theofanis Panagiotaropoulos, the corresponding author of Safavi et al.). In addition, Biyu Jade He's group was able to decode perceptual content from frontal areas in binocular rivalry (Wang et al., 2013). However, this result did not use a no-report paradigm, so the frontal representation could have been linked to the cognitive processes underlying reporting.

However, a group at the Max Planck Institute for Biological Cybernetics in Tübingen recorded from grids of microelectrodes ("Utah" arrays) placed in the frontal cortex of monkey in a binocular rivalry setup with gratings moving up in one eye and down in the other eye. This group found that they could decode whether the gratings the monkey was perceiving were moving up or down, as indexed by optokinetic nystagmus, thus confirming the result of the Safavi study (Dwarakanath et al., 2020; Kapoor, 2019; Kapoor, Safavi, & Logothetis, 2018; Panagiotaropoulos, Dwarakanath, & Kapoor, 2020). Most impressively, Kapoor, et al. (2022) found that the same decoder worked both for replay (i.e. physical alternation of the stimulus) and rivalry. This result used a no-report paradigm and the monkeys had not been previously trained on reporting the motions of gratings.

Do these results as impressive as they are show that frontal cortex is part of the neural basis of perception? No, for a simple but crucial reason, a problem I have called the "bored monkey Problem" (Block, 2020). The monkeys in these experiments spend hours looking at gratings going up and down without any task other than fixating the stimulus (pointing their eyes at it). If you were in this perceptual situation, you would inevitably have some cognitive states—thinking, wondering, questioning, musing, and the like—concerning the grating moving up when it is moving up and the grating moving down when it is moving down. The microelectrode arrays could be tapping postperceptual cognitive processing concerning which way the gratings are moving as well as or rather than the perceptions of the gratings themselves.

The same point applies to earlier "no-report" experiments involving humans. Erik Lumer and Geraint Rees scanned subjects who were viewing binocular rivalry stimuli but without any report (Lumer & Rees, 1999). The stimuli were a face shown to one eye and a moving grating shown to the other eye. The experimenters had no way of knowing exactly when the transitions were occurring but they observed regular alternations between the different circuits connected to face processing and motion processing. Those circuits included prefrontal areas. The authors concluded (p. 1669), "that functional interactions between visual and prefrontal cortex may contribute to conscious vision." In a recent article arguing for a frontal component of the neural basis of consciousness

(Michel & Morales, 2020), Jorge Morales and Matthias Michel cite this study in arguing for the conclusion that "multiple studies using binocular rivalry have consistently found that conscious perception correlates with PFC [NB: prefrontal cortex] activity whereas unconscious perception does not." However, these subjects experienced 6 trials of 41 seconds of binocular rivalry while in a scanner and another 6 trials of 41 seconds in which the different stimuli presented to the two eyes were designed to merge instead of being rivalrous. It would not be surprising if these subjects were thinking when experiencing a face that they were seeing a face or something about the face, and thinking about the grating when they were seeing a grating. These cognitive episodes could be responsible for the prefrontal activations.

Thus there is a flaw in the reasoning behind the "no-report" paradigm. Eliminating report is only successful in isolating the neural basis of perception if it eliminates postperceptual cognitive processing such as thought and judgment about the reportable properties that is systematically correlated with one of the perceptual representations. So what we really need to do is to replace the "no-report" paradigm with a "no-postperceptual-cognition" paradigm. But this may seem manifestly impossible. When subjects see things, they are free to make perceptual judgments and think about what they see. You can't stop subjects from thinking. We seem to be at an impasse.

The "bored monkey problem" has been disputed by (Panagiotaropoulos et al., 2020): They say:

> Block also argues that our results [they refer to (Kapoor et al., 2020; Panagiotaropoulos, Kapoor, & Logothetis, 2012)] showing decoding of conscious contents from prefrontal neural ensembles using no-report BR [i.e., binocular rivalry] are problematic due to the "bored monkey problem": macaques participating in passive, no-report BR are bored during the experiment and therefore engage in postperceptual, higher-order thoughts reliably aligned to the rivaling stimuli and therefore decodable in cognitive brain areas such as the PFC. In this case, prefrontal populations could reflect postperceptual processing rather than pure conscious representations. However, this would suggest that postperceptual thinking is reproducible, and stimulus aligned across trials. This seems an unlikely combination of events in the brains of bored macaques, given also the absence of active reports that could associate stimuli with specific actions (e.g., button presses) and thoughts. It is unclear why the macaques would engage in such reliable postperceptual cognitive thinking to fight or due to boredom.

Unlike Panagiotaropoulos et al. I have no experience with monkeys, however their objection seems to me flawed. They say it is unlikely that postperceptual thinking would be "reproducible, and stimulus aligned across trials." But the bored monkey problem does not require that the monkeys are always thinking "Now it is going up" when the grating is going up and "Now it is going down" when it is going down. It would be enough reproducibility and stimulus alignment to show up in studies such as theirs if the monkeys did this frequently and if the monkeys were rarely thinking "Now it is going down" when it is going up and rarely thinking "Now it is going up" when it is going down. Is that really so unlikely?

The "bored monkey problem" has recently been confirmed in human subjects by Claire Sergent and her colleagues (2021). Sergent et al. used a simple auditory detection task in which sounds were embedded in noise. In some sessions, subjects were asked to detect the sound, but in other sessions though the same auditory stimuli were present, subjects were given non-auditory tasks or no task at all.

At random times, subjects were interrupted with a mind-wandering task in which they were asked to classify what was on their minds as between the sound, the non-auditory task, their own thoughts, or nothing. They almost never reported nothing and most of the reports were of the non-auditory task or their own thoughts. In 19% of the cases they reported what was on their minds was the sounds. Sergent, et al. found that widespread frontal and parietal activation (what they term activation of the "global playground" as contrasted with the "global workspace") was correlated with mind-wandering reports of sounds being on the subjects' minds. Note that subjects could be consciously perceiving the sound even when what was most prominently in their minds was the visual or amodal task or their own thoughts. The fact that reports of the sound being on their minds correlated with the global playground activations suggests that the awareness of sounds was sufficiently present to cognition that it may be the presence to cognition that was responsible for frontal activation. Thus I consider this result a dramatic confirmation of the bored monkey problem.

The main significance of the Sergent, et al. article from the point of view of this book is the mind-wandering result. But I would be remiss if I did not mention the methodological advance that led to the global playground. Recall that in the no-report paradigm as just discussed, optokinetic nystagmus was calibrated in previous experiments involving reporting responses and then applied in a no-response paradigm. What Sergent, et al. hypothesized is that no indicator of perception is required. Brain activations with a threshold stimulus show what they term "bifurcation" dynamics because on almost all trials subjects are either fully conscious of the stimulus or not conscious of it at all, with very different brain processes in the two cases. Thus the widespread activations can be assumed to be the conscious cases. That idea is what allows for the isolation of the global playground, and since the global playground activations are not contaminated by the bifurcation dynamics, trials divide into those with widespread activations in parietal and to some extent prefrontal cortex and those trials without widespread activation. Since the dynamics themselves provide the differential activations, no other substitute for report is required. That allowed Sergent, et al. to escape the strictures of binocular rivalry, using instead presentation of stimuli at threshold where it was independently known that sometimes there is conscious perception and sometimes not. The widespread activation indexed by their procedure only minimally reflects executive processes as one would expect given the fact that the methodology involves no connection to report. Thus I think they are right that the "global playground" activation is a better bet as a theory of consciousness than the more extensive "global workspace" activations. However, the correlation with mind-wandering reports suggest that global playground activations reflect thought rather than conscious perception, thus confirming the bored monkey problem.

Let us now move to a solution to the bored monkey problem to be found in an experiment by Jan Brascamp, Randolph Blake, and Tomas Knapen (2015). (To avoid misunderstanding, note that this experiment did not involve nystagmus.) Brascamp et al. reasoned that detection of frontal transitions in binocular rivalry might have to do with the attraction of attention to perceptual transitions, so they designed stimuli for which the transitions would be "inconspicuous," not drawing attention. The stimuli were randomly moving dots. Every 300 ms there were transitions in which each dot was replaced by a dot at a different position moving in a random direction. In one condition, the dots in the two eyes were of different colors, whereas in the other condition, the dots were of the same color. See Figure 7.1.

The key idea is this: For the condition in which the eyes are shown *different* color dots, subjects noticed the rivalrous change of dominant eye because the color changed. However, for the condition in which the dots were of the *same* color, the subjects rarely noticed the change of dominant eye. The reason is that

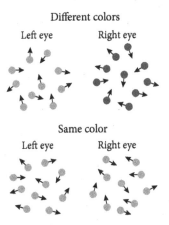

Figure 7.1 Quasi-random motion stimuli used in binocular rivalry experiments by Brascamp et al. (2015). The alternation between the blue and red dots at the top is very noticeable, but the alternation of the same-color dots is not because the dot pattern is ever-changing. This figure requires color. There is a free pdf on the Oxford University Press web site that has the color version of this and all the other figures. Thanks to Jan Brascamp for this figure.

they had a hard time detecting whether a sudden change was due to a change of dominant eye or to one of the frequent changes in which each dot is replaced by a dot in a different place moving in a different direction. So they were unlikely to notice the rivalry transitions as standing out from the constant changes. Thus the conscious changes due to a change in dominant eye were "inconspicuous" and could be expected not to draw attention and not be noticed. (Subjects are generally not aware of which of their eyes is dominating the perception in binocular rivalry.) The idea here is that one does not notice—in the sense of bringing under a concept—everything that one consciously sees. Thus Brascamp et al. had created a case of binocular rivalry in which the rivalry did not draw attention.

Note that the fact that subjects were unlikely to notice the transitions from one dominant eye to the other as standing out from the constant changes is compatible with the subject *perceptually representing* first the array shown to one eye, then the different array shown to the other eye. At any given time, the arrays shown to the two eyes differed in the direction of motion and the extent to which its motion cohered with the motion of other dots. The experimenters were able to confirm, using a number of different methods, that perceptual binocular rivalry was occurring for the same color patterns at the bottom of Figure 7.1—that is, that the two displays triggered different perceptual contents.

One such method involved a separate experiment varying the dot density in the two eyes. When the two eyes receive different inputs, there are only two alternative perceptual situations: (1) the percept can reflect some kind of combination or merger of the two inputs or (2) the percept can reflect rivalrous alternation of the sort described earlier. When they asked for reports of density they tended to get responses indicating the density that was input to one of the eyes rather than any sort of combination or merger of the two eyes.

Thus there was little merging in their procedure, providing evidence for real perceptual rivalry. They further confirmed perceptual rivalry by exploiting known temporal regularities of rivalry. Subjects were consciously experiencing repeated shifting of the patterns, but as noted earlier, they had no way of distinguishing between the transitions that reflected rivalry and those that reflected the regular change of patterns.

Were the rivalrous switches inaccessible or unreportable? No! They were accessible but mostly not accessed. The rivalrous switches were (mostly) indistinguishable from the switches that were happening every 300 ms, so the rivalrous switches did not stand out and were not noticed. The authors say (p. 1674), "Based on the sensitivity index, d', detection of switches in the same color condition could not be distinguished from chance, demonstrating just how inconspicuous these switches are." That is, the subjects were (approximately) at chance on distinguishing the rivalrous switches from the run-of-the-mill switches that were happening all the time. All switches—rivalrous and nonrivalrous—were noticeable, accessible, and reportable, but the subjects mostly could not pick out the rivalrous switches from the ones that were happening every 300 ms.

I mentioned that the methodology of subtracting fMRI scans of replay (real transitions) from rivalry (internally generated transitions) is geared toward detecting the causes of changes rather perceptual contents themselves, because the contents are the same in both cases. As I also mentioned, if the rivalrous contents are different, subtraction of replay from rivalry should detect the difference because of the strengthening and weakening characteristic of rivalry transitions and the traveling waves of transition. Brascamp et al. did not subtract replay from rivalry, but their methodology is importantly similar since they compared epochs containing a rivalry transition with epochs containing only the regular 300 ms transitions. And the same point applies to their methodology.

Using fMRI, Brascamp et al. could detect frontal differences in the case of different color dots but not in the case when the dots were of the same color. As they say, frontal differences in activation for the inconspicuously different stimuli were "altogether undetectable in our procedure," supporting the Einhäuser conclusion (p. 1677). Brascamp et al. conclude that "when viewing a conflicting or ambiguous stimulus, a switch in perception may arise in the visual system, but noticing the change may rely on brain regions dedicated to behavioral responses" (2015, p. 1677). The upshot is that it may be *noticing* that brings in frontally represented concepts—the perceptions in cases that do not draw attention are based in perceptual areas in the back and middle of the head.

Brascamp et al. used univariate fMRI, a technique in which voxel activations are averaged. This known to be less sensitive than multivariate fMRI, in which activations in individual voxels are examined. Odegaard et al. (Odegaard, Knight, & Lau, 2017a) have argued that failure to find frontal differences with fMRI may miss real effects that would be detected by other means. They mention that ECog recordings, in which there is direct intracranial electrophysiological recording in human surgical epileptics (in which the skull is opened and electrode grids are placed on the cortex), showed differential frontal activity even when subjects were not required to report the stimulus. Odegaard et al. are right that ECog may pick up changes missed by fMRI, but using patients to test rivalry even without report does not satisfy the point made here that the subjects may be thinking about the transitions and about the dominant stimuli even when not required to report on them (the bored monkey problem). Still, the basic point that Odegaard et al. were making does apply to the Brascamp et al. experiment, since the rivalry changes in that experiment, involving only the direction and coherence of motion of dots, might require temporal and spatial resolution too fine-grained for fMRI. It would be great if the no-cognition paradigm could be combined with ECog.

Ian Phillips and Jorge Morales (Phillips & Morales, 2020) have recently written a critique of my article in *Trends in Cognitive Sciences* that used arguments similar to those made in this section. (What I say in this section differs from the article in that in this chapter I am not focusing on consciousness.) My article made a negative and a positive point. The negative point was that the "no-report" paradigm is problematic because of the bored monkey problem. Phillips and Morales (P&M) do not dispute this negative point. What they do dispute is my positive point: that Brascamp et al. (2015) have evaded the bored monkey problem. One innovation introduced by Brascamp is to use stimuli that have two related useful properties. The first is that the stimuli do not afford any ready-to-hand cognitive categories for characterizing them other than "moving dots." Subjects can't say to themselves: "There is the face again." Phillips and Morales say (p. 165), "Nothing in Brascamp et al.'s methodology prevents observers engaging in extensive cognitive processing" both in the rivalry transitions and the similar real "objective") transitions. But they are neglecting the fact that the stimuli do not naturally draw cognitive processing in *either* the rivalry case *or* the real case.

The second useful property of these stimuli is that they are subjectively different from each other without being conspicuously different. Phillips and Morales (2020) say (p. 167), "Yet indiscriminable stimuli look the same." But although the stimuli are not noticeably different, they are subjectively different: They differ from each other in the directions of movement of each dot and in the overall directions of motion of the dots. Indeed, they are sufficiently perceptually different to trigger conscious rivalry.

I mentioned (Block, 2019f) that rivalry occurs in fruit flies and can occur in unconscious perception. Phillips and Morales conclude that the rivalry in Brascamp et al. might be "invisible." But one cannot generalize in this way from rivalry when subjects do not consciously see the stimuli to when they do see the stimuli. Rivalry is dominance of one whole neural coalition over another. I know of no evidence that in the case of consciously seen stimuli, rivalry can somehow result in slicing off the conscious part of the coalition. The competing stimuli are *subjectively* but not *noticeably* different. Not being noticeably different, rivalry transitions are less likely to draw more attention than real transitions—as confirmed by Brascamp et al.

But would the differences between the neural representations of such stimuli be decodable in the brain at all, given how similar they are? Recall that the explanation of binocular rivalry is that pools of neurons that represent each of the stimuli are mutually inhibitory. In the presence of neural noise, one pool wins out. The dominant pool of neurons then weakens due to adaptation, the other pool taking over in the winner-takes-all process of perception, then the cycle repeats. If this weakening and strengthening of content representations were happening in prefrontal cortex, it would be detectable, either with fMRI or with electrophysiological methods (microelectrodes inserted into the cortex). Not finding differences between the rivalrous changes and the real changes is evidence against prefrontal cortex differences and hence against cognitive theories of conscious contents. This point interacts with the issue of the not-noticeably different stimuli: With readily characterizable (e.g., face/house) stimuli, weakening and strengthening in visual cortex could have caused a *cognitive* reflection of that weakening and strengthening in prefrontal cortex, misleading us as to the role of consciousness in prefrontal cortex.

Returning to the comparison of the rivalrous transitions with the nonrivalrous real transitions, Phillips and Morales concede that failure to find prefrontal cortex differences between rivalrous and real transitions shows that the causes of rivalry transitions are not to be found in prefrontal cortex. But they go on to say that the conscious contents may nonetheless be in prefrontal cortex. They use this point to conclude that methodologies that compare real with rivalrous transitions—including subtracting replay from rivalry—"cannot discriminate rival hypotheses concerning NCC's."

But as I mentioned earlier, the neural bases of transitions and contents are linked. If perceptual contents are based in prefrontal cortex, the strengthening and weakening of content-representations that is intrinsic to binocular rivalry would make rivalrous transitions neurally different from real transitions, and, as also noted above, the gradual transitions of rivalry with their traveling waves also differentiates the rivalrous transitions from the real changes. Contents and differences in content have consequences for transitions. So, failure to find differences between rivalrous transitions and real transitions in cognitive areas of prefrontal cortex disconfirms prefrontalist theories of perceptual content.

Another "no-report" paradigm

I will very briefly describe a second kind of "no-report," "no-differential attention," and possibly "no-thought" paradigm that provides neural evidence for the noncognitive nature of perception. As with the previous section, this technique was originally introduced to find the neural basis of consciousness, but the method applies equally well to the question of whether perception is conceptual.

As mentioned earlier, fMRI is much better at distinguishing activity in one area of the brain from another than in temporal resolution. The next technique has the opposite profile, excellent temporal discrimination with poor spatial discrimination. The technique utilizes a web of electrodes placed on the scalp that measure the brain activations in response to a stimulus, "event-related potentials," or ERPs. As with the previous case described, when subjects make reports it appears that perception correlates highly with widespread frontal and parietal (middle of the brain) activity that occurs well after activity in the perceptual areas in the back of the brain (Dehaene, 2014). Earlier in this chapter I discussed the "global playground" theory and the "global neuronal workspace" theory of conscious perception, in which conscious perception is a cognitive phenomenon of "ignition" in the global neuronal workspace that involves activation of machinery of reporting, reasoning, decision-making, and other cognitive functions in frontal and parietal areas. Dehaene and his colleagues have found that ignition starts roughly 270 ms after the stimulus, whereas before 270 ms, only perceptual areas in the back of the head are activated.

As mentioned at the beginning of this chapter, I have objected (Block, 2007a, 2011c) that what previous studies measured was contaminated by the cognitive processes underlying deciding what the task requires, remembering what has happened, figuring out what response to give, and organizing a report. A series of studies by Michael Pitts (Pitts, Martinez, & Hillyard, 2011; Pitts, Metzler, & Hillyard, 2014; Schelonka, Graulty, Canseco-Gonzalez, & Pitts, 2017) confirms this claim. In one experiment, Pitts and his group presented subjects with stimuli that contained a ring with small disks on it. The subjects' task was to detect a slight dimming in one of the disks. See Figure 7.2 for an illustration. This focused a subject's attention on the periphery of their visual fields. Meanwhile the background of the ring contained a multitude of line segments that were constantly changing orientations. Sometimes the line segments formed geometrical figures such as squares or triangles. The subjects completed 240 trials of detecting dimming of the disk before the experimenters asked about perception of the geometrical figures. This is the methodological advance: Don't ask about a perception until long after the stimulus. The task was calibrated so that about half the subjects would be aware of the geometrical figures. Pitts gave subjects questionnaires to probe whether they had seen the specific figures that were formed in the background of their experiments and retained the information in "incidental memory." The result was that for those who were at least moderately confident at having seen the figures, the ERP traces that correlated best with conscious perception came just before "ignition" and global broadcasting. Thus, they probably saw the figures before they could have judged that the figures were there. As with binocular rivalry, the stimuli stay constant but perceptual representation of the stimuli varied.

What I just described is Phase 1 of Pitts's paradigm. In Phase 2, the subjects do the same task, but of course now that they have been asked about the background in the center of the screen, they are attending to it. In Phase 3, the task changes to reporting the lines in the center of the screen. See Figure 7.3. So, putting together all three phases, they have data that varies both whether the central stimulus (the display of lines) is being attended to (1 vs. 2 and 3), whether the central stimulus is seen consciously (half the subjects in 1 and almost all in 2 and 3 vs. the other half in 1), and whether the central stimulus is task-relevant (1 and 2 vs. 3). Phase 1 allows a determination of the difference between conscious perception vs. no conscious perception in inattention conditions. And comparing

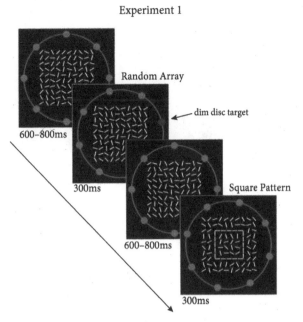

Figure 7.2 An illustration of Michael Pitts's paradigm. In Phase 1, the task is to detect a slightly dimmed disk as in the second figure. This task focuses attention on the periphery and inhibits attention to the center. In the meantime, the lines in the middle are constantly changing, occasionally forming a geometrical pattern. The displays are constructed so that about half the subjects will be aware of the occasional patterns. This figure requires color. There is a free pdf on the Oxford University Press web site that has the color version of this and all the other figures. Thanks to Michael Pitts for this figure.

Phase 1 with Phase 2 allows determination of the difference between attentive conscious perception and inattentive conscious perception. And bringing in Phase 3 reveals the neural bases of report. Overall, this paradigm supports the claim that the neural basis of the cognitive processes involved in categorizing the stimulus, maintaining that categorization in working memory, and deploying the maintained information in deciding what to report is in the late frontal activations that underlie cognition, whereas the neural basis of perceptual consciousness itself is in perceptual areas in the back of the head that very likely do not involve conceptualization and cognition.

As I mentioned earlier (Chapter 3), there have now been a number of papers that have shown that conscious perception can occur without the P3b and so without global broadcasting when the perception is not task-relevant (Cohen, Ortego, et al., 2020; Dembski et al., 2021; Sergent, et al., 2021). As I mentioned,

322 THE BORDER BETWEEN SEEING AND THINKING

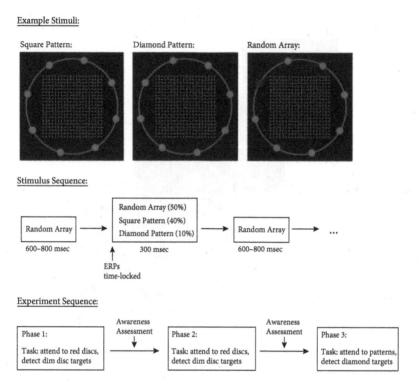

Figure 7.3 The three different phases in Pitts's paradigm. Thanks to Michael Pitts for this figure.

Dembski et al. also survey a range of results that show that what does correlate with conscious perception in an EEG signal is the "perceptual awareness negativity" that occurs much earlier (120 ms to 200 ms after stimulus presentation) and that is based in the brain circuits that process the relevant modality, visual areas for sight and auditory areas for hearing.

What is important for this chapter is not the fact that the neural basis of conscious perception is activated prior to global broadcasting but the fact that perception of the figures occurs prior to the activation of conceptual networks in the global workspace. As I mentioned earlier, the global workspace theory is a better theory of conceptualization than of consciousness, and the global playground theory is a still better theory of conceptualization.

Of course, the reasoning here depends on a prior classification of brain activations as perceptual and cognitive, but as before, these classifications lead to a coherent picture of what is going on in perception.

The Pitts methodology avoids mixing up the neural basis of access with the neural basis of consciousness and conceptualization of the stimuli by only asking for reports after many trials (240 in the first phase). The disadvantage of that technique is that one does not know how many times the subjects did consciously see the stimulus. Subjects were asked for estimates and most estimated more than 100 times, but one doesn't know how seriously to take that (Pitts, Lutsyshyna, & Hillyard, 2018). Another issue with the method is that it does not allow testing first conscious perception and then unconscious perception. Ideally, both orders would be used.

There is plenty of evidence that cognitive processing is largely based in frontal areas of the brain. For example, in maintenance of working memory, frontal areas (specifically on the side of the brain) control what the subject is remembering (Goldman-Rakic, 1987). I mentioned above that working memory is based in frontal areas and parietal (middle of the head) areas. And much of our conceptual life depends on working memory. Of course, all that evidence is based on prior assessments of what processes count as cognitive. So, any conclusion from neuroscience that the difference between rivalrous states is perceptual rather than cognitive essentially depends on which other phenomena are perceptual and which are cognitive.

Another interesting pair of results using the ERP methodology concerns color. Forder et al. (2017) found an effect of color category on preattentive passive color perception. Forder et al. picked stimuli on the blue/green border that subjects are known to disagree about. Some of their subjects classified the border color as blue, some as green. The color category activations occurred at about 100 ms after the stimulus. They also found a later effect at 220 ms to 260 ms. These effects are both too fast for cognition, so they may reflect low-level and high-level perception.

An earlier experiment from the same lab (He, Witzel, Forder, Clifford, & Franklin, 2014) found only the later of the two categorical effects. The earlier experiment required attention to the colors with a color-related task, whereas the later experiment involved passive and inattentive registration of colors. This is an intriguing difference that may be explained by low-level categorical effects in passive inattentive vision vs. higher level effects with attentive task-relevant performance.[1] The comparison between Forder et al. and He et al. suggests the same

---

[1] He et al. describe effects that occur past 200 ms as "postperceptual," but by that term they seem to mean "post-early-vision." (Pylyshyn says that early vision is the modular part of vision.) For example, they characterize perception as involving "early stages of color processing (e.g., at visual cortex)" (p. A322). And they state their results by comparing early perceptual processing with postperceptual processing as if there was no category of mid to late perceptual processing. ("the category effects at early perceptual stages of processing disappear and only post-perceptual category effects remain.") Also, they characterize attention as postperceptual ("This means that there is still some uncertainty about whether cross-linguistic differences in color category effects are due to differences in perception or post-perceptual processes such as attention," p. A323). But it is unclear whether there can even be perception without attention, and it is unclear whether attention can be separated from perception. Bottom-up (exogenous) attention peaks at 100 ms, well under the 200 ms mentioned by

picture as the one from the Brascamp et al. article: that conscious perception can occur well before the frontal effects that may involve the neural basis of concepts and cognition.

I will summarize the line of thought of this chapter. The "no-report" paradigm has been much discussed in the context of finding the neural basis of consciousness. The search for the neural basis of consciousness has been bedeviled by the problem of separating out the neural basis of consciousness from the neural basis of the reports that are needed to provide evidence that a conscious state has occurred. The leading idea of this chapter has been that the same issue bedevils the effort to find the neural basis of perception—even independently of issues of consciousness. Reports are required as evidence that perception has taken place and to identify the contents of perception, but then how do we know whether the neural bases so identified are the neural bases of perception itself rather than the neural bases of the perceptual judgments that underlie reports?

We saw one kind of no-report paradigm in Chapter 6 in which infant color perception was probed by the behavior of free eye movements to a patch that is seen as a different color. But to find the neural basis of perceptual contents we need an experimental paradigm that reveals perceptual content. One such paradigm uses reports that come before the perception, in which reports are used to calibrate an indicator of perception. The indicator discussed here was optokinetic nystagmus, an eye movement that indicates the direction in which a grating is seen to move. A second paradigm involved reports that come after hundreds of stimulus-response pairs in which the tasks are a distraction from the perception the experimenter is really interested in. Both of these paradigms provided evidence against the inclusion of prefrontal cortex as part of the neural basis of perception. And as we will see in Chapter 13, those results provide evidence against cognitive and conceptual theories of consciousness.

Thus far, I have been considering the positive case for nonconceptual perceptual categorization. I turn now to the negative case—that is, the case against arguments for conceptual perception.

He et al. Although endogenous attention is cognitively controlled, decades of research by Marisa Carrasco has shown very similar processes for exogenous and endogenous attention (Carrasco, 2011). Further, attentional effects have been shown in unconscious perception (Norman, Heywood, & Kentridge, 2015).

Brogaard and Gatzia claim that color experience is the result of postperceptual processes, but they also seem to be limiting vision to early vision. For example, they also regard the experience of faces as produced postperceptually, regarding the fusiform face area as a postperceptual area: "The experiences of hues, unlike the experience of an approximate wavelength and a relative contrast, involve post-perceptual processes and can be compared with experiences of faces, the content of which is computed by ventral areas in the close vicinity" (2017b, p. 205).

8

Evidence that is wrongly taken to show that perception is conceptual

I have mentioned two kinds of evidence for the nonconceptuality of perception: The first—evidence that I did not discuss in detail—involved the fine-grained nature of perceptual representation as compared with conceptual representation (Evans, 1982). The second involved the visual abilities of infants, insects, and wasps without evidence of conceptual abilities that are linked to the visual abilities (Burge, 2010a; Peacocke, 2001a). There is also evidence that has been taken to support conceptual representation in perception. The purpose of this chapter is negative—to rebut this evidence.

Fast perception

The experimental results that have been taken to support conceptual perception all involve the apparently conceptual use of fast perception.

Molly Potter and her colleagues presented subjects with a series of 6 or 12 pictures presented very quickly (Potter et al., 2014). (This paradigm is called RSVP, for rapid serial visual presentation.) Either immediately before or immediately after the series, the subjects were presented with a brief description, for example "Flowers" in Figure 8.1. Other sample descriptions were "swan," "traffic jam," "boxes of vegetables," "children holding hands," "boat out of water," "campfire," "bear catching fish," and "narrow street." Subjects had to answer yes or no (by pressing buttons) indicating whether or not the description fitted one of the pictures. When the response was "Yes," subjects had to decide which of two pictures had been presented. Subjects were counted as having gotten a match if they picked the right picture. (See the two pictures in Figure 8.1, top right.)

A key feature of this paradigm is that each picture "masks" the previous picture. As mentioned in a number of earlier chapters, masking is a well-known visual phenomenon in which a stimulus presented soon after another stimulus makes the first stimulus harder to see by interrupting visual processing. In this experiment, the pictures were presented very quickly, as many as 12 in a tiny fraction of a second (156 ms—shorter than the time of a blink). So, what the subjects are seeing is a brief flurry of pictures that is over almost immediately.

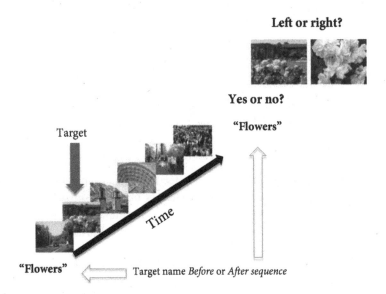

Figure 8.1 Sequence from Potter et al. (2014, p. 273). Reprinted with permission from Springer Nature.

One issue in these experiments is what the effect of a mask is on the processing of the previous stimulus and in particular whether the mask prevents further perceptual processing. (To get ahead of the story, the mask does not prevent further processing.)

The main result was that subjects were above chance in knowing which descriptions matched the pictures they had seen, even for the shortest exposures, 13 ms and 27 ms. And it didn't matter much where the target picture was in the series. That shows that subjects could not have been pursuing a strategy of focusing on the first picture without looking at subsequent pictures.

A second result was that accuracy was similar for 6 pictures and 12 pictures, so the memory capacity would seem much larger than typical measures of "working memory" according to "slot" models of working memory (Block, 2011c). The more items in the RSVP stream, the worse the performance. But if only a few items were recalled (e.g., roughly 4 items, as dictated by many slot models), one would expect the performance with 6 items in the RSVP stream to drop by half when there are 12 items. But the performance does not drop that much, suggesting that subjects retained some information from most of the twelve. (See the section on slot models in Chapter 1.) A further result was that there was a smooth accuracy curve from 13 ms at the lowest to 80 ms at the highest, suggesting that there was no difference in kind between the performance at different presentation times. Finally, since subjects had to match pictures with descriptions, there is a strong case that the matching was conceptual. That is, there is a strong case for the subjects having conceptualized the pictures (and formed the concepts expressed by the words) prior to the matching.

Eric Mandelbaum and Henry Shevlin (Mandelbaum, 2017; Shevlin, 2016) have argued on the basis of this and some other similar experiments that the output of the perception module must be conceptual because the recognition occurs too fast for conceptual cognition to be deployed. (I will focus on Mandelbaum's version of the argument.) To explain the result, it must be assumed of course that some traces of the stimuli persist in the brain. Mandelbaum's and Shevlin's conceptual interpretation tacitly assumes that those traces are not further processed but are already at the conceptual level by the time the mask arrives.

It should be noted that this conclusion is not endorsed by Potter et al. They were mainly concerned with arguing that because of the short recognition times, there was not enough time for feedback from higher areas, so the recognition had to be purely feed-forward, with no contribution from top-down feedback.[1]

There are many possible theories about what is going on here, but one general principle is that what counts in this debate is not the brevity of the stimuli, but *for how long the stimuli are processed.*

I'll mention two hypotheses, both involving Potter's use of Jeremy Wolfe's "carwash" metaphor. (The carwash model is not mentioned in the works by Mandelbaum or Shevlin that I am criticizing.) The analogy is to a carwash that has separate stages, wash, buff, dry, polish, for example. The thought is that if two cars occupy the same stage at the same time, e.g., both occupy the drying stage at once, the drying of one or both will suffer. Similarly, the processing of two stimuli can suffer if they occupy the same stage of processing. But one car can be washed while another is simultaneously buffed and another simultaneously polished.

1. **Nonconceptual carwash model.** As one car progresses in the carwash, another car starts, interfering with the second only if they occupy the same stage, for example both in the polishing stage at the same time (Moore & Wolfe, 2001). What exits from the carwash are nonconceptual percepts. But there is plenty of time for the subject to conceptualize the percepts in order to match the pictures to the descriptions. There is 200 ms between the last picture and the description (e.g., "Flowers") and the subjects have as much time as they want to answer. Processing continues in the 200 ms interval

---

[1] Note that if Potter et al. are right, this puts pressure on the predictive coding approach discussed in the "Bayesian inference" section of Chapter 4, because it is hard to see how there would be time for the predictive processes postulated by that approach. Indeed, on any Bayesian picture, the processing of these stimuli would have to be mainly "bottom-up," since given the wide variation in subject matter of the pictures, priors will be of little use in distinguishing one description from another.

and while the subject is deciding what button to push. Conceptualization occurs during this period. On this model, perception is nonconceptual. The conceptual matching is done postperceptually.
2. **Conceptual carwash model:** Same as the previous interpretation except that what emerges from the carwash are conceptualized percepts.

Note that both of these explanations are inconsistent with the tacit assumption of Mandelbaum's argument that the traces of the stimuli are not processed once the next picture in the series is shown. That assumption is needed in order to argue that the time of processing is too short to go beyond perception. The whole idea of the carwash model is that there is further processing of these traces, but that the processing of two representations in the same stage at the same time interfere. Without support for the assumption that the traces of the stimuli are not processed after being masked by the next picture, the argument for conceptual perception falters.

Potter et al. ask, "How can conceptual understanding persist long enough to be matched to a name presented 200 ms after the offset of the final masking picture, given that the target might have been any of the six or 12 pictures just viewed?" (p. 276) They answer their own question as follows:

> The answer to this question may lie in the carwash metaphor of visual processing (Moore & Wolfe, 2001; Wolfe, 2003), in which each stimulus is passed from one level of processing to the next. In such a model, multiple stimuli can be in the processing pipeline at once. At the end of this pipeline, the stimuli, having now been processed to the level of concept, may persist in local recurrent networks that sustain activation for several pictures in parallel, at least briefly. In such a model, concepts are presumably represented in a multidimensional, sparsely populated network in which visual masks may not be effective if they are not also conceptually similar to the item being masked.

Note that on Potter's version of the carwash model, the masking of each picture in the RSVP series by the next picture weakens the processing of that picture but does not stop the processing. That is, it does not stop the processing unless the processing of the stimulus has reached the conceptual stage and the mask is "conceptually similar to the item being masked."

What does the Potter story have to say about the difference between the conceptual and nonconceptual version of the carwash? Well, nothing. Potter et al. say that the line of representations in the carwash are processed to the point of conceptualization, but they don't say whether that occurs before or after the end of perceptual processing. So, Potter's story doesn't distinguish between the two hypotheses.

A later paper, "Failure to Detect Meaning in RSVP at 27 ms per Picture," provides evidence for the nonconceptual carwash (Maguire & Howe, 2016). Maguire and Howe show that masks of lines and edges eliminate the positive results from the 13 ms and 27 ms stimuli, but not the 53 ms stimuli. Lines and edges are more effective for the shorter presentation times, but scenes are more effective than lines and edges at the later stimulus times (53 ms and 80 ms). Maguire and Howe suggest that the explanation is that different masks are effective at impinging different stages of processing. In terms of the carwash metaphor, lines and edges work well for times between stimulus and mask such that the stimulus is still being processed by very early vision, in which it is known that lines and edges are registered. Thus, we have evidence that lines and edges in early vision are still being processed by the time the 27 ms mask catches up with the processing of the last stimulus—presumably substantially after the 27 ms mark. For longer stimuli, the mask hits when the stimulus is being processed at higher level areas. As they note, this sort of picture is suggested by Potter (1976). It turns out however, that the masking at 82 ms with the *same rough texture as a natural scene* was almost as good as a mask by a natural scene (Loschky, Hansen, Sethi, & Pydimarri, 2010). The higher order statistics of the natural scene and the scene texture are the same, suggesting that it is the texture of the mask that counts at the stage that the 82 ms mask is impacting.

As mentioned earlier, it is now well established that we see "ensemble" properties such as averages or extent of variation. If the kind of perception involved in the Potter study was ensemble perception, the Loschky result just mentioned would only show that the ensemble properties of a textured mask have the same masking import as the ensemble properties of a scene mask. But the Potter results are not primarily about ensemble properties. Detecting properties such as presence of boxes of vegetables or a boat out of water is not a matter of ensemble perception.

Given the fact that the Potter results concern perception of shapes, one could expect masks with shapes to have a larger effect on shape processing stages of perception. This reasoning suggests that processing even well after 82 ms after the stimulus has not fully reached the level of shapes, since the shapes are only slightly more effective than textures as masks. This suggests that even well after 82 ms after the stimulus, the processing is still at an early stage of vision in which shapes are not yet processed. (I say "well after 82 ms" because one has to add the time it takes for the mask to be processed to the level of shapes before it can interfere with the processing of shapes of the original stimulus.) Further, the fact that the content of the mask seems unimportant and that the stimulus is not subject to "conceptual masking" is good evidence that the processing even well after 82 ms has not gotten to a conceptual level. This is good evidence that the

Potter results cannot be regarded as indicating any supposed conceptual aspect to perception.

Similar points apply to two other studies that are similar to Potter's (Grill-Spector & Kanwisher, 2005; Keysers, Xiao, Földiák, & Perrett, 2001). Grill-Spector and Kanwisher used "noise" masks, which Maguire and Howe (2016) show are the least effective for short presentations of the four kinds of masks that they examined, so we should not put much stock in their shortest presentation times. I have gone into more detail for Potter than for Grill-Spector and Kanwisher because their masks were probably more effective.

Mandelbaum, following Fodor's claim that perceptual outputs are "shallow" (1983), suggests that the concepts involved in perception are "basic-level" concepts. (See footnote 2, this chapter, for a definition of "basic level.") Grill-Spector and Kanwisher found that subjects were slower at matching pictures to terms for categories that are subordinate to basic-level categories (ROSE instead of FLOWER), and he takes that as evidence that perception categorizes things at the basic level. But that result can just as easily be explained in terms of the nonconceptual carwash. For example, on the nonconceptual carwash model, the postperceptual basic-level categorization is faster because . . . well, part of the definition of the basic level is that conceptualization at that level is faster and more accurate. The reason "flower" is regarded as a basic-level term rather than "rose" is in part because applying "flower" is faster than applying "rose" for normal people. It is often said that specialists are more likely to have what for most people are subordinate categories as basic-level categories. For example, a florist might have "rose" rather than "flower" as a basic-level term. All this means is that the cluster of properties that define the basic level single out a different level for some terms in the case of specialists.

Another problem with Mandelbaum's argument is that many of the descriptions used in these experiments involve non-basic-level terms. The basic level is a kind of object, not action. Basic-level terms are nouns, and the phenomena that define the basic level apply to nouns but not verbs. But these experiments use phrases that contain verbs, e.g., "children holding hands" or "bear catching fish."

In sum, Mandelbaum's argument for conceptual perception tacitly assumes that in experiments such as Potter's there is no further processing after the mask, but there is ample evidence against this assumption.

Mandelbaum also appeals to studies of ultrafast responses to certain kinds of pictures: faces and scenes by Simon Thorpe's group. Kirchner and Thorpe (2006) showed subjects pairs of pictures, one of which contained an animal. Their task was to move their eyes to the side of the screen of a picture with an animal. This was a "forced choice" procedure in that the subjects had to move their eyes one way or the other. The median time to move the eyes to the side in correct trials was 228 ms. The longer reaction times were much more accurate than the shorter ones, but about half the subjects did better than chance for times as short as 150 ms. Kirchner and Thorpe argue that the "minimum reaction time" (a measure they acknowledge is controversial) was 120 ms over all conditions and that it takes about 20–25 ms to program the eye movement, leaving 95–100 ms for the "underlying visual processing."

However, one involvement of concepts and cognition in this task may be to establish a perceptual set. The subjects may construct a perceptual set that in effect involves a directive to look in the direction of an animal. The response to the stimulus can then be based on a nonconceptual perceptual categorization that interacts with the perceptual set that is formed on the basis of conceptual reasoning.

Kirchner and Thorpe concede that the visual representations that drive their subjects' responses occur prior to scene segmentation and selection of the part of the image in which there is a target. As Kirchner and Thorpe note, the subjects have a perceptual set to move the eyes to the right or the left given a face/animal. So these results are at best weak support for conceptual perception.

Later in this chapter, I will describe experiments by Long and Konkle that suggest that there are certain cues that can be present in low-level and mid-level vision that can allow subjects to make responses that seem to reflect basic-level object recognition but actually reflect a "frame" prior to such object recognition. These cues can indicate the difference between animals and vehicles for example, and may well be involved in the Thorpe experiments. One such cue is degree of curvature. It turns out that animals and smaller things have more curvature than artifacts and bigger things, allowing for faster discrimination between animals and nonanimals and discrimination on the basis of prototypical size of artifacts. See the discussion at the end of the chapter, especially surrounding Figure 8.2. So the Thorpe results may be based on low-level perception.

One notable feature of both Mandelbaum's reasoning and Potter's use of the carwash model is a modularist assumption: that vision is a module whose outputs are the only representations available to cognitive processes. However, there is good evidence that both perceptual and cognitive processes can reach into perceptual processing with access to certain aspects of mid-level vision, notably whether the perceptual representations are of large or small artifacts and whether they are of artifacts or not. This may be an important part of the explanation of ultrafast perception and is the subject of the next section.

Mandelbaum suggested a different argument for conceptual perception, based on another experiment of Potter's (in the question period of my talk at the CUNY Graduate Center, February 6, 2019). In 1975, Potter and Faulconer published a paper titled "Time to Understand Pictures and Words" that has been interpreted

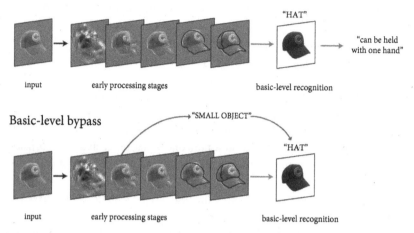

Figure 8.2 At the top, the "Basic-level bottleneck" account shows the standard assumption that categorization requires high-level visual analysis. At the bottom, the "Basic-level bypass" approach indicates that perceptual categorization of a small object as small can directly act on mid-level visual representations. From (Long, 2017, p. 8). Thanks to Bria Long for this diagram.

by some as showing that the time taken to understand pictures such as a picture of a carrot was the same as the time taken to understand words such as "carrot." Mandelbaum suggested that this experiment supports the conceptual perception view on the ground that going from a picture to a basic-level concept could only be as fast as going from a word to a basic-level concept if the basic-level concept was the output of perception. ("Basic level" is defined in this footnote.[2])

Here is what Potter and Faulconer did. They started with 48 pictures and 48 words and 18 "superordinate" terms like "food," "clothes," or "tool." (These terms are superordinate in the sense that they are a level above basic-level terms like "carrot," "hat," and "hammer.") Subjects were then asked to provide a yes/no answer to whether pictures of, for example, a carrot, pie, hat, coat, pliers, or wrench, fit into those categories. Subjects were slightly faster for pictures than for words.

---

[2] Many concepts can be organized into an inclusion structure. All floor lamps are lamps; all lamps are furniture; all furniture items are artifacts. Basic-level concepts—originally identified by Eleanor Rosch—are those, like the concept of a lamp, that are learned first by children, processed faster by adults, and are preferred by most people for use in thinking about things. Concepts at the basic level typically have implications for language structure and use (Murphy, 2016). They have more commonly known features than subordinate or superordinate concepts. They are usually expressed by count nouns, often monomorphemic count nouns. They come most naturally to both adults and children in categorizing things. Examples are the concept of a dog (DOG) as contrasted with LABRADOR or ANIMAL; FLOWER as contrasted with ROSE or PLANT. Which level is basic is not a fixed feature of conceptual structure but rather depends on familiarity and expertise.

Since the superordinate category was named in advance of the stimulus, it would make sense for a subject to activate that superordinate representation. For example, the subject might be given the category of food, the subject being asked if the item to be presented will be a food or a word for a kind of food. The result then is *not* that a picture of a carrot and the word "carrot" activate the concept of a carrot equally quickly. The result is that classifying the picture and the word as falling under the superordinate category occur equally quickly. There is no evidence from this experiment that the concept of a carrot is *ever even* activated in response to the picture of a carrot. Subjects could be simply directly classifying the picture as a picture of food. More generally, there is no evidence from this experiment that basic-level concepts are involved at all in subjects' answers concerning the pictures.

Cognitive access to mid-level vision

Mandelbaum (2017, p. 3) says, "non-conceptualists hold that first we perceive and then we categorize, in which case categorization should be slower than perception." However, if conceptualizing machinery can operate on *intermediate perceptual representations*, then it can operate in parallel with perception. That is, while the perceptual processing is moving toward a perceptual representation, cognition can operate on information from the internal stages of perception. Subjects can have ultrafast reactions to stimuli that depend on perceptual categorizations that skip basic-level object recognition and so provide no comfort for conceptualist views of perception. I now turn to evidence that in fact, conceptualizing machinery does have access to intermediate stages of perception.

A recent series of experiments by Bria Long, Talia Konkle, and their colleagues provides evidence that we have perceptual and cognitive access to mid-level vision that skips the stage of high-level vision, including object recognition at the basic level (Long & Konkle, 2017; Long et al., 2016, 2017). If they are right, another pillar of Fodorian modularity is brought into question, that cognition has no access to and cannot compute over representations internal to the perceptual modules. (See Chapter 9 on Fodorian modularity.)

Long and her colleagues made use of "texturizing" algorithms (the products of which are "texforms") that have been shown to mimic the kind of information available to peripheral vision in early stages of the visual system, V2 and V3.[3] These texturizing algorithms contain the kind of information available to

---

[3] Freeman and Simoncelli (2011) showed that these textures were "metamers" of the untexturized pictures from which they were derived in the sense that in peripheral vision, V2 and V3 did not distinguish between the "controlled" and paired texturized items. For philosophers who want more on these texturizing algorithms, see a brief presentation aimed at philosophers by Block (2013).

subjects in ensemble perception of summary statistics or gists. (Ensemble properties have been discussed a number of times in this book and were defined in Chapter 4 in the section "Atomic propositional representations." See Figure 8.3, for examples of texforms.)

Long and her colleagues used (their own version of) these texturizing algorithms because they obliterate the shape information required to conceptualize the pictures at the basic level (e.g., car) and at superordinate levels (e.g., vehicle), while preserving other kinds of information, specifically concerning whether the items are pictures of animals or artifacts and amazingly, differences in the prototypical size of the things pictured.[4]

Long et al. show that subjects could not identify (in the sense of giving the basic-level category of) the object represented in their "texforms," e.g., they cannot identify a car as a car. And they cannot identify it as a vehicle either. However, they also show that subjects are faster at picking out animal texforms among artifact texforms or artifact texforms among animal texforms than when target and distractors are both animal texforms or both artifact texforms. This suggests that we do have perceptual access to these intermediate level representations of object type while lacking knowledge of which object in that type it is (Long et al., 2017). In addition, subjects are faster at picking out large-object texforms among small-object texforms or smalls among larges than when the distractors are of the same type (Long et al., 2016).

To be clear: The pictures are all the same size, whether of small or large things. The small/large distinction is a matter of the prototypical size of what is represented, e.g., cup vs. car. Further investigation suggests that curvature is important, with animals and smaller things having more curvature than artifacts and bigger things. Another important feature is number of perceived surfaces, with bigger objects having more perceived surfaces.

The same basic point—that high-level vision can be bypassed in reacting to stimuli—is also shown with another texform experiment, this one using the "size-Stroop" paradigm. In the original Stroop paradigm, subjects are slower at naming the color of the word "red" if the color of the word is green than if the color is red. "Incongruency" hinders responses and in addition, congruency facilitates responses relative to a neutral word (that does not name a color). In the size Stroop effect, subjects are asked to judge which of two pictures on a screen is bigger. They are slower if the bigger picture is a cup and the smaller one is a car, though real-world size is irrelevant to the task. Long and Konkle (2017) found that the size Stroop effect worked with texforms. For example, subjects were slower at saying a big cup texform was bigger than a small car texform even though they had no

---

[4] The synthesized pictures that they produced are equalized for low-level features such as luminance, contrast, area, aspect ratio, and contour variance.

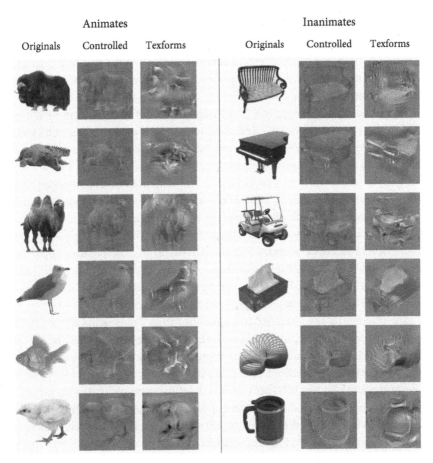

Figure 8.3 From (Long et al., 2017). See text for explanation. This figure is more informative in color. There is a free pdf on the Oxford University Press web site that has the color version of this and all the other figures. Thanks to Bria Long for this figure.

idea that one was a cup and the other a car. Again, this provides evidence that perception can go directly to prototypical size information, skipping high-level vision and skipping conceptual categorization at the basic level (and superordinate levels). That is, size information is automatically retrieved as part of the intermediate visual processing and can play a role in responses to the stimuli. (These results also suggest unconscious perception of prototypical size.)

Earlier, I mentioned transcranial magnetic stimulation (TMS), in which an electromagnetic pulse creates neural noise. Prototypical size of inanimate things is an organizing principle of visual cortex, with representations of big things in some areas and small things in others. (A partial explanation for this organization is that small inanimate things tend to be manipulable, whereas big inanimate things tend to be landmarks.) A TMS pulse to an area that prefers small prototypical size (near the lateral occipital complex) decreased the size Stroop effect, but this did not happen when a TMS pulse was administered to a conceptual area (Chiou & Lambon Ralph, 2016).

Long et al. (2017) ask (p. 16), "Why might the adult visual system be sensitive to these mid-level cues?" And they answer with evidence that mid-level cues may bypass basic-level recognition, "allowing conceptual properties about an object to be inferred prior to basic-level recognition" (p. 16). See Figure 8.2 for a depiction of the model supported by the evidence just described and the way it differs from standard pictures of vision and conceptualization of visual percepts. According to standard models, perceptual categorization requires processing through high-level vision. This is depicted in the top of Figure 8.2, the "Basic-level bottleneck" account, according to which no conceptualization of the stimulus occurs without high-level shape analysis. The evidence detailed here supports the "Basic-level bypass" model, in which perceptual categorization of a small object as small can bypass high-level vision.

The findings by Long and her colleagues fit with a "frame and fill" model, in which low-frequency representations in frontal cortex 100 ms after the signal arrives provides the frame, that frame being filled in by processing triggered by top-down attentional feedback (Bar et al., 2006; Calderone et al., 2013). What is meant by "low frequency"? That refers to the dimension of "spatial frequency." Spatial frequency is an index of amount of detail per degree of visual angle. I have appealed to it earlier in the context of stripes, a special case in which stripiness indexes spatial frequency. Pictures with lots of closely packed edges tend to have higher spatial frequencies. Low-frequency features are coarse-grained, whereas high-frequency features are fine-grained. See Figure 8.4 for superimposed low and high spatial frequency images.

There are many experimental indications that subjects can tell the difference between animal and nonanimal pictures very quickly based on low spatial frequency information (Bar, 2004). These low-frequency features are sent from very early vision to frontal cortex to be used in an initial "fast-feed-forward sweep" that may be prior to object perception and used by the visual system to regulate attention—as the basis for sending amplifying signals to some parts of the image and suppressive signals to other parts (Hochstein & Ahissar, 2002). The idea is that while the fast low-frequency information is sent to frontal cortex (especially the orbitofrontal cortex), the ventral stream is processing the high spatial frequency information much more slowly. Then the top-down attentional signals arrive, amplifying some ventral stream representations and inhibiting others.

Bellet, et al. (2022) showed they could decode perceptual representations in monkeys in prefrontal cortex (ventro-lateral, i.e. lower and side) as early as 50 ms. after the stimulus but these signals tended to die out by 200 ms. after the stimulus

Figure 8.4 Superimposed low frequency and high frequency images. From close up you see a bicycle (high frequency image) with a shadow, but from far away (or if you squint) you see a motorcycle (low frequency image). Any curve can be decomposed into component sine waves. The spatial frequency of the curve depends on the spatial frequencies of those sine waves. See the Wikipedia article on spatial frequency at https://en.wikipedia.org/wiki/Spatial_frequency. Thanks to Aude Oliva for the figure. See (Oliva et al., 2006). If you are reading in grayscale, Figure 1.1 is a better illustration of this point.

which suggests little or no global broadcasting and little or no conceptualization of the percept. So fast processing does not always result in conceptualization.

I won't go into this issue further, but I think the reader has enough information from what I have said to see that the arguments for conceptual perception that are based on fast perception founder on three main features of perception, the role of perceptual set; that perceptual processing can continue even after being masked; and that perceptual and cognitive categorization can make use of textural aspects of perception while the slow processing of fine-grained features is taking place.

I have been arguing that perception is constitutively iconic, nonconceptual and nonpropositional. Cognition can use perceptual materials that have these properties, but cognition does not have them constitutively. A thinker need not be able to use perceptual materials in thought.

I will now move to a discussion of cognitive penetration.

9

Cognitive penetration is common but does not challenge the joint

I'll start with a discussion of some recent history, then move to perceptual set and ambiguous stimuli. Then after a discussion of the role of attention in cognitive penetration, I'll move to E.J. Green's dimension restriction proposal and finally the role of mental imagery in cognitive penetration. In Chapter 10, I will describe a number of kinds of top-down effects that are not cases of cognitive penetration, then in Chapter 11, I will talk about cognitive architecture and the extent to which there is some truth in the modularity thesis.

Cognitive impenetrability: Recent history

In the 1940s, the "New Look" approach to perception argued that expectations can determine the contents of perception. For example, Jerome Bruner and Leo Postman (1949) gave subjects brief glimpses of playing cards, asking for identifications. Unknown to the subjects, some of the cards were "trick" cards, e.g., a black three of hearts and a red two of spades. Subjects required much longer presentations to give responses to the incongruous cards and often mistakenly identified them as normal cards. (For example, a black three of hearts might be identified as a three of spades.) These "New Look" results reverberated around intellectual life. Scientists, historians and philosophers wondered how science could be objective given that observation was "theory-laden" (Hanson, 1958; Kuhn, 1962).

In the later New Look years, the term "cognition" was often expanded to include perception. A landmark textbook of 1967 (Neisser, 1967, p. 4) defined the term this way (cf. also Linton, 2017):

> As used here, the term "cognition" refers to all the processes by which the sensory input is transformed, reduced, elaborated, stored, recovered, and used. It is concerned with these processes even when they operate in the absence of relevant stimulation, as in images and hallucinations. Such terms as *sensation, perception, imagery, retention, recall, problem-solving,* and *thinking,* among many others, refer to hypothetical stages or aspects of cognition.... Given such

a sweeping definition, it is apparent that cognition is involved in everything a human being might possibly do; that every psychological phenomenon is a cognitive phenomenon.

This usage of "cognition" reflected the view that perception was suffused with thought, and it still survives in the term "visual cognition," sometimes used to describe higher level perception, even though the ideology that supports the terminology would now be rejected by most of the psychologists who use the term.

But New Look experiments did not properly distinguish between perceptual judgment—a cognitive state—and perception itself. Recall that by "perceptual judgment" I mean a minimal immediate direct judgment about what is being perceived. A minimal perceptual judgment conceptualizes each representational aspect of a perception and no more. An immediate perceptual judgment conceptualizes a perception with no inferential step. A direct perceptual judgment is based on the perception with no intermediary.

Forty years after the rise of the New Look, Jerry Fodor and Zenon Pylyshyn famously argued that perception—or at least vision—is a modular system that is "informationally encapsulated" in the sense that perception uses information from the senses but cannot use or compute over representations of information in the rest of the mind (Fodor, 1983; Pylyshyn, 1999).[1] The informational encapsulation of perception contrasts with the "isotropy" of cognition in the sense that a cognitive state can in principle access anything the subject knows.

Peter Carruthers distinguishes narrow scope from wide scope encapsulation (Carruthers, 2006). Narrow scope encapsulation is encapsulation in more or less the Fodor/Pylyshyn sense: A narrow scope encapsulated system cannot access any information from outside the system. He contrasts this with wide scope encapsulation, which allows for the accessibility of some but not other items outside the system. According to Carruthers, cognition is encapsulated in the wide sense but not the narrow sense.

Fodor and Pylyshyn also argued that perception is cognitively impenetrable (1999, p. 343). As with informational encapsulation, there are many equally good notions of cognitive impenetrability. (This is "pluralism" about cognitive impenetrability; Gross, 2017; Stokes, 2013, 2015.) However, I think it is worth spelling out the idea behind Fodor's (1983) and Pylyshyn's (1984) notion of cognitive impenetrability. They took cognitive impenetrability to preclude effects in which

---

[1] Pylyshyn claimed to be talking about "early" vision only, but as many have noticed, he very often seems to be talking about vision rather than early vision. Early vision is often taken to include the processing of the low-level features just mentioned of shape, spatial relations, motion, texture, brightness, and color rather than high-level features like faceness, causation, and agency (Block, 2014c; Siegel, 2010). As I will explain, cognitive penetration of early vision can be produced reliably by ambiguous stimuli.

the content of a cognitive state has a direct content-appropriate influence on the content of a perceptual state in virtue of the contents of both states. Cognitive penetration in the sense under discussion is not just an effect of content but also an effect on content.

Arguably, a cognitively impenetrable system in the Fodor/Pylyshyn sense has to be informationally encapsulated, since if a perceptual system could access knowledge items in perceptual computations, affecting the computations, that effect would count as cognitive penetration. (There is an escape, though, if the accessed knowledge items weren't used for anything.) The converse however is not true: An informationally encapsulated system need not be immune to cognitive penetration. A quick way to see that point is that cognitive penetration need not involve knowledge at all. An informationally encapsulated system could still be penetrated by desire. If wanting the objects of one's affection to be beautiful made them look beautiful, that would be cognitive penetration but would not violate encapsulation in the usual sense of the term. More generally, informational encapsulation concerns whether a perceptual system can only receive information from the senses, or, alternatively, can access the cognitive database. But effects of cognition need not be of that kind.

The point of the "direct" in the Fodor/Pylyshyn notion of cognitive penetration would be to exclude cases in which a cognitive state influences perception by influencing something else, for example, pupil size (which is known to respond to cognitive factors; Rieger & Savin-Williams, 2012; Urai, Braun, & Donner, 2017). Fiona Macpherson mentions a case in which the belief in an alien invasion causes a migraine, which in turn causes the experience of flashing lights of the sort that one might suppose an alien invasion would produce (Macpherson, 2015). Such a case is ruled out by the directness condition because the belief has its effect via an intermediary, the migraine.

Fodor justifies a directness condition by noting that otherwise we could regard the effect on heart rate by the decision to do jumping jacks as a cognitive penetration of heart rate (1983). Heart rate is not a representational state, so an effect on it could not be appropriate to the content of that state, but Fodor is ignoring that, focusing on the indirectness. Directness conditions are notoriously difficult to spell out, since there are always intermediate links in a causal chain and it can be difficult to decide which ones to count as incompatible with directness. Certainly, Fodor and Pylyshyn expected some subpersonal states to be compatible with directness, so a natural construal of what they had in mind by "direct" would preclude only intermediate links that are person-level states. It should be noted that "direct" admits of other interpretations. One notion of directness would confine direct effects to those in which cognitive premises yield perceptual conclusions via a process of reasoning.

An alternative conception of cognitive penetration is that two perceivers perceiving and attending to the same distal stimulus under the same external conditions nonetheless have different perceptual contents as a result of a difference in cognitive or affective states (Macpherson, 2012; Siegel, 2012). This kind of characterization doesn't match the Fodor/Pylyshyn idea because it doesn't require directness or content appropriateness.

Here is an example of cognitive penetration in the MacPherson/Siegel sense that may not be cognitive penetration in the Fodor/Pylyshyn sense: A difference in perceptual set may make a difference in perceptual contents without any simultaneous direct content-appropriate effect of cognition on perception. For example, a symbol that looks roughly like '13' can look one way in the context "A_C" and another way in the context "12__14" (Bruner & Minturn, 1955). (See Figure 9.1.) And that suggests that a letter-related perceptual set could result in a different perception than a number-related perceptual set even when two perceivers are perceiving and attending to the same distal stimulus under the same external conditions at the same time. Arguably, this is not cognitive penetration in the Fodor/Pylyshyn sense because the perceptual set is induced by previous perceptions and is not a direct of effect of cognition on the current perception.

If this is regarded as an undesirable consequence, it could be avoided in a variety of ways, for example by increasing the spatial and temporal windows of what is counted as the stimulus. But there may be differences in perceptual set that cannot be handled in this way.

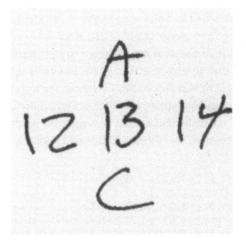

Figure 9.1 If read left to right, subjects tend to identify the middle symbol in arrays like this as "13" whereas if read up to down as a "B."

E. J. Green and Dustin Stokes have suggested replacing a Fodor/Pylyshyn directness condition with a condition stipulating an internal process (Green, 2017b; Macpherson, 2012; Stokes, 2013). Where I have stipulated a content-appropriate effect, others speak of a semantically coherent effect (Green, 2017b; Pylyshyn, 1999), an intelligible content relation (Macpherson, 2017), or that a cognitive content be utilized by perception (Gross, 2017). Wayne Wu (2017) jettisons the content condition altogether in favor of a correlational relation.

Of course, we are all familiar with disagreements about how to define important ideas such as empiricism or physicalism. And the notions I have been appealing to, iconic vs. discursive, conceptual and propositional states, are themselves lightning rods of controversy, some of it verbal. But the disagreement over cognitive penetration is different, since the warring factions cannot agree even on paradigm cases. I mentioned that Fodor heaps scorn on the idea that the decision to do jumping jacks cognitively penetrated heart rate. Gary Lupyan (2017) says that a similarly indirect effect on heart rate should count as cognitive penetration.[2] The theorists mentioned really seem to have different pictures of what a modular system is. And agreement about some cases masks differences about why a case falls on one side or the other. For example, some participants are thinking of penetration of perception and others of perceptual experience (Macpherson, 2017).

As I mentioned, Gross and Stokes (Gross, 2017; Stokes, 2013, 2015) suggest pluralism about "cognitive penetration" in which different definitions would be relevant to different debates, e.g., one notion if one's concern is how perception justifies belief, another if one's concern is cognitive or neural architecture. I am skeptical, however, whether intuitions about cognitive penetration will coincide even when we restrict the discussion to one of these concern-areas.

For example, even when it comes to cognitive architecture, there are different conceptions of "cognitive penetration." First, what is cognitive architecture? Architectural features of a system are supposed to be features of its most basic structure, features that govern how the system processes information and are not normally changed by that processing. Of course, the architecture of a mental system includes what modules there are and how they influence one another. The term "architecture" is usually understood to suggest the hardware side of a software/hardware distinction. See (Block, 1995b) and Chapter 1.

---

[2] He says, " But consider that it is also possible to speed one's heart rate simply by thinking certain thoughts.... No toe touches required. Suppose that influencing heart rate in this way is achieved by thinking about doing exercise. Would this not count as a genuine instance of heart rate being cognitive penetrable because it is the thoughts about exercise that are causing the heart rate increase rather than thoughts about increasing one's heart rate?" This case is just as indirect as Fodor's and also fails the content—appropriateness condition.

The disagreement mentioned above between Fodor and Lupyan persists despite their common focus on architecture. Gross, focusing on cognitive architecture, argues that feature-based attention is not an example of cognitive penetration because the cognitive state does not have the right semantic relation to the perception. For example, attending to redness does not involve anything like a reason for seeing redness. Even on Gross's condition, the effect of context on phonemic restoration described in Chapter 2 might well count as cognitive penetration. Consider the context mentioned earlier: "On the highway, he drives the car much _____." One has a reason to hear a word that is ambiguous between "factor" and "faster" as "faster." (There will be a reminder about this example in the next section.)

Macpherson (2012, but not 2017) excludes spatial attention from cognitive penetration. Raftopoulos also rejects attention as cognitive penetration but for a different reason—that its effect is insufficiently "direct" (Raftopoulos, 2009). Macpherson allows indirect effects so long as there is a semantic relation involved in each link in the causal chain (2017). It would be hard to avoid the conclusion that there is a substantial verbal element in the debates about cognitive penetration. (See Chalmers, 2011.)

The New Look suggested no fundamental difference between cognition and perception, but the modularists purported to find such a difference in the cognitive architecture of the brain—between cognitively impenetrable perceptual modules and the nonmodular swamp of cognition—and so the increasing resistance to modularism is often seen as going against a joint.

Over the last 10 years, the pendulum has shifted away from the modularist/cognitive impenetrability perspective. Popular theoretical ideas, e.g., the "predictive coding" framework (Clark, 2016; Hohwy, 2013), have been taken to show that perception is much less driven by sensory inputs and more driven by prediction than orthodox vision science has supposed. The recent successes of transformer models such as GPT-3 and PaLM that are based on predicting the next "word" as well as graphical versions of them such as Dall-e-2 reinforce the importance of prediction.

Many have thought that the causal interactions between prediction and sensory inputs are so extensive that there is no important distinction between cognition and perception. In a position paper on the predictive coding approach to perception, Andy Clark says, "the lines between perception and cognition [are] fuzzy, perhaps even vanishing" (2013, p. 190). In a debate (with Fiona Macpherson) about "cognitive penetration" of perception (Lupyan, 2015), Gary Lupyan says, "I am supporting a collapse of perception and cognition which makes the whole question of the penetrability of one by the other, ill-posed. But I would be thrilled if my arguments contribute to the eventual demise of this question."

Lupyan thinks there is no joint and that cognitive penetration is a confused notion. Many of us who think there is a joint think cognitive penetration in roughly the Fodor/Pylyshyn sense is a respectable notion, but we disagree about whether the joint depends on limits on cognitive penetration. Some who favor a joint—for example, Firestone and Scholl (2016a)—are modularists who take the joint to be based in the architecture of the mind, and in particular on the alleged cognitive impenetrability of perception. My view is different—that there is a joint but that its basis is not mainly architectural.

Among those who think that cognitive penetration at least makes sense, the evidence for cognitive penetration has often been met with resistance. The debate has often focused on "top-down" effects. The term presupposes a hierarchical theory of the mind in which there are higher and lower stages of perception and of cognition, with cognition conventionally regarded as higher than perception. (As I will explain later, there are "top-down" effects that are not effects of cognition on perception, but I will put that point aside for the moment.)

In a paper titled "Cognition Does Not Affect Perception: Evaluating the Evidence for 'Top-Down' Effects," Chaz Firestone and Brian Scholl review a wide range of apparent evidence for direct content-specific effects of cognition on perception, concluding that there are no effects of cognition "on *what we see* as a whole—including visual processing and the conscious percepts it produces." Their rationale is that this is what is important to a joint in nature. They say:

> What do we mean when we say that cognition does not affect perception, such that there are no top-down effects on what we see? The primary reason these issues have received so much historical and contemporary attention is that a proper understanding of mental organization depends on whether there is a salient "joint" between perception and cognition. Accordingly, we focus on the sense of "top-down" which directly addresses this aspect of how the mind is organized. (Firestone & Scholl, 2016a, Section 2)

Mistakenly, or so I have been arguing, both the Firestone and Scholl article and the responses take the issue of a joint to depend on whether or not there is cognitive penetration. One of the main claims of this book is that there is plenty of evidence for cognitive penetration in the sense described of direct effects of the content of cognition on the content of perception, although I also think there is truth in the Fodor/Pylyshyn modularity thesis in that violations of modularity may be tightly circumscribed. Perception is often dominated by the stimulus, whereas cognition uses a wide range of other information. The information involved in seeing an unambiguous figure as a cube comes almost entirely from the eyes, whereas the information involved in deciding whether to pick up the cube depends on what one knows about where it came from, what it is for, and so forth. The most dramatic cases of cognitive penetration are in situations in which the perceptual information does not decide between dramatically different but equally probable environmental situations. (I will refer to these as "ambiguous stimuli," though of course all stimuli can be produced by more than one environmental situation.)

The situations in which information from outside the sense organs influences whether one sees something as a cube in a certain orientation are mainly confined to ambiguous cases like the Necker cube (Figure 9.2, reproduced from Figure 1.3) and other ambiguous stimuli. But it should be noted that since the differing percepts of these cases can differ in shape and surface representations, the effect of cognition on perception can penetrate the early visual processing that computes shape and surface representation. Take for example the face/vase stimulus. When the face is dominant, different shapes are represented in the dominant percept than when the vase is dominant. The background is seen as shapeless and extending behind the shaped figure (Peterson & Cacciamani, 2013). Curves that are seen as concave become seen as convex and conversely. (See Chapter 2.)

However, on the underlying issue of whether there is a joint in nature between cognition and perception, it is the critics of Firestone and Scholl who are wrong. There is cognitive penetration of perception by cognition, but not of a sort that impugns the joint between perception and cognition. I also agree with Firestone and Scholl that a lot of the supposed cases of cognitive penetration that have

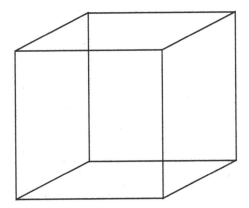

Figure 9.2 Necker cube, reproduced from Chapter 1 for conveenience. On initial viewing, especially from below, the left facing face is usually in the foreground. After staring at the stimulus, especially from above, that face will recede and the right facing face will be in the foreground. This is an example of a stimulus that is ambiguous in the sense that the perceptual information does not decide between dramatically different but equally probable environmental situations.

been headlined in popular science outlets in recent years are the result of highly flawed methodologies. It is claimed that vision discourages hill climbing when one is wearing a heavy backpack by making the hill look steeper, that objects look closer if you have a tool to reach them and heights look higher if you fear heights (Firestone, 2013; Firestone & Scholl, 2016a). The real cases of cognitive penetration that I will discuss later are less sensational.

Everyone has always realized that perception affects cognition, as when I believe what I see. Why should anyone have thought that the reverse direction of causation was so theoretically significant? The answer may be found in the appeal of Fodor's and Pylyshyn's modular picture of the mind and its consequence that perceptions have access only to information from sense organs whereas cognition has access to a wide range of information represented in many different faculties. If perception really is informationally isolated from cognition, that would ground a joint. But as I have argued, a joint between perception and cognition survives even if perception is not as informationally encapsulated as Fodor and Pylyshyn thought it was. Further, with a more adequate understanding of feature-based attention and the nature of mental imagery, elements of a modular picture can withstand giving up the cognitive impenetrability thesis.

I will argue that on many notions of cognitive penetration, including the Fodor-Pylyshyn notion, cognitive penetration is common and easy to reliably produce. I will give a number of examples of straightforward cognitive penetration, steering clear of the kind of work from social psychologists that has been so ably dissected by Firestone and Scholl and also Frank Durgin (Durgin et al., 2009; Firestone, 2013; Firestone & Scholl, 2013, 2016a, 2016b). The cases I will mention are ones in which the contents of perception are affected, changing the accuracy conditions of the perception.

Further, the cases of cognitive penetration I will mention include cases in which the influence of cognition on perception suggests an "epistemic downgrade" of the perception (Siegel, 2017). For example, if a person has a facial expression that is indeterminate between friendly and angry, my belief that the person is angry may lead me to perceive the face as angry. As Siegel notes, the epistemic value of my perception is therefore challenged. Further, there will be cases of the sort that the advocates of theory loaded perception were concerned with. If the color of the litmus paper is indeterminate as between red and blue, my belief that the liquid is an acid may result in my seeing it as more red than blue.

A recent paper (Montemayor & Haladjian, 2017, p. 1) on the perception/cognition border puts the alternatives this way: "The main thesis of this paper is that two prevailing theories about cognitive penetration are too extreme, namely, the view that cognitive penetration is pervasive and the view that there is a sharp and fundamental distinction between cognition and perception, which precludes any type of cognitive penetration." I am arguing for versions of both of the extreme views: that there is a fundamental distinction between perception and cognition and there is also pervasive cognitive penetration, though of limited kinds.

Perceptual set

One type of cognitive penetration occurs when a subject is prepared by context for a perceptual task. A recent experiment (Uithol, Bryant, Toni, & Mars, 2021) asked subjects to either answer a "basic-level" question about an upcoming animal picture, e.g., "Is this a frog?" or a "superordinate level" question, e.g., "Is this an amphibian?" The question was flashed on the screen for 2 seconds, and then 4 seconds elapsed before the subjects had to answer by pressing a button on one side for yes and the other side for no. Brain imaging (fMRI) in the 4-second interval showed differences at the earliest cortical areas, V1 and V2 between the two questions, revealing that perceptual set has an effect on perceptual processing. The relevance of this result to normal perception, though, remains to be seen.

Ambiguous stimuli

As I mentioned, many of the clearest cases of cognitive penetration involve ambiguous stimuli, stimuli that can be seen by normal observers in a number of ways, those ways being influenced by cognitive factors.

One type of case involves perceptual set. The middle symbol in Figure 9.1 tends to be identified one way if read left to right and another way read up to down. Jerome Bruner and his fellow advocates of the "New Look" assumed this was a perceptual effect (Bruner, 1957). I will be describing some cases of cognitive penetration of the perception of ambiguous figures, but I want to start with some notable cases of ambiguous figures whose perception is not cognitively penetrated. See Figure 9.3 for some examples in which knowledge does not appear to penetrate amodal completion in perception. Some cases will be mentioned below in this section in which cognition does affect amodal completion.

The Bayesian approach that is now widespread in perceptual sciences suggests that when the data are equivocal—that is, equally support different environmental situations—the likelihood function will not discriminate between these different environmental hypotheses, so there will be a larger role for representations of prior probabilities in determining the percept. (See Chapter 4.) But that approach does not tell us whether the priors are explicitly represented or whether, to the extent that they are represented, the representations are within the visual system or are part of cognition. If the representation of priors is within

Figure 9.3 Ambiguous stimuli in which knowledge does not penetrate perception. In the top picture, context might be expected to see the occluded figure as an octagon. One would not expect the middle figure to be seen as an impossibly elongated arm. Both from Keane, Lu, Papathomas, Silverstein, and Kellman (2012, p. 749). The former was originally from Kanizsa (1985). These two figures are printed with permission of Elsevier. In the bottom figure, the pattern above the square might lead us to see the occluded lion as a lion but instead one sees it as the back of an elongated deer. Thanks to Chaz Firestone for this figure.

the visual system and the Bayesian processes that use them are within the visual system, then the effect of priors on perception is not cognitive penetration.

I will go through some of the mechanisms that may be involved in the perception of ambiguous stimuli, arguing that those mechanisms that are known to obtain do not threaten a joint. In the next chapter, I will describe some other phenomena that have been thought to illustrate effects of cognition on perception. In some cases, for example, memory-color and figure-ground assignment, the top-down effects are effects within the visual system and not effects of cognition on perception.

Some cases of ambiguous stimuli give rise to perceptually unstable perceptions in which there is a cycle of first one percept, then another, then back to the first. These are "reversible" bistable figures. Examples were given earlier in the "Rivalry" section of Chapter 2 and others are exhibited in Figure 9.4. These stimuli can produce different percepts with different accuracy conditions. Reversal of such figures is influenced by eye movements, showing bottom-up effects. But these reversals also occur without eye movements and even with afterimages, as in Figure 2.10. The perception of ambiguous figures involves changes in early vision as well as late vision. As I noted earlier, attributions of surface layouts are often quite different in the different percepts of ambiguous stimuli, showing differences in relatively early vision. That is even true for the very well-known example given earlier of the Necker cube (Figure 9.2). If these repeating reversals are cases of cognitive penetration, then cognition penetrates early vision.

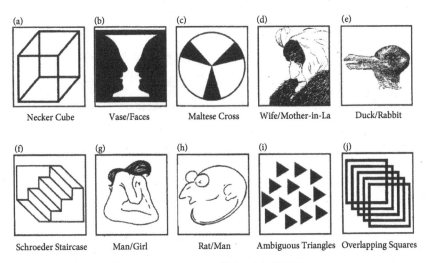

Figure 9.4 Bistable Figures. From Long and Toppino (2004).

Not all ambiguous stimuli yield bistable percepts. One type of example, illustrated in Figure 9.5, is ambiguous only in that one can see either meaningless blobs or else something meaningful (what that meaningful thing is will be revealed eventually, though many readers will be familiar with the stimulus). Another relatively stable perception of an ambiguous stimulus, described in detail in Chapter 2, is the perception involved in the phonemic restoration effect. Some case of the phonemic restoration effect are clear cases of a direct effect of cognition on perception. Others, typically the restoration of a syllable in the middle of a multisyllabic word, appear to be top-down effects within the language module itself and so not cases of cognitive penetration. I will briefly remind the reader of the discussion in Chapter 2.

Recall that in one version of the phonemic restoration effect, a single phoneme is replaced by a white noise sound that I represented as '#.' The clearest cases of an effect of cognition on perception were cases like "fa#tor" that can be heard as "faster" or "factor" depending on context. Some other examples of words that differ in one phoneme that are used in some of the experiments were "novel"/"nozzle" and "babies"/"rabies." In the phonemic restoration effect, the # sound is heard as a phoneme, but for these ambiguous stimuli, one might ask what determines which phoneme?

As I noted, context can strongly influence the perception. For example, this context would dispose the subject to hear "fa#ter" as "faster": "On the highway, he drives the car much _____." This result has a number of interpretations. One interpretation is that the effect is within the perceptual system because the unit of perception is the whole sentence, not just the word. Another is that it is a matter of perceptual set—to be discussed below. Another is that it is a case of priming. All of these factors could be involved. But I mentioned neurophysiological

Figure 9.5 A famous photograph by R. C. James is shown on the left. I won't say what it depicts, but if you want to know, look at the title of van Tonder and Ejima (2000) in the References. Both images are from that article, p. 149. Reprinted with Permission of SAGE Publications, Ltd.

evidence that the phonemic restoration effect is partly determined by cognitive areas of the brain and that suggests cognitive penetration.

I mentioned strong evidence in Chapter 2 that the phonemic restoration effect is an effect on perception rather than an effect on perceptual judgment. In addition, these effects, unlike some effects of attention, change the accuracy conditions of the perception. Seeing a word as "faster" is a perception with different accuracy conditions from seeing it as "factor."

The contextual effect just mentioned may be an effect of perceptual set on perception of the sort described earlier. As far as I know, it is not known whether perceptual set is best thought of as a perceptual effect involving either priming or an extended stimulus (large enough to include the context) or as a cognitive effect. However, in the case of reversible stimuli, there is some evidence that cognitive factors are involved. Reisberg found that occupying subjects' working memory with an irrelevant task (mental arithmetic, remembering 7 digits) slowed their reversals in rivalrous stimuli, suggesting a cognitive component in the reversals (Reisberg, 1983). Further evidence that cognition is affecting reversals is that frontal lobe damage decreases reversal rate (Long & Toppino, 2004). Even if these results show cognitive effects on perception, the mechanisms remain unclear. They may involve feature-based attention, a topic that will be discussed in detail later in this chapter.

Our perception of reversible figures can be partially accommodated by a modularist perspective in that they can be described as cases of bottom-up perception in which what cognition does is select one of the bottom-up channels. One channel is held in unconscious perception while the other is conscious. In some cases, the selection may work via spatial attention. For example, in the duck/rabbit illusion, the change may be effected by changing attentional focus from the mouth of one creature to the mouth of the other (Long & Toppino, 2004). It is difficult to see why such cases should be more of a challenge to a joint between cognition and perception than any other case of spatial attention.

Other cases may work via feature-based attention. In Figure 9.12, one attends to the conjoint features of horizontal/blue/yellow or else to vertical/green/red. In this case as in the duck/rabbit, it may be that one of two bottom-up channels is selected.

However, other cases may not fit this mold. In many cases of ambiguous stimuli, for example, the rat/man stimulus to be discussed later in this chapter, there is no reason to think the visual system is computing both percepts until a cognitive hint is given.

Another type of case in which effects of cognition seem to be at work is a famous photograph by R. C. James, on the left in Figure 9.5. As Van Tonder and Ejima note (2000), this photograph has often been used to argue for top-down effects on perception.

However, as Van Tonder and Ejima go on to show, there are substantial bottom-up components involved in the identification of the creature depicted on the photograph on the left. (I will refer to it as the "creature" rather than using the more specific description available in the title of the Van Tonder article in the References for readers who are not familiar with this stimulus.) They probed the reactions of subjects who had not seen the photograph before. Only one subject fully recognized what was depicted, but most saw a bulging convex body in the location of the creature. The image on the right of Figure 9.5 is obtained from the one on the left by rotating texture blobs within the body of the creature. The picture on the right was recognized as a bulging convex body 40% less often than the one on the left. As Van Tonder and Ejima note, this is evidence for a substantial bottom-up component to the recognition of the creature. They did not test this, but to me, the two images of Figure 9.5 look nearly indistinguishable. If that is right, once a viewer knows what is depicted, the bottom-up differences have little effect, showing the power of the top-down influence. See for yourself whether the two pictures look pretty much the same once you know what is depicted.

Recall the discussion of illusory contours in Chapter 2. The illusory contour effects pictured in Figures 2.15 and 6.8 occur independently of attention and independently of what the subject notices (Keane, 2018). The interpolation of illusory contours appears to be a product of many factors, one of which is what is called "relatability": whether the inducing edges can be joined by a smooth monotonically curving edge that does not bend more than 90° (Keane, 2018). Other factors include whether the edge elements in the stimulus are large enough to comprise a significant proportion of the total edge, that is, whether the real part of the apparent edge is not tiny in comparison to the illusory part; and whether the edge elements have the appropriate junction structure. For example, four appropriate "pac-men" arranged properly form an excellent illusory Kanizsa rectangle but four similarly arranged plus signs form much weaker illusory contours (Keane, 2018).

Given the Van Tonder and Ejima result, I would guess that the picture on the left of Figure 9.5 has better inducers for illusory contours than the picture on the right, providing part of the mechanism for a bottom-up component to the recognition of the ... umm ... creature.

I went into the somewhat underwhelming result concerning Figure 9.5 because it is one of very few actual experimental papers on this kind of topic and it does serve to remind one that the kinds of bottom-up and top-down factors that are operating cannot be ascertained without actual experimental data.

A result involving illusory modal contours illustrates both cognitive penetration and aspects of perception that are less susceptible to cognitive penetration

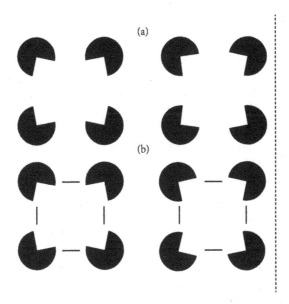

Figure 9.6 Illusory modal contours. The left side of A is termed a "fat" illusory contour, whereas the right side of A is termed a "thin" illusory contour. The lines in B hinder subjects in distinguishing fat from thin. From supplementary material of Zhou, Tjan, Zhou, and Liu (2008) using stimuli of the sort that originated in Ringach and Shapley (1996). Reprinted with permission from the *Journal of Vision*.

(Keane et al., 2012).[3] Keane et al. made use of two aspects of illusory contours. The left side of A in Figure 9.6 is termed a "fat" illusory contour, whereas the right side of A is termed a "thin" illusory contour. The lines in B hinder subjects in distinguishing fat from thin. Recall that pac-man edge inducers are considered "relatable" if the curve of completion does not bend by more than 90°. Keane et al. showed subjects stimuli that could be seen as fat or thin; in which there could be lines, as in Figure 9.6, or not; and in which the inducers were relatable or not. Another pair of conditions were that in half the cases subjects were encouraged to "group" the inducers by being shown templates with real edges where illusory edges could occur and by being told that the inducers belonged together. Subjects in the "ungroup" condition were told that the inducers did not belong together even though in some of the stimuli it might look as if they did. Subjects were given the task of distinguishing between fat and thin.

---

[3] As mentioned earlier, Figure 2.15 shows standard examples of modal and amodal illusory contours. The upward pointing triangle is "modally" completed in that the figure is seen as brighter than the background, whereas the edges of the triangle pointing down are amodally completed in that the subject has the impression of a complete triangle without any visible edge.

The main result indicating cognitive penetration was that discrimination of fat from thin was much better in the grouping condition than in the ungrouping condition. That shows that the examples of completed contours and/or grouping instructions had a large perceptual effect. It remains possible that the effect of the examples could have been within the perceptual system, but that seems unlikely since the effect persisted even when the examples were given every 20th trial and so did not have the kind of proximity to the stimulus that is typical of perceptual effects.

However, the grouping condition only had an effect on subjects' discriminations in the relatable condition, suggesting that cognitive penetration only works in a genuinely ambiguous case in which the stimulus could be seen either way. Further, the effect of the distractor lines (as in B in Figure 9.6) was independent of grouping/ungrouping, again suggesting a bottom-up component unaffected by cognition. Thus, we have examples of both cognitive penetration and aspects of perception that are not affected by cognition, at least in this experiment.

In sum, ambiguous stimuli provide good candidates for cognitive penetration, especially in the cases like the phonemic restoration effect, in which the perceptions are not reversible. However, it remains to be seen what the mechanisms of the effects are. I will argue that examination of the mechanisms that are known suggest these cases do not challenge the joint. Although this is the end of the section explicitly devoted to ambiguous stimuli, the rest of this chapter will mainly be about cognitive penetration of ambiguous stimuli and the mechanisms by which that happens. The next two sections will be about the role of attention in cognitive penetration. The next section is about the role of spatial attention and the one after it is about feature-based attention. It is feature-based attention that engenders the most convincing cases of cognitive penetration, but it will be useful to discuss spatial attention first.

Spatial attention

Let us start with a discussion of voluntary top-down ("endogenous") attention. This is the kind of attention involved when someone "pays attention" to something. Endogenous attention can be attention to an area of space, to an object, or to a feature or property. As we will see, the effects of top-down attention, especially on ambiguous stimuli, can make for radical shifts in the contents of perception as indexed by the accuracy conditions of perceptions.

One could think of endogenous attention as a mediating state, a state that cognition engenders and that in turn affects perception. One decides (a cognitive state) to pay attention (a mediating state) and that affects perception. On that interpretation, the effect of endogenous attention on perception would be indirect and so not cognitive penetration on the Fodor/Pylyshyn definition of cognitive penetration (Raftopoulos, 2009). However, one can also think of endogenous attention as a cognitive state in its own right, making effects of endogenous attention direct effects that do constitute cognitive penetration. Endogenous attentional states ("paying attention") typically have their own contents so it makes sense to treat them as cognitive states. I don't think there is any matter of fact as to which construal is best.

Firestone and Scholl try to disallow endogenous attention by a variant of the "indirectness" strategy. As mentioned earlier, Firestone and Scholl argued in the concluding sentence of their paper that it is "eminently plausible that there are no top-down effects of cognition on perception" (2016a). Their treatment of attention classifies it as an effect on "input" that only indirectly affects perception, and so does not constitute a case of cognitive penetration. Here is their main treatment: "In many such cases, changing what we see by selectively attending to a different object or feature ... seems importantly similar to changing what we see by moving our eyes (or turning the lights off). In both cases, we are changing the input to mechanisms of visual perception, which may then still operate inflexibly given that input." Their characterization applies better to spatial attention than to feature-based attention. But even in the case of spatial attention, the "input" analogy is strained.

Our understanding of attention has shifted in recent years. Early work on attention utilized a "spotlight" model in which an area of space was illuminated by the spotlight of attention. It was soon realized, however, that this metaphor was inadequate, since spatial attention modulates large areas of the visual field, amplifying in some areas and suppressing in others. The spotlight metaphor gave way to a "landscape of attention" metaphor (Datta & DeYoe, 2009).

Datta and DeYoe showed subjects stimuli that were divided into 18 areas. See Figure 9.7. Subjects fixated (pointed their eyes at) the dot in the center of the stimulus and either attended to the fixation point or to one of the 18 areas. To make sure that subjects attended to the right area, they were asked to report the color and orientation of the stripes of the indicated area. (For example, in the cued area in Figure 9.7, the stripes are blue and horizontal.)

While performing the task, the subjects' early visual areas were scanned. See Figure 9.8. Datta and Deyoe found they could decode where subjects were attending with close to 100% accuracy. What Figure 9.8 shows is attentional amplification in the brain areas whose receptive fields are middle southwest of the fixation point, intense inhibition in a number of the inner areas, and various intermediate degrees of amplification and inhibition in other areas.

What strains the "input" analogy is the presence of both inhibition and amplification, and the fact of different types of inhibition and amplification. In one kind, the outputs of cortical neurons are multiplied. In another, the normal baseline firing rate of the neurons is boosted. These effects concern different kinds of neural

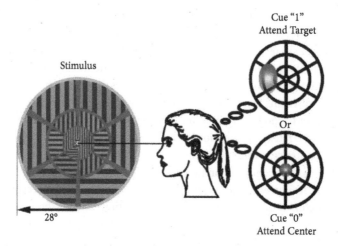

Figure 9.7 Subjects were asked to fixate on the dot in the center of the stimulus and either attend to the fixation point or to a cued area of the stimulus. They were asked to report the color and orientation of the stripes in the cued area to ensure attention to it. From Datta and DeYoe, 2009, p. 1038). This figure requires color. There is a free pdf on the Oxford University Press web site that has the color version of this and all the other figures. Reprinted with permission from Elsevier.

Figure 9.8 fMRI data on one trial, which reveals where the subject was attending. Warm colors represent amplificatory activity, cool colors represent inhibitory activity. Yellow is the highest, whitish blue is the lowest. From Datta and DeYoe, 2009, p. 1039). This figure requires color. There is a free pdf on the Oxford University Press web site that has the color version of this and all the other figures. Reprinted with permission from Elsevier.

processing and are not equivalent to any normal input modulation. Further strain on the input analogy is provided by distinct effects, shown by Marisa Carrasco, on apparent contrast, speed, size, color saturation, and spatial frequency, but not on certain other properties, for example, hue (Block, 2010, 2015a; Carrasco, 2011).[4]

---

[4] I should mention this critique (Beck & Schneider, 2017), though see Block (2015a, pp. 22–24) for some discussion of the same issues. Beck and Schneider claim that Carrasco's results can be accounted for by appeal to salience rather than changes in apparent size, speed, etc.

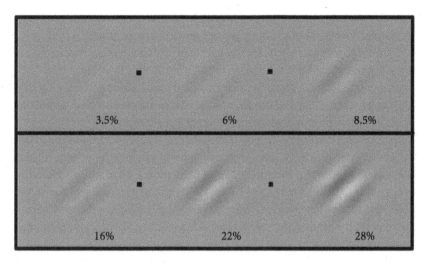

Figure 9.9 This figure sums up the effects of four experiments. Look at the two patches on the lower right, the 22% and the 28% patch. If one is fixating on and attending to the square dot in between them, the patch on the right looks, veridically, to be higher in contrast. But if one attends to the patch on the left, they look equal in contrast. Thanks to Marisa Carrasco for this diagram. (Cf. Carrasco, Ling, & Read, 2004.)

That is, the attended item looks more contrasty, bigger, faster, more saturated, and stripier. In addition, attention to one of two simultaneous light flashes makes the attended flash seem to occur 40 ms before the other flash (Spence & Parise, 2010). (Spatial frequency is explained in the caption and text surrounding Figure 1.1) The Carrasco effect works for prothetic properties like brightness, contrast, speed, and size, properties that have a "direction" of less and more and normally a zero point. There is no Carrasco effect for metathetic properties like pitch or orientation that are "circular" in the sense that continual changes of the same sort lead back to the starting point. Hue is metathetic and there is no Carrasco effect; color saturation is prothetic and there is a Carrasco effect.

Figure 9.9 shows data from four different comparisons. The circular grids are "Gabor patches," commonly used in psychophysical experiments. When attending to and fixating on the square dot on the lower right, the 28% patch looks higher in contrast than the 22% patch. When attending to the 22% patch, however, they look equal in contrast. It is disputed whether in these cases attention actually changes accuracy of the percepts. (This issue is discussed in detail in Beck & Schneider, 2017; Block, 2010, 2015a, 2015b; and Fink, 2015.) But attention does definitely change the accuracy of the comparative percept. The 22% and 28% patch are seen accurately as different with one distribution of attention, but inaccurately as the same with another distribution of attention. (These effects work for both voluntary and involuntary attention.)

I'm not sure whether there are any effects of spatial attention that could not be replicated by appropriate changes in the stimuli, but they would have to be very complex, changing speed in some cases, contrast in others, etc. Rather than being an effect on inputs, these attentional effects are cortical and at different cortical levels of the visual system for different visual properties.

On one understanding of "input," Firestone and Scholl are pinpointing a stage of processing involving the eye. Their examples of moving the eyes or turning the lights off suggest that interpretation. But on a more expansive understanding of input in which it includes inputs to various stages of processing in the hierarchical structure of the visual system, there might be much less disagreement. It is hard to see how that understanding would fit with the Fodor/Pylyshyn type of modularism, though.

In this section, I have not cited any clear cases of content-specific effects of cognition on perception. The purpose of this section has been to offer spatial attention as a possible mechanism of some of the effects cited earlier. For example, in the duck/rabbit ambiguous stimulus, attention to the duck mouth and the rabbit mouth is one mechanism that has been offered to explain the change of perception (Long & Toppino, 2004). Whether or not Firestone's & Scholl's treatment of spatial attention shows that it does not involve real cognitive penetration, I don't think their line of thought can defang feature-based attention, a subject to which I now turn.

Feature-based attention

In 1982, Anne Treisman, one of the pioneers of early work on attention, said, "attention cannot be distributed over a subset of items (e.g., the red ones) when these are spatially scattered among other items in a randomly mixed display" (quoted in Müller, 2014). This turned out to be mistaken, since it was found that there is a kind of nonspatial attention often called "feature-based" attention that operates across the whole visual field (Carrasco, 2011; Müller, 2014) and affects scattered items in a randomly mixed display on the basis of their properties. If I am looking for a red thing, the representation of redness all over the visual field is boosted and the representation of other colors is inhibited. Importantly, feature-based attention is an effect of content and on content. Feature-based attention works in part by amplifying neural responses to the extent that they are similar to the relevant feature and suppressing neural responses to the extent that they are less similar to the relevant feature (Treue, 2015).

There has been some skepticism in the literature about whether feature-based attention is a real phenomenon or is a misdescription of bottom-up priming (Awh, Bepolsky, & Theeuwes, 2012), but the skeptics ignored substantial literature showing feature-based attention independent of priming (Scolari, Ester, & Seremces, 2015; Treue, 2015). And later work by some of the skeptics concedes that feature-based attention is real (Bepolsky & Awh, 2016). Feature-based attention may not always be under full cognitive control (Green, 2017a). And it may in many cases be mediated by priming by a sample of the feature to be attended (Theeuwes, 2013). Past history of perception and of rewarded perception also play a role (Awh et al., 2012). (Priming is defined in footnote 7 in Chapter 3.)

Bayesian views sometimes purport to reduce attention to expectation. However, expectation can have an effect even for an unattended stimulus, and subjects can attend on the basis of a cue even when aware that it has no predictive utility (Gross, 2017; Summerfield & Egner, 2016). Expectation and feature-based attention act in quite different ways. Expectation tends to decrease spiking activity at least in inferotemporal cortex and V1, whereas feature-based attention increases spiking activity (Kok, Rahnev, Jehee, Lau, & de Lange, 2011; Kumar, Kaposvari, & Vogels, 2017). At least this holds if task relevance is used as an index of feature-based attention and predictability of a stimulus is used as an index of expectation. Further, feature-based attention works by increasing signal to noise ratio by suppressing noise, whereas expectation raises the baseline firing rate in signal-sensitive cells (Wyart, Nobre, & Summerfield, 2012).

One dramatic example of feature-based attention involves Figure 9.10. When you look at the figure, you can attend to the face or alternatively to the house, and these yield very different percepts.

This sort of stimulus is also used in binocular rivalry experiments, in which case it is viewed through glasses like those that used to be employed in 3D movies with red on one side and green on the other. What subjects see is first a face filling the whole visual field, then a house filling the whole visual field, etc. This is depicted in Figure 9.11. Again, feature-based attentional differences can affect the timing of the switches.

A similar case is illustrated in Figure 9.12. Attend to the blue and yellow horizontal stripes. Now attend to the red and green vertical stripes. Note the dramatic difference in appearance. From (Reavis, Kohler, Caplovitz, Wheatley, & Tse, 2013) with permission of Elsevier. What you see is quite different if you attend to the horizontal stripes than if you attend to the vertical stripes.

Feature-based attention appears to affect whether an object is consciously visible or not. Lupyan and Ward (2013) used a technique called "continuous flash suppression" to suppress conscious awareness of a stimulus, making the perception unconscious. In this technique, a rapidly alternating attention-grabbing

Figure 9.10 Stimulus used in binocular rivalry experiments. When viewed through glasses that are red on one eye and green on the other, what subjects experience is first a face, then a house, then a face, etc. This figure requires color. There is a free pdf on the Oxford University Press web site that has the color version of this and all the other figures. I thank David Carmel for this picture.

noise pattern presented to one eye reduces the probability of conscious awareness of a stimulus presented to the other eye for extended periods of time, reliably up to a few minutes.[5] Lupyan and Ward used this technique to suppress conscious awareness of objects while at the same time giving the subjects auditory cues.

---

[5] There has been disagreement over whether the unconscious perceptions created by this technique are really unconscious rather than weakly conscious. While the topic is mired in controversy, my take on it is that the controversies are due to a misunderstanding of the role of "controls." Experimenters have mistakenly tried to make sure that the very same features that lead to breaking through the cloak of continuous flash suppression do not also make a brief or degraded stimulus

COGNITIVE PENETRATION IS COMMON 361

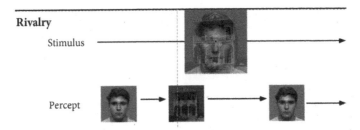

Figure 9.11 A rendering of what the subject sees in binocular rivalry stimulus situations of the sort depicted in Figure 9.10. The subject's whole visual field is filled by first one image then the other, and so on as long as the subject views the stimulus. Note that the time between percepts is not the same from one change to another. This figure requires color. There is a free pdf on the Oxford University Press web site that has the color version of this and all the other figures. Thanks to Frank Tong for this picture.

They found that cues that correctly named the object, e.g., the word 'kangaroo' when the subjects were seeing a picture of a kangaroo, made the subjects more likely to report that they were seeing something and also made them faster at doing so than when there was no cue. In contrast, mismatched word/cue pairs made the subjects less likely to report seeing something, and slower at so doing. They also investigated the suppression of geometric figures that were morphs of circles and squares, giving as cues the word 'circle' or the word 'square.' They found that the word 'square' increased sensitivity in proportion to the degree of squareness of the stimulus. Likewise for the word 'circle' and circularity. These results strongly suggest that feature-based attention can both increase and decrease activation of perceptual representations.

---

easier to see consciously without continuous flash suppression. However, the very salience-making features that promote consciousness in continuous flash suppression also promote consciousness for brief or degraded stimuli. The proper role of controls should be to avoid low-level confounds and decision effects. For example, Mudrik and colleagues (Mudrik, Breska, Lamy, & Deouell, 2011; Mudrik & Koch, 2013) showed that a picture of a man shaving with a fork broke through continuous flash suppression into conscious perception faster than a picture of the man shaving with a razor. The proper role of the controls in this case should be to ensure that the picture of a man shaving with a fork does not differ in measures of low-level salience from the picture of the man shaving with a razor. One should expect that the same increased high-level salience for shaving with a fork over shaving with a razor might make a brief or degraded fork-picture more likely to be perceived consciously than a brief or degraded razor-picture. (See Block & Phillips, 2016.)

Stein and colleagues (Stein & Peelen, 2021) have shown that at least some of the flash-suppressed properties also count as unconscious using a more demanding criterion. They presented subjects with flash-suppressed upright and inverted faces, finding that subjects could be consciously aware that they had seen a face and where it was without being consciously aware of the orientation of the face. This result suggests that the integration of features required to detect a face can occur unconsciously.

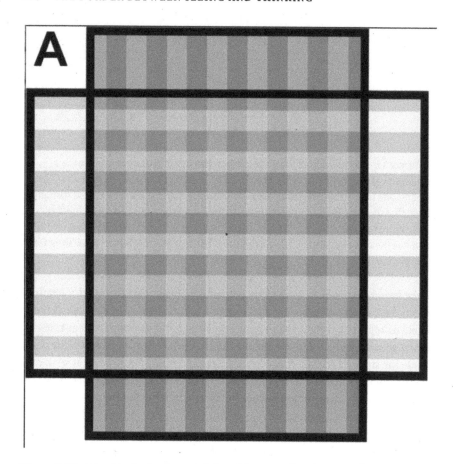

Figure 9.12 Attend to the horizontal stripes. Now attend to the vertical stripes. Note the dramatic difference in appearance. From Reavis, Kohler, Caplovitz, Wheatley, and Tse (2013) with permission of Elsevier. This figure is more useful with color. There is a free pdf on the Oxford University Press web site that has the color version of this and all the other figures.

A later paper replicated Lupyan and Ward's results and also did a similar experiment involving color, with similar results (Forder, Taylor, Mankin, Scott, & Franklin, 2016). However, Forder et al. found stronger evidence for the inhibitory effect of an incongruent cue (the word 'red' when the color in the suppressed eye is blue) than for an amplificatory effect of a congruent cue. These effects would count as cognitive penetration on many definitions of the term.

In their responses to critics (2016b), Firestone and Scholl acknowledge that feature-based attention is not like moving one's eyes. They say this (p. 62):

So, what about those cases of attention that *aren't* like moving your eyes? To be sure, we think such cases are rarer than many commentaries imagined. For example, attending to features, rather than locations, may not be analogous to moving one's eyes, but it is importantly analogous to seeing through a tinted lens —merely increasing sensitivity to certain features rather than others. Across the core cases of attending to locations, features, and objects, both classical and contemporary theorizing understands that, fundamentally, "attention is a *selective* process" that modulates "early perceptual *filters*" (Carrasco, 2011, p.1485–1486, emphasis added). This is what we mean when we speak of attention as constraining input: attention acts as a "filter" that "selects" the information for downstream visual processing, which may itself be impervious to cognitive influence.

This claim, that "fundamentally, "attention is a *selective* process" that modulates "early perceptual *filters*"" is misleading in that attention does not act *only* on early vision. One fundamental fact about feature-based attention is that it modulates the circuits that process the feature in question and those circuits can be at any level in the visual system, not just in early vision. As Carrasco notes, "Neurophysiological studies have also shown that shifting attention between different feature dimensions (e.g., color or orientation) modulates activity in cortical areas specialized for processing those dimensions" (2011, p. 1508). And a later review by Matthias Müller makes the same point: "attending to a certain feature, such as color or motion, selectively increases the response in cortical areas that process that particular feature, such as motion in human middle temporal complex (MT+) or color in V4" (2014, p. 123). Carrasco had used the same example: "a study combining fMRI and neuromagnetic recordings found that a moving stimulus elicited a larger neural response in the motion-sensitive area MT when movement was relevant than when color was relevant, whereas a color-change stimulus produced greater activity in the color-selective area V4/V8 when color was attended than when movement was relevant" (2011, 1509) These areas are usually considered "mid-level" rather than "early" vision, so it is implausible that these effects involve anything that could be called "changing the input."

The neuroscience of feature-based attention further bolsters the claim that it is cognitive penetration. Using three different kinds of brain imaging and a technique of "frequency tagging," Daniel Baldauf and Robert Desimone (2014) looked at brain responses to superimposed pictures of faces and houses. (Frequency tagging: The faces and houses flickered with different frequencies [2 Hz for faces, 1.5 Hz for houses] that provided a signature indicating which stimulus was being processed.) When subjects attended to the faces, they found enhanced responses in a face-sensitive area (the fusiform face area, or FFA) and when subjects attended to the house they found enhanced responses in an area that responds more to houses and places than faces (the parahippocampal place area, or PPA). These are high-level visual areas, and enhancement in them is not analogous to moving one's eyes or looking through a tinted lens—unless one could speak of a face-tinted or place-tinted lens. Further, Baldauf and Desimone showed that the effect of attending to a face—in terms of spectral power—was much stronger in the face-sensitive areas of high-level vision than in early visual areas. And the same applied—albeit to a slightly smaller degree—for attention to houses. More 2 Hz power in the FFA than in V1 strongly suggests a direct effect of face attention on the FFA, even if some of the effect is mediated by an effect on low-level vision. In another paradigm (albeit involving spatial rather than feature-based attention), effects on low-level vision were shown to occur after effects on high-level vision, suggesting that the effects on high-level vision were not mediated entirely by the effects on low-level vision (Buffalo, Fries, Landman, Liang, & Desimone, 2010).

The relevant parts of Figure 9.13 are the three squares on the lower left, those showing the spectral power of the signals in V1, the FFA, and the PPA. What the diagram shows is that the spectral power of the blue face representation

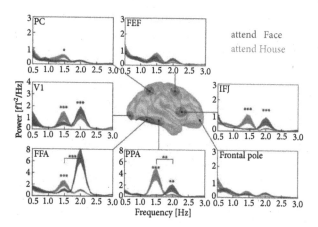

Figure 9.13 Data slide from Baldauf and DeSimone (2014, p. 425). The horizontal access shows the tagging frequency. Houses oscillated at 1.5 Hz, while faces oscillated at 2 Hz. Using this technique combined with various forms of brain imaging, the power of face and house signals in various brain areas could be identified. PC = parietal cortex, FEF = frontal eye field, V1 = the first visual area in the cortex, IFJ = inferior frontal junction, FFA = fusiform face area, PPA = parahippocampal place area. Reprinted with permission from the AAAS. This figure requires color. There is a free pdf on the Oxford University Press web site that has the color version of this and all the other figures.

indicating the condition of attending to the face is about four times greater in the FFA than in V1. Thus even if some of the amplification of the face signal in the FFA due to attention to the face derives from early vision, there is a substantial direct effect of the attention on the face representation in the FFA itself. A similar point applies to the PPA, though the magnitude of the effect is not as great.

The face and house areas are part of high-level vision, but there is also an effect on low-level vision, including an effect in the lowest visual area, V1, in this and other studies. These are neural effects, so there is more work to be done to show that they result in effects on the content of perception. But they do hint that these phenomena go counter to Pylyshyn's view that early vision is immune to cognitive penetration.

So Gary Lupyan (2015) is on the right track when he says that feature-based attention operates at all levels of the visual hierarchy (e.g., both orientations and faces) and so is not a matter of operation on input. (See the section of Chapter 2 on the visual hierarchy.) However, a closer look at the mechanisms of feature-based attention suggests that the spirit of Firestone and Scholl's position may be right. One type of attentional effect could be characterized as "boosting." This boosting can happen in a number of different ways, as mentioned earlier in this chapter. In one type of boosting effect, mentioned above in connection with spatial attention, it is as if the contrast of the stimulus is multiplied by a constant factor. In a somewhat different kind of boosting effect, the output of the perceptual neuron can be multiplied by a constant factor. In another kind of boosting effect, the baseline for firing of the neuron can be raised. (See sections 4.6 and 4.7 of Carrasco, 2011, and Chapter 2 of Wu, 2014, for accounts of how the "Normalization model of attention" explains why one effect occurs rather than another.) Another type of attentional effect is "tuning." In feature-based attention, attention to, for example, verticality changes the sensitivity of orientation-sensitive circuits toward verticality. Spatial attention is often seen as tuning for spatial area.

These effects do not involve interactions of the sort that are prototypical for cognitive states, e.g., where a premise from knowledge of paleontology plus another premise from knowledge of nuclear physics were combined to yield an astronomical explanation of the extinction of the dinosaurs. Feature-based attention does not use premises at all, and the interactions are not the reasoning that is typical of cognition. The effects are property based in the sense that what is attended to and what has the effects are attention to a specific property.

The mechanisms of feature-based attention are of the sort that operate in perception and are not reasoning. For example, coordinated oscillation is thought to be one of the mechanisms by which properties are bound together in a single percept (Seth, McKinstry, Edelman, & Krichmar, 2004). Suppose one sees a blue square moving to the right and a red triangle moving to the left. What makes the perception of blue and the perception of red parts of perceptions of different objects; and what puts the perception of blue and square and rightward motion together in one percept? Part of the answer to both questions appears to be that representations of properties of a single object are synchronized: they hum together. By the usual criteria of what counts as a perceptual process, one segment of the mechanism by which feature based attention works is perceptual. Of course, cognitive mechanisms are also at work (but not well understood) in mobilizing the attention to begin with. The critics of a joint have not presented evidence that suggests that any of these mechanisms are indeterminate as between cognition and perception. Further, attention affects a relatively small class of properties that are represented in the perceptual systems. (See Chapter 2 on how to determine which properties those are.) It would be surprising if there were feature-based attention for laziness, plasticity or incoherence. (Cf. Pylyshyn's discussion of transducible properties [1984].)

Of course, we don't know how the cognitive machinery works in which a desire to attend to a face rather than to a house issues in frontal areas sending attention signals. Those who are against a joint in nature owe us a reason to think that these unknown mechanisms do not divide neatly into cognitive and perceptual parts. Why am I taking separability of mechanisms to be so important to the joint? Contrary to the assumptions often made by advocates of Fodorian modularity, causation across a border is no bar to a joint in nature. There is a joint between living things and artifacts, but each affects the other; people create cars, and cars causally influence driver backaches and pride of ownership. There is a joint separating vertebrates and bacteria, but bacteria cause illnesses in people and people kill bacterial by taking antibiotics.

By contrast: it was once thought that there was a joint between the stomach and the brain—that is, that they were completely distinct organs with completely distinct functions. Everyone knew that they interacted—a full stomach can make you happy and anxiety influences the secretion of stomach acid. But recent research has established that the gut brain, a neural network of 200 million neurons is continuous with the central nervous system. The joint action of these parts of the nervous system are intertwined in anxiety, depression, autism, chronic pain, constipation, diarrhea, and many other disorders. Much of the neurotransmitter activity in the nervous system is localized in the gut, including 90% of serotonin and 50% of dopamine (Mayer, Knight, Mazmanian, Cryan, & Tillisch, 2014). When one examines the causal mechanisms of these disorders, it is difficult to see a fundamental difference between the two components of the nervous system. If you tried to divide the mechanisms by which the stomach and the brain affect one another, you would have to draw arbitrary lines. But as I have argued, the lines separating perception and cognition are not arbitrary.

Returning to the example of feature-based attention to direction of motion: As noted in Chapters 1 and 4, mid-level visual area MT+ is known to process optic flow, as would happen if you saw a cluster of moving dots. Different cells in MT+ respond to different directions. A number of feature-based attention studies use stimuli in which dots are moving in a variety of directions. Subjects can attend to one of those directions. Here is what happens when they do: There is increased gain in neurons that prefer the attended direction, there is suppression in neurons that prefer other directions, and there is a shift in tuning curves toward the preferred direction (Carrasco, 2011; Sneve, Sreenivasan, Alaes, Endestad, & Magnussen, 2015). Thus, there is a change in precision, focusing on the attended feature. Again, these are straightforwardly perceptual mechanisms.

E. J. Green raises the possibility that such effects might be due to low-level associations between words and visual features: Hearing the word "face" might make you visualize faces the way "salt" makes you think of pepper (Green, 2017b). If so, the effect would not be an effect on content but only on sound or orthography. There is some evidence for an effect of associations (Costello, Jiang, Baartman, McGlennen, & He, 2009). But later work (Pinto et al., 2015) suggests that even when preexisting associations are not present, there is a substantial effect of expectations on perception. (See also Lupyan & Ward, 2013.)

In some of antijoint work cited above (see, for example, the citations to work of Lupyan), it sometimes appears that it is feature-based attention rather than spatial attention that is supposed to cause problems for a joint, since feature-based attention is active at all levels of the visual system whereas spatial attention is focused on early stages. However, in the Baldauf and Desimone paper I just quoted, the authors are at pains to tell the reader how similar feature-based attention is in its mechanisms to spatial attention. They say, "The neural mechanism that enables attention to an object or feature seems intuitively more complex than spatial attention, which may only require a spatial-biasing signal that targets a relevant location. Yet the present study reveals some striking parallels in neural mechanisms" (2014, p. 426). They go on to describe how both spatial and feature-based attention work similarly: In both cases, frontal areas (generally thought to reflect cognition) send signals to the areas doing the actual sensory processing. The signals are oscillations: In effect, the frontal areas drive enhancement in the sensory processing areas by humming at the same frequency as the sensory areas.

Lupyan mentions a number of cases that can involve feature-based attention. He is responding to Firestone and Scholl's claim that supposed top-down effects

Figure 9.14 The Brick Wall illusion. There are two ways to see this picture and they are dramatically different from one another. Many observers report that it is very difficult to get one of the interpretations without being told what to look for. A hint is given in the text and there is a spoiler image at the end of the chapter. The spoiler is more powerful when viewed upside down. The spoiler works via blurring out details that aren't relevant to the hard-to-get interpretation. The source of this photo is unknown. Phil Plait discusses its origin (Plait, 2016). This figure works better with color. There is a free pdf on the Oxford University Press web site that has the color version of this and all the other figures.

can almost never be experienced for oneself and that this is anomalous: "In our field, experimental data about what we see are routinely accompanied by such demonstrations—in which interested observers can experience the relevant phenomena for themselves, often in dramatic fashion" (2016a, p. 11). To combat this charge, Lupyan describes a number of cases in which he says that knowledge can lead to a dramatic change in experience. He alleges that knowledge can be involved in perception of Figure 9.14. However, an effect of knowledge can be mediated by feature-based attention, so whether effects of knowledge really are cognitive penetration depends on whether feature-based attention is cognitive.

What one sees in the figure looks at first glance like an ordinary brick wall. I won't say more right now. Stare at it without blinking for 60 seconds. My experience is that the image changes after that. If you don't get the change, there is a spoiler at the end of the chapter. The spoiler works most powerfully upside down, but rightside up might do the trick.

I agree with Lupyan that the effect of switching from one interpretation of this image to the other is dramatic in that the two perceptions are very different from one another. I am pretty sure that this is a reversible figure, like the duck/rabbit and other items of Figure 9.4, though once one sees the construal that doesn't immediately appear, it can be hard to unsee it. It may be a case of a nonreversible ambiguous figure as with Figure 9.5.

As I noted earlier, the difference is that in the case of the reversible items like the duck/rabbit and other pictures of Figure 9.4, the different perceptions are more or less equally likely. In the case of nonreversible ambiguous figures like that of Figure 9.5, the visual system prefers a representation of a salient object (the creature) to the representation of an expanse of blobs, so once the visual system hits on that percept, it sticks.

This stickiness of perception, known as hysteresis, was investigated experimentally by Molly Potter using out of focus slides that slowly came into focus and then out of focus again (Potter, 1964). She found that the threshold of blurriness for recognizing an image was far higher going into focus than going out of focus. That is, once subjects recognized a picture, it they could maintain the recognition even with substantial defocus. The picture with its recognizable objects was much more salient than a collection of blurs. In short, the brick wall illusion is not such a case because both percepts are representations of recognizable objects. Neither is an expanse of blobs though one of the representations may still represent a much more salient object.

My overall point is that the effects of both kinds of ambiguous stimuli may be understood in terms of feature-based attention. I know of no evidence that the mechanisms of feature-based attention do not divide into the perceptual and the cognitive or that feature-based attention directly modulates conceptual representations (Block, 2016b; Ogilvie & Carruthers, 2016).

Dimension restriction

E. J. Green has suggested a way of preserving a version of the cognitive penetration condition (2020b). My disagreement with his proposal is similar to my disagreement with Firestone and Scholl in that I think he underestimates the efficacy of feature based attention. He says that although there is cognitive penetration by some of the usual definitions, none of them introduce a "new" feature dimension into perception. What is a feature dimension? Color is a feature dimension that allows for specific color features, for example a specific shade of red. He calls his proposal the (feature) dimension restriction hypothesis, or DRH. There are two ways of understanding the DRH proposal, one true but not that useful for distinguishing perception and cognition; and the other exciting and, I believe, false.

First the true understanding of the DRH: There are features that cannot be represented in perception even though they can be represented in cognition. We can perceptually represent the colors and shapes in a painting, but although we can cognitively represent the fact that it was painted by Rembrandt, we cannot represent this fact perceptually. More generally, we can cognitively but not perceptually represent dimensions of justice, altruistic action, logical form, and justified inference. In this sense of the suggestion, it amounts to the point that there are feature dimensions that are representable by cognition but not perception. Or, reversing the emphasis, some of the features of things in the world are observable and others are not. As I mentioned in Chapter 1, one can imagine a creature whose limited cognition was entirely restricted to properties it can perceptually represent and whose perception was not more fine-grained than its cognition. For that creature, what can be represented perceptually and cognitively would coincide. Nonetheless, that creature could still exemplify the basic differences between perception and cognition described here.

The exciting and probably false understanding of the DRH is that cognition cannot introduce into an individual perception a new feature that would not otherwise be represented in that very perception. Consider the rat-man ambiguous drawing in item h of Figure 9.4. Suppose an observer sees it as a rat and does not see it as a face. Then someone tells the observer that it can also be seen as a face, resulting in the observer knowing that it can be seen as a face, and that in turn results in the observer seeing it as a face. In this way, cognition can introduce a new feature into a perception that was not represented before the effect of the cognitive state.

As Green mentions, a reviewer for the article (who turns out to be me) noted the rat-man problem. Green replies in the published article. I will now describe his replies and my rejoinders. I will start with the first understanding of the DRH proposal: as saying that there are feature dimensions that are not perceptible and cannot be made perceptible by cognition. Green distinguishes between a relativized and nonrelativized interpretation of "perceptible," where the parameter of relativization is to the individual perceiver at a time. In the nonrelativized sense, the DRH would say that there are feature dimensions that no observer could possibly represent. Green says that there may be no dimension restrictions in this sense. For any dimension you might mention, perhaps there can be some evolutionary history that would allow a creature to perceptually represent that dimension. I am skeptical, but this disagreement isn't relevant, since as Green makes clear, he does not intend this interpretation of the DRH. (The reason for my skepticism is that to build a detector that detects justification, one would have to build in cognitive processing of a sort that would preclude perceptual recognition.)

Green also rejects the relativized interpretation on the ground that relativization to the person at a time is insufficiently fine grained: He notes that dimensions that are available to one perceptual process at a time may not be available to another perceptual process at that time. The example he gives is that visual search cannot access T-junctions and cross shapes that can be accessed by other perceptual processes.

So Green rejects both interpretations of the first horn of the dilemma. The upshot is that he embraces a version of the second horn of the dilemma, the exciting but false (according to me) claim that cognition cannot introduce into an individual perceptual process a new feature that would not otherwise be represented in that process. That is just what the rat-man case seems to show is wrong. So what about the rat-man example? He says (p. 352):

> Let's now extend the model to the rat-man image.... I conjecture that when you attend to the region corresponding to the man's eyes or glasses, this promotes the old man percept. When you attend to the regions corresponding to the rat's eyes or mouth, this promotes the rat percept. This is just a hypothesis, of course, but it is an empirically reasonable one. Moreover, there is strong evidence that eyes are among the most important features in face perception and recognition ... so it is plausible that attending to the eyes would preferentially activate high-level processes attuned to faces (e.g., those subserved by the FFA). But this is a selection effect. Cognition affects which objects or features get selected for further processing, and thus affects which high-level processes dominate at a time. But there is no reason to think that this enriches the dimensions computable by either early vision or high-level vision.

Green seems to think that if an effect is a "selection" effect, it does not impinge on the DRH. But why? Perhaps the idea is that selection would have to operate on dimensions that are already being computed over in the perception, so no new dimensions are introduced. But Green gives no evidence that when one is seeing the stimulus as a rat, there is already a face-dimension that is being computed over. There are some ambiguous stimuli in which arguably both ways of processing it are present in the visual system from the outset but I know of no evidence that this thesis is true for all ambiguous cases.

Perhaps, though, Green is thinking of the attention in this case as spatial attention. In that case, Green is giving the same response as the one canvassed earlier in this chapter by Firestone and Scholl, in which they claimed that attention works by changing the input to the perception. Recall that Firestone and Scholl had claimed that attention is no more a case of cognitive penetration than the fact that one moves one's eyes in looking for things. Perhaps Green is saying that the DRH only precludes "new" dimensions introduced into a perception, but dimensions introduced by changing the input are not new in the relevant sense.

I agree with Green that the alternation of reversible ambiguous figures is known to be influenced by spatial attention. It is known that for some reversible figures such as the Necker cube and the face/vase, where subjects attend influences reversals (Meng & Tong, 2004; Peterson & Gibson, 1991). As I mentioned earlier, in the duck/rabbit ambiguous stimulus, it has been suggested that attending to mouth or ears has an effect on seeing-as (Long & Toppino, 2004). Further, the brain basis for control of alternation is likely to be in areas of the superior parietal lobe that govern spatial attention. For example, as Green notes, cortical thickness, gray-matter density, and white-matter integrity in the superior parietal lobe correlate with alternation rate and transcranial magnetic stimulation applied to this area decreases alternation rate (Kanai, Bahrami, & Rees, 2010).

However, as I have been saying, the most impressive effects of cognition on perception derive from feature-based attention, not spatial attention. As I mentioned in my response to Firestone and Scholl, feature-based attention acts on the circuits that process the feature in question. Those circuits can affect any level of the visual system, and are not just "inputs." Recall that Baldauf and Desimone (2014) looked at brain responses to superimposed pictures of faces and houses, using frequency tagging. They found that the power of face responses was much higher in the mid-level face processing area than in V1, showing that although there was an effect on "input," there was also a direct effect on the face area. Another study showed that the effect on high-level vision occurred before the effect on low-level vision, again showing a direct effect on mid-level vision.

The effects of spatial attention mentioned in the paragraph before last derive from experiments on bistable perception in which both construals of an ambiguous figure vie with one another for dominance. First one dominates, then adaptation sets in, then the other dominates. The problem for the DRH posed by the rat-man case is that the defender of the DRH must rule out the possibility that one can see the picture one way for a period in cases in which the visual system has not computed the other way of seeing it. This point can be further bolstered

Figure 9.15 As with Figure 9.14, there are two ways to see this. Art by Johannes Stoetter, johannesstoetterart.com. Management & Permission to use this picture granted by WB-Production.com. The spoiler image for this picture is given at the end of the chapter. See https://youtu.be/8gw8MN1FjRY for videos that dramatically show the alternative interpretation. This figure works better with color. There is a free pdf on the Oxford University Press web site that has the color version of this and all the other figures.

by Figure 9.15, which contains another image that poses the same problem as the rat-man picture. The picture is designed to be seen, initially, as a parrot. One can stare at the picture for some time without seeing it another way. A cognitive hint, however, allows the viewer to see it another way. That other way is indicated at the end of the chapter.

Green also applies his account to irreversible ambiguous stimuli such as the Dalmation stimulus of Figure 9.5.

> This account may generalize to certain degraded images containing objects that suddenly "pop into place," like the Dalmatian image. . . . Studies suggest that there are low-level diagnostic features in the Dalmatian image (mainly texture differences) that aid our ability to detect the figure. When these are absent, finding the Dalmatian is considerably more difficult (van Tonder & Ejima 2000). I conjecture that when cognition aids in detecting the Dalmatian, it does so by attentionally selecting low-level features diagnostic of dogs (or perhaps mid-sized four-legged animals in general). Once selected, these features are prioritized by the processes responsible for object differentiation. When these processes decide that an object is present, the Dalmatian pops into place. But this is a selection effect, not an enrichment effect.

Here it is clearer that a selection effect is meant to be a matter of feature-based attention to low-level features.

Why does Green think that if the effect is a matter of attention to low-level features, that saves the DRH? Consider the case in which one perceives Figure 9.5 while seeing it as a collection of blobs and not seeing it as an animal. Then a cognitive hint allows one to see it as a dog, allegedly via attention to low-level features diagnostic of dogs. Perhaps Green's idea is that the low-level features are *already* part of the perception so no "new" features are introduced?

But since the feature-based attention results in the activation of the high-level feature *dog*, why isn't that a new feature, one that was not already part of the perception? Recall that attention can affect high-level circuits before it affects representations of low-level properties. So face-representing circuits in high-level visual areas might be activated before low-level circuits that compute texture and orientation.

Green's conjecture is clearly that—a conjecture. No one knows how irreversible cases like the Dalmatian work. One possibility is a direct effect attentional effect on high-level dog representations. Another possibility is the one Green describes. My disagreement with Green can be seen as a disagreement about the nature of attention. Green emphasizes two things that attention does: select and modulate. He says (p. 373), "Attention may either select among candidate inputs to a perceptual process or modulate the information computed over by a process (or both)." This is true for spatial attention. However, we have seen in a number of cases such as the rat-man case that feature-based attention can reconfigure a stimulus, introducing a new feature into a perception that was probably not already represented.

I conclude that there are many different sorts of cases of cognitive penetration involving feature-based attention, notably cases of ambiguous stimuli, but that there is no reason to believe that they challenge the joint in nature between cognition and perception.

Mental imagery

In this section, I am going to discuss a potential case of cognitive penetration that was mentioned earlier in the section of Chapter 1 titled "Conceptual engineering." The case may seem to be a curiosity of little general interest. I suspect—but can't show—that it is actually indicative of a phenomenon that is ubiquitous in our perceptual lives.

There is plenty of evidence that subjects can superimpose mental images on percepts. (See Block, 2008, 2016b; Howe & Carter, 2016; Macpherson, 2012.) I'll give more detail about the experiment I mentioned in Chapter 1. There are

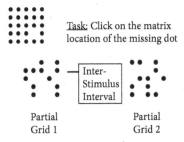

Figure 9.16 The task is to move the cursor to the missing dot. Partial Grid 1 appears briefly, and then Partial Grid 2 appears in the same location. If Partial Grid 1 and Partial Grid 2 are superimposed, they make a grid with a missing dot. Thanks to Vincent di Lollo for this figure.

certain tasks that are easy with vision. If presented with a 5 × 5 grid of dots with one dot missing, subjects can easily move a cursor to the missing dot. So far, we have just a perceptual task. Now consider a variant: part of the grid is presented briefly first, then another part in the same place. If the second partial grid is presented within a few milliseconds of the first, the subject can fuse them and click on the missing grid easily. This task is pictured in Figure 9.16.

Both variants just discussed are done perceptually with no imagery, but there is a further variant in which mental imagery is superimposed on perception. In that variant, Partial Grid 2 comes long after Partial Grid 1 has disappeared. Partial Grid 2 appears on the screen and stays there until after the response. The details of the results are diagrammed in Figure 9.17, which is explained in the caption of the figure. The important result is that if Partial Grid 2 comes a few seconds after Partial Grid 1 has disappeared, subjects can identify the missing dot with more than 90% accuracy on the dots in Partial Grid 1 (which is no longer on the screen). That is, mistakes of clicking on a square that had contained a dot on Partial Grid 1 are well under 10%. Subjects say they are forming an image of Partial Grid 1 and superimposing it on the one on the screen (Partial Grid 2). And the timing of the effect supports what they say. If Partial Grid 2 appears within a few ms after Partial Grid 1, subjects can fuse the two and are at nearly 100% accuracy. This is a perception, not mental imagery. But by a few hundred ms after Partial Grid 1 has disappeared, their responses have fallen to chance. Then by around 1–1.5 seconds, the accuracy climbs to 90%. Stephen Kosslyn has independently estimated that it takes about 1 to 1.5 seconds to generate a mental image (Kosslyn, 1994). Kosslyn also replicated this experiment using completely different methods with the same result (Lewis, Borst, & Kosslyn, 2011). In Kosslyn's version, the subjects memorized partial grids and were simply told to superimpose them on partial grids on the screen.

376 THE BORDER BETWEEN SEEING AND THINKING

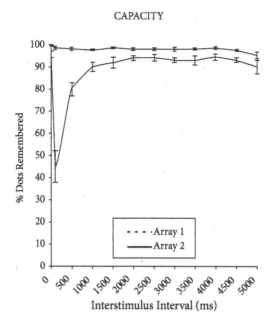

Figure 9.17 The horizontal axis represents the interstimulus interval between the first partial grid, Array 1, and Array 2, as diagrammed in Figure 9.16. The vertical axis represents number of dots remembered. Array 2 remains on the screen until the trial is over. Accuracy on Array 2—indicated by the solid (non-dashed) line—is measured as follows. Subjects click on a square to indicate that it is the square with the missing dot. If they click on a square that has a visible dot in it, that dot is counted as not remembered. Unsurprisingly, subjects rarely click on a square with a visible dot on it, so the accuracy for Array 2 is close to 100%, falling off towards the end as a result of fatigue. What is really surprising, is that accuracy on Array 1 in which the dots are remembered rather than being on the screen is almost as high as accuracy for Array 2. Thanks to James Brockmole for this figure.

We understand an aspect of how this works based on the fact that the processes involved in mental imagery are very similar to the processes involved in perception, even at the level of V1, the lowest cortical level. (See the section on mental imagery in Chapter 5 for more detail on this point.) Subjects viewed photographs of five works of art while in a brain scanner (fMRI). Algorithms were trained on low-level features of the stimuli so that it could be determined from the scans which photograph they were looking at. Next subjects were asked to imagine one or another of the works of art from the set presented. The brain imaging classifier could determine what they were imagining based on the earlier data (Howe & Carter, 2016; Naselaris, Olman, Stansbury, Ugurbil, & Gallant, 2015). We do not yet know how the intention to form an image results in one being formed. But what we do know about the process suggests perceptual mechanisms of the sort studied by perception scientists and so the mechanisms of the part we know about do not challenge the joint in nature.

As I mentioned earlier, this is cognitive penetration only if we count the representation that results from superimposing imagery on perception as itself a perception. (Recall that the result of superimposing imagery on perception is what I termed "quasi-perception" in Chapter 1. I am not sure that the question of whether quasi-perception is perception has a determinate answer. As I noted, for those (not including me) who think that cognitive penetration is incompatible with a joint, there is a case for excluding such quasi-perceptions from the category of perception. That case is based on the idea that we should clarify the concept of perception to home in on a joint if there is one.

As I also noted earlier, if we think of the intention to form the image as the cognitive state that is affecting perception, then the mental imagery itself would be an intermediary causal link and the effect on quasi-perception would not be

Figure 9.18 This is the spoiler image for Figure 9.14. It works as a spoiler as is, but its spoiling power is increased by turning the page upside down. The source of this photo is unknown. This figure works better with color. There is a free pdf on the Oxford University Press web site that has the color version of this and all the other figures.

Figure 9.19 Spoiler image for Figure 9.15. This is a body-painted human. See https://youtu.be/8gw8MN1FjRY for videos for this and similar images. Bodypainting Illusion Art by Johannes Stoetter, johannesstoetterart.com. Management & Permission to use this picture granted by WB-Production.com. This figure works better with color. There is a free pdf on the Oxford University Press web site that has the color version of this and all the other figures.

direct, so on the Fodor/Pylyshyn notion of cognitive penetration, the superimposition of imagery on perception would not be cognitive penetration.

If the combined imagery/perception states are cases of perception, then the role of imagery in perception might be greater than usually thought. Ian Phillips has argued for unconscious mental imagery (Phillips, 2014). The evidence for unconscious mental imagery is that reports of imagery vary wildly from person to person but are almost uncorrelated with performance on tasks that seem to require imagery (Schwitzgebel, 2011). One conclusion is that people are to a large extent unaware of their imagery. But if we are often unaware of mental imagery, it might be involved in perception to an extent that we are unaware of.

Bence Nanay (2010, 2016) makes the case that the sense one has in perception of the occluded parts of the cat behind the picket fence are actually filled in by a kind of amodal imagery. If perception of occluded objects involves a kind of combined imagistic/perceptual state, then imagistic perception would be normal.

So far, we have seen a number of kinds of top-down effects. In the shooter task discussed in Chapter 3, the top-down effect involved an effect of racial stereotype on perceptual judgment, but not perception. So that was not a case of cognitive penetration. The effects of attention on perception discussed in this chapter, especially the effects involving ambiguous stimuli, are genuine cases of cognitive penetration by almost any standard, but these cases have not been shown to impugn the joint. The imagery phenomena just discussed are different from both, since these phenomena involve a cognitive state that affects something, but whether that something is a perceptual state and whether the effect is direct may be indeterminate.

Mental imagery also affects perception via priming and adaptation, and these effects can be opposite in direction. (For some examples of the opposite effects of priming and adaptation, see Block, 2014c.) In binocular rivalry, imagining one of the two stimuli has been reported to make that stimulus more likely to dominate. Perceiving one of the two stimuli immediately prior to binocular rivalry has the opposite effect, making the stimulus less likely to dominate because of adaptation. (See Chapter 2 on adaptation.) Dijkstra et al. showed that the effect of imagery on binocular rivalry is highly variable, depending on the contrast of the stimuli and on features of the individual perceiver. (Dijkstra, Hinne, Bosch, & van Gerven, 2019). The overall lesson is that mental imagery has substantial effects on perception, but the effects are dependent on context and on features of the individual perceiver.

This chapter has been concerned with the extent to which various forms of modularity are violated by perception. But there is another issue: To the extent to which perception is modular, can that be used to characterize the perception/cognition border? There is a case to be made—but I won't make it here—that a modularity based border will wrongly put some cognitive systems on the perceptual side, notably the "core cognition" system to be discussed in Chapter 12. See (Nes, Sundberg, & Watzl, 2021).

10
Top-down effects that are probably not cases of cognitive penetration

Although I think cognitive penetration is common, I also think that many putative cases of cognitive penetration are actually top-down effects within the visual system. I move now to a discussion of some of these cases.

Figure/ground

Gary Lupyan uses figures like those in Figure 10.1 and Figure 10.2 below as part of his case against a joint in nature (2017).

In the left side of Figure 10.1, there is a preference for seeing the black center as figure and the white as surround. (Though if you keep staring at it, adaptation will inevitably produce a reversal.) Gestalt principles dictate that closed, symmetrical shapes that are largely convex, smaller than their surround, and enclosed by it are preferred as figure. Dark areas are also preferred when they contrast with the background of the display as here where the page is white. On the right side, the preference is less clear though perhaps there is a preference for the dark side as figure. In Figure 10.2, there is something like a reversal. The white sides of both figures are preferred—and the causally effective difference is that they are the silhouettes of familiar objects. Lupyan says (p. 8):

> Indeed, the idea that object knowledge affects figure-ground segregation appear downright paradoxical if one assumes that the process of figure-ground segregation is what provides the input to later object recognition processes.... But finding that recognition can precede and influence such "earlier" perceptual processes is exactly what one would expect if the goal of vision to provide the viewer with a useful representation of the input (Marr, 1982), and to do so as quickly as possible.... The relevance of such findings to CPP [NB: cognitive penetration of perception] is that they show that figure-ground segregation does *not* operate in a content-neutral way and is sensitive to at least some aspects of meaning.

Figure 10.1 In the figure on the left, gestalt principles dictate a preference for the black center part as figure because it contrasts more with the white background of the page. On the right side, there is a smaller preference for the black as figure. Thanks to Mary Peterson for this figure.

Figure 10.2 The inverted version of the previous figure. Here there is preference for the white areas because they have familiar silhouettes. Thanks to Mary Peterson for this figure.

His reasoning seems to be that meanings are involved in the earliest stages of perception so there is infiltration of cognition into all of perception.

However, this argument has three serious flaws, all shown by Mary Peterson's work. First, having seen a silhouette disposes the subject to see that outline as figure even if the outline has been seen only once and doesn't look like anything the subject would recognize. Peterson and her colleagues showed that a single exposure to a novel meaningless figure (that looked like a gerrymandered state border) was enough to increase the chances of that outline to be favored as figure

(Peterson & Lampignano, 2003). So past history has an impact on figure/ground assignment independently of any kind of cognitive assignment of meanings.

Second, when familiarity and meaningfulness of silhouettes clash, it is familiarity that determines what is figure and what is ground, independently of meaning (Peterson & Cacciamani, 2013; Peterson & Gibson, 1994). For example, in displays like the left side of Figure 10.1, telling the subject that the silhouette is an upside down version of the silhouette of a standing woman such as that of Figure 10.2 does not have any effect on making the subject more likely to see the white space in the left side of Figure 10.2 as figure, nor does it have any effect on how long the subject holds it as figure. The left sides of those two figures (the standing and upside down woman) are reproduced as A and B in Figure 10.3. C of Figure 10.3 contains scrambled segments of the upright woman silhouette. Telling subjects that C contains scrambled segments of the upright woman silhouette also has no effect on seeing the white in C as figure. What counts is not what the subject knows but what representations in the visual system are accessed by visual processing.

Further, and even more impressively, a visual associative agnosic who was unable to cognitively classify familiar objects showed the normal effects of familiarity without recognizing any of the silhouettes (Peterson, De Gelder, Rapcsak, Gerhardstein, & Bachoud-Lévi, 2000). (This patient had associative agnosia, in which patients can see shapes but cannot cognitively classify objects. This form of agnosia contrasts with visual form agnosia, in which patients can see

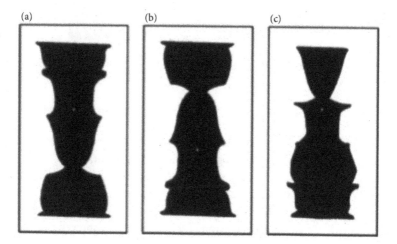

Figure 10.3 A is the same as the left side of Figure 10.2, the silhouette of a standing woman, B is the upside-down version, the same as the left side of Figure 10.1. C has scrambled contours from A. Thanks to Mary Peterson for this figure.

textures and colors but not shapes. Associative agnosics such as this patient can copy drawings, but visual form agnosics cannot copy well. See the discussion in Chapter 1.) And this same article discusses a comparison patient who could recognize the silhouettes but showed no familiarity effect on figure assignment. This is a double dissociation of knowledge and figure assignment and justifies the title of the article: "Object Memory Effects on Figure Assignment: Conscious Object Recognition Is Not Necessary or Sufficient."

A third point: Lupyan seems to be assuming—or maybe assuming that others assume—that since figure/ground segregation is "early," categorization effects penetrate early vision. However, Peterson's work shows that figure/ground segregation can take as long as 200 ms, which is outside the bounds of early vision. So categorization effects on figure/ground segregation allows for a substantial bottom/up component to perception.

I am arguing that figure assignment in these experiments need not depend on knowledge. Of course, it does depend on a form of what might be called "memory," and some may wish to use "knowledge" in an expansive sense, counting that "memory" as knowledge. However, knowledge in the sense that I am using here is part of cognition, a system of representation in which the representations function in reasoning as premises or conclusions. There is no reason to think that the kind of memory involved in figure assignment—memory that is baked into the object recognition system—has that kind of computational role.

I should say that figure/ground assignment can depend on cognition in the form of feature-based attention (Wagatsuma, Oki, & Sakai, 2013). See the discussion in Chapter 9 of feature-based attention. My point is not that cognition cannot affect figure and ground but rather that the effects are highly circumscribed.

Peterson also showed that the ground part of figure/ground displays such as the ones reproduced here can be processed unconsciously (Cacciamani, Mojica, Sanguinetti, & Peterson, 2014). For example, in Figure 10.4 (reproduced from Figure 2.12), subjects tend to see the black area as figure. It is favored by gestalt principles. But the white ground was nonetheless unconsciously processed, since subjects showed an effect on a task that required discrimination of words from nonwords for words that described the ground—"butterfly" in the case of Figure 10.4—even when they had no conscious appreciation of the identity of the backgrounds. If there is unconscious processing of the ground, that could give rise to feature-based attention to the ground features. That could in turn make the ground into figure.

Eric Mandelbaum uses some of these results about unconscious processing of ground, not to argue directly against a joint, as with Lupyan, but in order to provide an argument for conceptualism. You will recall that conceptualism is the view that at least some perceptual representations are conceptual. As noted earlier, conceptualism does threaten a joint. If perception can be conceptual, it

Figure 10.4 Gestalt principles favor the black central area as figure, but subjects nonetheless processed the content of the white background to the semantic level even if they showed no conscious recognition of what the white items are. (Cf. Cacciamani et al., 2014). Thanks to Mary Peterson for this figure.

would be hard to resist the idea that perception can be propositional. It is not clear how much of a joint would be left. The considerations raised above apply to Mandelbaum's argument, but there are some further wrinkles that I will address now.

Mandelbaum says (2017, p. 11):

> The modular non-conceptualist appears to have two problems. One is that the meanings of the silhouettes in the figure/ground images sometimes effect assignment of figure/ground (i.e., if only one of the silhouettes represents a common image, that silhouette is more likely to be seen as figure; Peterson and Gibson 1994). This appears to be an instance of top-down penetration, but not if object meanings are available before figure/ground assignment as part of the intramodular proprietary database. Since non-conceptualists do not posit such intramodular categorization information, this explanation isn't available to them. Perhaps the modular non-conceptualist would then be inclined to ditch the modularism in favor of being a top-down theorist. But in that case, they would run into a different problem: that of explaining how the effects happen before reentrant connections are available.

The first horn of Mandelbaum's dilemma for modular nonconceptualists is that the silhouettes of common images are more likely to be seen as figures, even when the silhouettes are not consciously recognized. He takes modularists to be committed to vision having its own database and assumes that that database will not have information about what he calls "object meanings"—what I would call cognitive categories of objects. So modularists are supposed to have a problem about how unconscious recognition can influence figure/ground assignment. However, as I mentioned in connection with Lupyan's point, there is no reason to think that cognitive categories are involved in figure assignment. The Peterson results I mentioned show effects of familiarity rather than cognitive categories on figure-ground assignment. So, the first horn is ineffective.

I am a nonconceptualist but also not a modularist, so the second horn is more relevant to me: How can this effect happen before reentrant connections are available. What Mandelbaum has in mind seems to be that figure/ground segregation is supposed to be the first stage of perception and so happens very quickly, before top-down effects can occur. On that view, there is a mystery for the nonconceptualist about how nonconceptual figure assignment can depend on cognitive categories. However, as just pointed out, the idea that figure/ground segregation is the first stage of perception has long been abandoned. Peterson's work shows that it happens within about 200 ms after stimulus presentation, leaving plenty of time for top-down feedback. Further, as emphasized earlier, contours shape the early processes of figure/ground segregation. This is a diachronic effect—perceptual learning. (See the earlier section in Chapter 1 on clarifying the concepts of perception and cognition.) This reshaping does not require any recognition of the familiar contour.

Memory color

There are many reports of effects of cognition on perception that do not stand up under scrutiny (Durgin et al., 2009; Firestone, 2013; Firestone & Scholl, 2013, 2016a, 2016b). After giving a list of problems with many putative effects of cognition on perception, Valenti and Firestone note, "In the entire literature on top-down effects of cognition on perception, one class of findings stands apart in straightforwardly overcoming many of the above weaknesses: a collection of results known as "memory color" effects (Valenti & Firestone, 2019).

One type of memory color effect presents subjects with a picture of a common object colored at random (a banana might be purple). Subjects are asked to adjust the color to look a neutral gray. They twiddle two knobs, one of which controls the red/green axis and the other of which controls the blue/yellow axis. The memory color effect is that in order to make a banana look gray, subjects adjust it 13%–22% toward the blue direction (Witzel & Hansen, 2015; Witzel, Olkkonen, & Gegenfurtner, 2017; Witzel, Valkova, Hanswen, & Gegenfurtner, 2011).

Further, this effect can be predicted by Bayesian modeling in terms of combining a stimulus with a memory representation of the color as shown in Figure 10.5. (See the caption to Figure 10.6 and Witzel et al., 2017). So, this looks like the kind of top-down effect that might well challenge a joint in which subjects'

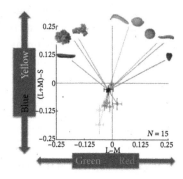

Figure 10.5 Subjects are presented with randomly colored common fruits and vegetables. They are asked to adjust a red/green knob and a yellow/blue knob to make the pictures look a neutral gray. The horizontal axis represents the green/red dimension and the vertical axis the yellow/blue dimension. What the diagram shows is that stereotypical yellow fruits such as bananas and lemons are adjusted so that they are objectively bluish with a bit of green added. The black circle and square near the center indicate the adjustments people make when the stimulus is a uniform disk/"noisy" pattern disk. The location of the black circle and square slightly in the blue/green direction shows a slight blue/green bias. Thanks to Maria Olkkonen for this figure. (See Olkkonen, Hansen, & Gegenfurtner, 2008.) This figure requires color. There is a free pdf on the Oxford University Press web site that has the color version of this and all the other figures.

knowledge of an object's typical color is enmeshed with perceptual processing of (a picture of) that object.

However, there is reason to think that memory color is not a general effect of knowledge on perception. The effect works for yellow and blue but not for paradigms of red and green. For example, there is a negative effect on hearts (Witzel & Hansen, 2015). That is, subjects adjust a picture of a heart so as to be slightly reddish rather than greenish to make it look gray. There are near zero effects for the classic red coke insignia, the typical red strawberry, and the classic red fire extinguisher, and only a weak effect for green ping pong tables. But there are strong positive effects for bananas, the classic yellow German mailbox, blue smurfs and Nivea tins, and the purple Milka container (Witzel et al., 2011). (As you can see from the diagram, there are effects for orange and green items so long as they have some admixture of blue and yellow.)

I mentioned an old experiment by Delk and Fillenbaum (1965) in which subjects were asked to adjust a background to match a heart shape. The background they choose is redder than if the shape is a circle or a square. The methodology of the studies by Gegenfurtner, Witzel, et al. are so far superior

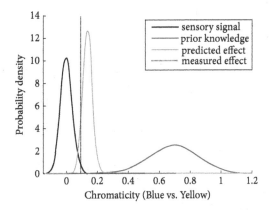

Figure 10.6 Bayesian treatment of the memory color effect modeled. The x-axis represents the blue-yellow channel, the y-axis the probability that a given stimulus will have a color at a point in that channel. The blue line represents the sensory signal of a gray item. (It is zero on the blue-yellow axis). The red curve represents the chromaticity of a typical banana. The idea is that the red curve represents the "knowledge" of a typical observer of the color of a banana. The gray curve combines the red and blue curves, and the dotted line is the point in the blue-yellow dimension that the subject reaches in order to make the banana look gray. The size of the top-down effect in this figure is 13.7%. Thanks to Chrisoph Witzel for this figure. (See Witzel et al., 2017; Witzel, Olkkonen, & Gegenfurtner, 2018.) This figure requires color. There is a free pdf on the Oxford University Press web site that has the color version of this and all the other figures.

to the Delk and Fillenbaum methods that I am inclined to doubt their result. Alternatively, the method used might have encouraged the use of mental imagery, superimposed on perception (Macpherson, 2012).

Returning to the discussion of the results by Gegenfurtner, Witzel, et al., even though subjects believe that both gray photos and gray drawings represent bananas, the effect is larger for fully textured photos. One hypothesis that the experimenters discuss is that the effect is based on associations within the visual system between on the one hand, shape and texture, and on the other hand color. One point in favor of that hypothesis is illustrated in Figure 10.7. This figure compares the memory color effect illustrated above in Figure 10.5 with the same experiment run with textureless depictions of the same common fruits and vegetables. As you can see, the textureless effects are tiny by comparison. Still, the shapes of the lemon and banana are shapes the subjects would know are meant to depict lemons and bananas. If the phenomenon is an effect of knowledge, why is the effect so much smaller for the pictures? (Cf. Deroy, 2013, on this point and Brogaard & Gatzia, 2017b, for a different view.)

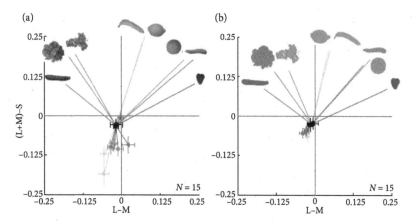

Figure 10.7 On the left we have the diagram from Figure 10.5. On the right we have a diagram representing the same experiment run with textureless pictures of the common fruits and vegetables. What is illustrated is that the memory color effects are much smaller without texture in the pictures. Thanks to Maria Olkkonen for this figure. (See Olkkonen et al., 2008.) This figure requires color. There is a free pdf on the Oxford University Press web site that has the color version of this and all the other figures.

Further evidence that memory color effects stem from within the visual system comes from a brain imaging study using "multivoxel pattern analysis," a technique in which smallish individual volumes of cortex are analyzed jointly. Bannert and Bartels (2013) showed subjects eight objects thought to have colors that are salient to their subjects (broccoli, lettuce, banana, tennis ball, strawberry, coke can, Nivea container, and blue traffic sign). The objects were presented to some subjects in color and other subjects in grayscale. While subjects viewed the grayscale objects, Bannert and Bartels were able to decode the colors of the objects in V1, providing further evidence that the memory color effect is real. More importantly, they were able to provide evidence that at least part of the cause of the color representations in V1 were coming from a mid-level visual area, V4+. Thus we have evidence that the effect is within the visual system.

In sum, there is no reason to think that the memory color effects are effects of cognition on perception and there is some reason to think these effects are a result of associations within vision itself.

I have been arguing that memory color effects, if they occur, may be effects within vision rather than effects of cognition on vision. But there is some reason to doubt that these effects are visual at all. One problem is that the effects are so large that they should be clearly visible, but they are not. A gray banana such as the one pictured in Figure 10.8 should look 13%–22% as yellow as a yellow

Figure 10.8 Gray banana. Thanks to Chaz Firestone for this image.

banana (Valenti & Firestone, 2019). A 22% effect would be 3–5 times over the threshold for discrimination (Valenti & Firestone, 2019). Take a look at Figure 10.8 for yourself. Does it look yellowish?

Valenti and Firestone (2019) note that the technique of adjusting an arbitrarily colored object to "look gray" allows for strategic responding. There are many shades of gray. When asked to make a banana "look gray," subjects may choose a shade of gray that does not have a hint of yellow, resulting in a bluish shade that still qualifies as gray (Zeimbekis, 2013). Valenti and Firestone note that such an effect could explain the fact that the memory color effects work for blue/yellow but not red/green once one notes that discrimination along the blue/yellow axis is worse than on the red/green axis. Subjects who try to make a strawberry gray will tolerate only a bit of green, whereas subjects who try to make a banana gray will tolerate a lot of blue because they are worse at discriminating how much blue they are adding.

Valenti and Firestone (2019) did experiments to confirm these ideas. Their experiments used an "odd one out" methodology illustrated in Figure 10.9. The three items in Figure 10.9 are colored gray, bluish, and bluish. Importantly the bluishness is exactly the shade that subjects adjusted the color of the banana to be to look neutral gray in Witzel's study (2016). (The stimuli were provided by Witzel.) The prediction of the memory color theory would be that the left disk and the banana both look gray, so the odd one out would be the right-most disk. The prediction of the no-memory color theory would be that the odd one out would be the left gray disk, since that was actually a different color from the others. As you can see from the graph, the memory color option was rarely picked whereas the no-memory color option was picked in the majority of cases. Twenty-seven percent of subjects picked the middle picture, which was predicted by neither theory. Valenti and Firestone suggest that subjects who did not look closely enough to see any difference in color just chose the one that was different in shape. Valenti and Firestone also looked at bluish banana, gray disk, gray banana; bluish disk, gray banana, gray disk; and gray banana, bluish disk, bluish banana. In each case, the memory color theory was strongly disconfirmed.

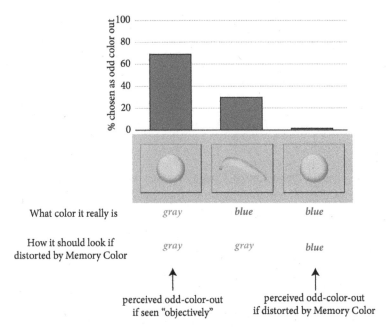

Figure 10.9 An illustration of one of the stimuli from Valenti and Firestone (2019, p. 6). The colors are gray, blue, blue, and subjects favored the gray one as the "odd one out" instead of the blue disk as the odd one out as predicted by the memory color theory. Reprinted with permission of Elsevier. This figure requires color. There is a free pdf on the Oxford University Press web site that has the color version of this and all the other figures.

Valenti and Firestone suggest a criticism: that the instructions focused subjects on the color of pixels on the screen instead of the objects like bananas. They did another version that was the same as the previous one except that after the subjects made their "odd one out" judgment, the pictures disappeared and subjects had to remember which locations had contained bananas. The idea behind this manipulation was that they would have to focus on the objects and not just the pixels. The results were the same. Valenti and Firestone did another series of experiments, replicating (Delk & Fillenbaum, 1965) and once again showing that the effects are not effects on perception. The upshot of the whole series of experiments is that all or most memory color effects appear to be effects on perceptual judgment rather than on perception itself.

One concern I have about the Valenti and Firestone approach is that the stimuli are insufficiently ambiguous. I have seen one demo of a memory color effect (by Rosa Lafer-Sousa and Michael Cohen) that has not yet been published but that seemed pretty strong. It involved a black and white American flag in very

very dim light that seemed to have reddish stripes. My view is that the jury is still out on memory color.

It is often assumed that effects of memory on color perception show cognitive penetration. For example, Berit Brogaard and Dimitria Gatzia say,

> We know from color science that color experiences are not purely perceptual: which hue we experience depends on a variety of factors besides the spectral properties of the object, the illumination, and the intrinsic makeup of our visual system, including the environment we evolved in, the background of the object, our prior encounters with the object in question, the characteristic color of the object, etc.... If it turns out that our color experiences are indeed directly affected by color-related beliefs, knowledge, or memory acquired after the maturity of the sensory system, then it follows that color experience is cognitively penetrable. (2017b, p. 194)

However, even if memory color effects are effects on perception (contrary to Valenti & Firestone) a dependence on prior encounters with the type of object does not show cognitive penetration, since whether cognitive penetration is involved depends on what kind of trace of those encounters is mediating the effect. That is, whether an effect of memory on perception is a case of cognitive penetration depends on what kind of memory is involved. If the memory in question is coded in associations within vision, the effect is not cognitive penetration or cognitive anything.

Of course, someone might want to use the word "knowledge" to include stored associations in the visual system. I am not arguing that the cognitive sense of "knowledge" used here is the only legitimate use of the term. To remind the reader, cognition and knowledge are here understood in terms of propositional and conceptual representations that function in inference, reasoning, action-planning, problem solving, evaluating, deciding, and the like—where reference to "and the like" is meant to indicate a natural family of propositional conceptual processes.

Pete Mandik has argued that certain illusions show perception is conceptual. One is memory color, just discussed. The other has to do with the fact that the color we see something as having has to do with our visual appreciation of the shapes of the objects and the context of lighting as indicated by the distribution of light and shadow over various objects. As he puts it, "there's scientific evidence that the colors objects visually appear to have depends (sometimes and perhaps all the time) on their visual shape and what categories the seen objects are seen as belonging to" (2017, p. 230). However, the explanation of memory color may well apply to these cases.

There is another kind of case in which familiarity with objects influences perception. Retinal motion is a guide to speed in the world, but real-world objects at different distances can be moving at vastly different speeds while impinging on the retina in the same way. The visual system has been shown to use prototypical size in these computations. Martín et al. compared appreciation of visual speed of a tennis ball and a basketball with subjects who were familiar with both and found an effect of prototypical size (Martin, Chambeaud, & Barraza, 2015). However, since object-size is known to be represented within the visual system (Long et al., 2016), this could well be an effect within the visual system.

Memory color probably is not a case of cognitive penetration, but I discussed many cases of cognitive penetration in the last chapter, the most dramatic of which have to do with ambiguous stimuli. But I have argued that none of the genuine cases of cognitive penetration that I know about impugn a joint.

Why would cognitive penetration impugn a joint? If what we know could freely affect what we see, that would make one wonder whether the differences in iconicity, conceptuality, and propositionality already pinpointed are real, or if real, are as important as one might have thought from what I have said so far. Differences like iconic/discursive, nonconceptual/conceptual and nonpropositional/propositional, if real, should have architectural consequences in some kinds of computational separation. And such architectural consequences do seem to be manifested in the cases of known illusions and apparent motion discussed earlier.

To summarize the top-down effects discussed so far:

- Spatial attention: These are effects of cognition on perception, but may not always change accuracy conditions of the perceptions as explained in connection with Carrasco's results.
- Feature-based attention: These cognitive effects on perception do change accuracy conditions, but so far it appears that the mechanisms by which they work divide into the cognitive and the perceptual, so these cases may not challenge a joint
- Ambiguous stimuli: Many of these cases involve dramatic changes in accuracy conditions (e.g., duck vs. rabbit), and in representations even in early vision. Even the Necker cube involves very different surface representations. In the case of reversible figures, there may be competing bottom-up perceptions. The role of cognition may be in choosing between them. Nonreversible figures are better bets for cognitive infiltration of perception. However, to the extent that the mechanisms of these effects involve spatial attention or feature-based attention, the issues really reduce to the cases discussed in Chapter 9.

- Mental imagery: These cases are also dramatic effects of cognition on perception-like representations, but a case against a joint on the basis of mental imagery has not been made.
- Figure-ground effects: These are dramatic effects, but in many classic cases are modulated not by knowledge but by familiarity or by a non-cognitive form of memory. The only clear cases of cognitive penetration of figure/ground perception are due to feature-based attention.
- Memory color: These cases are probably not cases of cognitive effects on color perceptions but rather they are either effects on perceptual judgment rather than perception, or, if they are effects on perception, they are effects of associations within the visual system.
- I also discussed the shooter task in Chapter 3. The evidence presented suggested that at least one version of the task involved an effect on perceptual judgment rather than perception.

Summing up, some of these cases involve cognitive effects on perception but have not been shown to threaten a joint. Others do not involve cognitive effects on perception at all. There are different ways for top-down effects to coexist with a joint in nature.

Opponents of a joint in nature between perception and cognition often put the question like this: "Is what we perceive influenced by our current goals, knowledge, and expectations?" Or like this: "The same sensory input or set of inputs can produce different perceptual experiences depending on the attentional state of the viewer?" (These are from p. 2 of Lupyan, 2017.) But as we have seen, a yes answer to these questions need not impugn the joint.

What is the upshot of the cases of cognitive penetration just discussed for the architecture of the mind? Are there no perceptual modules? That is the topic of the next chapter (11).

11
Modularity

I have been arguing that perception is nonconceptual, iconic, and nonpropositional. The purpose of this chapter is to examine how much truth there is in the modularity approach to cognitive architecture. One dimension of modularity is informational encapsulation. The classic example is that illusions continue to fool the eye even when one knows that they are illusions, as illustrated in Figure 11.1.

Jesse Prinz argues for sensory representations in both perception and cognition—the difference being that the computational processes of perception are different from those of for example working memory (Prinz, 2006b). I have been arguing for a contrary view based on the fact that perceptual representations are and cognitive representations are not iconic, nonconceptual and nonpropositional. But there is also an architectural dimension of the difference between perception and cognition.

Jerry Fodor (1983) characterized modules in terms of a list of nine diagnostic properties that are supposed to apply to input systems but not to central cognition.[1] Those properties are: domain specificity, mandatory operation, limited central accessibility, fast processing, informational encapsulation, "shallow" outputs, fixed neural architecture, characteristic and specific breakdown pattern, and characteristic ontogenetic pace and sequencing. Each module was supposed to have its own "database" and its own algorithms, which were available to the computations of that module but not to other modules.

As you recall from Chapter 9, an informationally encapsulated module cannot use information from central cognition—or from other modules. Fodor initially suggested very fine-grained modules, for example, distinct modules for color, 3D shape, spatial relations, faces of conspecifics, and visual guidance of actions (1983, p. 47). Subsequently, modularists have tended to regard vision—at least early vision—as itself a module.

As mentioned earlier, Fodor emphasized informational encapsulation. But as the multimodal nature of perception has become clearer, modularists have de-emphasized informational encapsulation in favor of an emphasis on cognitive penetration (in which the contents of cognition influence the contents of

---

[1] As Fodor notes, Chomsky used the term "module" in a different way, for a body of representation (Samuels, 2012).

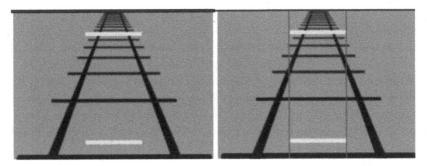

Figure 11.1 The top yellow line looks longer than the bottom yellow line even when one knows that and even sees that they are the same length. This image is in the public domain in the United States because it was solely created by NASA. NASA copyright policy states that "NASA material is not protected by copyright unless noted." From the Wikipedia article "Subjective Constancy."

perception), thereby allowing for information sharing among perceptual modalities while excluding direct content-specific effects of cognition on perception.

Many writers have used a weaker notion of module oriented around functional specialization and especially domain specificity (Coltheart, 1999; Ogilvie & Carruthers, 2015, 2016). Domain specificity is a matter of restrictions on the class of inputs that the module processes. In a recent *Nature Reviews Neuroscience* article, the neuroscientists Robert Spunt and Ralph Adolphs say, "We concur with others[2] that domain specificity should be the defining characteristic of a module; however, we go further in suggesting that informational encapsulation and cognitive impenetrability are not only unnecessary but in fact counter-productive for producing domain specificity" (2017, p. 565). They term their view "new look modularity." They call it "modularity" because they think there are modules defined by domain specificity, and "new look" because, as with the New Look figures like Bruner discussed in Chapter 1, they advocate cognitive penetration and violations of informational encapsulation. However, the cases of cognitive penetration that they discuss are diachronic, the effect of cognition on shaping the perceptual systems.

They say that domain specificity can arise because the mechanisms that process that domain only receive inputs of a certain sort, as for example with face perception that only receives inputs from the eyes. Another mechanism that they describe is that a system may be domain-specific because its computational machinery is specialized, as with language. The specialization of face areas for faces might arise in that way. And the specialization of the visual word form area may

---

[2] They reference Coltheart (1999).

be due to an interaction between experience, restricted inputs, and restricted computational properties.

But these effects are diachronic and are excluded by Fodor and Pylyshyn, whose modularity thesis concerned synchronic cognitive penetration, that is, perception rather than perceptual learning. Further, as I argued in Chapter 1 in the section on clarifying the concepts of perception and cognition, there is a rationale for clarifying the concepts of perception and cognition so as to home in on a joint if there is one. As I argued, that could militate for excluding diachronic effects from cognitive penetration.

It should be noted that although diachronic effects on perception do exist, they are greatly overestimated by writers who do not properly separate perceptual and post-perceptual effects. For example, a review article on the effects of language on color categorization (Regier & Kay, 2009, p. 439) says this:

> Does language affect perception? As noted above, several studies suggest that the answer is 'yes', at least in connection with color. These studies have shown that there is 'categorical perception' (CP: faster or more accurate discrimination of stimuli that straddle a category boundary) for color, and that differences in color category boundaries between languages predict where CP will occur... Moreover, several of these studies, and others... have shown that color CP disappears with a concurrent verbal interference task, confirming that color CP is language based.

However, if the language had really altered the visual system's category boundaries in these cases, the verbal interference tasks would not eliminate the effect. The very evidence cited by Regier and Kay to show diachronic cognitive penetration shows the opposite (Cf. Winawer, et al., 2007).

Ryan Ogilvie and Peter Carruthers also advocate a version of modularity in which domain specificity looms large and cognitive penetration is of little consequence. They define vision this way: "One can perfectly well characterize the visual system functionally, as the set of brain-mechanisms specialized for the analysis of signals originating from the retina" (2015). This sort of characterization of vision in terms of domain-specificity looks less like it gets to the heart of vision when one notes that as pointed out earlier, spatial perception, including visual perception, is characteristically multimodal, even at the level of the first cortical stage of visual processing (Murray et al., 2016). The spatial component of what is often thought of as the visual system is shared among all the spatial senses and is specialized for the analysis of signals containing spatial information from all the sense organs, not just the retina. So domain-specificity does not look like a good way of characterizing a module, at least if the different senses are supposed to be modular.

Earlier, I mentioned transcranial magnetic stimulation (TMS), in which an electromagnetic pulse is applied to the scalp, injecting noise into the cortical areas beneath and temporarily disabling that chunk of cortex. Sathian et al. (2001) used a setup in which blindfolded subjects felt the direction and texture of ridges with their index finger. A TMS pulse in somatosensory cortex disabled tactile perception of both texture and direction. Subjects said they felt pressure but not texture and direction. But a pulse in the occipital lobe, the part of the cortex most specialized for vision, disabled tactile perception of direction. Subjects said that they could feel the texture but did not know in which direction the ridges were pointing. "Visual" brain areas are often activated in tactile perception, and it has been reported that localized injuries in occipital cortex can cause both visual and tactile agnosia—inability to recognize objects (Sathian, Prather, & Zhang, 2004). Although much of what is usually thought of as visual machinery is really specialized for spatial analysis (Green, 2020b), it would be a mistake to think that there is anything that could be called a spatial module.

Carruthers is an advocate of the "massive" modularity view that jettisons cognitive impenetrability, focusing on, in addition to domain specificity, automaticity, fixed neural realization, and inaccessibility to the rest of cognition (Carruthers, 2006; Sperber, 2001). Massive modularists hold that in addition to the input system modules, there are many cognitive modules, notably modules concerned with various aspects of reasoning and decision-making. In addition, they hold that there is not much in the mind that is not modular (Samuels, 2012). In Chapter 9, I mentioned Carruthers's distinction between wide- and narrow-scope informational encapsulation. Carruthers holds that cognitive modules are wide-scope encapsulated in the sense that their access to the knowledge base is limited. Cognitive modules can use "fast and frugal" heuristics to compute over part of the knowledge base.

At the neural level, there are known to be a number of cortical areas, indicated in Figure 11.2, that respond most to certain stimuli. Although many controversies in this area rage, Spunt and Adolphs describe the evidence for "preferred domains" as "practically indisputable" (Spunt & Adolphs, 2017, p. 564). One controversy has to do with whether these specializations arise as a result of the application of general learning mechanisms to the acquisition of expertise or whether they are designed for the particular function. Another dispute concerns whether the areas that respond to, for example, faces, really are specialized for faces as opposed to the recognition of items that differ slightly in holistic configural features.

Many of Fodor's nine characteristics of modules have some truth to them even if they do not always co-occur (Prinz, 2006b). As we have just discussed, domain specificity has something to it. Also, it is true that, by and large, cognition does not have access to information that is internal to perceptual systems. However,

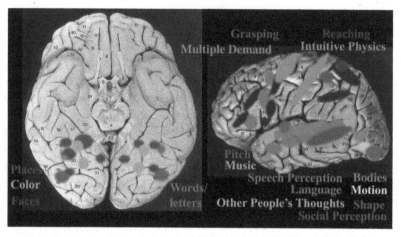

Figure 11.2 Specialized brain areas. The labeled colored patches indicate areas that are active when people are perceiving items of those categories. An earlier version can be found in (Kanwisher, 2010). As Kanwisher notes, these areas can be found in virtually all normal subjects with a short fMRI scan. This figure requires color. There is a free pdf on the Oxford University Press web site that has the color version of this and all the other figures. Thanks to Nancy Kanwisher for this figure.

as we saw in connection with the work by Bria Long in Chapter 8, there seems to be cognitive access to the ensemble computation stage of intermediate levels of the visual system. This is revealed in the fact that texturized pictures of animals look different from texturized pictures of artifacts and that texturized pictures of small artifacts look different from texturized pictures of large artifacts even when the pictures are the same size and even when subjects have no idea what is being represented (Long et al., 2017).

Automaticity, fast processing, and shallow outputs go together and can be characterized via Rodney Brooks's (and Errol Morris's) phrase, "fast, cheap and out of control" (Robbins, 2015). The fast processing condition does apply to perceptual systems with a few exceptions such as binocular fusion. However, perception is not distinctive in this respect, since all System 1 processing, including System 1 cognitive processing, is fast.

The shallow output feature is supposed to be associated with being computationally cheap and having informational content that is not very specific. Fodor was an advocate of conceptual outputs of perception and for him shallowness meant that the outputs of perception were basic-level concepts like the concept of a dog rather than the more specific and supposedly less computationally cheap concept of a Labrador retriever. (By the criterion of generality, the concept of an animal would be even cheaper, but that is not at the basic level.) As has often been pointed out, the criteria that specify the basic level are highly plastic. For example, for a dog expert, the category of Labrador retriever might be at the basic level and for a chair salesman, the category of dining room chair might be at the basic level. It is not at all clear that these occupations change perception in tandem with the cognitive changes implicated in the basic level.

Sine wave speech also illustrates another flaw in one of the nine criteria, mandatory processing. The idea of mandatory processing was supposed to be that modules aren't under cognitive control. So long as the signals are getting to the module, it processes the input. Thus, the language module automatically processes speech, and so long as the eyes are open, the visual module automatically processes visual information, etc. However, in the case of sine wave speech, one has a choice about whether to treat as the sine wave sound as speech or as noise: the sounds are ambiguous between words and meaningless sounds (Remez, Rubin, Pisoni, & Carrell, 1981). (The reader can hear examples by doing a search for "sine wave speech.") If one listens for speech, one hears words. You can verify this for yourself by googling some examples. YouTube has many examples.

Being fast, cheap, and out of control are properties often linked to cognitive impenetrability (Robbins, 2015). Speed is partly a function of automaticity, since there is supposed to be no time-consuming decision process about whether to process an input. It is because input systems do not have access to information in cognition that they can use fast computation that doesn't take up the resources that would be required to yield very specific representations.

As I have been pointing out, cognitive impenetrability is wrong as applied to perception. I noted that some of the most impressive cases of cognitive penetration involve ambiguous stimuli. These are impressive because the different percepts of ambiguous stimuli often involve different surface representations, showing penetration of early vision, contrary to Pylyshyn. When bottom-up factors are not decisive, there is room for the influence of top-down factors. However, in the case of reversible ambiguous stimuli, it may be that the role of the top-down factors is to choose between bottom-up percepts, showing that the role of penetration is limited. It is unclear however whether the perception of ambiguous figures that are not reversible can be thought of that way. Examples of nonreversible ambiguous pictures are Figure 9.5 and possibly the brick wall illusion of Figure 9.14. An auditory analog may be sine wave speech.

Fixed neural architecture was shown to be wrong by Mriganka Sur's lab, when they rewired the ferret auditory cortex to be a visual cortex. But something of the idea of fixed neural architecture was confirmed when the rewired auditory cortex turned out to have roughly the "pinwheel" structure of ocular dominance columns typical of the earliest visual cortex (Sharma, Angelucci, & Sur, 2000).

400   THE BORDER BETWEEN SEEING AND THINKING

Some of the other structures of visual cortex were reproduced in auditory cortex, though in a somewhat disorganized form.

In talking of characteristic ontogenetic pace and sequencing, Fodor is really referring to the claim of innateness of modules. I think it is fair to say that there is as much disagreement about this matter now as there was in 1983 when Fodor's book was published. Carey (2009) makes a powerful case for innateness of many systems, including perceptual systems, in humans as well as in animals. Prinz (2002, 2006b) makes the opposite case.

However, new techniques have provided strong evidence for innate mental capacities, especially in animals. One of the most powerful techniques is controlled rearing, in which the experimenter controls everything the newborn animal sees. I'll give a simple example of amodal completion from the early work of Giorgio Vallortigara and Lucia Regolin, who have pioneered the use of newly hatched chicks in discovering the innate capacities of the chicks. One line of work makes use of imprinting.

Vallortigara and Regolin get eggs that are about to hatch from farmers, then they hatch the eggs in a controlled environment. Chicks imprint on a moving object they see immediately on hatching and then they prefer to huddle with that object if presented with a choice. See Figure 11.3.

If imprinted on an object, newborn chicks that have never seen an occluded object prefer to huddle with an occluded version of that object rather than a broken one, suggesting an innate capacity for amodal completion. (See Figure 11.4 and Carey, 2009, pp. 58–59.) Similar studies with chicks that have not ever

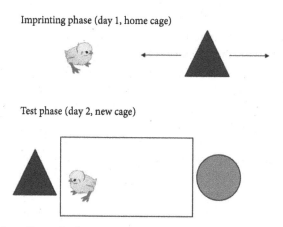

Figure 11.3 A newborn chick is imprinted on a moving object represented by the triangle. (The arrows represent movement.) Then, later when given a choice of huddling next to that object or a different object, the chick prefers the original object. Thanks to Susan Carey for this figure.

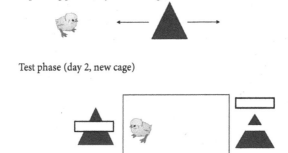

Figure 11.4 The chick is imprinted on an object and then if given a choice between that object occluded and another object with a gap plus the occluder, the chick prefers the occluded object. Thanks to Susan Carey for this figure.

seen an object go behind an occluder show that they search behind the occluding object the first time they see it, revealing an innate aspect of object-permanence. Similar methods show that chicks have a visual appreciation of the kind of contact causality to be discussed in the next chapter.

There have also been many neuroscience discoveries that tilt toward innateness. For example, face-selective cortical areas have been found in 4-month-old human infants (Spunt & Adolphs, 2017), suggesting an innate component to the face areas indicated in Figure 11.2.

Fodor's criterion of characteristic and specific breakdown pattern seems to have been interpreted by him to mean that there are specific brain areas, lesions in which cause specific deficits in modules. It is certainly true that perception and language are subject to specific lesion-caused deficits. Evidence is accumulating that specializations that seemed to be localized to specific cortical areas are better understood as a function of circuits involving many brain areas. Even face perception, once thought to be localized to the fusiform face area, is now known to be subserved by six cortical face patches that are linked together in a face-processing system (Chang & Tsao, 2017; Moeller et al., 2017; Tsao, Moeller, & Freiwald, 2008).

I mentioned in Chapter 9 that the most flagrant cases of cognitive penetration involve ambiguous stimuli in which cognition can tilt the perception one way or another. See Figure 9.5 for a notable example of an "irreversible" ambiguous stimulus and Figure 9.4 for "reversible" ambiguous stimuli. In the example of Figure 9.5, being told what the picture depicts can change the way it looks, including changing amodal contours. I mentioned the distinction between amodal and modal contours in Chapter 2 and Chapter 9. To save the reader the trouble of looking back to the Kanizsa Triangle from those chapters, I am reproducing

Figure 11.5 Kanizsa Triangle. Reprinted from earlier chapters for convenience. From the Wikipedia article "Illusory Contours."

it below as Figure 11.5. The triangle with the vertex pointing down has modal edges because of the apparent brightness difference between the triangle and the white background. In the case of the triangle with the vertex pointing up, one sees the black lines as completed behind the modal triangle but there is no apparent brightness difference. The completed edges are amodal.

Chapter 9 mentioned that cognitive penetration is involved in both amodal and modal contour interpolation. However, a recent article points out that Fodor's other criteria of modularity are met by modal and amodal interpolation (Keane, 2018).

Interpolation is domain specific in that it is devoted to completing contours that are partially specified in very specific ways. The edges must be aligned in specific ways; as mentioned earlier, they must be "relatable" in the sense of joinable by a smooth monotonically changing curve with no turn of more than 90°; they must not be blurry; and they must obey certain grouping conditions. Interpolation is fast, taking between 50 ms and 150 ms. When the bottom-up conditions are in place, interpolation is obligatory, independent of knowledge and attention. The elongated arm of Figure 9.3 illustrates the independence from knowledge. Interpolation is innate in chicks as illustrated above, but also in humans, though the ability to process speed and motion must be in place, and that takes about 2 months (Keane, 2018). The mechanisms of interpolation resist introspective access. We do not know the rules for interpolation by introspection; they are only revealed by experiments. The representations of interpolation are shallow in that they are confined to edges and surfaces. Finally, there are localized neural mechanisms of interpolation.

The upshot of all this is that Fodor's nine characteristics of modules do apply moderately well in some cases. Ironically, the one that Fodor and Pylyshyn thought was most important, cognitive impenetrability, survives less well than the others. Fortunately, the joint in nature between cognition and perception is not mainly dependent on modularity since the joint involves nonarchitectural elements having to do with format, state and content.

As I mentioned in Chapter 1, the phenomena that are most challenging for a joint in nature between perception and cognition include our appreciation of numerosity and causation. I now turn to that topic.

12
Core cognition and perceptual analogs of concepts

As noted earlier, joints in nature can survive borderline cases. I mentioned that glasses are rigid in the manner of solids but have the amorphous structure of liquids. The joint between liquids and solids is not impugned by glasses, because there is a difference in kind between the crystalline structure of solids and the amorphous structure of liquids. This difference in kind is revealed by the fact that glasses flow, albeit slowly at some temperatures and that when they break, they do not exhibit the "shear" properties of solids.

But Nick Shea has argued against a joint between cognition and perception, alleging that "core cognition" is not just a borderline case, but has properties that are fundamental to perception and also properties that are fundamental to cognition. He argues, specifically with regard to "core cognition," that "their borderline nature raises the possibility it may be impossible to distinguish them from perceptual states in such a way that the perception-cognition distinction does important explanatory work" (2014, p. 85).

If there are phenomena that have fundamental properties of both perception and cognition, they might be candidates for conceptual perception, and that would impugn the joint by impugning my claim that an important feature of the joint is that perception is constitutively nonconceptual and cognition is not. (Nonconceptual cognition is not so worrying since my claim is that cognition is not constitutively conceptual, propositional or iconic; and that claim does not rule out cases of nonconceptual cognition.)

Another form of potential damage to the joint has to do with the explanatory unity of the properties that characterize perception, iconic format, nonconceptuality, and nonpropositionality. As noted earlier, if there could be a category of mentality that for example is nonconceptual but also propositional, that would show that something is wrong with the picture I am presenting.

Perception of causation

Some of the phenomena Shea mentions reflect high-level perception, that is, perceptual representation of properties that go beyond those that are the direct

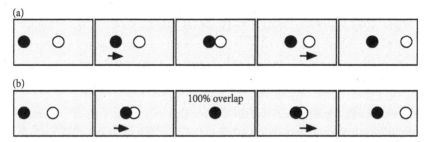

Figure 12.1 Top (a): classic Michotte causal launch, in which the dark disk is seen to cause the lighter disk to move. Bottom (b): Noncausal pass, in which the dark disk is normally seen to pass through the white disk, exchanging colors with it. Thanks to Brian Scholl for this figure. (Cf. Choi & Scholl, 2006.)

product of sensory transduction—shape, spatial relations, motion, texture, brightness and color. (See Chapter 2 for more on the difference between high-level and low-level perception.) I presented evidence in Chapter 2 that we perceive the high-level property of approximate numerosity. In this section, I will describe convincing evidence that we also visually perceive causal relations. Of course we also have *concepts* of numerosity and of causal relations. My strategy will be to argue that appealing to percepts of causal relations and also concepts of causal relations, we can explain the phenomena of core cognition having to do with causation: We do not need a third type of mental representation intermediate between percepts and concepts.

Shea mentions experiments on causation of a sort diagrammed in Figure 12.1a involving moving disks on a screen. In the 1930s, Albert Michotte (1946/1963) created stimuli in which disks on a screen can look as if one disk is causing another to move—like shadows of billiard balls hitting one another.[1] See Figure 12.1. (You can find a video illustration at http://perception.yale.edu/DemoFiles/Causality-Basics/Causality-Basics-launching.mov.)

Shea discusses the difference between two kinds of cases that fit Figure 12.1a, but which involve variation in whether there is or is not a delay between the movement of the first and second disk, the result being that for substantial delays, the interaction no longer looks causal. (The delay is between the third and fourth rectangle in Figure 12.1a.) Referencing the difference between causal and noncausal sequences, Shea says:

---

[1] Michotte says that Hume thought no mark of causation can be directly perceived, countering that, "if Hume had been able to carry out an experiment such as ours, there is no doubt that he would have been led to revise his views on the psychological origin of the popular idea of causality" (Michotte, 1946/1963, p. 256; Wagemans, van Lier, & Scholl, 2006).

The experienced difference between the two settings is input driven and partially encapsulated (e.g., against the knowledge that both are a matter of lights on a computer screen and neither is causal), but it is widely disputed whether a causal relation is something that can be perceived, as opposed to being contributed by cognition (Siegel, 2009). (Shea, 2014, p. 87)

However, I will argue in the rest of this section that the current state of evidence—specifically involving three recent articles (two of which came out after Shea's article)—shows it should no longer be disputed that we see causal relations in the sense of visually representing causation of a certain kind.

Of course, not all kinds of causation are observable, for example causation by omission. And the evidence I will be talking about is silent on many kinds of observable causation, as, for example, when a flame causes metal to glow (Rips, 2017). What has been shown is that we perceptually represent at least one kind of contact causation that could be described as billiard-ball-causality. Here I will focus on that kind of causation. In the rest of this section, I will explain a number of lines of research that establish that we can perceive causation.

Known Illusion

A sequence like that in Figure 12.1a looks causal even when subjects know it is not. Indeed, so long as the white disk does not move faster than the dark disk, it looks as if every bit of the white disk's motion is determined by the dark disk (Kominsky & Scholl, 2020). These experiments typically involve shapes presented on computer screens. Subjects all know that the shapes are just a matter of computer controlled pixels and so do not have the kind of physical instantiations required for the kind of causality portrayed but the sequences still look causal. This is a classic "known illusion" that is typical of perception (Helton, 2017; Quilty-Dunn, 2015). As with the Müller-Lyer illusion and the illusion of Figure 11.1, one visually represents the situation as having properties that one knows it does not have.

Adaptation

Causal sequences have adaptive effects on other causal sequences. Again, see Chapter 2 for an extensive discussion of adaptation and its perceptual nature. Rolfs et al. (2013) used stimuli like those in Figure 12.1a and b. Although sequences like that in in Figure 12.1a look causal so long as there are no substantial delays or gaps, whether sequences like that in Figure 12.1b look causal depends on the degree of overlap between the black and white disks. If the overlap is zero, then we have the same sequence as in in Figure 12.1a and it looks causal. However, if the overlap is 100%, as depicted in in Figure 12.1b, the sequence normally looks as if the black disk passes through the white disk and changes color, moving to the right. This is seen as noncausal, the first disk having no effect on the second disk. (Recall that 'causal' here refers to one kind of causation.) However, if the degree of overlap is roughly 50%, the sequence is ambiguous. It can be seen as causal or as a noncausal pass. (Of course such bistable perceptions are themselves characteristic of perception as noted in Chapter 2.) Such a bistable display can be seen at http://perception.yale.edu/DemoFiles/Causality-CausalCapture/Causality-CausalCapture-pass.mov. If you see a display as causal but keep looking at repeated presentations, inevitably you will see it as a pass.

Rolfs et al. presented subjects with repeated causal sequences like that in in Figure 12.1a and found that after seeing many causal sequences, subjects were significantly less likely to see an ambiguous sequence as causal. This is the classic "repulsive" effect of adaptation, which as argued in Chapter 2 stems from perception. There was no repulsive effect if the black disk moved past the white disk before the white disk started to move, a sequence that does not look causal. There was also a repulsive effect of being exposed to versions of Figure 12.1a, in which the white disk moves at more than twice the speed of the black disk. These cases look as if the black disk is causing some but not all of the motion of the white disk.

Retinotopic

The adaptation effects just described are retinotopic. (Recall that two items are in the same retinotopic location when they project to the same part of the retina and in the same spatiotopic location when they are perceived as in the same area of space. Retinotopic effects move with the eye.) There were only slight adaptive effects unless the two displays were at the same retinotopic location. As mentioned earlier, there are no known cases of cognitive effects that are retinotopic (Rolfs et al., 2013; Scholl & Gao, 2013). Also as explained earlier, retinotopic effects are dependent on the many retinotopic areas in visual cortex. (But what shows those areas are visual rather than cognitive? See Chapter 2 for a response to this sort of circularity concern.)

The Rolfs et al. retinotopic adaptation results were replicated by Kominsky and Scholl (2020). These results have met with some skepticism on the part of commentators who conflate perception and conception of causality. Arnold et al.

(Arnold, Petrie, Gallagher, & Yarrow, 2015) say (p. 7) that the retinotopic adaptation of causality

> ... seems surprising, as people will readily infer a causal relationship between two events when those events are widely separated either in space or time. For instance, people may report the sensation that their own footfall has caused a distant light to turn on/off if the two events happen to coincide in time. Alternatively, people readily report that a bolt of lightning has caused subsequent thunder, which might not be heard until seconds later. Such a malleable approach to inferring causality does not sit comfortably with the suggestion that mechanisms that detect such relationships are located at low-levels of the visual hierarchy, and have retinotopically-mapped receptive fields. (Rolfs et al., 2013)

However, our inference that a bolt of lightning causes thunder is conceptual and cognitive and so has no bearing on the perception of causality. As Kominsky and Scholl say, it conflates causal perception and causal reasoning. The sense that a footfall causes a light to turn on may be explained in the same way—or it may have a perceptual component.

Categorical perception

Perception of causation is categorical in a number of respects. Categorical perception is explained in Chapter 6. Michotte showed in the 1930s that small differences in the delay between the third and fourth rectangle in Figure 12.1a make for big differences between seeing the event as causal and seeing it as two motions that are not causally related. This is categorical perception: A small difference in the objective parameter makes a big difference in the percept (Butterfill, 2009; Harnad, 1987b).

In the experiment by Rolfs et al. described above, they varied the overlap between the black and white disks in Figure 12.1b. As mentioned earlier, the more the overlap, the more likely the sequence was to be seen as a noncausal pass. However, these curves were significantly nonlinear. In particular, small differences in the vicinity of 50% overlap made very large differences in the probability of the sequences being seen as causal. Again we have the signature of categorical perception. The categorical perception of causation is important because categorical perceptual representations are perceptual analogs of concepts that have played an outsized role in influencing thinkers to think that what are really purely perceptual phenomena are somehow intermediate between perception and cognition.

Habituation

The difference between adaptation and habituation is described in footnote 3 in Chapter 6. Briefly, adaptation is an aftereffect in which a stimulus subsequent to the adapting stimulus is seen differently because sensitivity is decreased as thresholds rise. Habituation is loss of interest. The baby looks at (for example) its feet instead of at the screen. Habituation does not argue as strongly for the perceptual nature of the states, but it is some evidence, especially in infants. Six-month-old infants who habituated to A launching B recovered interest to B launching A. But if you add temporal gaps to make the sequences look non-causal, you get very little dishabituation (Leslie & Keeble, 1987). The changes in spatiotemporal properties were the same in the causal reversal as in the noncausal reversal. This result suggests that 6-month-olds see the Michotte causal sequences as substantially different from noncausal sequences.

Pop-out

Certain kinds of causal sequences "pop out" in the presence of other causal sequences. As argued in Chapter 2, pop-out is an indicator of perception. See Figure 2.13 and Figure 4.3 for other examples of pop-out.

In the sequence in Figure 12.1a, if the two disks move at the same speed (that is, the left disk moves at a constant speed until it touches the right disk and then that disk moves off at that same speed), the event is seen as causal, and it is seen as causal even if the left disk moves at a higher speed than the right disk. This type of causation is usually called "launching." However, if the second disk moves off at three times the speed of the first (1:3), it is seen as causal but as also involving a source of movement in the right disk itself. If the right disk moves at substantially more than twice the speed of the left disk, the sequence is called "triggering."

Kominsky et al. (2017b) used a "visual search" task of the sort mentioned in connection with the discussion involved with Figure 2.13 and Figure 4.3. Subjects saw three videos at once, two launchings with identical speeds (either 1:1 or 3:3) and one that was 3:1 on some trials and 1:3 on others. In seeing the three videos, the 1:3 triggering popped out but the 3:1 did not. The index of pop-out was speed of finding the event, as in the cases discussed earlier.

Kominsky et al. (2017b) also did a habituation study with 8-month-old infants. Infants who were habituated to 1:1 events strongly dishabituated to 1:3 events but not to 3:1 events, suggesting a perceptual similarity between 1:1 and 3:1 but not between those and 1:3 events. (As a control, they showed there were no such disparities in noncausal events—such as the ones with spatial or temporal offsets described above.)

The following can be shown in Newtonian mechanics: In a collision in which a moving object hits a stationary object and the mass of the stationary object is negligible compared to that of the moving object, and kinetic energy and momentum are conserved, the velocity imparted to the stationary object will approach a value of double that of the original moving object. No matter how massive the moving object and how light the stationary object, the imparted motion cannot exceed double the original velocity. The calculation is explained by Kominsky et al. (2017a). Amazingly the visual system may have evolved so as to respect that piece of Newtonian mechanics.

These visual search and habituation results indicate a categorical difference between launching and triggering. However, Kominsky and Scholl (2020) did not find a categorical difference between launching and triggering using the adaptation technique described above. As Kominsky and Scholl note, visual search and habituation may be more sensitive measures than adaptation because adaptation is sensitive to categorical joints in the visual system whereas habituation and visual search are more sensitive to differences *within* perceptual categories. For example, there is a categorical difference between straight and curved lines, but nonetheless a very curved line is easy to find among mildly curved lines. Launchings of 3:1, 1:1, and 1:3 all look causal even though subjects can distinguish between them. That can explain why they all adapt one another even though 1:3 pops out in visual search because of the self-generated motion.

Shea argues—of our appreciation of causation in Michotte-style experiments—that "it may be impossible to distinguish them from perceptual states in such a way that the perception-cognition distinction does important explanatory work" (p. 14), but it should no longer be controversial that we have straightforwardly perceptual appreciation of causation. In sum, this section has provided evidence that causal relations can be perceived and that that perception is categorical.

Core cognition

Let us now return to the question of this chapter of whether core cognition impugns the joint between perception and cognition because it has properties that are fundamental to both perception and cognition.

Susan Carey and Elizabeth Spelke (Carey, 2009; Carey & Spelke, 1994) introduced the landmark theoretical idea of "core cognition" (sometimes called "core knowledge"). Core cognition concerns at least three domains: physical objects/causal interactions, number, and agency/goal directed action. The first of these comprises the phenomena involving causation described in the last section. According to Carey's characterization (I will mainly be discussing her version rather than Spelke's), in each of these domains there are innate, domain-specific perceptual analyzers that identify items in the domain; innate conceptual roles with conceptual content; continuity throughout development; and a shared evolutionary history with other mammals and in some cases, other nonmammalian vertebrates.

Some of the items in the list of properties of the last sentence seem very perceptual, e.g., domain-specific perceptual analyzers. But some seem clearly cognitive, e.g., conceptual content. Here is what Shea (2014, p 86) has to say about this combination of the perceptual and the cognitive.

> Susan Carey has emphasized another set of examples which she calls the systems of "core cognition" (Carey, 2009). These systems are intermediate between the paradigmatically perceptual and the paradigmatically cognitive. Two of her flagship cases concern numerosity. Carey (2009) marshals an impressive array of evidence for the existence of two different relatively low-level systems that are involved in representing quantities. The first is the object-file system, which individuates small arrays of objects in parallel and keeps track of which is which as they move. While the numerosity of these sets is not represented explicitly, numerosity is implicit in the way the system operates: comparing arrays via 1-1 correspondence and keeping track of the addition or subtraction of small numbers of objects from the set. The second is the analogue magnitude system, which is capable of keeping track of the approximate number of items in a large set (Dehaene, 2011).
>
> Carey argues that these processes deserve their own category in the psychological inventory. They are neither clearly perceptual nor clearly cognitive. They operate amodally, on a variety of modal inputs, but the calculations they perform are informationally encapsulated and relatively independent of what is going on in the rest of cognition.[2]

Two of the systems of core cognition are concerned with number, and one of those is the "analog magnitude system" that governs appreciation of approximate numerosity. But we have seen that approximate numerosity can be perceived. In

---

[2] Burge also seems to regard core cognition as probably post-perceptual. (See footnote 7 in Burge, 2019, and p. 1 of Burge, 2010c.)

fact, you should have perceived it when you looked at Figure 2.3 and Figure 2.4 in Chapter 2! So, approximate numerosity—like causation—is represented perceptually as well as conceptually. In the passage just quoted, Shea says that the systems of core cognition are "are neither clearly perceptual nor clearly cognitive." No: The perception of causation is paradigmatically perceptual, albeit a case of paradigmatic *high-level* perception. And the same is true for the perception of numerosity. Of course we also have concepts of causation and numerosity that play a role in cognition.

My response then to the idea that core cognition is neither perceptual nor cognitive is that it is both—that is, there is pure perception of objects, numerosity, and causation, but also automatic or nearly automatic conceptualization of those perceptions, resulting in the characteristics of cognition, for example innate conceptual role.

Judging from her replies to her critics (Carey, 2011a), Carey might agree. Burge (2011) argued against what he took to be Carey's view that "object representations are exclusively nonperceptual." (p. 125). Carey replied that although she has argued for conceptual object representations in young children, adults have perceptual object representations and young children may have them too.

I am not denying that core cognition is a single system albeit a system that involves disparate parts. The system comprising perception and cognition of causation may have a single genetic blueprint that involves both perception and cognition, notably certain inferences regarding causation.

Let's take a closer look at a supposed case of inference in object perception (one of the core domains).

For example, consider the study diagrammed in Figure 12.2, in which an occluded appreciation of causation leads to dishabituation when the occluder is removed and expectations are contradicted. As Carey says about this case,

> even though contact between the two objects was not visible during the habituation trials, infants treat the contact test event as familiar based on the partially occluded habituation event. For this to be so, infants must form an inference or expectation about the unseen causal interaction occurring during habituation. Thus, as young as there is evidence that infants perceive causality in Michotte's launching events, they recruit these representations even when not part of a data-driven perceptual process. (Carey, 2009, p. 226).

Dishabituation, as you will recall from the earlier discussion, is recovery of interest. As was shown in detail in Chapter 6, infants can habituate and dishabituate to color without having any conceptual abilities with regard to color. Recall that infants saw a red ball come out from one side of screen, going back behind it; and

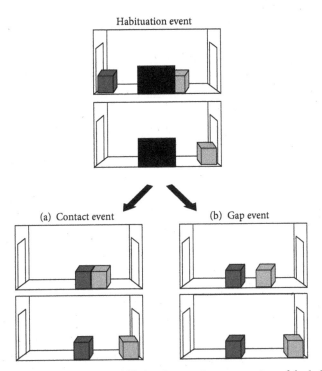

Figure 12.2 Subjects (8-month-old babies) viewed a presentation of the habituation event in the top panel, in which a moving object comes in from the left, goes behind a screen and another object emerges from the right. The motions are consistent with a smooth path. Then the screen is raised and they see either the situation on the lower right or the lower left. If there is a gap between the incoming and outgoing objects (no contact), as on the right, subjects dishabituate (Muentener & Carey, 2010) Thanks to Susan Carey for this diagram.

a green ball from the other side that returns behind the screen. When the screen was lifted, the infants were not surprised to see just one ball. In this and many other cases presented in Chapter 6, infants that habituated to color were unable to use color in forming expectations or inferring which side of the screen an interesting event would appear on. So, dishabituation in this case may not indicate any conceptual abilities of the sort involved in inference.

A further point is that the reaction of surprise as events unfold need not reflect a prediction or inference or expectation about what will happen. Jenny Judge argues that at least in the case of musical surprise, an ongoing model of the situation can produce a reaction of surprise when the current model is disconfirmed. The model is constantly updated and when an update now conflicts with what is being heard now, the surprise reaction is triggered. The key distinction here is between the consequences of a model for a later time at which there is a present-tense representation and the use of those consequences to make a future-tense prediction. Judge argues that at each present period the model is updated, but that process of updating for the present moment needn't involve any actual future-tense prediction (Judge, 2018).

In sum, some cases of what look like expectation can be handled entirely by the perceptual system. In other cases, cognition is involved, but neither of these cases require anything other than perception and cognition. That is the basic point of this chapter, but I will say a bit more about how perception and cognition are related to each other.

As noted in Chapter 5, an object-file is a representation that maintains reference to an object over time and stores and updates information about the object (Green & Quilty-Dunn, 2021; Kahneman et al., 1992; Quilty-Dunn, 2017). Chapter 5 makes the case that working memory representations can use perceptual materials but are cognitive representations. Carey and her colleagues (Carey, 2009; Feigenson et al., 2002) have shown that working memory can use conceptual representations that include iconic perceptual materials, representing varying environmental magnitudes via varying mental magnitudes. Babies that are shown graham cracker pieces that vary in size deposited in two containers will crawl toward the container with more cracker.

Carey presents evidence that the same working memory representations support both numerosity cognition and cognition in which amount of stuff is at issue. (See Chapter 5: the section "Object files in working memory.") The difference depends on contextual factors that make one or another aspect of the task salient. These are cognitive representations, but similar factors are involved in perceptual representations. When objects are presented, one after another in a habituation experiment, similar contextual variables determine whether the infant habituates to size or number (Carey, 2009, pp. 84–85, 142–146). From my point of view, these experiments dramatize the fact that perceptual materials are used both in perception and in working memory cognition.

Carey (2009) mentions that the core cognition system that handles number shows sensitivity to arithmetical operations. For example, if infants view a series of displays of different numbers of dots in which there were always twice as many red dots as blue dots, they begin to habituate (i.e., look at displays for less time) but they then dishabituate (look longer) if the ratio of red and blue dots is reversed. This shows they are sensitive to ratios. But this kind of sensitivity might also be accomplished by perceptual systems. Anecdotally, people think that it can look as if there are roughly twice as many red things than blue things. Habituation is quite different from adaptation (as I annoyingly keep reminding the reader) and I don't know specific work on adaptation to ratios, but I would be surprised if we—and other animals—did not adapt to ratios. One reason to believe that ratios can be perceived is that pigeons are sensitive to ratios of reinforcers (Landon & Davison, 2001). Many creatures that forage are able to make comparisons between quantities of food in various locations and also quantities of competing consumers of the food. These comparisons may be perceptual. Alternatively, they may be postperceptual cognitive operations on perceptually given quantities. In neither case is there a challenge to the joint.

If infants are shown 5 objects moving behind a screen, then another 5 objects, then if the screen is removed revealing just 5 objects, the infants look longer than if it reveals 10 objects. This result suggests sensitivity to facts of addition. A similar study shows sensitivity to facts of subtraction. Again, these may be sensitivities within the perceptual systems. Newborn chicks preferentially move toward larger sets of objects hidden behind screens. If objects are visibly transferred from behind one screen to the other, the chicks can keep track of which screen hides more of them, showing a kind of sensitivity to both addition and subtraction (Rugani, Fontanari, Simoni, Regolin, & Vallortigara, 2009). Similar abilities have been shown in vervet monkeys (Tsutsumi, Ushitani, & Fujita, 2011), and even in bees (Cepelewicz, 2021a; Howard, Avarguès-Weber, Garcia, Greentree, & Dyer, 2019a and 2019b). These abilities may be perceptual or they may be postperceptual. To create a problem for the joint in nature between perception and cognition, some evidence would have to be adduced that these sensitivities to arithmetical relations cannot be handled entirely by two categories, perception and cognition.

Experiments on kindergartners and first graders who have not learned about multiplication or division show that they are nonetheless sensitive to multiplicative/divisive relationships (Barth, Baron, Spelke, & Carey, 2009). Children were shown examples in which blue dots are halved in number while a "magic" sound indicates a transition. Then in the experimental manipulation, they are shown a cloud of blue dots that go behind a box. Then the "magic" sound is played while the experimenter says that the sound magically changes them. Then they are shown a cloud of red dots and asked whether there are more of the hidden blue dots or more red dots. Children are about 70%–80% accurate at this depending on the comparison ratios between the red and blue dots. Together with similar results for doubling, these results show sensitivity to facts about multiplication and division. The children are clearly engaging in a cognitive task using perceptual representations of approximate numerosity. Again, there is no indication in such experiments that the explanation requires anything other than perception and cognition.

Adults have perceptual representations of colors and for at least some colors, we also have conceptual representations. As was noted earlier, 4- to 11-month-old infants have color percepts without color concepts. In the case of causation and numerosity, we do not know whether infants have both the percepts and the concepts, and it is possible that the sensitivity to arithmetical relations just

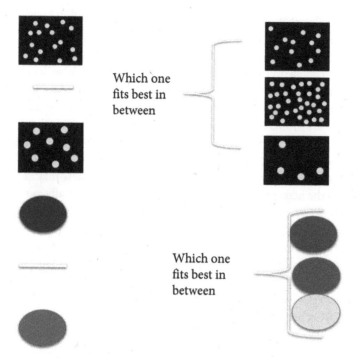

Figure 12.3 Similar tasks involving conceptualized numerosities and conceptualized colors. This figure requires color. There is a free pdf on the Oxford University Press web site that has the color version of this and all the other figures.

mentioned is conceptual rather than perceptual. But no reason has been given to think that anything more than perception and cognition are needed to explain the phenomena.

Consider the tasks of Figure 12.3. The first asks which of the numerosities on the right fits between (in the gap) the numerosities on the left. If one has to do it quickly, without counting, perceptual appreciation of approximate numerosities could be used in a concept. (On the left, the numerosities are 16 and 8; so, the top (12) cluster would fit in between. The second task asks which color fits in the gap. Similarly, conceptualized percepts would naturally play a role. The point I am making is that these two problems involve similar thought processes involving conceptualized percepts. The thought processes are similar despite the fact that there is a "core cognition" system for approximate numerosity but not color. The major difference is that in the case of numerosities, we have nearly automatic conceptualization, perhaps even in infancy, whereas in the case of color we do not. But both illustrate how cognitive tasks can involve perceptual representations.

In sum, core cognition may be a heterogeneous mixture of pure perception and pure cognition.

13
Consciousness

Oversimplifying, we can say that theories of the neural basis of consciousness tend to divide on whether consciousness is rooted in the "front" or the "back" of the brain. However, "front" and "back" are vague terms, and both camps often regard parts of the parietal cortex as part of the neural basis of consciousness. The real neocortex-location issue is whether certain regions (not all) in front of the central sulcus are necessary for perceptual consciousness. The position I will call "prefrontalism" says yes, advocates of the "back" say no. Prefrontalists emphasize dorsolateral, medial prefrontal, anterior cingulate, and orbitofrontal regions of prefrontal cortex. But front/back is really a surrogate for the more fundamental issue of whether consciousness is cognitive or whether it is noncognitive—mainly sensory (in a wide sense that includes imagery, dreaming, and hallucination). It is because activations in some areas of prefrontal cortex appear to be necessary for cognitive function that it looms so large in these debates. (What is meant by cognition here is thought-based mentality, notably reasoning, deciding, evaluating, reporting, and working memory.) Advocates of the "back of the head" view of consciousness can allow that if thought has its own kind of phenomenal consciousness, it might be based in cognitive regions of prefrontal cortex. The important difference between cognitivist and noncognitivist views is that we noncognitivists say that perceptual consciousness does not require cognitive processing.[1]

I used the terms "necessary" and "rooted in" to describe the relation between consciousness and certain brain areas. More specifically, the relation is constitution. The issue is whether certain prefrontal areas are constitutively necessary for perceptual consciousness. The distinction alluded to is that between constitutive and contingent causal factors (Adams & Aizawa, 2008; Block, 2005a). Blood flow in the brain is contingently causally necessary for conscious experience since it is the brain's energy supply but in principle some other form of energy could take its place. It is neural processing itself or some aspect of it that is constitutive of conscious experience.

This "front of the head" vs. "back of the head" debate maps onto popular theories of consciousness. Prefrontalists are represented by the global workspace

---

[1] Some of the material in this chapter is adapted from my earlier work (Block, 2019f, 2020).

theory (Dehaene, 2014) and the higher order theory (Brown, Lau, & LeDoux, 2019; Lau & Rosenthal, 2011) of consciousness. According to the global workspace theory, sensory activations compete among themselves, with dominant neural coalitions in sensory areas triggering workspace neurons in frontal and parietal cortex, forming an active reverberating network that makes sensory information available to reasoning, reporting, decision-making, and other cognitive processes. According to higher order theories of consciousness, what makes a perception conscious is that there is an accompanying cognitive state about the perception.

Meanwhile, the back of the head accounts are represented by the integrated information theory (Tononi & Edelman, 1998) and the recurrent processing theory (Lamme, 2016). According to the recurrent processing account, consciousness is a matter of the formation of feedback loops with certain neural properties. According to the integrated information theory, a system is conscious to the extent that it is both differentiated and integrated. These theories do not characterize consciousness as closely linked to cognition. For integrated information theory, the back of the head focus has to do with the prevalence there of gridlike structures. For recurrent processing theories, the back of the head focus derives from the fact that sensory areas are located there.

This debate between advocates of the front and the back is widely recognized to be the focus of current controversy about consciousness. Indeed, the Templeton World Charity Foundation is funding an "adversarial collaboration" to—among other things—resolve the issue between advocates of the front and back of the neocortex (Ball, 2019). The prefrontalists recently published a manifesto (Dehaene et al., 2017) in *Science*, arguing that if we are to make conscious machines, we should base them on the computations that underlie human consciousness. The computations they describe are those advocated by global workspace and higher order theorists.

As described in detail in Chapter 7, there have been many studies that have shown representations of perceptual contents in prefrontal cortex, even in no-report experiments in which perceptual contents are indicated by involuntary eye movements. As mentioned, one of the most impressive studies (Kapoor, et al., 2022) trained a decoder to detect the percept in prefrontal cortex in binocular rivalry. They then found that the same decoder worked for "replay", the case in which the stimulus was switched back and forth to mimic the experience of rivalry. And a decoder trained on replay also worked for rivalry. Unsurprisingly, such results have been taken to support cognitive theories of consciousness. (See, for example, https://twitter.com/vishneuro/status/1506291906451546114.)

As noted in Chapter 7, these results are problematic as support for cognitive theories of consciousness because the prefrontal decoding of perceptual information can derive from perceptual information that has been conceptualized in thought.

I called this the bored monkey problem: that the subjects of the experiement may be thinking about their percepts. In the case of monkeys, they have thousands of trials and nothing else to do. As noted in Chapter 7, this speculation has been confirmed in (Sergent, et al., 2021). Sergent, et al. used infrequent probes in a mind-wandering test. They found that there was a high correlation between reports of thinking about the stimulus and prefrontal activations (as manifested in broadcasting in the "global playground", a variant of the global workspace).

In sum, some experimental results that have been widely taken to favor cognitive theories of consciousness do not in fact support such theories.

Phenomenal consciousness vs. access consciousness

In previous work on consciousness, I have been concerned to distinguish phenomenal consciousness from access consciousness. This distinction is important for this book because one way of framing the upshot of the point about nonconceptual color perception in Chapter 6 is that it shows phenomenal consciousness of color in infants without access consciousness.

Phenomenal consciousness is "what it is like" to see blue or hear a bell (Nagel, 1974). In this chapter I will be mainly discussing perceptual phenomenal consciousness, whose specific phenomenal nature can be described as perceptual phenomenology.

Access-consciousness can be understood in two different ways, (1) dispositionally, as a matter of *availability* to cognitive processes, or, (2) occurrently, in terms of representations *actually being encoded* by the machinery of thought and reasoning. I started out with the dispositional sort of characterization—dispositional in the sense in which solubility and fragility are dispositions—saying (1990, p. 597), "There is one sense of 'consciousness' that is particularly relevant for our concerns, one in which a state is conscious to the extent that it is accessible to reasoning and reporting processes. In connection with other states, it finds expression in speech." I noted that something like this idea is used in ordinary discussion and in Freudian approaches where a state is unconscious to the extent that it is not available to reasoning and reporting but is only revealed in dreams and slips. As I noted, there is nothing in this Freudian approach that rules out unconscious images being phenomenally conscious.

A problem with the dispositional approach is that it is not clear it has a role in the science of consciousness. For that reason, I focused on finding a non-ad-hoc information-processing image of phenomenal consciousness. The motivation for finding such an information-processing shadow of phenomenal consciousness was to pose the question of whether phenomenal consciousness could be identified with its information-processing shadow. One problem with cognitive accessibility for that purpose is that unconscious perception often involves representations that are cognitively accessible in the sense that they *would* be cognitively accessed with a change in the distribution of attention. I tried using the dispositional notion of "poised" for reasoning and reporting (Block, 1995c) on the ground that a representation that requires a shift of attention for cognitive access is not poised for reasoning and reporting.

However, there was an additional problem with poise: Since conscious states and events such as toothaches and perceptions are occurrences, it is unsatisfactory to identify them with dispositions. Their information processing images should also be occurrent. A slightly tweaked version would be to use "becomes poised" instead of "poised," since becoming poised is an occurrence. However, I moved to a more theory-loaded notion of access consciousness in terms of being "broadcast for free use in reasoning and for direct "rational" control of action" (2002a). Another occurrent notion of access-consciousness that avoids any commitment to the global workspace would be: A representation is conscious to the extent that it is encoded by the machinery of thought and reasoning. (See Chalmers, 1996, 1997, on these and related ideas.) Stanislas Dehaene, the leading advocate of the global neuronal workspace, also adopts an actual encoding notion of access consciousness (Dehaene & Changeux, 2004).

In an article titled "In Praise of Poise," Daniel Stoljar argues that I was wrong to move away from the notion that appeals to poise (Stoljar, 2019). I said that conscious states are occurrences, not dispositions. Stoljar counters that we can avoid the problem of treating access-consciousness as a pure disposition if we characterize it as poise grounded in attention. This is Stoljar's proposed definition of access-consciousness: "For any subject S and any psychological state X of S, X is an access conscious state if and only if (a) X is poised for use by S in the rational control of S's thought and action, (b) S attends to the content of X, and (c) clause (a) is true because clause (b) is true, that is, S attends to the content of X to a degree sufficient to make (a) true." This definition defines an occurrent state (because of the grounding in an act of attention). I like that feature of it although I think the appeal to attention may be problematic if there can be a form of access-consciousness that does not require attention. (See Block, 2019d.)

The nonconceptual perceptions of the infants described in Chapter 6 are not access conscious either in the dispositional or occurrent senses. The child's color perception discussed in Chapter 6 is not disposed to play a role in reasoning in reporting because there can be no cognitive access to the perceptions without training.

I can imagine someone claiming that if the nonconceptual and nonpropositional perceptions were conceptualized, then they would play a role in reasoning and so they are access-conscious in the dispositional sense. But this claim is based on a familiar kind of distortion of dispositional concepts. To get an idea of the distortion, note that we can speak of a normal child-bearing age biological female (i.e. a person with a womb, whatever their gender identity) as having the capacity to become pregnant or even the disposition to become pregnant. We would not normally think of a normal biological male as able to become pregnant or as being disposed to become pregnant, even though a womb might be surgically hooked up inside the normal biological male's body by some future medical procedure. To say on this ground that a normal biological male is disposed to become pregnant or has the capacity to become pregant would be distort the concepts. Similarly, although training can impart concepts of color, the normal untrained infant of the ages discussed earlier is not disposed to reason with color.

To conceptualize a perceptual representation in the way required would be to turn it into a perceptual judgment. Access-conscious perceptions in the occurrent sense are really conceptualized perceptual judgments rather than perceptions. Phenomenal consciousness has been claimed by me and others to "overflow" access consciousness in both the occurrent and dispositional senses as indicated in Chapter 1 to describe the results of the experimental paradigm of Victor Lamme and his colleagues at the University of Amsterdam. That is, a phenomenally conscious perception at a time is alleged to encompass conscious perception of more "items" than perceptual judgments at that time (Block, 1995c). These conclusions have not convinced all readers but the infant color work of Chapter 6 allows for a quite different argument for phenomenal-consciousness without access-consciousness.

The infants' color perceptions are not "accessible to reasoning and reporting processes" because the concepts required for access are missing—and not just missing as a matter of chance but for a systematic reason. So they are not poised for reasoning and reporting and hence not access-conscious even in the relatively relaxed "poised" sense. Further, the infant subjects of color experience cannot cognitively represent to themselves that they have color experience, and since they don't notice color they cannot have cognitive pointers to their color experience, so no form of higher order representation applies. The upshot is that the case described in Chapter 6 challenges both the global workspace and higher order approaches to consciousness.

Peter Carruthers has noted that a form of the overflow argument can be stated without bringing in consciousness at all (as I pointed out in Chapter 1) (Carruthers, 2015, 2017). He concludes that if overflow is a matter of information processing then it cannot be used to show that phenomenal consciousness overflows access-consciousness. He says (Carruthers, 2017, p. 69), "What Block takes to be a contrast between rich phenomenal experience, on the one hand, and more limited-content access-consciousness, on the other, might rather be the difference between rich stimulus-driven perception (which is both access-conscious and phenomenally conscious) and limited-content working memory (which is likewise both access-conscious and phenomenally conscious)."

Carruthers' argument depends on using a highly dispositional notion of access-consciousness that I have never endorsed. It is not true that all 12 items in the Sperling array or all 8 items in the Lamme array are access-conscious since they are not all encoded in the global workspace or in working memory. Nor are they all "poised" to be used in reasoning, problem solving, and the like. It takes attention to promote one of these representations to the level of "poise."

As I mentioned in Chapter 6, there is one obvious way for cognitive theorists to resist this argument: to deny that infants' color perception is phenomenally conscious in the first place. As I mentioned, there is no direct evidence that infant color perception is in fact conscious. However, the habituation paradigm provides strong *indirect* evidence for conscious color perception. Recall that after repeated viewing of the same color, the infants look less and less often at the screen until there is a detectable color change. Then they look at the screen more often. That process is very plausibly a reflection of decreasing level of interest. The infant would rather look at his or her feet than at the screen. I have never heard of any evidence for decreasing or increasing level of interest as part of a person's unconscious mental life. I don't know of any reported instance of habituation in blindsight or any other unconscious perception paradigm. A similar point applies to another one of the methods of gauging infants' color perception mentioned in Chapter 6, the fact that a person viewing a uniformly colored screen will tend to move fixation to a different colored disk. As I mentioned, this behavior is used to ascertain which disks look different to the subject. Plausibly, moving one's eyes to something that looks different is a reflection of interest in the item because it looks different. The same behavior is standard in adults as well. Remember that this is a voluntary movement. (See Figure 6.4.)

Infants between 6 and 11 months old have phenomenal consciousness of color without access consciousness of color. What about adults? I argued that adults have non-conceptual perception of color, but do they exhibit phenomenal without access consciousness of color? No not normally. Adults have color concepts so they can be poised to cognitively process color information. A similar point applies to the fact that perceptual representations are non-propositional shown in Chapter 5. Although perceptual representations cannot function in inference, they are easily conceptualized by people who have the relevant concepts.

In sum, the points about color perception in 6- to 11-month-old infants presented in Chapter 6 provide evidence against cognitive theories of consciousness. I will now discuss the global workspace and higher order views in more detail, filling in some of the missing steps in the argument just given.

Global workspace

The global workspace theory is a cognitivist and conceptualist theory because the very global workspace activation that its proponents take to constitute consciousness actually ensures that the globally broadcast representations are part of a conceptually activated network.[2] (See the discussion in Chapters 1 and 4 involving Figure 1.2 for more on the global workspace.)

The distinction mentioned earlier in this chapter between occurrent and dispositional gives rise to two different kinds of theories that appeal to the global workspace. Stanislas Dehaene advocates consciousness as *encoding* in the global workspace as distinct from *availability* to the global workspace (Dehaene & Changeux, 2004; Dehaene et al., 2017). The effect of that is to require that consciousness be conceptual. For example, there are a million colors, but it is said that people can recognize under 100 specific shades. If there are 100 different options for conceptual color encodings in the global workspace, that kind of global workspace account will underestimate the fineness of grain of color experience. (See the discussion of Gareth Evans's argument near the beginning of Chapter 6.) This is one of the reasons that I regard the global workspace model as a much better model of conceptualization of perception than of perceptual consciousness.

In Chapter 6, I mentioned Claire Sergent's (2021) "global playground" isolated in a no-report paradigm. The global playground subtracts from the global workspace some of the brain activations that play a role in reporting a perception, but still includes the prefrontal basis of the cognitive states involved in thinking about the stimulus, as shown by Sergent's mind-wandering probes. It is better than the global workspace as a theory of perceptual concepts since it subtracts reporting activations. But it has the same flaw as the global workspace as a theory of consciousness since it includes the cognitive basis of perceptual judgement.

Jesse Prinz claims that consciousness is attended intermediate level representation where the intermediate level in the visual system is in between the zero-crossings of low-level vision and the "high"-level contents such as that

---

[2] I mentioned the "prefrontalist" manifesto (Dehaene et al., 2017). Some of us who favor a back-of-the-head basis for consciousness have responded (Boly et al., 2017; Carter et al., 2018).

Nixonish look that so many different photos of Nixon from different angles all have in common. The intermediate level allows for the million different color representations. Prinz requires availability to the global workspace of those attended intermediate-level representations but does not link consciousness to the actual encodings in the frontal systems that maintain the perceptual activations, so he escapes the grain problem (2012, pp. 99–106). But Prinz's requirement of availability to the global workspace makes his view problematic in the light of the argument for nonconceptual perception from Chapter 6. The child's nonconceptual color perception is conscious but not available to the global workspace because of the child's lack of color concepts.

In sum, the global workspace and the global playground theories of consciousness, as well as Prinz's theory, are challenged by the arguments for nonconceptual and nonpropositional perception.

Higher order thought

A higher order state is a state that is about another mental state. A perception of the environment is a first-order state. A thought about a perception is a second-order state. A thought about a thought about a perception is a third-order state, and so on.

There are two approaches to higher order thought (HOT) theories of consciousness. The "double representation" approach says that the HOT involves a distinct coding of the perceptual content. Suppose that one has a perceptual representation of red. In normal circumstances, if it is a conscious perception of red, it will be "accompanied" (according to this version of the HOT theory) by a thought to the effect that one has an experience as of red (Brown et al., 2019; Rosenthal, 1997). (More on the relation of accompaniment below.)

So on this version of the HOT approach, there are two representations of red, one perceptual, one cognitive and conceptual. (See Block, 2011b, 2011d; Rosenthal, 2011; Weisberg, 2011.) Now, however, it is mysterious how a perception can be conscious according to this version of HOT theory. To see the problem, consider a HOT to the effect that I myself am seeing green. Let's say that this thought lasts two seconds and that there are two perceptions of green that occur at different times during those two seconds. Suppose further, that if we had asked the subject to press a button when they saw green, the time of the button press would pinpoint one of the perceptions as conscious but not the other. Note that what I am supposing here is that a certain counterfactual is true, not that the subject was ever asked to press a button when seeing green. The point of making this evidence counterfactual is that it provides evidence that one but not the other perception is conscious without elaborating the example in a way that would make it part of the example that the identifying information made it into the HOT. I am supposing that the HOT does not contain any information that would decide between the two perceptions. So the two perceptions equally satisfy the HOT, but only one is conscious, thus revealing an inadequacy in the HOT theory.

It might be natural to suppose that temporal or causal information could decide the issue. But this is so only if the HOT has temporal or causal content, and it isn't clear what that content would be. Further, any such additional content added to the HOT would allow for *another* case in which there are two first order states that equally satisfy *that* content.

The example uses the supposition that the perceptions are at different times, but that feature of the example is not necessary. The conscious perception could be of one maximally fine-grained shade of red and the unconscious perception could be of another maximally fine-grained shade of red. They could be simultaneous. We can see a million shades but only have concepts of a small minority of those. Even if it were possible to put together descriptions of such shades on the order of "1003 shades to blue from reddish blue," I think we could agree that a normal HOT would not contain such descriptions. The problem for the HOT account is that it has no way to explain how one of the perceptions could be conscious and the other not.

Indeed, the two perceptions could be simultaneous AND have the same content. As was mentioned in Chapter 2 in the section on the visual hierarchy, humans and other primates have two visual systems, a dorsal system that is dedicated to fast and inflexible spatial computations, is used to guide action and is mostly or totally unconscious; and a conscious ventral system that is slower, more flexible, and functions to produce a model of the world useful for planning. (A popular treatment of the distinction can be found in Goodale & Milner, 2005. A treatment aimed at philosophers: Clark, 2001. A revised version: Milner & Goodale, 2008). There are often—even usually—simultaneous representations of the spatiotemporal aspects of the same events in both systems. So there could be a ventral and dorsal representation with the content: round object moving up. How could the content of a HOT that lacks singular terms distinguish between simultaneous perceptions with the same content? Nonetheless one is conscious and the other not.

An obvious suggestion is that we can adopt a causal/historical account of what makes a HOT be about a perception. We have two perceptions that equally satisfy the descriptive content of the HOT, but one and not the other causes the HOT. But that gives rise to the problem of how a thought to the effect that I am smelling vomit could make a perception of crimson a conscious perception. The perception of crimson could cause the HOT while a simultaneous first-order smell-representation of vomit does not cause any higher order state. The consequence would be that the perception of crimson is a conscious perception and the perception of vomit is not, even though the subject experiences the perception of crimson as if it were the perception of vomit. One could build in a content restriction, but then we would be back where we started with the fact that a descriptivist view based on content is inadequate.

The difficulty for the HOT theory is that it is unclear what relation has to obtain between a HOT and a perception for the perception to be conscious. The relation is often described as accompaniment: "The core of the theory, then, is that a mental state is a conscious state when, and only when, it is accompanied by a suitable HOT" (Rosenthal, 1997, p. 741). But as just pointed out, a HOT could accompany two perceptions, one of which is conscious and the other not.

The HOT theorist can say both perceptions are conscious or that it is indeterminate which is conscious. (Richard Brown and Jake Berger seemed inclined this way when I brought up this issue in the NYU mind discussion group in November 2019.) However, I don't think this case can be so easily brushed off. The crucial feature of the case is that there is a fact as to which one is conscious and which is not (e.g., the ventral perception is conscious, the dorsal one is not). What the case reveals is a disconnect between the HOT and the perceptions that are conscious or not.

Problems for the HOT theory are sometimes approached by using intuitions to shape a more complex causal condition. But the HOT theory is supposed to be an empirical theory not a conceptual analysis based on "intuitions." As David Rosenthal puts it, "The HOT model is an empirical hypothesis about what it is for a mental state to be a conscious state, so it is no difficulty that one can imagine things that would falsify it" (Rosenthal, 2002b, p. 659).

This cluster of problems is avoided on the second version of the HOT view, in which there is a thought or at least a cognitive state that makes a perception conscious but that thought does not itself have any perceptual content (Cleeremans, 2014; Cleeremans et al., 2020; Lau, 2019; 2022; Odegaard, Knight, & Lau, 2017b). Lau sometimes refers to the higher order state as a pointer to a first-order state. The pointer theory is cognitive in that the pointer is a thought but it is not conceptualist since there is no concept of red involved in the thought that is supposed to make a perception of red conscious. In Lau's and Cleeremans's version of the HOT theory, the content of the higher order state has to do with the level of reliability of the first-order state as a guide to the world.

The first version of the higher order theory—the one in which there are two representations of red, one conceptual representation in the HOT and one nonconceptual representation in the perception—is most clearly refuted by the considerations in Chapter 6. For the representation in thought has to be conceptual (since what it is to be conceptual is to be used in thought), whereas the infants have no color concepts. The pointer version is not as clearly incompatible with the point in Chapter 6 about the nonconceptual nature of children's conscious perceptions of color, but the fact that these infants cannot *notice* color does conflict with the pointer version. Since these children's cognitive states do not appear to take account of color at all, why should we supposed that they have cognitive pointers to them? In sum, higher order theories are cognitive theories of consciousness and so are subject to the arguments developed in Chapter 6.[3]

Alleged evidence for higher order thought theories of consciousness

Hakwan Lau and Richard Brown have written an article making the empirical case for the HOT approach (Lau & Brown, 2019). In this section I consider their claims.[4]

Much of the battle over first-order vs. higher order theories of conscious experience concerns intuitions concerning the word "consciousness"—or, more charitably, the concept of consciousness.

Advocates of higher order theories focus on the founding intuition that a conscious state is one that one is conscious of oneself as being in. This "transitivity principle" in effect reduces consciousness to consciousness-of. It appears at first glance that consciousness is a monadic property of a state, but according to the transitivity principle, that is an illusion, since what makes a state conscious is supposed to be a relation of something else to that state, specifically the relation of consciousness-of. In recent years, I have suggested that first-order theories can accommodate this intuition via a "same order" account in which conscious states include a kind of awareness of themselves. I have also taken seriously the idea that the founding intuition is too superficial to give us any insight. We say that a song is something one sings, that a dance is something one dances and a jump is something one jumps (Sosa, 2003). These relations are superficial in that they do not provide any substantive insight into what singing, dancing, or jumping is. Similarly, the fact that we say a conscious state is one we are conscious of is a superficial relation.

It may appear that the higher order approach can acknowledge nonconceptual unconscious perception. On this picture of the higher order view, what an appropriate HOT does is transform a nonconceptual first order unconscious

---

[3] Cognitive and conceptualist theories are typically committed to the claim that there is no real "explanatory gap" and so count as "Type-A" theories in Chalmers's scheme (Chalmers, 2003).

[4] This section is adapted from my response to Lau and Brown (Block, 2019b). That response came out in a festschrift edited by Adam Pautz and Daniel Stoljar (Pautz & Stoljar, 2019). I am grateful to Adam Pautz and Daniel Stoljar for their helpful comments on earlier versions of some of this material.

perceptual state into a combined higher order/first order conceptual state. However, that is not the right picture of the higher order view.

I can explain this point by describing a bizarre feature of higher order views such as that of Rosenthal and Weisberg (Rosenthal, 2005; Weisberg, 2010). A thought to the effect that I am having an experience of something green color can occur without any first-order visual representation of any color of anything (Block, 2011b, 2011d; Neander, 1998). One could close one's eyes and think such a thought. The only way higher order views can accommodate this fact is by regarding a nonexistent "intentional inexistent" state as conscious in these cases. This forces higher order advocates to reinterpret the transitivity principle, since there is nothing for one to be conscious of in the case of an "empty" HOT. As David Rosenthal, puts it, "Conscious states are states we are conscious of ourselves as being in, whether or not we are actually in them" (2002a, p. 415). And again, "So erroneous HOTs will in this case result in there being something it's like for one to be in a state that one is not actually in" (2009, p. 209). What is revealed by this point is that what is essential to conscious perception on the higher order theory is only higher order and conceptual.

I have found discussions on this topic rather unproductive—even more so than most intuition-based disagreements in philosophy. So, I welcome the fact that Hakwan Lau and Richard Brown have focused their discussion on actual cases that raise genuine empirical issues (Lau & Brown, 2019). By discussion of these and other real cases, we stand a better chance of adjudicating between first-order and higher order theories.

Lau and Brown describe three cases that they think are ones in which there is conscious perception (or at least perception-like experience) but no relevant first-order perceptual representation is present—or where there may be a first-order representation but it is too weak to account for the conscious perception. I will go through these cases one by one.

Rare Charles Bonnet Syndrome

Lau and Brown define "Rare Charles Bonnet Syndrome" as a syndrome of visual hallucination with destruction of the first visual cortical area, V1. In the cases they describe, *partial* damage to early visual cortex including area V1 is accompanied by vivid visual hallucinations. These hallucinations often occupy the whole visual field, including the part of the visual field served by the damaged part of V1. The left side of V1 processes visual signals in the right visual field, but loss of the left side of V1 is compatible with preserved hallucinations in the right visual field.

According to Lau and Brown, this phenomenon poses a problem for first-order theories because there is no first order physical state that can realize the conscious experiences. Lau and Brown are adverting to the idea that I and others have emphasized that the first-order realizer of conscious visual percepts involve feedback loops from higher visual areas to early visual processing, including the first visual area, V1 (Block, 2007a; Lamme, 2003).

My response will appeal to the distinction mentioned earlier in this chapter between causal and constitutive factors in conscious experience (Adams & Aizawa, 2008; Block, 2005a). To take a nonmental example, dry fuel causally contributes to fire, but is not constitutive of fire. What is constitutive is rapid exothermic oxidation. If you have rapid exothermic oxidation, you have fire whether or not the fuel is wet. Moving to consciousness: As mentioned earlier, blood flow in the brain is a contingent causal factor in the production of conscious experience, because blood carries oxygen necessary for neural processing. Neural processing itself is constitutive of consciousness—what conscious experience is. Even if blood flow stops, there can be brief consciousness before the neurons die for lack of oxygen.

My account of consciousness is biologically based and has always focused mainly on activations in the circuits that process the relevant contents. For example, as noted in Chapters 1, 4, and 9, we know that neural activity in MT+ is part of the circuit that underlies (and is the constitutive basis of) conscious experience of motion. We know that neural activity in the fusiform face area and other face patches is part of the constitutive basis of conscious face experience.

I have entertained the idea that recurrent loops from content areas such as MT+ or the fusiform face area to lower visual areas may be necessary for conscious experience. But I have not committed to whether these loops are causally necessary or constitutively necessary. Further, I have never said that an intact V1 was necessary for conscious experience. I normally refer to "lower visual areas," as here (2007a, p. 496), where I said: "However, mere activation over a certain threshold in V5 is not enough for the experience as of motion: the activation probably has to be part of a recurrent feedback loop to *lower areas*" [italics added]. In the same paper (2007a, p. 499), I suggested, "Perhaps V2 or other lower visual areas can substitute for V1 as the lower site in a recurrent loop."

In (2007a, p. 499), I considered other cases of conscious experience with damaged V1. I said:

> Blindsight patients who have had blindsight for many years can acquire some kinds of vision in their blind fields despite lacking V1 for those areas. One subject describes his experience as like a black thing moving on a black background.... Afterimages in the blind field have been reported.... Stoerig (2001)

notes that blindsight patients are subject to visual hallucinations in their blind fields even immediately after the surgery removing parts of V1.

I considered another suggestion due to Petra Stoerig (2001, p.190), keyed to the fact that the damage to V1 in these cases is only partial: "this may be due to a high-level of excitation that spreads to other higher cortical areas that have their own feedback loops to other areas of V1 or to other areas of early vision such as V2" (2007a, p. 499). Here is how Stoerig (p. 190) puts it: "In the case of hallucinations, the spontaneous extrastriate cortical activation [extrastriate cortex is above the level of V1 in the visual hierarchy described in Chapter 2] is quite strong, and may therefore spread to other structures, subcortical and cortical, in the ipsi- and contralesional hemisphere." (If damage is on the left, the ipsilateral hemisphere is the left one and the contralateral hemisphere is the right one.)[5]

Importantly, the cases of rare Charles Bonnet syndrome that Lau and Brown describe are all cases of partial destruction of V1. Two of them are descriptions of damage to one side of the visual cortex. The third describes damage to "most of the primary visual cortex" (primary visual cortex = V1), suggesting that some of V1 was preserved (Duggal & Pierri, 2002, p. 291). Suppose as in one of Stoerig's cases we have visual experience of motion in the left visual field in the absence of the right half of V1, the part that processes the left visual field. That activation could spread from the right part of the motion area to the left part of it, and then down to the intact part of V1.

To summarize: My biological theory of consciousness has focused on content areas such as MT/V5 for motion content. I have also speculated that loops to lower areas are important, but I have usually marked those references as somewhat speculative. So, rare Charles Bonnet syndrome does not go counter to anything I and other advocates of recurrent loops have said, since we have not required V1. Further, in cases of partial damage to V1, other pathways to the remaining part of V1 may take over.

Lau and Brown note that I am not committed to feedback to V1, but they think that feedback to V1 fits with my philosophical position:

---

[5] Some have questioned whether blindsight is genuinely unconscious as opposed to weakly conscious (Block & Phillips, 2016; Phillips, 2015). Recent work has used better procedures in identifying blindsight, but there is still a great deal of controversy about whether blindsight is unconscious (Garric, Caetta, Sergent, & Chokron, 2020; Phillips, 2020a, 2020b). Phillips (2020a) has argued that a signal detection approach reveals that blindsight involves weak conscious perception. Matthias Michel and Hakwan Lau (Michel & Lau, 2021) note that the key issue is not total abolition of conscious perception in blindsight but rather a *relative* dissociation: that subjects can respond to more features of the stimulus than they can consciously see. For example, blindsight patients who are reporting on a tilted grid may have conscious awareness of something rather than nothing, e.g., a featureless blob, but are nonetheless able to report on whether the grid is tilted to the right or the left even if they have no conscious awareness of the lines. Thus even if blindsight is not totally unconscious, there is strong reason to believe it involves unconscious perception. (This view comports with my contribution to this debate: Peters et al., 2017. See also Burge, 2020, footnote 45.)

... on Block's view, it is the *biological substrate* of the first-order representation that is critical for conscious phenomenology. Presumably, the feedback-to-V1 view is attractive to him because the recurrent processing reflected by the feedforward and feedback waves of neural activity seems to give a flavor of a specialized biological phenomenon. If Block is to abandon this view, he would need to specify what is special about extrastriate activity that allows them to support conscious phenomenology. Is it not just normal neural coding, that sometimes can reflect unconscious processing too?

Of course, they are right that the biological point of view should seek an account of the difference between conscious and unconscious perception. Our failure to find any remotely plausible explanatory account is part of the phenomenon that is labeled "the hard problem of consciousness" (Chalmers, 1996) and the "explanatory gap" (Levine, 1983). However, there are some proposals as to what the difference comes to in human brains. One proposal is that it is just a matter of level of activation. Another proposal is that feedback to lower visual areas is required but not necessarily feedback to V1. These are not very explanatory proposals, and we should hope for more.

The descriptions of rare Charles Bonnet syndrome in the articles that Lau and Brown refer to reveal vivid hallucinations, but it is not clear that they are as fine-grained as normal perception. The description by Contardi et al. (2007, p. 272) is this: "she usually referred to seeing coloured 'Lilliputian' figures of women and children, either static or moving, but usually running in meadows or even lying in bed with her, or, occasionally, brightly coloured countryside scenes." The description by Ashwin and Tsaloumas (2007) is "he noticed vivid images of lions and cats in the right visual field. Over the next few days he described as seeing flock of birds, pack of hounds, chessboards and brightly coloured scarves in the same area" (p. 184). Similar descriptions are given by Duggal and Pierri (2002). Nothing in these descriptions suggests, for example, that the hallucinators have experiences as of different shades of color of the sort one finds in a paint store despite the claim of Joseph LeDoux and Richard Brown (LeDoux & Brown, 2017) that the experiences of these hallucinators are "rich."

Of course, hallucinations may always be caused by higher level cognitive activity. Presumably the Lilliputian figures are not something the patient had ever seen. But that does not mean that they are constitutively cognitive. Recall the distinction made repeatedly in this chapter between constitutive and merely contingent causal factors. Blood flow is a contingent causal factor, but neural processing is constitutive. The cognitive activity may have its effect by causing activations in the perceptual areas that are themselves constitutive of the hallucinatory experience.

One problem for cognitive theories of consciousness of the sort that L&B are advocating is that the cognitive system that according to them generates conscious experience is simply too coarse-grained to explain the fact that normal human perceivers can consciously see a million colors even though they have concepts of only a tiny fraction of those colors. It has often been noted that our experiences are more finely differentiated than our concepts of those experiences as indexed by our ability to identify the experiences (Evans, 1982; Peacocke, 1992a; Tye, 2006). For example, even people with perfect pitch can recognize fewer than 100 pitches but can distinguish among more than a thousand pitches (Raffman, 1995). Potentially, cases of hallucination can provide further evidence for the coarse grain of purely top-down experiences and so add to the growing evidence against cognitive theories of conscious experience.

Peripheral vision

Lau and Brown (p. 179) put the criticism of my view on the basis of peripheral vision as follows:

> In Peripheral Vision, it is not clear how the relevant first-order representations can exist, because even at the retinal level, the relevant input is not rich enough. One can perhaps argue that the color sensation and vividness of details in the first-order representation is created from top-down mechanisms, but one needs to substantiate such empirical claims. In our own introspective experience, even if we open our eyes for a brief period to new scene, we get the phenomenological feeling that the periphery is not exactly monochrome and devoid of details.

And later they say that, "under rigorous laboratory testing, it seems that we do not actually experience any determinate color in the periphery." I mentioned one kind of problem about this view having to do with impressions of colorfulness and sharpness in the periphery and I will not repeat these points here. Instead, I will amplify some remarks in (2007b, p. 534).

First, it is a fallacy to focus so strongly on retinal receptors. What counts is color representations in the circuits that subserve actual perception, not the direct input feeding to those circuits. Indirect inputs to color processing include memory traces of colors of specific objects and integration over both time and space. Further, retinal activity in a laboratory setting may underestimate retinal activity in naturalistic situations. For example, it has been found that peripheral processing is substantially greater when subjects are walking than when they are seated in a stationary experiment (Cao & Händel, 2019). Walking increases contrast sensitivity in the periphery compared to the fovea. Of course this effect does not depend on any change in retinal receptors. The point about walking suggests that there may be more color processing in the periphery in naturalistic situations than in laboratory situations.

Second, it is a myth that there are insufficient color receptors in the periphery of the retina to see vivid colors. Discrimination of one hue from another is as good at 50° as in the fovea if the color stimuli are large enough (Mullen, 1992). And there is some color sensitivity out to 80° to 90°. I called this a myth (2007b, p. 534). and a recent article describes it as a "widespread misconception even among vision scientists" (Tyler, 2015, p. 1). This misconception was recently repeated yet again (Cohen, Dennett, & Kanwisher, 2016).

Christopher Tyler (2015) estimates that one-third of the cells in the peripheral retina are color-sensing cone cells. However, vision in the periphery involves integration over wider areas (Block, 2012, 2013; Pelli & Tillman, 2008). Integration over wider areas could produce vivid color experience. See Figure 13.1 (reproduced from Chapter 3 for convenience) for an illustration of the size of the integration windows.

Tyler argues that color perception in the periphery is more vivid than in the fovea. Of course, that depends on how large the items are in the fovea and the periphery. Figure 13.2 is a display in which the colored circles have been increased in size in the periphery to more than match the decrease in cone density. (See also the discussion in Haun, Koch, Tononi, & Tsuchiya, 2017.)

Third, it is well known that there is integration of color information over time within visual cortex. Indeed, there is some evidence that colors are processed one at a time so that the multicolored scenes we are aware of requires integrating many different color-processing episodes in a brief period (Huang & Pashler, 2007; Huang, Treisman, & Pashler, 2007). Seeing peripheral colors over time could be due to previous less peripheral fixations. Again, these are first-order effects.

Fourth, "Memory color" effects are widely accepted, though in the light of the work by Valenti and Firestone described in Chapter 10, perhaps wrongly so. In a paradigm that was described earlier, subjects presented with a picture of a common object colored at random (a banana might be purple) are asked to adjust the color to look a neutral gray. They adjust two knobs, one of which controls the red/green axis and the other of which controls the blue/yellow axis. The alleged memory color effect is revealed by the fact that in order to make a banana look gray, subjects move the dial 15%–20% to the blue direction See the discussion in connection with Figure 10.5 and Figure 10.6.

In sum, there are many mechanisms that can explain vivid color phenomenology in the periphery due to activations in the visual system despite the relative paucity of color receptors in the peripheral retina.

434   THE BORDER BETWEEN SEEING AND THINKING

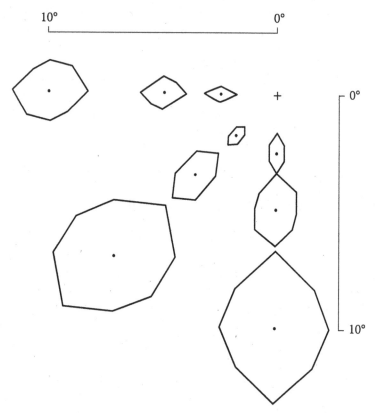

Figure 13.1 Integration windows. The fixation point is the '+'. The diagram illustrates the size and shape of windows within which stimuli are integrated. These windows increase in size with eccentricities. Reproduced from Chapter 3 for convenience. (Cf. Pelli & Tillman, 2008.) Thanks to Denis Pelli for this diagram.

The problems that I have been pointing out are exhibited dramatically in Figure 13.3 (from Lau & Rosenthal, 2011). In the caption, Lau and Rosenthal speak of low spatial and color sensitivity in the periphery of vision along with the main attention being devoted to the center of the visual field. They say (p. 369), "Based on these findings [the ones just mentioned], one might expect our conscious visual experience to be similar to what is shown in (a). However, there is a compelling subjective impression that peripheral vision is less impoverished: in particular, subjective vision is more similar to what is depicted in (b) rather than (a)." However, once one takes into account (1) there are peripheral color receptors, (2) temporal integration, (3) spatial integration, and (4) effects of prior experience as is reflected in memory color and top-down "filling-in" effects of cognition on perception, we can see that this reasoning is defective.

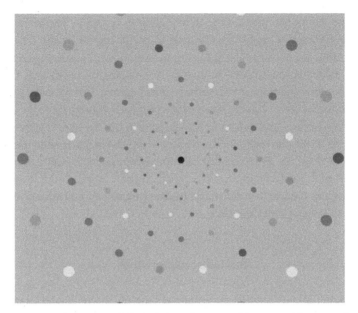

Figure 13.2 Fixate the central black disk at about 12 inches away. The outer disks should be as vivid in color as the inner ones. From Tyler (2015). This figure requires color. There is a free pdf on the Oxford University Press web site that has the color version of this and all the other figures.

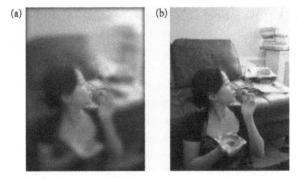

Figure 13.3 From Lau and Rosenthal (2011, p. 369). Reprinted with permission from Elsevier. The point of this figure is easier to see in color. There is a free pdf on the Oxford University Press web site that has the color version of this and all the other figures.

Lau and Rosenthal mention top-down filling-in (p. 369): "Furthermore, the subjective richness of qualitative character in peripheral vision could be due to memory from previous visual fixations at such locations. If so, the apparent richness of qualitative character is due to top-down 'filling in,' rather than detailed first-order representations at the moment of perception. This again fits well with the higher-order view." Their mistake in this passage is inattention to the distinction between causal and constitutive factors. (See the discussion above for an explanation of this distinction.) The efficacy of top-down filling-in in increasing the level of detail in representations in the visual system is well documented (Churchland & Ramachandran, 1996; Spillman et al., 2006). This is a causal effect of cognition on first-order perceptual representation and does nothing to promote the higher order approach.

Inattentional Inflation

Rahnev et al. (2011) created an experimental situation in which subjects were just as good at discriminating the orientation of an unattended high contrast grating as with an attended low contrast grating. They increased the contrast of the unattended stimulus so as to compensate for the lower apparent contrast induced by lack of attention. They titrated contrast and attention so as to lead to equal discrimination performance in the low attention and high attention conditions. Despite equal discrimination performance in the two cases, subjects gave higher visibility ratings to the unattended grating than to the attended grating. Lau and his colleagues were also able to achieve similar results using masking.

In another paper by the same group (Rahnev, Bahdo, deLange, & Lau, 2012) that yielded similar results, the subjects' judgments were confidence judgments rather than visibility judgments. Rahnev et al. (2012) used a 4-point scale in which 1 represented low confidence and 4 was high confidence. In another paper by this group titled "Direct Injection of Noise to the Visual Cortex Decreases Accuracy but Increases Decision Confidence" (Rahnev, Maniscalco, Luber, Lau, & Lisanby, 2012), an electromagnetic pulse was delivered to the visual cortex. As the authors note, electromagnetic pulses of this sort increase variation in neural activity without increasing strength. The effect was to decrease perceptual accuracy but to increase confidence.

Lau and Brown argue as follows, focusing on the attention version of the experiment:

1. The first-order states were about the same in strength as evidenced by the equal performance on discriminating the gratings (the measure of performance is the "sensitivity," d' (pronounced 'd-prime'));

2. But as reflected in the differing visibility judgments, the unattended case was higher in consciousness;
3. To explain the higher degree of consciousness in the unattended case we cannot appeal to a first-order difference, since there is no such difference (given the equal discrimination mentioned in premise 1). So the only available explanation has to appeal to a (postulated) higher order difference in judgments of visibility.

Premise 2 says that the unattended case was higher in "degree of consciousness." I doubt whether this claim has any clear meaning. Cars on the highway are less visible in a hazy day than on a sunny day, but there is no reason to think the experience of the driver is less conscious for all that. But this is not my main concern about premise 2. My main concern is that when subjects report visibility, they may be mixing in the phenomenology of confidence with the phenomenology of perceptual qualities such as contrast. For example, if two percepts are the same in d' but the unattended one is rated as higher in "strength," the explanation might be that the subject is in effect saying to themselves, "Something is stronger about this perception and the only way I have to report this is to move the visibility slider higher."

There are two broad classes of ways to understand what subjects may be reporting in these experiments.

Perceptual interpretation: The phenomenology of inflation is perceptual. Perhaps the unattended grids look higher in contrast or more vivid.

Certainty interpretation: The phenomenology of inflation is the phenomenology of certainty or confidence. The experience of seeing the unattended grids involves a greater feeling of confidence.

Note that on the certainty interpretation, the phenomenology of inflation might be cognitive phenomenology rather than perceptual phenomenology.

Here is the problem for Lau and Brown: if the phenomenology of inflation is cognitive phenomenology, first-order views are unaffected, since they do not suggest that first-order representations in the visual system are responsible for cognitive phenomenology. The first order views under discussion concern perceptual phenomenology rather than cognitive phenomenology. Recall that the argument against first-order views from these experiments was supposed to be that the equal discrimination abilities suggest the first-order activations in the attended and unattended cases are the same, so first-order views can't explain the phenomenological difference between them. But first-order views of cognitive phenomenology do not appeal to first-order perceptual activations, so the Lau and Brown reasoning is undermined.

Lau and Brown say that using changes in visibility ratings as evidence for changes in phenomenology is standard in the field: If "higher visibility ratings is not good enough evidence that phenomenology changed, what else can count as good evidence? To deny that is to deny the common standard of interpretation of experiments in this field."

They are certainly right that visibility ratings are widely taken to index phenomenology. But they do not consider the question of *phenomenology of what*? The phenomenology indexed could be the phenomenology of higher confidence. The problem with Lau and Brown's appeal is that both the perceptual phenomenology and cognitive phenomenology hypotheses fit the "common standard of interpretation." The question is whether there is any reason to prefer the perceptual interpretation that would be required for the Lau and Brown argument.

The explanation in Rahnev (2011) of the effect suggests the cognitive interpretation. The explanation is that attention to a stimulus makes representations of the stimulus more stable, thereby decreasing variation in the strength of the representation. As a result, the representation of the unattended stimulus is more variable in strength than the representation of the attended stimulus. Rahnev et al. put their result by saying (p. 1514) that an "important idea of the model is that attention reduces the trial-by-trial variability of an internal perceptual signal, which subsequently reduces the probability with which the signal exceeds the decision criterion." But higher variability promotes more crossing a threshold of confidence than lower variability, and hence there is a higher likelihood of *judging* the stimuli to be visible. This is an effect on the criterion for judgment—the judgment that one has seen the grating—not on perception itself.

Here is an analogy: Suppose there are two political demonstrations, one on your left, the other on your right. You want to judge which is louder. You listen for noises that are so loud that it is painful to hear them. Unknown to you, the average noise level is the same but the one on the right is more unruly—that is, there is more variability. So, the demonstration on the right is more likely to cross the threshold for really loud noises and you are more likely to judge it as louder even though the average noise levels are the same.

Here is my point: Rahnev's model of the phenomenon suggests that it is a judgment phenomenon, a phenomenon of judgments crossing a confidence line. I would say—from my first-order point of view—that it is a phenomenon in which the judgments in the unattended case differ without any known difference in actual perceptual consciousness. A higher order theorist might say that the difference in judgments constitutes a difference in perceptual consciousness, backing up premise 2 in the sense of "consciousness" required for the argument, namely perceptual consciousness. They may think that the criterion is a matter of the threshold for consciousness. But this little dialogue shows that the justification of premise 2 interpreted as concerning perceptual consciousness presupposes the higher order conclusion and cannot be used to argue for it. The title of the paper is "Attention Induces Conservative Subjective Biases in Visual Perception," and that is what the paper shows.

The question-begging nature of the argument is apparent in Lau and Brown's justification for premise 2: "However, as in standard models of perception . . . subjective perception happens when the signal crosses a threshold or criterion." If the difference between the attended and unattended case is in the feeling of confidence, then "subjective perception" would be wrong.

Note that my argument is not that the evidence strongly favors the cognitive phenomenology interpretation. I think that the threshold-crossing explanation of the phenomenon weakly favors that interpretation. My main point, though, is that the experiment leaves open the possibility of cognitive phenomenology as the difference.

A further problem with the reasoning of Rahnev et al. has been pointed out by Lee, Denison, and Ma (in preparation). As they note, d' is a statistic that describes the average of responses over a series of trials, not a single trial. The statistic d' is the signal-to-noise ratio where the signal is the first-order signal. But very different first-order signals can all be compatible with the same d' if the noise is different, as will of course happen with different levels of attention. So equalizing for d' is very much not the same as equalizing for first-order representational strength.

Lee et al. also note that Rahnev et al. suppose a fixed criterion. As they persuasively argue, that assumption is illicit and probably false. They get a better fit with the data with a variable criterion model based on work by Denison, Adler, Carrasco, and Ma (2018) in the context of a postperceptual decision-making framework. They note that when the stimuli include a number of intermediate cases instead of just two extremes, subjects are better able to understand the decision-making process, and when that is done, evidence emerges for the phenomena being rooted in suboptimal reporting rather than a change in perception.

In conversation, Richard Brown notes that Rahnev et al. gave subjects rewards for more optimal metacognitive judgments, but that the rewards failed to put a dent in the inattentional inflation. (A metacognitive judgment of perception is optimal insofar as one's confidence tracks whether one's discriminations are right.) In the "Supplementary Information" section of the article, the authors describe variants of the experiment in which they reward subjects for responding optimally, by explaining that the payoff structure promotes unbiased responding and by giving them trial-by-trial feedback, a procedure that is said to diminish suboptimal decision biases. However, as Greyson Abid has pointed out, cognitive biases might be similarly resistant to feedback (Abid, 2019).

A similar dialectic applies to Lau and Brown's discussion of temporary inactivation of frontal cortex due to electromagnetic pulses from transcranial magnetic stimulation (TMS) (in Lau & Rosenthal, 2011). They say (p. 369):

> Rounis et al. [Here they refer to (Rounis, Maniscalco, Rothwell, Passingham, & Lau, 2010). I am substituting (author, date) references for their numbers.] reported that TMS targeted at the dorsolateral prefrontal cortex both lowered subjective reports of visual awareness and impaired metacognitive ability . . . the effect was salient in the subjective reports, whereas task performance was unimpaired. . . . However, because subjective reports are more direct measures of visual awareness compared to task performance [Lau, 2008, Figure 2], this is in agreement with the claim proposed by the higher-order view that the prefrontal cortex is crucial for conscious awareness, and in particular the subjective aspects (i.e., not only task performance).

Again, they give no evidence that it is "visual awareness" that is at issue in this experiment as opposed to cognitive phenomenology.

I can add that from the point of view of a first-order theory such as mine, these results are unsurprising. Dorsolateral prefrontal cortex is a known cognitive and metacognitive area, so the fact that disturbances of it have a negative effect on metacognitive accuracy is to be expected. These may be effects on cognition and cognitive phenomenology rather than effects on anything visual.

Although I am skeptical about inattentional inflation in perceptual phenomenology, I acknowledge that people can have very impaired access to unattended aspects of the visual scene. In the 1970s, McConkie and colleagues (McConkie & Rayner, 1975; McConkie & Zola, 1979) used eye-trackers to change aspects of the visual scene that the subject was not fixating. The result was that subjects missed vast changes in text being read outside of a fixation area. I was a subject in one of these experiments and thought that the apparatus must be broken since I didn't notice any changes! Michael Cohen and colleagues have since updated this procedure with naturalistic pictures that change in various ways outside the fixation point. Cohen and colleagues varied the circle around the fixation point in which the pictures are unchanged, but even with very narrow circles, subjects often did not notice when the foveal area was vibrantly colored but outside the fixation circle the colors changed to grayscale (Cohen, Ostrand, Frontero, & Pham, 2020; Cohen & Rubenstein, 2020).

One mechanism that may be involved here is various forms of "filling-in" as with the phonemic restoration effect discussed in Chapter 1 and the modal and amodal contour completion discussed in Chapters 6 and 11. But putting filling-in to one side, Cohen's results may simply reflect lack of cognitive access to aspects of one's own phenomenology. Note that I am not saying that the black and white periphery is inaccessible, just that with attention to the foveal area it is not accessed, much as the gorilla that walks across the stage in one of the more famous change blindness setups is not accessed—at least not accessed as a gorilla. In that experiment, subjects are asked to count passes between members of the white-shirted team, ignoring passes between members of the black-shirted team. As a result of inattention to blackness, they often do not notice a black gorilla that moves across the fixation point. But anecdotally many subjects report having seen something black and having ignored it. Using signal detection methods, Nartker et al. found that in a classic "inattentional blindness paradigm, subjects were able to answer questions about the properties of the items they supposedly did not see suggesting that they may have had degraded conscious perception of it (Nartker, Firestone, Egeth, & Phillips, 2021). The upshot is that to notice the gorilla one may have to conceptualize it as a gorilla. Similarly, to notice the black and white periphery in Cohen's experiment one may have to conceptualize it as black and white. My suggestion is that subject *do not* so conceptualize it, not that they *cannot* so conceptualize it. (Note: most lottery tickets do not win, but it is not true that any given one of them cannot win.)

The main point of this chapter came at the beginning, where I reminded the reader that Chapter 6 showed that from 6 to 11 months, infants have color perception without color cognition. I further argued that the infants' perceptions are conscious. If that is right, cognitive theories of consciousness are wrong. This point applies straightforwardly to standard versions of the HOT theory, in which perceptual content is expressed in the HOT. The infants cannot have the relevant HOT because they lack the necessary color concepts. The application to the "pointer" version of the HOT account depends on the less well confirmed point that 6- to 11-month-old infants do not notice colors.

In the case of the global workspace theory, consciousness requires encoding of perceptual content in the global workspace, rendering it vulnerable to my point because encoding requires concepts they do not have.

Lau and Brown assume that inattentional inflation and inflation in peripheral vision are instance of the same phenomenon. However, as I pointed out in Chapter 1, peripheral inflation is probably a perceptual phenomenon, at least in part. Recall that Galvin and colleagues (1997) showed that when subjects matched the appearance of peripheral with foveally viewed edges, an objectively blurred edge in the periphery tended to be matched with a sharper edge in the fovea. This experiment does not require a signal-detection framework, since matching is arguably a perception-dominated process with no bias to either matching or not matching. If, as I've argued and as has been argued more persuasively by Lee et al. (in preparation), the explanation of inattentional inflation is a matter of suboptimal reporting, then peripheral and inattentional inflation are quite different phenomena.

Hakwan Lau and his colleagues regard inflation as a kind of illusion. For example, Knotts et al. liken inflation to the "uniformity illusion," in which a foveal texture is seen as uniform across the visual field even when the textures in the periphery are not the same as those in the fovea (Knotts, Odegaard, Lau, & Rosenthal, 2019). But as I pointed out in Chapter 1, perception can only give us information about properties it is sensitive to (Anstis, 1998; Haun, 2021). In foveal vision, we can't see spatial frequencies above 50 cycles per degree. In peripheral vision, our sensitivity is lower, but that is not a defect any more than it is a defect of foveal vision to not be sensitive to 70 cycles per degree. Nor is it a defect of color vision that it is not sensitive to ultraviolet or infrared light.

Prefrontalism and electrical stimulation of the brain

Some recent studies have involved intracranial brain stimulation in which microelectrodes are placed on the surface of the brains of epilepsy patients whose brains are being mapped for purposes of finding the sources of epileptic seizures that have been resistant to drugs. The patients often volunteer for studies in which electrical impulses are delivered to their brains and the patients report on their experiences. To control for the possibility that the patients may have theories about what the experimenters want to hear, the trials in which there is stimulation are accompanied by control trials in which they use sham stimulation that uses procedures that are similar to real stimulation.

The prefrontalist theories of consciousness just discussed all predict that such stimulation of prefrontal cortex, especially lateral prefrontal cortex, should have an effect on ongoing perceptual experience, that is, the perceptual experiences that the subjects are having of the hospital, lab, and personnel. The "double representation" approach (in which the contents of conscious perception are represented both in perceptual areas and in the prefrontal areas that subserve higher order thought) predicts that prefrontal stimulation (especially in lateral prefrontal cortex) should disturb the perceptual contents that subjects are currently experiencing in some way. For example, if the patient is looking at the doctor's face or at the recording apparatus, those perceptions should be in some way distorted or otherwise affected by stimulation that injects static into the representations of HOT. For example, if the HOT represents a certain set of colors, textures, motions, and angles, injecting static into it should in some way change what is represented and therefor change experience if the theory of consciousness is right.

What about the "pointer" version of the higher order theory Cleeremans, 2014; Cleeremans et al., 2020; Lau, 2019; 2022; Odegaard, Knight, & Lau, 2017b)? Recall that this version of the theory prescinds from double representation by construing the higher order activations as pointers to a perceptual state. The pointers are sometimes supposed to have their own contents pertaining to whether the perception is reliable or not. On this view, stimulation to prefrontal cortex might result in changing which perceptual state the pointer points to, or it might result in changing the reliability content, giving a perception the feel of a hallucination, or it might disrupt the monitoring process in some other way. In all these cases, subjects should be able to report the perceptual changes. What would not be expected is completely novel hallucinations with no effect on current perceptions since the injection of noise would not produce so much structure.

Similar points apply to global workspace theories since they postulate that lateral prefrontal cortex is crucial to maintaining and broadcasting specific perceptual contents. Stimulation to this area should in some way alter or impede global broadcasting, perhaps changing its content or changing which content is globally broadcast.

All these prefrontalist views predict alteration of current ongoing perception by stimulation to prefrontal cortex (PFC). By "ongoing perception" I mean the percepts that the patient has at the time of stimulation, for example perception of the doctor's face. However, reviews of the stimulation literature indicate that such effects are never reported (Fox et al., 2020; Raccah, Block, & Fox, 2021).

There is one study of two patients in which stimulation of lateral PFC caused visual hallucinations (Blanke, Landis, & Seeck, 2000). There is some indication, though, that the states caused might have been more cognitive than perceptual. In any case, the crucial point is that there are no reported alterations of ongoing perception.

Stimulation of orbitofrontal cortex produces experiences of smell and taste, somatosensory experience, and changes of mood. Stimulation of anterior cingulate cortex also improves mood, the urge to laugh, the feeling of perseverance, and sometimes other emotional experiences. But no changes in ongoing visual experience have been reported.

One reason that there are fewer reports of experience from stimulation to prefrontal cortex than posterior areas of the brain is that coding schemes in the PFC are "dense" compared to the "sparse" coding in posterior areas. That is, whereas in perceptual areas individual neurons can represent edges or faces, in PFC representation is spread over larger circuits. Further, PFC circuits might "multiplex" more than sensory circuits with the effects of activation depending on context. These points suggest that it should be difficult to produce structured hallucinations by stimulating PFC, but, the fact remains that the prefrontalist theories predict changes in ongoing perceptual experience, and those changes are not observed to happen.

As mentioned earlier, many studies have shown that perceptual contents can be decoded from prefrontal cortex. I have argued that they reflect postperceptual cognition (the bored monkey problem) rather than perceptual consciousness. However, a recent study (Bellet et al., 2022) showed decoding of perceptual contents as early as 50 ms. after the stimulus. The authors regard this result as in contradiction to Raccah et al. (2021). They say

> Furthermore, our results also contradict the interpretation of a recent study investigating extensively the causal effect of intracranial electrical stimulation on conscious perception in humans (Fox et al., 2020). This study and a recent review suggest that electrical stimulation of PFC rarely elicits exogenous sensations (Raccah et al., 2021).

However, these very fast results reflect a wave of purely feedforward processing that is almost certainly unconscious, whereas the results of Raccah et al. (2021) concerned conscious perception. See Chapter 8 for more details.

I will now discuss other approaches to consciousness, "overflow," biological reductionism, naïve realism, teleological approaches, the "fading qualia" argument, and finally the relation between consciousness and free will.

Overflow

In Chapter 1, I described the work by Victor Lamme and colleagues at the University of Amsterdam on "overflow." As I noted, their experiment was replicated using quite different materials with the same result (Freeman & Pelli, 2007). If you don't recall Lamme's experiment, I suggest you go back to Chapter 1 and review it. As I noted, putting consciousness to one side, what that work clearly shows is that the capacity of perception (whether conscious or unconscious) is higher than that of cognition. I noted that the question of whether there is more capacity in conscious perception than in cognition can be divided into two questions:

1. Is there a greater capacity in perception than cognition?
2. Is the excess capacity conscious?

As explained in Chapter 1, the answer to the first question is clearly yes. What about the second question?

As I argued above, the global workspace model is an excellent model of conceptualization (and the global playground model is even better). Encoding in the global workspace conceptualizes a percept. The advocate of the global workspace model can accept that there are nonconscious percepts that are maintained in perceptual areas but do not trigger ignition, but that only a few of them are conceptualized and encoded in the global workspace.

Stanislas Dehaene refers to the kind of representation that is strongly maintained in the back of the head but loses out in the competition to be broadcast as "preconscious" (Dehaene et al., 2006). As Dehaene notes, the strength of the preconscious activations in his attentional blink experiment could not be distinguished from the strength of the conscious activations. Here is how Dehaene and his colleagues describe the result (p. 205):

> In a recent study of the attentional blink, we observed that up to about 180 ms after stimulus presentation, the occipito-temporal event-related potentials [NB—a measure of brain circuit activation] evoked by an invisible word were large and essentially indistinguishable from those evoked by a visible word.... Yet on invisible trials, the participants' visibility ratings *did not deviate from the lowest value, used when no word was physically present*. Thus, intense occipito-temporal activation can be accompanied by a complete lack of conscious report. (italics added).

I added the italics since I think we have to consider the possibility that the stimuli that could not be reported without a change of attention may be conscious after all. The infants' color perceptions can't be reported by them either, but we have an account of why not in terms of failure of conceptualization. Report is not the criterion for consciousness.

In any case, the advocate of the global workspace view of consciousness can accept a kind of overflow—overflow of perception (whether conscious or not) over cognition. Similar points apply to both forms of the higher order viewpoint. Both can allow for more unconscious perception than can be encoded in cognitive states.

But the cost for the cognitive theorists is that they are stuck with the doctrine that nonconceptualized percepts are not conscious. So for example, the color perceptions of an 11-month-old would not be conscious. As I argued above, habituation suggests conscious perception. Even 4- to 6-month-olds will stop looking at the screen if the same color is flashed again and again, and their interest recovers if the color changes. That does not sound like unconscious perception. Further, even 4- to 6-month-old infants will move their eyes to a disk of a different color. Why do they do that if they do not consciously see the disk? This is not a knock-down argument against cognitive theorists, but it does have some weight.

Biological reductionism

I hold that phenomenal consciousness is reducible to its physical basis. This "section" is brief because much of the rest of the chapter is concerned with this issue.

The best candidates for this reduction involve neurobiology. For example, in the creatures that seem to have consciousness (e.g., primates, octopi), neurons operate via electrical signals triggering the release of neurotransmitters, and the neurotransmitters in turn engender further electrical signals. Neurons operate in a chemical soup, with direct effects from one neuron to another mediated by chemicals. The release of chemicals is not confined to the synapse but can also happen in dendrites (Tao et al., 2019). I will be appealing to this electrochemical nature of known cases of consciousness as an example of a candidate for neurobiological reduction of consciousness.[6]

Direct awareness

Some views of phenomenal consciousness take it to involve a direct awareness relation to a peculiar entity like a sense datum or to object or properties in the environment. This direct awareness is supposed to be a primitive unanalyzable acquaintance relation that is not a matter of representation. According to these direct realist/naïve realist views, the phenomenal character of a perceptual experience is object-constituted in the sense that a perceptual experience of a tomato depends for its existence and individuation on the tomato. Any experience that is of a different tomato will have a different phenomenal character, even if it is phenomenally indistinguishable and even if the different tomato is exactly the same in all its properties and causes exactly the same activations in the brain. And a veridical and subjectively indistinguishable hallucinatory experience would have to be different in phenomenal character as well. (I have encountered disbelief on the part of scientists that anyone really holds this view. For scientists reading this, I am describing a real viewpoint, albeit one that many scientists find bizarre. Naïve realist writing is famously obscure. Susanna Siegel has written a very clear account and critique of some of their views [Siegel, 2019].)

Direct/naïve realism is explicitly antirepresentational (Brewer, 2011; Campbell, 2002; Fish, 2009; Martin, 2002; McDowell, 1994; Travis, 2004) though, implausibly, direct/naïve realists often allow perceptual representation in unconscious perception (Travis, 2004). I say "implausibly" because a natural view would be that when an unconscious perception becomes conscious, what happens is that an unconscious representation becomes a conscious representation. But

---

[6] Susanna Schellenberg (2017, p. 16) describes my view this way: "Block analyzes qualia in terms of neural states. So for Block the final level of analysis is not qualia but rather neural states. In that sense his view is more powerful than views on which the final level of analysis is qualia." The term "analysis" can be understood in different ways, but if it is armchair analysis that is meant, I don't think there is any interesting analysis of the concept of qualia. My view is that qualia can be empirically reduced to physical states. Just as water is not analyzed as H_2O, qualia are not analyzed as physical.

direct/naïve realism cannot allow that. In addition, there is a good case for perceptual states that are partly conscious and partly unconscious (Block, 2016a; Block & Phillips, 2016; Phillips, 2015). It is difficult to see how to make sense of that from a direct realist point of view.

As Chris Hill points out (Hill, 2009, 2019), vision science has no room for such an acquaintance relation and the success of vision science argues against it. Further, as noted in Chapter 1, the treatment in vision science of illusion presupposes representation.

The direct realism point of view is often justified by appeal to the "openness to the world" of perceptual experience (McDowell, 1994). Martin Heidegger famously expressed this by saying, "Much closer to us than any sensations are the things themselves. We hear the door slam in the house and never hear acoustic sensations or mere sounds" (1977, p. 156). G. E. Moore's (1903) doctrine of "transparency" or "diaphanousness" is supposed to combine openness with the claim that one cannot be aware of the experiences themselves (Crane, 2006; Martin, 2002; Siewart, 2003; Stoljar, 2004).

There is a view about belief that has a similar motivation to naïve realism about perception. Naïve realists say you cannot directly introspect conscious perceptions—what you get when you try is ever more attentive perception of the objects perceived. You "see through" the perception to the world. Gareth Evans held that when you try to introspect your beliefs, you end up considering what is the case about the world (Evans, 1982). How do I know whether I believe the moon is made of green cheese? I ask myself what the moon is made of, considering the moon and its composition, not my own mind.

In a class on this topic, Carolina Flores noted that followers of Evans (many of them naïve realists) do not conclude, though, that beliefs are not representations. Why then do naïve realists conclude that perception is not representational? One factor may be that the plausibility of belief being direct awareness of the world is nil, because all will agree that our cognitive awareness of the world is mediated by perception.

Enactivism is another antirepresentational view of conscious perceptual experience. The enactive view of perceptual experience says that perceptual experience is a kind of activity rather than a kind of representation (Hurley, 1998; Hutto & Myin, 2014; Noë, 2004; O'Regan, 2011; Orlandi, 2011; Thompson & Varela, 2001). This approach has many problems, but perhaps the most relevant for present purposes is that it has trouble explaining what is in common to

- Perceiving something red (but not green),
- Imaging something red (but not green), and
- Dreaming of something red (but not green)

that can help to explain the overlap in phenomenology that can occur among these experiences as of red (Block & O'Regan, 2012). A further problem arises if one tries to promote enactivism from a theory of perceptual experience to a theory of perception itself. It is hard to see what kind of activity (or laws of activity) could be in common between conscious and unconscious perception of red. (For more on what is wrong with enactivism, see Block, 2005a; de Vignemont, 2011; Matthen, 2014.)

Enactivism and naïve realism argue for an antirepresentational point of view on the basis of a general philosophical position, but some theorists, for example, Orlandi, make an empirical case (2014). (See Mole & Zhao, 2016, for an empirical refutation of Orlandi's antirepresentational view.)

I have been assuming in this book that perception has representational content that can be thought of in terms of accuracy conditions of perceptual representation. As I noted in Chapter 1, I have discussed direct realist views elsewhere and won't revisit those discussions here (2010) except to mention some of the issues in this chapter. But even assuming that perception has representational content, the issue arises as to whether that content can be constituted by its objects.

As noted in Chapter 3, "particularists" about perception (Schellenberg, 2011, 2017; Schellenberg, 2018; Tye, 2009, 2014c) acknowledge the representational content of perception but hold that the representational content of perception is constituted by its object. The motivation is the same as that of direct realists, the intuition that the experience of the tomato involves the tomato itself. Opposed to this point of view is the claim that perceptual contents are general, for example, the "existentialist" (Hill, 2013, 2019) view that the content of my perception of the tomato is that there is a red round thing in front of me. Other generalist views are Colin McGinn's view that we ascribe clusters of properties (McGinn, 1999) and Mark Johnston's "sensory profile" account (Johnston, 2004).

A case can be made that token perceptions are object-constituted (Burge, 2005; McDowell, 2010). Burge combines such a view with a view of the phenomenology of perception as based in perceptual types that are not object-constituted. Such types are common to the perception of this tomato, a perception of an exactly similar tomato and a hallucination of a tomato and so the phenomenology of perception can be grounded in such types. These views are sometimes characterized as "dual content" views (Hill, 2013).

I prefer the dual content view, because it accommodates the transparency intuitions while giving a neat account of why the phenomenology of perception does not have to differ in veridical and hallucinatory cases. There is nothing extravagant about the dual contents because everyone has to allow for the contents of both tokens and types.

Though I prefer the dual content view, I have little sympathy for the appeal to intuitions that it is based on. Although I like some intuitions better than others,

I don't think we can rely on any of them. I said that I accept the intuition that the particular token perception of the tomato that I am touching would have to be distinct from the possible perception I would have been having were I to have touched a different but exactly similar tomato. But what is that intuition really worth? It may involve a disguised appeal to theoretical assumptions. In the philosophy of perception, intuitions are apt to be influenced by disguised introspections. This is especially plausible in the case of the diaphanousness intuition. We are best off if we can get an empirical handle on the issues in philosophy of perception and that is what I have been trying to do in this book.

Teleological approaches

Philosophers have often favored reductions of the representational content of perception to notions involving covariation and teleology. For example, Michael Tye (2000) advocates the view that what it takes for a type of perceptual state to represent that P is for it to be tokened, in optimal circumstances, if and only if, and because, P is the case. However, as Alex Byrne (2003) has noted, this sort of optimality view (advocated in very different variants by Fred Dretske (1995) and Jerry Fodor (1990) runs into trouble with visual illusions, given that they obtain in circumstances in which vision is functioning optimally, working as it was designed to work.

Of course, visual illusions are a by-product of a system that has accuracy as one of its goals, but is subject to limited resources. There is, however, another well-known problem with the teleological approach, namely, that accuracy is not the only aim of perceptual systems. Teleological approaches analyze misrepresentation in terms of malfunction, but proper function can come at the expense of accuracy. An amusing example that fancifully illustrates the point outside of the domain of perception is the tweet of 2018 often attributed to Donald Trump (in response to Michael Wolff's *Fire and Fury*), "I am a very stable genius."[7] One could speculate that the function of "I am a very stable genius" was to bolster his self-confidence when he was feeling stupid and unstable or was worried that others thought that. On a crude teleosemantic theory that dictated that the truth condition of a statement is the condition in which it fulfills its function, the truth condition of "I am a very stable genius" would not be that the speaker is a very stable genius.

---

[7] Although that sentence was widely quoted, I was unable to find it on Trump's twitter feed. I saw a tweet on January 6, 2018: "Actually, throughout my life, my two greatest assets have been mental stability and being, like, really smart."

The crude theory just mentioned is an "output"-oriented teleological theory in that the functions mentioned have to do with the use of the representations. Neander holds an "input"-based teleological theory that holds that the accuracy condition of a representation is the condition that is supposed to cause it.

Moving back to the topic of perception and to a more realistic example, consider Christopher Peacocke's hypothetical case (1993) in which a prey animal systematically visually underestimates the distance to predators. For example, a predator that is 30 feet away might be represented as 20 feet away. Peacocke hypothesizes that this kind of underestimation could have an evolutionary advantage in promoting escape despite the disadvantage in accuracy. More generally, there are trade-offs between accuracy and other relevant variables that can determine an overall function that deviates from accuracy, so a teleosemantic theory that identifies accuracy with evolutionary function will get accuracy conditions wrong.

Recent teleosemantic accounts (Neander, 2017; Shea, 2018) have attempted to work around this problem in ways that are too far from the concerns of this book to be discussed in detail. I will very briefly describe Nicholas Shea's (2018) approach. If the sole use of the prey animal's distance representations were in the context of avoiding predators, then, according to Shea, the Peacocke example is misdescribed: the alleged 20-foot estimate would indeed have the 30-foot accuracy condition. That is, there could be no daylight between accuracy conditions and proper function and no systematic underestimates.

However, systematic underestimates could occur if there is a second use of distance perception, say in guiding reaching. In that case, "If behavioural dispositions to act on a set of representations are formed in one context, and are relatively developmentally fixed, then it may make sense to 'trick' the system when deploying it in other contexts, if the behaviours appropriate to the new context would be different" (2018, p. 172). So, according to Shea, the best content-based explanation of both behaviors would dictate that this is a case in which the system is "tricked" into relying on a false representation in the predator context.

However, that reply raises the problem of the nature of the accuracy condition for the reaching behavior. Shea makes use of a variety of roughly teleosemantic relations in addition to natural selection ("survival," design, learning). His technique could be uncharitably described as using a number of different forms of roughly teleosemantic conditions on the supposition that the deviations of the different measures from accuracy will be of different sorts and so would on the average yield real accuracy conditions. But that does not avoid the fundamental problem that none of the teleosemantic forces has a constitutive connection to accuracy and so the result of combining them cannot be expected to have a constitutive connection to accuracy.

I've been discussing teleological approaches to perceptual representation without discussing their relevance to consciousness. One relevance depends on a "representationist" (or "representationalist") approach to perceptual consciousness in which the phenomenal character of a conscious perception is grounded in its representational content (Dretske, 1995; Tye, 2014b, 2018). The teleological approaches are concerned in the first instance with representational content: If consciousness is grounded in representational content, that fact can be used to motivate a teleological approach to consciousness. I have discussed representationism elsewhere (Block, 2009, 2010, 2015a), and the view will also be discussed in the next section on the fading qualia argument.

Fading qualia

David Chalmers has argued that although phenomenal consciousness and access consciousness are metaphysically distinct, they are nomologically correlated, i.e., correlated as a consequence of laws of nature (Chalmers, 1997). His chief argument has been the "fading qualia" argument and another argument that uses the same ideas, the "dancing qualia" argument (Chalmers, 1995, 1996). (I'll just talk about the first of these.) A version of the fading qualia argument has also been defended on different grounds by Michael Tye (2018). This argument depends on a conception of consciousness and cognition as tightly coupled. I believe that the view I have argued for in which perception is constitutively distinct in format and content from cognition provides the materials for seeing what is wrong with that argument.[8]

The example used in the fading qualia argument may derive from John Haugeland (1980), but the best version is that of Chalmers (1995). There are two stages.

- Stage 1.0 is a normal brain (on the left in Figure 13.4). At Stage 1.1, the cell body of one neuron is replaced by a silicon chip that process inputs from dendrites and outputs to axons just as real cell bodies do. At Stage 1.2, another neuron is similarly modified, and so on for all the neurons in the brain. At the end of Stage 1 we have a hybrid brain, combining elements of our electrochemical mechanisms with digital chips.
- Stage 2.0: all cell bodies have been replaced, but the electrical impulses in axons still produce neurotransmitters that flow across synapses to dendrites

---

[8] This section is adapted from Block, 2019c, which came out in a festschrift edited by Adam Pautz and Daniel Stoljar (Pautz & Stoljar, 2019). I am grateful to Adam Pautz and Daniel Stoljar for their helpful comments on earlier versions of some of this material.

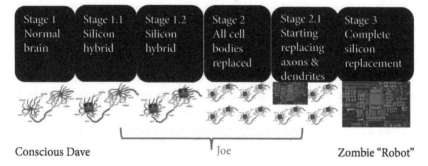

Figure 13.4 The silicon replacement scenario. It starts with Conscious Dave and ends with the zombie, Robot. Somewhere in the middle (Joe) there must be some kind of change in consciousness that is not reflected in perceptual judgments, since by hypothesis, the judgments do not change as the replacement goes on.

in other neurons. Starting with Stage 2.1, the "awkward axons and dendrites that mediate the connection between the chips" are simply replaced with standard digital connections, and by the time all these replacements have happened, at Stage 3.0, there are "no biochemical mechanisms playing an essential role."

Tye and Chalmers think the silicon replacement does not change phenomenology. I think phenomenology depends on the nature of our biological machinery. As mentioned earlier, the idea of the brain as analogous to the electrical circuits in a computer is wrong, since it neglects the chemical aspect of the brain. For example, in *C. elegans*, a much studied worm, two neurons that run the length of the worm's body have a double use, mediating both escape from harsh touch and also proprioception. Harsh touch causes the neuron to "fire," leading to escape, but proprioception works differently. Proprioception is mediated by the release of a chemical (a neuropeptide, NLP-12) from the dendrites without firing of the neuron (Tao et al., 2019). It may be said that chemical action can be simulated. Whether or not that is true, it is a familiar point that simulation of a rainstorm is not wet or windy. Similarly, it may be that simulation of conscious processing does not yield conscious processing.

Tye thinks that silicon replacement does not change phenomenology because evolutionary history is (allegedly) preserved. Chalmers thinks that there is a nomological correlation between functional organization and phenomenology.

The gradualness of the silicon-replacement is crucial to Chalmers's and Tye's argument. The starting point is Conscious Dave with his rich conscious experience, and the ending point is the silicon-brained being—following Chalmers, we can call him Robot. Robot is assumed to be a zombie with no consciousness at all.

This is the reduction assumption: The point of the argument is to derive an unacceptable consequence from it and so reject the possibility of a zombie. A sample intermediate case—somewhere in the middle of the transformation—is Joe. Dave, Joe, and Robot are assumed to be functionally identical, an assumption questioned by Peter Godfrey-Smith, who notes that there would have to be fine-grained differences, a problem that I will put to one side (Godfrey-Smith, 2016a).

Consciousness disappears during the gradual replacement of Conscious Dave's neurons, dendrites, and axons by silicon simulators. According to Chalmers, the two possibilities for intermediate cases are suddenly disappearing qualia and fading qualia. According to suddenly disappearing qualia, the replacement of a single neuron destroys consciousness altogether. Chalmers gives a broadly empirical argument that this option would require an unprecedented brute discontinuity in laws of nature. My own view is that there is a closely related more specific empirical reason for the same conclusion: It is fundamental to the way the brain works that everything is accomplished by ensemble activity in neural circuits, not individual neurons. There has never been an accepted neural model of any brain process (as far as I know) in which the destruction of a single neuron has massive effects. In sum, I agree with Chalmers that the suddenly disappearing qualia option has very little empirical plausibility.

The second option is that the intermediate case, Joe, has faint versions of all Conscious Dave's experiences, e.g., he sees tepid pink where I see bright red. But, of course, it is built-in to the example that what he says and judges about his experiences is the same as what Dave says and judges about his quite different experiences, or at least that the words that he utters are the same as the words that Dave utters. (I will ignore the possibility that Joe's words have different meanings from Dave's.) So, what Joe says and judges is systematically wrong about his experience. And that according to Chalmers (1995) is empirically implausible.

> There is a significant implausibility here. This is a being whose rational processes are functioning and who is in fact *conscious*, but who is completely wrong about his own conscious experiences. Perhaps in the extreme case, when all is dark inside, it is reasonable to suppose that a system could be so misguided in its claims and judgments—after all, in a sense there is nobody in there to be wrong. But in the intermediate case, this is much less plausible. In every case with which we are familiar, conscious beings are generally capable of forming accurate judgments about their experience, in the absence of distraction and irrationality. For a sentient, rational being that is suffering from no functional pathology to be so systematically out of touch with its experiences *would imply a strong dissociation between consciousness and cognition* [italics added]. We have little reason to believe that consciousness is such an ill-behaved phenomenon, and good reason to believe otherwise.... Unless we are prepared to accept this

massive dissociation between consciousness and cognition [italics added], the original system must have been conscious after all. (Chalmers, 1995, Section 3; approximately the same passage is found in Chalmers, 1996, p. 257)

One could doubt whether damaging the mechanisms of consciousness would result in decreasing the apparent color saturation of color percepts, but I will put that kind of worry aside, accepting that Joe is substantially wrong in some way or another about his own experience. One could also raise the question of whether the silicon simulation is really possible. There are many mechanisms of neural information transfer that on the face of it may be difficult or impossible to simulate in real time in a small space. As I have been emphasizing, neurons affect other neurons in part by many types of complex mechanisms, e.g., slow profusion of neurotransmitters into extracellular fluid. And some transfers of information work via direct connections between neurons ("gap junctions") through which many types of molecules can ooze from one neuron to another—rather than via a neuron firing. But I will put these issues aside and assume that the scenario that Chalmers describes is indeed possible.

What to think about Joe is the crux of the issue. Chalmers's argument again is broadly empirical. He says of Joe that his "rational processes are functioning," and speaking of Joe, he says: "For a sentient, rational being that is suffering from no functional pathology to be so systematically out of touch with its experiences would imply a strong dissociation between consciousness and cognition."

The possibility of a strong dissociation between consciousness and cognition is the crux of the argument. I think such a strong dissociation is possible— Chalmers and Tye deny it. It is certainly counterintuitive to suppose that a person's cognitions about their own consciousness could be wildly wrong. But to just point out that Joe as just described is counterintuitive is no argument at all. This is the crux of my argument since it shows the fading qualia argument is question-begging.

Chalmers does have further elaboration but it does require a long diversion about the notion of functional pathology. I will devote the rest of this section to the topic of functional pathology though with a heavy heart since it has no close connection to consciousness and cognition in my view.

What does it mean to say that Joe suffers from no functional pathology? There is an important ambiguity in this notion. One of the normal functional roles of experiences as of pink is to enable introspective judgments that one is seeing something pink, but Joe does not instantiate this normal introspective relation. Instead Joe makes false judgments to the effect that he is seeing something bright red. And we may suppose that Joe insistently denies seeing something pink. Joe has phenomenal states that—pathologically—do not have the kind of effects on belief as in a functionally normal person. Joe's introspection is systematically unreliable—so why isn't that functional pathology?

Chalmers says, "In conversation, he seems perfectly sensible," but what Joe says seems perfectly sensible only if one neglects the fact that, by Chalmers's and Tye's own stipulation, what he says about his own experience is systematically mistaken. Chalmers says Joe "is a fully rational system whose cognitive mechanisms are functioning just as well as mine," but that is true only if one neglects the fact that, by Chalmers's and Tye's stipulation, his introspection does not work. Failure of introspection is a functional pathology in one sense of the term.

Of course, there is another notion of "functional pathology" that does not take into account the phenomenal character of the functional state. Joe's functional organization is isomorphic to Conscious Dave's functional organization. Joe is functionally normal in that purely causal sense, a sense that ignores phenomenal character.

So, there is one functional regularity that all should agree is preserved in Joe and another functional regularity that is not preserved. I cannot see a theory-neutral rationale for preferring one to the other. Chalmers's rationale for focusing on the phenomenology-neutral notion would seem to be *functionalism itself*. Joe is "functionally normal" in that his functional organization is isomorphic to that of a normal person. But to appeal to functionalism in a defense of functionalism is question-begging. That is, the rationale would be that the phenomenal character of a state is assumed to be determined by its function. If functionalism is right about cognition, the effect of insisting on the functionalist notion of functional pathology is to assume that consciousness and cognition cannot radically diverge—precisely what is at issue in the argument.

However, instead of the blanket term "functional pathology," Chalmers might simply have given a list of mental states and conditions that in cases with which we are familiar, make introspection unreliable, e.g., distraction, self-deception, etc. And none of those circumstances are in play in Joe, the intermediate case. We could regard "functional pathology" as an abbreviation of "distraction, self-deception, and . . . ," where the meaning of the " . . . " is "other conditions that make introspection unreliable."

But why isn't the pathology that Joe has one of the conditions that make introspection unreliable? The decision not to include it in the list is question-begging. Further, a list-like notion of "functional pathology"—based on armchair considerations—is greatly inferior to one based on mechanisms, and to find the mechanisms you have to leave the armchair. There are many cases of failure of reliability of a person's judgments about their own experience that have nothing to do with "cases with which we are familiar" in daily life. Perhaps the most dramatic case is anosognosia, in which patients systematically deny a deficit—even while complaining about other deficits (Marcel, 2004). A particularly interesting case is "anosognosia for hemiplegia" (Block, 2011a; Fotopoulou, Pernigo, Maeda, Rudd, & Kopelman, 2010; Marcel, 2004). Hemiplegia is paralysis of one side of the body. In anosognosia for hemiplegia, subjects who are told to raise their arm and fail to do it seem incapable of appreciating that they are experiencing the arm not moving. In some cases of anosognosia, denial of a deficit may be due to hallucination, but as Fotopoulou et al. argue, that is probably not the case for this condition. So, the subject may be experiencing the arm not moving while simultaneously claiming it is moving.

I have seen quite a few videos of these patients and no patient I have seen has been asked while trying to move his arm, "Are you having the experience as of moving your arm?" The patients and doctors who question them do not put their points in the ways philosophers might want them to. But, patients do say they are moving their arms when they can see perfectly well that the arms are not moving.

Now these patients do have a pathology that would put them on the irrationality list: They fall when they try to walk because they do not know that one leg is paralyzed. However, if what I have been saying is right about fundamental properties of perception being distinct from fundamental properties of paradigm cognition, this sort of irrationality is not required for a disconnect between perception (conscious or unconscious) and cognition. The mechanisms of rationality are primarily mechanisms of reasoning, evaluating, thinking, and deciding. A disconnect between consciousness and cognition need not involve problems with these mechanisms. In particular, Joe's cognition might be functioning in a functionally normal way aside from the isolation of Joe's cognitive system from phenomenology. There is nothing in the nature of cognition that precludes that possibility.

No good notion of functional pathology can be framed without considering mechanisms by which experience produces judgments and behavior, and to find them we must leave the armchair. Thus, I think that the methodology used by both Chalmers and Tye is flawed.

I will now approach this same point from a slightly different direction. It will be useful to proceed using the example of the quantum approach to consciousness. I do not take this approach very seriously, nor do very many neuroscientists take it seriously, but it will be useful to illustrate the point.

Stuart Hameroff and Roger Penrose have proposed that consciousness depends on quantum processes inside tiny microtubules that are part of the skeleton of cells and are located inside neuronal cell bodies, axons and dendrites (Hameroff & Penrose, 2014). Microtubules are part of the cytoskeleton of the cell that maintains the shape of the cell. Whatever one thinks of this theory, it is not refuted by Chalmers's thought experiment. Robot as Chalmers describes it would lack consciousness according to the Hameroff-Penrose account because of the lack of microtubules in the silicon chips. (I am assuming that they hold that quantum processes of the sort in microtubules are necessary for consciousness so a silicon device that simulates us need not have such processes.) And intermediate cases would also be deficient in microtubules though not totally devoid of them. So, at some point in the progression from Conscious Dave to zombie Robot, the deficit in microtubules could be expected to result in a deficit in consciousness even though that intermediate case (Joe) is guaranteed by the terms of the thought experiment to walk and talk and would be more generally functionally just like Conscious Dave.

Of course, Hameroff and Penrose may take the line that no mechanism that lacks microtubules can possibly duplicate the functional organization of a conscious human. I am tempted to say the same about the biological mechanisms I envision as the ground of consciousness. But let us put that issue aside and assume that the zombie Robot is possible.

I doubt that even with this concession, Hameroff and Penrose would regard their view as refuted by Chalmers's argument—nor should they. What they should say is that in "every case with which we are familiar," our conscious utterances and consciously controlled behavior are caused by microtubule activity. So how can the postulation of a *different* mechanism by which a robot's utterances and behavior are caused by something else refute the microtubule account of *us*? Our introspections are accurate. Joe, lacking as he does, some of the quantum mechanisms that ground consciousness and that are necessary for consciousness, has inaccurate introspections. Whatever oddity there is in the consideration of Joe derives from constructing a case in which what third parties can observe stays the same whereas the mental states that the observables tell us about change.

Suppose I text myself "Just ran out of milk" to remind myself to buy milk. The text is evidence that I used to have milk. But if the world had come into existence a fraction of a second ago complete with all the evidence of the past (as Russell once considered) then all evidence of the past—including my text—is misleading. Cases with which we are familiar provide no precedent for such massive unreliability, but the absurdity does not show any impossibility of the claim that the world came into existence a fraction of a second ago.

As I said, I do not accept the microtubule account, so how can I use it to defend my account? My account is much vaguer—that there is something about our biological makeup—perhaps its electrochemical character—that underlies conscious phenomenology. So, the objection to Chalmers and Tye based on my account would be the same as the one given for the microtubule theory—except in its appeal to something so specific as quantum activity in microtubules.

Tye's version of the argument is importantly different from Chalmers's. He does not appeal to empirical plausibility—to the presumed reliability of our cognitive appreciation of our own phenomenology—but rather to "plausibility" in a sense he does not explain but that seems to be some sort of armchair intuition. For example, about Robot, he says of the idea that Robot's phenomenal beliefs are all wrong,

> this is very implausible. It requires us to accept that the being at the end of the replacement process is radically mistaken about his own phenomenal life even

though he is fully rational. This is difficult to swallow. A more reasonable hypothesis is that rational conscious beings are not so mistaken. (p. 558)

Although Tye and Chalmers both appeal to the rationality of the subject of the thought experiment, there is a difference: At every crucial point, Tye appeals to "plausibility." I counted 10 occurrences of variants of the word, not counting other words with the same use like "swallow" or considerations of what it is "reasonable to say." This argument has the same weaknesses as Chalmers's argument plus the additional weakness of supposing the argument from familiar cases is all a matter of plausibility rather than an empirical consideration of the nature of consciousness.

Although I have emphasized that Tye is giving an armchair argument whereas Chalmers (1995) appeals to the broadly empirical, Chalmers's argument has strong a priori elements. See especially the very interesting dialogue involving comments on a paper by Miguel Sebastian (2014) at: https://consciousnessonline.wordpress.com/2013/02/15/what-panpsychists-should-reject-on-the-incompatibility-of-panpsychism-and-organizational-invariantism/.

In that thread (on Consciousness Online), Adam Pautz notes that since on Chalmers's view, there are possible worlds in which there are fading qualia, it has to be a contingent truth that in our world there can be no fading qualia. But to the extent to which the arguments for the impossibility of fading qualia in the actual world are a priori, then the claim that there can be no fading qualia in the actual world would be a strange case of the contingent a priori. This point is more apt in application to Tye's version than to Chalmers's version of the argument, since Chalmers does appeal to broadly empirical considerations.

Tye introduces one further wrinkle. He supposes that the word "pain" as used by you expresses a "concept that rigidly picks out a state whose essence is its phenomenal character." ("Water" rigidly picks out the same substance [H_2O] in each world in which water exists. In this it differs from "watery stuff," a description that picks out substances in worlds that are like water with respect to superficial properties even if they have different molecular structures.)

After your neurons are replaced by silicon chips, the word "pain" as used by the zombie that results from the replacement rigidly picks out a nonphenomenal state. So, a new concept has been introduced. He then argues that the introduction of this new concept would be puzzlingly unlike all other cases of concept introduction, concluding (Tye, 2018, p. 561):

> It seems to me, then, that the most reasonable thing to say that is that there is just a single concept expressed by "pain" and that during the replacement process the beliefs do not change and neither does the phenomenology. So, if we wish to respect our initial intuitions and we also wish to avoid getting embroiled in

puzzles and problems that arise once we take the view that the phenomenology changes with the gradual silicon chip replacement, we should accept that, notwithstanding the absence of sameness in electrochemical mechanisms, there is sameness in phenomenology.

Suppose that Robot does not lack consciousness altogether but simply has a different kind of consciousness from us. And suppose further that Joe has a kind of consciousness that bears some similarity to ours and some to Robot's. In that case, the phenomenal "pain"-concept used by Robot and Joe would be different from ours. (I am thinking of phenomenal concepts as encompassing some sort of "sample" of a phenomenal state [Balog, 2009b; Block, 2006; Papineau, 2002].) We can use this account to explain why Conscious Dave's, Joe's, and Robot's phenomenal concepts differ from one another. And if Robot completely lacks consciousness, as the argument supposes, the "sample" would be a sample of nothing, making Robot's "phenomenal concept" if it can be called that, very different from ours.

In short, Robot's and Joe's concepts would have samples that are unlike ours. The fact that this would be unlike other cases of the introduction of a phenomenal concept seems to me to count against it not at all. And the same applies to the limiting case in which the sample is a nonphenomenal state.

Before I end the chapter on consciousness, I will discuss one more topic: the relation between consciousness and free will. Although this topic is not usually discussed in the context of the nature of perception, I will be arguing that attention to perception clarifies a major controversy about conscious decision.[9]

Consciousness and free will

There is neural evidence that has been taken to support the claim that phenomenally conscious decision is "epiphenomenal" in the sense that it has no causal effects on bodily movements (Libet, Gleason, Wright, & Pearl, 1983; Passingham & Lau, 2006). In these experiments, unconscious neural events leading up to the conscious decision are found *prior* to any consciousness that a decision has been made. Some commentators conclude from this sort of evidence that the conscious decision to act is not causally efficacious in producing action. This section will concern what is wrong with this reasoning. But first, what is a conscious decision?

---

[9] A somewhat shortened version of the next section was published as Block, 2022. Thanks to Amber Hopkins, Uri Maoz, Claire Simmons, and Walter Sinnott-Armstrong for comments on an earlier version.

What is a conscious decision?

A decision in one sense of the term is the formation of an intention. A phenomenally conscious decision in one sense of the term is then a phenomenally conscious formation of an intention. To say that forming the intention is phenomenally conscious in this sense is to say that there is something it is like to form the intention, that the formation of the intention has a phenomenal "feel." That phenomenal feel can take the form of an awareness of making a choice. Or it can be a matter of being phenomenally conscious of the decision *as a decision*, in which case the subject must possess the concept of a decision. It seems, though, that there are plenty of conscious decisions that don't feel like anything at all. We make many minor choices every day. Does it always feel like something to make them? Perhaps there is only a feeling of choice when there is some kind of deliberation about the choice. Still, our mundane everyday choices are conscious in the sense of "access-consciousness."

Access-consciousness as you will recall is immediate global availability to cognitive processing whether that cognitive processing is or is not itself phenomenally conscious (Block, 2002a). An access-conscious state is immediately available to reasoning, planning, evaluating, problem-solving, reporting, memory, and other cognitive processes. If there are Freudian repressed states, they are unconscious in the access sense whether or not they have any phenomenal feel.

I just introduced three senses of "conscious decision," (1) a phenomenally conscious decision, (2) a decision that is phenomenally conscious as a decision, (3) an access-conscious decision. Of these three senses, the first two involve a phenomenal feel. And it is the presence of the phenomenal feel involved in such conscious decisions that give rise to the problem to be discussed here. That problem is this: Some evidence has been taken to support the claim that phenomenally conscious decisions are "epiphenomenal" in the sense that they have no causal effects on bodily movements (Libet et al., 1983; Passingham & Lau, 2006). In these experiments, unconscious neural events leading up to the decision and consciousness of it are alleged to be found *prior* to consciousness of the decision; indeed some experiments suggest that the consciousness of the decision can occur at least in part after the action (Lau, Rogers, & Passingham, 2006). (Whether or not these experiments really do establish the conclusions they are taken to establish is not my concern here; my concern is what follows from these claims if they are true.) Some commentators conclude from this sort of evidence that the conscious decision to act is not causally efficacious in producing the action, because the unconscious neural events are sufficient to cause the action. This reasoning is my target.

I will explain why this reasoning is mistaken in terms that apply to *all mental events*. The main examples will concern conscious vision, because we understand the psychology and neuroscience of vision much better than we understand any other aspect of the mind. In particular, there are dramatic cases in which unconscious and conscious states have *conflicting* contents. The lessons from such examples will then be applied to the case of conscious decisions. My technique will be to sketch some examples that show that the conscious and unconscious aspects of a mental event can have different and opposed effects on behavior. When the behavior fits with the conscious aspect, we can sometimes be sure that it is causally efficacious even if the unconscious parts precede the conscious parts. The upshot will be that even in the cases where the influence of the conscious and unconscious aspects of the mental events point in the same direction, they may make somewhat independent contributions to the behavioral effect. In what follows, the detail about conscious vision may make the reader wonder whether the topic of conscious decision has somehow been forgotten, so bear with me.

Are conscious perceptions epiphenomenal?

All conscious mental events, including conscious perceptions, involve unconscious processing. Visual perception, conscious and unconscious, is typically processed by the lateral geniculate nucleus and the first cortical visual area, V1. (For some kinds of unconscious perception, the pathways involve the superior colliculus and the pulvinar, bypassing the lateral geniculate nucleus-to-V1 route.) There is good reason to believe that representations at the level of the lateral geniculate nucleus and V1 are not part of the neural basis of consciousness. (Some of this evidence is summarized in Koch, 2004; Koch, Massimini, Boly, & Tononi, 2016.)

If a grating of black and white bars is very finely spaced, it looks like a uniform gray field. More specifically, a grating consisting of parallel black bars separated by equal sized white bars of more than 50 black-white pairs per degree of visual angle (i.e., a "spatial frequency" of more than 50 cycles per degree—cyc/deg—of visual angle) looks like a uniform gray field. In Figure 13.5, the three circles look the same if the spatial frequency of the pair on the left exceeds 50 cyc/deg of visual angle, which you can arrange by standing far enough back from the figure.

However, even when the viewer is far enough away that these three circles look the same, they have different effects on the retina and in the early part of the visual system, as Shang He and Donald MacLeod (2001) showed. The limit of resolution of 50 cyc/deg is sometimes attributed to the fact that the lens of the eye blurs very fine gratings, but as He and MacLeod note, that does not tell us whether, if fine gratings could *somehow* be presented directly to the retina, the retina could resolve the gratings. He and MacLeod approached this question via

Figure 13.5 Items of this sort can look to have solid colors to viewers for whom the distance from the beginning of one black bar to the beginning of another in the grid subtends one-fiftieth or less of a degree of visual angle. In that sense, these fine gratings are "invisible" to that viewer.

the observation that visible gratings produce a number of orientation-specific aftereffects. In particular, if one looks at a visible tilted grating for a period—say one minute—then gratings presented immediately afterward that are close in orientation to the original grating appear somewhat rotated away from the orientation of the original grating. This illusion, the tilt aftereffect, is described in Chapter 2 along with other "repulsive" effects of adaptation. An additional and more basic orientation-specific aftereffect is that gratings at the same orientation of the original grating are harder to see. For example, the degree of contrast of the bars required to detect the grating increases. Both effects are said to depend on the fact that orientation-specific cells early in the cortical processing of vision become "fatigued" in the original period of firing, a process known as adaptation to that orientation. See Chapter 2 for the limitations of the "fatigue" account.

He, Cavanagh, and Intriligator (1996) showed that if grids are made invisible by another method that I will not describe, the invisible lines cause orientation-specific aftereffects. However, no one had been able to do a direct test of whether gratings which are too fine to see produce orientation-specific aftereffects such as the tilt aftereffect because of the fact just mentioned that the lens of the eye blurs out very fine details. He and MacLeod used an amazing method to avoid the lens of the eye: They were able to project the grids directly to the retina through the side of eye, bypassing the lens, by using laser interferometry. (Technically, what they projected were lines made up of interference fringes caused by interference among different frequencies of light.) Using this method, they projected gratings that are too fine to see directly onto the retina, showing that "invisible" gratings produce aftereffects of the same magnitude as visible gratings, revealing that the "invisible" gratings are indeed represented in the visual system, including in the retina and early vision. As He and MacLeod also note, this result is further confirmed by recordings from monkey visual systems. (See also Rajimehr, 2004.)

An analogous result obtains for color flicker. If two colors alternate at frequencies above 10 Hz (10 cycles per second), viewers see a single fused color rather than flickering colors (so long as the two colors have the same luminance). For example, red and green flickering above 10 Hz looks nonflickering and yellow. (Combining red and green lights—an "additive" mixture, as is used in your computer screen—produces yellow. By contrast, pigments subtract colors, e.g., red pigment subtracts blue and green, which is why mixing pigments results in different colors from mixing lights.) The phenomenon in which red and green fast flickering creates yellow is called heterochromatic flicker fusion. However, retinal cells respond to flicker way above the frequency that the subject can see—as high as 40 Hz, and a waystation between the retina and the cortex (the lateral geniculate nucleus) responds to frequencies that are almost as high. In the first cortical visual area, V1, all cells responded to 15 Hz flicker and most to 30 Hz flicker (Gur & Snodderly, 1997). In sum, the retina and early vision registers flicker that the subject does not see as flicker.

These are among many items of evidence for the conclusion that the retina and the earliest stages of visual processing in the cortex are not part of the minimal physical basis of conscious experience. The retina and V1 both register differences in gratings that are not consciously experienced and register color differences that are not consciously experienced. One way to see the point is in terms of the significance of 50 cyc/deg for the retina and V1 as opposed to conscious vision. Variations in orientation of gratings of more than 50 cyc/deg make a difference in the retina and V1 of the same sort as variations of orientation of less than 50 cycles per degree, but only the latter make a difference in conscious experience. The contrast between gratings under 50 and over 50 cyc/deg is no more significant at the level of the retina and V1 than the contrast between under and over 40 cyc/deg, but 50 cyc/deg is the magic number when it comes to visual experience. The upshot is that the retina and V1 are poor candidates for being part of the minimal physical basis of conscious vision (Koch, 2004; Rees et al., 2002).

A further piece of the case against the retina and V1 as part of the physical basis of visual experience is that although the retina and V1 do respond to very fine gratings, higher areas in the visual system do not. John-Dylan Haynes and Geraint Rees (2005) used fMRI brain scanning (functional magnetic resonance imaging) to measure responses to visible and invisible gratings in V1, V2, and V3. (The invisible gratings were rendered invisible by a technique honed by Steve Macknik known as the standing wave of invisibility—in which a central item is "masked" by items that appear before and after it to both sides of the central item.) Haynes and Rees were able to predict the orientation of the grating the subject was seeing from the activity in V1 whether or not the subjects said they saw the grating. They were able to predict the orientations at a greater than chance level even when subjects were at chance in choosing which orientation they saw. (The subject doesn't know the orientation but the information is in V1.) It should be noted that this is a direct measure of the sensitivity of V1 to invisible gratings rather than the indirect measure involving adaptation mentioned earlier. Moving to the question of higher areas, Haynes and Rees were not able to predict the orientation of invisible gratings from activations in V2 or V3. (And responses even to visible gratings decreased in the higher areas.)

The upshot is that differences in activations in the retina and V1 that do not make a difference in other areas do not make a difference to simultaneous conscious experience. That is, if the retina and V1 vary while other areas in the brain are constant in activation, experience is constant too, suggesting that it is activity in those other areas that is the minimal physical basis of conscious experience.

It is important to realize that this is really a burden of proof argument. It is possible that some other kind of difference in the retina or V1 that does not change other areas would show a different result, but the burden is on anyone who thinks there are such differences to find them. Further, it is conceivable that some mechanism could be part of the physical basis of consciousness even though no difference in its operation makes a difference to consciousness without some other difference. That is, it is conceivable that a mechanism could be part of the minimal physical basis of consciousness, but its effects be "partnership" effects in every case. But again, the burden is on the advocate of such a possibility to find even the slightest bit of evidence for it. The paradigms used in vision science to date provide considerable evidence that the retina is not part of the minimal physical basis of any contents of consciousness. The burden is on those who disagree to isolate contents and discover evidence concerning those contents that challenge that consensus.

The major theories of consciousness that are relevant to this issue agree that processing in the lateral geniculate nucleus and V1 *precedes* conscious processing. I will explain with respect to three of the major theories of consciousness.

(1) The global workspace theory dictates that conscious processing of a stimulus begins—at the earliest—270 ms after the stimulus, long after the stimulus is extensively processed in the lateral geniculate nucleus and V1 (Dehaene et al., 2006). (2) Higher order thought takes somewhat *more* time than global broadcasting, so theories of consciousness based on HOT (Brown et al., 2019; Rosenthal, 1986) also allow for substantial unconscious processing prior to conscious processing. (3) The recurrent processing approach to consciousness also dictates that conscious processing occurs well after stimuli are extensively processed in the lateral geniculate nucleus and V1 (Lamme, 2003; Pitts et al., 2014). According to Victor Lamme's version of the recurrent processing account, conscious perception requires processing in the lateral geniculate nucleus and V1, then processing in higher visual areas, and then, finally, feedback to V1. And

there is independent evidence for the need for the feedback to V1 (Block, 2007a; Silvanto, Cowey, Lavie, & Walsh, 2005). So on this account, conscious perception requires first activations in V1 and then a second round of activations in V1.

So, as with decision, unconscious visual processing precedes conscious visual processing. Nonetheless, conscious perceptions are often causally efficacious in producing actions. But how do we know whether it is in virtue of the conscious aspect of the perception that the action occurred, i.e., that the conscious aspect of the perception is causally efficacious?

A conscious perception has conscious and unconscious aspects, and when a conscious perception causes something, it will not always make sense to ask which aspects are causally efficacious. An iceberg displaces an amount of water equal to the weight of the whole iceberg, so it is the whole iceberg that is causally efficacious in that respect, not just the part below water. If the above-water part of an iceberg hits a ship, we cannot conclude that the below-water part was not causally efficacious, since without the below-water part there would be no above-water part to hit the ship. The same point applies to conscious mental events—without their unconscious part there would be no conscious part.

There is a complication however. When one event causes another, some of the properties of the cause may be causally efficacious in producing the effect and others not. When the brick flying through the air breaks the window, it is in virtue of its mass and velocity that the window breaks, not in virtue of its color: The color is causally inefficacious in breaking the window. See Chapter 3 for some discussion of this issue.

Still, in many cases we can ask whether the conscious part is causally efficacious, that is, whether it was at least partly in virtue of the conscious part that the effect happened. In some cases the answer is demonstrably yes.

It is well known that unconscious perceptual processing can influence behavior. In one experiment (Debner & Jacoby, 1994), subjects were presented with a strongly masked word and then asked to complete a word stem, but not with the word they saw if they saw a word. (Masking can make a stimulus hard to consciously see if the timing is right.) If the word "reason" is presented consciously (lightly masked), then the subject can succeed in avoiding the presented word in completing the stem, for example, by completing "rea___" with "reader." But if "reason" is presented unconsciously (strongly masked), then the subject is more likely than baseline to complete the stem "rea___" with "reason."

Similar "opposite" effects of conscious and unconscious processing occur in visual perception. Suppose a subject has the task of pressing the button marked "yellow" if the stimulus is yellow and a button marked "red & green" if the stimulus is flickering red and green. If the stimulus is a red/green flickering stimulus at 12 Hz, the subject will consciously see yellow and so can be expected to press the "yellow" button. But if the stimulus had been degraded or masked and so was entirely unconscious, the stimulus would have registered in unconscious processing as red and green flickering, so the yellow color would not have been perceptually registered and if the resulting unconscious perceptual processing had an effect on behavior, it would incline the subject to the "red & green" rather than the "yellow" button.

When the colored stimulus flickers at 12 Hz, resulting in pressing the "yellow" button, we can conclude that the conscious part was causally efficacious, since the unconscious part by itself would not have influenced the subject's behavior in the direction of the "yellow" button. Similarly, if the stripe density of a stimulus is 60 cycles per degree, a subject will classify it as uniform gray on the basis of conscious perception. But if the perception had had no conscious part, the visual system would have registered it as striped rather than uniform, so it would have inclined the subject to the striped response—to the extent that the unconscious perceptual processing would have causally influenced a response. So, in the conscious case, we can conclude that the conscious aspect was causally efficacious.

The counterfactual test I am using has to be applied carefully. If the exposed part of an iceberg caused damage to a ship sufficient to sink it, we can ask what would have happened had the top part of the iceberg not been there so that the iceberg was entirely below water. The ship might have been sunk anyway though through a different causal path. Still, if the result goes the other way—if the iceberg would not have sunk the ship had it not had the above-water part—then we can reasonably conclude that the above-water part was causally efficacious.

The resulting picture of the relation between conscious and unconscious mental events is that when a conscious mental event is causally efficacious, we can sometimes ask whether it is causally efficacious in virtue of its conscious aspect. I have just given examples that show that the conscious and unconscious aspects can have different and opposed effects on behavior in at least some cases. In these cases, it is particularly obvious that the conscious aspect of the mental event is causally efficacious. But even in the case where the influence of the conscious and unconscious aspects of the mental events point in the same direction, they may make somewhat independent contributions to the behavioral effect.

Back to phenomenally conscious decisions

Conscious decisions (I'm talking about phenomenally conscious decisions here) are conscious mental events, and so the points just made about *all conscious mental events* apply to them. If the subject is choosing between salad and chocolate cake, the unconscious aspect of the decision might incline the subject to the chocolate cake whereas the conscious aspect might incline the subject to the salad. If the subject chooses the salad, then the conscious aspect was presumably causally efficacious. However, if the conscious and unconscious aspects inclined the subject to the same decision, *both* may be causally efficacious. With decision as with perception, the unconscious and conscious aspects of the decision can point in the same direction but make somewhat independent contributions, in which case again the conscious aspects are causally efficacious. An unconscious part of a mental event always precedes conscious aspects, but the conscious aspects may nonetheless be causally efficacious.

With decision, as with perception, we can expect that there will be differences between the kinds of contents that will typically be unconscious and those that will typically be conscious. An unfortunate legacy of the Libet style experiments is a focus in the neuroscience of decision on very simple contents that can be either conscious or unconscious, basically go/no go contents. The field would be better off with an increased emphasis on the contents of decision and on which ones can be expected to be conscious and which unconscious.

This chapter has mainly concerned cognitive theories of consciousness, with a focus on whether the points made in Chapter 6 about color perception without color cognition refute these cognitive theories. In addition, I argued in the last section that a consideration of the relation between conscious perception and its unconscious underpinnings clarifies the role of consciousness in decision.

14
Conclusions

As I mentioned in Chapter 1, the view that perception is constitutively iconic, nonconceptual, and nonpropositional is far from new, having been debated pro and con for many years, with many philosophers and many scientists on both sides of the debate. The purpose of this book has been to clarify these debates and to sketch actual experimental evidence for the positive side. This book has been all about evidence.

In the first paragraph of this book I mentioned sixteen questions that the book would be concerned with. I'll list the questions here and my answers to them.

1. **What is the difference between seeing and thinking?**
   Perception is constitutively nonpropositional, nonconceptual, and iconic, and cognition does not constitutively have any of these properties.
2. **Is the border between seeing and thinking a joint in nature in the sense of a fundamental explanatory difference?**
   Yes.
3. **Is it a difference of degree?**
   No.
4. **Does thinking affect seeing, i.e., is seeing "cognitively penetrable"?**
   Yes, the most dramatic cases being perception of ambiguous stimuli.
5. **Do we visually represent faces, causation, numerosity, and other "high-level" properties or only the colors, shapes, and textures on the basis of which we see that high-level properties are instantiated?**
   We visually represent high-level properties in both conscious and unconscious vision.
6. **Is high-level perception or object perception conceptual or propositional?**
   I think not but the case is less strong than for low-level perception.
7. **Is perception iconic or more akin to language in being discursive?**
   Iconic.
8. **Is seeing singular? That is, does seeing necessarily function to single something out?**
   There is no fact of the matter. Some visual states are not very plausibly construed as singular.

9. **Which is more fundamental, visual attribution or visual discrimination?**

   Both are fundamental, and there is no strong reason for thinking that one is more fundamental.

10. **Is all seeing seeing-as?**

    Yes, since all seeing involves visual attribution.

11. **What is the difference between the format and content of perception and do perception and cognition have different formats?**

    The format is the structure of the representational vehicle; the content is the way it represents the world to be. Perception and cognition have different constitutive formats: perception is iconic, cognition discursive. I argued that although perception has finer grained content than cognition, a perception and a thought in principle can share the same content, e.g., a representation of sky blue.

12. **Is perception probabilistic, and if so, why are we not normally aware of this probabilistic nature of perception?**

    Perception may not be probabilistic, though probabilistic models of perception are useful if treated in an "as-if" mode. Instrumentalism about the probabilistic features of idealized models is motivated by the fact that the behavioral capacities that Bayesian rationality would provide are evolutionarily selected for but the Bayesian implementations at the algorithmic level may not be.

13. **Is there evaluative perception**

    Surprisingly, there is no good evidence for evaluative perception.

14. **Are the basic features of mind known as "core cognition" a third category in between perception and cognition?**

    No, core cognitive representations are an amalgam of perception and cognition (as are, in my view, emotions).

15 **Are there perceptual categories that are not concepts?**

    Yes, see Chapter 6.

16. **Where does consciousness fit in with regard to the difference between seeing and thinking? In particular, does the nonconceptual and nonpropositional nature of perception have consequences for the nature of consciousness?**

    The noncognitive nature of perception precludes cognitive theories of consciousness. In particular, there is an argument from one of the cases of nonconceptual perception to the conclusion that there is phenomenal consciousness without access-consciousness.

To elaborate on some of the main conclusions:

1. There is strong positive evidence for a joint in nature between cognition and perception. I emphasized the distinction between format, content and

representational state, noting that there is no such thing as nonconceptual content; rather what is nonconceptual is perceptual states. The joint consists in three properties that are constitutive of perception but not cognition: iconic format, nonconceptual, and nonpropositional states. Note however, that the three properties are not sufficient for perception since, for example, the perceptual simulations used in cognition have those constitutive properties. (See footnote 3 in Chapter 1 for more on why the three properties are not sufficient.)
2. Some of the indicators of perception discussed in Chapter 2 may be more basic to perception than others. In particular, I discussed the fact that perceptions compete with one another. One principle governing this competition is "divisive normalization." I discussed a special case of divisive normalization in which the perception of a disk and surrounding donut interact, making the disk look lower in contrast than it would otherwise look if it shares features with the donut. As I noted, there is evidence that this basic computation of vision does not apply to visual working memory, the scratch pad of cognition. And that suggests a fundamental difference between perception and working memory.
3. That joint is compatible with cognitive penetration, direct content-specific effects of the content of cognition on the content of perception. And there are often such direct effects, notably in the case of ambiguous stimuli, i.e., when different categorizations of a stimulus are more or less equally probable.
4. But the known mechanisms by which cognitive penetration works do not impugn a joint in nature between cognition and perception. Indeed, they support the joint to the extent that known mechanisms separate into the perceptual and the cognitive.
5. Many supposed intermediate cases between cognition and perception involve nonconceptual perceptual analogs of concepts. Some core cognition phenomena may be perceptual, some cognitive.
6. At least some conscious perception is nonconceptual and nonpropositional, and that fact poses problems for cognitive theories of consciousness. In particular, children between 6 months and 11 months have phenomenal consciousness of color without access consciousness of color.

After laying out a three-layer methodology in Chapter 1, I considered various markers of perception in Chapter 2. I then moved to two kinds of seeing-as in Chapter 3, non-conceptual and conceptual seeing-as, arguing that the joint falls between them. I gave an example from the racial bias literature explaining how to tell conceptual and nonconceptual seeing-as apart. I then discussed Bayesian approaches, arguing that they do not support genuine inference in perception.

Chapter 3 also argues that there is no fact of the matter as to whether perception is constitutively singular in content. That chapter also argues that both attribution and discrimination are fundamental to perception and neither is prior.

My argument for the nonpropositional nature of perception started from the fact that perception does not involve logically complex contents—for example, one cannot perceptually ascribe negations or disjunctions of properties. One can see something as nonblue by seeing it as red, but one cannot see anything simply as not-blue. One can see something as intermediate or indeterminate between red and blue (e.g., purple) but not as having the disjunctive property of simply being red or being blue. Similar points hold for other logical connectives. I considered the objection that perception may be propositional but that the propositions are always atomic because the information available via perception supplies only information suitable for atomic propositions. I countered that stimuli can involve disjunctive, conditional, and conjunctive information. I then discussed whether there can be perception of absences, arguing that to the extent that there is perceptual representation of absences or emptiness, it does not involve true negation.

My argument for the iconic format of perception involved a notion of iconicity as analog tracking and mirroring. Analog tracking and mirroring obtains when there is a set of environmental properties and a set of representations of those environmental properties such that:

1. Certain differences in representations function as responses to differences in environmental properties in a way that is sensitive to the degree of environmental differences. For example, as objects like the ones depicted in Figure 5.2 are rotated, perceptual representations function to alter in a way that corresponds to that rotation and is sensitive to that degree of rotation.
2. Certain differences in representations function to alter the situation that is represented in a way that depends on the degree of representational change.
3. Certain relations (including temporal relations) among the environmental properties are mirrored by representations that instantiate analogs of those relations.

As I noted, iconic representations often represent integral dimensions in the environment via integral representational dimensions. I discussed a few of the many items of evidence that the mental imagery and perceptual systems overlap considerably in representations and mechanisms. Then I went through a few representative items of evidence that perceptual imagery makes use of an analog of spatial properties in the brain to represent spatial properties in the world. The special category of perceptual object representations came in for a lot of discussion since they have been said by some to be discursive. I discussed evidence to the contrary from apparent motion, object-based attention, object-based visuospatial neglect and inhibition of return. Finally, I rebutted arguments from E. J. Green and Jake Quilty-Dunn concerning object-perception.

An experimental argument for the nonconceptual nature of perception is that for some perceptual contents, children under 11 months old do not normally use them in reasoning. I argue that those perceptual states are nonconceptual, and that there is reason to think that all perception is nonconceptual. My main argument worked from an example, that 6- to 11-month-old infants have color discrimination that is almost the equal of adults, but without color concepts. The argument against color concepts relied on evidence that without special training, these infants fail to use color perception in reasoning even though they are able to use spatial and kind properties in similar tasks. The point of this argument is to put the proponents of conceptual perception in the position of having to justify the idea that some perception is nonconceptual and some conceptual. That view would have to be justified as against the view that (1) all perception is nonconceptual and (2) in some cases, conceptualization in perceptual judgment is nearly automatic. I also looked at evidence from neuroscience that perception is nonconceptual, including evidence from binocular rivalry and inattentive perception. Since there is good reason to think that the color perception of children under 11 months is conscious but not poised for cognitive access, they are a case of phenomenal consciousness without access consciousness.

After making the positive case for perception being constitutively iconic in format, nonconceptual, and nonpropositional, I turned to the negative case, especially arguments against conceptual perception. I first discussed one case of putative ultrafast perceptual categorization, arguing that a careful look at the carwash model shows that these experiments do not actually support ultrafast perception, since the carwash model allows for perceptual categorization long after the initial presentations. I also discussed experimental paradigms that do show a kind of ultrafast perception, arguing that they do not support conceptual perception because they can be explained by a combination of perceptual set and perceptual access to intermediate stages of processing.

Many top-down effects are effects of higher levels on lower levels within perceptual modules. In particular, top-down effects on figure/ground organization and perception of color fit this characterization. However, many top-down effects are genuine cases of cognitive penetration, notably the role of cognition in connection with perceiving ambiguous stimuli. The competing perceptions of ambiguous stimuli differ in surface representations and so have an impact on early or at least early-ish perception. In addition, when an ambiguous stimulus that is perceived initially as a nonface is then perceived as a face, new representational properties are introduced, contrary to modularist suggestions.

In the case of feature-based attention and mental imagery, known mechanisms do not appear to be hard to classify as perceptual or cognitive, pulling the teeth of these cases with regard to a joint. Ambiguous stimuli divide into reversible and nonreversible cases. For reversible cases, there may be automatic bottom-up processing of both percepts, with cognition playing the role of selecting between them via feature-based or even spatial attention. Nonreversible ambiguous stimuli such as sine-wave speech and the Dalmation of Figure 9.5 are better candidates for cognitive infiltration of perception. They deserve further study.

Fodor characterized modules in terms of nine diagnostic properties. The two that have loomed largest in subsequent discussion have been cognitive impenetrability and domain specificity. Both have something to them, but in the case of domain-specificity, it applies to perceptual systems only if limited to synchronic rather than diachronic effects. Another of Fodor's diagnostic properties, innate structure, has also proven to be importantly right. Limited central accessibility turns out to be partly wrong.

Core cognition poses the greatest threat to a joint because core capacities are foundational in our mental lives and allegedly have properties that are fundamental to both perception and cognition, undermining the explanatory unity of the properties I claim are fundamental to perception. Further, phenomena that have fundamental properties of both perception and cognition might be candidates for conceptual perception, and that would impugn the joint by impugning one of the properties that I have said is basic to the joint.

I considered two core faculties, our appreciation of causation and approximate numerosities. I argued that we have categorical perception of causation and that perceptual categories are easy to conflate with concepts, but they can be distinguished on the basis of psychological and neurophysiological evidence. I argued that in the case of both causation and numerosity, we have nearly automatic conceptualization of perception, making it difficult to empirically separate the perception and its conceptualization, but that there is no good evidence for a single faculty that combines both perception and cognition. In the end, it looks as if core cognition combines purely perceptual and purely cognitive abilities.

Overall, what I have tried to do in this book is to try to avoid the use of "intuitions" that are the foundation of so much of philosophy of perception, substituting an appeal to empirical facts.

References

Abdul-Malak, D., & Durgin, F. (2009). Dividing the legs of sheep: Does Burr's Australian stockman strategy work? *Journal of Vision, 9*(8), 980.

Abid, G. (2019). Deflating inflation: The connection (or lack thereof) between decisional and metacognitive processes and visual phenomenology. *Neuroscience of Consciousness, 2019*(1), 1–7. https://doi.org/10.1093/nc/niz015

Abid, G. (2021). Recognition and the perception-cognition divide. *Mind & Language*.

Adam, K. C. S., & Serences, J. T. (2019). Working memory: Flexible but finite. *Neuron, 103*(2), 184–185.

Adam, K. C. S., Vogel, E. K., & Awh, E. (2017). Clear evidence for item limits in visual working memory. *Cognitive Psychology, 97*, 79–97. https://doi.org/10.1016/j.cogpsych.2017.07.001

Adams, F., & Aizawa, K. (2008). *The bounds of cognition*. Oxford, UK: Blackwell.

Afraz, A., & Cavanagh, P. (2009). The gender-specific face aftereffect is based in retinotopic not spatiotopic coordinates across several natural image transformations. *Journal of Vision, 9*(10), 10–10. https://doi.org/10.1167/9.10.10

Afraz, S.-R., & Cavanagh, P. (2006). Is the "face aftereffect" retinotopic or spatiotopic? *Journal of Vision, 6*(6), 882–882. https://doi.org/10.1167/6.6.882

Alais, D., O'Shea, R. P., & Blake, R. (2010). Visual sensitivity underlying changes in visual consciousness. *Current Biology, 20*, 1362–1367.

Alberti, L. (1991). *On painting* (C. Grayson, Trans.). London, UK: Penguin. Original work published in 1435.

Algom, D., & Fitousi, D. (2016). Half a century of research on Garner interference and the separability–integrality distinction. *Psychological Bulletin, 142*(12), 1352–1383. https://doi.org/10.1037/bul0000072

Alkire, M. T. (2008). General anesthesia and consciousness. In S. Laureys (Ed.), *The neurology of consciousness: Cognitive neuroscience and neuropathology* (pp. 118–134). Amsterdam, Netherlands: Elsevier.

Allen, E. C., Beilock, S. L., & Shevell, S. K. (2012). Individual differences in simultaneous color constancy are related to working memory. *Journal of the Optical Society of America A, 29*(2), A52–A59. https://doi.org/10.1364/JOSAA.29.000A52

Alston, W. (1967). Religion. In Paul Edwards (Ed.), *The encyclopedia of philosophy* (Vol. 7, pp. 140–145). New York, NY: Macmillan.

Alvarez, G., & Oliva, A. (2008). The representation of simple ensemble visual features outside the focus of attention. *Psychological Science, 19*, 392–398.

Alvarez, G. A., & Franconeri, S. L. (2007). How many objects can you track? Evidence for a resource-limited attentive tracking mechanism. *Journal of Vision, 7*(13), 14.11–10. https://doi.org/10.1167/7.13.14

Amalric, M., Wang, L., Pica, P., Figueira, S., Sigman, M., & Dehaene, S. (2017). The language of geometry: Fast comprehension of geometrical primitives and rules in human adults and preschoolers. *PLoS Computational Biology, 13*(1), e1005273–e1005273. https://doi.org/10.1371/journal.pcbi.1005273

Amodio, D. (2014). The neuroscience of prejudice and stereotyping. *Nature Reviews Neuroscience, 15*, 670–682.

Anken, J., Tivadar, R. I., Knebel, J.-F., & Murray, M. M. (2018). Brain mechanisms for perceiving illusory lines in humans. *NeuroImage, 181*, 182–189. https://doi.org/10.1016/j.neuroimage.2018.07.017

Anobile, G., Arrighi, R., Togoli, I., & Burr, D. (2016). A shared numerical representation for action and perception. *eLIFE*. https://doi.org/10.7554/eLife.16161

Anstis, S. (1998). Picturing peripheral acuity. *Perception, 27*, 817–825. https://doi.org/10.1068/p270817

Arend, L., & Reeves, A. (1986). Simultaneous color constancy. *Journal of the Optical Society of America A, 3*(10), 1743–1751. https://doi.org/10.1364/JOSAA.3.001743

Ariely, D. (2001). Seeing sets: Representation by statistical properties. *Psychological Science, 12*, 157–162.

Aristotle. (1955). On dreams. In W. D. Ross (Ed.), *Aristotle: Parva naturalia* (pp. 458a33–b25). Oxford, UK: Clarendon Press.

Arnold, D. H., Petrie, K., Gallagher, R., & Yarrow, K. (2015). An object-centered aftereffect of a latent material property: A squishiness visual aftereffect, not causality adaptation. *Journal of Vision, 15*(9), 4–4. https://doi.org/10.1167/15.9.4

Ashwin, P., & Tsaloumas, M. (2007). Complex visual hallucinations (Charles Bonnet syndrome) in the hemianopic visual field following occipital infarction. *Journal of the Neurological Sciences, 263*, 184–186.

Aslin, R. N. (2007). What's in a look? *Developmental Science, 10*(1), 48–53. https://doi.org/10.1111/j.1467-7687.2007.00563.x

Astle, D. E. (2009). Going from a retinotopic to a spatiotopic coordinate system for spatial attention. *Journal of Neuroscience, 29*(13), 3971–3973. https://doi.org/10.1523/jneurosci.5929-08.2009

Audi, R. (2018). Moral perception defended. In A. Bergqvist & R. Cowan (Eds.), *Evaluative perception* (pp. 58–79). Oxford, UK: Oxford University Press.

Aulet, L., Chiu, V., Prichard, A., Spivak, M., Lourenco, S., & Berns, G. (2019). Canine sense of quantity: Evidence for numerical ratio-dependent activation in parietotemporal cortex. *Biology Letters, 15*(12), 1–5. https://doi.org/10.1098/rsbl.2019.0666

Aulet, L. S., & Lourenco, S. F. (2021). Numerosity and cumulative surface area are perceived holistically as integral dimensions. *Journal of Experimental Psychology: General, 150*(1), 145–156. https://doi.org/10.1037/xge0000874

Awh, E., Bepolsky, A., & Theeuwes, J. (2012). Top-down versus bottom-up attentional control: A failed theoretical dichotomy. *Trends in Cognitive Sciences, 16*(8), 437–443.

Ayer, A. J. (1936/1971). *Language, truth and logic*. London/Harmondsworth, UK: Victor Gollanz/Penguin.

Baddeley, A. (2011). Working memory: Theories, models, and controversies. *Annual Review of Psychology, 63*(1), 1–29. https://doi.org/10.1146/annurev-psych-120710-100422

Baddeley, A. D., & Hitch, G. J. (1974). Working memory. In G. A. Bower (Ed.), *The psychology of learning and motivation: Advances in research and theory* (pp. 47–89). New York, NY: Academic Press.

Bahrami, B. (2003). Object property encoding and change blindness in multiple object tracking. *Visual Cognition, 10*(8), 949–963. https://doi.org/10.1080/13506280344000158

Baker, N., & Kellman, P. J. (2018). Abstract shape representation in human visual perception. *Journal of Experimental Psychology: General, 147*(9), 1295–1308. https://doi.org/10.1037/xge0000409

Balcetis, E., & Dunning, D. (2010). Wishful seeing: Desired objects are seen as closer. *Psychological Science, 21,* 147–152.

Baldauf, D., & Desimone, R. (2014). Neural mechanisms of object-based attention. *Science, 344*(6182), 424–427.

Ball, B. (2017). On representational content and format in core numerical cognition. *Philosophical Psychology, 30*(1–2), 119–139. https://doi.org/10.1080/09515089.2016.1263988

Ball, P. (2019, March 6). Neuroscience readies for a showdown over consciousness ideas. *Quanta Magazine.*

Balog, K. (2009a). Jerry Fodor on non-conceptual content. *Synthese, 170,* 311–320.

Balog, K. (2009b). Phenomenal concepts. In B. McLaughlin, A. Beckermann, & S. Walter (Eds.), *The Oxford handbook of philosophy of mind* (pp. 292–312). Oxford, UK: Oxford University Press.

Balota, D. A., & Black, S. (1997). Semantic satiation in healthy young and older adults. *Memory and Cognition, 25*(2), 190–202.

Bannert, M., & Bartels, A. (2013). Decoding the yellow of a gray banana. *Current Biology, 23,* 2268–2272.

Bar, M. (2004). Visual objects in context. *Nature Reviews Neuroscience, 5*(8), 617–629. https://doi.org/10.1038/nrn1476

Bar, M., Kassam, K. S., Ghuman, A. S., Boshyan, J., Schmid, A. M., Dale, A. M., ... Halgren, E. (2006). Top-down facilitation of visual recognition. *Proceedings of the National Academy of Sciences, USA, 103*(2), 449–454. https://doi.org/10.1073/pnas.0507062103

Barbot, A., & Carrasco, M. (2018). Emotion and anxiety potentiate the way attention alters visual appearance. *Scientific Reports, 8*(1), 5938. https://doi.org/10.1038/s41598-018-23686-8

Barrett, L. F., & Bar, M. (2009). See it with feeling: Affective predictions during object perception. *Philosophical Transactions of the Royal Society of London B: Biological Sciences, 12*(1471-2970 [Electronic]), 1325–1334.

Barth, H., Baron, A., Spelke, E., & Carey, S. (2009). Children's multiplicative transformations of discrete and continuous quantities. *Journal of Experimental Child Psychology, 103*(4), 441–454. https://doi.org/10.1016/j.jecp.2009.01.014

Bartolomeo, P., Hajhajate, D., Liu, J., & Spagna, A. (2020). Assessing the causal role of early visual areas in visual mental imagery. *Nature Reviews Neuroscience, 21*(9), 517–517. https://doi.org/10.1038/s41583-020-0348-5

Bayne, T. (2009). Perception and the reach of phenomenal content. *Philosophical Quarterly, 59,* 385–404.

Bayne, T. (2016). VI—Gist! *Proceedings of the Aristotelian Society, 116*(2), 107–126. https://doi.org/10.1093/arisoc/aow006

Bayne, T., Brainard, D., Byrne, R. W., Chittka, L., Clayton, N., Heyes, C., ... Webb, B. (2019). What is cognition? *Current Biology, 29*(13), R608–R615. https://doi.org/10.1016/j.cub.2019.05.044

Bayne, T., & McClelland, T. (2019). Ensemble representation and the contents of visual experience. *Philosophical Studies, 176*(3), 733–753. https://doi.org/10.1007/s11098-018-1037-3

Bays, P. M. (2018). Reassessing the evidence for capacity limits in neural signals related to working memory. *Cerebral Cortex, 28*(4), 1432–1438. https://doi.org/10.1093/cercor/bhx351

Beck, J. (2012). The generality constraint and the structure of thought. *Mind, 121*(483), 563–600.

Beck, J. (2014). *Marking a perception–cognition boundary: The criterion of stimulus-dependence.* Paper presented at the Society for Philosophy and Psychology, Vancouver.

Beck, J. (2015). Analogue magnitude representations: A philosophical introduction. *British Journal for the Philosophy of Science, 66,* 829–855.

Beck, J. (2018). Marking the perception–cognition boundary: The criterion of stimulus-dependence. *Australasian Journal of Philosophy, 96*(2), 319–334.

Beck, J. (2019). Perception is analog: The argument from Weber's law. *Journal of Philosophy, 116*(6), 319–349.

Beck, J., & Schneider, K. (2017). Attention and mental primer. *Mind and Language, 32*(4), 463–494.

Begby, E. (2011). Review of origins of objectivity. *Notre Dame Philosophical Reviews, 2.* http://ndpr.nd.edu/news/24627-origins-of-objectivity/

Bellet, J., Gay, M., Dwarakanath, A., Jarraya, B., van Kerkoerle, T., Dehaene, S., & Panagiotaropoulos, T. I. (2022). Decoding rapidly presented visual stimuli from prefrontal ensembles without report nor post-perceptual processing. *Neuroscience of Consciousness, 2022*(1), 1–12.

Benda, J., & Herz, A. (2003). A universal model for spike-frequency adaptation. *Neural Computation, 15*(11), 2523–2564.

Bengson, J. (2013). Presentation and content: A critical study of Susanna Siegel, *The contents of visual experience* (Oxford, UK: Oxford University Press, 2010). *Nous, 47*(4), 795–807. https://doi.org/10.1111/nous.12049

Bepolsky, A., & Awh, E. (2016). The role of context in volitional control of feature-based attention. *Journal of Experimental Psychology: Human Perception and Performance, 42*(2), 213–224.

Berkeley, G. (1734). *Treatise concerning the principles of human knowledge.* London, UK: Jacob Tonson.

Bermudez, J. (1994). Peacocke's argument against the autonomy of nonconceptual content. *Mind and Language, 9,* 402–418.

Bermudez, J., & Cahen, A. (2015). Nonconceptual mental content. In E. Zalta, U. Nodelman, C. Allen, & R. Anderson (Eds.), *Stanford encyclopedia of philosophy.* Stanford: Stanford University.

Bermudez, J. L. (2007). Review: Negation, contrariety, and practical reasoning: Comments on Millikan's "Varieties of meaning." *Philosophy and Phenomenological Research, 75*(3), 663–669.

Beschin, N., Cubelli, R., Della Sala, S., & Spinazzola, L. (1997). Left of what? The role of egocentric coordinates in neglect. *Journal of Neurology, Neurosurgery and Psychiatry, 63*(4), 483–489.

Biederman, I. (1987). Recognition-by-components: A theory of human image understanding. *Psychological Review, 94*(2), 115–147.

Bilalić, M. (2018). The double take of expertise: Neural expansion is associated with outstanding performance. *Current Directions in Psychological Science, 27*(6), 462–469. https://doi.org/10.1177/0963721418793133

Bilalić, M., Langner, R., Erb, M., & Grodd, W. (2010). Mechanisms and neural basis of object and pattern recognition: A study with chess experts. *Journal of Experimental Psychology: General, 139*(4), 728–742. https://doi.org/10.1037/a0020756

Bilalić, M., Turella, L., Campitelli, G., Erb, M., & Grodd, W. (2012). Expertise modulates the neural basis of context dependent recognition of objects and their relations. *Human Brain Mapping, 33*(11), 2728–2740. https://doi.org/10.1002/hbm.21396

Billock, V. A., Gleason, G. A., & Tsou, B. H. (2001). Perception of forbidden colors in retinally stabilized equiluminant images: An indication of softwired cortical color opponency? *Journal of the Optical Society of America. A., Optics, Image Science, and Vision, 18*(10), 2398–2403.

Bisiach, E., & Luzzatti, C. (1978). Unilateral neglect of representational space. *Cortex, 14*(1), 129–133. doi:http://dx.doi.org/10.1016/S0010-9452(78)80016-1

Blake, R., & He, S. (2005). Adaptation as a tool for probing the neural correlates of visual awareness: progress and precautions. In C. Clifford & G. Rhodes (Eds.), *Fitting the mind to the world: Adaptation and after-effects in high-level vision* (pp. 281–307). Oxford, UK: Oxford University Press.

Blake, R., & Logothetis, N. (2002). Visual competition. *Nature Reviews Neuroscience, 3*, 13–27.

Blanke, O., Landis, T., & Seeck, M. (2000). Electrical cortical stimulation of the human prefrontal cortex evokes complex visual hallucinations. *Epilepsy and Behavior, 1*(5), 356–361. https://doi.org/10.1006/ebeh.2000.0109

Block, N. (1980). What is functionalism? In N. Block (Ed.), *Readings in the philosophy of psychology* (pp. 171–184). Cambridge, MA: Harvard University Press.

Block, N. (1981). *Imagery*. Cambridge, MA: MIT Press.

Block, N. (1983a). Mental pictures and cognitive science. *Philosophical Review, 93*, 499–542.

Block, N. (1983b). The photographic fallacy in the debate about mental imagery. *Nous, 17*, 651–662.

Block, N. (1986). Advertisement for a semantics for psychology. *Midwest Studies in Philosophy, 10*, 615–678.

Block, N. (1987). Functional role and truth conditions. *Proceedings of the Aristotelian Society, 61*, 157–181.

Block, N. (1990). Consciousness and accessibility. *Behavioral and Brain Sciences, 13*(4), 596–598.

Block, N. (1994). Consciousness. In S. Guttenplan (Ed.), *A companion to philosophy of mind* (1st ed., pp. 210–218). Oxford, UK: Blackwell.

Block, N. (1995a). How many concepts of consciousness? *Behavioral and Brain Sciences, 18*(2), 272–284.

Block, N. (1995b). The mind as the software of the brain. In D. Osherson, L. Gleitman, S. M. Kosslyn, E. Smith, & S. Sternberg (Eds.), *An invitation to cognitive science* (pp. 377–425). Cambridge, MA: MIT Press.

Block, N. (1995c). On a confusion about a function of consciousness. *Behavioral and Brain Sciences, 18*(2), 227–247.

Block, N. (1997a). Anti-reductionism slaps back. *Philosophical Perspectives, 11*, 107–133.

Block, N. (1997b). Biology versus computation in the study of consciousness. *Behavioral and Brain Sciences, 20*(1), 159–166.

Block, N. (2002a). Concepts of consciousness. In D. Chalmers (Ed.), *Philosophy of mind: Classical and contemporary readings* (pp. 206–218). New York, NY: Oxford University Press.

Block, N. (2002b). The harder problem of consciousness. *Journal of Philosophy, 99*(8), 1–35.

Block, N. (2003a). Mental paint. In M. Hahn & B. Ramberg (Eds.), *Reflections and replies: Essays on the philosophy of Tyler Burge* (pp. 165–200). Cambridge, MA: MIT Press.

Block, N. (2003b). Spatial perception via tactile sensation. *Trends in Cognitive Sciences, 7*(7), 285–286.

Block, N. (2005a). Review of Alva Noë, Action in Perception. *Journal of Philosophy, 102*(5), 259–272.

Block, N. (2005b). Two neural correlates of consciousness. *Trends in Cognitive Sciences, 9*(2), 46–52.

Block, N. (2006). Max Black's objection to mind-body identity. *Oxford Studies in Metaphysics 2*, 3–78.

Block, N. (2007a). Consciousness, accessibility, and the mesh between psychology and neuroscience. *Behavioral and Brain Sciences, 30*, 481–548.

Block, N. (2007b). Overflow, access and attention. *Behavioral and Brain Sciences, 30*, 530–542.

Block, N. (2008). Consciousness and cognitive access. *Proceedings of the Aristotelian Society, 108*(3), 289–317.

Block, N. (2009). Wittgenstein and qualia. In M. Baghramian (Ed.), *Permutations: Essays on Hilary Putnam*. Oxford, UK: Oxford University Press.

Block, N. (2010). Attention and mental paint. *Philosophical Issues: A Supplement to Nous, 20*, 23–63.

Block, N. (2011a). The Anna Karenina theory of the unconscious. *Neuropsychoanalysis, 13*(1), 34–37.

Block, N. (2011b). The higher order approach to consciousness is defunct. *Analysis, 71*(3), 419–431.

Block, N. (2011c). Perceptual consciousness overflows cognitive access. *Trends in Cognitive Sciences, 15*(12), 567–575.

Block, N. (2011d). Response to Rosenthal and Weisberg. *Analysis, 71*(3), 443–448.

Block, N. (2012). The grain of vision and the grain of attention. *Thought, 1*(3), 170–184.

Block, N. (2013). Seeing and windows of integration. *Thought, 2*, 29–39.

Block, N. (2014a). Consciousness, big science and conceptual clarity. In G. Marcus & J. Freeman (Eds.), *The future of the brain: Essays by the world's leading neuroscientists* (pp. 161–176). Princeton, NJ: Princeton University Press.

Block, N. (2014b). The defective armchair: A reply to Tye. *Thought, 3*(2), 159–165.

Block, N. (2014c). Seeing-as in the light of vision science. *Philosophy and Phenomenological Research, 89*(3), 560–573.

Block, N. (2015a). The puzzle of perceptual precision. In J. Windt & T. Metzinger (Eds.), *MIND anniversary collection* (pp. 1–52). Frankfurt am Main, Germany: Barbara-Wengeler-Stiftung.

Block, N. (2015b). Solely generic phenomenology. In J. Windt & T. Metzinger (Eds.), *MIND anniversary collection* (pp. 1–10). Frankfurt am Main, Germany: Barbara-Wengeler-Stiftung.

Block, N. (2016a). The Anna Karenina principle and skepticism about unconscious perception. *Philosophy and Phenomenological Research, 93*(2), 452–459. https://doi.org/10.1111/phpr.12258

Block, N. (2016b). Tweaking the concepts of perception and cognition. *Behavioral and Brain Sciences, 39,* 21–22.

Block, N. (2018). If perception is probabilistic, why does it not seem probabilistic? *Philosophical Transactions of the Royal Society B: Biological Sciences, 373*(1755), 1–10.

Block, N. (2019a). The direct realist approach to illusion: Reply to Bill Brewer. In A. Pautz & D. Stoljar (Eds.), *Blockheads! Essays on Ned Block's philosophy of mind and consciousness* (pp. 35–39). Cambridge, MA: MIT Press.

Block, N. (2019b). Empirical science meets higher-order views of consciousness: Reply to Hakwan Lau and Richard Brown. In A. Pautz & D. Stoljar (Eds.), *Blockheads! Essays on Ned Block's philosophy of mind and consciousness* (pp. 199–213). Cambridge, MA: MIT Press.

Block, N. (2019c). Fading qualia: A response to Michael Tye. In A. Pautz & D. Stoljar (Eds.), *Blockheads! Essays on Ned Block's philosophy of mind and consciousness*. Cambridge, MA: MIT Press.

Block, N. (2019d). Poise, dispositions, and access consciousness: Reply to Daniel Stoljar. In A. Pautz & D. Stoljar (Eds.), *Blockheads! Essays on Ned Block's philosophy of mind and consciousness* (pp. 537–544). Cambridge, MA: MIT Press.

Block, N. (2019e). Tyler Burge on perceptual adaptation. In A. Pautz & D. Stoljar (Eds.), *Blockheads! Essays on Ned Block's philosophy of mind and consciousness* (pp. 71–78). Cambridge, MA: MIT Press.

Block, N. (2019f). What is wrong with the no-report paradigm and how to fix it. *Trends in Cognitive Sciences, 23*(12), 1003–1013.

Block, N. (2020). Finessing the bored monkey problem. *Trends in Cognitive Sciences, 24*(3), 167–168. https://doi.org/10.1016/j.tics.2019.12.012

Block, N. (2022). Do conscious decisions cause physical actions? In U. Maoz & W. Sinnott-Armstrong (Eds.), *Free will: Philosophers and neuroscientists in conversation*. Oxford, UK: Oxford University Press.

Block, N., & O'Regan, K. (2012). Discussion of J. Kevin O'Regan's "Why red doesn't sound like a bell: Understanding the feel of consciousness." *Review of Philosophy and Psychology, 3,* 89–108.

Block, N., & Phillips, I. (2016). Debate on unconscious perception. In B. Nanay (Ed.), *Current controversies in philosophy of perception*. London: Routledge, Taylor & Francis Group.

Bloem, I. M., & Ling, S. (2019). Normalization governs attentional modulation within human visual cortex. *Nature Communications, 10*(1), 5660. https://doi.org/10.1038/s41467-019-13597-1

Bloem, I. M., Watanabe, Y. L., Kibbe, M. M., & Ling, S. (2018). Visual memories bypass normalization. *Psychological Science, 29*(5), 845–856. https://doi.org/10.1177/0956797617747091

Blough, P. (1992). Detectability and choice during visual search: Joint effects of sequential priming and discriminability. *Animal Learning and Behavior, 20,* 293–300.

Boghossian, P., & Williamson, T. (2020). *Debating the a priori*. Oxford, UK: Oxford University Press.

Boly, M., Massimini, M., Tsuchiya, N., Postle, B. R., Koch, C., & Tononi, G. (2017). Are the neural correlates of consciousness in the front or in the back of the cerebral cortex?

Clinical and neuroimaging evidence. *Journal of Neuroscience, 37*(40), 9603–9613. https://doi.org/10.1523/jneurosci.3218-16.2017

Bonato, M., Saj, A., & Vuilleumier, P. (2016). Hemispatial neglect shows that (before) is (left). *Neural Plasticity, 2016*, 1–11.

Bornstein, M. (1985). On the development of color naming in young children: Data and theory. *Brain and Language, 26*, 72–93.

Bouchacourt, F., & Buschman, T. J. (2019). A flexible model of working memory. *Neuron, 103*(1), 147–160.e148. https://doi.org/10.1016/j.neuron.2019.04.020

Boyd, R. (1989). What realism implies and what it does not. *Dialectica, 43*(1-2), 5–29.

Boyd, R. (1991). Realism, anti-foundationalism and the enthusiasm for natural kinds. *Philosophical Studies, 61*(1), 127–148. https://doi.org/10.1007/BF00385837

Bracci, S., & Op de Beeck, H. (2016). Dissociations and associations between shape and category representations in the two visual pathways. *Journal of Neuroscience, 36*(2), 432. https://doi.org/10.1523/JNEUROSCI.2314-15.2016

Brady, T. F., Konkle, T., & Alvarez, G. (2011). A review of visual memory capacity: Beyond individual items and toward structured representations. *Journal of Vision, 11*(5), 1–34.

Brascamp, J., Blake, R., & Knapen, T. (2015). Negligible fronto-parietal BOLD activity accompanying unreportable switches in bistable perception. *Nature Neuroscience, 18*(11), 1672–1678.

Brascamp, J., Sterzer, P., Blake, R., & Knapen, T. (2018). Multistable perception and the role of the frontoparietal cortex in perceptual inference. *Annual Review of Psychology, 69*(1), 77–103. https://doi.org/10.1146/annurev-psych-010417-085944

Breedlove, J. L., St-Yves, G., Olman, C. A., & Naselaris, T. (2020). Generative feedback explains distinct brain activity codes for seen and mental images. *Current Biology, 30*(12), 2211–2224.e2216. https://doi.org/10.1016/j.cub.2020.04.014

Brewer, B. (2005). Perceptual experience has conceptual content. In M. Steup (Ed.), *Contemporary debates in epistemology* (pp. 89–112). Oxford, UK: Oxford University Press.

Brewer, B. (2011). *Perception and its objects*. Oxford, UK: Oxford University Press.

Brewer, B. (2019). Attention and direct realism. In A. Pautz & D. Stoljar (Eds.), *Blockheads! Essays on Ned Block's philosophy of mind and consciousness* (pp. 19–34). Cambridge, MA: MIT Press.

Briscoe, R. (2015). Cognitive penetration and the reach of phenomenal content. In J. Zeimbekis & A. Raftopoulos (Eds.), *The cognitive penetrability of perception: New philosophical perspectives* (pp. 174–199). Oxford, UK: Oxford University Press.

Brockmole, J. R., Wang, R. F., & Irwin, D. E. (2002). Temporal integration between visual images and visual percepts. *Journal of Experimental Psychology: Human Perception and Performance, 28*(2), 315–334.

Brogaard, B. (2013). Do we perceive natural kind properties? *Philosophical Studies, 162*, 35–42.

Brogaard, B. (2014). Seeing as a non-experiential mental state: The case from synesthesia and visual imagery. In R. Brown (Ed.), *Consciousness inside and out: Phenomenology, neuroscience, and the nature of experience* (Vol. 6, pp. 377–394). Dordrecht, Netherlands: Springer.

Brogaard, B., & Gatzia, D. (2017a). Cortical color and the cognitive sciences. *Topics in Cognitive Science, 9*, 135–150.

Brogaard, B., & Gatzia, D. (2017b). Is color experience cognitively penetrable? *Topics in Cognitive Science, 9*, 193–214.

Broggin, E., Savazzi, S., & Marzi, C. A. (2012). Similar effects of visual perception and imagery on simple reaction time. *Quarterly Journal of Experimental Psychology*, 65(1), 151–164. https://doi.org/10.1080/17470218.2011.594896

Bronfman, Z., Brezis, N., Jacobson, H., & Usher, M. (2014). We see more than we can report: 'Cost free' color phenomenality outside focal attention." *Psychological Science*, 25(7), 1394–1403.

Brouwer, G. J., & Heeger, D. J. (2013). Categorical clustering of the neural representation of color. *Journal of Neuroscience*, 33(39), 15454–15465. https://doi.org/10.1523/JNEUROSCI.2472-13.2013

Brown, H., & Friston, K. (2012). Free-energy and illusions: The cornsweet effect. *Frontiers in Psychology*, 3, 1–13.

Brown, R., Lau, H., & LeDoux, J. (2019). Understanding the higher-order approach to consciousness. *Trends in Cognitive Sciences*, 23(9), 754–768. https://doi.org/10.1016/j.tics.2019.06.009

Bruner, J., & Minturn, A. (1955). Perceptual identification and perceptual organization. *Journal of General Psychology*, 53, 21–28.

Bruner, J., & Postman, L. (1949). On the perception of incongruity: A paradigm. *Journal of Personality*, 18, 206–223.

Bruner, J. S. (1957). On perceptual readiness. *Psychological Review*, 64(2), 123–152. https://doi.org/10.1037/h0043805

Buffalo, E., Fries, P., Landman, R., Liang, H., & Desimone, R. (2010). A backward progression of attentional effects in the ventral stream. *Proceedings of the National Academy of Sciences*, 107(1), 361–365.

Burge, T. (2005). Disjunctivism and perceptual psychology. *Philosophical Topics*, 33(1), 1–78.

Burge, T. (2009). Five theses on de re states and attitudes. In J. Almog & P. Leonardi (Eds.), *The philosophy of David Kaplan*. Oxford, UK: Oxford University Press.

Burge, T. (2010a). *Origins of objectivity*. Oxford, UK: Oxford University Press.

Burge, T. (2010b). Origins of perception. *Disputatio*, 4(29), 1–38.

Burge, T. (2010c). Steps toward origins of propositional thought. *Disputatio*, 4(29), 39–67.

Burge, T. (2011). Border crossings: Perceptual and post- perceptual object representation. *Behavioral and Brain Sciences*, 34(3), 125.

Burge, T. (2014). Reply to Block: Adaptation and the upper border of perception. *Philosophy and Phenomenological Research*, 89(3), 573–583.

Burge, T. (2018). Iconic representation: Maps, pictures, and perception. In S. Wuppuluri & F. Doria (Eds.), *The map and the territory: Exploring the foundations of science, thought and reality* (pp. 79–100). Cham, Switzerland: Springer.

Burge, T. (2019). Psychological content and egocentric indexes. In A. Pautz & D. Stoljar (Eds.), *Blockheads! Essays on Ned Block's philosophy of mind and consciousness* (pp. 41–69). Cambridge, MA: MIT Press.

Burge, T. (2020). Entitlement: The basis for empirical epistemic warrant. In P. J. Graham & N. J. L. L. Pedersen (Eds.), *Epistemic entitlement* (pp. 37–142). Oxford, UK: Oxford University Press.

Burge, J., & Burge, T. (2022). Shape, perspective, and what is and is not perceived: Comment on Morales, Bax, and Firestone (2020). *Psychological Review*. Prepublication copy at: *psyArXiv*, February 25. https://doi.org/ 10.1037/rev0000363

Burke, L. (1952). On the tunnel effect. *Quarterly Journal of Experimental Psychology*, 4(3), 121–138. https://doi.org/10.1080/17470215208416611

Burr, D., & Ross, J. (2008). A visual sense of number. *Current Biology, 18*(6), 425–428.

Burton, N., Jeffery, L., Calder, A. J., & Rhodes, G. (2015). How is facial expression coded? *Journal of Vision, 15*(1), 15.11.11. https://doi.org/10.1167/15.1.1

Butler, A., Oruc, I., Fox, C. J., & Barton, J. J. S. (2008). Factors contributing to the adaptation aftereffects of facial expression. *Brain Research, 1191*, 116–126.

Butterfill, S. (2009). Seeing causes and hearing gestures. *Philosophical Quarterly, 59*(236), 405–428.

Byrne, A. (2001). Intentionalism defended. *Philosophical Review, 110*, 199–240.

Byrne, A. (2003). Consciousness and nonconceptual content. *Philosophical Studies, 113*, 261–274.

Byrne, A. (2005). Perception and conceptual content. In E. Sosa & M. Steup (Eds.), *Contemporary debates in epistemology* (pp. 231–250). Oxford, UK: Blackwell.

Byrne, A. (2019). Schellenberg's capacitism. *Analysis, 79*(4), 713–719. https://doi.org/10.1093/analys/anz037

Byrne, A., Hilbert, D. R., & Siegel, S. (2007). Do we see more than we can access? *Behavioral and Brain Sciences, 30*(5/6), 501–502.

Cacciamani, L., Mojica, A., Sanguinetti, J., & Peterson, M. (2014). Semantic access occurs outside of awareness for the ground side of a figure. *Attention, Perception and Psychophysics, 76*(8), 2531–2547.

Calderone, D. J., Hoptman, M. J., Martinez, A., Nair-Collins, S., Mauro, C. J., Bar, M., ... Butler, P. D. (2013). Contributions of low and high spatial frequency processing to impaired object recognition circuitry in schizophrenia. *Cerebral Cortex, 23*(8), 1849–1858. https://doi.org/10.1093/cercor/bhs169

Camp, E. (2009). Putting thoughts to work: Concepts, systematicity, and stimulus-independence. *Philosophy and Phenomenological Research, 78*(2), 275–311.

Camp, E. (2018). Why maps are not propositional. In A. Grzankowski & M. Montague (Eds.), *Non-propositional intentionality* (pp. 19–45). Oxford, UK: Oxford University Press.

Campbell, J. (2002). *Reference and consciousness.* Oxford, UK: Oxford University Press.

Campbell, J. (2011). Tyler Burge: Origins of objectivity. *Journal of Philosophy, 108*(5), 269–285.

Campbell, J., & Cassam, Q. (2014). *Berkeley's puzzle: What does experience teach us?* Oxford, UK: Oxford University Press.

Cao, L., & Händel, B. (2019). Walking enhances peripheral visual processing in humans. *PLOS Biology, 17*(10), e3000511. https://doi.org/10.1371/journal.pbio.3000511

Cao, R. (2018). *Why computation isn't enough: Essays in neuroscience and the philosophy of mind* (PhD dissertation). New York University, New York.

Cappelen, H. (2018). *Fixing language: An essay on conceptual engineering.* Oxford, UK: Oxford University Press.

Caramazza, A., & Hillis, A. E. (1990). Spatial representation of words in the brain implied by studies of a unilateral neglect patient. *Nature, 346*(6281), 267–269. https://doi.org/10.1038/346267a0

Carandini, M., & Heeger, D. J. (2012). Normalization as a canonical neural computation. *Nature Reviews Neuroscience, 13*(1), 51–62. https://doi.org/10.1038/nrn3136

Carey, S. (2009). *The origin of concepts.* Oxford, UK: Oxford University Press.

Carey, S. (2011a). Authors' response. *Behavioral and Brain Sciences, 34*(3), 152–167.

Carey, S. (2011b). The origin of concepts: A précis. *Behavioral and Brain Sciences, 34*(3), 113–167.

Carey, S., & Spelke, E. (1994). Domain-specific knowledge and conceptual change. In L. Hirschfeld & S. Gelman (Eds.), *Mapping the mind: Domain specificity in cognition and culture*. New York, NY: Cambridge University Press.

Carlson, T. A., & He, S. (2004). Competing global representations fail to initiate binocular rivalry. *Neuron, 43*(6), 907–914. https://doi.org/10.1016/j.neuron.2004.08.039

Carrasco, M. (2011). Visual attention: The past 25 years. *Vision Research, 51*, 1484–1525.

Carrasco, M., Ling, S., & Read, S. (2004). Attention alters appearance. *Nature Neuroscience, 7*, 308–313.

Carruthers, P. (2006). *The architecture of the mind*. Oxford, UK: Oxford University Press.

Carruthers, P. (2009). Invertebrate concepts confront the generality constraint (and win). In R. Lurz (Ed.), *The philosophy of animal minds* (pp. 89–107). Cambridge, UK: Cambridge University Press.

Carruthers, P. (2014). The fragmentation of reason. In P. Quintanilla, C. Mantilla, & P. Cépeda (Eds.), *Cognición social y lenguaje. La intersubjetividad en la evolución de la especie y en el desarrollo del niño*. Lima: Pontificia Universidad Católica del Perú.

Carruthers, P. (2015). *The centered mind: What the science of working memory shows us about the nature of human thought*. Oxford, UK: Oxford University Press.

Carruthers, P. (2017). Block's overflow argument. *Pacific Philosophical Quarterly, 98*, 65–70.

Carter, O., Hohwy, J., Van Boxtel, J., Lamme, V., Block, N., Koch, C., et al. (2018). Conscious machines: Defining questions. *Science, 359*(6374), 400. https://doi.org/10.1126/science.aar4163

Castaldi, E., Piazza, M., Dehaene, S., Vignaud, A., & Eger, E. (2019). Attentional amplification of neural codes for number independent of other quantities along the dorsal visual stream. *eLIFE* 2019(8), e45160. https://doi.org/10/75554/eLife.45160

Cavanagh, P. (2011). Visual cognition. *Vision Research, 51*(13), 1538–1551. https://doi.org/10.1016/j.visres.2011.01.015

Cavedon-Taylor, D. (2017). Touching voids: On the varieties of absence perception. *Review of Philosophy and Psychology, 8*(2), 355–366. https://doi.org/10.1007/s13164-016-0302-7

Celeghin, A., Diano, M., Bagnis, A., Viola, M., & Tamietto, M. (2017). Basic emotions in human neuroscience: Neuroimaging and beyond. *Frontiers in Psychology, 8*(1432), 1–13.

Cepelewicz, J. (2021a, August 9). Animals count and use zero: How far does their number sense go? *Quanta Magazine*.

Cepelewicz, J. (2021b, August 24). The brain doesn't think the way you think it does. *Quanta Magazine*.

Cesana-Arlotti, N., Martín, A., Téglás, E., Vorobyova, L., Cetnarski, R., & Bonatti, L. L. (2018). Precursors of logical reasoning in preverbal human infants. *Science, 359*(6381), 1263.

Chalmers, D. (1995). Absent qualia, fading qualia, dancing qualia. In T. Metzinger (Ed.), *Conscious experience* (pp. 309–328). Paderborn: Ferdinand Schoningh.

Chalmers, D. (1996). *The conscious mind: In search of a fundamental theory*. Oxford, UK: Oxford University Press.

Chalmers, D. (1997). Availability: The cognitive basis of experience. *Behavioral and Brain Sciences, 20*(1), 148–149.

Chalmers, D. (2003). Consciousness and its place in nature. In S. Stich & T. Warfield (Eds.), *Blackwell guide to the philosophy of mind* (pp. 102–142). Oxford: Blackwell.

Chalmers, D. (2006). Perception and the fall from Eden. In T. Gendler & J. Hawthorne (Eds.), *Perceptual experience* (pp. 49–125). Oxford, UK: Oxford University Press.

Chalmers, D. (2011). Verbal disputes. *Philosophical Review, 120*(4), 515–566.

Chalmers, D. (2012a). *Constructing the world.* New York, NY: Oxford University Press.

Chalmers, D. (2012b). Twentieth excursus: Reference magnets and the grounds of intentionality. In D. Chalmers (Ed.), *Constructing the world.* Extended edition. Internet: David Chalmers.

Chambers, D., & Reisberg, D. (1985). Can mental images be ambiguous? *Journal of Experimental Psychology: Human Perception and Performance, 11*, 317–328.

Chang, L., & Tsao, D. Y. (2017). The code for facial identity in the primate brain. *Cell, 169*(6), 1013–1028.e1014. https://doi.org/10.1016/j.cell.2017.05.011

Chen, J., Sperandio, I., Henry, M. J., & Goodale, M. A. (2019). Changing the real viewing distance reveals the temporal evolution of size constancy in visual cortex. *Current Biology, 29*(13), 2237–2243. e2234. https://doi.org/10.1016/j.cub.2019.05.069

Chiou, R., & Lambon Ralph, M. A. (2016). Task-related dynamic division of labor between anterior temporal and lateral occipital cortices in representing object size. *Journal of Neuroscience, 36*(17), 4662–4668. https://doi.org/10.1523/jneurosci.2829-15.2016

Choi, H., & Scholl, B. (2006). Perceiving causality after the fact: Postdiction in the temporal dynamics of causal perception. *Perception, 35*, 385–399.

Chopin, A., Mamassian, P., & Blake, R. (2012). Stereopsis and binocular rivalry are based on perceived rather than physical orientations. *Vision Research, 63*, 63–68. https://doi.org/10.1016/j.visres.2012.05.003

Christophel, T., Klink, P., Spitzer, B., Roelfema, P., & Haynes, J. (2017). The distributed nature of working memory. *Trends in Cognitive Sciences, 21*(2), 111–124.

Churchland, P. (1986). *Neurophilosophy: Toward a unified science of the mind-brain.* Cambridge, MA: MIT Press.

Churchland, P. M. (1981). Eliminative materialism and the propositional attitudes. *Journal of Philosophy, 78*, 67–90.

Churchland, P. S., & Ramachandran, V. S. (1996). Filling-in: Why Dennett is wrong. In K. Akins (Ed.), *Perception* (pp. 65–91). Oxford, UK: Oxford University Press.

Clark, A. (2001). Visual experience and motor action: Are the bonds too tight? *Philosophical Review, 110*, 495–519.

Clark, A. (2013). Whatever next? Predictive brains, situated agents, and the future of cognitive science. *Behavioral and Brain Sciences, 36*(3), 233–253. https://doi.org/10.1017/S0140525X12000477

Clark, A. (2016). *Surfing uncertainty: Prediction, action, and the embodied mind.* Oxford, UK: Oxford University Press.

Clark, A. (2018). Beyond the 'Bayesian blur': Predictive processing and the nature of subjective experience. *Journal of Consciousness Studies, 25*(3–4), 71–87.

Clarke, S. (2022). Beyond the icon: Core cognition and the bounds of perception. *Mind and Language, 37*(1), 94–113.

Cleeremans, A. (2014). Connecting conscious and unconscious cognition. *Cognitive Science, 38*(6), 1286–1315.

Cleeremans, A., Achoui, D., Beauny, A., Keuninckx, L., Martin, J.-R., Muñoz-Moldes, S., . . . de Heering, A. (2020). Learning to be conscious. *Trends in Cognitive Sciences, 24*(2), 112–123. https://doi.org/10.1016/j.tics.2019.11.011

Clifford, A., Franklin, A., Davies, I., & Holmes, A. (2009). Electrophysiological markers of color categories in the infant brain. *Brain and Cognition, 71*, 165–172.

Clifford, C., Wenderoth, P., & Spehar, B. (2000). A functional angle on some after-effects in cortical vision. *Proceedings of the Royal Society B, 267*, 1705–1710.

Cohen, M., & Dennett, D. (2011). Consciousness cannot be separated from function. *Trends in Cognitive Sciences, 15*(8), 358–364.

Cohen, M., Dennett, D., & Kanwisher, N. (2016). What is the bandwidth of perceptual experience? *Trends in Cognitive Sciences, 20*(5), 324–335.

Cohen, M. A. (2019). What is the true capacity of visual cognition? *Trends in Cognitive Sciences, 23*(2), 83–86. https://doi.org/10.1016/j.tics.2018.12.002

Cohen, M. A., Alvarez, G. A., Nakayama, K., & Konkle, T. (2017). Visual search for object categories is predicted by the representational architecture of high-level visual cortex. *Journal of Neurophysiology, 117*(1), 388–402. https://doi.org/10.1152/jn.00569.2016

Cohen, M. A., Ortego, K., Kyroudis, A., & Pitts, M. (2020). Distinguishing the neural correlates of perceptual awareness and post-perceptual processing. *Journal of Neuroscience, 40*(25), 4925–4935. https://doi.org/10.1523/JNEUROSCI.0120-20.2020

Cohen, M. A., Ostrand, C., Frontero, N., & Pham, P.-N. (2020). Characterizing a snapshot of perceptual experience. *Journal of Experimental Psychology: General, 150*(9), 1695–1709. https://doi.org/10.1037/xge0000864

Cohen, M. A., & Rubenstein, J. (2020). How much color do we see in the blink of an eye? *PsyArXiv.* https://doi.org/10.31234/osf.io/enywt

Colombo, M., & Seriès, P. (2012). Bayes in the brain: On Bayesian modelling in neuroscience. *British Journal for the Philosophy of Science, 63*, 697–723.

Coltheart, M. (1980). Iconic memory and visible persistence. *Perception and Psychophysics, 27*(3), 183–228.

Coltheart, M. (1999). Modularity and cognition. *Trends in Cognitive Sciences, 3*(3), 115–120.

Connolly, K. (2011). Does perception outstrip our concepts in fineness of grain? *Ratio, 24*, 243–258

Conson, M., Polito, F., Di Rosa, A., Trojano, L., Cordasco, G., Esposito, A., & Turi, M. (2020). "Not only faces": Specialized visual representation of human hands revealed by adaptation. *Royal Society Open Science, 7*(12), 200948. https://doi.org/10.1098/rsos.200948

Constantinescu, A. O., O'Reilly, J. X., & Behrens, T. E. J. (2016). Organizing conceptual knowledge in humans with a gridlike code. *Science, 352*(6292), 1464–1468. https://doi.org/10.1126/science.aaf0941

Contardi, S., Rubboli, G., Giulioni, M., Meichelucci, R., Pizza, F., Gardella, E., ... Tassinari, C. (2007). Charles Bonnet syndrome in hemianopia, following antero-mesial temporal lobectomy for drug-resistant epilepsy. *Epileptic Disorders, 9*(3), 271–275.

Cornelissen, F. W., & Brenner, E. (1995). Simultaneous colour constancy revisited: An analysis of viewing strategies. *Vision Research, 35*(17), 2431–2448.

Correll, J., Park, B., Judd, C., & Wittenbrink, B. (2002). The police officer's dilemma: Using ethnicity to disambiguate potentially threatening individuals. *Journal of Personality and Social Psychology, 83*, 1314–1329.

Correll, J., Urland, G., & Ito, T. (2006). Event-related potentials and the decision to shoot: The role of threat perception and cognitive control. *Journal of Experimental Social Psychology, 42*, 120–128.

Correll, J., Wittenbrink, B., Crawford, M. T., & Sadler, M. S. (2015). Stereotypic vision: How stereotypes disambiguate visual stimuli. *Journal of Personality and Social Psychology, 108*(2), 219–233. https://doi.org/10.1037/pspa0000015

Costello, P., Jiang, Y., Baartman, B., McGlennen, K., & He, S. (2009). Semantic and subword priming during binocular suppression. *Consciousness and Cognition, 18*(2), 375–382. https://doi.org/10.1016/j.concog.2009.02.003

Crane, T. (1988). The waterfall illusion. *Analysis, 48*, 142–147.

Crane, T. (1992). The nonconceptual content of experience. In T. Crane (Ed.), *The contents of experience*. Cambridge, UK: Cambridge University Press.

Crane, T. (2000). The origins of qualia. In T. Crane & S. Patterson (Eds.), *History of the mind-body problem* (pp. 169–194). New York, NY: Routledge.

Crane, T. (2006). Is there a perceptual relation? In T. Gendler & J. Hawthorne (Eds.), *Perceptual experience* (pp. 126–146). Oxford, UK: Oxford University Press.

Crane, T. (2009). Is perception a propositional attitude? *Philosophical Quarterly, 59*(236), 452–469.

Culham, J. C. (2012). New ideas on how drivers perceive speed emerge from the fog. *eLIFE, 1*, e00281–e00281. https://doi.org/10.7554/eLife.00281

Curtin, C. (2007, February 22). Fact or fiction? Glass is a (supercooled) liquid. *Scientific American*. https://www.scientificamerican.com/article/fact-fiction-glass-liquid/#

Cussins, A. (1990). The connectionist construction of concepts. In M. Boden (Ed.), *The philosophy of AI*. Oxford, UK: Oxford University Press.

Datta, R., & DeYoe, E. (2009). I know where you are secretly attending! The topography of human visual attention revealed with fMRI. *Vision Research, 49*, 1037–1044.

Davidson, D. (1968). On saying that. *Synthese, 19*(1–2), 130–146.

Davidson, D. (1999). The emergence of thought. *Erkenntnis, 51*, 511–521.

Davies, M. (1992). Perceptual content and local supervenience. *Proceedings of the Aristotelian Society, 92*, 21–45.

Davies, M. (1996/7). Externalism and experience. In N. Block, O. Flanagan, & G. Güzeldere (Eds.), *The nature of consciousness: Philosophical debates* (pp. 309–327). Cambridge, MA: MIT Press.

Davies, M., & Humberstone, L. (1980). Two notions of necessity. *Philosophical Studies: An International Journal for Philosophy in the Analytic Tradition, 38*(1), 1–30.

Davies, W. (2020). Colour relations in form. *Philosophy and Phenomenological Research*, n/a(n/a). https://doi.org/10.1111/phpr.12679

De Agrò, M., Rößler, D. C., Kim, K., & Shamble, P. S. (2021). Perception of biological motion by jumping spiders. *PLOS Biology, 19*(7), e3001172. https://doi.org/10.1371/journal.pbio.3001172

de Bellis, E., Schulte-Mecklenbeck, M., Brucks, W., Herrmann, A., & Hertwig, R. (2018). Blind haste: As light decreases, speeding increases. *PloS One, 13*(1), e0188951–e0188951. https://doi.org/10.1371/journal.pone.0188951

de Gardelle, V., Sackur, J., & Kouider, S. (2009). Perceptual illusions in brief visual presentations. *Consciousness and Cognition, 18*, 569–577.

de Vignemont, F. (2011). A mosquito bite against the enactive approach to bodily experiences. *Journal of Philosophy, 108*(4), 188–204.

de Vignemont, F. (2018). *Mind the Body: An Exploration of Bodily Self-Awareness*. Oxford, UK: Oxford University Press.

de Vignemont, F. (2021). Fifty shades of affective colouring of perception. *Australasian Journal of Philosophy, 2021*, 1–15. https://doi.org/10.1080/00048402.2021.1965176

Debner, J. A., & Jacoby, L. L. (1994). Unconscious perception: Attention, awareness and control. *Journal of Experimental Psychology: Learning, Memory and Cognition, 20*, 304–317.

Dehaene, S. (2000). *How we learn: Why brains learn better than any machine... for now*. New York, NY: Viking.

Dehaene, S. (2011). *The number sense: How the mind creates mathematics* (2nd ed.). Oxford, UK: Oxford University Press.

Dehaene, S. (2014). *Consciousness and the brain: Deciphering how the brain codes our thoughts*. New York, NY: Viking.

Dehaene, S., & Changeux, J.-P. (2004). Neural mechanisms for access to consciousness. In M. Gazzaniga (Ed.), *The cognitive neurosciences* (Vol. 3, pp. 1145–1158). Cambridge, MA: MIT Press.

Dehaene, S., Changeux, J.-P., Nacchache, L., Sackur, J., & Sergent, C. (2006). Conscious, preconscious, and subliminal processing: A testable taxonomy. *Trends in Cognitive Sciences, 10*, 204–211.

Dehaene, S., & Cohen, L. (2011). The unique role of the visual word form area in reading. *Trends in Cognitive Sciences, 15*(6), 254–262. https://doi.org/10.1016/j.tics.2011.04.003

Dehaene, S., Kersberg, M., & Changeux, J.-P. (1998). A neuronal model of a global workspace in effortful cognitive tasks. *Proceedings of the National Academy of Sciences, 95*, 14529–14534.

Dehaene, S., Lau, H., & Kouider, S. (2017). What is consciousness, and could machines have it? *Science, 358*, 486–492.

Delk, J., & Fillenbaum, S. (1965). Differences in perceived color as a function of characteristic color. *American Journal of Psychology, 78*, 290–293.

Dembski, C., Koch, C., & Pitts, M. (2021). Perceptual awareness negativity: A physiological correlate of sensory consciousness. *Trends in Cognitive Sciences, 25*(8), 660–670. https://doi.org/10.1016/j.tics.2021.05.009

Dener, E., Kacelnik, A., & Shemesh, H. (2016). Pea plants show risk sensitivity. *Current Biology, 26*(13), 1763–1767. https://doi.org/10.1016/j.cub.2016.05.008

Denison, R. N., Adler, W. T., Carrasco, M., & Ma, W. J. (2018). Humans incorporate attention-dependent uncertainty into perceptual decisions and confidence. *Proceedings of the National Academy of Sciences, USA, 115*(43), 11090–11095. https://doi.org/10.1073/pnas.1717720115

Dennett, D. C. (1984). *Elbow room: The varieties of free will worth wanting*. Cambridge, MA: MIT Press.

Dennett, D. C. (1991). *Consciousness explained*. Boston, MA: Little Brown.

Deroy, O. (2013). Object-sensitivity versus cognitive penetrability of perception. *Philosophical Studies, 162*, 87–107.

Deroy, O., Fairvre, N., Lunghi, C., Spence, C., Aller, M., & Noppeney, U. (2016). The complex interplay between multisensory integration and perceptual awareness. *Multisensory Research, 29*(6–7), 585–606. https://doi.org/10.1163/22134808-00002529 1-22

Deutsch, D., Henthorn, T., Fau-Lapidis, R., & Lapidis, R. *Illusory transformation from speech to song*. *Journal of the Acoustical Society of America 129*(4), 2245–2252.

Dickinson, J. E., Morgan, S. K., Tang, M. F., & Badcock, D. R. (2017). Separate banks of information channels encode size and aspect ratio. *Journal of Vision, 17*(3), 27–27. https://doi.org/10.1167/17.3.27

Dijkerman, H. C., Milner, A. D., & Carey, D. P. (1998). Grasping spatial relationships: Failure to demonstrate allocentric visual coding in a patient with visual form agnosia. *Consciousness and Cognition, 7*(3), 424–437. https://doi.org/10.1006/ccog.1998.0365

Dijkstra, N., & Fleming, S. (2021). Fundamental constraints on distinguishing reality from imagination. *PsyArXiv*. https://doi.org/10.31234/osf.io/bw872

Dijkstra, N., Hinne, M., Bosch, S. E., & van Gerven, M. A. J. (2019). Between-subject variability in the influence of mental imagery on conscious perception. *Scientific Reports*, 9(1), 15658. https://doi.org/10.1038/s41598-019-52072-1

Dils, A., & Boroditsky, L. (2010). Visual motion aftereffect from understanding motion language. *Proceedings of the National Academy of Sciences, 107*, 16396–16400.

Doeller, C. F., Barry, C., & Burgess, N. (2010). Evidence for grid cells in a human memory network. *Nature, 463*(7281), 657–661. https://doi.org/10.1038/nature08704

Donis, F. (1999). The oblique effect in pigeons (*Columba livea*). *Journal of Comparative Psychology, 113*(2), 107–115.

Donkin, C., Kary, A., Tahir, F., & Taylor, R. (2016). Resources masquerading as slots: Flexible allocation of visual working memory. *Cognitive Psychology, 85*, 30–42. https://doi.org/10.1016/j.cogpsych.2016.01.002

Drayson, Z. (2017). Modularity and the predictive mind. In T. Metzinger & W. Wiese (Eds.), *Philosophy and predictive processing*. Frankfurt am Main, Germany: MIND Group.

Dretske, F. (1969). *Seeing and knowing*. Chicago, IL: University of Chicago Press.

Dretske, F. (1981). *Knowledge and the flow of information*. Cambridge, MA: MIT Press.

Dretske, F. (1988). *Explaining behavior: Reasons in a world of causes*. Cambridge, MA: MIT Press.

Dretske, F. (1995). *Naturalizing the mind*. Cambridge, MA: MIT Press.

Dretske, F. (2007). What change blindness teaches about consciousness. *Philosophical Perspectives, 21*, 215–230.

Dretske, F. (2010). What we see: The texture of conscious experience. In B. Nanay (Ed.), *Perceiving the world* (pp. 54–67). Oxford, UK: Oxford University Press.

Drew, A., Torralba, M., Ruzzoli, M., Morís Fernández, L., Sabaté, A., Szabina Pápai, M., & Soto-Faraco, S. (2021). Conflict monitoring and attentional adjustment during binocular rivalry. *European Journal of Neuroscience*. https://doi.org/10.1111/ejn.15554

Duggal, H., & Pierri, J. (2002). Charles Bonnet syndrome: Neurobiological insights. *Indian Journal of Psychiatry, 44*(3), 289–292.

Durgin, F. (2008). Texture density adaptation and visual number revisited. *Current Biology, 18*(18), R855–R856.

Durgin, F. H., Baird, J. A., Greenburg, M., Russell, R., Shaughnessy, K., & Waymouth, S. (2009). Who is being deceived? The experimental demands of wearing a backpack. *Psychonomic Bulletin and Review, 16*(5), 964–969.

Durgin, F. H., DeWald, D., Lechich, S., Li, Z., & Ontiveros, Z. (2011). Action and motivation: Measuring perception or strategies? *Psychonomic Bulletin and Review, 18*(6), 1077–1082. https://doi.org/10.3758/s13423-011-0164-z

Durie, B. (2005, January 29). Senses special: Doors of perception. *New Scientist*.

Dwarakanath, A., Kapoor, V., Werner, J., Safavi, S., Fedorov, L. A., Logothetis, N. K., & Panagiotaropoulos, T. I. (2020). Prefrontal state fluctuations control access to consciousness. *bioRxiv*, 2020.2001.2029.924928. https://doi.org/10.1101/2020.01.29.924928

Eberhardt, J., Goff, P., Purdie, V., & Davies, P. (2004). Seeing black: Race, crime, and visual processing. *Journal of Personality and Social Psychology, 87*(6), 876–893.

Echeverri, S. (2017). Visual reference and iconic content. *Philosophy of Science, 84*, 761–781.

Egan, F. (2014). How to think about mental content. *Philosophical Studies, 170*, 115–135.

Egan, F. (2018). The nature and function of content in computational models. In M. Sprevak & M. Colombo (Eds.), *The Routledge handbook of the computational mind* (pp. 247–258). London, UK: Routledge.

Emberson, L. (2016). Gaining knowledge mediates changes in perception (without differences in attention): A case for perceptual learning. *Behavioral and Brain Sciences, 39*, e240.

Emberson, L. L., & Amso, D. (2012). Learning to sample: Eye tracking and fMRI indices of changes in object perception. *Journal of Cognitive Neuroscience, 24*(10), 2030–2042. https://doi.org/10.1162/jocn_a_00259

Endress, A., & Potter, M. (2015). Large capacity temporary visual memory. *Journal of Experimental Psychology: General, 214*(143), 548–565.

Endress, A. D., & Siddique, A. (2016). The cost of proactive interference is constant across presentation conditions. *Acta Psychologica, 170*, 186–194. https://doi.org/10.1016/j.actpsy.2016.08.001

Endress, A. D., & Szabo, S. (2017). Interference and memory capacity limitations. *Psychological Review, 124*(5), 551–571. https://doi.org/10.1037/rev0000071

English, M. C., & Visser, T. A. (2014). Exploring the repetition paradox: The effects of learning context and massed repetition on memory. *Psychonomic Bulletin and Review, 21*(4), 1026–1032. https://doi.org/10.3758/s13423-013-0566-1

Ester, E. F., Sprague, T. C., & Serences, J. T. (2017). Category learning biases sensory representations in human visual cortex. *bioRxiv*. https://doi.org/10.1101/170845

Ester, E. F., Sprague, T. C., & Serences, J. T. (2020). Categorical biases in human occipitoparietal cortex. *Journal of Neuroscience, 40*(4), 917. https://doi.org/10.1523/JNEUROSCI.2700-19.2019

Evans, G. (1982). *The varieties of reference*. Oxford, UK: Oxford University Press.

Evans, J., & Stanovich, K. (2013). Dual-process theories of higher cognition: Advancing the debate. *Perspectives on Psychological Science, 8*(3), 223–241.

Fang, M. W. H., Ravizza, S. M., & Liu, T. (2019). Attention induces surround suppression in visual working memory. *Psychonomic Bulletin and Review, 26*(6), 1925–1932. https://doi.org/10.3758/s13423-019-01624-7

Farah, M. (2004). *Visual agnosia* (2nd ed.). Cambridge, MA: MIT Press.

Farennikova, A. (2013). Seeing absence. *Philosophical Studies, 166*(3), 429–454.

Feigenson, L., Spelke, E., & Carey, S. (2002). Infants' discrimination of number vs. continuous extent. *Cognitive Psychology, 44*, 33–66.

Field, H. (1978). Mental representation. *Erkenntnis, 13*, 9–18.

Fink, S. B. (2015). Phenomenal precision and some posible pitfalls: A commentary on Ned Block. In T. Metzinger & J. Windt (Eds.), *MIND anniversary collection* (pp. 1–14). Frankfurt am Main, Germany: Barbara-Wengeler-Stiftung.

Finke, R., & Pinker, S. (1982). Spontaneous imagery scanning in mental extrapolation. *Journal of Experimental Psychology: Learning, Memory, and Cognition, 8*(2), 142–147.

Finke, R. A. (1989). *Principles of mental imagery*. Cambridge, MA: MIT Press.

Firestone, C. (2013). How "paternalistic" is spatial perception? Why wearing a heavy backpack doesn't—and couldn't—make hills look steeper. *Perspectives on Psychological Science, 8*(4), 455–473.

Firestone, C., & Scholl, B. (2013). "Top-down" effects where none should be found: The El Greco fallacy in perception research. *Psychological Science, 25*(1), 38–46.

Firestone, C., & Scholl, B. J. (2015). Enhanced visual awareness for morality and pajamas? Perception vs. memory in "top-down" effects. *Cognition, 136*, 409–416. https://doi.org/10.1016/j.cognition.2014.10.014

Firestone, C., & Scholl, B. (2016a). Cognition does not affect perception: Evaluating the evidence for "top-down" effects. *Behavioral and Brain Sciences, 39*, e229. https://doi.org/10.1017/S0140525X15000965

Firestone, C., & Scholl, B. (2016b). Seeing and thinking: Foundational issues and empirical horizons. *Behavioral and Brain Sciences, 39*, e229.

Firestone, C., & Scholl, B. J. (2016c). "Moral perception" reflects neither morality nor perception. *Trends in Cognitive Sciences, 20*(2), 75–76. https://doi.org/10.1016/j.tics.2015.10.006

Fish, W. (2009). *Perception, hallucination and illusion*. Oxford, UK: Oxford University Press.

Fish, W. (2013). High level properties and visual experience. *Philosophical Studies, 162*, 43–55.

Fitch, W. T. (2014). Toward a computational framework for cognitive biology: Unifying approaches from cognitive neuroscience and comparative cognition. *Physics of Life Reviews, 11*(3), 329–364. https://doi.org/10.1016/j.plrev.2014.04.005

Flombaum, J., & Scholl, B. (2006). A temporal same-object advantage in the tunnel effect: Facilitated change detection for persisting objects. *Journal of Experimental Psychology: Human Perception and Performance, 32*(4), 840–853.

Fodor, J. (1975). *The language of thought*. Cambridge, MA: Harvard University Press.

Fodor, J. (1980). Methodological solipsism as a research strategy in cognitive psychology. *Behavioral and Brain Sciences, 3*, 63–109.

Fodor, J. (1983). *Modularity of mind: An essay on faculty psychology*. Cambridge, MA: MIT Press.

Fodor, J. (1987). *Psychosemantics: The problem of meaning in the philosophy of mind*. Cambridge, MA: MIT Press.

Fodor, J. (1990). Psychosemantics, or, Where do truth conditions come from? In W. Lycan (Ed.), *Mind and Cognition*. Hoboken, NJ: Wiley-Blackwell.

Fodor, J. (1998). *Concepts: Where cognitive science went wrong*. Oxford, UK: Oxford University Press.

Fodor, J. (2007). The revenge of the given. In B. McLaughlin & J. Cohen (Eds.), *Contemporary debates in philosophy of mind* (pp. 105–117). Oxford, UK: Blackwell.

Fodor, J. (2015). Burge on perception. In E. Margolis & S. Laurence (Eds.), *The conceptual mind: New directions in the study of concepts* (pp. 203–221). Cambridge, MA: MIT Press.

Fodor, J., & Pylyshyn, Z. (1988). Connectionism and cognitive architecture. *Cognition, 28*, 3–71.

Forder, L., He, X., & Franklin, A. (2017). Colour categories are reflected in sensory stages of colour perception when stimulus issues are resolved. *PloS One, 12*(5), e0178097. https://doi.org/10.1371/journal.pone.0178097

Forder, L., He, X., Witzel, C., & Franklin, A. (2014). Speakers of different colour lexicons differ only in post-perceptual processing of colour. *Perception, 43*(37th European Conference on Visual Perception, Belgrade, Serbia, 24–28 August 2014), 145.

Forder, L., Taylor, O., Mankin, H., Scott, R. B., & Franklin, A. (2016). Colour terms affect detection of colour and colour-associated objects suppressed from visual awareness. *PloS One, 11*(3), e0152212. https://doi.org/10.1371/journal.pone.0152212

Foster, D. H. (2003). Does colour constancy exist? *Trends in Cognitive Sciences, 7*(10), 439–443. https://doi.org/10.1016/j.tics.2003.08.002

Fotopoulou, A., Pernigo, S., Maeda, R., Rudd, A., & Kopelman, M. (2010). Implicit awareness in anosognosia for hemiplegia: Unconscious interference without conscious re-representation. *Brain, 133*(12), 3564–3577.

Fougnie, D., & Alvarez, G. (2011). Object features fail independently in visual working memory: Evidence for a probabilistic feature-store model. *Journal of Vision, 11*(12), 3.

Fougnie, D., Cormiea, S., Kanabar, A., & Alvarez, G. (2016). Strategic trade-offs between quantity and quality in working memory. *Journal of Experimental Psychology: Human Perception and Performance, 42*(8), 1231. doi:http://dx.doi.org/10.1037/xhp0000211

Fox, K. C. R., Shi, L., Baek, S., Raccah, O., Foster, B. L., Saha, S., . . . Parvizi, J. (2020). Intrinsic network architecture predicts the effects elicited by intracranial electrical stimulation of the human brain. *Nature Human Behaviour, 4*(10), 1039–1052. https://doi.org/10.1038/s41562-020-0910-1

Francis, G. (2015). Excess success for three related papers on racial bias. *Frontiers in Psychology, 6*, 512. https://doi.org/10.3389/fpsyg.2015.00512

Frank, E. T., Wehrhahn, M., & Linsenmair, K. E. (2018). Wound treatment and selective help in a termite-hunting ant. *Proceedings of the Royal Society B: Biological Sciences, 285*(1872), 20172457. https://doi.org/10.1098/rspb.2017.2457

Frank, M. C., Everett, D. L., Fedorenko, E., & Gibson, E. (2008). Number as a cognitive technology: Evidence from Pirahã language and cognition. *Cognition, 108*(3), 819–824.

Frankland, S. M., & Greene, J. D. (2020a). Concepts and compositionality: In search of the brain's language of thought. *Annual Review of Psychology, 71*(1), 273–303. https://doi.org/10.1146/annurev-psych-122216-011829

Frankland, S. M., & Greene, J. D. (2020b). Two ways to build a thought: Distinct forms of compositional semantic representation across brain regions. *Cerebral Cortex, 30*(6), 3838–3855. https://doi.org/10.1093/cercor/bhaa001

Franklin, A. (2006). Constraints on children's color term acquisition. *Journal of Experimental Child Psychology, 94*, 322–327.

Franklin, A. (2015). Infant color categories. In L. Ronier (Ed.), *Encyclopedia of color science and technology*. Heidelberg, Germany: Springer-Verlag (Online). https://doi.org/10.1007/978-3-642-27851-8

Franklin, A., Drivonikou, A., Bevis, L., Davies, I., Kay, P., & Regier, T. (2008). Categorical perception of color is lateralized to the right hemisphere in infants, but to the left hemisphere in adults. *Proceedings of the National Academy of Sciences, 105*(9), 3221–3225.

Franklin-Hall, L. (2015). Natural kinds as categorical bottlenecks. *Philosophical Studies, 172*, 925–948.

Frässle, S., Sommer, J., Jansen, A., Naber, M., & Einhäuser, W. (2014). Binocular rivalry: Frontal activity relates to introspection and action but not to perception. *Journal of Neuroscience, 34*(5), 1738–1747.

Freeman, A. W., & Li, D. F. (2009). Conditions required for binocular rivalry suppression. *Attention, Perception, and Psychophysics, 71*(1), 174–182. https://doi.org/10.3758/app.71.1.174

Freeman, J., & Pelli, D. (2007). An escape from crowding. *Journal of Vision, 7*(2), 1–14.

Freeman, J., & Simoncelli, E. (2011). Metamers of the visual stream. *Nature Neuroscience, 14*(9), 1195–1201.

French, C., & Gomes, A. (2019). How naïve realism can explain both the particularity and the generality of experience. *Philosophical Quarterly, 69*(274), 41–63.

French, C., & Phillips, I. (2020). Austerity and illusion. *Philosophers' Imprint, 20*(15), 1–19.
Fridland, E. (2014). Skill, nonpropositional thought, and the cognitive penetrability of perception. *Journal for General Philosophy of Science, 46*(1), 105–120. https://doi.org/10.1007/s10838-015-9286-8
Frisby, J. (1979). *Seeing: Illusion, brain and mind*. Oxford, UK: Oxford University Press.
Frith, C. (2017, September 22). Our illusory sense of agency has a deeply important social purpose. *Aeon*. https://aeon.co/ideas/our-illusory-sense-of-agency-has-a-deeply-important-social-purpose?utm_source=Aeon+Newsletter&utm_campaign=d0bdc9ed1a-EMAIL_CAMPAIGN_2017_09_19&utm_medium=email&utm_term=0_411a82e59d-d0bdc9ed1a-69465649
Fritsche, M., & de Lange, F. P. (2019). Reference repulsion is not a perceptual illusion. *Cognition, 184*, 107–118. https://doi.org/10.1016/j.cognition.2018.12.010
Fulkerson, M. (2020). Emotional perception. *Australasian Journal of Philosophy, 98*(1), 16–30. https://doi.org/10.1080/00048402.2019.1579848
Gallistel, C. R. (2011). Mental magnitudes. In S. Dehaene & E. Brannon (Eds.), *Space, time and number in the brain* (pp. 3–12). Oxford, UK: Oxford University Press.
Gallistel, C. R., & Gelman, I. I. (2000). Non-verbal numerical cognition: From reals to integers. *Trends in Cognitive Sciences, 4*(2), 59–65.
Gallistel, C. R., Krishan, M., Liu, Y., Miller, R., & Latham, P. E. (2014). The perception of probability. *Psychological Review, 121*(1), 96–123.
Galvin, S. J., O'Shea, R. P., Squire, A. M., & Govan, D. G. (1997). Sharpness overconstancy in peripheral vision. *Vision Research, 37*(15), 2035–2039. https://doi.org/10.1016/S0042-6989(97)00016-3
Ganson, T. (2021). An alternative to the causal theory of perception. *Australasian Journal of Philosophy, 99*(4), 683–695. https://doi.org/10.1080/00048402.2020.1836008
Gantman, A., Devraj-Kizuk, S., Mende-Siedlecki, P., Van Bavel, J. J., & Mathewson, K. E. (2020). The time course of moral perception: An ERP investigation of the moral pop-out effect. *Social Cognitive and Affective Neuroscience, 15*(2), 235–246. https://doi.org/10.1093/scan/nsaa030
Gantman, A. P., & Van Bavel, J. J. (2014). The moral pop-out effect: Enhanced perceptual awareness of morally relevant stimuli. *Cognition, 132*(1), 22–29. https://doi.org/10.1016/j.cognition.2014.02.007
Gantman, A. P., & Van Bavel, J. J. (2015). Moral perception. *Trends in Cognitive Sciences, 19*(11), 631–633. https://doi.org/10.1016/j.tics.2015.08.004
Gantman, A. P., & Van Bavel, J. J. (2016). See for yourself: Perception is attuned to morality. *Trends in Cognitive Sciences, 20*(2), 76–77. https://doi.org/10.1016/j.tics.2015.12.001
Garner, W., & Felfoldy, G. (1970). Integrality of stimulus dimensions in various types of information processing. *Cognitive Psychology, 1*(3), 225–241. https://doi.org/10.1016/0010-0285(70)90016-2
Garner, W. R. (1974). *The processing of information and structure*. New York, NY: Wiley.
Garric, C., Caetta, F., Sergent, C., & Chokron, S. (2020). Making sense of blindsense: A reply to Phillips. *Cortex, 127*, 393–395. https://doi.org/10.1016/j.cortex.2020.03.004
Garrison, K. E., & Handley, I. M. (2017). Not merely experiential: Unconscious thought can be rational. *Frontiers in Psychology, 8*, 1096–1096. https://doi.org/10.3389/fpsyg.2017.01096
Gauker, C. (2011). *Words and images: An essay on the origin of ideas*. Oxford, UK: Oxford University Press.

Gazzaniga, M., Ivry, R., & Mangun, G. (2002). *Cognitive neuroscience: The biology of the mind*. New York, NY: W. W. Norton.
Gelman, S. (2003). *The essential child: Origins of essentialism in everyday thought*. Oxford, UK: Oxford University Press.
Gerbino, W., & Fantoni, C. (2017). Action valence and affective perception. *Behavioral and Brain Sciences, 39*, e243. https://doi.org/10.1017/S0140525X15002605
Giardino, V., & Greenberg, G. (2015). Introduction: Varieties of iconicity. *Review of Philosophy and Psychology, 6*(1), 1–25. https://doi.org/10.1007/s13164-014-0210-7
Gibson, J. J. (1979). *The ecological approach to visual perception*. Boston, MA: Houghton Mifflin.
Glüer, K. (1999). Sense and prescriptivity. *Acta Analytica, 23*, 111–128.
Glüer, K. (2009). In defence of a doxastic account of experience. *Mind and Language, 24*(3), 297–327. https://doi.org/10.1111/j.1468-0017.2009.01364.x
Godfrey-Smith, P. (2016a). Mind, matter, and metabolism. *Journal of Philosophy, 113*(10), 481–506.
Godfrey-Smith, P. (2016b). *Other minds: The octopus, the sea and the deep origins of consciousness*. New York, NY: Farrar, Straus and Giroux.
Godfrey-Smith, P. (2017). The evolution of consciousness in phylogenetic context. In K. Andrews & J. Beck (Eds.), *The Routledge handbook of philosophy of animal minds*. London: Taylor & Francis.
Goldman-Rakic, P. (1987). Circuitry of primate prefrontal cortex and regulation of behavior by representational memory. In F. Plum (Ed.), *Handbook of physiology, the nervous system, higher functions of the brain* (pp. 373–417). Rockville, MD: American Physiological Society.
Goldstone, R. (1994). Influences of categorization on perceptual discrimination. *Journal of Experimental Psychology: General, 123*(2), 178–200.
Goldstone, R., & Hendrickson, A. (2010). Categorical perception. *WIREs Cognitive Science, 1*(1), 69–78.
Golkowski, D., Larroque, S. K., Vanhaudenhuyse, A., Plenevaux, A., Boly, Di Perri, C., Ranft, A., ... Ilg, R. (2019). Changes in whole brain dynamics and connectivity patterns during sevoflurane- and propofol-induced unconsciousness identified by functional magnetic resonance imaging. *Anesthesiology, 130*(6), 898–911. https://doi.org/10.1097/ALN.0000000000002704
Goodale, M., & Milner, D. (2005). *Sight unseen: An exploration of conscious and unconscious vision*. Oxford, UK: Oxford University Press.
Goodman, J. (2013). Inexact knowledge without improbable knowing. *Inquiry, 56*(1), 30–53.
Goodman, N. (1976). *Languages of art: An Approach to a theory of symbols*. Indianapolis, IN: Hackett.
Gopnik, A., Glymour, C., Sobel, D. M., Schulz, L. E., Kushnir, T., & Danks, D. (2004). A theory of causal learning in children: Causal maps and Bayes nets. *Psychological Review, 111*(1), 3–32. https://doi.org/10.1037/0033-295X.111.1.3
Gordon, R., & Irwin, D. (2000). The role of physical and conceptual properties in preserving object continuity. *Journal of Experimental Psychology: Learning, Memory, and Cognition, 26*(1), 136–150.
Gordon, R. D., Vollmer, S. D., & Frankl, M. L. (2008). Object continuity and the transsaccadic representation of form. *Perception and Psychophysics, 70*(4), 667–679. https://doi.org/10.3758/PP.70.4.667

Gottlieb, J., & Rezaei, A. (under review). Conscious perception and perceptual capacities.

Green, E. J. (2017a). *Comments on Firestone and Prinz*. Paper presented at the American Philosophical Association, Eastern Division, Baltimore, Maryland.

Green, E. J. (2017b). *Keeping cognitive penetration in check*. Paper presented at the NYU Consciousness Discussion Group, NYU Department of Philosophy.

Green, E. J. (2021). Binding and differentiation in multisensory object perception. *Synthese, 198*(5), 4457–4491.

Green, E. J. (2020a). The perception-cognition border: A case for architectural division. *The Philosophical Review, 129*(3), 323–393.

Green, E. J. (2020b). Representing shape in sight and touch. *Mind and Language, n/a*(n/a). https://doi.org/10.1111/mila.12352

Green, E. J., & Quilty-Dunn, J. (2017). What is an object file? *British Journal for the Philosophy of Science*. https://doi.org/10.1093/bjps/axx055

Green, E. J., & Quilty-Dunn, J. (2021). What is an object file? *The British Journal for the Philosophy of Science 72*(3), 665–699.

Gregory, R. (1974). Choosing a paradigm for perception. In E. Carterette & M. Friedman (Eds.), *Historical and philosophical roots of perception* (pp. 255–283). New York, NY: Academic Press.

Grice, H. P. (1957). Meaning. *Philosophical Review, 66*(3), 377–388.

Grice, H. P. (1961). The causal theory of perception. *The Aristotelian Society: Proceedings, Supplementary Volume, 35*, 121–152.

Griffiths, T. L., Chater, N., Norris, D., & Pouget, A. (2012). How the Bayesians got their beliefs (and what those beliefs actually are): Comment on Bowers and Davis (2012). *Psychological Bulletin, 138*(3), 415–422.

Griffiths, T. L., & Tenenbaum, J. B. (2006). Optimal predictions in everyday cognition. *Psychological Science, 17*(9), 767–773. https://doi.org/10.1111/j.1467-9280.2006.01780.x

Grill-Spector, K., & Kanwisher, N. (2005). Visual recognition as soon as you know it is there, you know what it is. *Psychological Science, 16*(2), 152–160.

Groening, J., Venini, D., & Srinivasan, M. V. (2017). In search of evidence for the experience of pain in honeybees: A self-administration study. *Scientific Reports, 7*, 45825. https://doi.org/10.1038/srep45825 https://www.nature.com/articles/srep45825#supplementary-information

Gross, S. (2017). Cognitive penetration and attention. *Frontiers in Psychology, 8*, 1–12.

Gross, S. (2018). Perceptual consciousness and cognitive access from the perspective of capacity-unlimited working memory. *Proceedings of the Royal Society B, 373*(1755), 20170343. doi:http://dx.doi.org/10.1098/rstb.2017.0343

Gross, S. (2020). Probabilistic representations in perception: Are there any, and what would they be? *Mind and Language, 35*(3), 377–389. https://doi.org/10.1111/mila.12280

Gross, S. (forthcoming). Is there an empirical case for semantic perception? In *Linguistic Understanding: Perception and Inference* (Special issue). *Inquiry*.

Gross, S., & Flombaum, J. (2017). Does perceptual consciousness overflow cognitive access? The challenge from probabilistic, hierarchical processes. *Mind and Language, 32*(3), 358–391. https://doi.org/10.1111/mila.12144

Grush, R. (2007). A plug for generic phenomenology. *Behavioral and Brain Sciences, 30*(5/6), 504–505.

Gu, S., Wang, F., Patel, N., Bourgeois, J., & Huang, J. (2019). A model for basic emotions using observations of behavior in Drosophila. *Frontiers in Psychology, 10*(781), 1–13. https://doi.org/10.3389/fpsyg.2019.00781

Gupta, A. (2013). The relationship of experience to thought. *The Monist, 96*(2), 252–294.

Gur, M., & Snodderly, D. M. (1997). A dissociation between brain activity and perception: Chromatically opponent cortical neurons signal chromatic flicker that is not perceived. *Vision Research, 37*(4), 377–382.

Gutkin, B., & Zeldenrust, F. (2014). Spike frequency adaptation. *Scholarpedia, 9*(2), 30643.

Haberman, J., Brady, T., & Alvarez, G. (2015a). Individual differences in ensemble perception reveal multiple, independent levels of ensemble representation. *Journal of Experimental Psychology: General, 144*(2), 432–446.

Hajonides, J. E., Nobre, A. C., van Ede, F., & Stokes, M. G. (2021). Decoding visual colour from scalp electroencephalography measurements. *NeuroImage, 237,* 118030. https://doi.org/10.1016/j.neuroimage.2021.118030

Halberda, J. (2018). Logic in babies. *Science, 359*(6381), 1214.

Hameroff, S., & Penrose, R. (2014). Consciousness in the universe: A review of the "Orch OR" theory. *Physics of Life Reviews, 11*(1), 39–78.

Hamlin, J. K., Wynn, K., & Bloom, P. (2007). Social evaluation by preverbal infants. *Nature, 450*(7169), 557–559. https://doi.org/10.1038/nature06288

Hanif, H. M., Perler, B. L., & Jason, J. S. B. (2013). The visual representations of words and style in text: An adaptation study. *Brain Research, 1518,* 61–70. https://doi.org/10.1016/j.brainres.2013.04.036

Hanson, N. (1958). *Patterns of discovery: An inquiry into the conceptual foundations of science.* Cambridge, UK: Cambridge University Press.

Harman, G. (1973). *Thought.* Princeton, NJ: Princeton University Press.

Harnad, S. (1987a). *Categorical perception.* Cambridge, UK: Cambridge University Press.

Harnad, S. (1987b). Categorical perception: A critical overview. In S. Harnad (Ed.), *Categorical perception: The groundwork of cognition* (pp. 1–28). Cambridge, UK: Cambridge University Press.

Harrison, S. A., & Tong, F. (2009). Decoding reveals the contents of visual working memory in early visual areas. *Nature, 458*(7238), 632–635. https://doi.org/10.1038/nature07832

Haugeland, J. (1980). Programs, causal powers and intentionality. *Behavioral and Brain Sciences, 3,* 432–433.

Haugeland, J. (1991). Representational genera. In J. Haugeland (Ed.), *Having thought: Essays in the metaphysics of mind.* Cambridge, MA: Harvard University Press.

Haun, A., Koch, C., Tononi, G., & Tsuchiya, N. (2017). Are we underestimating the richness of visual experience? *Neuroscience of Consciousness, 2017*(1), niw023https://doi.org/10.1093/nc/niw023

Haun, A. M. (2021). What is visible across the visual field? *PsyArXiv.* https://doi.org/10.31234/osf.io/wdpu7

Hayashi, R., Yamaguchi, S., Narimatsu, T., Miyata, H., Katsumata, Y., & Mimura, M. (2017). Statokinetic dissociation (Riddoch phenomenon) in a patient with homonymous hemianopsia as the first sign of posterior cortical atrophy. *Case Reports in Neurology, 9*(3), 256–260. https://doi.org/10.1159/000481304

Haynes, J.-D., & Rees, G. (2005). Predicting the orientation of invisible stimuli from activity in human primary visual cortex. *Nature Neuroscience, 8*(5), 686–691.

He, S., Cavanagh, P., & Intriligator, J. (1996). Attentional resolution and the locus of visual awareness. *Nature, 383*, 334–338.

He, S., & MacLeod, D. I. A. (2001). Orientation-selective adaptation and tilt after-effect from invisible patterns. *Nature, 411*, 473–476.

He, X., Witzel, C., Forder, L., Clifford, A., & Franklin, A. (2014). Color categories only affect post-perceptual processes when same- and different-category colors are equally discriminable. *Journal of the Optical Society of America, 31*(4), A322–A331.

Heck, R. (2000). Nonconceptual content and the space of reasons. *Philosophical Review, 109*, 483–523.

Heck, R. (2007). Are there different kinds of content? In J. Cohen & B. McLaughlin (Eds.), *Contemporary debates in philosophy of mind* (pp. 117–138). Oxford, UK: Blackwell.

Heeger, D. J. (1992). Normalization of cell responses in cat striate cortex. *Visual Neuroscience, 9*(2), 181–197. https://doi.org/10.1017/S0952523800009640

Heidegger, M. (1977). The origin of the work of art. In D. F. Krell (Ed.), *Martin Heidegger: Basic writings*. New York, NY: Harper and Row.

Helmholtz, H. v. (1866). *Treatise on physiological optics*. Rochester, NY: Optic Society of America.

Helton, G. (2016). Recent issues in high-level perception. *Philosophy Compass, 11*(12), 851–862.

Helton, G. (2017). Visually perceiving the intentions of others. *Philosophical Quarterly*, pqx051–pqx051. https://doi.org/10.1093/pq/pqx051

Herrington, J. D., Taylor, J. M., Grupe, D. W., Curby, K. M., & Schultz, R. T. (2011). Bidirectional communication between amygdala and fusiform gyrus during facial recognition. *NeuroImage, 56*(4), 2348–2355. https://doi.org/10.1016/j.neuroimage.2011.03.072

Hershler, O., & Hochstein, S. (2006). With a careful look: Still no low-level confound to face pop-out. *Vision Research, 46*(18), 3028–3036.

Hesse, J. K., & Tsao, D. Y. (2020a). The macaque face patch system: A turtle's underbelly for the brain. *Nature Reviews Neuroscience, 21*(12), 695–716. https://doi.org/10.1038/s41583-020-00393-w

Hesse, J. K., & Tsao, D. Y. (2020b). A new no-report paradigm reveals that face cells encode both consciously perceived and suppressed stimuli. *eLIFE, 9*, e58360. https://doi.org/10.7554/eLife.58360

Hill, C. (2009). *Consciousness*. Cambridge, UK: Cambridge University Press.

Hill, C. (2013). Visual awareness and visual qualia. In T. Horgan, M. H. Sabates, & D. Sosa (Eds.), *Supervenience in mind*. Cambridge, MA: MIT Press.

Hill, C. (2019). Perceptual existentialism sustained. *Erkentniss, 86*(6), 1391–1410.

Hill, C. (2021). Perceptual awareness of particulars. In B. McLaughlin & J. Cohen (Eds.), *Contemporary debates in philosophy of mind*. Oxford, UK: Blackwell.

Hirsh, I. J. (1959). Auditory perception of temporal order. *Journal of the Acoustical Society of America, 31*(6), 759–767. https://doi.org/10.1121/1.1907782

Hochberg, J. E., Triebel, W., & Seaman, G. (1951). Color adaptation under conditions of homogeneous visual stimulation (Ganzfeld). *Journal of Experimental Psychology, 41*(2), 153–159.

Hochmann, J.-R. (2010). *Categories, words and rules in language acquisition* (PhD dissertation). SISSA, Trieste.

Hochstein, S., & Ahissar, M. (2002). View from the top: Hierarchies and reverse hierarchies in the visual system. *Neuron, 36*(5), 791–804.

Hofstadter, D. R. (1979). *Godel, Escher, Bach: An eternal golden braid*. New York, NY: Basic Books.

Hohwy, J. (2013). *The predictive mind*. Oxford, UK: Oxford University Press.

Hohwy, J., Roepstorff, A., & Friston, K. (2008). Predictive coding explains binocular rivalry: An epistemological review. *Cognition, 108*(3), 687–701.

Hollingworth, A., & Henderson, J. M. (2002). Accurate visual memory for previously attended objects in natural scenes. *Journal of Experimental Psychology: Human Perception and Performance, 28*(1), 113–136. https://doi.org/10.1037/0096-1523.28.1.113

Howard, S., R., Avarguès-Weber, A., Garcia, J., E., Greentree, A., D., & Dyer, A., G. (2019a). Symbolic representation of numerosity by honeybees (Apis mellifera): Matching characters to small quantities. *Proceedings of the Royal Society B: Biological Sciences, 286*(1904), 20190238. https://doi.org/10.1098/rspb.2019.0238

Howard, S. R., Avarguès-Weber, A., Garcia, J. E., Greentree, A. D., & Dyer, A. G. (2019b). Numerical cognition in honeybees enables addition and subtraction. *Science Advances, 5*(2), eaav0961. https://doi.org/10.1126/sciadv.aav0961

Howe, P., & Carter, O. (2016). Hallucinations and mental imagery demonstrate 'top-down' effects on visual perception. *Behavioral and Brain Sciences, 39*, e248. https://doi.org/10.1017/S0140525X15002502

Hoy, R. (1989). Startle, categorical response, and attention in acoustic behavior of insects. *Annual Reviews of Neuroscience, 12*, 355–375.

Huang, L., & Pashler, H. (2007). A boolean map theory of visual attention. *Psychological Review, 114*(3), 599–631.

Huang, L., Treisman, A., & Pashler, H. (2007). Characterizing the limits of human visual awareness. *Science, 317*, 823–825.

Huberle, E., & Karnath, H. O. (2006). Global shape recognition is modulated by the spatial distance of local elements—evidence from simultanagnosia. *Neuropsychologia, 44*(6), 905–911.

Hurley, S. (1998). *Consciousness in action*. Cambridge, MA: Harvard University Press.

Huttenlocher, P. R., & Dabholkar, A. S. (1997). Regional differences in synaptogenesis in human cerebral cortex. *Journal of Comparative Neurology, 387*, 167–178.

Hutto, D., & Myin, E. (2014). Neural representations not needed: No more pleas, please. *Phenomenology and the Cognitive Sciences, 13*(2), 241–256.

Irwin, D. (1992). Memory for position and identity across eye movements. *Journal of Experimental Psychology: Learning, Memory, and Cognition, 18*(2), 307–317.

Irwin, D. E., & Andrews, R. V. (1996). Integration and accumulation of information across saccadic eye movements. In I. Toshio & J. L. McClelland (Eds.), *Attention and performance. Vol. 16: Information integration in perception and communication* (pp. 125–155). Cambridge, MA: MIT Press.

Jacob, P., & de Vignemont, F. (2010). Spatial coordinates and phenomenology in the two visual systems model. In N. Gangopadhyay, M. Madary, & F. Spicer (Eds.), *Perception, action, and consciousness: Sensorimotor dynamics and two visual systems*. Oxford, UK: Oxford University Press.

Jacob, P., & Jeannerod, M. (2003). *Ways of seeing: The scope and limits of visual cognition*. Oxford, UK: Oxford University Press.

Jacobs, C., Schwarzkopf, D. S., & Silvanto, J. (2018). Visual working memory performance in aphantasia. *Cortex: A Journal Devoted to the Study of the Nervous System and Behavior, 105*, 61–73. https://doi.org/10.1016/j.cortex.2017.10.014

Jacobs, L. F., Arter, J., Cook, A., & Sulloway, F. J. (2015). Olfactory orientation and navigation in humans. *PloS One, 10*(6), e0129387–e0129387. https://doi.org/10.1371/journal.pone.0129387

Jacobson, H. (2021). The role of valence in perception: An ARTistic treatment. *Philosophical Review, 130*(4), 481–531.

James, L., & Vila, B. (2016). The reverse racism effect: Are cops more hesitant to shoot black suspects? *Criminology and Public Policy, 15*(2), 457–479.

James, W. (1890). *Principles of psychology*. New York, NY: Henry Holt.

Javadi, A. H., & Wee, N. (2012). Cross-category adaptation: Objects produce gender adaptation in the perception of faces. *PloS One, 7*(9), e46079–e46079. https://doi.org/10.1371/journal.pone.0046079

Jazayeri, M., & Movshon, J. A. (2006). Optimal representation of sensory information by neural populations. *Nature Neuroscience, 9*, 690. https://doi.org/10.1038/nn1691 https://www.nature.com/articles/nn1691#supplementary-information

Jeannerod, M., & Jacob, P. (2005). Visual cognition: A new look at the two-visual systems model. *Neuropsychologia, 43*(2), 301–312.

Jeffery, L., Burton, N., Pond, S., Clifford, C., & Rhodes, G. (2018). Beyond opponent coding of facial identity: Evidence for an additional channel tuned to the average face. *Journal of Experimental Psychology: Human Perception and Performance, 44*(2), 243–260. doi:http://dx.doi.org/10.1037/xhp0000427

Jiang, F., Blanz, V., & O'Toole, A. J. (2007). The role of familiarity in three-dimensional view-transferability of face identity adaptation. *Vision Research, 47*(4), 525–531. https://doi.org/10.1016/j.visres.2006.10.012

Jin, D., Dragoi, V., Sur, M., & Seung, S. (2005). Tilt aftereffect and adaptation-induced changes in orientation tuning in visual cortex. *Journal of Neurophysiology, 94*, 4038–4050.

Johnson-Laird, P. (2008). *How we reason*. Oxford, UK: Oxford University Press.

Johnston, M. (2004). The obscure object of hallucination. *Philosophical Studies, 120*, 113–183.

Johnston, R. A., Milne, A. B., Williams, C., & Hosie, J. (1997). Do distinctive faces come from outer space? An investigation of the status of a multidimensional face-space. *Visual Cognition, 4*(1), 59–67. https://doi.org/10.1080/713756748

Jonas, E., & Kording, K. P. (2017). Could a neuroscientist understand a microprocessor? *PLoS Computational Biology, 13*(1), e1005268–e1005268. https://doi.org/10.1371/journal.pcbi.1005268

Jordan, K., Clark, K., & Mitroff, S. (2010). See an object, hear an object file: Object correspondence transcends sensory modality. *Visual Cognition, 18*(4), 492–503.

Judge, J. (2018). The surprising thing about musical surprise. *Analysis, 78*(2), 225–234. https://doi.org/10.1093/analys/anx139

Kahneman, D., Slovic, P., & Tversky, A. (1982). *Judgment under uncertainty: Heuristics and biases*. Cambridge: Cambridge University Press.

Kahneman, D., Treisman, A., & Gibbs, B. (1992). The reviewing of object files: Object-specific integration of information. *Cognitive Psychology, 24*, 175–219.

Kanai, R., Bahrami, B., & Rees, G. (2010). Human parietal cortex structure predicts individual differences in perceptual rivalry. *Current Biology: CB, 20*(18), 1626–1630. https://doi.org/10.1016/j.cub.2010.07.027

Kanizsa, G. (1985). Seeing and thinking. *Acta Psychologica, 59*(1), 23–33.

Kanwisher, N., & Wojciulik, E. (1998). Implicit but not explicit feature binding in a Balint's patient. *Visual Cognition, 5*(1–2), 157–181. https://doi.org/10.1080/713756779

Kanwisher, N. (2010). Functional specificity in the human brain: A window into the functional architecture of the mind. *Proceedings of the National Academy of Sciences, USA, 107*(25), 11163–11170. https://doi.org/10.1073/pnas.1005062107

Kapoor, V. (2019). *Neuronal discharges in the prefrontal cortex reflect changes in conscious perception during a no report binocular rivalry paradigm.* Paper presented at the Association for the Scientific Study of Consciousness 23, London, Ontario.

Kapoor, V., Dwarakanath, A., Safavi, S., Werner, J., Besserve, M., Panagiotaropoulos, T. I., & Logothetis, N. K. (2020). Decoding the contents of consciousness from prefrontal ensembles. *bioRxiv.* https://doi.org/10.1101/2020.01.28.921841

Kapoor, V., Safavi, S., & Logothetis, N. K. (2018). *Spiking activity in the prefrontal cortex reflects spontaneous perceptual transitions during a no report binocular rivalry paradigm.* Paper presented at the 11th FENS Forum of Neuroscience, Berlin. Poster retrieved from https://ep70.eventpilot.us/web/page.php?page=IntHtml&project=FENS18&id=abstract_37575

Kapoor, V., Dwarakanath, A., Safavi, S., Werner, J., Besserve, M., Panagiotaropoulos, T. I., & Logothetis, N. K. (2022). Decoding internally generated transitions of conscious contents in the prefrontal cortex without subjective reports. Nature Communications, *13*(1), 1535.

Kaski, D. (2002). Revision: is visual perception a requisite for visual imagery? *Perception, 31*(6), 717–731. https://doi.org/10.1068/p3360

Kawashima, T., & Matsumoto, E. (2018). Negative cues lead to more inefficient search than positive cues even at later stages of visual search. *Acta Psychologica, 190*, 85–94. https://doi.org/10.1016/j.actpsy.2018.07.003

Kean, S. (2020). This man can read letters but numbers are a blank. *Science, 369*(6503), 494. https://doi.org/10.1126/science.369.6503.494

Keane, B. P. (2018). Contour interpolation: A case study in modularity of mind. *Cognition, 174*, 1–18. https://doi.org/10.1016/j.cognition.2018.01.008

Keane, B. P., Lu, H., Papathomas, T. V., Silverstein, S. M., & Kellman, P. J. (2012). Is interpolation cognitively encapsulated? Measuring the effects of belief on Kanizsa shape discrimination and illusory contour formation. *Cognition, 123*(3), 404–418. https://doi.org/10.1016/j.cognition.2012.02.004

Keijzer, F. (2013). The Sphex story: How the cognitive sciences kept repeating an old and questionable anecdote. *Philosophical Psychology, 26*(4), 502–519.

Keil, F. (1989). *Concepts, kinds and cognitive development.* Cambridge, MA: MIT Press.

Keysers, C., Xiao, D., Földiák, P., & Perrett, D. (2001). The speed of sight. *Journal of Cognitive Neuroscience, 13*(1), 90–101.

Kibbe, M. M., & Leslie, A. M. (2019). Conceptually rich, perceptually sparse: Object representations in 6-month-old infants' working memory. *Psychological Science, 30*(3), 362–375. https://doi.org/10.1177/0956797618817754

Kim, S., Burr, D., & Alais, D. (2019). Attraction to the recent past in aesthetic judgments: A positive serial dependence for rating artwork. *Journal of Vision, 19*(12), 19–19. https://doi.org/10.1167/19.12.19

Kimura, A., Wada, Y., Yang, J., Otsuka, Y., Dan, I., Masuda, T., . . . Yamaguchi, M. K. (2010). Infants' recognition of objects using canonical color. *Journal of Experimental Child Psychology, 105*(3), 256–263. https://doi.org/10.1016/j.jecp.2009.11.002

Kirchner, H., & Thorpe, S. (2006). Ultra-rapid object detection with saccadic eye movements: Visual processing speed revisited. *Vision Research, 46*, 1762–1776.

Kitagawa, N., & Ichihara, S. (2002). Hearing visual motion in depth. *Nature, 416*(6877), 172–174.

Kitcher, P. (2007). Does "race" have a future? *Philosophy and Public Affairs, 35*(4), 293–317.

Klauer, K. C., & Musch, J. (2003). Affective priming: Findings and theories. *Psychology of Evaluation: Affective Processes in Cognition and Emotion, 7*, 49.

Klein, R., & Ivanoff, J. (2008). Inhibition of return. *Scholarpedia, 3*(10), 3650.

Klink, P. C., Boucherie, D., Denys, D., Roelfsema, P. R., & Self, M. W. (2017). Interocularly merged face percepts eliminate binocular rivalry. *Scientific Reports, 7*(1), 7585. https://doi.org/10.1038/s41598-017-08023-9

Kloth, N., Rhodes, G., & Schweinberger, S. R. (2017). Watching the brain recalibrate: Neural correlates of renormalization during face adaptation. *NeuroImage, 155*, 1–9. doi:http://dx.doi.org/10.1016/j.neuroimage.2017.04.049

Knau, H., & Spillmann, L. (1997). Brightness fading during Ganzfeld adaptation. *Journal of the Optical Society of America. A, Optics, Image Science, and Vision,14*(6), 1213–1222.

Knotts, J. D., Odegaard, B., Lau, H., & Rosenthal, D. (2019). Subjective inflation: Phenomenology's get-rich-quick scheme. *Current Opinion in Psychology, 29*, 49–55. https://doi.org/10.1016/j.copsyc.2018.11.006

Koch, C. (2004). *The quest for consciousness: A neurobiological approach*. Englewood, CO: Roberts and Company.

Koch, C., Massimini, M., Boly, M., & Tononi, G. (2016). Neural correlates of consciousness: Progress and problems. *Nature Reviews Neuroscience, 17*(5), 307–321. https://doi.org/10.1038/nrn.2016.22

Kok, P., Rahnev, D., Jehee, J. F. M., Lau, H. C., & de Lange, F. P. (2011). Attention reverses the effect of prediction in silencing sensory signals. *Cerebral Cortex, 22*(9), 2197–2206. https://doi.org/10.1093/cercor/bhr310

Kominsky, J. F., & Scholl, B. J. (2020). Retinotopic adaptation reveals distinct categories of causal perception. *Cognition, 203*, 104339. https://doi.org/10.1016/j.cognition.2020.104339

Kominsky, J. F., Strickland, B., Wertz, A. E., Elsner, C., Wynn, K., & Keil, F. C. (2017). Categories and constraints in causal perception. *Psychological Science, 28*(11), 1649–1662. https://doi.org/10.1177/0956797617719930

Konkle, T., & Oliva, A. (2012). A real-world size organization of object responses in occipitotemporal cortex. *Neuron, 74*(6), 1114–1124.

Konkle, T., Wang, Q., Hayward, V., & Moore, C. (2009). Motion aftereffects transfer between touch and vision. *Current Biology, 19*, 745–750.

Kosslyn, S. (1980). *Image and mind*. Cambridge, MA: Harvard University Press.

Kosslyn, S. (1983). *Ghosts in the mind's machine*. New York, NY: Norton.

Kosslyn, S. (1994). *Image and brain: The resolution of the imagery debate*. Cambridge, MA: MIT Press.

Kosslyn, S., Pinker, S., Schwartz, S., & Smith, G. (1979). On the demystification of mental imagery. *Behavioral and Brain Sciences, 2*, 535–581.

Kosslyn, S., Thompson, W. L., & Ganis, G. (2006). *The case for mental imagery*. Oxford, UK: Oxford University Press.

Kouider, S., de Gardelle, V., & Dupoux, E. (2007). Partial awareness and the illusion of phenomenal consciousness. *Behavioral and Brain Sciences, 30*(5–6), 510–511.

Kouider, S., de Gardelle, V., Sackur, J., & Dupoux, E. (2010). How rich is consciousness? The partial awareness hypothesis. *Trends in Cognitive Sciences, 14*, 301–307.

Kounios, J., Kotz, S. A., & Holcomb, P. J. (2000). On the locus of the semantic satiation effect: Evidence from event-related brain potentials. *Memory and Cognition, 28*(8), 1366–1377.

Kourtzi, Z., & Kanwisher, N. (2000). Activation in human MT/MST by static images with implied motion. *Journal of Cognitive Neuroscience, 12*, 48–55.

Kriegel, U. (2019). The perception/cognition divide: One more time, with feeling. In C. Limbeck-Lilienau & F. Stadler (Eds.), *The philosophy of perception* (pp. 149–170). Berlin, Germany, and Boston, MA: De Gruyter.

Kripke, S. (1972). Naming and necessity. In D. Davidson & G. Harman (Eds.), *Semantics of natural language* (pp. 253–355). Boston, MA, and Dordrecht, Netherlands: Reidel.

Kripke, S. (1982). *Wittgenstein on rules and private language*. Cambridge, MA: Harvard University Press.

Kristjánsson, Á., & Tse, P. U. (2001). Curvature discontinuities are cues for rapid shape analysis. *Perception and Psychophysics, 63*(3), 390–403. https://doi.org/10.3758/BF03194407

Kuhl, B. A., & Anderson, M. C. (2011). More is not always better: Paradoxical effects of repetition on semantic accessibility. *Psychonomic Bulletin and Review, 18*(5), 964–972. https://doi.org/10.3758/s13423-011-0110-0

Kuhn, T. (1962). *The structure of scientific revolutions*. Chicago, IL: University of Chicago Press.

Kulvicki, J. (2004). Isomorphism in information-carrying systems. *Pacific Philosophical Quarterly, 85*(4), 380–395.

Kulvicki, J. (2015). Analog representation and the parts principle. *Review of Philosophy and Psychology, 6*, 165–180.

Kumar, S., Kaposvari, P., & Vogels, R. (2017). Encoding of predictable and unpredictable stimuli by inferior temporal cortical neurons. *Journal of Cognitive Neuroscience, 29*(8), 1445–1454. https://doi.org/10.1162/jocn_a_01135

Kwak, Y., & Curtis, C. E. (2022). Unveiling the abstract format of mnemonic representations. *Neuron, 110*.

Lamme, V. (2003). Why visual attention and awareness are different. *Trends in Cognitive Sciences, 7*, 12–18.

Lamme, V. (2004). Separate neural definitions of visual consciousness and visual attention: A case for phenomenal awareness. *Neural Networks, 17*(5–6), 861–872.

Lamme, V. (2006). Towards a true neural stance on consciousness. *Trends in Cognitive Sciences, 10*(11), 494–501.

Lamme, V. (2016). The crack of dawn: Perceptual functions and neural mechanisms that mark the transition from unconscious processing to conscious vision. In T. Metzinger & J. Windt (Eds.), *Open MIND, 2 volume set* (Vol. 1). Frankfurt am Main: MIND Group. https://doi.org/10.15502/9783958570092

Lamme, V. A. F. (2018). Challenges for theories of consciousness: Seeing or knowing, the missing ingredient and how to deal with panpsychism. *Philosophical Transactions of the Royal Society B: Biological Sciences, 373*(1755), 20170344.

Lande, K. (2022). Seeing and visual reference. *Philosophy and Phenomenological Research, 2021*, 1–32. https://doi.org/10.1111/phpr.12859

Landman, R., Spekreijse, H., & Lamme, V. A. F. (2003). Large capacity storage of integrated objects before change blindness. *Vision Research, 43*, 149–164.

Landon, J., & Davison, M. (2001). Reinforcer-ratio variation and its effects on rate of adaptation. *Journal of the Experimental Analysis of Behavior*, 75(2), 207–234.

Lapate, R. C., Samaha, J., Rokers, B., Postle, B. R., & Davidson, R. J. (2020). Perceptual metacognition of human faces is causally supported by function of the lateral prefrontal cortex. *Communications Biology*, 3(1), 360. https://doi.org/10.1038/s42003-020-1049-3

Latour, B. (1998). Ramses II est-il mort de la tuberculose? *La Recherche*, 307(March), 84–85.

Lau, H. (2008). Are we studying consciousness yet? In L. Weiskrantz & M. Davies (Eds.), *Frontiers of consciousness: Chichele lectures* (pp. 245–258). Oxford, UK: Oxford University Press.

Lau, H. (2019). Consciousness, metacognition, and perceptual reality monitoring. *PsyArXiv*. Retrieved from https://doi.org/10.31234/osf.io/ckbyf

Lau, H. (2022). *In consciousness we trust: The cognitive neuroscience of subjective experience*. Oxford, UK: Oxford University Press.

Lau, H., & Brown, R. (2019). The emperor's new phenomenology? The empirical case for conscious experiences without first-order representations. In A. Pautz & D. Stoljar (Eds.), *Themes from Block*. Cambridge, MA: MIT Press.

Lau, H., Rogers, R., & Passingham, R. (2006). Manipulating the experienced onset of intention after action execution. *Journal of Cognitive Neuroscience*, 19(1), 81–90.

Lau, H., & Rosenthal, D. (2011). Empirical support for higher-order theories of conscious awareness. *Trends in Cognitive Sciences*, 15(8), 365–373.

Lawrence, D. H. (1950). Acquired distinctiveness of cues: Selective association in a constant stimulus situation. *Journal of Experimental Psychology*, 40(2), 175–188.

Lea, S. E. G., Earle, D. C., & Ryan, C. M. E. (1999). The McCollough effect in pigeons: Tests of persistence and spatial-frequency specificity. *Behavioural Processes*, 47(1), 31–43. https://doi.org/10.1016/S0376-6357(99)00047-9

Leahy, B. P., & Carey, S. E. (2020). The acquisition of modal concepts. *Trends in Cognitive Sciences*, 24(1), 65–78. https://doi.org/10.1016/j.tics.2019.11.004

Lebrecht, S. (2012). *"Micro-valences": Affective valence in "neutral" everyday objects* (PhD dissertation). Brown University, Providence RI.

Lebrecht, S., Bar, M., Barrett, L., & Tarr, M. (2012). Micro-valences: Perceiving affective valence in everyday objects. *Frontiers in Psychology*, 3, 107.

LeDoux, J., & Brown, R. (2017). A higher-order theory of emotional consciousness. *Proceedings of the National Academy of Sciences*, 114(10), E2016–E2025. doi:www.pnas.org/cgi/doi/10.1073/pnas.1619316114

Lee, J. L., Denison, R., & Ma, W. J. (in preparation). Re-thinking the fixed-criterion model of perceptual decision-making. http://psyarxiv.com/ys8mb/

Lee, T., & Nguyen, M. (2001). Dynamics of subjective contour formation in the early visual cortex. *Proceedings of the National Academy of Sciences*, 98(4), 1907–1911.

Lee, T. S., & Mumford, D. (2003). Hierarchical Bayesian inference in the visual cortex. *Journal of the Optical Society of America. A, Optics, Image Science, and Vision*, 20(7), 1434–1448.

Leonard, M., Baud, M., Sjerps, M., & Chang, E. (2016). Perceptual restoration of masked speech in human cortex. *Nature Communications*, 7, 13619. https://doi.org/10.1038/ncomms13619

Leslie, A. M., & Keeble, S. (1987). Do six-month-old infants perceive causality? *Cognition*, 25(3), 265–288. https://doi.org/10.1016/S0010-0277(87)80006-9

Leslie, S.-J. (2013). Essence and natural kinds: When science meets preschooler intuition. *Oxford Studies in Epistemology, 4*, 108–166.
Levine, J. (1983). Materialism and qualia: The explanatory gap. *Pacific Philosophical Quarterly, 64*, 354–361.
Levine, J. (2010). Demonstrative thought. *Mind and Language, 25*, 169–195.
Lewis, D. (1971). Analog and digital. *Nous, 5*(3), 321–327.
Lewis, D. (1984). Putnam's paradox. *Australasian Journal of Philosophy, 62*(3), 221–236. https://doi.org/10.1080/00048408412340013
Lewis, D. (1986). *On the plurality of worlds.* Oxford, UK: Blackwell.
Lewis, K., Borst, G., & Kosslyn, S. (2011). Integrating images and percepts: New evidence for depictive representation. *Psychological Research, 75*(4), 259–271.
Libet, B., Gleason, C. A., Wright, E. W., & Pearl, D. K. (1983). Time of conscious intention to act in relation to onset of cerebral activity (readiness-potential): The unconscious initiation of a freely voluntary act. *Brain, 106*(0006-8950 [Print]), 623–642.
Linton, P. (2017). *The perception and cognition of visual space.* London: Palgrave Macmillan.
Liu, B., Hong, A., Rieke, F., & Manookin, M. B. (2021). Predictive encoding of motion begins in the primate retina. *Nature Neuroscience, 24*(9), 1280–1291. https://doi.org/10.1038/s41593-021-00899-1
Loar, B. (2003). Phenomenal intentionality as the basis of mental content. In M. Hahn & B. Ramberg (Eds.), *Reflections and replies: Essays on the philosophy of Tyler Burge* (pp. 229–257). Cambridge, MA: MIT Press.
Locke, J. (1690). *An essay concerning human understanding.* London, UK: Edward Mory at the Sign of the Three Bibles in St. Paul's Church-Yard.
Logothetis, N., & Leopold, D. (1999). Multistable phenomena: Changing views in perception. *Trends in Cognitive Sciences, 3*(7), 254–264.
Logue, H. (2021). Abstract and particular content: The best of both theories. In B. McLaughlin & J. Cohen (Eds.), *Contemporary debates in philosophy of mind.* Oxford, UK: Blackwell.
Long, B. (2017). *Mid-level features elicit cognitive and neural representations of object size.* (PhD dissertation). Harvard University, Cambridge, MA.
Long, B., & Konkle, T. (2017). A familiar-size Stroop effect in the absence of basic-level recognition. *Cognition, 168*, 234–242. https://doi.org/10.1016/j.cognition.2017.06.025
Long, B., Konkle, T., Cohen, M. A., & Alvarez, G. A. (2016). Mid-level perceptual features distinguish objects of different real-world sizes. *Journal of Experimental Psychology, General, 145*(1), 95–109. https://doi.org/10.1037/xge0000130
Long, B., Moher, M., Konkle, T., & Carey, S. (2019). Animacy and object size are reflected in perceptual similarity computations by the preschool years. *Visual Cognition, 27*(5–8), 435–451. https://doi.org/10.1080/13506285.2019.1664689
Long, B., Störmer, V., & Alvarez, G. (2017). Mid-level perceptual features contain early cues to animacy. *Journal of Vision, 17*(6), 20. https://doi.org/10.1167/17.6.20
Long, G., & Toppino, T. (2004). Enduring interest in perceptual ambiguity: Alternating views of reversible figures. *Psychological Bulletin, 130*(5), 748–768. https://doi.org/10.1037/0033-2909.130.5.748
Loschky, L., Hansen, B., Sethi, A., & Pydimarri, T. (2010). The role of higher order image statistics in masking scene gist recognition. *Attention, Perception, and Psychophysics, 72*, 427–444.

Lumer, E. D., & Rees, G. (1999). Covatiation of activity in visual and prefrontal cortex associated with subjective visual perception. *Proceedings of the National Academy of Sciences, 96*(4), 1669–1673.

Lupyan, G. (2015). Cognitive penetrability of perception in the age of prediction: Predictive systems are penetrable systems. *Review of Philosophy and Psychology, 6*(4), 547–569. https://doi.org/10.1007/s13164-015-0253-4

Lupyan, G. (2017). Changing what you see by changing what you know. *Frontiers in Psychology, 8*, 553.

Lupyan, G., & Clark, A. (2015). Words and the world: Predictive coding and the language-perception-cognition interface. *Current Directions in Psychological Science, 24*(4), 279–284.

Lupyan, G., Rahman, A., Boroditsky, L., & Clark, A. (2020). Effects of language on visual perception. *Trends in Cognitive Sciences, 24*(11), 930–944.

Lupyan, G., & Ward, E. J. (2013). Language can boost otherwise unseen objects into visual awareness. *Proceedings of the National Academy of Sciences, USA, 110*(35), 14196–14201. https://doi.org/10.1073/pnas.1303312110

Lycan, W. G. (2014). The intentionality of smell. *Frontiers in Psychology, 5*(436). https://doi.org/10.3389/fpsyg.2014.00436

Ma, W. J., Husain, M., & Bays, P. M. (2014). Changing concepts of working memory. *Nature Neuroscience, 17*(3), 347–356.

Macpherson, F. (2012). Cognitive penetration of colour experience: Rethinking the issue in light of an indirect mechanism. *Philosophy and Phenomenological Research, 84*(1), 24–62.

Macpherson, F. (2015). Cognitive penetration and predictive coding: A commentary on Lupyan. *Review of Philosophy and Psychology, 6*(4), 571–584. https://doi.org/10.1007/s13164-015-0254-3

Macpherson, F. (2017). The relationship between cognitive penetration and predictive coding. *Consciousness and Cognition, 47*, 6–16.

Maguire, J., & Howe, P. (2016). Failure to detect meaning in RSVP at 27 ms per picture. *Attention, Perception and Psychophysics, 78*(5), 1405–1413. https://doi.org/10.3758/s13414-016-1096-5

Maier, M., & Abdel Rahman, R. (2018). Native language promotes access to visual consciousness. *Psychological Science, 29*(11), 1757–1772. https://doi.org/10.1177/0956797618782181

Maley, C. (2011). Analog and digital, continuous, and discrete. *Philosophical Studies, 155*, 117–131.

Maloney, L. T., & Mamassian, P. (2009). Bayesian decision theory as a model of human visual perception: Testing Bayesian transfer. *Visual Neuroscience, 26*(1), 147–155. https://doi.org/10.1017/s0952523808080905

Mamassian, P., Landy, M., & Maloney, L. (2002). Bayesian modeling of visual perception. In R. Rao, B. Olshausen, & M. Lewicki (Eds.), *Probabilistic models of the brain: Perception and neural function* (pp. 13–36). Cambridge, MA: MIT Press.

Mandelbaum, E. (2017). Seeing and conceptualizing: Modularity and the shallow contents of perception. *Philosophy and Phenomenological Research, 97*(2), 267–283.

Mandik, P. (2012). Color-consciousness conceptualism. *Consciousness and Cognition, 21*, 617–631.

Mandik, P. (2017). The myth of color sensations, or how not to see a yellow banana. *Topics in Cognitive Science, 9*, 228–240.

Marcel, A. (2004). Anosognosia for plegia: Specificity, extension, partiality and disunity of bodily unawareness. *Cortex, 40*, 19-40.

Marchi, F., & Newen, A. (2015). Cognitive penetrability and emotion recognition in human facial expressions. *Frontiers in Psychology, 6*, 828.

Margolis, E., & Laurence, S. (2012). The scope of the conceptual. In E. Margolis, R. Samuels, & S. Stich (Eds.), *The Oxford handbook of philosophy of cognitive science*. Oxford, UK: Oxford University Press.

Marino, A., & Scholl, B. (2005). The role of closure in defining the "objects" of object-based attention. *Perception and Psychophysics, 67*(7), 1140-1149.

Marr, D. (1982). *Vision: A computational investigation into the human representation and processing of visual information.* San Francisco, CA: WH Freeman.

Martin, A., Chambeaud, J. G., & Barraza, J. F. (2015). The effect of object familiarity on the perception of motion. *Journal of Experimental Psychology: Human Perception and Performance, 41*(2), 283-288. https://doi.org/10.1037/xhp0000027

Martin, J., & Dokic, J. (2013). Seeing absence or absence of seeing? *Thought, 2*, 117-125.

Martin, M. (2020). The diversity of experiences. *Philosophy and Phenomenological Research, 100*(3), 728-737.

Martin, M. G. F. (1992). Perception, concepts, and memory. *Philosophical Review, 101*, 745-763.

Martin, M. G. F. (2002). The transparency of experience. *Mind and Language, 17*, 376-425.

Martin, M. G. F. (2004). The limits of self-awareness. *Philosophical Studies, 120*, 37-89.

Matsumiya, K., & Shiori, S. (2008). Haptic movements enhance visual motion aftereffect. *Journal of Vision, 8*(6), 172. https://doi.org/10.1167/8.6.172

Matthen, M. (2005). Visual concepts. *Philosophical Topics, 33*(1), 207-233.

Matthen, M. (2014). Debunking enactivism: A critical notice of Hutto and Myin's radicalizing enactivism. *Canadian Journal of Philosophy, 44*(1), 118-128. https://doi.org/10.1080/00455091.2014.905251

Matthen, M. (2016). Is perceptual experience normally multimodal? In B. Nanay (Ed.), *Current controversies in philosophy of perception* (pp. 121-136). New York, NY: Routledge.

Maule, J., & Franklin, A. (2019). Color categorization in infants. *Current Opinion in Behavioral Sciences, 30*, 163-168. https://doi.org/10.1016/j.cobeha.2019.08.005

Mayer, E. A., Knight, R., Mazmanian, S. K., Cryan, J. F., & Tillisch, K. (2014). Gut microbes and the brain: Paradigm shift in neuroscience. *Journal of Neuroscience, 34*(46), 15490-15496. https://doi.org/10.1523/jneurosci.3299-14.2014

McBurney, D. (2010). Evolutionary approach: Perceptual adaptations. In B. Goldstein (Ed.), *Encyclopedia of perception* (pp. 405-407). Los Angeles, CA: Sage.

McClamrock, R. (1991). Marr's three levels: A re-evaluation. *Minds and Machines, 1*(2), 185-196.

McCloskey, M. (2009). *Visual reflections: A perceptual deficit and its implications.* Oxford, UK: Oxford University Press.

McConkie, G. W., & Rayner, K. (1975). The span of the effective stimulus during a fixation in reading. *Perception and Psychophysics, 17*, 578-586.

McConkie, G. W., & Zola, D. (1979). Is visual information integrated across successive fixations in reading? *Perception and Psychophysics, 25*, 221-224.

McDowell, J. (1994). *Mind and world.* Cambridge, MA: Harvard University Press.

McDowell, J. (2010). Tyler Burge on disjunctivism. *Philosophical Explorations, 13*(3), 201-213.

McDowell, J. (2019). Comments on Brewer, Gupta, and Siegel. *Philosophical Issues, 29*(1), 338–347.

McFadyen, J., Mermillod, M., Mattingley, J. B., Halász, V., & Garrido, M. I. (2017). A rapid subcortical amygdala route for faces irrespective of spatial frequency and emotion. *Journal of Neuroscience, 37*(14), 3864–3874. https://doi.org/10.1523/JNEUROSCI.3525-16.2017

McGinn, C. (1999). *Knowledge and reality.* Oxford, UK: Oxford University Press.

McGrath, M. (2014). Propositions. In E. Zalta (Ed.), *The Stanford encyclopedia of philosophy.* Stanford, CA: Metaphysics Research Lab, Stanford University.

McKee, S. P., & Nakayama, K. (1984). The detection of motion in the peripheral visual field. *Vision Research, 24*(0042-6989 [Print]), 25–32.

Meck, W., & Church, R. M. (1983). A mode control model of counting and timing processes. *Journal of Experimental Psychology: Animal Behaviour Processes, 9*(0097-7403 [Print]), 320–334.

Meng, M., & Tong, F. (2004). Can attention selectively bias bistable perception? Differences between binocular rivalry and ambiguous figures. *Journal of Vision, 4*(7), 539–551. https://doi.org/10.1167/4.7.2

Mentch, J., Spiegel, A., Ricciardi, C., & Robertson, C. E. (2019). GABAergic inhibition gates perceptual awareness during binocular rivalry. *Journal of Neuroscience, 39*(42), 8398. https://doi.org/10.1523/JNEUROSCI.0836-19.2019

Miceli, G., Fouch, E., Capasso, R., Shelton, J., Tomaiuolo, F., & Caramazza, A. (2001). The dissociation of color from form and function knowledge. *Nature, 4*(6), 662–667.

Michel, M., & Lau, H. (2021). Is blindsight possible under signal detection theory? Comment on Phillips (2020). *Psychological Review, 128*(3), 585–591.

Michel, M., & Morales, J. (2020). Minority reports: Consciousness and the prefrontal cortex. *Mind and Language, 35*(4), 493–513. https://doi.org/10.1111/mila.12264

Michotte, A. (1946/1963). *The perception of causality.* Oxford, UK: Basic Books.

Miller, S., Ngo, k., & van Swinderen, B. (2012). Attentional switching in humans and flies: rivalry in large and miniature brains. *Frontiers in Neuroscience, 5*(188), 1–17.

Millikan, R. G. (2004). *Varieties of meaning.* Cambridge, MA: MIT Press.

Milner, D., & Goodale, M. (2008). Two visual systems re-viewed. *Neuropsychologia, 46*, 774–785.

Milton, F., Fulford, J., Dance, C., Gaddum, J., Heuerman-Williamson, B., Jones, K., ... Zeman, A. (2021). Behavioral and neural signatures of visual imagery vividness extremes: Aphantasia versus hyperphantasia. *Cerebral Cortex Communications, 2*(2), tgab035. https://doi.org/10.1093/texcom/tgab035

Miracchi, L. (2017). Perception first. *Journal of Philosophy, 114*(12), 629–627. https://doi.org/10.5840/jphil20171141244

Mitroff, S., Scholl, B., & Wynn, K. (2005). The relationship between object files and conscious perception. *Cognition, 96*, 67–92.

Mody, S., & Carey, S. (2016). The emergence of reasoning by the disjunctive syllogism in early childhood. *Cognition, 154*, 40–48. https://doi.org/10.1016/cognition.2016.05.012

Moeller, S., Crapse, T., Chang, L., & Tsao, D. Y. (2017). The effect of face patch microstimulation on perception of faces and objects. *Nature Neuroscience, 20*(5), 743–752. https://doi.org/10.1038/nn.4527 http://www.nature.com/neuro/journal/v20/n5/abs/nn.4527.html#supplementary-information

Mole, C., & Zhao, J. (2016). Vision and abstraction: An empirical refutation of Nico Orlandi's non-cognitivism. *Philosophical Psychology, 29*(3), 365–373. https://doi.org/10.1080/09515089.2015.1081163

Mollon, J. (1974). After-effects and the brain. *New Scientist, 61*(886), 479–482.

Montague, M. (2018). The sense/cognition distinction. *Inquiry*, 1–17. https://doi.org/10.1080/0020174X.2018.1562371

Montemayor, C., & Haladjian, H. (2017). Perception and cognition are largely independent, but still affect each other in systematic ways: Arguments from evolution and the consciousness-attention dissociation. *Frontiers in Psychology, 8*(40), 1–15.

Moore, C., & Wolfe, J. (2001). Getting beyond the serial/parallel debate in visual search: A hybrid approach. In K. Shapiro (Ed.), *The limits of attention: Temporal constraints on human information processing* (pp. 178–198). Oxford, UK: Oxford University Press.

Moore, G. E. (1903). The refutation of idealism. *Mind, 12*, 433–453.

Moradi, F., Koch, C., & Shimojo, S. (2005). Face adaptation depends on seeing the face. *Neuron, 45*(1), 169–175. https://doi.org/10.1016/j.neuron.2004.12.018

Morales, J., Bax, A., & Firestone, C. (2020). Sustained representation of perspectival shape. *Proceedings of the National Academy of Sciences, 117*(26), 14873. https://doi.org/10.1073/pnas.2000715117

Morales, J., & Firestone, C. (2020). Seeing what's not there: The perception of absences. *CUNY Cognitive Science talks*. New York, NY: CUNY.

Morey, C. C. (2018). The case against specialized visual-spatial short-term memory. *Psychological Bulletin, 144*(8), 849–883. https://doi.org/10.1037/bul0000155

Morrison, J. (2015). Anti-atomism about color representation. *Nous, 49*(1), 94–122.

Moyer, R., & Landauer, T. (1967). Time required for judgments of numerical inequality. *Nature, 215*, 1519–1520.

Mudrik, L., Breska, A., Lamy, D., & Deouell, L. (2011). Integration without awareness: Expanding the limits of unconscious processing. *Psychological Science, 22*(6), 764–770.

Mudrik, L., & Koch, C. (2013). Differential processing of invisible congruent and incongruent scenes: A case for unconscious integration. *Journal of Vision, 13*(13), 1–14.

Muentener, P., & Carey, S. (2010). Infants' causal representations of state change events. *Cognitive Psychology, 61*(1095-5623 [Electronic]), 63–86.

Mullen, K. T. (1992). Colour vision as a post-receptoral specialization of the central visual field. *Vision Research, 31*(1), 119–130.

Müller, M. (2014). Neural mechanisms of feature-based attention. In G. Mangun (Ed.), *Cognitive electrophysiology of attention: Signals of the mind* (pp. 123–135). Amsterdam: Elsevier.

Munton, J. (2016). Visual confidences and direct perceptual justification. *Philosophical Topics, 44*(2), 301–326.

Munton, J. (2021). How to see invisible objects. *Nous, n/a*(n/a). https://doi.org/10.1111/nous.12360

Murphy, G. L. (2016). Explaining the basic-level concept advantage in infants ... or is it the superordinate-level advantage? *Psychology of Learning and Motivation, 64*, 57–92. doi:http://dx.doi.org/10.1016/bs.plm.2015.09.002

Murphy, H. (2017, December 8). Why we "hear" some silent GIF. *New York Times*.

Murray, M., Thelen, A., Thut, G., Romei, V., Martuzzi, R., & Matusz, P. (2016). The multisensory function of the human primary visual cortex. *Neuropsychologia, 83*, 161–169.

Naber, M., & Brascamp, J. (2015). Commentary: Is the frontal lobe involved in conscious perception? *Frontiers in Psychology, 6*, 1736.

Nagel, T. (1974). What is it like to be a bat? *Philosophical Review, 83*(4), 435–450.

Nagel, W. (1906). Observations on the color sense of a child. *Journal of Comparative Neurology and Psychology, 16*, 217–230.

Nakashima, R., Iwai, R., Ueda, S., & Kumada, T. (2015). Egocentric direction and position perceptions are dissociable based on only static lane edge information. *Frontiers in Psychology, 6*, 1837. https://doi.org/10.3389/fpsyg.2015.01837

Nakayama, K., He, Z. J., & Shimojo, S. (1995). Visual surface representation: A critical link between lower-level and higher-level vision. In S. M. Kosslyn & D. Osherson (Eds.), *Visual cognition: An invitation to cognitive science* (Vol. 2, pp. 1–70). Cambridge, MA: MIT Press.

Nanay, B. (2009). Perceptual representation. In B. Goldstein (Ed.), *Encyclopedia of perception* (pp. 790–793). Thousand Oaks, CA: Sage.

Nanay, B. (2010). Perception and imagination: Amodal perception as mental imagery. *Philosophical Studies, 150*(2), 239–254. https://doi.org/10.1007/s11098-009-9407-5

Nanay, B. (2016). Imagination and perception. In A. Kind (Ed.), *The Routledge handbook of philosophy of perception* (pp. 124–134). London, UK: Routledge.

Nartker, M., Firestone, C., Egeth, H., & Phillips, I. (2021). What we've been missing about what we've been missing: Above-chance sensitivity to inattentional blindness stimuli. *Journal of Vision, 21*(9), 2909–2909. https://doi.org/10.1167/jov.21.9.2909

Naselaris, T., Olman, C., Stansbury, D., Ugurbil, K., & Gallant, J. L. (2015). A voxel-wise encoding model for early visual areas decodes mental images of remembered scenes. *NeuroImage, 105*, 215–228.

Neander, K. (1998). The division of phenomenal labor: A problem for representational theories of consciousness. *Philosophical Perspectives, 12*, 411–434.

Neander, K. (2017). *A mark of the mental: In defense of informational teleosemantics*. Cambridge, MA: MIT Press.

Neisser, U. (1967). *Cognitive psychology*. Englewood Cliffs, NJ: Prentice-Hall.

Nes, A., Sundberg, K., & Watzl, S. (2021). The perception/cognition distinction. *Inquiry*, 1–31. https://doi.org/10.1080/0020174X.2021.1926317

Neta, R. (2013). What is an inference? *Philosophical Issues, 23*(1), 388–407. https://doi.org/10.1111/phis.12020

Newcombe, N. S., Levine, S. C., & Mix, K. S. (2015). Thinking about quantity: The intertwined development of spatial and numerical cognition. *Wiley Interdisciplinary Reviews: Cognitive Science, 6*(6), 491–505. https://doi.org/10.1002/wcs.1369

Newen, A. (2021). *Challenging the perception/cognition divide*. Paper presented at the Workshop on Perception and Belief, Bochum, Germany.

Newen, A., & Bartels, A. (2007). Animal minds and the possession of concepts. *Philosophical Psychology, 20*(3), 283–308. https://doi.org/10.1080/09515080701358096

Newen, A., & Vetter, P. (2016). Why cognitive penetration of our perceptual experience is still the most plausible account. *Consciousness and Cognition, 47*, 26–37.

Newen, A., Welpinghus, A., & Juckel, G. (2015). Emotion recognition as pattern recognition: The relevance of perception. *Mind and Language, 30*(2), 187–208. https://doi.org/10.1111/mila.12077

Nie, Q., Müller, H., & Conci, M. (2017). Hierarchical organization in visual working memory: From global ensemble to individual object structure. *Cognition, 159*, 85–96.

Nieder, A. (2016). The neuronal code for number. *Nature Reviews Neuroscience, 17*, 366–382.

Noë, A. (2004). *Action in perception.* Cambridge, MA: MIT Press.

Noles, N., Scholl, B., & Mirtroff, S. (2005). The persistence of object file representations. *Perception and Psychophysics, 67*(2), 324–334.

Noordhof, P. (2018). Evaluative perception as response-dependent representation. In A. Bergqvist & R. Cowan (Eds.), *Evaluative perception* (pp. 81–108). Oxford, UK: Oxford University Press.

Norman, L., Akins, K., & Kentridge, R. (2014). Color constancy for an unseen surface. *Current Biology, 24*(23), 2822–2826.

Norman, L., Heywood, C., & Kentridge, R. (2015). Exogenous attention to unseen objects? *Consciousness and Cognition, 35*, 319–329.

O'Callaghan, C. (2016). Enhancement through coordination. In B. Nanay (Ed.), *Current controversies in philosophy of perception* (pp. 109–120). New York, NY: Routledge.

O'Regan, J. K. (2011). *Why red doesn't sound like a bell: Understanding the feel of consciousness.* New York, NY: Oxford University Press.

O'Shaughnessy, B. (2012). Seeing an aspect and seeing under an aspect. In J. Ellis & D. Guevara (Eds.), *Wittgenstein and philosophy of mind* (pp. 37–60). Oxford, UK: Oxford University Press.

Odegaard, B., Knight, R., & Lau, H. (2017a). Should a few null findings falsify prefrontal theories of conscious perception? *bioRxiv.* https://doi.org/10.1101/122267

Odegaard, B., Knight, R. T., & Lau, H. (2017b). Should a few null findings falsify prefrontal theories of conscious perception? *Journal of Neuroscience, 37*(40), 9593. https://doi.org/10.1523/JNEUROSCI.3217-16.2017

Ogilvie, R., & Carruthers, P. (2015). Opening up vision: The case against encapsulation. *Review of Philosophy and Psychology, 7*(4), 1–22. https://doi.org/10.1007/s13164-015-0294-8

Ogilvie, R., & Carruthers, P. (2016). Firestone and Scholl conflate two distinct issues. *Behavioral and Brain Sciences, 39*, e255.

Okazawa, G., Tajima, S., & Komatsu, H. (2015). Image statistics underlying natural texture selectivity of neurons in macaque V4. *Proceedings of the National Academy of Sciences, USA, 112*(4), E351–360. https://doi.org/10.1073/pnas.1415146112

Oliva, A., Torralba, A., & Schyns, P. (2006). Hybrid images. *ACM Transactions on Graphics (TOG)—Proceedings of ACM SIGGRAPH 2006, 25*(3), 527–532.

Olkkonen, M., Hansen, T., & Gegenfurtner, K. (2008). Color appearance of familiar objects: Effects of object shape, texture, and illumination changes. *Journal of Vision, 8*(5), 1–16.

Openshaw, J., & Weksler, A. (2019). A puzzle about seeing for representationalism. *Philosophical Studies, 177*(9), 2625–2646. https://doi.org/10.1007/s11098-019-01331-y

Orlandi, N. (2011). The innocent eye: Seeing-as without concepts. *American Philosophical Quarterly, 48*, 17–31.

Orlandi, N. (2014). *The innocent eye: Why vision is not a cognitive process.* Oxford, UK: Oxford University Press.

Orlandi, N., & Lee, G. (2018). How radical is predictive processing? In M. Colombo, E. Irvine, & M. Stapleton (Eds.), *Andy Clark & critics.* Oxford, UK: Oxford University Press.

Overgaard, M., & Fazekas, P. (2016). Can no-report paradigms extract true correlates of consciousness? *Trends in Cognitive Sciences, 20*(4), 241–242.

Özgen, E., & Davies, I. R. L. (2002). Acquisition of categorical color perception: A perceptual learning approach to the linguistic relativity hypothesis. *Journal of Experimental Psychology: General, 131*(4), 477–493. https://doi.org/10.1037/0096-3445.131.4.477

Paffen, C. L. E., Naber, M., & Verstraten, F. A. J. (2008). The spatial origin of a perceptual transition in binocular rivalry. *PLoS One, 3*(6), e2311.

Palmer, S. (1999). *Vision science: From photons to phenomenology*. Cambridge, MA: MIT Press.

Palmer, S., Brooks, J., & Lai, K. (2007). The occlusion illusion: Partial modal completion or apparent distance? *Perception, 36*, 650–669.

Palumbo, R., D'Ascenzo, S., Quercia, A., & Tommasi, L. (2017). Adaptation to complex pictures: Exposure to emotional valence induces assimilative aftereffects. *Frontiers in Psychology, 8*, 1–8.

Panagiotaropoulos, T. I., Dwarakanath, A., & Kapoor, V. (2020). Prefrontal cortex and consciousness: Beware of the signals. *Trends in Cognitive Sciences, 24*(5), 343–344. https://doi.org/10.1016/j.tics.2020.02.005

Panagiotaropoulos, T. I., Deco, G., Kapoor, V., & Logothetis, N. K. (2012). Neuronal discharges and gamma oscillations explicitly reflect visual consciousness in the lateral prefrontal cortex. *Neuron, 74*, 924–935.

Papineau, D. (2015). Can we really see a million colours? In P. Coates & S. Coleman (Eds.), *The nature of phenomenal qualities* (pp. 275–297). Oxford: Oxford University Press.

Papineau, D. (2002). *Thinking about consciousness*. New York, NY: Oxford University Press.

Pardo-Vazquez, J. L., Castiñeiras-de Saa, J. R., Valente, M., Damião, I., Costa, T., Vicente, M. I., . . . Renart, A. (2019). The mechanistic foundation of Weber's law. *Nature Neuroscience, 22*, 1493–1502. https://doi.org/10.1038/s41593-019-0439-7

Passingham, R., & Lau, H. (2006). Free choice and the human brain. In S. Pockett, W. Banks, & S. Gallagher (Eds.), *Does consciousness cause behavior?* (pp. 53–72). Cambridge, MA: MIT Press.

Pautz, A. (2009). What are the contents of experiences? *Philosophical Quarterly, 59*, 483–507.

Pautz, A. (2011). Can disjunctivists explain our access to the sensible world? *Philosophical Issues, 21*, 384–433.

Pautz, A. (2017a). Experiences are representations: An empirical argument. In B. Nanay (Ed.), *Current controversies in the philosophy of perception* (pp. 23–42). London, UK: Routledge.

Pautz, A. (2017b). The perceptual representation of objects and natural kinds: Comments on speaks. *Philosophy and Phenomenological Research, 95*(2), 470–477. https://doi.org/10.1111/phpr.12414

Pautz, A. (2020). The puzzle of the laws of appearance. *Philosophical Issues, 30*(1), 257–272. https://doi.org/10.1111/phis.12184

Pautz, A. (2021). *Perception*. London, UK: Routledge.

Pautz, A., & Stoljar, D. (Eds.). (2019). *Blockheads! Essays on Ned Block's philosophy of mind and consciousness*. Cambridge, MA: MIT Press.

Payne, B. (2001). Prejudice and perception: The role of automatic and controlled processes in misperceiving a weapon. *Journal of Personality and Social Psychology, 81*(2), 181–192.

Peacocke, C. (1983). *Sense and content*. Oxford, UK: Oxford University Press.

Peacocke, C. (1986). The inaugural address: Analogue content. *Proceedings of the Aristotelian Society, Supplementary Volumes, 60*, 1–17.

Peacocke, C. (1989). Perceptual content. In J. Almog, J. Perry, & H. Wettstein (Eds.), *Themes from Kaplan* (pp. 297–329). New York, NY: Oxford University Press.

Peacocke, C. (1992a). Scenarios, concepts, and perception. In T. Crane (Ed.), *The contents of experience: Essays on perception* (pp. 105–135). Cambridge, UK: Cambridge University Press.

Peacocke, C. (1992b). *A study of concepts*. Cambridge, MA: MIT Press.

Peacocke, C. (1993). Externalist explanation. *Proceedings of the Aristotelian Society, 67*, 203–230.

Peacocke, C. (1994). Nonconceptual content: Kinds, rationales and relations. *Philosophy and Phenomenological Research, 9*, 419–429.

Peacocke, C. (2001a). Does perception have a nonconceptual content? *Journal of Philosophy, 98*, 239–264.

Peacocke, C. (2001b). Phenomenology and nonconceptual content. *Philosophy and Phenomenological Research, 62*(3), 609–615.

Peacocke, C. (2002). Postscript to Peacocke 1994. In Y. Gunther (Ed.), *Essays on nonconceptual content* (pp. 107–132). Cambridge, MA: MIT Press.

Peacocke, C. (2019). *The primacy of metaphysics*. Oxford, UK: Oxford University Press.

Pearson, J. (2019). The human imagination: The cognitive neuroscience of visual mental imagery. *Nature Reviews Neuroscience, 20*(10), 624–634. https://doi.org/10.1038/s41583-019-0202-9

Pearson, J. (2020). Reply to: Assessing the causal role of early visual areas in visual mental imagery. *Nature Reviews Neuroscience, 21*(9), 517–518. https://doi.org/10.1038/s41583-020-0349-4

Pelli, D., Palomares, M., & Majaj, N. (2004). Crowding is unlike ordinary masking: Distinguishing feature integration from detection. *Journal of Vision, 4*, 1136–1169.

Pelli, D., & Tillman, K. (2008). The uncrowded window of object recognition. *Nature Neuroscience, 11*(10), 1129–1135.

Perdreau, F., & Cavanagh, P. (2011). Do artists see their retinas? *Frontiers in Human Neuroscience, 5*, 171. https://doi.org/10.3389/fnhum.2011.00171

Perky, C. W. (1910). An experimental study of imagination. *American Journal of Psychology, 21*(3), 422–452. https://doi.org/10.2307/1413350

Perry, C. J., Barron, A. B., & Cheng, K. (2013). Invertebrate learning and cognition: Relating phenomena to neural substrate. *Wiley Interdisciplinary Reviews: Cognitive Science, 4*(5), 561–582. https://doi.org/10.1002/wcs.1248

Peters, M., & Lau, H. (2015). Human observers have optimal introspective access to perceptual processes even for visually masked stimuli. *eLIFE, 4:e09651*. http://dx.doi.org/10.7554/eLife.09651

Peters, M. A. K., Kentridge, R. W., Phillips, I., & Block, N. (2017). Does unconscious perception really exist? Continuing the ASSC20 debate. *Neuroscience of Consciousness, 2017*(1). https://doi.org/10.1093/nc/nix015

Peterson, M., & Cacciamani, L. (2013). Toward a dynamical view of object perception. In Z. Pizlo & S. Dickinson (Eds.), *Shape perception in human and computer vision: An interdisciplinary perspective* (pp. 443–457). London, UK: Springer.

Peterson, M., De Gelder, B., Rapcsak, S., Gerhardstein, P., & Bachoud-Lévi. (2000). Object memory effects on figure assignment: Conscious object recognition is not necessary or sufficient. *Vision Research, 40*, 1549–1567.

Peterson, M., & Gibson, B. (1994). Object recognition contributions to figure-ground organization: Operations on outlines and subjective contours. *Perception and Psychophysics, 56*(5), 551–564.

Peterson, M., & Lampignano, D. (2003). Implicit memory for novel figure-ground displays includes a history of cross-border competition. *Journal of Experimental Psychology: Human Perception and Performance, 29*(4), 808–822.

Peterson, M. A., & Gibson, B. S. (1991). Directing spatial attention within an object: Altering the functional equivalence of shape description. *Journal of Experimental Psychology: Human Perception and Performance, 17*(1), 170–182. https://doi.org/10.1037/0096-1523.17.1.170

Peterson, M. F., & Eckstein, M. P. (2013). Individual differences in eye movements during face identification reflect observer-specific optimal points of fixation. *Psychological Science, 24*(7), 1216–1225. https://doi.org/10.1177/0956797612471684

Petzold, A., & Sharpe, L. (1998). Hue memory and discrimination in young children. *Vision Research, 38*(23), 3759–3772.

Phillips, B. (2019). The shifting border between perception and cognition. *Nous, 53*(52), 316–346.

Phillips, I. (2011a). Attention and iconic memory. In C. Mole, D. Smithies, & W. Wu (Eds.), *Attention: Philosophical and psychological essays* (pp. 204–227). Oxford, UK: Oxford University Press.

Phillips, I. (2011b). Perception and iconic memory: What Sperling doesn't show. *Mind and Language, 26*(4), 381–411.

Phillips, I. (2014). Lack of imagination: Individual differences in mental imagery and the significance of consciousness. In J. Kallestrip & M. Sprevack (Eds.), *New waves in philosophy of mind* (pp. 278–300). London, UK: Palgrave Macmillan.

Phillips, I. (2015). Consciousness and criterion: On Block's case for unconscious seeing. *Philosophy and Phenomenological Research, 93*(2), 419–451.

Phillips, I. (2018). Unconscious perception reconsidered. *Analytic Philosophy, 59*(4), 471–514.

Phillips, I. (2020a). Blindsight is qualitatively degraded conscious vision. *Psychological Review, 128*(3), 558. https://doi.org/10.1037/rev0000254

Phillips, I. (2020b). Making sense of blindsense: A commentary on Garric et al., 2019. *Cortex, 127*, 388–392. https://doi.org/10.1016/j.cortex.2019.11.016

Phillips, I., & Morales, J. (2020). The fundamental problem with no-cognition paradigms. *Trends in Cognitive Sciences, 24*(3), 165–167.

Picon, E., Dramkin, D., & Odic, D. (2019). Visual illusions help reveal the primitives of number perception. *Journal of Experimental Psychology: General, 148*(10), 1675–1687. https://doi.org/10.1037/xge0000553

Pilotti, M., Antrobus, J. S., & Duff, M. (1997). The effect of presemantic acoustic adaptation on semantic "satiation." *Memory and Cognition, 25*(3), 305–312.

Pinto, Y., Sligte, I. G., Shapiro, K., & Lamme, V. (2013). Fragile visual short-term memory is an object-based and location-specific store. *Psychonomic Bulletin and Review.* https://doi.org/10.3758/s13423-013-0393-4

Pinto, Y., van Gaal, S., de Lange, F. P., Lamme, V. A., & Seth, A. K. (2015). Expectations accelerate entry of visual stimuli into awareness. *Journal of Vision, 15*(8), 13. https://doi.org/10.1167/15.8.13

Piqueras-Fiszman, B., & Spence, C. (2012). The Influence of the color of the cup on consumers' perception of a hot beverage. *Journal of Sensory Studies, 27*(5), 324–331.

Pitts, M., Martinez, A., & Hillyard, S. A. (2011). Visual processing of contour patterns under conditions of inattentional blindness. *Journal of Cognitive Neuroscience, 24*(2), 287–303.

Pitts, M., Metzler, S., & Hillyard, S. (2014). Isolating neural correlates of conscious perception from neural correlates of reporting one's perception. *Frontiers in Psychology, 5*(1078), 1–16.

Pitts, M. A., Lutsyshyna, L. A., & Hillyard, S. A. (2018). The relationship between attention and consciousness: an expanded taxonomy and implications for "no-report" paradigms. *Philosophical Transactions of the Royal Society B: Biological Sciences, 373*, 1755.

Plait, P. (2016, May 18). A fantastic optical illusion: Just another brick in the wall? *Slate*.

Planton, S., van Kerkoerle, T., Abbih, L., Maheu, M., Meyniel, F., Sigman, M., . . . Dehaene, S. (2021). A theory of memory for binary sequences: Evidence for a mental compression algorithm in humans. *PLoS Computational Biology, 17*(1), e1008598. https://doi.org/10.1371/journal.pcbi.1008598

Potter, M. (1964). Inference in visual recognition. *Science, 144*(3617), 424–425.

Potter, M. (1976). Short-term conceptual memory for pictures. *Journal of Experimental Psychology: Human Learning and Memory, 2*, 509–522.

Potter, M., Wyble, B., Hagmann, C., & McCourt, E. (2014). Detecting meaning in RSVP at 13 ms per picture. *Attention, Perception and Psychophysics, 76*, 270–279.

Potter, M. C., & Faulconer, B. A. (1975). Time to understand pictures and words. *Nature, 253*(5491), 437–438. https://doi.org/10.1038/253437a0

Pratte, M. S. (2018). Iconic memories die a sudden death. *Psychological Science, 29*(6), 877–887. https://doi.org/10.1177/0956797617747118

Pratte, M. S. (2019). Swap errors in spatial working memory are guesses. *Psychonomic Bulletin and Review, 26*(3), 958–966. https://doi.org/10.3758/s13423-018-1524-8

Pratte, M. S., Park, Y. E., Rademaker, R. L., & Tong, F. Accounting for stimulus-specific variation in precision reveals a discrete capacity limit in visual working memory. *Journal of Experimental Psychology: Human Perception and Performance, 43*(1), 6.

Pretto, P., Vidal, M., & Chatziastros, A. (2008). Why fog increases the perceived speed. *Proceedings of the 9th Driving Simulation Conference (DSC Europe 2008)* (pp. 223–235). Paris: Actes.

Prinz, J. (2002). *Furnishing the mind: Concepts and their perceptual basis*. Cambridge, MA: MIT Press.

Prinz, J. (2006a). Beyond appearances: The content of perception and sensation. In T. Gendler & J. Hawthorne (Eds.), *Perceptual experience* (pp. 434–459). Oxford, UK: Oxford University Press.

Prinz, J. (2006b). Is the mind really modular? In R. Stainton (Ed.), *Contemporary debates in cognitive science* (pp. 22–36). Oxford, UK: Blackwell.

Prinz, J. (2012). *The conscious brain*. New York, NY: Oxford University Press.

Prinz, J. (2013). Siegel's get rich quick scheme. *Philosophical Studies, 163*, 827–835.

Putnam, H. (1974). Reductionism and the nature of psychology. *Cognition, 2*, 131–146.

Putnam, H. (1975). The meaning of "meaning." *Minnesota Studies in the Philosophy of Science, 7*, 131–193.

Pylyshyn, Z. (1973). What the mind's eye tells the mind's brain: A critique of mental imagery. *Psychological Bulletin, 80*, 1–24.

Pylyshyn, Z. (1984). *Computation and Cognition*: MIT Press.

Pylyshyn, Z. (1989). The role of location indexes in spatial perception: A sketch of the FINST spatial-index model. *Cognition, 32*(1), 65–97. https://doi.org/10.1016/0010-0277(89)90014-0

Pylyshyn, Z. (1999). Is vision continuous with cognition? The case for cognitive impenetrability of visual perception. *Behavioral and Brain Sciences, 22*, 341–365.

Pylyshyn, Z. (2002). Mental imagery: In search of a theory. *Behavioral and Brain Sciences, 25*, 157–182.

Pylyshyn, Z. (2003). Return of the mental image: Are there pictures in the brain? *Trends in Cognitive Sciences, 7*, 113–118.

Pylyshyn, Z. (2007a). Multiple object tracking. *Scholarpedia, 2*(10), 3326.

Pylyshyn, Z. (2007b). *Things and places: How the mind connects with the world*. Cambridge, MA: MIT Press.

Quian Quiroga, R. (2017). How do we recognize a face? *Cell, 169*(6), 975–977. https://doi.org/10.1016/j.cell.2017.05.012

Quilty-Dunn, J. (2015). Believing in perceiving: Known illusions and the classical dual-component theory. *Pacific Philosophical Quarterly, 96*(4), 550–575. https://doi.org/10.1111/papq.12115

Quilty-Dunn, J. (2016a). Iconicity and the format of perception. *Journal of Consciousness Studies, 23*(3–4), 255–263.

Quilty-Dunn, J. (2016b). Seeing objects: A case study in the under-intellectualization of perception. In J. Quilty-Dunn, *Syntax and semantics of perceptual representation* (PhD Thesis). New York, NY: City University of New York

Quilty-Dunn, J. (2017). *Syntax and Semantics of Perceptual Representation* (PhD thesis). City University of New York Graduate Center, New York.

Quilty-Dunn, J. (2019a). Is iconic memory iconic? *Philosophy and Phenomenological Research, n/a*(n/a). https://doi.org/10.1111/phpr.12625

Quilty-Dunn, J. (2019b). Perceptual pluralism. *Nous, 54*(4), 807–838. https://doi.org/10.1111/nous.12285

Quilty-Dunn, J. (2020). Concepts and predication: From perception to cognition. *Philosophical Issues, 30*(1), 273–292.

Quilty-Dunn, J., & Green, E. J. (forthcoming). Perceptual attribution and perceptual reference. *Philosophy and Phenomenological Research, 00*, 1–26.

Quinn, P. C., & Bhatt, R. S. (1998). Visual pop-out in young infants: Convergent evidence and an extension. *Infant Behavior and Development, 21*(2), 273–288. https://doi.org/10.1016/S0163-6383(98)90006-6

Raccah, O., Block, N., & Fox, K. C. R. (2021). Does the prefrontal cortex play an essential role in consciousness? Insights from intracranial electrical stimulation of the human brain. *Journal of Neuroscience, 41*(10), 2076–2087.

Radonjic, A., Cottaris, N. P., & Brainard, D. H. (2015). Color constancy in a naturalistic, goal-directed task. *Journal of Vision, 15*(13), 3–3. https://doi.org/10.1167/15.13.3

Raffman, D. (1995). On the persistence of phenomenology. In T. Metzinger (Ed.), *Conscious experience* (pp. 293–308): Paderborn: Ferdinand Schoningh.

Raftopoulos, A. (2009). *Cognition and perception: How do psychology and neural science inform philosophy?* Cambridge, MA: MIT Press.

Raftopoulos, A. (2010). Can nonconceptual content be stored in visual memory? *Philosophical Psychology, 23*(5), 639–668.

Rahnev, D. (2019). The Bayesian brain: What is it and do humans have it? *Behavioral and Brain Sciences, 42*, e238. https://doi.org/10.1017/S0140525X19001377

Rahnev, D., Bahdo, L., deLange, F., & Lau, H. (2012). Pre-stimulus hemodynamic activity in dorsal attention network is negatively associated with decision confidence in visual perception. *Journal of Neurophysiology, 108*(5), 1529–1536.

Rahnev, D., & Denison, R. (2018). Suboptimality in perceptual decision making. *Behavioral and Brain Sciences, 41*, 1–107. https://doi.org/10.1101/060194

Rahnev, D., Maniscalco, B., Graves, T., Huang, E., de Lange, F. P., & Lau, H. (2011). Attention induces conservative subjective biases in visual perception. *Nature Neuroscience, 14*, 1513–1515.

Rahnev, D., Maniscalco, B., Luber, B., Lau, H., & Lisanby, S. (2012). Direct injection of noise to the visual cortex decreases accuracy but increases decision confidence. *Journal of Neurophysiology, 107*, 1556–1563.

Rajimehr, R. (2004). Unconscious orientation processing. *Neuron, 41*, 663–673.

Reavis, E. A., Kohler, P. J., Caplovitz, G. P., Wheatley, T. P., & Tse, P. U. (2013). Effects of attention on visual experience during monocular rivalry. *Vision Research, 83*, 76–81. https://doi.org/10.1016/j.visres.2013.03.002

Redshaw, J., & Suddendorf, T. (2016). Children's and apes' preparatory responses to two mutually exclusive possibilities. *Current Biology, 26*(13), P1758–1762.

Rees, G., Kreiman, G., & Koch, C. (2002). Neural correlates of consciousness in humans. *Nature Reviews Neuroscience, 3*, 261–270.

Reeves, A., & Lemley, C. (2012). Unmasking the perky effect: Spatial extent of image interference on visual acuity. *Frontiers in Psychology, 3*, 296. https://doi.org/10.3389/fpsyg.2012.00296

Reid, V. M., Dunn, K., Young, R. J., Amu, J., Donovan, T., & Reissland, N. (2017). The human fetus preferentially engages with face-like visual stimuli. *Current Biology, 27*(12), 1825–1828.e1823. https://doi.org/10.1016/j.cub.2017.05.044

Reiland, I. (2014). On experiencing high-level properties. *American Philosophical Quarterly, 51*(3), 177–184.

Reis, K. S., Heald, S. L. M., Veillette, J. P., Van Hedger, S. C., & Nusbaum, H. C. (2021). Individual differences in human frequency-following response predict pitch labeling ability. *Scientific Reports, 11*(1), 14290. https://doi.org/10.1038/s41598-021-93312-7

Reisberg, D. (1983). General mental resources and perceptual judgments. *Journal of Experimental Psychology: Human Perception and Performance, 9*(6), 966–979.

Remez, R. E., Rubin, P. E., Pisoni, D. B., & Carrell, T. D. (1981). Speech perception without traditional speech cues. *Science, 212*(4497), 947–949.

Rennig, J., Bilalić, M., Huberle, E., Karnath, H.-O., & Himmelbach, M. (2013). The temporo-parietal junction contributes to global gestalt perception-evidence from studies in chess experts. *Frontiers in Human Neuroscience, 7*, 513–513. https://doi.org/10.3389/fnhum.2013.00513

Rescorla, M. (2015a). Bayesian perceptual psychology. In M. Matthen (Ed.), *The Oxford handbook of the philosophy of perception* (pp. 694–716). Oxford, UK: Oxford University Press.

Rescorla, M. (2015b). Review of Nico Orlandi's "The Innocent Eye." *Notre Dame Philosophical Reviews.* January 10, 2015. https://ndpr.nd.edu/reviews/the-innocent-eye-why-vision-is-not-a-cognitive-process/

Rescorla, M. (2019). The language of thought hypothesis. In E. Zalta (Ed.), *The Stanford encyclopedia of philosophy*. Stanford, CA: Stanford University.

Rescorla, M. (2020). A realist perspective on Bayesian cognitive science. In A. Nes & T. Chan (Eds.), *Inference and consciousness* (pp. 40–73). London, UK: Routledge.

Reynolds, J. H., & Heeger, D. J. (2009). The normalization model of attention. *Neuron, 61*, 168–185.

Rhodes, G., Louw, K., & Evangelista, E. (2009). Perceptual adaptation to facial asymmetries. *Psychonomic Bulletin and Review, 16*(3), 503–508. https://doi.org/10.3758/pbr.16.3.503

Rhodes, G., Peters, M., Lee, K., Morrone, M. C., & Burr, D. (2005). Higher-level mechanisms detect facial symmetry. *Proceedings of the Royal Society B: Biological Sciences, 272*(1570), 1379–1384. https://doi.org/10.1098/rspb.2005.3093

Rice, M. (1980). *Cognition to language: Categories, word meaning, and training*. Baltimore, MD: University Park Press.

Richard, A. M., Lee, H., & Vecera, S. P. (2008). Attentional spreading in object-based attention. *Journal of Experimental Psychology: Human Perception and Performance, 34*(4), 842–853.

Rieger, G., & Savin-Williams, R. (2012). The eyes have it: Sex and sexual orientation differences in pupil dilation patterns. *PLoS One, 7*(8), 1–10.

Regier, T., & Kay, P. (2009). Language, thought, and color: Whorf was half right. *Trends in Cognitive Sciences, 13*(10), 439–446.

Ringach, D. L., & Shapley, R. (1996). Spatial and temporal properties of illusory contours and amodal boundary completion. *Vision Research, 36*(19), 3037–3050.

Rips, L. (2017). Core cognition and its aftermath. *Philosophical Topics, 45*(1), 157–179.

Robbins, P. (2015). Modularity of mind. In E. Zalta (Ed.), *Stanford encyclopedia of philosophy*. Stanford, CA: Stanford.

Rock, I. (1983). *The logic of perception*. Cambridge, MA: MIT Press.

Rogers, M. R., Witzel, C., Rhodes, P., & Franklin, A. (2020). Color constancy and color term knowledge are positively related during early childhood. *Journal of Experimental Child Psychology, 196*, 104825. https://doi.org/10.1016/j.jecp.2020.104825

Rolfs, M., Dambacher, M., & Cavanagh, P. (2013). Visual adaptation of the perception of causality. *Current Biology, 23*(3), 250–254.

Roller, J., Laganapan, A., Meijer, J.-M., Fuchs, M., & Zumbusch, A. (2021). Observation of liquid glass in suspensions of ellipsoidal colloids. *Proceedings of the National Academy of Sciences, 118*(3), e2018072118. https://doi.org/10.1073/pnas.2018072118

Rolls, E. T. (2010). The affective and cognitive processing of touch, oral texture, and temperature in the brain. *Neuroscience Biobehavioral Review, 34*(2), 237–245. https://doi.org/10.1016/j.neubiorev.2008.03.010

Rosenberg, R., & Feigenson, L. (2012). *Extreme feature loss in infants' object chunking*. Paper presented at the International Conference on Infant Studies, Minneapolis, MN.

Rosenthal, D. (1986). Two concepts of consciousness. *Philosophical Studies, 49*(3), 329–359.

Rosenthal, D. (1997). A theory of consciousness. In N. Block, O. Flanagan, & G. Güzeldere (Eds.), *The nature of consciousness: Philosophical debates*. Cambridge, MA: MIT Press.

Rosenthal, D. (2002a). Explaining consciousness. In D. Chalmers (Ed.), *Philosophy of mind: Classical and contemporary readings* (pp. 406–421). Oxford, UK: Oxford University Press.

Rosenthal, D. (2002b). How many kinds of consciousness? *Consciousness and Cognition, 11*, 653–665.

Rosenthal, D. (2005). *Consciousness and mind*. New York, NY: Oxford University Press.

Rosenthal, D. (2009). Higher order theories of consciousness. In B. McLaughlin & A. Beckermann (Eds.), *Oxford handbook of the philosophy of mind* (pp. 239–252). Oxford, UK: Clarendon Press.

Rosenthal, D. (2011). Exaggerated reports: Reply to Block. *Analysis, 71*(3), 431–437.

Roskies, A. (2008). A new argument for nonconceptual content. *Philosophy and Phenomenological Research, 76*(3), 633–659.

Rounis, E., Maniscalco, B., Rothwell, J., Passingham, R., & Lau, H. (2010). Theta-burst transcranial magnetic stimulation to the prefrontal cortex impairs metacognitive visual awareness. *Cognitive Neuroscience, 1*(3), 65–175.

Rugani, R., Fontanari, L., Simoni, E., Regolin, L., & Vallortigara, G. (2009). Arithmetic in newborn chicks. *Proceedings of the Royal Society B: Biological Sciences, 276*(1666), 2451–2460. https://doi.org/10.1098/rspb.2009.0044

Sablé-Meyer, M., Fagot, J., Caparos, S., van Kerkoerle, T., Amalric, M., & Dehaene, S. (2021). Sensitivity to geometric shape regularity in humans and baboons: A putative signature of human singularity. *Proceedings of the National Academy of Sciences, 118*(16), e2023123118. https://doi.org/10.1073/pnas.2023123118

Safavi, S., Kapoor, V., Logothetis, N., & Panagiotaropoulos, T. (2014). Is the frontal lobe involved in conscious perception? *Frontiers in Psychology, 5*, 1063.

Sainsbury, M. (2019). Loar on lemons: The particularity of perception and singular perceptual content. In A. Sullivan (Ed.), *Sensations, thoughts, language: Essays in honor of Brian Loar*. London, UK: Routledge.

Salzman, C. D., Murasugi, C., Britten, K., & Newsome, W. T. (1992). Microstimulation in visual area MT: effects on direction discrimination performance. *Journal of Neuroscience, 12*(6).

Samuel, A. G. (1997). Lexical activation produces potent phonemic percepts. *Cognitive Psychology, 32*(2), 97–127. https://doi.org/10.1006/cogp.1997.0646

Samuel, A. G. (2001). Knowing a word affects the fundamental perception of the sounds within it. *Psychological Science, 12*(4), 348–351. https://doi.org/10.1111/1467-9280.00364

Samuels, R. (2012). Massive modularity. In E. Margolis, R. Samuels, & S. Stich (Eds.), *Oxford handbook of philosophy of cognitive science*. Oxford, UK: Oxford University Press.

Sanborn, A. N., & Chater, N. (2016). Bayesian brains without probabilities. *Trends in Cognitive Sciences, 20*(12), 883–893. https://doi.org/10.1016/j.tics.2016.10.003

Sathian, K., Prather, S. C., & Zhang, M. (2004). Visual cortical involvement in normal tactile perception. In G. Calvert, C. Spence, & B. Stein (Eds.), *The handbook of multisensory processes*. Cambridge, MA: MIT Press.

Sathian, K., & Zangaladze, A. (2001). Feeling with the mind's eye: The role of visual imagery in tactile perception. *Optometry and Vision Science, 78*(5), 276–281.

Saxe, R. R., Whitfield-Gabrieli, S., Scholz, J., & Pelphrey, K. A. (2009). Brain regions for perceiving and reasoning about other people in school-aged children. *Child Development, 80*(4), 1197–1209. https://doi.org/10.1111/j.1467-8624.2009.01325.x

Schellenberg, S. (2011). Perceptual content defended. *Nous, 45*(4), 714–750.

Schellenberg, S. (2017). Perceptual consciousness as a mental activity. *Nous, 53*(1), 114–133.

Schellenberg, S. (2018). *The unity of perception: Content, consciousness, evidence*. Oxford, UK: Oxford University Press.

Schellenberg, S. (2019). Accuracy conditions, functions, perceptual discrimination. *Analysis, 79*(4), 739–754. https://doi.org/10.1093/analys/anz057

Schelonka, K., Graulty, C., Canseco-Gonzalez, E., & Pitts, M. A. (2017). ERP signatures of conscious and unconscious word and letter perception in an inattentional blindness paradigm. *Consciousness and Cognition, 54*, 56–71. https://doi.org/10.1016/j.concog.2017.04.009

Schiffer, S. (1981). Truth and the theory of content. In H. Parret & J. Bouveresse (Eds.), *Meaning and understanding.* New York, NY: De Gruyter.

Schneegans, S., & Bays, P. M. (2017). Neural architecture for feature binding in visual working memory. *Journal of Neuroscience, 37*(14), 3913–3925. https://doi.org/10.1523/jneurosci.3493-16.2017

Scholl, B. (2001). Objects and attention: the state of the art. *Cognition, 80*, 1–46.

Scholl, B., & Flombaum, J. (2010). Object persistence. In B. Goldstein (Ed.), *Encyclopedia of perception* (Vol. 2, pp. 653–657). Thousand Oaks, CA: Sage.

Scholl, B., & Leslie, A. (1999). Explaining the infant's object concept: Beyond the perception/cognition dichotomy. In E. Lepore & Z. Pylyshyn (Eds.), *What is cognitive science?* (pp. 1–4)9. Oxford, UK: Blackwell.

Scholl, B., & Pylyshyn, Z. (1999). Tracking multiple items through occlusion: Clues to visual objecthood. *Cognitive Psychology, 38*(2), 259–290. https://doi.org/10.1006/cogp.1998.0698

Scholl, B. J., & Gao, T. (2013). Perceiving animacy and intentionality: Visual processing or higher-level judgment? In M. D. Rutherford & V. A. Kuhlmeier (Eds.), *Social perception: Detection and interpretation of animacy, agency, and intention* (pp. 197–229). Cambridge, MA: MIT Press.

Schubert, T. M., Rothlein, D., Brothers, T., Coderre, E. L., Ledoux, K., Gordon, B., & McCloskey, M. (2020). Lack of awareness despite complex visual processing: Evidence from event-related potentials in a case of selective metamorphopsia. *Proceedings of the National Academy of Sciences*, 202000424. https://doi.org/10.1073/pnas.2000424117

Schurgin, M., & Flombaum, J. (2018). Visual working memory is more tolerant than visual long-term memory. *Journal of Experimental Psychology: Human Perception and Performance, 44*(8), 1216–1227.

Schut, M., Fabius, J., Van der Stoep, & Van der Stigchel, S. (2017). Object files across eye movements: Previous fixations affect the latencies of corrective saccades. *Attention, Perception, and Psychophysics, 79*, 138–153.

Schwartz, L., & Yovel, G. (2019). Learning faces as concepts rather than percepts improves face recognition. *Journal of Experimental Psychology: Learning, Memory, and Cognition, 45*(10), 1733–1747. https://doi.org/10.1037/xlm0000673

Schwitzgebel, E. (2011). *Perplexities of consciousness.* Cambridge, MA: MIT Press.

Scolari, M., Ester, E., & Seremces, J. (2015). Feature- and object-based attentional modulation in the human visual system. In K. Nobre & S. Kastner (Eds.), *The Oxford handbook of attention.* Oxford, UK: Oxford University Press.

Scott, T. R., & Powell, D. A. (1963). Measurement of a visual motion aftereffect in the rhesus monkey. *Science, 140*(3562), 57–59.

Searle, J. (1980). Author's response. *Behavioral and Brain Sciences, 3*, 450–457.

Sebastian, M. (2014). What Panpsychists should reject: on the incompatibility of panpsychism and organizational invariantism. *Philosophical Studies, 172*(7), 1833–1846.

Seiple, W., & Holopigian, K. (1996). Outer-retina locus of increased flicker sensitivity of the peripheral retina. *Journal of the Optical Society of America A, 13*(3), 658–666. https://doi.org/10.1364/JOSAA.13.000658

Sekuler, R. (1965). The first recorded observation of the after-effect of seen motion. *American Journal of Psychology, 78*(4), 686–688.

Sellars, W. (1956). Empiricism and the philosophy of mind. *Minnesota Studies in the Philosophy of Science, 1*, 253–329.

Sellars, W. (1997). *Empiricism and the philosophy of Mind (with an introduction by Richard Rorty and a study guide by Robert Brandom)*. Cambridge, MA: Harvard University Press.

Sergent, C., Corazzol, M., Labouret, G., Stockart, F., Wexler, M., King, J. R., . . . Pressnitzer, D. (2021). Bifurcation in brain dynamics reveals a signature of conscious processing independent of report. *Nature Communications, 12*(1), 1149.

Seth, A. K., McKinstry, J. L., Edelman, G. M., & Krichmar, J. L. (2004). Visual binding through reentrant connectivity and dynamic synchronization in a brain-based device. *Cerebral Cortex, 14*(11), 1185–1199. https://doi.org/10.1093/cercor/bhh079

Setogawa, T., Eldridge, M. A. G., Fomani, G. P., Saunders, R. C., & Richmond, B. J. (2021). Contributions of the monkey inferior temporal areas TE and TEO to visual categorization. *Cerebral Cortex, 31*(11), 4891–4900. https://doi.org/10.1093/cercor/bhab129

Shallice, T., & Jackson, M. (1988). Lissauer on agnosia. *Cognitive Neuropsychology, 5*(2), 153–156. https://doi.org/10.1080/02643298808252931

Sharma, J., Angelucci, A., & Sur, M. (2000). Induction of visual orientation modules in auditory cortex. *Nature, 404*, 841–847.

Shea, N. (2014). Distinguishing top-down from bottom-up effects. In S. Biggs, M. Matthen, & D. Stokes (Eds.), *Perception and its modalities* (pp. 73–91). Oxford, UK: Oxford University Press.

Shea, N. (2018). *Representation in cognitive science*. Oxford, UK: Oxford University Press.

Shea, N. (2020). Representation in cognitive science: Replies. *Mind and Language, 35*(3), 402–412. https://doi.org/10.1111/mila.12285

Shekhar, M., & Rahnev, D. (2018). Distinguishing the roles of dorsolateral and anterior PFC in visual metacognition. *Journal of Neuroscience, 38*(22), 5078–5087. https://doi.org/10.1523/jneurosci.3484-17.2018

Shepard, R. (1978). The mental image. *American Psychologist, 33*(2), 125–137.

Shepard, R., & Chipman, S. (1970). Second-order isomorphism of internal representations: Shapes of states. *Cognitive Psychology, 1*(1), 1–17.

Shepard, R. N. (1987). Toward a universal law of generalization for psychological science. *Science, 11*(0036-8075 [Print]), 1317–1323.

Shevlin, H. (2016). *Consciousness, perception, and short-term memory* (PhD dissertation). City University of New York, New York.

Sider, T. (2011). *Writing the book of the world*. Oxford, UK: Oxford University Press.

Siegel, S. (2006). Subject and object in visual experience. *Philosophical Review, 115*, 355–386.

Siegel, S. (2009). The visual experience of causation. *Philosophical Quarterly, 59*(236), 519–540.

Siegel, S. (2010). *The contents of visual experience*. Oxford, UK: Oxford University Press.

Siegel, S. (2012). Cognitive penetrability and perceptual justification. *Nous, 46*(2), 201–222.

Siegel, S. (2014). Affordances and the contents of perception. In B. Brogaard (Ed.), *Does perception have content?* (pp. 39–76): Oxford University Press.
Siegel, S. (2016). The contents of perception. In E. N. Zalta (Ed.), *The Stanford encyclopedia of philosophy* (Vol. Spring, 2016). Stanford: Center for the Study of Language and Information.
Siegel, S. (2017). *The rationality of perception*. Oxford, UK: Oxford University Press.
Siegel, S. (2019). The uneasy heirs of acquaintance. *Philosophical Issues, 29*(1), 348–365.
Siegel, S., & Byrne, A. (2016). Rich or thin? In B. Nanay (Ed.), *Current controversies in philosophy of perception* (pp. 59–80). New York, NY, and London, UK: Routledge.
Siewart, C. (2003). Is experience transparent? *Philosophical Studies, 117*, 15–41.
Silvanto, J., Cowey, A., Lavie, N., & Walsh, V. (2005). Striate cortex (V1) activity gates awareness of motion. *Nature Neuroscience, 8*(2), 143–144.
Silver, M. A., & Kastner, S. (2009). Topographic maps in human frontal and parietal cortex. *Trends in Cognitive Sciences, 13*(11), 488–495. https://doi.org/10.1016/j.tics.2009.08.005
Silver, M. A., Ress, D., & Heeger, D. J. (2005). Topographic maps of visual spatial attention in human parietal cortex. *Journal of Neurophysiology, 94*(2), 1358–1371. https://doi.org/10.1152/jn.01316.2004
Sims, C. R. (2018). Efficient coding explains the universal law of generalization in human perception. *Science, 360*(6389), 652.
Sinha, P., Crucilla, S., Gandhi, T., Rose, D., Singh, A., Ganesh, S., . . . Bex, P. (2020). Mechanisms underlying simultaneous brightness contrast: Early and innate. *Vision Research, 173*, 41–49. https://doi.org/10.1016/j.visres.2020.04.012
Siuda-Krzywicka, K., Boros, M., Bartolomeo, P., & Witzel, C. (2019). The biological bases of colour categorisation: From goldfish to the human brain. *Cortex, 118*, 82–106. https://doi.org/10.1016/j.cortex.2019.04.010
Siuda-Krzywicka, K., Witzel, C., Chabani, E., Taga, M., Coste, C., Cools, N., . . . Bartolomeo, P. (2019). Color categorization independent of color naming. *Cell Reports, 28*(10), 2471–2479.e2475. https://doi.org/10.1016/j.celrep.2019.08.003
Siuda-Krzywicka, K., Witzel, C., Taga, M., Delanoe, M., Cohen, L., & Bartolomeo, P. (2019). When colours split from objects: The disconnection of colour perception from colour language and colour knowledge. *Cognitive Neuropsychology, 37*(5–6), 325–339. https://doi.org/10.1080/02643294.2019.1642861
Skelton, A., Catchpole, G., Abbott, J., Bosten, J., & Franklin, A. (2017). Biological origins of color categorization. *Proceedings of the National Academy of Sciences, 114*(21), 5545–5550. https://doi.org/10.1073/pnas.1612881114
Sligte, I. G. (2011). *A new definition of visual short term memory* (PhD dissertation). University of Amsterdam, Amsterdam.
Sligte, I. G., Scholte, H. S., & Lamme, V. (2008). Are there multiple visual short term memory stores? *PloS One, 3*(2), e1699.
Sligte, I. G., Scholte, H. S., & Lamme, V. (2009). V4 activity predicts the strength of visual short-term memory representations. *Journal of Neuroscience, 29*(23), 7432–7438.
Sligte, I. G., Vandenbroucke, A. R., Scholte, H. S., & Lamme, V. A. (2010). Detailed sensory memory, sloppy working memory. *Frontiers in Psychology, 1*, 175. https://doi.org/10.3389/fpsyg.2010.00175
Sligte, I. G., Wokke, M. E., Tesselaar, J. P., Scholte, H. S., & Lamme, V. (2011). Magnetic stimulation of the dorsolateral prefrontal cortex dissociates fragile visual short term memory from visual working memory. *Neuropsychologia, 49*, 1578–1588.

Sloman, A. (1978). *The computer revolution in philosophy*. Hassocks, Sussex: Harvester.
Smith, A. D. (2002). *The problem of perception*. Cambridge, MA: Harvard University Press.
Smith, B. (2015). The chemical senses. In M. Matthen (Ed.), *The Oxford handbook to philosophy of perception*. Oxford, UK: Oxford University Press.
Smortchkova, J. (2020). After-effects and the reach of perceptual content. *Synthese, 198*(8), 7871–7890. https://doi.org/10.1007/s11229-020-02554-x
Sneve, M., Sreenivasan, K., Alaes, D., Endestad, T., & Magnussen, S. (2015). Short-term retention of visual information: Evidence in support of feature-based attention as an underlying mechanism. *Neuropsychologia, 66*, 1–9.
Sober, E. (1976). Mental representations. *Synthese, 33*(1), 101–148.
Soja, N. (1994). Young children's concept of color and its relation to the acquisition of color words. *Child Development, 65*, 918–937.
Sokolowski, H. M., Fias, W., Bosah Ononye, C., & Ansari, D. (2017). Are numbers grounded in a general magnitude processing system? A functional neuroimaging meta-analysis. *Neuropsychologia, 105*(Supplement C), 50–69. https://doi.org/10.1016/j.neuropsychologia.2017.01.019
Solomon, S., & Kohn, A. (2014). Moving sensory adaptation beyond suppressive effects in single neurons. *Current Biology, 24*, R1012–R1022.
Sosa, E. (1984). Body-mind interaction and supervenient causation. *Midwest Studies in Philosophy, 84*, 630–642.
Sosa, E. (2003). Privileged access. In Q. Smith & A. Jokic (Eds.), *Consciousness: New philosophical perspectives* (pp. 238–251). Oxford, UK: Oxford University Press.
Speaks, J. (2005). Is there a problem about nonconceptual content? *Philosophical Review, 114*(3), 359–398.
Speaks, J. (2017). Reply to critics. *Philosophy and Phenomenological Research, 95*(2), 492–506. https://doi.org/10.1111/phpr.12415
Spelke, E. (1990). Principles of object perception. *Cognitive Science, 14*, 29–56.
Spence, C., & Parise, C. (2010). Prior-entry: A review. *Consciousness and Cognition, 19*(1), 364–379. https://doi.org/10.1016/j.concog.2009.12.001
Sperber, D. (2001). In defense of massive modularity. In E. Dupoux (Ed.), *Language, brain and cognitive development: Essays in honor of Jacques Mehler* (pp. 47–57). Cambridge, MA: MIT Press.
Sperling, G. (1960). The information available in brief visual presentations. *Psychological Monographs, 74*(498 [whole issue]), 1–29.
Sperling, G., van Santen, J., & Burt, P. (1985). Three theories of stroboscopic motion perception. *Spatial Vision, 1*, 47–56.
Spillman, L., Otte, T., Hamburger, K., & Magnussen, S. (2006). Perceptual filling-in from the edge of the blind spot. *Vision Research, 46*, 4252–4257.
Spunt, R. P., & Adolphs, R. (2017). A new look at domain specificity: Insights from social neuroscience. *Nature Reviews Neuroscience, 18*(9), 559–567. https://doi.org/10.1038/nrn.2017.76
Stalnaker, R. (2014). *Context*. Oxford, UK: Oxford University Press.
Stein, T., & Peelen, M. V. (2021). Dissociating conscious and unconscious influences on visual detection effects. *Nature Human Behaviour, 5*, 612–624. https://doi.org/10.1038/s41562-020-01004-5
Steinman, R. M., Pizlo, Z., & Pizlo, F. J. (2000). Phi is not beta, and why Wertheimer's discovery launched the Gestalt revolution. *Vision Research, 40*(17), 2257–2264. https://doi.org/10.1016/S0042-6989(00)00086-9

Stevens, S. S. (1939). Psychology and the science of science. *Psychological Bulletin*, 36(4), 221–263. https://doi.org/10.1037/h0056886

Stoerig, P. (2001). The neuroanatomy of phenomenal vision: A psychological perspective. In P. C. Marijuan (Ed.), *Cajal and consciousness: Scientific approaches to consciousness on the centennial of Ramon y Cajal's textura* (Vol. 929, pp. 176–194): Annals of the New York Academy of Sciences (special issue).

Stokes, D. (2013). Cognitive penetrability of perception. *Philosophy Compass*, 8/7, 646–663.

Stokes, D. (2015). Towards a consequentialist understanding of cognitive penetration. In J. Zeimbekis & A. Raftopoulos (Eds.), *The cognitive penetrability of perception: New philosophical perspectives* (pp. 75–100). Oxford, UK: Oxford University Press.

Stokes, D. (2018). Rich perceptual content and aesthetic properties. In A. Bergqvist & R. Cowan (Eds.), *Evaluative perception*. Oxford, UK: Oxford University Press.

Stokes, M. B., & Payne, B. K. (2010). Mental control and visual illusions: Errors of action and construal in race-based weapon misidentification. In R. Adams Jr., K. Ambady, K. Nakayama, & S. Shimojo (Eds.), *The science of social vision* (pp. 295–305). New York, NY: Oxford University Press.

Stoljar, D. (2004). The argument from diaphanousness. In M. Ezcurdia, R. Stainton, & C. Viger (Eds.), *New essays in the philosophy of language and mind* (Supplemental volume of *The Canadian Journal of Philosophy*, pp. 341–390). Calgary: University of Calgary Press.

Stoljar, D. (2009). Perception. In *Central issues of philosophy* (pp. 51–67). Oxford, UK: Wiley-Blackwell.

Stoljar, D. (2019). In praise of poise. In A. Pautz & D. Stoljar (Eds.), *Blockheads! Essays on Ned Block's philosophy of mind and consciousness* (pp. 511–535). Cambridge, MA: MIT Press.

Storrs, K. R. (2015). Are high-level aftereffects perceptual? *Frontiers in Psychology*, 6(157). https://doi.org/10.3389/fpsyg.2015.00157

Stott, J. R. R. (2013). Orientation and disorientation in aviation. *Extreme physiology and medicine*, 2(1), 1–11. https://doi.org/10.1186/2046-7648-2-2

Strong, C. A. (1930). *Essays on the natural origin of mind*. London, UK: Macmillan.

Suchow, J., Fougnie, D., Brady, T. F., & Alvarez, G. (2014). Terms of the debate on the format and structure of visual memory. *Attention, Perception and Psychophysics*, 76(7), 2071–2079. https://doi.org/10.3758/s13414-014-0690-7

Suhler, C. L., & Churchland, P. S. (2009). Control: Conscious and otherwise. *Trends in Cognitive Sciences*, 13(8), 341–347. https://doi.org/10.1016/j.tics.2009.04.010

Summerfield, C., & Egner, T. (2016). Feature-based attention and feature-based expectation. *Trends in Cognitive Sciences*, 20(6), 401–404.

Sun, Y., Wang, X., Huang, Y., Ji, H., & Ding, X. (2021). Biological motion gains preferential access to awareness during continuous flash suppression: Local biological motion matters. *Journal of Experimental Psychology: General*, 151(2), 309–320. https://doi.org/10.1037/xge0001078

Susilo, T., McKone, E., & Edwards, M. (2010). Solving the upside-down puzzle: Why do upright and inverted face aftereffects look alike? *Journal of Vision*, 10(13), 1–16.

Suzuki, S. (2005). High-level pattern coding revealed by brief shape aftereffects. In C. W. G. Clifford, & G. Rhodes (Eds.) *Fitting the mind to the world: Adaptation and after-effects in high-level vision*. Advances in Visual Cognition. Oxford, UK: Oxford University Press.

Suzuki, W. A. (2010). Untangling memory from perception in the medial temporal lobe. *Trends in Cognitive Sciences, 14*(5), 195–200. https://doi.org/10.1016/j.tics.2010.02.002

Svalebjørg, M., Øhrn, H., & Ekroll, V. (2020). The illusion of absence in magic tricks. *i-Perception, 11*(3), 2041669520928383. https://doi.org/10.1177/2041669520928383

Szabo, Z. (1995). Berkeley's triangle. *History of Philosophy Quarterly, 12*(1), 41–63.

Tamber-Rosenau, B. J., Fintzi, A. R., & Marois, R. (2015). Crowding in visual working memory reveals its spatial resolution and the nature of its representations. *Psychological Science, 26*(9), 1511–1521. https://doi.org/10.1177/0956797615592394

Tanigawa, H., Majima, K., Takei, R., Kawasaki, K., Sawahata, H., Nakahara, K., . . . Hasegawa, I. (2022). Decoding distributed oscillatory signals driven by memory and perception in the prefrontal cortex. Cell Reports, *39*(2), 110676.

Tao, L., Porto, D., Li, Z., Fechner, S., Lee, S. A., Goodman, M. B., . . . Shen, K. (2019). Parallel processing of two mechanosensory modalities by a single neuron in *C. elegans*. *Developmental Cell, 51*(5), 617–631.e3. https://doi.org/10.1016/j.devcel.2019.10.008

Tarr, M., & Pinker, S. (1989). Mental rotation and orientation-dependence in shape recognition. *Cognitive Psychology, 21*, 233–282.

Tarr, M. J., & Hayward, W. G. (2017). The concurrent encoding of viewpoint-invariant and viewpoint-dependent information in visual object recognition. *Visual Cognition, 25*(1–3), 100–121. https://doi.org/10.1080/13506285.2017.1324933

Taylor, H. (2020). Fuzziness in the mind: Can perception be unconscious? *Philosophy and Phenomenological Research, 101*(2), 383–398. https://doi.org/10.1111/phpr.12592

Taylor, H. (2022). Consciousness as a natural kind and the methodological puzzle of consciousness. *Mind and Language*.

Teeuwen, R. R. M., Wacongne, C., Schnabel, U. H., Self, M. W., & Roelfsema, P. R. (2021). A neuronal basis of iconic memory in macaque primary visual cortex. *Current Biology, 31*(24), 5401–5414. https://doi.org/10.1016/j.cub.2021.09.052

Teng, C., & Kravitz, D. J. (2019). Visual working memory directly alters perception. *Nature Human Behaviour, 3*(8), 827–836. https://doi.org/10.1038/s41562-019-0640-4

Teufel, C., & Nanay, B. (2017). How to (and how not to) think about top-down influences on visual perception. *Consciousness and Cognition, 47*, 17–25. doi:http://dx.doi.org/10.1016/j.concog.2016.05.008

Theeuwes, J. (2013). Feature-based attention: It is all bottom-up priming. *Philosophical Transactions of the Royal Society B, 368*(1628), 1–11.

Theodoni, P., Panagiotaropoulos, T., Kapoor, V., Logothetis, N., & Deco, G. (2011). Cortical microcircuit dynamics mediating binocular rivalry: The role of adaptation in inhibition. *Frontiers in Human Neuroscience, 5*(145), 1–19. https://doi.org/10.3389/fnhum.2011.00145

Thierry, G., Athanasopoulos, P., Wiggett, A., Dering, B., & Kuipers, J.-R. (2009). Unconscious effects of language-specific terminology on preattentive color perception. *Proceedings of the National Academy of Sciences, 106*(11), 4567. https://doi.org/10.1073/pnas.0811155106

Thoen, H. H., How, M. J., Chiou, T.-H., & Marshall, J. (2014). A different form of color vision in mantis shrimp. *Science, 343*(6169), 411. https://doi.org/10.1126/science.1245824

Thompson, E., & Varela, F. (2001). Radical embodiment: Neural dynamics and consciousness. *Trends in Cognitive Sciences, 5*(10), 418–425.

Tian, X., & Huber, D. E. (2010). Testing an associative account of semantic satiation. *Cognitive Psychology, 60*(4), 267–290. https://doi.org/10.1016/j.cogpsych.2010.01.003

Tibbetts, E. A., Agudelo, J., Pandit, S., & Riojas, J. (2019). Transitive inference in Polistes paper wasps. *Biology Letters, 15*(5), 20190015. https://doi.org/10.1098/rsbl.2019.0015

Tipper, S., Jordan, H., & Weaver, B. (1999). Scene-based and object-centered inhibition of return: Evidence for dual orienting mechanisms. *Perception and Psychophysics, 61*(1), 50–60.

Tipper, S. P., & Behrmann, M. (1996). Object-centered not scene-based visual neglect. *Journal of Experimental Psychology: Human Perception and Performance, 22*(5), 1261–1278.

Tononi, G., & Edelman, G. M. (1998). Consciousness and complexity. *Science, 282*, 1846–1851.

Tootell, R. B. H., Reppas, J. B., Dale, A. M., Look, R. B., Sereno, M. I., Malach, R., . . . Rosen, B. R. (1995). Visual motion aftereffect in human cortical area MT revealed by functional magnetic resonance imaging. *Nature, 375*, 139. https://doi.org/10.1038/375139a0

Travis, C. (2004). The silence of the senses. *Mind, 113*(449), 57–94.

Treisman, A. (1998). Feature binding, attention and object perception. *Philosophical Transactions of the Royal Society of London B: Biological Sciences, 353*(1373), 1295–1306. https://doi.org/10.1098/rstb.1998.0284

Treisman, A., & Gormican, S. (1988). Feature analysis in early vision: Evidence from search asymmetries. *Psychological Review, 95*(1), 15–48.

Tremoulet, P., Leslie, A., & Hall, D. (2000). Infant individuation and identification of objects. *Cognitive Development, 15*, 499–522.

Treue, S. (2015). Object- and feature-based attention: Monkey physiology. In K. Nobre & S. Kastner (Eds.), *The Oxford handbook of attention*. Oxford, UK: Oxford University Press.

Tsao, D. Y. (2019). Face values. *Scientific American, 2029*(February), 23–29.

Tsao, D. Y., Moeller, S., & Freiwald, W. A. (2008). Comparing face patch systems in macaques and humans. *Proceedings of the National Academy of Sciences, USA, 105*(49), 19514–19519. https://doi.org/10.1073/pnas.0809662105

Tsuchiya, N., Wilke, M., Frässle, S., & Lamme, V. (2015). No-report paradigms: Extracting the true neural correlates of consciousness. *Trends in Cognitive Sciences, 19*(12), 757–770.

Tsutsumi, S., Ushitani, T., & Fujita, K. (2011). Arithmetic-like reasoning in wild vervet monkeys: A demonstration of cost-benefit calculation in foraging. *International Journal of Zoology, 2011*, 806589. https://doi.org/10.1155/2011/806589

Tucker, C. (2010). Why open-minded people should endorse dogmatism. *Philosophical Perspectives, 24*, 529–545.

Tye, M. (1991). *The imagery debate*. Cambridge, MA: MIT Press.

Tye, M. (1995a). Blindsight, orgasm and representational overlap. *Behavioral and Brain Sciences, 18*, 268–269.

Tye, M. (1995b). *Ten problems of consciousness*. Cambridge, MA: MIT Press.

Tye, M. (2000). *Consciousness, color, and content*. Cambridge, MA: MIT Press.

Tye, M. (2002). Representationalism and the transparency of experience. *Nous, 36*(1), 137–151.

Tye, M. (2005). On the nonconceptual content of experience. In M. E. Reicher & J. C. Marek (Eds.), *Experience and analysis* (pp. 221–235). Vienna, Austria: Obvahpt.

Tye, M. (2006). Nonconceptual content, richness, and fineness of grain. In T. Gendler & J. Hawthorne (Eds.), *Perceptual experience* (pp. 504–530). Oxford, UK: Oxford University Press.

Tye, M. (2009). *Consciousness revisited*. Cambridge, MA: MIT Press.
Tye, M. (2010). Attention, seeing and change blindness. *Philosophical Issues, 20*, 410–437.
Tye, M. (2014a). Does conscious seeing have a finer grain than attention? *Thought, 3*, 154–158.
Tye, M. (2014b). Transparency, qualia realism and representationalism. *Philosophical Studies, 170*, 39–57.
Tye, M. (2014c). What is the content of a hallucinatory experience? In B. Brogaard (Ed.), *Does perception have content?* (pp. 291–308). Oxford, UK: Oxford University Press.
Tye, M. (2018). Homunculi heads and silicon chips: The importance of history to phenomenology. In A. Pautz & D. Stoljar (Eds.), *Themes from Block*. Cambridge, MA: MIT Press.
Tye, M. (2019). How to think about the representational content of visual experience. In C. Limbeck & F. Stadler (Eds.), *The philosophy of perception, Proceedings of the Austrian Ludwig Wittgenstein Society*. Berlin, Germany: De Gruyter.
Tyler, C. (2015). Peripheral color demo. *i-Perception, 6*(6), 1–5.
Uithol, S., Bryant, K. L., Toni, I., & Mars, R. B. (2021). The anticipatory and task-driven nature of visual perception. *Cerebral Cortex, 31*(12), 5354–5362. https://doi.org/10.1093/cercor/bhab163
Urai, A., Braun, A., & Donner, T. (2017). Pupil-linked arousal is driven by decision uncertainty and alters serial choice bias. *Nature Communications, 8*, 14637. https://doi.org/10.1038/ncomms14637
Valenti, J. J., & Firestone, C. (2019). Finding the "odd one out": Memory color effects and the logic of appearance. *Cognition, 191*, 103934. https://doi.org/10.1016/j.cognition.2019.04.003
Valentine, T. (1991). A unified account of the effects of distinctiveness, inversion, and race in face recognition. *Quarterly Journal of Experimental Psychology, A, 43*(2), 161–204. https://doi.org/10.1080/14640749108400966
Valentine, T., Lewis, M. B., & Hills, P. J. (2016). Face-space: A unifying concept in face recognition research. *Quarterly Journal of Experimental Psychology, 69*(10), 1996–2019. https://doi.org/10.1080/17470218.2014.990392
Vallortigara, G. (2021). *Born knowing: Imprinting and the origins of knowledge*. Cambridge, MA: MIT Press.
van Bergen, R. S., Ma, W. J., Pratte, M. S., & Jehee, J. F. (2015). Sensory uncertainty decoded from visual cortex predicts behavior. *Nature Neuroscience, 18*(12), 1728–1730.
Van Gulick, R. (2007). What if phenomenal consciousness admits of degrees? *Behavioral and Brain Sciences, 30*(5/6), 528–529.
van Tonder, G., & Ejima, Y. (2000). Bottom-up clues in target finding: Why a Dalmatian may be mistaken for an elephant. *Perception, 29*, 149–157.
van Zandvoort, M. J. E., Nijboer, T. C. W., & de Haan, E. (2007). Developmental colour agnosia. *Cortex, 43*(6), 750–757. https://doi.org/10.1016/S0010-9452(08)70503-3
VanRullen, R. (2006). On second glance: Still no high-level pop-out effect for faces. *Vision Research, 46*(17), 3017–3027.
Varshney, L., & Sun, J. (2013). Why do we perceive logarithmically? *Significance, 10*(1), 28–31.
Völter, C., & Call, J. (2017). Causal and inferential reasoning in animals. In J. Call (Ed.), *APA handbook of comparative psychology. Vol. 2: Perception, learning, and cognition* (Vol. 2, pp. 643–671). American Psychological Association.

Wackermann, J., Pütz, P., & Allefeld, C. (2008). Ganzfeld-induced hallucinatory experience, its phenomenology and cerebral electrophysiology. *Cortex, 44*(10), 1364–1378.

Wagatsuma, N., Oki, M., & Sakai, K. (2013). Feature-based attention in early vision for the modulation of figure–ground segregation. *Frontiers in Psychology, 4*(123). https://doi.org/10.3389/fpsyg.2013.00123

Wagemans, J., van Lier, R., & Scholl, B. (2006). Introduction to Michotte's heritage in perception and cognition research. *Acta Psychologica, 123*, 1–19.

Wagner, K., & Barner, D. (2016). The acquisition of color words: How children perceive, abstract, categorize, and label color. In Mark Aronoff (Ed.), *Oxford research encyclopedia of linguistics*. https://oxfordre.com/linguistics/view/10.1093/acrefore/9780199384655.001.0001/acrefore-9780199384655-e-28

Walker, E. Y., Cotton, R. J., Ma, W. J., & Tolias, A. S. (2020). A neural basis of probabilistic computation in visual cortex. *Nature Neuroscience, 23*(1), 122–129. https://doi.org/10.1038/s41593-019-0554-5

Walker, R. (1995). Spatial and object-based neglect. *Neurocase, 1*(4), 371–383. https://doi.org/10.1080/13554799508402381

Wang, J., & Feigenson, L. (2021). Dynamic changes in numerical acuity in 4-month-old infants. *Infancy, 26*(1), 47–62. https://doi.org/10.1111/infa.12373

Wang, M., Arteaga, D., & He, B. (2013). Brain mechanisms for simple perception and bistable perception. *Proceedings of the National Academy of Sciences, 110*(35), E3350–E3359.

Warren, R. M. (1968). Verbal transformation effect and auditory perceptual mechanisms. *Psychological Bulletin, 70*(4), 261–270.

Warren, R. M. (1970). Perceptual restoration of missing speech sounds. *Science, 167*(3917), 392–393.

Webster, M. (2011). Adaptation and visual coding. *Journal of Vision, 11*(5), 1–23.

Webster, M. (2012). Evolving concepts of sensory adaptation. *F1000Reports Biology, 4*(21), 1–7.

Webster, M. (2015). Visual adaptation. *Annual Reviews of Vision Science, 1*, 547–567. https://doi.org/10.1146/annurev-vision-082114-035509

Webster, M., & MacLin, O. (1999). Figural aftereffects in the perception of faces. *Psychonomic Bulletin and Review, 6*(4), 647–653.

Weisberg, J. (2010). Misrepresenting consciousness. *Philosophical Studies*. https://doi.org/10.1007/s11098-010-9567-3

Weisberg, J. (2011). Abusing the notion of what-it's-like-ness: A response to Block. *Analysis, 71*(3), 438–443.

Weiskrantz, L. (1986/2009). *Blindsight: A case study spanning 35 years and new developments.* Oxford, UK: Oxford University Press.

Wertheimer, M. (1912). Experimentelle Studien über das Sehen von Bewegung. *Zeitschrift für Psychologie, 61*, 161–265.

Wexley, K., Yukl, G., Kovacs, S., & Sanders, R. (1972). Importance of contrast effects in employment interviews. *Journal of Applied Psychology, 56*(1), 45–48.

Whitwell, R., Sperandio, I., Buckingham, G., Chouinard, P., & Goodale, M. (2020). Grip constancy but not perceptual size constancy survives lesions of early visual cortex. *Current Biology, 30*(18), 3680–3686. https://doi.org/10.1016/j.cub.2020.07.026

Wilcox, T. (1999). Object individuation: Infants' use of shape, size, pattern, and color. *Cognition, 72*, 125–166.

Wilcox, T., & Biondi, M. (2015). Object processing in the infant: lessons from neuroscience. *Trends in Cognitive Sciences, 19*(7), 406–413. https://doi.org/10.1016/j.tics.2015.04.009

Wilcox, T., Hirshkowitz, A., Hawkins, L., & Boas, D. (2014). The effect of color priming on infant brain and behavior. *NeuroImage, 85,* 302–313.

Wilcox, T., & Woods, R. (2009). Experience primes infants to individuate objects: Illuminating learning mechanisms. In A. Woodward & A. Needham (Eds.), *Learning and the infant mind* (pp. 117–143). New York, NY: Oxford University Press.

Winawer, J., Witthoft, N., Michael, C. Frank, Wu, L., Alex, R. Wade, & Boroditsky, L. (2007). Russian blues reveal effects of language on color discrimination. *Proceedings of the National Academy of Sciences, 104*(19): 7780–7785.

Winawer, J., Huk, A., & Boroditsky, L. (2010). A motion aftereffect from visual imagery of motion. *Cognition, 114*(2), 276–284.

Wittgenstein, L. (1953). *Philosophical investigations.* New York, NY: Macmillan.

Witzel, C. (2016). An easy way to show memory color effects. *i-Perception, 7*(5), 2041669516663751. https://doi.org/10.1177/2041669516663751

Witzel, C. (2019). Misconceptions about colour categories. *Review of Philosophy and Psychology, 10*(3), 499–540. https://doi.org/10.1007/s13164-018-0404-5

Witzel, C., & Hansen, T. (2015). Memory effects on color perception. In A. Elliot, M. Fairchild, & A. Franklin (Eds.), *Handbook of color psychology* (pp. pp. 641–659). Cambridge, UK: Cambridge University Press.

Witzel, C., Olkkonen, M., & Gegenfurtner, K. (2017). Memory colours affect colour appearance. *Behavioral and Brain Sciences,39,* E262. https://doi.org/10.1017/S0140525X15002587

Witzel, C., Olkkonen, M., & Gegenfurtner, K. R. (2018). A Bayesian model of the memory colour effect. *i-Perception, 9*(3), 2041669518771715. https://doi.org/10.1177/2041669518771715

Witzel, C., Valkova, H., Hanswen, T., & Gegenfurtner, K. (2011). Object knowledge modulates colour appearance. *i-Perception, 2,* 13–49.

Wokke, M., Vandenbroucke, A., Scholte, H., & Lamme, V. (2012). Confuse your illusion. *Psychological Science, 24*(1), 63–71. https://doi.org/10.1177/0956797612449175

Wolfe, J. M. (2001). Asymmetries in visual search: An introduction. *Perception and Psychophysics, 63*(3), 381–389.

Wolfe, J. M., & Horowitz, T. S. (2017). Five factors that guide attention in visual search. *Nature Human Behaviour, 1,* 0058. https://doi.org/10.1038/s41562-017-0058

Wood, J. N. (2009). Distinct visual working memory systems for view-dependent and view-invariant representation. *PloS One, 4*(8), e6601. https://doi.org/10.1371/journal.pone.0006601

Wood, J. N., & Spelke, E. S. (2005). Chronometric studies of numerical cognition in five-month-old infants. *Cognition, 97*(1), 23–39. https://doi.org/10.1016/j.cognition.2004.06.007

Wooldridge, D. E. (1963). *The machinery of the brain.* New York, NY: McGraw-Hill.

Wu, C.-C., & Wolfe, J. M. (2018). A new multiple object awareness paradigm shows that imperfect knowledge of object location is still knowledge. *Current Biology, 28*(21), 3430–3434.e3433. https://doi.org/10.1016/j.cub.2018.08.042

Wu, W. (2014). *Attention.* Abingdon, UK, and New York, NY: Routledge.

Wu, W. (2017). Shaking up the mind's ground floor: The cognitive penetrability of visual attention. *Journal of Philosophy, 114*(1), 5–32.

Wyart, V., Nobre, A. C., & Summerfield, C. (2012). Dissociable prior influences of signal probability and relevance on visual contrast sensitivity. *Proceedings of the National Academy of Sciences, 109*(9), 3593. https://doi.org/10.1073/pnas.1120118109

Xie, W., & Zhang, W. (2017). Dissociations of the number and precision of visual short-term memory representations in change detection. *Memory and Cognition, 45*(8), 1423–1437. https://doi.org/10.3758/s13421-017-0739-7

Xing, Y., Ledgeway, T., McGraw, P. V., & Schluppeck, D. (2013). Decoding working memory of stimulus contrast in early visual cortex. *Journal of Neuroscience, 33*(25), 10301–10311. https://doi.org/10.1523/JNEUROSCI.3754-12.2013

Xu, F., & Carey, S. (1996). Infants' metaphysics: The case of numerical identity. *Cognitive Psychology, 30*, 111–153.

Xu, F., Carey, S., & Welch, J. (1999). Infants' ability to use object kind information for object individuation. *Cognition, 70*, 137–166.

Xu, Z., Adam, K. C. S., Fang, X., & Vogel, E. K. (2018). The reliability and stability of visual working memory capacity. *Behavior Research Methods, 50*(2), 576–588. https://doi.org/10.3758/s13428-017-0886-6

Yamamoto, S. (2018). *Perceptual content and perceptual justification* (PhD dissertation). Brown University, Providence, RI.

Yantis, S. (2005). How visual salience wins the battle for awareness. *Nature Neuroscience, 8*, 975. https://doi.org/10.1038/nn0805-975

Zeimbekis, J. (2013). Color and cognitive penetrability. *Philosophical Studies, 165*(1), 165–175.

Zhang, W., & Luck, S. J. (2008). Discrete fixed-resolution representations in visual working memory. *Nature, 453*, 233–237.

Zhao, J., Kong, F., & Wang, Y. (2013). Attentional spreading in object-based attention: The roles of target–object integration and target presentation time. *Attention, Perception, and Psychophysics, 75*(5), 876–887. https://doi.org/10.3758/s13414-013-0445-x

Zhao, Y.-J., Kay, K. N., Tian, Y., & Ku, Y. (2021). Sensory recruitment revisited: Ipsilateral V1 involved in visual working memory. *Cerebral Cortex 32*(7), 1470–1479. https://doi.org/10.1093/cercor/bhab300

Zhou, J., Tjan, B. S., Zhou, Y., & Liu, Z. (2008). Better discrimination for illusory than for occluded perceptual completions. *Journal of Vision, 8*(7), 26–26. https://doi.org/10.1167/8.7.26

Zorzi, M., Bonato, M., Treccani, B., Scalambrin, G., Marenzi, R., & Priftis, K. (2012). Neglect impairs explicit processing of the mental number line. *Frontiers in Human Neuroscience, 6*(125), 1–12.

Zosh, J. M., & Feigenson, L. (2009). Beyond "what" and "how many": Capacity, complexity and resolution of infants' object representations. In L. Santos & B. Hood (Eds.), *The origins of object knowledge* (pp. 25–51). New York, NY: Oxford University Press.

Zwislocki, J. J. (2009). Stevens' power law. In J. J. Zwislocki (Ed.), *Sensory neuroscience: Four laws of psychophysics* (pp. 1–80). Boston, MA: Springer US.

Author Index

For the benefit of digital users, indexed terms that span two pages (e.g., 52-53) may, on occasion, appear on only one of those pages.

Figures are indicated by *f* following the page number

Abid, Greyson, 117, 274, 439
Adolphs, Ralph, 395-96, 397
Alberti, Leon Battista, 223
Alston, William, 22
Alvarez, George, 232-34, 233*f*, 235-36
Andrews, Rachel V., 262-63
Aristotle, 61-62
Arnold, Derek H., 407-8
Audi, Robert, 158
Ayer, A.J., 208

Baldauf, Daniel, 363-64, 364*f*, 365, 367
Balog, Kati, 202n.7
Balota, David A., 102-3
Bar, Moshe, 162-63
Barbot, Antoine, 162
Barrett, Lisa Feldman, 51, 162-63
Bartels, Andreas, 168, 169
Bax, Axel, 32
Bayne, Tim, 5, 6, 10, 13-14, 123
Beck, Jacob, 41-43, 224, 225
Begby, Endre, 11
Behrens, Timothy E.J., 56
Bengson, John, 137
Berkeley, George, 175, 196, 220, 268
Bermúdez, José Luis, 183
Biondi, Marisa, 281
Black, Sheila, 102-3
Blake, Randolph, 315-17, 315*f*
Bloem, Ilona M., 113-14, 120
Bloom, Paul, 165
Boghossian, Paul, 57-58
Boyd, Richard, 22
Brascamp, Jan, 106-7, 309-10, 311, 315-17, 315*f*
Briscoe, Robert, 10
Brogaard, Berit, 391
Brown, Richard, 427-42, 464-65
Bruner, Jerome, 338, 347
Burge, Tyler, 11, 19-20, 28, 78, 82-83, 85-86, 87, 117, 121-42, 121n.2, 122*f*, 144, 147, 169, 177, 179, 183, 284, 448

Burke, Luke, 256
Burton, Nichola, 86
Byrne, Alex, 4-5, 9-10, 28, 167-68, 174, 269-70, 449

Camp, Elisabeth, 169, 222, 302
Campbell, John, 292
Carey, Susan, 14-15, 38, 187, 188*f*, 203-4, 246-47, 276-77, 276n.3, 289-91, 290*f*, 400, 410-16
Carlson, Thomas A., 191-92, 192*f*
Carrasco, Marisa, 162, 323-24n.1, 355-58, 357*f*, 363
Carruthers, Peter, 339, 396, 397, 421-22
Cavanagh, Patrick, , 13, 201, 406-9
Cepelewicz, Jordana, 51-52
Chalmers, David, 24, 29, 180, 451-59
Chang, Le, 95-97
Christophel, Thomas B., 285
Church, Russell M., 225
Churchland, Patricia, 51-52, 66, 133
Churchland, Paul, 51-52
Clark, Andy, 119, 194-95, 201, 205, 212-13, 343
Cleeremans, Axel, 442-43
Cohen, Michael, 440-41
Constantinescu, Alexandra. O., 56
Contardi, Sara, 431
Crane, Tim, 28, 177-79
Curtis, Clayton E., 197, 251, 256-57

Darwin, Charles, 292
Datta, Ritobrato, 355, 356*f*
Davidson, Donald, 173
Davies, Will, 149
De Vignemont, Frédérique, 157-58, 165
Dehaene, Stanislas, 7-8, 7*f*, 53-54, 224, 256-57, 285, 319-20, 417-18, 420, 423-24, 445, 464-65
Delk, John L., 386-87, 390
Dener, Efrat, 208-9, 209*f*
Denison, Rachel, 205, 439

Dennett, Daniel, 66, 248
Deroy, Ophelia, 77–78
Desimone, Robert, 363–65, 364f, 367
Deutsch, Diana, 103
DeYoe, Edgar A., 355, 356f
Dijkstra, Nadine, 228, 379
Doeller, Christian F., 55–56
Dretske, Fred, 25, 29
Durgin, Frank, 43–44, 346

Egan, Frances, 30
Einhäuser, Wolfgang, 309–10
Ejima, Yoshimichi, 351–52
Ekroll, Vebjørn, 182–83, 183f
Ester, Edward F., 273–74, 273f
Evans, Gareth, 27, 196, 269, 302, 447

Farennikova, Anya, 182, 183
Faulconer, Barbara A., 331–33
Feigenson, Lisa, 89, 246–47, 286
Fillenbaum, Samuel, 386–87, 390
Finke, Ronald, 81, 227, 230–31, 231f
Firestone, Chaz, 32, 81, 119, 160–61, 185–86, 344–46, 355, 358, 362–63, 365, 385, 388–91, 390f
Fitch, Tecumseh, 53
Fleming, Steve, 228
Flombaum, Jonathan I., 38–39, 239, 256, 259, 280n.4
Flores, Carolina, 447
Fodor, Jerry, 3, 37–38, 46, 46n.10, 49, 53, 168, 196, 201–2, 202n.7, 211, 218–20, 221, 265, 302, 339–41, 394–403, 473
Fougnie, Daryl, 232–34, 233f, 235–36, 302–3
Fox, Kieran C.R., 443–44
Frankland, Steven, 55–56
Franklin, Anna, 274–78, 283, 291, 323–24
Frässle, Stefan, 309–10
Freeman, Jeremy, 333n.3
Fridland, Ellen, 45
Frisby, John, 61–62
Frith, Chris, 201
Fulkerson, Matthew, 158

Gallistel, Randy, 204
Galvin, Susan J., 31
Garner, Wendell R., 234–35
Gatzia, Dimitria, 391
Gegenfurtner, Karl R., 385–87
Gibson, J.J., 30
Godfrey-Smith, Peter, 17–18, 19
Goldstone, Robert L., 271–73, 272f

Goodale, Melvyn A., 138
Goodman, Jeremy, 150
Gordon, Robert D., 262–63
Green, E.J., 20, 22, 87, 215, 216, 232–34, 235–37, 248, 252–54, 261, 367, 370–74
Greene, Joshua, 55–56, 122
Gregory, Richard, 201
Grice, H. Paul, 30, 138–41
Griffiths, Thomas L, 206, 212
Gross, Stephen, 38, 39–40, 103n.7, 210–12, 342–75

Hajonides, Jasper E., 296–97
Haladjian, Harry H., 346–47
Hall, D. Geoffrey, 288–89, 289f
Hameroff, Stuart, 456–57
Hamlin, J. Kiley, 165
Haugeland, John, 29, 29n.5
Hayes, Cecilia, 13–14
Haynes, John-Dylan, 285, 463–64
He, Biyu Jade, 311–12
He, Sheng, 191–92, 192f, 461–63
He, Xun, 323–24, 323–24n.1
Heck, Richard, 171, 174, 269–70
Heeger, David, 113
Heidegger, Martin, 447
Helton, Grace, 98, 99–100
Henderson, John M., 263
Hendrickson, Andrew T., 271–73, 272f
Hill, Christopher, 96–97, 128, 138–39, 141, 447, 448
Hillyard, S.A., 320–21, 321f, 322–23, 322f
Hochmann, Jean-Remy, 287–88
Hohwy, Jakob, 106–7, 119
Hollingworth, Andrew, 263

Irwin, David E., 261–63

Jacobs, Christianne, 257–58
Jacobson, Hilla, 164, 165
James, William, 249
Johnston, Mark, 448
Jordan, Kerry E., 252–54, 253f, 259–60
Judge, Jenny, 413–14

Kahneman, Daniel, 237, 248–49
Kapoor, Vishal, 311–12, 313–14
Kay, Paul, 396
Keane, Brian P., 352–54, 402
Keeble, Stephanie, 147–48
Keil, Frank C., 410
Kirchner, Holle, 330–31
Knapen, Tomas, 315–17, 315f

Koch, Christoph, 7, 91–92, 308
Kominsky, Jonathan, 69, 406–10
Konkle, Talia, 89–90, 111, 333–37
Kosslyn, Stephen, 223, 226–27, 226f, 251, 252, 257
Kouider, Sid, 257
Kripke, Saul, 127
Kulvicki, John, 223
Kwak, Yuna, 197, 251, 256–57

Lamme, Victor, 8–9, 34–38, 36f, 112, 249–50, 254–55, 308, 418, 444, 464–65
Lande, Kevin, 132–33
Landman, Rogier, 34–35, 249, 254–55
Latour, Bruno, 167
Lau, Hakwan, 255, 256–57, 317, 427–43
Leahy, Brian, 203–4
Lebrecht, Sophie, 163–64
Lee, Geoff, 150, 213–14
Lee, Jenn Laura, 439
Leopold, David A., 107–8
Leslie, Alan M., 147–48, 288–90, 289f
Lewis, David, 26–27
Libet, Benjamin, 459–67
Ling, Sam, 113–14, 120
Loar, Brian, 127
Logothetis, Nikos K., 107–8, 311–12
Long, Bria, 111, 332f, 333–37
Lumer, Erik, 312–13
Lupyan, Gary, 49, 201, 205, 342, 342n.2, 343–44, 359–62, 365, 367–69, 380–81
Luzon, Bar, 141

Ma, Wei Ji, 439
MacLeod, Donald, 461–63
MacPherson, Fiona, 49, 340–41, 343
Maloney, Lawrence, 205
Mamassian, Pascal, 205
Mandelbaum, Eric, 20, 278–79, 327, 330–32, 333, 383–85
Mandik, Pete, 391
Marin, Michael, 131
Marr, David, 201, 205–6, 217
McCloskey, Michael, 32
McCollough, Celeste, 72–73
McConkie, George, 440–41
McDowell, John, 28, 193–94, 266, 269–70, 292, 447, 448
Meck, Warren H., 225
Michel, Matthias, 312–13, 430n.5
Michotte, Albert, 405 n.1, 405f, 406, 408
Miller, George, 54
Milner, David, 138

Mitroff, Stephen R., 252–54, 253f, 259–60
Montemayor, Carlos, 346–47
Moore, George Edward, 447
Moradi, Farshad, 91–92
Morales, Jorge, 32, 185–86, 312–13, 317–19
Morrison, John, 149
Munton, Jesse, 132–33, 193–94

Nakayama, Ken, 132, 217, 240–41, 240f, 255–56
Nanay, Bence, 378
Neander, Karen, 32
Neisser, Ulric, 338–39
Newen, Albert, 52, 79–81, 168, 169

Odegaard, Brian, 317, 442–43
Ogilvie, Ryan, 396
Olkkonen, Maria, 385–87, 386f, 387f, 388f
Orlandi, Nico, 202, 213–14, 448

Palmer, Stephen, 94
Panagiotaropoulos, Theofanis I., 311–12, 313–14
Papineau, David, 149
Pautz, Adam, 4–5, 10, 24, 28, 29, 193–94, 198–200, 458
Payne, Keith, 122–23
Peacocke, Christopher, 168, 225, 266, 269–70, 450
Pearson, Joel, 228–29
Pelli, Denis, 133–34, 133f, 134f
Penrose, Roger, 456–57
Perky, Cheves West, 228
Peters, Megan, 255
Peterson, Mary, 72f, 108–9, 381–83, 381f, 382f, 384–85, 384f
Petzold, Axel, 292
Phillips, Ian, 19–20, 92n.6, 165, 217, 317–19, 378, 430n.5
Picon, Edwina, 148–49
Pinker, Steven, 230–31, 231f
Pitts, Michael, 320–21, 321f, 322f, 322–23, 464–65
Postman, Leo, 338
Potter, Mary C., 38–39, 325–33
Potter, Molly, 369
Pouget, Alexandre, 206, 212
Pratte, Michael, 40–41, 41f, 249–50
Pressnitzer, Daniel, 314–15
Prinz, Jesse, 4–5, 9, 168, 394, 400, 423–24
Putnam, Hilary, 23–24, 39
Pylyshyn, Zenon, 46, 49, 124–25, 146–47, 218, 221, 248, 252, 339–41, 339n.1

Quilty-Dunn, Jake, 20, 37–38, 41n.8, 42–43, 122, 168–69, 215, 216–17, 232–34, 235–37, 248, 252–54, 253f, 258–59, 260–61, 263, 302–3

Raccah, Omri, 443–44
Rahnev, Dobromir, 205, 436, 438–39
Ramachandran, Vilayanur Subramanian (V.S.), 66, 133
Rayner, Keith, 440–41
Rees, Geraint, 308, 312–13, 463–64
Regier, Terry, 396
Regolin, Lucia, 400–1
Rescorla, Michael, 206–8, 209–10
Rhodes, Gillian, 81–82
Robbins, Philip, 398, 399
Rock, Irving, 201, 202
Rolfs, Martin, 406–9
Rolls, Edmund, 158–59
Rosch, Eleanor, 332n.2
Rosenthal, David, 424–27, 428, 434–36, 435f, 440, 464–65
Russell, Bertrand, 170–71

Safavi, Shervin, 311–12
Sainsbury, Mark, 128, 140–41
Samuel, Arthur, 65, 66–68
Schellenberg, Susanna, 123–42, 144, 145–46, 146n.6, 151, 446n.6, 448
Schelonka, Kathryn, 317–21, 321f, 322f
Scholl, Brian, 69, 160–61, 218, 241, 242f, 280n.4, 289–90, 344–46, 355, 358, 362–63, 365, 406–8, 410
Schurgin, Mark W., 259
Schwitzgebel, Eric, 303
Searle, John, 29, 29n.5
Sergent, Claire, 314–15, 423
Sethi, Umrao, 292
Sharma, Jitendra, 399–400
Sharpe, Lindsay T., 292
Shea, Nicholas, 211–12, 404–10, 411–12, 450
Shemesh, Hagai, 208–9, 209f
Shepard, Roger, 145, 176f, 222–23, 230f
Shevlin, Henry, 101, 327
Siegel, Susanna, 4–5, 27–28, 58, 62–64, 77, 153, 156, 178, 179, 299, 341, 346
Silvanto, Juha, 257–58
Simoncelli, Eero P., 333n.3
Sinha, Pawan, 118–19
Siuda-Krzywicka, Katarzyna, 295–96
Skelton, Alice E., 277–78, 277f

Sligte, Ilja, 250
Smortchkova, Joulia, 75–77, 81, 90, 91–92
Spelke, Elizabeth, 14–15, 218, 246–47, 411
Spence, Charles, 303
Sperling, George, 249
Spunt, Robert, 395–96, 397
Stevens, Stanley Smith, 151
Stoerig, Petra, 430
Stokes, Dustin, 342
Stokes, Mark G., 296–97
Stoljar, Daniel, 268, 420
Strong, Charles Augustus, 266
Sur, Mriganka, 399–400
Suzuki, Wendy, 307
Svalebjørg, Mats, 182–83, 183f

Thorpe, Simon, 330–31
Treisman, Anne, 358
Tremoulet, Patrice, 288–89, 289f
Tsao, Doris, 95–97
Tsuchiya, Naotsugu, 308
Tye, Michael, 9–10, 134–35, 139–40, 170–71, 211, 297–98, 448, 449, 451–59
Tyler, Christopher, 433, 435f

Valenti, J.J., 385, 388–91, 390f
Vallortigara, Giorgio, 400–1
Van Rullen, Rufin, 11, 184–85
Van Tonder, Gert Jakobus, 351–52
Vetter, Petra, 80–81
Von Helmholtz, Herman, 201, 201n.6

Ward, Emily J., 359–62
Warren, Richard M., 64–65, 101–2
Webster, Michael A., 86
Weiskrantz, Larry, 44, 135
Wilcox, Teresa, 279–82, 283–84, 287
William of Ockham, 53
Williamson, Timothy, 57–58, 152
Wittgenstein, Ludwig, 219–20, 265
Witzel, Christoph, 295–96, 385–87
Wolfe, Jeremy, 40n.7, 183–84, 184f, 185, 327–28
Wood, Justin, 250
Wooldridge, Dean, 18–19, 18–19n.2
Wu, Chia-Chien, 40n.7

Yamamoto, Stephen, 94
Yarrow, Kielan, 407–8

Zola, David, 440–41

Subject Index

For the benefit of digital users, indexed terms that span two pages (e.g., 52–53) may, on occasion, appear on only one of those pages.
Figures are indicated by *f* following the page number

adaptation. *See* auditory perception: adaptation in; visual perception: adaptation in
agnosia
   apperceptive or visual form (*see* visual perception: disorders of)
   associative (*see* cognition: disorders of)
alexia. *See* visual perception: disorders of
analog magnitude representation. *See* analog mirroring
analog mirroring, 221–23, 224–25, 232, 239f, 239–41, 242, 243, 244, 411, 471–72. *See also* representation: iconic; representation: numerosity
   neuroscience of, 224–25
analog tracking. *See* analog mirroring
anosognosia. *See* cognition: disorders of
attended intermediate level representation (AIR) theory, 9, 423–24
attention, 162, 323–24, 323–24n.1
   change blindness and, 279–81, 280n.4, 440–41
   cognitive penetration and (*see* modularity thesis: attention and)
   consciousness and, 27, 316–17, 320–22, 321f, 322f, 420, 445 (*see also* visual perception: rivalry in)
   disorders of, 244–46, 245f (*see also* visual perception: disorders of)
   endogenous, 354–55
   exogenous, 117
   infant, 117, 280–81
   inhibition of return in, 243
   models of, 355–57, 356f
   neuroscience of, 355–57, 356f, 363–65, 364f, 367
   noticing vs., 280, 440–41 (*see also* attention: change blindness and)
   object-based, 186, 241–43, 242f
   psychophysics of, 355–58, 357f, 365, 367, 436–37
   unconscious, 359–61, 360–61n.5

auditory perception, 64–69, 271–73, 272f
   adaptation in, 64–65, 66–68, 102–3
   ambiguous stimuli in, 65, 66–67, 350–51, 399
   discrimination in, 149–50
   neuroscience of, 65–66, 314
belief
   analytic vs. synthetic, 57–58
   concepts in, 167–68
   de re versus de dicto, 43, 134–35
   direct awareness of, 447
   perceptual (*see* perceptual judgment; perceptual belief in)
bistable stimuli. *See* visual perception: rivalry in
blindsight, 135, 429–30, 430n.5
bored monkey problem. *See* perceptual neuroscience: mind-wandering in

cognition, 13, 14
   adaptation in, 97–104
   animal, 17–19, 18–19n.2, 53–54, 55, 172, 187–88, 188f
   architecture of, 342–43, 344, 399–400 (*see also* modularity thesis)
   capacity of, 37
   in children (*see* cognition: infant)
   consciousness and (*see* consciousness: cognitivist theories of)
   core, 14–15, 165, 404–16, 469, 470, 473 (*see also* representation: numerosity; visual perception: of causation)
   cross-cultural, 55, 269, 294–95
   demonstratives in (*see* cognition: singular content in)
   developmental, 53–54, 55
   disorders of, 5–6, 8, 10, 169–70, 295–96, 382–83, 397, 455–56
   iconic representation in (*see* representation: iconic)

cognition (cont.)
  infant, 165, 187–88, 188f, 203–4, 290–91 (see also cognition: core)
  insect (see animal)
  markers of, 61–120
  mental imagery in, 197–98
  neuroscience of, 55–56, 100, 113–15, 279, 285, 296–97, 309–10, 323
  nonconceptual, 123, 169, 302
  nonlinguistic, 183
  phenomenology of, 460–61, 466–67
  propositional, 168, 172–76, 267–68
  representational contents of, 22, 172–76
  singular content in, 124, 126, 127
  system 1 and 2, 99–100
  visual, 13, 15, 21–22n.3 (see also working memory)
cognitive penetration. See modularity thesis
Computational Theory of Mind, 52–53
computer vision, 16, 25, 57, 94
concepts, 12, 28, 166–72, 174–75, 196, 267–68
  basic-level, 330, 331–33, 332n.2, 332f, 334, 398–99 (see also modularity thesis: conceptual vs. nonconceptual versions of)
  constitutive properties of, 166, 302–5, 398–99
  demonstrative, 269–70, 297
  development of, 293–98
  infant, 286, 287–88, 291–92, 294, 297
  in perception (see perception: conceptual)
  proto- (see concepts: infant)
  recognitional, 270, 274
conceptual engineering. See kinds: conceptual engineering of
conditioning
  classical, 18
  operant, 18
consciousness, 417–67, 469, 470
  animal, 19
  cognitivist theories of, 417–19, 421, 422, 442–44, 445, 451–59 (see also global workspace theory; consciousness: higher-order theories of)
  contents of, 35–37, 421–22, 444–45
  dispositionalist approaches to, 419–22, 423–24
  enactivist theories of, 447–48
  epiphenomenalist views of, 459–67
  functionalist views of, 451–59
  higher-order theories of, 417–18, 424–43, 464–65
  infant, 292–93, 422
  integrated information theory of, 418
  neuroscience of, 7–9, 417, 428–31, 440, 442–44, 445–46, 446n.6, 461–66
  noncognitivist theories of, 8–9, 417 (see also consciousness: integrated information theory of; consciousness: recurrent processing theory of; perceptual neuroscience)
  perceptual (see perception: phenomenology of)
  prefrontalist theories of (see consciousness: cognitivist theories of)
  recurrent processing theory of, 8–9, 417–18, 430–31, 464–65
  transitivity principle of (see consciousness: higher-order theories of)
constancy. See perception: constancies in; perception: constitutive properties of
content. See representation
contextual representation. See auditory perception: ambiguous stimuli in; perception: ambiguous stimuli in

direct awareness. See naïve realism
discursive representation. See representation: propositional
divisive normalization, 113–15, 241, 470

eliminativism, 51–52
epistemology of perception. See perceptual judgment

first-order recurrence. See consciousness: recurrent processing theory of
first-order theory. See consciousness: noncognitivist theories of
fragile visual short-term memory, 34–38, 249–50
  format of, 40–41, 249–50
  psychophysics of, 34–35

global workspace theory, 7–8, 9, 156, 159–60, 257, 309, 319–22, 417–18, 420, 423–24, 441, 443, 444–45, 464–65 (see also consciousness: cognitivist theories of)

hallucination, 21–22n.3
  Rare Charles Bonnet Syndrome, 428–32
  veridical, 141, 448–49

iconic memory, 39–41, 248–49, 287
  neuroscience of, 249
  psychophysics of, 40–41, 249
illusion, 30
  absence (*see* visual perception: of absence)
  apparent motion, 135, 238–41, 238*f*, 239*f*, 258–59
  brick wall, 367–69, 368*f*
  Cornsweet, 201 (*see also* perception: inference in)
  illusory contours, 16–17, 111–13, 352–54
  McCollough effect (*see* visual perception: adaptation in; visual perception: norm-based)
  McGurk effect, 303
  Michotte causal launch, Chapter 12.F1, 405–6 (*see also* perception: of causation)
  motion aftereffect (*see* visual perception: adaptation in; visual perception: multichannel)
  Muller-Lyer, 12
  Necker cube, 13, 104–5, 104*f*, 105*f*, 345*f* (*see also* perception: ambiguous stimuli in; visual perception: rivalry in)
  oculogravic, 303
  phi phenomenon (*see* illusion: apparent motion)
  plug/hat, 148–49, 148*f*
  reductive theories of content and, 449–50
  sharpness overconstancy (*see* subjective inflation: peripheral)
  simultaneous contrast illusion, 118–19
  of sound, 303–4
  speech to song, 103
  tilt aftereffect (*see* visual perception: adaptation in; visual perception: multichannel)
  tunnel effect, 132–33, 256, 279–80, 287 (*see also* visual perception: motion)
  veridical, 138–39 (*see also* hallucination: veridical)
  visual perception, Opponent-process theory of
  waterfall (*see* visual perception: adaptation in; visual perception: multichannel)
imaginings. *See* mental imagery
intentionalism. *See* representationism
intentionality, 16
  intrinsic and derived, 29
item effect. *See* working memory: capacity of

kinds, 20–21, 22, 366–67
  conceptual engineering of, 44–53
  folk psychological, 51–52
  functional, 23, 24, 26
  natural, 23, 26, 50
  perception of (*see* perception: kind)
  rigidity of, 24, 458–59
  semantics of, 24, 26–27

language of thought, 53–56
language perception. *See* auditory perception; visual perception: linguistic

machine vision. *See* computer vision
mental imagery, 15, 21, 21–22n.3, 48–49, 50, 197–98, 199, 226–31
  aphantasia and, 257–58
  modularity thesis and (*see* modularity thesis: mental imagery and)
  neuroscience of, 227–28, 376–77
  perception vs., 228–29, 376–79
  phenomenology of, 228
  psychophysics of, 226–27, 226*f*, 229–31, 230*f*, 231*f*
  working memory and (*see* working memory: mental imagery in)
mental rotation, 176*f*, *See also* representation: iconic
method of phenomenal contrast. *See* visual perception: phenomenology of
micro-valences, 163–64. *See also* perception: evaluative; visual perception: emotion
minimal immediate direct perceptual judgment. *See* perceptual judgment
misrepresentation. *See* illusion
modularity thesis, 3, 45–49, 69, 153–54, 327, 331, 333, 338–79, 380–93, 394–403, 468, 470, 472
  attention and, 343, 351, 354–69, 371–74, 473
  conceptual vs. nonconceptual versions of, 327–30, 384–85, 398–99, 472
  domain specificity and, 395–96, 397, 473
  encapsulation and, 339, 394–95, 411 (*see also* cognition: architecture of)
  impenetrability and, 339–43, 342n.2, 473 (*see also* perceptual learning; visual perception: expert)
  massive, 397
  mental imagery and, 374–79
  neuroscience of, 347, 398*f*
  perceptual expectations and, 338–39, 343, 359

moral pop-out effect. *See* pop-out: moral
multichannel adaptation. *See* visual perception: multichannel; visual perception: adaptation in; visual perception: opponent process theory of
multiple object tracking, 40n.7, 146, 190, 190*f*, 216, 218, 246, 261, 411

naïve realism, 27, 29, 32, 125n.3, 446–49
New Look psychology. *See* modularity thesis: perceptual expectation and

object files. *See* attention: object-based; multiple object tracking; visual perception: object; working memory: object representation in
object-specific preview benefit, 252–64. *See also* attention: object-based; multiple object tracking; perception, object; working memory, object representation in
olfactory perception, 2, 100
   adaptation in, 100
   neuroscience of, 100
opponent process system. *See* visual perception: opponent process theory of; visual perception: adaptation in; visual perception: color in; visual perception: norm-based
overflow. *See* consciousness: contents of

partial report superiority. *See* fragile visual short-term memory; iconic memory; working memory: capacity of
parts principle. *See* analog mirroring; representation: iconic
perception
   ambiguous stimuli in, 189, 219–21, 260, 345–46, 345*f*, 347–54, 358–69, 399–400, 401–2
   animal, 304, 452 (*see also* visual perception: animal)
   associative effects in, 46n.10, 94–95, 160–61n.7, 367, 387–88, 391, 430
   auditory (*see* auditory perception)
   Bayesian theories of, 143–44, 200–14, 347–49, 385–86, 387*f* (*see also* predictive processing)
   bias in, 152–57
   binding in, 157–58, 181, 181n.1 (*see also* perception: cross-modal)
   capacities in, 131, 145–46, 146n.6 (*see also* perception: discrimination in)
   categorical, 145, 265–305, 396, 408–9, 410, 469 (*see also* perception: language and; visual perception: categorical)
   causal efficacy of, 129–30, 465–66
   causal theories of, 138–41
   of causation, Cchapter 12.S1, 468
   conceptual, 166, 196–98, 201–2, 298–99, 301, 325–37, 383–85, 404, 424–27, 432, 472
   constancies in, 17, 20, 21–22n.3, 78, 117, 137–38, 173, 201–2, 281–84
   constitutive properties of, 21–22, 21–22n.3, 24–26, 50, 81–82, 120, 123–24, 128, 142–52, 166–214, 215–64, 468, 470 (*see also* representation: conceptual; representation: nonconceptual; representation: nonpropositional; representation: propositional)
   cross-cultural, 277–78, 277*f*
   crossmodal, 87–90, 303–4, 397
   demonstrative (*see* perception: singular content in; cognition: demonstratives in)
   determinacy of, 219–21
   dimensions of, 234–37, 370–74
   discrimination in, 142–52, 271, 274–75, 275*f*, 469
   dual component theory of, 51
   evaluative, 157–65, 469 (*see also* visual perception: emotion)
   evolutionary functions of, 119
   existential content in, 124, 128–29, 132, 138–42, 179
   format of (*see* representation: iconic; perception: constitutive properties of)
   generalization in (*see* perception: categorical)
   hysteresis in, 369, 373–74 (*see also* visual perception: recognition in)
   inference in, 166–214 (*see also* representation: functional role of)
   of kind, 286, 289–91, 290*f*
   language and, 292, 293–96, 396
   markers of, 115–18
   Marr's levels of, 195–206, 210
   modes of, 165, 170–71, 211–12
   nonconceptual, 265–305, 327–28 (*see also* representation: nonconceptual)
   object, 146–47, 215–16, 237–46, 252–64, 412–13, 413*f*, 414, 468 (*see also* illusion: apparent motion; multiple object tracking; visual perception: figure-ground segmentation in)

object-involving content in, 125–26, 126n.4, 131–32, 446–49
olfactory (*see* olfactory perception)
overintellectualization of, 144
phenomenology of, 90, 170–71, 234, 255–56, 419–23, 461–66
probabilistic representation in, 204–14, 469 (*see also* representation: of probability)
property instances in, 128–30, 144
propositional, 176–77, 182–87, 189–90, 468
relational, 189–90
singular content in, 123–42, 215–18, 269–70, 468
spatial, 89, 90, 128–29
strong singular content in (*see* perception: object-involving content in)
tropes in (*see* perception: property instances in)
unconscious, 419–20, 424–26, 427–28, 446–47, 464–66 (*see also* visual perception: unconscious)
visual (*see* visual perception)
perceptual attribution. *See* seeing-as
perceptual expectation, 287–91, 289f, 290f, 293, 413–14
  modularity and (*see* modularity thesis: perceptual expectation and)
  role of visual short-term memory in, 288–89
perceptual judgment, 12, 13, 28, 42–44, 62–64, 75, 77–78, 94, 104–6, 109, 121–22, 152–57, 192–93, 282–83, 339, 421
  infant, 117, 283
  neuroscience of, 52
  perceptual belief in, 16, 28, 134–35
  perceptual justification in, 28, 43–44, 56, 57–58, 193–94, 297–98, 346
  phenomenology of, 299–300
perceptual learning, 45–48, 299
perceptual neuroscience
  methodological puzzle of, 306–7, 324
  mind-wandering in, 312–14, 315, 317–18
  no-report paradigms in, 306–7, 308–24
  nonconceptual representation in, 306–24
  visual, 5, 6–7, 68, 69–70, 73, 79–80, 83–84, 95–96, 100, 106, 112, 113–15, 117, 202–3, 213, 296–97, 307, 335–37, 461–66

perceptual particulars. *See* perception: singular content in
perceptual predication. *See* seeing-as
perceptual prediction. *See* perceptual expectation
perceptual reference. *See* perception: singular content in
perceptual seeming. *See* perceptual judgment: perceptual justification in
perceptual set, 331, 341, 347, 350–51
pop-out
  of causation, 409–410
  moral, 159–61
  in visual search, 109–11, 183–85, 184f, 409
predictive coding, 84, 106–7, 194–95, 327n.1 (*see also* perception: Bayesian theories of; perception: inference in)
  light-from-above prior in, 202
  modularity thesis vs., 343
priming, 160–61n.7, 359
  affective, 164
  semantic, 160–61, 359–62
problem of circularity, 34, 61, 62–64, 66, 307–8. *See also* perceptual neuroscience: methodological puzzle of

representation, 2, 27–28, 30–33
  accuracy conditions on, 28, 32, 178–79, 449–51
  atomic, 188–90, 221
  conceptual (*see* concepts)
  discursive (*see* representation: conceptual; representation: propositional)
  distributed, 52
  format of (*see* representation: conceptual; representation: iconic; representation: propositional; representation: vehicles of vs. contents of)
  functional role of, 77, 116–17, 116f, 178, 211–12, 215–21, 268–69, 454–56 (*see also* representation: structure of; representation: vehicles of vs. contents of)
  holistic, 232–34, 235–37
  iconic, 1–2, 53, 56, 173, 175, 196, 215–64, 468, 471–72
  in neural networks, 53–54
  individuation conditions of, 123–42, 269–70
  neuroscience of, 52–53, 80
  nonconceptual, 173, 174–75, 472

representation (*cont.*)
  nonpropositional, 176–79, 471
  numerosity, 73, 74*f*, 87–89, 88*f*, 90, 115, 148–49, 148*f*, 245–46, 247, 411–12, 414–16, 416*f*, 468 (*see also* perception: crossmodal)
  perceptual (*see* visual perception: representational contents of)
  perspectival, 32, 117–18, 200
  of probability, 204–14
  propositional, 28, 41n.8, 51, 121–22, 167, 170–71, 172–76, 180–82, 267 (*see also* representation: conceptual)
  recursive, 53–55
  reductive accounts of, 30, 449–51
  reusability criterion for, 211
  sensitivity vs., 204–14
  structure of, 180–82, 221 (*see also* representation: vehicles of vs. contents of)
  truth conditions, 28
  vehicles of vs. contents of, 173–74, 176, 211–12, 218–19, 469–70
representationism, 9–10, 27

seeing-as, 11, 25, 29, 121–65, 294
  cognitive, 122–23
  perceptual, 121–122–123, 469
seeing-that, 25
sensation vs. perception, 78, 137, 284. *See also* visual perception: constitutive properties of
signal detection theory, 73–75, 436–37, 438–39. *See also* attention: psychophysics of; visual perception: psychophysics of
Spelke objects. *See* multiple object tracking; visual perception: object
Stevens's power law, 151. *See also* perception: discrimination in; seeing-as; Weber-Fechner Law
stimulus-dependence, 41–43
Stroop effect, 334–36, 335*f*
subjective inflation
  inattentional inflation, 436–42
  peripheral, 31–32, 432, 434–36, 435*f*, 441–42

transsaccadic memory. *See* working memory: transsaccadic
tree structures. *See* representation: recursive

veridicality conditions. *See* representation: accuracy conditions

visual perception
  of absence, 182–86, 184*f*
  adaptation in, 61–64, 69–83, 85–101, 102–3, 103n.7, 119–20, 234, 406–8
  of affect (*see* visual perception: emotion)
  amodal and modal completion in, 132–33, 182–83, 183*f*, 185–86, 300*f*, 304, 347, 348*f*, 352–54, 353n.3, 353*f*, 401–2, 402*f* (*see also* illusion: illusory contours; visual perception: filling-in of)
  amodal and modal interpolation in (*see* visual perception: amodal and modal completion in)
  animal, 17–18, 19–20, 106, 107*f*, 110*f*, 111, 266–67, 400–1, 400*f*, 401*f*, 414–15
  attention in, 90–92, 162, 336
  Bayesian theories of, 213–14
  binding in (*see* visual perception: crowding in)
  capacity of, 34–41
  categorical, 12, 45, 46, 265–305, 333, 336
  in cognition (*see* cognition: visual)
  cognitive penetration of (*see* modularity thesis)
  of color, 62, 63*f*, 70–71, 150, 169–70, 199–200, 265–305, 323–24, 385–93, 415–16, 416*f*, 433, 435*f* (*see also* Stroop effect; visual perception: opponent-process theory of)
  concepts in, 15, 17, 42–43, 45, 51, 77–78, 79, 96–97, 121–22, 149–50
  criterion effects on (*see* visual perception: psychophysics of)
  crowding in, 133–35, 133*f*, 134*f*
  dimensions of, 90–91, 370–74
  disorders of, 32, 68, 138, 146n.6 (*see also* attention: disorders of; blindsight; hallucination)
  dynamical systems models of, 106–9
  emotion, 75–79, 76*f*, 82n.4, 86, 89–90, 162
  ensemble, 85, 135–36, 189–90, 329, 333–35, 335*f*
  expert, 79–80, 94 (*see also* perceptual learning)
  explanatorily deep properties of (*see* constitutive properties of)
  facial, 91–94, 93*f*, 95–97, 468 (*see also* visual perception: emotion; visual perception: gender)
  familiarity in (*see* visual perception: recognition in)

figure-ground segmentation in, 108–9, 108f, 136, 137, 146–47, 380–85
filling-in of, 66, 132–33, 436
foveal versus peripheral, 31, 132, 434f, 435f
ganzfeld, 136–37, 136n.5, 145
of gender, 75–78, 76f, 82n.4, 192–94, 193f
gist (*see* visual perception: ensemble)
grain of, 31, 44
habituation in, 147–48, 267, 275–77, 276n.3, 409, 410, 412–13, 413f, 414–15, 422 (*see also* visual perception: infant)
high- and low-level, 3–5, 6, 8, 9–11, 13, 77, 82–84, 85–97, 162–63, 191–92, 194–95, 200, 298–302, 323–24, 323–24n.1, 327–30, 331, 339n.1, 363–65, 374, 468 (*see also* visual perception: mid-level)
iconic (*see* representation: iconic)
illusions of (*see* illusion)
infant, 89, 115, 116–17, 116f, 246–47, 265–305, 401, 410, 412–13, 413f, 415
innateness of (*see* visual perception: animal; visual perception: infant)
insect (*see* animal)
laws of, 3
linguistic, 68
markers of, 61–120
metamers of, 95, 333–34, 333n.3
mid-level, 333–37
of motion, 6–7, 9, 17, 69–70, 128–29, 132–35, 195, 202–3, 206–7 (*see also* illusion: apparent motion; perception: object)
multichannel, 71–72, 73, 86–87
necessary conditions of (*see* visual perception: constitutive properties of)
neuroscience of (*see* perceptual neuroscience)
nonconceptual, 19
norm-based, 71, 85–86, 300–1 (*see also* visual perception: adaptation in)
numerosity representation in (*see* representation: numerosity)
opponent-process theory of, 51–52, 71–73, 180, 278 (*see also* visual perception: norm-based)
peripheral, 132–35, 432–36 (*see also* subjective inflation: peripheral)
perspectival (*see* representation: perspectival)

phenomenology of, 6–7, 8, 15–17, 44, 62–64, 75–77, 118–19, 134–35, 139, 141, 299–300, 300f
psychophysics of, 73–77, 85, 86, 91, 110f, 115–16, 336–37, 337f, 461–62, 462f (*see also* Stevens's power law; visual perception: adaptation in; Weber-Fechner Law)
pure, 15, 17–20, 80–81
recognition in, 325–28, 326f, 336, 380, 381f, 382, 392
representational contents of, 22, 27–29
retinotopy in, 69–70, 73–75, 78n.3, 88–89, 101, 407–8
rich versus thin, 4–5
rivalry in, 104–9, 182, 191–95, 308–13, 315–19, 315f, 349, 349f, 351, 359, 360f, 361f, 362f
spatiotopy in, 69–70, 73–75, 88f, 88–89
template theories of, 94–95
unconscious, 16, 19–20, 29, 91–92, 92n.6, 146n.6, 260, 383–84, 461–64
ventral and dorsal streams of, 83–84
visual search
 efficiency of, 115–16
 indirect, 185
 pop-out in (*see* pop-out: in visual search)
visual simulation. *See* mental imagery
visuospatial neglect. *See* attention: disorders of

warrant. *See* perceptual judgment: perceptual justification in
Weber's Law. *See* Weber-Fechner Law
Weber-Fechner Law, 115, 151, 224. *See also* perception: markers of
working memory, 15–16, 50, 250–52, 284–86
 capacity of, 37–38, 326–27
 chunking in, 54–55, 285–86
 concept possession and, 168–69
 conceptualization in, 197, 256–57, 258, 286
 format of, 40–41, 232–34, 233f, 236, 247, 250–52, 254–55, 41412.P44 (*see also* fragile visual short-term memory; iconic memory)
 fragile (*see* fragile visual short-term memory)
 iconic representation in (*see* working memory: format of)

working memory, (*cont.*)
  infant, 286–93
  mental imagery in, 254–55, 257–58, 374–75, 376f
  models of, 38–41, 247
  neuroscience of, 15n.1, 54–55, 113–14, 250, 251, 285, 323
  object representation in, 246–47, 254–55, 258–64
  phenomenology of, 256
  pool model (*see* working memory: models of)
  psychophysics of, 40–41, 54–55, 114, 251, 261–62, 263
  slot model (*see* working memory: models of)
  transsaccadic, 261–63
  unconscious, 37
  variable precision (*see* working memory: models of)